12 days
due
Read

THE FRONTISPIECE on the next page represents the CÆSARIAN INFLUENCES behind the post-war dictators. EUROPA, the woman, is mounted on ZEUS, the supreme deity of the Greeks, — bringer of victories and god of moral law and social virtues. At the sides of the picture are the fasces inclosing the axes carried in front of the Roman consuls as SYMBOLS OF POWER. In the center is the generally accepted St. Helena death mask of NAPOLEON I. Dominating the entire picture, he represents the spirit of middle-class law, order, and national unity. "LE TITRE D'EMPEREUR NE SE PERD PAS" is Napoleon's own expression of the concept of absolutism which seems to actuate his twentieth-century successors.

The drawing was made for this book by Fortunino Matania.

"LE TITRE D'EMPEREUR
NE SE PERD PAS." ‹ ‹ ‹

EUROPE
SINCE NAPOLEON

BY

FRANKLIN CHARLES PALM

UNIVERSITY OF CALIFORNIA

WITH THE ASSISTANCE OF

FREDERICK E. GRAHAM

SAN JOSE STATE TEACHERS COLLEGE

GINN AND COMPANY

BOSTON · NEW YORK · CHICAGO · LONDON
ATLANTA · DALLAS · COLUMBUS · SAN FRANCISCO

2818

The Athenæum Press

GINN AND COMPANY · PRO-
PRIETORS · BOSTON · U.S.A.

PREFACE

EUROPE SINCE NAPOLEON is an attempt to provide a history in which factual detail is subordinated to interpretation. Those facts not integrally vital have been cast aside, and events have been so interlocked as to endow men and movements with a consistent unity.

The rise of the middle classes, the bourgeoisie, to dominance over western Europe has been made the theme of this book. For today the bourgeoisie rule the world,— its governmental, economic, social, cultural, and religious activities. This middle-class system was definitely established during the latter half of the nineteenth century, but it was rising in influence many years before, most strikingly after the close of the Napoleonic wars in 1815. Therefore this volume begins with that date. Inasmuch as the new order has experienced since 1870 the greatest change, that period has been given relatively more space than the early one. Imperialism, the expansion of the bourgeois ideal, the international anarchy which culminated in the World War, the world conflict itself, the post-war reaction, and the great depression,— all these, therefore, have been given special emphasis. For similar reasons the narrative is not confined to Europe but extends to the continents which the bourgeois civilization has gradually engulfed,— Asia, Africa, Australia, and the Americas.

A textbook of such a general nature can make no pretense to any high degree of originality. It is hoped, however, that a freshness of approach will be found in this volume. Nowhere else, it is believed, is the theme of bourgeois influence so sharply and continuously stressed. Not to be found in most similar histories, too, are such full treatments of the rise of the bourgeoisie in the Americas, Pope Pius IX, the diplomatic background of the World War, and the revolt of Asia as appear in this.

My indebtedness extends to so many authorities that it would be impracticable to print an exhaustive list. Many of them, however, will be found in the bibliographical appendixes at the end of the work.

Responsibility for the general plan of this book and for the views expressed is assumed by me. In the preparation of the volume, however, Mr. Graham is responsible for a major part of the material found in Chapters XXIII–XXV, XXXI–XXXIX.

To those persons who aided in the preparation of this work an expression of appreciation is due. Professors Herbert Eugene Bolton and James Westfall Thompson of the University of California and Professor William H. Poytress of San Jose State College proffered excellent suggestions. Mr. Victor Norman and Mr. Theodore Ginsburg read the manuscript and proof, and gave valuable assistance in improving the matter and style. Miss Mary Ross, Mr. Frederick A. Rice, Mr. Edward Willis, and Mr. Harry Smulowitz read various parts and made pertinent criticisms. Mr. Bernerd Weber aided in some of the mechanical work of preparing the manuscript. Finally, a word of gratitude is extended to the publishers for their more than usual coöperation in preparing the book for publication.

FRANKLIN C. PALM

BERKELEY, CALIFORNIA

CONTENTS

PART V. THE RISE OF INDUSTRIAL POWERS, 1878–1914

PART VI. IMPERIALISM: DIFFUSION OF WESTERN CIVILIZATION

PART VII. INTERNATIONAL ANARCHY

PART VIII. THE AFTERMATH: BOURGEOIS CONSERVATISM AND THE NEW REVOLUTION

LIST OF MAPS

EUROPE SINCE NAPOLEON

PART I. THE RISE OF THE MIDDLE CLASSES

CHAPTER I

The Founding of the New Order

THE Age of Bourgeois Achievement — such was the history of Europe in the century after Napoleon. During that period feudalism, still discernible on the political atlas, was obliterated by the superimposed engraving of a new and revolutionary formula of society, Capitalism. Chiseling the new order with sure strokes was a changed leadership: disregarded was the sovereignty of noble birth, praised was the dignity of position attained by self-enterprise; down went the surplice and the jeweled hilt, up rose the voice of the market place. The exit of Napoleon was the cue for the entrance of the middle classes. Feudal polity became capitalistic policy, the liege lord and serf became employer and employee, the reciprocal tradition of fealty in exchange for protection became the conception of labor and pay. And that the accomplishments of the new classes were of enduring excellence was truly attested, as we shall see, by the glorious

---

NOTE. STEAM TRANSPORTATION, *introduced in the first half of the nineteenth century, aided industrial development and the rise of the middle classes. The picture above is from an old print.*

3

material and cultural monuments of the nineteenth century. Across the map of Europe the moving finger of history traced the word *Bourgeoisie.*

Western bourgeois civilization was not a modern creation. It had its origins in the unrecorded past; in ancient times it attained momentum as it combined with Greek, Roman, and western Oriental cultures; in the medieval period it swept along Teutonic and Latin influences. By the seventeenth century this rapidly developing civilization reached its contemporary mold, "a form of culture of a sedentary population grouped around the state as a central institution, having a symbolic form of writing and an economic structure which makes fairly extensive use of the division of labor." Finally, in the last hundred years, Western civilization has expanded to pronounced supremacy with the hegemony of the middle classes and the triumph of capitalism.

The terms *bourgeoisie* and *middle classes* are used synonymously in this book. They refer to the commercial, industrial, and professional groups as distinguished from the nobility, the peasants, and the wage-earners. Today, however, the term *middle classes* is used in a different sense; it now applies more particularly to professional groups, farmers, small entrepreneurs, and at times even to high-salaried and skilled workers.

In the Middle Ages society had been divided into several main classes: ecclesiastics, lords, freemen, townsmen, and serfs. The first two were the privileged groups; they had the right to own property; at times they controlled nearly all the wealth of western Europe. Both were exempt from taxation, the churchmen justifying their immunity by the labor of saving souls, the nobles earning their freedom by protecting their dependents. Of the taxpaying classes, which included freemen and townsmen, the serfs were bound to the estate by feudal law. In return for devoting a part of their time in the service of their lord the serfs received the use of an allotted amount of land, from which they attempted to obtain a living for their families. Theirs was the privilege of making both ends meet — when they could.

The revival of commerce and industry and the rise of

towns were accompanied by social readjustments within the working classes. From the laborers emerged freemen, who bought and sold goods, owned ships, and made articles which they or others exchanged. Before long certain individuals possessed warehouses, boats, and stores. Hiring other men for wages, these petty capitalists developed business enterprises from which they derived considerable profits. Below them were the men they employed for wages, the artisans; above were the privileged groups who dominated the peasants and serfs. As long as agriculture remained the chief occupation, the landowning aristocrats ruled Western society. With the rapid development of commerce the way was prepared for their decline. By the nineteenth century the rising middle classes had usurped their supremacy and a new order supplanted the old.

Contributing to this change were a number of events. Of these the Crusades (1096–1291) were especially important. By bringing the West into contact with the luxuries and culture of the Orient and by weakening the nobility through the failure of many *The Rise of the Middle Classes* to return, the attempts to regain the Holy Land resulted in a decisive setback to the old order. Moreover, the trips to the East stimulated interest in material things. In time merchants developed a lucrative trade, carrying goods across northern Italy to the West and returning with other commodities to the East. Establishing towns and cities, the middle classes became strong enough to extract from their feudal lords charters which recognized their independence. Guilds, "associations of all persons living in a town engaged in a particular craft or trade," were formed. These organizations provided coöperative facilities for the development of medieval commerce. Meanwhile the numerous plagues, epidemics, and famines which afflicted Europe during the Middle Ages depleted the ranks of the privileged classes. Thus opportunities were afforded for influential members of the bourgeoisie to occupy positions of administrative importance.

The formation of strong monarchies also facilitated the rise of the business man. Eager to end the numerous wars, to abolish the many tariffs and tolls which hindered the development of commerce, and to see political and social order reestablished, he supported his king's attempts to extend the royal prerogative at the expense of feudal lords. As monarchs increased their power, they created armies and navies strong enough to protect traders on land and sea. Many of the rulers promoted economic development by maintaining peace, order, and security and by encouraging the growth of commerce and industry. Consequently the middle classes gladly supported the authority of the king and willingly paid increased taxes.

Another force which stimulated the growth of the bourgeoisie was the Commercial Revolution. The discovery of America and the remarkable development of trade and industry which new markets and resources opened up, together with the great influx of gold and silver into Europe, led to the establishment of the modern capitalistic system. Whereas in the Middle Ages most of the small supply of precious metals was held by the church, in the sixteenth and seventeenth centuries gold and silver became the common media of exchange. Barter virtually disappeared. Men by possessing precious metals were enabled, for example, to build warehouses and construct boats, by hiring workmen for wages. The number of persons engaging in various enterprises and securing their livelihood by wages in the form of gold and silver steadily increased. The Commercial Revolution resulted in a remarkable development of trade and industry. Trade in the everyday commodities of life began to displace the exchange of articles of luxury, which hitherto had held a dominant place in commerce. The increase of trade which followed paved the way for the rise of a powerful and ambitious class of business and professional men, capable of directing governments as well as business enterprises. Such wealthy houses as the Medici of Florence and the Welsers and Fuggers of Germany wielded great influence in the sixteenth century through their financial assistance to kings and scholars.

In a way the Renaissance, between the fourteenth and sixteenth centuries, was a bourgeois movement. Individualism and emphasis upon worldly things, bases of a middle-class régime, were fundamental reasons for the attempts of Renaissance men to imitate the ancients in art and in living. Wealthy individuals of that time, such as the Medici in Florence, took keen delight in becoming patrons of the learning which would sanction mundane rather than spiritual ways of living. "The Greeks and the Roman freemen enjoyed the material and sensual sides of life. Why should we not do likewise and develop a great materialistic civilization?"

Perhaps the theological warriors, who were chiefly responsible for the religious struggles of this period, thought they were attacking extreme worldliness when they assaulted Rome. Instead they provided a religious justification for the individualism and the materialism of the Renaissance. Martin Luther (1483–1546) preached religious individualism and advocated justification by faith rather than by sacramental observances; to him salvation was an affair between God and man. A later reformer, John Calvin (1509–1564), strengthened economic as well as religious individualism by his theory of predestination, which declared that some are saved and others doomed. His followers concluded that it remained for the individual to see that he was one of the elect and that this end could best be achieved by avoiding wickedness through carrying out the teachings of the Bible and engaging in hard work. Such action often resulted in the accumulation of wealth. Thus the test of salvation tended to become economic success as well as moral perfectibility.

The outstanding result of the Protestant Revolt was the subordination of religion to politics as a pivotal factor in social life. Henceforth the individual owed allegiance to the state as well as to the church. During the sixteenth and seventeenth centuries, as the influence of ecclesiastical authorities diminished, the power of absolute kings increased. Consequently a change occurred in the attitude of most men toward life. In medieval times religion had caused them to rely upon faith and rewards in the future world to compensate for the trials and tribulations in the present. The Protestant Revolt, in setting up the material standard as a means of preservation, enabled men to combine religious and economic salvation. Somewhat later the religious phase declined, business materialism becoming an end in itself. Then men began to emphasize the worldly side of their existence rather than the spiritual. A new standard for judging life had appeared, one which broke the backbone of medieval society. Any man could climb into the elect group through the acquisition of property. Existence on this earth became far more attractive as men began to appreciate and to strive for those things which make up the life abundant. Business, politics, and war emerged as the dominant interests.

These changes soon undermined the old feudal society. More and more the nobles and clergy found it difficult to defend their temporal privileges. Where formerly they had had certain responsibilities which justified their claims to exemption from taxes, the rise of the absolute monarchy deprived the nobles of the right to protect the peasants. Thereafter many of them degenerated into courtiers, little better than parasites, living on the bounty of kings. Capable rulers, such as Louis XIV (1643–1715), often preferred to select able business leaders rather than nobles as their ministers, for these men knew how to promote the economic development of the state. Adopting the mercantilistic view that treasure was a prime source of power, they tried to increase the supply by regulating and subsidizing agriculture, commerce, industry, and colonial expansion. But the old order was not adapted to a capitalist régime. Three defects and abuses present in absolute monarchy — feudal society, paternalism, and mercantilism — aroused much criticism.

The Idea of Progress

By the eighteenth century an iconoclastic revolt developed against the old system. Such seventeenth-century scientists as Descartes, Newton, and Bacon and such eighteenth-century publicists as Voltaire, Rousseau, and Adam Smith led the opposition. Through their research, they evolved a scientific method and a philosophical point of view which tended to weaken the bases not only of the privileged classes, but also of the absolute government itself. Affirming a belief in social progress, many of them asserted that the decadent absolute monarchies and the degenerate feudalism would have to give way to a new order. They advanced the "natural-law concept" and denounced the theory of divine right, social inequalities, and religious intolerance.

Notable thinkers of the past had prepared the way for the general acceptance of this concept of mutual growth. Roger Bacon in the thirteenth century and Bodin, Francis Bacon, Descartes, and Newton in the sixteenth and seventeenth centuries had "indirectly called attention to the idea of progress as a guiding principle in seeking solutions for the difficult problems which were harassing the minds of men." The rise of this progressive idea, however, is in a large measure an account of the middle-class struggle for ascendancy in the state, in which was disregarded the idea of providence, — the basis of the aristocratically organized society of the Middle Ages. In its place was substituted the belief in growth, which "included the gradual enlightenment of man's nature, the evolution of his intelligence, the expansion of his moral sense, and the improvement of his well-being."

Influenced by this view, men first strove for intellectual and religious liberty, later for political rights, and eventually for economic freedom. A series of upheavals resulted from the attempts of the bourgeoisie to realize these aims. The middle classes were largely responsible for the sixteenth-century religious wars, the Civil War (1642–1649) and the Glorious Revolution (1688) in England, and revolutions in America in 1776 and in France in 1789. Desirous of well-being, the middle classes fostered the conception of the dignity of the individual as achieved through self-determination and self-expression. This assumption was primarily utilitarian, an outgrowth of the Puritan idea that an individual should mold his own destiny. The inevitable result was the acceptance of the idea of success, measured in commercial enterprise and in the attainment of economic liberty.

In adopting this concept of progress men were at first cosmopolitan. They did not think in terms of national entities. According to intellectuals, such as Kant and Schiller, humanity would be benefited by obedience to the dictates of social expediency; thereby man in the future would enter upon his rightful heritage and enjoy the inalienable rights of life, liberty, and the pursuit of happiness. These beliefs spread rapidly and were highly characteristic of the middle classes. Art, science, and literature, religion and politics, the family and the state, — all were examined by the interpreters of social progress with a view to bringing them into conformity with the new thought. The middle classes presently discovered that they could not extend their business interests properly as long as the numerous regulations which maintained the old order remained. Reaching the conclusion that economic factors dominated all aspects of earthly existence, they believed that political, social, economic, religious, and intellectual institutions and beliefs which stood in the way of economic advancement should be modified or abolished. Opposition to the barrier of classes became more pronounced. The destruction of social inequalities and the creation of an ideal civil society became one of their chief aims. Thus they hoped to supplant the old régime through the development of national governments under their control.

As bitter opponents of the established order the business men accepted suggestions which would enable them to gain their ends. They welcomed, therefore, the ideas of an eighteenth-century English economist, Adam Smith (1723–1790). In 1776 he published the *Wealth of Nations*, which soon became their economic bible. Maintaining that the true strength of a nation lay in the prosperity of its citizens, Smith contended that unrestricted enterprise promoted the accumulation of riches by the individual. In direct opposition to mercantilism he asserted that restrictions were useless and even harmful: each man knew best how to acquire wealth; and if he were permitted to adopt a policy of self-interest, the nation would become rich. The individual, therefore, should be allowed freedom in business, unhampered by governmental regulation. This *laissez faire* doctrine, as it was called, constituted the expression of economic liberty.

The Doctrine of Laissez Faire

Smith, however, merely expressed an idea which arose out of many intellectual streams of thought. From the theologians came the doctrine that there was no need for the state to interfere in everyday life. From the political teachings of Locke and Rousseau emanated the belief that the state had no right to intervene in economic matters. The French Physiocrats even maintained that it was inexpedient for the government to become involved in business affairs.

Everywhere the commercial classes welcomed these principles. Many property-owners also joined in their support. In France the peasants enthusiastically backed a movement to overthrow those feudal restrictions which prevented them from selling grain in the highest market. Turgot (1727–1781), who inspired some of Smith's ideas, was an outstanding exponent of individualism, claiming that all regulations should be removed from agriculture as well as industry. Certain publicists even went so far as to assert that governmental interference was not only unwise but immoral. Man had natural rights, which it was criminal to deny. Every individual, for example, had the right to make money, unhampered by political and social restrictions. At the same time private property was sacred and inviolable. Thus the bourgeois philosophy justified the accumulation of riches by an individual. No rules or regulations should stand in the way of a man engaged in the production of wealth. Once wealth was in his possession, no one should have the right to deprive him of it against his will.

There was a danger to capitalism in the whole-hearted acceptance of individualism. The workers soon announced that these so-called rights included that of possessing employment and of receiving an increased share of the fruits of their labor. Thereupon the employers invoked the concept of "natural laws" to defend their position against the laborers. According to this philosophy, inasmuch as natural physical laws had been formulated for the movements of the stars, the planets, and in fact all forms of nature, did it not follow that certain natural laws should determine social conditions? Natural laws explained why certain nations and individuals were wealthy and others poor. Poverty would always exist. If poor men were given larger wages, they would have larger families and more mouths to feed; then poverty would persist. Man-made regulations, maintained the orthodox advocate of this philosophy, could not overcome the law of supply and demand. It was a natural law. But then how could wage-earners be saved from poverty if some were predestined to be rich and others poor? The exponents of *laissez faire* left the solution to the individual. Bourgeois individualism made economic salvation possible through the practice of thrift, self-denial, and hard work. Other things being equal, a man who followed these precepts could enter the paradise of the middle classes. If by cleverness, shrewdness, or good luck he obtained a large share of the wealth of a nation, then as a rich man he was entitled to a place in a special section of paradise reserved for moneyed aristocrats.

At first, economic liberty was designed in theory to benefit all deserving men. Later, in the nineteenth century, the capitalists, in exploiting the wage-earners, used this idea to justify their opposition to state legislation on behalf of the workers. Antagonized, the latter criticized the middle classes and denounced an individualism which seemingly fostered social and economic inequalities. In its stead many laborers favored socialism, anarchism, and other doctrines, agitating for a new order instead of modification of the old.

Early political and economic theories were but manifestations of the rise and domination of the middle classes. A *Economic Revolutions* Technological Revolution, by which the apparently unlimited productive power of steam, electricity, and chemical processes transformed the life of the people, made possible this great social phenomenon of the last two centuries.

In 1769 James Watt secured the first patent for a steam engine. There soon followed locomotives, steamboats, and engines in factories. Meanwhile, "from the workshop and the laboratory the discoveries of the mind were carried to the four corners of the earth." By the side of feudal lords and kings, who had ruled Europe since the fall of Rome, appeared business men — new competitors. Increasing in number, wealth, and power because of the Technological Revolution and the factory system, by 1815 they were "ready to become the real directors of the political and economic drama."

With this transformation brought about by technology came a complete change in the system of economy. The feudal régime disappeared. In place of a social structure in which the status or occupation of each individual had been determined by birth and law, and under which production was carried on to meet immediate needs, or for local exchange at a "just price," there arose the new system of production known as *capitalism*. This term does not mean capital goods, such as wines, machinery, and railways, nor is it synonymous with *manufacturing*, for it also includes the whole scheme of agricultural economy. It is not, moreover, restricted to machine industry, having begun to flourish before machinery had come into extensive use in the production of goods. Capitalism may be considered as a system of production in which the primary concern is profit for the entrepreneur. Unlike primitive agriculture and handicraft, which produced for local use or exchange at a just price, capitalism produces to sell on the most advantageous terms, that is, with the maximum amount of profit to the owners. The scope of its operations seems almost unlimited. Indeed, under the capitalistic system the volume of goods turned out, the amount of wealth accumulated, the number of men and women employed, would seem to be capable of almost unlimited expansion. It *Capitalism* was this system which facilitated the rise of the middle classes during the nineteenth century.

Two important developments insured the supremacy of the capitalistic system. These were the Agricultural and the Industrial Revolutions, both resulting largely from the technological transformation.

Before these two revolutions the economic life of the world for many centuries had been much the same. Great movements such as the Renaissance and the Commercial Revolution had not seriously modified the daily life of the common man. Indeed, the unsurpassed achievements of the Renaissance artists, the ~~beginnings~~ of modern science, and the establishment of Christian sects in the sixteenth century did not drastically affect his daily existence. On the continent the feudal régime in the country and the guild in the towns, although both were decadent, still dominated his life.

During the early modern period the desire for luxuries such as tea, coffee, sugar, spices, jewels, and tobacco led to the creation of great trading companies and the rise of commercial states. Such concerns as the Dutch, the English, and the French East India companies struggled to obtain the lion's share of the products of the East. In the Americas, Europeans established monopolies and attempted to secure the support and protection of their governments. Home states became interested in overseas possessions not merely as sources of raw materials but also because of the markets which they afforded for European goods. By granting financial aid to trading companies, by establishing regulations directed against their competitors, and by engaging in colonial wars nations tried to control and to increase their colonies. During the seventeenth and eighteenth centuries the leading powers in western Europe fought for overseas possessions. Trade increased, although it was small compared to that of the present.

Down to the middle of the eighteenth century, only small-scale manufacturing existed. Under the guild system, which predominated throughout the Middle Ages, production, not extensive as yet, was carried on in small groups. A master gathered around him a band of craftsmen and apprentices "who were all employed together in the friendly operation of a common workshop." By the fifteenth and sixteenth centuries a different type of organization appeared in certain industries. This new kind of industrial order was called the domestic or putting-out system. It "involved the intervention of a capitalist or organizer between craftsman and consumer — a man who owned the raw materials, and often the tools, hired the workmen for wages and made his living by marketing the goods at a profit."

Under the domestic system there were no large factories,

such as existed in the early twentieth century, employing hundreds or thousands of men. Nearly all articles of daily use, including clothing, were manufactured around the fireside. Certain goods were made to sell. For example, a man with capital might own the materials and tools with which to make cloth. Knowing where to obtain the raw products and where to dispose of the finished articles, and with capital to buy the former, he could parcel the work out to families, pay them wages, and later sell the finished product to the consumer. In some parts of Europe there were weavers who, owning tools and materials, worked in their own cottages and disposed of the goods which they produced to merchants in markets. The latter either sold or exported such commodities.

The gradual development of urban life which accompanied the moderate increase of commerce and of industry did not modify Western society to any extent; for agriculture was still the chief occupation, and on the farm one found less change than in the city. The peasant generally raised enough to supply his family and to pay his dues and taxes as his ancestors had done for centuries. Some farmers, however, developed a desire for luxuries, and in order to earn money for these things they had to raise a surplus of wheat or some other commodity to sell. Though a small amount of trade developed, the position of the average peasant was little changed by 1750. In many parts of Europe he was still a serf, dependent upon his lord. Usually, in the eighteenth century, he was isolated, primarily because of the difficulties of traveling: bad roads, river tolls, and highway robbers.

By the middle of the eighteenth century certain developments caused the breakdown of this isolation. Between 1750 and 1800 population increased at a remarkable rate, because of the increase of the food supply and the decrease of the death rate. The latter was attributable partly to a number of medical discoveries, as, for example, vaccination for smallpox (1796), and partly to a renewed interest in the problem of health. Better sanitary conditions, more comfortable modes of dress, and the decreasing aversion toward baths were all conducive to an extension of the average life. More people

made necessary a further increase in the production of food as well as in the expansion of trade and industry. Soon the need became urgent for greater production of necessities of life. The Agricultural and Industrial Revolutions, first gaining a hold in England, furnished the solution for a situation which threatened to become acute.

The growth of population, especially in the towns and cities of England, brought about an increased demand for food and changed the self-supporting farms into "factories of bread and meat." This occurred during the latter part of the eighteenth century and resulted from the Agricultural Revolution, which had two important phases: a reform in methods and the establishment of a new system of land tenure.

The Agrarian Revolution

Before the eighteenth century agricultural processes had changed very little. For centuries it had been the custom to sow seeds broadcast. This was a wasteful method, as many seeds failed to take root and others were too close together to grow. In the middle of the eighteenth century the invention of the drill, which deposited seeds in straight furrows with sufficient space between to assure growth, increased a farmer's potential wheat crop. Study of soils also resulted in the introduction of clovers into the rotation of crops, because these were found to add atmospheric nitrogen to the soil. By this improved rotation, which changed the crops each year in a four-year cycle, the farmer was able to use all his land without impoverishing it.

The introduction of artificial fertilizers was a step forward. Manure had long been used to restore the fertility of exhausted soil. In the nineteenth century science produced artificial means of nurturing exhausted or poor soils. These, together with irrigation and drainage, increased not only the crops but also the extent of the lands upon which products could be successfully raised.

Scientific methods were applied to other phases of farm life. Careful breeding improved cattle. The increased number and size of domestic animals were important, inasmuch as men remained meat-eaters despite the gain in population. Farm

tools were improved. In the eighteenth century the drill, the horse hoe, and the threshing machine were invented. A climax in agrarian development was reached when the famous Bell reaper appeared in 1826. These various machines revolutionized agriculture.

This agricultural revolution completely changed the English landowning system. For centuries most farmers had owned or rented lands consisting of strips located in various parts of local estates. This situation made it difficult for the great landowners to introduce the new methods of farming and stock-raising. Therefore, aided by Parliamentary support, they gradually took over the land which had been tilled by the peasants. They then consolidated and inclosed their holdings and proceeded to drain and fertilize the soil, rotate crops, and introduce careful breeding of cattle and sheep. The small farmer suffered as a result of the inclosure movement. Frequently he could not show clear title to his strips and was forced off the land. Moreover, he often was too poor to purchase tools, farm buildings, seeds, and stock. Giving up his property he became a worker in the factories, or a landless agricultural laborer. Meanwhile he could voice his discontent only in such ballads as:

> The law locks up the man or woman
> Who steals the goose from off the common;
> But leaves the greater villain loose
> Who steals the common from the goose.

The great landlord, however, with sufficient capital, was able to create farms capable of utilizing the new methods of agriculture.

This reorganization of agriculture played an important part in the development of capitalistic farming. New scientific methods and machinery enabled the proprietors to get along with a reduced number of hired laborers, to increase their crops, and to become wealthy. At the same time the agricultural revolution inflicted but a temporary hardship on most of the peasants. Without land many of them flocked to the cities looking for work. This they secured; for an increased supply of labor helped to make possible another revolution in England, more important, so far as the rise of the new régime was concerned, than the changes in agriculture, — the Industrial Revolution.

With the increase in population, in food, and in goods, the middle-class men enjoyed a higher standard of living. But still they were not satisfied. They desired *The Industrial Revolution* more varied foods, better clothes, and more beautiful buildings. The lower classes too developed more wants. They demanded more substantial food, and cotton and linen clothing. Expanding markets led to increased trade; and increased trade, to an urge for better highways and faster transportation. The result was the Industrial Revolution.

This upheaval, which later spread to the Continent, originated in England for certain definite reasons. In the first place, Englishmen — living on an island and involved in the political, territorial, and military problems of Europe only when their interests were at stake — were able to concentrate on economic affairs. Furthermore, they were less hampered in their commercial and industrial undertakings by political authority than were the Europeans. The middle classes and the landowners obtained virtual control over the government in the seventeenth century and were in a position to develop their economic interests without interference. Moreover, England, an insular kingdom, had been interested in trade by sea for centuries. She possessed a merchant marine, an overseas empire, and facilities for banking and investment. With gold, abundant raw materials, and available markets she had the necessary foundations upon which to construct a great industrial state.

The demand for goods increased during the revolutionary period on the Continent (1789–1815), as industry there was at a standstill. Consequently England had a virtual monopoly of markets. In fact, while Napoleon was trying to ruin British manufacture and trade by the blockade system, he enabled England to become the only nation capable of furnishing food, clothes, and supplies to her allies as well as to her enemies.

Although deficient in timber, England had the iron and coal needed in industrial expansion. She also had a damp climate, favorable for the manufacture of textiles. Moreover, as stated before, the eviction of tenants from the lands provided England with the labor supply required for mechanical work. These factors created not merely the urge to manufacture but more than that — the need to discover some way of producing more goods than men were able to make by hand. Englishmen during this period turned to machinery for increased production, instituting the great transition from man power to machine power.

Human energy could not hope to do the work of the mechanical devices which were soon enthroned in the realm of industry. Spinning-machines to make yarn, run by water power and later by steam, facilitated an increased output of manufactured goods. With the development of mechanical power came factories, making possible the production of greater quantities of goods in huge shops instead of in private homes as under the domestic system. Arkwright, called the father of the factory system, not only used machines but anticipated contemporaneous specialization by having men work in factories on particular phases of the production of certain articles.

A marked gain in the output of manufactured goods was the result of the discipline and supervision of men in factories. Indeed the factory, whether worked by steam power or water power, constituted the early phase of the Industrial Revolution. To it may be ascribed the greatly increased production, first of woolen, cotton, and iron goods, and later of most other manufactured articles, the necessities and luxuries of today. The utilization of steam power did not result merely in the development of factories and the increased output of manufactured articles; it also made goods cheaper, increased the demand, and revolutionized transportation and communication.

Of all the inventions of the nineteenth century perhaps the most dramatic was the railroad. As early as the reign of Charles I of England (1625–1649) wagons had been drawn on tracks by horses. But the discovery of the steam engine caused a number of men to contemplate the construction of a locomotive which would take the place of horses on public vehicles. George Stephenson, convinced that this idea was feasible, built a steam engine capable of drawing a wagon on a track at the "tremendous speed" of ten miles an hour. By 1830 he was ready to give his locomotive a real test. The Liverpool and Manchester Railway was opened, and his engine, the *Rocket*, drawing the first train, made almost thirty miles an hour. This "rapid trip" marked the beginning of a transportation system which closely linked the city and country. Eventually the spread of these steel bands became a powerful factor in promoting national consolidation. Furthermore, the steamship carried on where the railroads left off. Owing to the work of Robert Fulton and others in the first part of the nineteenth century, steam came to be utilized to propel ships.

The rise of the factory system and the invention of the locomotive, the steamship, and the telegraph changed the whole face of the world. Producers and consumers, living thousands of miles apart, were brought close together. Business men were able to communicate with each other quickly, and they built factories, developed mines, and exchanged goods with increasing rapidity. Invaded by these eager generals of industry with their armies of workers, small country villages became large industrial cities in a few years. A verse from a comic song of 1828 on the growth of Birmingham, England, describes this change :

> I remember one John Growse,
>   A buckle-maker in Brummagem :
> He built himself a country house,
>   To be out of the smoke of Brummagem :
> But though John's country house stands still,
> The town itself has walked up hill,
> Now he lives beside of a smoky mill,
>   In the middle of the streets of Brummagem.[1]

[1] J. A. Langford, *A Century of Birmingham Life*, Vol. II, pp. 524–525 (James Dobbs, " I can't find Brummagem ").

But the Industrial Revolution did more than change the appearance of Brummagem. It insured the rule of the middle classes and the rise of the common man. The first steps in this direction were taken in the eighteenth century. At that time institutions *The Rise of the Un-privileged Classes* protected royalty, nobility, clergy, and, in the city republics, the ruling bourgeois aristocracy — groups which at the most never exceeded 10 per cent of the total population. Usually the law or custom saw to it that families retained large estates and lucrative government posts and handed them down to their eldest sons. Legislation also prohibited the division of lands or of property, thus providing legal machinery to insure the survival of large estates; for upon this depended the privileged position of the nobles. All members of a nobleman's family were favored. The estate went to the eldest son; the younger sons received offices in the army, the government, or the church. Kings, nobles, clergy, and bourgeois aristocrats virtually possessed a monopoly of property and of offices. Legally other people had few rights. Feudal law, Roman law, and church law all recognized the privileges of the man higher up.

At no time in the modern period, however, were the lower classes absolutely destitute of certain rights and liberties. As far back as Anglo-Saxon England one discovers that many commoners had political and legal prerogatives in their hundred courts and in their courts of the shire. The period of strong government which followed the Norman conquest of England in 1066 diminished the prestige of these institutions. Nevertheless, they did not disappear. Some became a recognized part of the common law, and as such could not be abolished.

In the seventeenth century the attempts of the Stuart kings to override the common law and to disregard the rights and privileges of Englishmen proved unsuccessful. In fact, a successful alliance of traders and landowners against these despotic rulers culminated in the "Glorious Revolution" of 1688. As a result of this popular victory the rights of Englishmen were not only confirmed legally but also extended.

Certain classes, notably the great landowners and traders, thenceforth played an important rôle in English national politics. Through their representatives in Parliament they virtually selected their rulers and defined "the rights of Parliament to control taxation, the army, and its own proceedings." This political change marked a definite stage in the rise of the new régime.

A further step in the direction of social democracy was taken when, in 1776, a new American republic of the thirteen revolting colonies was established. Upsetting English political and economic control, the colonists created a government under which all men were free and equal politically and socially. This victory effectively terminated the possibility of an old régime in the Americas. Little did the crowned heads of Europe realize that the American uprising was but the first of a series of revolutions which would sweep away the vestiges of the old system and replace it with a new order directed by the bourgeoisie.

The French Revolution, however, with its dynamic principles Liberty, Fraternity, and Equality, soon disillusioned and soured many moderate reformers. Alarmed at its destructive tendencies and stunned by its excesses, they made ineffectual attempts to check it. Despite their opposition the genius of the Revolutionary leaders, particularly of Napoleon Bonaparte, resulted in a decisive defeat of the old régime.

During the Revolution (1789–1799) a new political and social order began to evolve in France. Ability rather than birth became the prerequisite to individual advancement. (A commoner might become a bishop, a judge, an officer, or a government official.) After the abolition of primogeniture all heirs shared equally in the father's estate. The privileges of guilds were obliterated; no longer were certain trades monopolized by a few families. Moreover, the secularization of church property and the reduction of church revenues prevented a religious career from being a haven for the younger sons of nobles who sought lucrative offices. Henceforth the church of God was not a feudal institution with a privileged clergy composed chiefly of representatives of the nobility. All classes in

France were equal — legally, politically, and socially. The chief inequality was that of wealth.

The disintegration of large estates, both lay and ecclesiastical, during the Revolution brought into existence thousands of small farms, whose owners constituted the majority of the population of France. As property-owners and beneficiaries of the Revolutionary reforms the latter became stanch advocates of the political, social, and legal changes brought about by the Revolution. Later, however, as conservative landowners, they resisted all attempts to carry the idea of equality to its logical end — common ownership of property. Instead, the peasantry supported the middle classes in opposing both the reactionary efforts to restore the old régime and the socialist movements which they believed would deprive them of their holdings. In other words, France, the land of small property-owners, became the bulwark of the bourgeois system as a result of the Revolution. Subsequent revolutions merely served to confirm the supremacy of the middle classes and the emancipation of the peasantry.

In France attempts were made during the early part of the Revolution to establish universal suffrage and thus to attain true political equality. The propertied classes, however, fearful of the proletariat, succeeded in thwarting such a democratic tendency. Nevertheless the Declaration of the Rights of Man, drafted by the French National Assembly in August, 1789, recognized complete manhood suffrage as a fundamental right.

The Revolutionary principles, with their emphasis upon individualism, led to higher standards and rewards for personal efficiency and talent. More and more statesmen, generals, and diplomats came from the lower ranks of society. Before the revolutions they never could have hoped to rise, whereas now they could even aspire to be kings and world-conquerors. A product of the French Revolution, the bourgeois Napoleon I, as head of the French state, sought to create a great empire in which men, though denied political liberty, should enjoy legal equality, and in which careers should be determined by talent. The geographical location of France, together with a series of other obstructive factors, made it

impossible for Napoleon to realize his ideas. In his attempts
to dominate the Continent and to create a world empire he
encountered the opposition of the greater part of Europe.
The disastrous invasion of Russia (1812) and the defeats of
Leipzig (1813) and Waterloo (1815) finally doomed the Napoleonic scheme.

Nevertheless the Revolutionary principles survived. For a
while they encountered strong opposition in Europe. There
the old régime was still firmly intrenched. Moreover, the
French Revolution, with its violence, bloodshed, and confusion, created at first a feeling of panic. To many the old régime
stood for law and order; the introduction of new beliefs meant
chaos and anarchy. To them the attacks upon the Church
signified the establishment of a "Godless Age"; and they
concluded that the French Revolution had resulted in little
or nothing except blood and misery. Reactionary writers
strengthened this opinion by emphasizing the Reign of Terror
and by ignoring the beneficial results of the Revolution. After
1815, determined aristocrats, alarmed over the violent consequences of the Revolution, bitterly opposed its spread. Believing that the Revolutionary ideals had advanced too far
in Europe, they desired to retain at least the *status quo* and
to return in so far as possible to the "good old days." Such
was the attitude of most conservative statesmen in 1815,
especially of their leader, Prince Metternich of Austria.

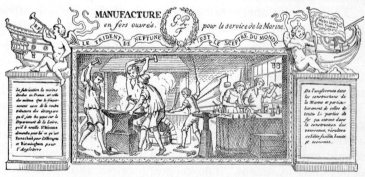

An Iron Manufacturer's Card, *taken from an early engraved advertisement*

CHAPTER II

The World in 1815

OUR world of today is an economic unit. We are dependent upon lands thousands of miles away for many things which we eat and wear; we have interests in those regions in the form of investments, farms, industries, and mines. The telegraph, the radio, the airplane, and the steamship have made neighbors of peoples who a century ago would have been strangers. News of a disaster, a revolution, or a war spreads rapidly, and the repercussions may be felt throughout the entire world.

A hundred years ago conditions were very different. Much of the world had not been explored by civilized man. Southern and central Africa were still the "black spots" of a dark continent. Slave-traders visited the western coast, where they established small trading posts; and sailors, on their trips around the Cape of Good Hope, occasionally stopped at the remote Dutch settlement there. The forbidding coasts, the inaccessible jungles, the extreme heat,— all prevented the white men from establishing permanent homes. Only black tribes were able to flourish in such an environment.

Economically and politically the shores of northern Africa in 1815 belonged much more to Europe than to Africa. Scarcely anywhere else in the world do the *Africa in 1815* lands around an inland sea form so definite a unity as those about the Mediterranean. North Africa, isolated from the rest of the continent by the Sahara Desert, has always been connected with the countries of southern Europe. For centuries there have been close relationships between Syria, the Balkan Peninsula, Italy, Spain, and Africa from Egypt to Morocco. The split which divided these regions into Moslem and Christian religious creeds could not destroy this geographical unity. In the early Middle Ages the followers of

25

Mohammed crossed from north Africa into Spain and southern France, where they tried to establish their culture in western Europe. During the Crusades the Christians became the aggressors. They too failed in their efforts to dominate the Mediterranean world. In 1798 Napoleon made an unsuccessful attempt to utilize Egypt as the starting-point of a French empire which should extend to the Orient. After 1815, however, most European states were inclined to neglect north Africa. Nevertheless certain law-abiding citizens, especially in France, retained an interest in this region because of the fertility of the lands and the existence of good harbors. Their interest was also kept alive by the piratical princes who had established their lairs in Algiers, Tunis, and other points along the coast. These pirates laid waste the shores of Spain and of Italy and continually endangered the safety of commerce throughout the Mediterranean. "Even Napoleon at Elba trembled at the thought of attacks by Corsairs." Many years were to elapse before the European conquest would terminate the activities of these marauders of north Africa.

For centuries the Orient had been the goal of European missionaries, traders, and adventurers. In 1815, however, *Asia in 1815* most of Asia was extremely remote or practically unknown. Asia Minor and the regions along the African and Asiatic shores of the Mediterranean Sea belonged to the Sultan of Turkey. In the Middle East, Persia and Afghanistan (backward countries ruled by Moslem dynasts) were almost inaccessible to Westerners. The confines of central Asia were virtually impenetrable. In the Far East, China and Japan were practically closed to foreigners, European ships being allowed to touch only at the Chinese port of Canton. Europe never lost interest in the enigmatical Orient. Before the nineteenth century the construction of a canal between the Mediterranean and the Red Sea to provide a short water route to the East had been considered. For lack of a shorter route, traders from western Europe, in their quest for the much-sought goods of the Orient, were eagerly and continually venturing forth on long and stormy trips around Africa.

In 1815 the English and the Dutch were the important colonial powers in Asia. They possessed virtually a monopoly of the trade routes between the two continents. The English had the right of way in India and Australia, and the Dutch owned important islands in the East Indies. Russians also were expanding in Asia, the absence of a natural boundary in the east facilitating penetration. Long before 1815 they had pushed across to the Pacific, establishing numerous settlements on the cold Siberian plains. Russia was a huge, shifting empire, partly European and partly Asiatic, a human avalanche threatening to slide either way.

Turning to the New World, one discovers a unique situation. Western Europe was losing its grip on the Americas. England had relinquished the thirteen colonies; France had sold her empire in Louisiana; and a series of revolutions was depriving Spain of her vast overseas possessions in the New World.

The New World in 1815

In the Americas the peoples were assuming a new attitude toward their respective countries. Separated from Europe by the broad Atlantic Ocean, in possession of vast fertile lands and untold mineral wealth, the inhabitants as a whole demanded the right to grow without European interference. Their desire for independence showed itself not only in the revolt of the thirteen colonies but also in revolutionary movements in Canada and Hispanic America. These upheavals checked European expansion in the Western Hemisphere and eventually resulted in independence for most of the revolting colonies.

In short, Europe's contact with other continents in 1815 consisted primarily in the control and regulation of trade. Some military expeditions were sent to more backward regions, but these were aimed chiefly at the protection of commerce rather than at the establishment of political dependencies. Europeans were interested in colonies only as places where they could obtain products which, on account of unfavorable conditions, could not be produced in Europe. The need for markets, for opportunities for the investment of surplus capital, and for land upon which to settle surplus populations was not yet strong enough to result in the Europeanization of the world.

The French Revolution and the Napoleonic period brought about important changes in the relative importance of colonial empires. During the preceding centuries vari-

Colonial Empires in 1815

ous naval powers had struggled for supremacy in the Americas, Africa, and Asia. By 1815, however, England had taken possession of a large part of the French colonial empire and had deprived the Dutch and the Spanish of much of their commercial power and most of their strategic trading-stations. Mistress of the seas, she was now in a position to create the largest empire in history. She had rivals, however. Russia planned to enlarge her already extensive empire in Asia. The United States threatened to dominate the Americas. France was soon to fix her eyes again on north Africa. Nevertheless, England, through her control of the seas, of Gibraltar, of Canada, of Capetown, of India, as well as of important lands in the Pacific, possessed a decisive advantage over all her rivals. As long as she could retain her superiority and at the same time maintain the balance of power in Europe, commercial, industrial, and colonial supremacy was hers.

Although in 1815 England was the dominant world power, the old spirit of aggressive imperialism seemed on the wane. Many of her citizens questioned the value of colonies, asserting that they were liabilities. "We defy anyone," wrote J. R. McCulloch in the *Edinburgh Review* (1825), "to point out a single benefit, of any sort whatever, derived by us from the possession of Canada, and our colonies in North America. They are productive of heavy expense to Great Britain, but of nothing else." In 1828 Benjamin Disraeli, in his *Voyage of Captain Popanilla*, described the discovery of an uninhabited island consisting of a bare rock. Its fortification was ordered immediately; a president and council, a bishop, a judge, and an agent for dealing with the original inhabitants were appointed. Why, asked Captain Popanilla, was this small rock crammed "full of clerks, soldiers, lawyers and priests?" The guide replied, "I am the last man in the world to answer ques-

tions, but I believe we call it the colonial system." The loss
of the thirteen colonies and her own remarkable industrial
development, accompanied by serious social and economic
problems, were partly responsible for the decline in Great
Britain of interest in her colonies.

Lack of attention to imperial activities in the early nineteenth century was primarily due to the fact that ownership of
colonies was a mercantilistic survival out of harmony with the
needs of a nation unable to supply its expanding internal consumption. Only after England had exhausted its home markets and had partly solved its internal problems was imperialism revived. Then, as we shall see, colonies were acquired in
order that the mother country might obtain markets, raw
materials, places to invest capital, and resources necessary for
the continued expansion of its capitalistic structure.

Neither were the Continental powers especially interested
in colonies at this time. They were preoccupied with international politics and domestic problems. Previously the leading countries had attempted to enlarge and consolidate their
territories and at the same time to expand overseas. During the administrations of Henry IV, of Richelieu, and of
Louis XIV, in early modern France, the frontiers had been
pushed to the Pyrenees Mountains, the Alps, the Spanish
Netherlands, and toward the Rhine. Meanwhile a French
empire was established in Asia and in the New World. During
the eighteenth century most of these overseas acquisitions
were lost. Later, Napoleon, continuing the territorial policies
of his predecessors, acquired for France her natural frontier,
the Rhine, and planned the establishment of a magnificent
world empire. In his attempts to achieve these ends he overturned the balance of power, fought the leading nations in
Europe, including England, but was himself eventually overthrown. Despite these reverses France remained a powerful
state. In the early nineteenth century she was the one Mediterranean power able to create an empire. Spain, in the
process of losing the greater part of her domain, had sunk to
the level of a third-rate nation, and Portugal was practically
a satellite of England. Italy was merely "a geographical

expression," since the nation was split up into small states, of which many were under foreign control.

The Napoleonic wars did not permanently modify the status of all the small nations of Europe. In the Alps the Swiss people, speaking French, Italian, or German, man-

Europe in 1815

aged to preserve the independence which they had won centuries before. Across from England the Dutch, the Danes, and the Swedes remained free peoples.

Both Belgians and Norwegians, however, were placed under foreign control. Like their Dutch neighbors, the Belgians were separated from the British Isles by a narrow body of water. They were also not far distant from Paris, the capital of their powerful neighbor to the south. Long the object of international rivalries, Belgium had been ruled successively by Spaniards, Austrians, and French. In 1815, however, Great Britain was determined to remove Belgium from the hands of the great states. To achieve this end Belgium and Holland were united so as to present strong opposition to French ambitions. The diplomats of Europe hoped thereby to checkmate France and to maintain the balance of power. Similarly, Norway was subjected to foreign rule. She was taken from Denmark, which had supported Napoleon, and handed over to Sweden as a reward for the latter's assistance against the French conqueror.

By 1815 the map of central Europe had been greatly altered. The Holy Roman Empire, a collection of about three hundred semi-independent states under the weak sway of a "phantom emperor," had been abolished by Napoleon in 1806. Besides destroying this medieval institution Napoleon had consolidated many of the small German states, thus greatly reducing their number. In 1815 these were loosely united into a new confederation presided over by the Hapsburg emperor, the hereditary ruler of the Austrian empire. By this organization, which created the appearance but not the reality of unity, the ancient Austrian dynasty kept up the traditional territorial and political decentralization of middle Europe.

Meanwhile the rival house of Hohenzollern emerged from the Napoleonic wars with a larger and more powerful Prussian kingdom in northern Germany. In a position to challenge Hapsburg supremacy in middle Europe, this ambitious family was soon able to take advantage of the movement for German national unity which arose out of opposition to Napoleon.

To the east of Prussia and Austria lay the Slavic empire of Russia, isolated from central and western Europe by historical developments rather than by geographical or racial factors. The vast Russian plain, inhabited on the west by Germans, Jews, Poles, and other peoples, actually extended into Prussia and Austria. Gradually an arbitrary dividing line, called a frontier, emerged, leaving Russians, Poles, Jews, and Germans on both sides. Marginal to Western culture, Russia remained as much a part of Asia as of Europe. The lack of natural frontiers toward Asia had enabled Tatars and other Eastern invaders to sweep over Russia in the Middle Ages. Cultural influences from the Byzantine Empire, especially the Greek Orthodox faith, gave it an Eastern tinge. In 1815 Russia still remained an Oriental state, located partly in Europe but stretching far into Asia.

At that time Russia was practically a landlocked country. Despite the fact that, a century before, Peter the Great had acquired the Baltic provinces and founded the city of St. Petersburg, Russia lacked an "open window," the harbor of the new capital being icebound at least half the year. Thwarted in the Baltic, Russia turned to the Near East in her attempt to obtain a satisfactory seaport. To accomplish this aim she had to overcome first the opposition of the declining Ottoman Empire and later the hostility of Great Britain.

The primary object of Russian foreign policy in the Near East was the control of Constantinople. Overlooking the strategic straits which connect the Black Sea and the Mediterranean, and located on the narrow peninsula which virtually commands three continents, — Europe, Asia, and Africa, — this capital of the great Ottoman Empire was one of the jewel cities of the world. Once there, Russia could free thousands of brother Slavs who were ruled by the alien Turks. Also, once in possession of the city, the original capital of the Greek Orthodox religion, she could make it the center of a vast

Slavic empire. But other European nations, especially England, Austria, and France, preferred to keep the Turks in control of the city rather than allow Russia to seize it and to create an empire which would menace them by land and by sea. As we shall see, the powers found it increasingly difficult to hold back the colossal empire of the north.

The spread of revolutionary ideals, especially nationalism, did more than anything else to upset the equilibrium of the *Significance of Nation-* Balkans. As Slavic peoples and other national *alism* groups there embraced these principles, they became restless under Turkish rule. The resulting disorders led to the intrusion of foreign interests and the growth of international rivalries in the Balkans. Revolutionary sentiment there, as elsewhere, was largely responsible for the important political and territorial changes in the nineteenth century which greatly altered the world of 1815.

But what is nationalism? It may be characterized as the chief form of modern political loyalty to that new type of state called the nation. The term *nation* is derived from the Latin word *natio*, meaning "birth," "race," "people." According to diplomacy and to international law, a nation is an independent country or sovereign state. Its citizens may be a group of individuals who are often, though fallaciously, supposed to be members of a common race and who speak the same language. The term *nation* actually applies to a relatively large group of individuals who may or may not enjoy political independence, but who are agreed among themselves and differ from others in ideals, traditions, and institutions.

Nationalism is loyalty to the state or nation of which one is a member,— a loyalty embracing a desire for the independence, security, prosperity, and greatness of one's country. Usually, nationalism involves the tendency on the part of a group of people to strive for uniformity of language, of religion, of economic interests, and of other customs and institutions. A characteristic manifestation of nationalism has been the popular desire to enlarge a state through the inclusion of all regions in which the "national" language is prevalent or lands considered to be historically, geographically, ethnically, or economically part of the "nation." In the nineteenth century, however, the main emphasis was upon language-nationalism. This was especially true of the Italian and German patriots who desired to create unified and independent nations comparable to England and France.

Nationalism was one of the political results of eighteenth-century individualism. The French Revolution had emphasized the "rights of man" and made possible the rise of Napoleon, a confirmed middle-class individualist. But this famous Corsican adventurer, dazzled by the classical concept of world unity, made himself the missionary of a militant nationalism which aimed at a federated cosmopolitan world state. He failed, and his real project, a universal empire, disappeared into thin air.

Gradually nationalism became firmly fixed in the public mind as a guiding motive of public policy. Politicians took great pains to exploit it to their own advantage. It was soon apparent that nationalism, like individualism, was a middle-class ideal. Both rested on the principle of competition and were antagonistic toward the coöperative ideals of the Middle Ages and of modern socialism. Thus the middle classes, convinced that economic individualism was the secret of success, soon cleverly used nationalism as the means by which they as Frenchmen, Englishmen, or Germans, for example, might advance their private economic interests under the guise of devotion to the national ideal.

Eventually the concept of nationalism replaced absolutism as the principal check on unfettered individualism. Private judgment was denounced as unsound; the opinion of the majority was believed more reliable than that of the wisest councils of individuals or of monarchs. There resulted a growing emphasis upon the rights of nations, which were ruled by the majorities. Politically, the individual had to subordinate himself to the state, and real individualism disappeared. Thus two of the important contributions of the French Revolution, nationalism and individualism, helped to destroy the chief features of the old régime: social privilege and absolutism. Once the older order was overthrown and the new one inaugurated, those in power, the bourgeoisie, used nationalism as a means of checking other groups whenever the latter threatened their designs. Welding diverse interests, nationalism became the cohesive force of the body politic. To the people of the Western world it seemed the most inspiring doctrine of all and one of the most valuable assets of the new régime.

By 1815 it was impossible to disregard nationalism. The patriotic movements that had formerly stirred up the French, the Poles, the Portuguese, the Spaniards, the Italians, and the Germans in their opposition to Napoleon now influenced them to claim freedom and unity for all of their nationality. These demands could no longer be ignored, as the new political, economic, and social systems introduced into Europe during the Revolutionary and Napoleonic periods enabled the middle classes to gain political control of their governments. Their supremacy hastened the formation of new national states. After these countries were established, the bourgeois exponents of Western civilization were in a position to lead their nations in the conquest and Europeanization of the entire world.

"*La gloire de* NAPOLÉON *pas égalée — elle ne sera jamais effacée.*"

The drawing is from a rebus of 1840

PART II. EXPANSION OF REVOLUTIONARY IDEAS

CHAPTER III

The Congress of Vienna, 1815: Triumph of Conservatism

URING the Revolutionary conflicts, 1792–1815, various war aims were expressed. French liberals believed that a new Europe would emerge, inhabited by free peoples living in independent republics and maintaining peace by means of a European confederation. The rise of Napoleon did not nullify this ideal; it substituted the concept of a powerful French empire which was to supplant the old régime and, supported by neighboring dependent states, was to lead in the development of the new order. At first many individuals accepted this idealistic program. To Germans living in the Rhineland region, for example, France was the great emancipator, under whose leadership they might attain national independence and political and social freedom.

NOTE. *The picture at the top of the page shows a* BOURBON COACH *being burned in a Paris revolution. From a contemporary engraving in the Musée Carnavalet.*

From the beginning of the wars, however, the defenders of the old régime considered the French Revolution a menace to the established order in Europe. Fearing a general European revolution and the spread of political and of social liberalism and nationalism, they formed coalitions to suppress this threat. At first they met with little success. The French Revolutionists, as crusaders, were difficult to check. Napoleon's rise and the creation of the empire changed the situation. Aristocrats could now appeal to their subjects to support them in a struggle against this conqueror who failed to recognize the rights of princes, of states, or of nationalities. They declared that if he were to rule Europe, all peoples would be forced to submit to his will. He was pictured as the "beast of Paris," just as, later, William II, during the World War, was called the "beast of Berlin." Both liberals and conservatives in conquered countries were moved by this fear of a cruel despotism and attracted by promises of a constitution and other reforms offered by local rulers. As a result they joined in a series of concerted efforts to overthrow the conqueror.

Upon the fall of Napoleon the conservatives came into control. Resolved to restore absolutism and legitimate monarchs, determined never to permit a Bonaparte to govern France, and opposed to such revolutionary and bourgeois principles as constitutionalism, legal equality, equitable taxation, religious toleration, and intellectual liberty, they re-created as far as they were able the Europe of 1789.

The Age of Conservatism

A literary and artistic, as well as a political and social, reaction developed. Writers defended privilege and feudalism, stressing the importance of continuity and tradition in politics as well as in society. Opposition arose against any attempts to restore the pseudo-classicism of the Revolution. Many writers, inspired by a romanticism based upon emotion and idealized history, found in the customs, art, and beliefs of the Middle Ages the best examples of what constituted a perfect social order. Stressing divine right, but at the same time emphasizing nationalism as expressed in medieval legends, folksongs, and sagas, some romanticists actually visualized the reëstablishment of the perfect civilization which, according to these idealists, had existed in medieval times.

Conservative and practical statesmen realized that the great majority of people in 1815 wanted peace above all else and were not especially interested in the past or in the creation of an earthly paradise for the future. Famines, pestilences, crime, and disease — the results of great wars — caused churchmen, business men, wage-earners, and peasants to place emphasis upon the present and to demand law, order, and peace. Peace could be attained, believed the conservatives, provided the pre-Revolutionary conditions, under which people were happy and contented and lived in harmony with one another, could be restored. Foremost in the pacifist and reactionary movement was Prince Metternich, chancellor of the Austrian empire, "Gibraltar of the old Régime."

This able diplomat believed himself "to be God's lieutenant on earth, entrusted with the task of resisting new ideas." In Metternich's opinion revolution was "the disease that must be cured, the volcano which *Prince Metternich* must be extinguished, the gangrene which must be burned out with the hot iron, the hydra-headed monster with jaws open to swallow up the social order." "Sovereigns alone," he declared, "are entitled to guide the destinies of their peoples, and they are responsible to none but God." "What the European peoples want is not liberty but peace." Soon recognized as the leading exponent of the old order, he was reputed to be able to smell a liberal across a field of Bermuda onions. There are indications, however, that Metternich's conservatism was often inspired by political expediency.

Born at Coblenz in 1773 of a distinguished family, many members of which had served the Holy Roman Empire, Metternich was reared in the conservative and aristocratic surroundings of the Hapsburg court. From the beginning he developed for revolution and liberalism a hatred which became personal when Napoleon rudely seized the family estates. He shrewdly prepared the way for his career by marrying the granddaughter of the clever old Austrian chancellor, Count Kaunitz. This fortunate alliance not only brought

him large estates but also paved the way for his social and
diplomatic rise in Vienna. He represented his Hapsburg lord
at various times in Dresden, Berlin, St. Petersburg, and Paris.
In France he frequently found it difficult to cope with Napoleon's slippery minister, Prince Talleyrand; yet his good
looks, his clever wit, his aristocratic charms, and his popularity
with the ladies, especially Napoleon's sister, enabled him to
exert great influence at the court of the French emperor. At
that time he prepared himself for the clever diplomatic
maneuvers which were to make Austria the dominant European power after Napoleon's fall, and the great citadel of the
old régime.

Before the collapse of the Napoleonic edifice, Metternich
realized that liberalism must be checked. Quick to see, in
1813, that Napoleon's fall was imminent, he brought about
the intervention of Austria in the wars of liberation which
culminated in the defeat and first abdication of the French
emperor. Having won the confidence of the allies through
the part which he played in Napoleon's overthrow, Metternich
was able to pose as the leader destined to bring peace to war-
torn Europe.

Wisely he arranged that the peace congress should meet at
Vienna. As host he was able to occupy a strategic position
from the beginning. Aided by his Hapsburg
master, he provided a continuous round of
balls, banquets, theatricals, musicals, drives,
and hunts, which almost bankrupted the Austrian government. The money, however, was well spent. There was little
formality, and there were no fixed rules of procedure or officers at this congress; there were few plenary sessions, and no
motions or votes were taken at these meetings. Instead "at
a ball, kingdoms were enlarged or sliced up — at a dinner an
indemnity granted — a constitution sketched while hunting;
occasionally a *bon mot*, or a witty idea, brought an agreement where conferences and notes failed." The work at
this assemblage was done by a small committee usually composed of the representatives of England, Prussia, Russia, and
Austria, the "Big Four" which had been chiefly responsible

The Congress of Vienna

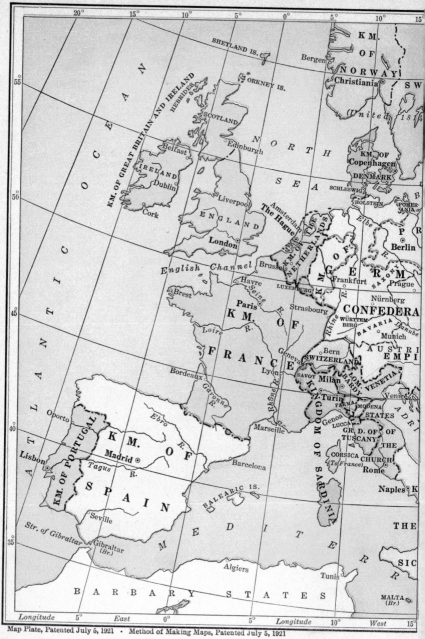

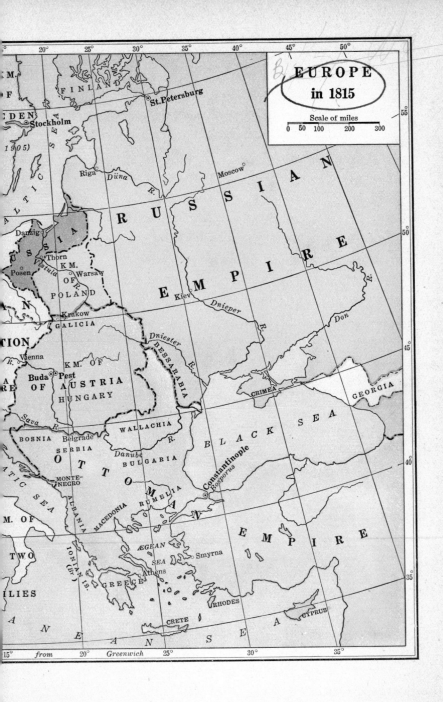

EUROPE
in 1815

Scale of miles

0   50   100   200   300

FINLAND

St. Petersburg

KM.
OF

DEN
Stockholm

(1905)

Riga   Düna   Moscow

R U S S I A N

Danzig

USSIA   Thorn
Posen   KM.
OF
POLAND   Warsaw

E M P I R E

Krakow   Kiev
GALICIA   Dnieper
R.   Don
Dniester
Vienna   KM. OF   BESSARABIA
Buda Pest   AUSTRIA
OF   HUNGARY
Sava R.   CRIMEA   GEORGIA
BOSNIA   Belgrade   WALLACHIA
SERBIA   R.   B L A C K   S E A
O   Danube
T   BULGARIA   Constantinople
MONTE-   T   Bosporus
NEGRO   O   Danube
ALBANIA   M   RUMELIA
A   N   E M P I R E
MACEDONIA
ÆGEAN
SEA   Smyrna
M. OF   Athens
TWO   GREECE
RHODES
ILIES   CRETE   CYPRUS

15°   from   20°   Greenwich   25°   30°   35°

for the overthrow of Napoleon. In this committee Viscount Castlereagh of England and Prince Metternich of Austria dominated the situation.

Vienna was a lively city during the congress. Every European country was represented except Turkey. Hundreds of distinguished-looking men, wearing magnificent uniforms adorned with gold lace and carrying bright swords, crowded the streets. The emperors of Austria and Russia, the kings of Prussia, Bavaria, and Württemberg, numerous lesser princes, and all the outstanding diplomats of Europe were present. A multitude of adventurers, representatives of various racial, religious, and economic groups, added much to the bustle and excitement in Vienna, although they contributed little as far as the peace settlement was concerned.

The leading diplomats talked loudly about peace, but knew that the distribution of territory, involving the reëstablishment of the balance of power, the conservation of the old régime, and the aggrandizement of *The Chief Aims of the Diplomats* their individual states, constituted their chief aims. Many of these matters had been at least partially settled before the representatives of the powers met at Vienna. As soon as Napoleon had abdicated, the allies, meeting at the French capital, had drawn up the Treaty of Paris, May 30, 1814. In it they had recognized the reëstablishment of the French monarchy and the restoration of the Bourbon king, Louis XVIII, to the throne. They also limited the boundaries of France to those which she had in 1792, and returned most of her colonies. In this treaty the powers further agreed to establish a German federation, to recognize the independence of Switzerland, to place a large part of Italy under Austrian control, and to allow Holland to annex the territory of the Austrian Netherlands, which is now Belgium. A future congress at Vienna, they decided, was to determine other territorial and dynastic problems, to establish a just balance of power, and to create permanent peace.

From the first the representatives of the victorious powers realized that a compromise policy alone would result in the maximum benefits. They felt that the preservation of the

status quo was advisable, rather than the complete reëstablishment of the old régime. With this idea in mind they permitted the new king of France to grant a charter to his people, allowing them limited constitutional liberties. No attempt was made to restore the nobles and clergy to their former privileged positions. The allied diplomats cleverly re-created only the framework of the old régime in France, believing that a more complete restoration might be inaugurated later.

At the Congress of Vienna (September, 1814, to June, 1815) the representatives of the great powers agreed that the establishment of a permanent peace should be their prime objective. To achieve this end they decided to follow the principle of legitimacy as far as possible in restoring the European territorial situation of 1789. Wherever old boundaries could not be reëstablished, in view of the necessity of granting rewards or inflicting punishments, compensation should be given if possible. The allies also agreed to hold periodic meetings after the congress ended, in order to see that the terms of the peace were carried out and maintained. As interpreted later by diplomats, this last arrangement merely signified that the allies would maintain the settlement by preventing the return of Napoleon.

The Prussian, Russian, and Austrian diplomats, especially Metternich, were interested in another objective. To them the *status quo* meant the suppression of further liberal movements. Conservatism, they believed, should be the aim of the leading powers during and after the Congress of Vienna. As we shall see, however, England subsequently refused to sanction this point of view.

At the congress all powers, large and small, were actuated chiefly by one motive, namely, the promotion of their particular interests. Inasmuch as the four great countries agreed to decide questions among themselves, and merely announced the results to the smaller states, the representatives of the latter were forced to restrict their attention to the social side of the congress.

Talleyrand, the French representative, who was ignored by the allies, shrewdly took up the cause of the little powers in

opposing the dictatorship of the Big Four. He held that international law required that the small states, Spain, Portugal, and Sweden, should be represented. In reply Humboldt of Prussia stated briefly, "Might is right; we do not recognize the law of nations to which you have appealed." Napoleon's return to France from exile was followed by the famous Hundred Days, culminating in the disastrous defeat at Waterloo on June 18, 1815. The angry allies determined to punish France by limiting her frontiers to those of 1790, by depriving her of part of Savoy, and by levying an indemnity upon her.

From the beginning of the peace negotiations the three great conservative states Austria, Russia, and Prussia were especially interested in the suppression of liberalism in Europe, and in the advancement *Peace Settlements* of their frontiers. Great Britain, however, was more concerned with the restoration of an equilibrium in Europe which would prevent France from dominating the Continent, closing its markets to British trade, and depriving England of her supremacy overseas.

To the satisfaction of England the allies quickly agreed that Holland and the Austrian Netherlands should be united to form the Kingdom of the Netherlands under the House of Orange. Thus was created a barrier to a French advance in the north. With the Dutch king as its grand duke, Luxembourg was involved in a personal union with Holland. Switzerland was declared independent, as were all the small Italian states which had existed before the invasion of Napoleon, with the exception of the ancient republics of Venice and Genoa. Genoa was awarded to the king of Sardinia, and Venetia to Austria as an indemnity for the latter's losses in the Netherlands. Austria also recovered the duchy of Milan and, by means of her holdings in Northern Italy and of her indirect influence in the Kingdom of the Two Sicilies to the south, was in a position not only to keep France out of Italy but also to dominate that peninsula.

France was thus surrounded by buffer states. She could not expand toward the Rhine, nor become a Mediterranean power through conquest of Italy, since the latter remained politically decentralized under Austrian supervision. England, the persistent enemy of Napoleon, the builder of repeated coalitions, and the pay-mistress of the allies for many years, was satisfied. France had been weakened and political stability had been reëstablished in western Europe.

England's allies were so engrossed in territorial disputes over middle Europe that they allowed her to retain many of the conquests which she had made at the expense of France and her allies and dependencies, especially Holland. She kept Heligoland in the North Sea, Malta and the Ionian Islands in the Mediterranean, Cape Colony in South Africa, and Ceylon and other islands in the East. In a position to prevent any rival from threatening her sea power, and with industries at home untouched by invasions and even increased through the changes brought about by the Industrial Revolution, she was able to take advantage of peace by reviving and expanding her commerce and industry. Meanwhile European nations, busily engaged in rehabilitating the devastated lands and in settling the vexatious political and social questions which arose out of the French Revolution, purchased British goods. Great Britain became the foremost industrial and capitalistic power of the world.

At first the Continental allies did not find it difficult to effect territorial adjustments. West Pomerania was taken from Sweden and given to Prussia. As compensation for this loss and for the earlier cession of Finland to Russia in 1809, Sweden received Norway from Denmark. Prussia procured certain territories along the west bank of the Rhine, whereas Austria regained most of her possessions in central Europe.

With the exception of the Hapsburgs, however, few in 1815 desired the revival of the Holy Roman Empire. Napoleon not only had destroyed this old political union, but also had further consolidated the three-hundred-odd states into about thirty-nine. These states desired to retain their sovereignty. The result of the particularistic or states-right feeling was the creation of the Germanic Confederation, a loose organization of the thirty-nine states with a diet consisting of delegates representing the reigning prince of each realm, presided over by Austria. According to the agreement, members could not enter into an alliance with foreign powers, either against the Confederation as a whole or against a fellow member. The constitution was placed under the guarantee of Europe, and by means of traditional and interested support which the lesser princes gave to Austria the Confederation soon came to be directed from Vienna. To England's satisfaction the Confederation decentralized middle Europe and thus was another factor in the reëstablishment of the Continental equilibrium. The creation of the Confederation also strengthened the prestige of Austria in central Europe. She assumed the influential position formerly held by France. Thenceforth, led by Metternich, Austria became the defender of the old régime and of the peace of Europe as against liberalism and war.

The disposition of Polish territory, which Napoleon had converted into the grand duchy of Warsaw, proved a difficult problem. Alexander I was bent on restoring the kingdom of Poland as a separate state over which he was to rule as king, thus joining Poland in a personal union with Russia. The king of Prussia, although interested in Poland, was willing to support the Czar on condition that Prussia should be compensated for her losses in the east by annexing the lands of the king of Saxony, who had supported Napoleon even after his repudiation by other members of the Confederation of the Rhine. Austria and England bitterly opposed Russia's and Prussia's plans to increase their domains in central Europe, realizing that a decentralized middle Europe consisting of weak states would enable Austria to maintain the *status quo* by dominating this section of the continent.

Talleyrand was quick to take advantage of this controversy. Fearing the rise of a strong Prussia across the Rhine, he preached the principle of legitimacy and supported Austria in her efforts to thwart Russian and Prussian designs in Poland and Saxony, even offering Austria military aid in the event of war. Austria gladly accepted Talleyrand's backing. Thus France, through an alignment with Austria and Great Britain as against Russia and Prussia, became once more one of the leading powers of Europe, although but recently she had been the disturber of peace, the *enfant terrible* of Europe.

A compromise finally was reached in the struggle over Poland and Saxony. Russia was allowed to create a kingdom of Poland out of the grand duchy of Warsaw. Polish Posen, Thorn, and Danzig, in addition to over one half of Saxony and compensation in the Rhineland for "sacrifices" of Polish territory, were given to Prussia. The rest of Saxony was restored to its legitimate ruler. Austria obtained south Galicia, but Cracow was declared a free city. These and other principal territorial changes decreed by the Congress of Vienna were destined to endure, with slight alterations, for nearly fifty years.

It is difficult to discover in any of these negotiations the operation of any lofty principle. Scant attention was paid to the views of the smaller states ; the settlement, *Achievements and Defects of the Settlement* for example, ignored the national claims of Norway and Belgium by uniting them respectively with Sweden and Holland. Self-interest seemed to be the keynote then as now. It is true that the diplomats used noble words. Phrases such as "reconstruction of the social order," "regeneration of the political system of Europe," "a durable peace based upon a just division of power," which were commonly heard in those years, recall the more recent propaganda of 1917–1918 concerning "a war to end wars," and "a war to make the world safe for democracy." Later these phrasemakers were to be seen scrambling for spoils and adopting the very measures which previously they had so fervently denounced. In 1815 diplomats regarded subjects as mere children and monarchs as the divinely appointed instruments of God.

At the same time one must not be too critical of these negotiators. They abolished the slave trade, consigning the enforcement of this agreement to each state. They also drew up a doctrine for international river navigation throughout Europe. As peacemakers they represented neither the best nor the worst of the old régime. France certainly did not receive harsh treatment, and the establishment of political equilibrium averted a general European conflict for forty years.

Two treaties, signed at Paris on November 20, 1815, supplemented the work of Vienna and marked the return to a much-desired peace. The first bound France *The Quadruple and* to carry out the new arrangements which had *Holy Alliances* been imposed in consequence of the return of Napoleon, to recede to the frontiers of 1790, to pay an indemnity, and to return to their rightful owners pictures and other works of art stolen by Napoleon. The second created an alliance. Having arranged the map of Europe as they desired, the statesmen representing Austria, Russia, Prussia, and Great Britain decided to provide against any future revolutionary uprisings which might undo their work. This last agreement generally is called the Quadruple Alliance.

According to its terms the four allied powers bound themselves to carry out the changes brought about by the treaties, including that of Vienna, and to maintain the terms of these settlements for twenty years, by armed force if necessary. Furthermore, they decided to "renew their meetings at fixed periods" and to discuss such matters "of common interest" as might seem necessary to preserve order in Europe. This last agreement could perhaps be said to contain the germ of future international government. Certainly it was important, since it indicated the realization on the part of statesmen that some form of international organization was necessary if the balance of power was to be preserved without recourse to war. In forming this Quadruple Alliance the member nations realized that they must consider the interests of the lesser powers as well as their own.

The Quadruple Alliance was not the only design for the preservation of peace by international agreement. On September 26, 1815, Alexander I of Russia offered his unique solution, the Holy Alliance. The Czar was a handsome man with noble and melancholy features. "Enamoured of solitude and sometimes falling on his knees to pray in the depths of a cemetery, chewing the cud of melancholy reflections on his walks, he felt himself called upon to make good the harm done by the Emperor [Napoleon I], and conceived 'the idea of a holy European League of which he would be more than

Agamemnon.'" In his dreamy, idealistic way Alexander tried to bind all monarchs together in a Christian union of charity, peace, and love.

Alexander had a practical purpose in proposing this scheme. By it he hoped to arouse the various nationalities, especially the Slavs, and to influence leading rulers to recognize the principle of self-determination. He believed that nationalities of an advanced stage of cultural development merited independence, and he proposed an alliance which should direct this national movement.

This scheme, called the Holy Alliance, stirred up considerable ridicule. Metternich described it as a "sonorous nothing." Nevertheless the Continental rulers, with the exception of the Pope and the Sultan of Turkey, who were not invited, attached their signatures to the document. The Prince of Wales, regent of Great Britain, despite his desire to do so, was "unable to sign it." Apparently English statesmen feared that an alliance of this kind might embroil Great Britain in the internal affairs of European and American countries. Therefore Castlereagh, England's foreign minister, labeled the scheme "a piece of sublime mysticism and nonsense"; but this so-called "mutual admiration society for the prevention of cruelty to legitimate monarchs" was founded, although it never became important.

England soon discovered that her allies planned to make the Quadruple Alliance a means by which the political and social as well as territorial *status quo* should be preserved throughout the world. Such a program was bound to lead to trouble. England was determined that no alliance, holy or otherwise, should involve her in the internal affairs of other states unless the equilibrium of power or her own imperial interests were affected. Austria, however, insisted that the Quadruple Alliance had been established to prevent the dangerous spread of such liberal tendencies as constitutionalism and self-determination, although Alexander at first believed such changes inevitable. Metternich contended that the Quadruple Alliance did commit its members to armed interference to suppress internal revolutions in any country, provided the congress deemed it expedient. A conflict between these views was unavoidable.

Despite the differences in interpretation the Quadruple Alliance functioned well for a time. The statesmen of the great powers coöperated in seeing that France maintained peace and paid her obligations. At the first meeting at Aix-la-Chapelle (1818) the allies decided that French conduct had been satisfactory and that consequently their armies should evacuate her soil. Further, France was admitted to the international *bloc* of great powers, which thus became the Quintuple Alliance, although her revolutionary past caused her allies still to regard her with some suspicion.

The great powers, however, found it difficult to coöperate on all international problems. In 1818 Alexander, fearing the spread of liberalism which threatened his con-

The Limitations of the Quadruple Alliance

trol, favored a union of legitimate rulers against revolutions. Later, when the Spanish colonies in South America revolted, he recommended intervention.

England refused to become involved in this matter. In the throes of a grave economic crisis, she was willing, even eager, to turn the revolt of the Spanish colonies to account in order to dump her goods in their markets. In fact, she welcomed the rebellion in view of Spain's monopolistic colonial policies which had hitherto prevented English traders from carrying on an extensive commerce with Hispanic America. Revolutions there meant increased commerce for England. Therefore the opposition of Castlereagh, who represented English trading interests, prevented the Alliance from crushing the revolts. The other powers, dependent upon the British fleet to settle overseas trouble, were helpless. Castlereagh and Metternich, however, finally satisfied the nervous Alexander by agreeing to a vague moral union.

Alexander at first insisted that the alliance oppose all revolutionary movements. In 1820 a military uprising broke out in Spain. When the Spanish king's life was threatened, the ruler very wisely

Revolution in Spain

agreed to a democratic constitution. Alexander was astounded, feeling that if this foolishness were to spread, no monarch would be safe. Therefore he demanded a meeting of all the allies to devise ways and means of destroying the Spanish constitution.

Castlereagh in a lengthy state paper again outlined the British foreign policy, asserting that His Majesty's government was committed to prevent the restoration of the Napoleonic dynasty and to maintain the agreements of Vienna for twenty years. He considered that the Spanish revolution was an internal affair, not dangerous to other countries, and that Great Britain would not be justified in sanctioning any attempt to suppress it by force. He did not mention the fact that a revolution in Spain would aid similar uprisings in South America, and that the establishment of numerous independent states in the Americas would enable the British to develop their commerce there. Furthermore, he wisely refrained from indicating that France had any aspirations in Hispanic America which might run counter to British interests. Instead this clever statesman placed the whole issue on a higher plane by declaring that Great Britain owed her own constitution and her present dynasty to an internal revolution. He did not, therefore, deny to other countries the right of changing their form of government. Moreover, the British people, as represented by Parliament, must be consulted before the government could act. Because of the fact that neither the people nor Parliament had been informed of any agreements other than those contracted at Vienna, Great Britain would fulfill only those obligations.

After the Spanish insurrection, revolutions occurred in Naples, Piedmont, and Portugal, with the people demanding "constitutions" and other political "rights."

Revolutions in Italy, Portugal, and Greece Austrian interests in Italy were threatened by the first two revolts. As a result Metternich concurred with Alexander in a plan to call a congress to settle this revolutionary menace. This time Castlereagh declined to attend personally and sent subordinate officials. When Metternich, Alexander, and the Prussian representatives at the Congress of Troppau (1820) decided to make Europe safe for all monarchs by outlawing revolutions and suppressing them by force if necessary, Castlereagh proclaimed all these gentlemen deficient in common sense. France likewise refused to approve this policy.

At the Congress of Laibach (1821) Alexander, now full of high-sounding sentiments, appointed Metternich to establish law and order in Naples and Piedmont. He notified the Greeks of his opposition to their revolt against the Turks.

Gradually the temperamental Czar changed his views. He decided that the Greek revolution was actually more of a national revolt for independence than a struggle to attain democracy. Consequently Alexander developed a profound interest in the aspirations of his coreligionists and of his brother Slavs in Greece. To him this uprising represented a different kind of revolution. Russia evidently was still interested in Constantinople and the Straits.

Alexander's attitude toward Greece resulted in a very significant diplomatic change. Metternich, who opposed all revolutions, was now joined by Castlereagh, who disapproved of this particular one, inasmuch as he feared that Russia might aid the Greeks and thereby increase her influence in the Balkans. They met in 1821 at Hanover and decided to summon one more congress, at which they hoped to prevent Alexander from taking any active measures against the Turks. Castlereagh was willing to see Hispanic American states obtain their freedom through revolution in order that England might trade with them, but he was opposed to the Greek revolution, fearing the growth of Russian influence in the Near East.

The Congress of Verona convened in 1822. Before it met, the revolutionary developments in Spain and the death of Castlereagh changed the entire complexion of the meeting. In the first place, Canning, who succeeded Castlereagh as the British representative, decided to destroy the congress system as a whole. It was his belief that England could benefit more from individualism in international affairs than through international coöperation. Secondly, France was about to intervene in Spain despite British objections. Consequently the congress was forced to consider the Spanish affair first. Canning clarified his government's position by asserting that Great Britain could not be a party to any proposed intervention. France, however, proceeded to suppress the Spanish revolution and to reëstablish the old régime in 1823.

Nevertheless the French government was not unfriendly toward the movement for independence in Hispanic America. *Great Britain and the* Backed by the commercial classes, who feared *Hispanic-American* that Great Britain might obtain a monopoly *Revolutions* of trade, certain French officials encouraged the establishment of Bourbon monarchies in the Americas. For instance, in 1818 they seriously considered the offer of an Argentine dictator to place the duke of Orleans on the throne of the United Provinces of La Plata.

In 1823 the king of Spain appealed to Metternich, who called a congress to deal with the situation in South America. This was exactly what Great Britain did not want and what France desired, the latter having joined Spain in opposing British interests in Hispanic America. England refused to send representatives to this proposed meeting. Other nations found themselves helpless. Lacking an international navy, they were unable to carry out their plans to crush the revolutions in Hispanic America. At this time Great Britain practically informed the European states that she would not intervene in Continental affairs unless the maintenance of the equilibrium of power were at stake. Furthermore, she gave them to understand that she would not permit her overseas interests to be threatened by European designs. To all intents she withdrew from the Quadruple Alliance, thus reducing its power and substituting for the concert of Europe the old policy described by Canning of "Every nation for itself, and God for us all!"

Perhaps this dispute over the situation in Hispanic America might be considered partially responsible for the collapse of one of the earlier attempts to establish international government. At least it marked the failure of the leading nations who had overthrown Napoleon to coöperate in ruling the world. At the same time one must realize that the system came to an end because the Quadruple Alliance became the

defender of absolutism and of an obsolete political system.
The European powers were trying to maintain a régime which
no longer had a place in modern society. Even though Austria
and Russia, the leaders, were little affected by the French
Revolution, the influence of that great event remained west
of the Rhine long after Napoleon's fall. In the United States
of America also liberalism had produced a healthy young
plant which conservative powers could not touch.

A Cartoonist in 1819 thus pictured the CENSORSHIP OF THE PRESS
under Metternich

CHAPTER IV

The Spread of the Revolutionary Movement, 1815-1848

IN 1814 Metternich and other reactionaries desired the restoration of absolutism in France. Alexander I of Russia, however, still affected by a curious liberalism, insisted that the Bourbon king, Louis XVIII, grant a charter establishing a constitutional government. Although Louis XVIII, a true Bourbon, "had forgotten nothing and learned nothing," he consented to this proposal. Wiser than his rabid ministers and other reactionaries, called the ultra-royalists, who demanded a complete return to the old régime, he could see that the latter was out of date. Probably he had visions of sometime becoming the George Washington of Bourbonism. However, unlike the frisky old Henry IV, he was not a real leader.

The Restoration in France 1815–1830

The constitutional government which was created consisted of a bicameral parliament: a Chamber of Peers, appointed for life by the king, and a Chamber of Deputies, elected for a term of five years. An age and property qualification restricted the franchise to only 100,000 out of 29,000,000 citizens, of which not more than 12,000 men were eligible to become deputies. Consequently the government was controlled by the large property owners. Compared to the political systems of other European countries it was probably liberal. The charter, in addition to creating a parliament, also contained provisions assuring the French people that they were not to lose the liberties or rights gained during the revolution. All persons were declared equal before the law; all were eligible to civil and to military positions, and thus there was to be no monopoly of the public service by one class, as there had been before the revolution. No one was to be arrested or prosecuted save by due process of law; no one was to be denied religious toleration or freedom

The Monarchy

of the press and of speech; and no attempt was to be made to annul the changes in land titles made during the revolution. Those who had purchased confiscated lands of the crown, clergy, and nobility were assured legal possession.

Freedom of press and of discussion, replacing the strict censorship of the empire, gave Frenchmen an opportunity to relieve themselves of long-suppressed ideas *Romanticism* and emotions. The new government was therefore ushered in by a "war of words." Monarchists (some favoring absolutism, others constitutionalism), Bonapartists (followers of Napoleon), and republicans (petty bourgeoisie and workers) expressed their beliefs with great abandon. Meanwhile ultramontanes (religious internationalists), Gallicans (religious nationalists), and enemies of the church revived the religious question with intense enthusiasm. Certain romanticists extolled the common people and the nation. Turning to medieval times for instances of patriotism and happiness, they found in this idealized period the most ennobling examples of real liberty, peace, and brotherhood. The nationalistic religion spread rapidly throughout Europe during the early nineteenth century.

After 1815 romanticism reached its height, affecting men engaged in all branches of literary and artistic work. To one ardent writer the future welfare of the world depended on the victory of romanticism over classicism. The chief characteristic of classicism was boredom, whereas "Romanticism," he wrote, "is the art of presenting to the world literary works which in the actual conditions of life and state of belief are best calculated to give the greatest possible pleasure." Musicians were affected by the romantic movement. Hector Berlioz (1803–1869), for instance, "more impassioned than any other member of the new school, possessed by the desire to astonish and terrify the bourgeois musicians of the Conservatoire, who lulled themselves sanctimoniously with the sober harmonies" of the classicists, composed music full of sinister vibration "in an orgy of fierce fanaticism — it was his way of showing hatred for the Philistines, the classicists, and society itself."

Many conservatives in France favored a return to the "good old days" and painted a different picture. Such intellectual *The Reactionaries* defenders of the old régime as the writers Bonald and De Maistre attacked the French Revolution and the eighteenth-century philosophers. These men maintained that Rousseau, in claiming that "man is naturally good and is corrupted by society," paved the way for massacres, the reign of terror, and the cruel wars of the revolutionary era. In their opinion "Man is naturally bad; original sin is the ultimate truth, and man is saved by society." Authority therefore is necessary; without the power of the king, the clergy, and the nobles, chaos and anarchy result.

The practical exponents of this idea returned to France after the fall of Napoleon. These were the nobles who had lost their lands. Determined to obtain revenge for what they had suffered, and acting through certain reactionary ministers, they reduced the army, bribed or gagged the press, abolished the tricolor flag, and shot the brave Marshal Ney. Soon it was reported that the king planned to restore to the *émigrés* and to the church the property confiscated during the revolution.

Between 1820 and 1824 the assassination of a nephew and heir to the throne, and the growth of radical sentiment throughout Spain and in Italy, caused the compromising Louis XVIII to support the ultra-royalists. Rising to power, these champions of the Metternichian system prepared the way for the restoration of the old régime by suspending the guarantee of personal liberty found in the charter, limiting the suffrage, and placing education in the hands of the church. In 1823 an army was sent to Spain to crush the revolution and to restore the Bourbons. These reactionaries apparently planned to coöperate with Prussia, Russia, and Austria in the suppression of all uprisings.

Despite the attempts of the ultra-royalists to destroy the constitutional government and to terrorize its followers, Louis XVIII remained firm in his promise to maintain the constitution. Supported by a number of moderate liberals, he managed to hold the extreme reactionaries in check. Furthermore, during the king's administration France experienced a remarkable economic growth. Trade and industry were revived, and the Industrial Revolution, developing in France and creating an increasingly wealthy middle class, tended to strengthen the government, although in reality it eventually led to the abolition of the old régime.

The death of Louis XVIII in 1824 and the accession of his brother as Charles X of France brought to a head the struggle between the enemies and the friends of the new régime. The new king was "the incarnation of the reckless and stubborn old reactionary aristocrat." *Reign of Charles X* Believing in the doctrine of divine right and saturated with a spirit of medieval mysticism, he felt that he, the anointed and the chosen of God, was destined to save the land from Voltairianism. As the convinced leader of the reactionaries in France he was reported to have said, "It is only Lafayette and I who have not changed since 1789." Sixty-seven years of age when he became king, he decided to restore the old régime before it was too late. To him this meant a king by divine right, a unified church, and a feudal aristocracy.

Frenchmen interested in contemporary problems were either amused or disgusted when they first heard of the king's medieval views. Before long, however, they became bored. "Let us shut the Bourbons up in the charter," said Thiers, the liberal French statesman, "and close the doors tightly; they will inevitably jump out of the window." Soon Charles X discovered that he would be unable to return the land to the *émigrés*. Therefore, in 1825, he had parliament vote them a billion francs for the losses they had suffered during the revolution. To pay the nobles, the government had to fund the public debt, to reduce the interest rate, and to allot the amount saved to the aristocrats. Inasmuch as the bonds were owned by members of the middle classes, this act made Charles X very unpopular among a powerful group of people. The bourgeois citizens were soon on the alert for a chance to take matters into their own hands.

Charles accorded them an opportunity. After his minister, Polignac, had inaugurated a foreign policy which nearly involved his country in a war with Great Britain over Belgium, this same foolish diplomat persuaded Charles X to suppress parliament. Thereupon the king issued the famous July Ordinances of July 26, 1830. These restricted the freedom of the press, dissolved the new chamber before it had even met, issued a new law disfranchising three fourths of the voters, and proclaimed another election of deputies.

This tyranny alienated all classes in France except the ultra-royalists. Aroused by the ordinances, printers and journalists, eager to check the power of the Bourbons, incited the Parisians to revolt. They were assisted by the old veterans, Talleyrand and Lafayette, who for once agreed upon a common program, namely, a constitutional monarchy of the English type.

The Revolution of 1830

The uprising was brief and successful. For three days the revolutionists took advantage of the narrow and crooked streets in Paris to harass and check the government troops. Finally Charles X abdicated in favor of his nine-year-old grandson, the Count of Chambord. Wisely, the ex-king left Paris for London. In 1836 he died in Austria in full expectation of joining the saints whom he had loved and served.

The revolution of 1830 was especially important, as it marked the end of divine-right monarchy and of ultra-royalist supremacy. Henceforth the people, or at least some of them, were to designate the kind of government to be established and the ruler to be at the head. The overthrow of Charles X also gave the middle classes their first opportunity to assume political power on the Continent. Their rise had been so sudden that they were not prepared to handle the crisis. Consequently the revolution of 1830 did not result in the creation of a republic. Led by the journalist Thiers and an influential banker named Laffitte, the bourgeois liberals succeeded in effecting the establishment of a constitutional monarchy.

Laffitte was chosen to offer the crown to Louis Philippe, duke of Orleans and liberal member of the Bourbon family.

It is reported that he did this in a typically businesslike way, giving Louis Philippe his choice between a passport and a kingship. Willingly Louis Philippe selected the crown, becoming king of the French — not king of France. Subtly he acknowledged that *Louis Philippe the Bourgeois King* the people had conferred sovereignty upon him, but in reality he knew it came to him from the aristocratic representatives of the middle classes.

At this crucial moment the aged Lafayette made his last important public appearance. On October 5, 1789, he had staged a balcony scene at Versailles with Marie Antoinette and helped to save her from the mob only for the guillotine; now he appeared with the outstanding royal candidate, Louis Philippe. Placing his arm around the royal shoulders, Lafayette assured the mob that Louis Philippe was but a servant of the people.

Louis Philippe was ambitious. He considered himself the representative of an illustrious line of monarchs and strove to retain the social prestige of the royal family. At the same time he desired to be regarded as a middle-class monarch and a democratic king. To emphasize this pretension he carried his famous green cotton umbrella, sent his sons to the public schools, graciously commended the writings of Voltaire and of Rousseau, and bowed freely and gracefully on all public occasions.

The new monarch's aim was to please everybody. He desired to be a symbol of all that was good in France. In his habits he was simple and above reproach. Apparently he seemed possessed of all the essential qualities of the victorious middle classes, such as domestic virtues, thrift, and urbanity. Nevertheless he embodied the historic past as the son of his liberal and "illustrious father," who had voted in the Convention for the death of Louis XVI. In order to be considered a product of the revolution, he restored the tricolor flag and the national guard. Furthermore, in his attempts to glorify the past he proclaimed Napoleon a great French leader and had his bones carried from St. Helena and laid to rest at the Invalides. He also placed in the Palace of Versailles pictures of the leading battles of French history and solemnly dedicated the chateau "to all the glories of France." Unfortunately for Louis Philippe, such acts caused ultra-royalists and Bonapartists to revive their propaganda with the hope that the absolutism of the empire might be restored.

Frenchmen were proud of the past, but at the same time they lived for the present. Patriotic, logical, and not bound to tradition as were their English neighbors, they allowed Louis Philippe to remain in power so long as he did not limit the rights won by the revolution. Politically his administration was a failure almost from the beginning. His government proved anything but democratic. Although the cabinet was responsible to parliament, a property qualification for voting excluded the workingmen and enabled a few wealthy bourgeois to control the legislative body. Thus in reality he ruled a conservative middle-class monarchy.

Louis Philippe's reign was notable chiefly because it was the period in which the Industrial Revolution, retarded by the Revolutionary Era (1789–1815), was re-

The Reign of Louis Philippe

vived. Encouraged by the government, a remarkable economic development occurred. France, with Lyons as the center, became the greatest silk-manufacturing country in Europe. Lack of sufficient coal and the poor quality of iron ore, however, seriously delayed French development in the iron-and-steel industry. In transportation there was material progress. For building a national system of railways, radiating from Paris, the administration adopted a comprehensive scheme, to be carried out by chartered companies aided by government subsidies. Several important lines were constructed under this program. Foreign commerce also increased during the July Monarchy. Although France was still backward in industrial and commercial development as compared to England, her agriculture, together with her manufacture of luxuries, established her as one of the most important nations in Europe.

Louis Philippe also discussed the creation of an empire which should include Belgium, all of Algeria and Egypt in Africa, and California in the Americas. He visualized a France which should surpass the monarchy of Louis XIV. Foreign opposition, however, prevented the ruler from acquiring Belgium. In Africa he was more successful. The report that Algerians molested French trade and hampered French business enterprise, together with the fact that the French government had lent money to Algerian bankers, was sufficient reason for continued intervention. His administration marked a definite stage in the development of modern bourgeois imperialism.

In educational affairs the governmental policies of Louis Philippe were essentially middle-class. In order that young people might contribute to the creation of a prosperous state, public schools were encouraged. A law was passed in 1833 establishing elementary education. Thenceforth every commune was bound to maintain, either alone or in conjunction with one or several other communes, at least one primary elementary school under the management of a lay or clerical teacher. Education was to be free, though not compulsory for the people of each locality. Considerable opposition developed to this legislative act. "It is vine-dressers we want, not readers," a peasant informed a school inspector. Nevertheless Guizot, Louis Philippe's premier, insisted that the work begun in the seventeenth century should be completed.

France remained peaceful and prosperous during the reign of this ponderous king; yet the people were not satisfied. They were disgusted by the reports of bribery which involved the ruler and his ministers, and they were vexed with the government's *The Weak Foreign Policies of Louis Philippe* weak foreign policy. France, they asserted, was degenerating into a satellite of Great Britain, and they cited the government's failure to establish French control in Spain and in Belgium because of English opposition as proof of this assertion. Moreover, Louis Philippe lowered French prestige on the Continent by refusing to help the Poles and Italians in their struggles for freedom. By abandoning the Egyptian leader, Mehemet Ali, in his struggle with the Turkish Sultan (1840), he lost a rare opportunity of developing French interests in the Orient. "What has this policy of business before

glory or honor obtained for us?" patriotic Frenchmen asked.
Most nations, they asserted, despised France. Many leaders
of the Catholic church considered the July Monarchy a complete failure. The government was doomed, despite the fact
that France enjoyed real economic prosperity.

As Napoleon had made noblemen of his soldiers, Louis
Philippe created a new aristocracy called the "July Nobles,"
bestowing titles upon bankers, manufacturers,
The New Bourgeois and successful speculators. From that time on
Aristocracy the wealthy capitalists replaced the landed
aristocrats as the dominant group in France.

The middle classes even invaded the army. During the
Revolutionary Era the feudal character of this organization
had been abolished. Men fought for their country, not for
the king or for a feudal lord. The duty of a citizen to defend
his state superseded the voluntary quest of adventure or of
material reward. The middle classes, nevertheless, were not
able to control the regular army until the time of the Third
Republic. During the years when they were rising to power
the army was composed for the most part of dissatisfied
adherents of the old nobility.

One military institution, however, was not dominated by
the aristocrats; this was the National Guard, established
during the French Revolution by the bourgeois Parisians,
"not at all . . . as a protection against the court, but as a
shield against the robbers." By 1848 this organization was
ruled by business men and became the focus of bourgeois
vanity. Service in this soldiery permitted a citizen to reconcile the pursuit of gold with the display of showy costume,
and fostered his belief in himself as the patriotic prop of
national prosperity. Wealth helped considerably in the Guard,
especially as members supplied their own uniforms; and when
under the Republic of 1848 certain crack regiments in bear-
skin shakos protested the admission of the proletariat to their
ranks, they expressed the snobbishness of caste actuated by
money rather than by blood.

The "citizen king" attempted to win the friendship of the
wage-earners. His life became one continual parade. In the

evenings, for example, a loafing, rowdy crowd around the railings of the palace made itself hoarse with shouts of "The King! The King!" Louis Philippe was obliged to appear on the balcony and sing the Marseil- *The "Democratic" King* laise while the crowd beat time with hands and feet. What would the immaculate Charles X have thought of such a spectacle? Perhaps he would have said what a certain deputy, a commoner, whispered: "Really, one cannot dine with the King any longer; he keeps such bad company."

Louis Philippe's crude attempts to attain popularity displeased all elements save his few aristocratic capitalistic supporters. Many proud French noblemen, aroused by the monarch's undignified behavior, *Opposition to the July Monarchy* were absolutely disgusted when they beheld the middle classes striving to assert the social superiority which money alone had won for them. Intellectuals like George Sand despised the "citizen king's" bourgeois respectability.

At first the bourgeoisie had accepted the king, believing that he would adopt a broad, liberal national policy; but soon they saw developing a new class system, in which the wealthy element set up a government as aristocratic as that of the old nobility. Unable to vote, the great mass of people could exercise no power. The moneyed and propertied class, however, replaced the blooded stock, claiming that all persons would benefit through equality of opportunity. Their unprivileged brothers could not see things in the same light. The wealthy few, the followers of Louis Philippe, soon discovered that instead of being the aggressors, attacking the defenders of the old régime, they had been converted into repressors, resisting the attempts of the masses to rise through political democracy.

From the first the king had encountered the opposition of the republicans. He managed to obtain the support of most moderate liberals by establishing a constitu- tional government, but by 1835 the rising tide *The Attempt to estab- lish a Strong Monarchy* of opposition, including an imperialist party bent on the restoration of the Napoleonic dynasty, aroused his fear. Like the Bourbons he determined on a policy of suppression. Freedom of the press was limited, and secret societies had to submit their constitutions for approval by the government. This reactionary policy only served to drive many moderate liberals into the republican camp.

Managing to rid himself of the opposition for a time, Louis Philippe exercised his personal power by selecting his cabinet irrespective of the wishes of parliament. Thiers, his premier, who believed that the king should reign but not rule, was compelled to resign, and the conservative Guizot (1787–1874) assumed his place. Thin and puny, with a pale complexion and emaciated features, he did not give the impression of being a man who could sway a mob. His enthusiasm when he spoke, however, caused people to forget his commonplace appearance. Guizot was a firm advocate of a government controlled by property owners. He believed that extension of the suffrage to the workingmen was foolish. "Work, get rich, and then you can vote" was his advice. A true disciple of Adam Smith, this French statesman saw to it that his government kept its hands off all internal political and social problems. Meanwhile the rich became richer and the masses became more destitute and dissatisfied. "Behold, gentlemen, the whole system of Government!" said a deputy in 1847, "Nothing, nothing, nothing!" Social problems now intensified the unrest.

During the reign of Louis Philippe thousands of wage-earners in the large cities of France were compelled to work *Increase of Opposition* long hours in unsanitary buildings for meager pay. They soon demanded that the government act to alleviate these conditions. Louis Philippe, however, ignored their requests and opposed their attempts to organize. Consequently the workers either became ardent republicans, determined to establish a real political and social democracy, or extreme socialists, bent on economic equality.

The attacks of the intellectuals on existing social and economic conditions were especially significant. Of these thinkers the very radical were, first, the followers of Saint-Simon, advocate of a utopia created under the leadership of men of wealth and men of science; next, those of Fourier, exponent of utopian communities; and, lastly, those of Proudhon, teacher of anarchism. All united in opposition to the government.

On the literary side, Honoré de Balzac (1799–1850) was the outstanding critic of the middle-class régime as established during the reign of Louis Philippe. Seeing little that was good in this new social order, Balzac, in his *Cousin Bette*, *Droll Stories*, and *Eugénie Grandet*, has given us a stimulating but exaggerated picture of bourgeois society. Although in his portrayal of the middle classes his studies are largely of the meaner and baser types, nevertheless his books are unequaled in literature for the vivid pictures they give of the cruel struggle from which there is no escape.

It was remarkable that the July Monarchy endured as long as it did. Opposed by the legitimists (supporters of the Bourbons), Bonapartists, republicans, wage-earners, and intellectuals, it could rely only on a small portion of the population of France. By 1848 the opposition became so general that a local insurrection in Paris brought about its end.

Between 1815 and 1848 the revolutionary movement spread to other parts of Europe. In Belgium it was especially important. The Congress of Vienna (1815) had handed Belgium over to Holland, in order to create a strong buffer state to the north of *The Revolution in Belgium* France. The Dutch and the Belgians, however, could not get along with one another, differing as they did in language, in religion, and in economic interests. The people of Holland spoke Dutch and were dominantly Protestants,— traders, and farmers. The Belgians, on the other hand, spoke French or Flemish and were Catholics and industrialists. Consequently they later demanded independence.

At first Holland opposed the attempt of the Belgians to be free, appealing to the five great powers to intervene on the ground that the territorial settlement of Vienna was threatened. But the powers found it difficult to act. Prussia, Austria, and Russia were occupied at home in combating revolutionary movements, while France wanted to have Belgium. Great Britain alone was in a position to intervene, as she was able to subordinate her internal problems to foreign questions. She opposed any move on the part of France to annex Belgium, favoring independence for the latter.

On November 18, 1830, the Belgian national congress met at Brussels and declared the House of Orange deposed, the throne vacant, and the future government of Belgium a limited and hereditary monarchy. Whereupon Talleyrand was sent by Louis Philippe to England to see what compensation France might gain from the change. He obtained little satisfaction. To save her face, France accepted an arrangement by which Belgium's neutrality would be guaranteed by the five great powers. After nine years of delay, during which Holland refused to accept this arrangement, the treaty was finally signed by England, France, Austria, Prussia, and Russia on April 19, 1839. This Belgian incident marked another breach in the Vienna settlement. Again the principles of nationalism and constitutionalism were victorious. The defenders of the old régime in western Europe were fighting a losing battle.

In certain parts of the Continent, however, the liberal movements between 1815 and 1848 were less successful, notably in Spain and Portugal. By the beginning of the nineteenth century these states were on the verge of losing their overseas colonial empires and were little better than vassals of France. Before Napoleon's expulsion from Spain the Spaniards drew up the constitution of 1812. Modeled after the French constitution of 1791, it asserted the sovereignty of the people and established a legislative assembly called the Cortes. Henceforth this constitution was the *Magna Carta* of the liberals.

Revolutionary Movements in the Iberian Peninsula, 1815–1848

The conservatives, however, regained the upper hand. Backed by the nobles and the clergy, King Ferdinand VII declared the constitution null and void, abolished the Spanish legislative body, and reestablished the old absolute government. But he failed to check the restless elements. Conservatives and liberals, hating each other, were soon ready to participate in a revolution. Threatened with bankruptcy and confronted with rebellion in the Americas, Spain soon found herself in a precarious position. A crisis was reached in 1820, when an uprising occurred in the army which had been raised to put down

Reactionary Rule of Ferdinand VII

the revolution overseas. This revolt spread into various parts of Spain. The cowardly Ferdinand now promised to support the constitution and begged the liberals to lay down their arms. Nevertheless, obtaining French aid in 1823, he plotted the overthrow of the constitutional government. Finally he was able to reëstablish an absolutism which shocked even the. conservative Metternich.

In 1823 Great Britain, influenced by commercial considerations, opposed the extension of the Metternichian system to the Americas. The United States also blocked attempts of the conservative powers to help Spain recover her empire. In the celebrated *Loss of Colonies and Civil War* Monroe Doctrine of 1823 the president of the United States proclaimed that "we should consider any attempt on their part to extend their system to any portion of this hemisphere as dangerous to our peace and safety." This policy helped to end European expansion in the new world. Ferdinand lost his colonies, and after ruling for nineteen years (1814–1833) as a cruel, unscrupulous, and treacherous king, set aside the Bourbon law of inheritance which fixed the royal succession only in the male side, and bequeathed his crown to his youthful daughter, Isabella II. Civil war followed, with Ferdinand's brother Don Carlos contesting the succession. Again Spain was torn by factional struggles which endured long past 1848. Liberalism was no longer the chief issue.

The history of Portugal in the early nineteenth century resembled that of Spain. The French, entering that country during the Napoleonic age, drove out the royal family, the members of which took refuge in *Triumph of Reaction in Portugal* their vast colony, Brazil. Great Britain then came to the rescue of Portugal, expelled the French, and made that country a satellite. Commercial relations and the strategic geographical location of Portugal on the Atlantic probably explain the British action. Soon tired of British control, the Portuguese in 1820 overthrew the regency established by England, and recalled the Portuguese king, John VI, from Brazil. Disturbed by the departure of the man they had accepted as their ruler, the Brazilians proclaimed their independence, while in Portugal the reactionaries, led by the king's younger son, Don Miguel, tried to overthrow King John.

Upon the death of John VI, in 1826, Pedro I of Brazil, his heir and now emperor of Brazil, granted the Portuguese people a parliamentary government and surrendered his crown to his seven-year-old daughter, Maria, on condition that she marry her uncle, Don Miguel. The latter disregarded these arrangements and proceeded to rule Portugal in true Metternichian fashion. Thus in the thirties Portugal, like Spain, was in theory a constitutional monarchy governed by a woman, but actually Don Miguel maintained absolute rule.

This situation was of great international importance. Both Great Britain and France were concerned with developments *International Signifi-* in Spain and Portugal. England, as in the *cance of Situation in* past, desired either to control these nations *Spain and Portugal* or to see them maintain their independence. France, on the other hand, wished to enhance her influence in the Iberian Peninsula, so that she might develop her Oriental and American ambitions and become a great world power.

At first both Great Britain and France coöperated in their support of the Spanish and Portuguese queens. In 1846 a rupture occurred between the two states. The cause of the trouble was the question of the marriages of Queen Isabella and her sister. Louis Philippe had arranged that Isabella should marry the duke of Cadiz and that her sister should become the wife of Louis' son, the duke of Montpensier. The French government, however, had promised the British authorities that the queen's sister should not wed a French prince until Isabella were married and had children. Nevertheless the marriages took place; and, to make matters worse, the duke of Cadiz was reported to be sterile. Surely Louis Philippe did not hope to carry out in 1846 the policy of Louis XIV, and to remove the Pyrenees Mountains by enabling his son to inherit both thrones! Whatever his purpose, the revolution of 1848, resulting in the overthrow of Louis Philippe, terminated another French attempt at dynastic aggrandizement.

Italy, more than any other country, suffered as a result of the Congress of Vienna. Despite common opposition to Napoleon the Italians were forced to submit to the harsh terms of a settlement arranged by *Revolutionary Developments in Italy* their victorious allies. These powers, disregarding the Italian desire for national unity, made that land again a "geographical expression." Most of the small states which had been independent before the Napoleonic invasion were given back their sovereignty. The king of Piedmont (House of Savoy) was restored to his throne, and he in turn reëstablished the privileged nobility and clergy. Ferdinand was placed at the head of the Kingdom of the Two Sicilies in the south, and in return for this favor he promised to make no foreign alliance and to grant no liberties to the people without Austrian consent. Parma, Modena, Lucca, Tuscany, the Papal States, Monaco, and San Marino were also recreated. Genoa and Venice alone were not restored, but were given to Piedmont and Austria respectively. Inasmuch as the states were small and weak, Austria was awarded a commanding position there in return for the loss of the Austrian Netherlands to Holland. She was given outright the richest part of the Po Valley, later the imperial provinces of Lombardy and Venetia, and Austrian princes and princesses were granted control over the duchies of Modena, Parma, and Tuscany.

Becoming a sea power as a result of the acquisition of Venetia, Austria was soon in a position to dominate the Adriatic Sea and to develop imperialistic ambitions. In the south, by virtue of an offensive and defensive treaty, Ferdinand, king of Naples, was virtually a satellite of the emperor of Austria. In fact, the king of Piedmont and the Pope were the only really independent princes on the Italian peninsula.

At first liberalism gained little headway in Italy. The rulers possessed practically autocratic power and tried earnestly to extinguish all the revolutionary ideas introduced by Napoleon. Constitutions, the Napoleonic code, gaslight, vaccination, and other innovations were abolished. In Turin French plants and vines were torn from the botanical gardens, and French furniture in the royal palace was destroyed. Italy, politically, socially, and economically, returned to the old régime, enforced by the Inquisition and by the vigilant police. Heavy taxation, industrial stagnation, illiteracy, and foreign control made the future appear dark.

Attempts of petty Italian despots to maintain conservatism caused much discontent. Despite their opposition new ideas, new habits, and new conventions persisted.

Growth of Nationalism

The Italians who had fought in the Napoleonic wars had become conscious of a national unity which oppression could not obliterate. Hence the middle-class doctrine of liberty in education, in religion, and in business, as well as in government, permeated Italy. There could be but one logical result: union and independence.

Secret societies played an important rôle in the events which led to the unification of Italy. The Carbonari, organized in various parts of Italy to work for unity, paved the way for the revolutions which started in Naples in 1820. This uprising was followed by a similar one in Piedmont, which was backed by the heir to the throne, Charles Albert of Savoy. These revolts, however, were easily repressed by Austria, and reaction became more brutal than ever.

Early in the nineteenth century appeared Joseph Mazzini (1805–1872), founder of the Young Italy movement. During his youth he felt keenly the unhappy situation of his beloved Italy. Favoring an ideal republic in which Italians could unite to create a superior political and social order not only in Italy but also throughout Europe, he soon became an ardent nationalist leader. Shortly after the European revolutions of 1830 he formed the society of "Young Italy," which within two years numbered sixty thousand members. Many of his followers suffered martyrdom in the local uprisings which followed, and Mazzini eventually failed in his attempt to create an independent Italian republic.

After 1830 it became evident that a different leader was essential if Italy were to be liberated from Austrian tyranny. Many patriots therefore favored a federation headed by the Pope, who might well represent Italian as well as religious unity. The Holy See wisely discouraged this movement, realizing that the head of the universal church must not be directly involved in a national movement. Finally there appeared an acceptable leader around whom all Italians could rally.

Charles Albert of the House of Savoy ascended the throne of Piedmont in 1831. Discredited by the failure of the constitutional movement in 1821, he was accused of being clerical and therefore antinational. This was not true. In a short time patriots recognized that he had the cause of Italy at heart and, like Dante and Machiavelli, dreamed of freeing Italy from foreign control. Surrounded by the selfish, corrupt, and jealous rulers of the small Italian states, he became to Italian patriots "the hero of freedom and light — the possible savior of Italy." Backed by his subjects, he also aroused the interest of such liberal nations as England and France, who favored a constitutional monarchy.

In 1846 Pius IX (1846–1878) ascended the papal throne. As a cardinal, in 1840 he had openly opposed reactionary oppression in Italy. As Pope, one of the first things he did was to pardon all political offenders and suspects. Metternich was dumfounded. "We were prepared for everything but a Liberal Pope," he exclaimed when he heard that Pius had appeared in 1848 on a balcony and, in addressing a crowd, had said "God bless Italy."

Between 1815 and 1848 the revolutionary movement spread rapidly throughout western Europe. It even reached the Russian borderlands, where the Poles decided to fight for freedom.

In 1492 Poland was one of the largest states in Europe. Including territory which stretched from the Baltic almost to the Black Sea, and from the Oder to the *Poland to 1815* Dnieper River, it controlled important water routes between these widely separated bodies of water. Governed by weak rulers whose power was limited by the nobles and by foreign intervention, the Polish state underwent a process of disintegration which resulted in the partition of that unfortunate country in the eighteenth century by Russia, Prussia, and Austria. This disaster merely served to increase the national feeling among the Poles. Working constantly for freedom, they had visions of achieving this end during the Napoleonic wars, but they were speedily disillusioned. Again in 1815, when Alexander I of Russia, receiving the major part of Poland, conceived the generous and sentimental plan of restoring the Polish kingdom and of making himself its ruler, the Poles entertained new dreams of freedom. The personal union of Russia and Poland, however, with Alexander as emperor of one and king of the other, was not satisfactory. Furthermore, Austria and Prussia refused to return their Polish possessions to the new kingdom. The Polish tragedy persisted.

Alexander gave the Poles under his control a constitution and tried unsuccessfully to govern them. But "the Russian oil and the Polish vinegar refused to mix." *Opposition to Russia* The Poles considered themselves a superior people. Further, their aristocrats resented Russian control. Polish leaders from the beginning refused to coöperate with Alexander in his attempts to establish a constitutional government. Failing in his efforts to maintain a diet, the Czar, after 1820, did not call another for five years. In 1825, because of the growth of secret societies, he practically nullified its power.

After the death of Alexander I (1825) the Poles started on another revolution in 1830, proclaiming the deposition of Czar Nicholas as king of Poland. At first the new Czar found it difficult to concentrate his troops against Poland. By the fall of 1831, however, the revolution was quelled, an iron rule was imposed upon the people, and Poland became a part of Russia. This revolution was unfortunate for both the Poles and the Russians. Before this time some form of constitutional government had existed; thenceforth autocracy enforced by the sword was triumphant. Liberal France and England remonstrated with Russia over her treatment of the Poles, but to no avail. Yet Poland, helpless and disarmed as she was, remained unconquerable.

After 1815 Austria, the dominant Continental power, became the conservative bulwark in central Europe. Lacking national, racial, or social unity, its peoples depended wholly upon the maintenance of the *status quo* and the House of Hapsburg as the single unifying force. Supported by a loyal nobility, an extensive bureaucracy, and a powerful church, this dynasty now led the *Repression in Central Europe (1815–1848)* opposition against all change. Indeed, its representative, Francis I (1792–1835), dedicated his life to the maintenance of the old régime.

He sincerely despised learning which he, moreover, regarded as dangerous for the state, the source of revolutionary ideas. "I do not want scholars — I want good subjects," he once told a delegation of professors. Books to him were stuff and nonsense; philosophy, art, literature, even religion if tainted with mysticism, were collectively referred to as "those things," and were assigned to the jurisdiction of the police. He even distrusted technical progress; he was opposed to railroads because he feared that they might bring the revolution into the country.[1]

From the first Francis accepted the patriarchal concept of the monarchy, believing that he was the "father of his people." In his last will he advised his son not to shift the foundations of the edifice of state. "Reign, and change nothing," he wrote; "plant yourself firmly and unswervingly in the soil of the principles by whose constant observance I not only guided the Monarchy through storm and stress, but also secured for it the high place which it occupies in the world."

The Hapsburgs were not able to make use of this favored position, because their Austrian and Hungarian possessions lacked unity. The dominant nationalities were the Germans in Austria (pure Austrians) and *Various Nationalities under Hapsburg Rule* the Magyars in Hungary. In parts of both countries were many representatives of various Slavic nationalities, as well as some Jews. In western Austria, where lay the ancient possessions of the Hapsburgs, the inhabitants were chiefly German. To the north Bohemia, inhabited by the Czechs, could not forget that she had lost her freedom in the sixteenth century when absorbed by Austria. To the east lay the Hungarian kingdom, now belonging to the Hapsburgs. Once a proud, independent state, defending Christendom

[1] Bagger, *Francis Joseph*, p. 39.

against the attacks of the Turks, the Magyars resented Austrian domination. To the south were the purely Italian provinces. All these peoples helped to make the Hapsburg empire a "national cockpit."

To rule this heterogenous collection of peoples was a herculean task. Emperor Francis I had the assistance of the capable Metternich, who believed that so long

Metternich's Reactionary Policies as nationalism, constitutionalism, and other liberal ideas could be kept out, the old régime could be maintained. He also realized that the Danube basin was a geographical and economic unit; therefore the political unity of the various nationalities, however diverse, within the empire, was necessary in order to maintain "their mutual welfare, created by natural circumstances." In his opinion, constitutions and national independence, if granted, would open the gates to anarchy; autocracy must be preserved, if only as a police power.

Metternich's efficient methods temporarily prevailed. To check national movements, he set various groups to watch one another. To exclude revolutionary ideas, a cordon of tariffs and censors was erected around the empire. The mails were opened and searched at the frontiers; the press was controlled by the government; and education was placed in the hands of the conservative church. Music, art, and the drama were censored; foreigners, professors, and students were watched; and all societies were suppressed. Indeed, Metternich was congratulated by friends for keeping the study of science and of history out of the schools. Determined to preserve the supremacy of the Hapsburg dynasty in central Europe by maintaining the established order, this energetic minister refused to distinguish between liberalism and radicalism. Anything new he considered dangerous.

He soon discovered that his task of defending the *status quo,* not only in Austria and Hungary, the personal possessions of the Hapsburgs, but also throughout central Europe, was exceedingly difficult. Since 1815 many Germans in the various states of that region had favored the establishment of constitutional government and the creation of a German nation.

These ideas were especially popular in Prussia, the largest of the German states not under Hapsburg control.

Wars and the benevolent despotism of her Hohenzollern monarchs had made Prussia in the eighteenth century the most powerful kingdom in north-central Europe. At that time the Hohenzollerns were the only rulers in a position to question Hapsburg supremacy. *The Regeneration of Prussia* Since the death of the greatest representative of this dynasty, Frederick II (1740–1786), however, the Prussians had seemed content to live upon the reputation gained for them by that capable ruler. Hapsburg leadership was not opposed. Suddenly the Napoleonic invasions and the defeat suffered at the battle of Jena (1806) roused the Prussians from their lethargy. They realized that their beloved land was no longer the great and powerful state of the preceding century.

A transformation now followed. Those Germans who rose as a result of the struggle against nature and man, who, surrounded by enemies, had created under the paternal and military guidance of their Hohenzollern rulers a powerful and a prosperous state, experienced a remarkable regeneration. Realizing that something must be done if Prussia was to regain her position of authority in north-central Europe, they brought about a remarkable reform of the Prussian state between 1806 and 1848.

Conservatives as well as liberals united in seeking vengeance for the national humiliation suffered at Jena. Philosophers, who previously had been writing about a federation of European states or about mankind, began to write about Prussia. All classes — nobles, clergy, middle-class men, and peasants — stood ready to sacrifice for the common cause of the state. Musicians, philosophers, scientists, traders, and students of the various German states, inspired by this nationalistic zeal, expressed their patriotism by writing stimulating books, making wonderful discoveries, and composing beautiful music. Fichte and Hegel, the philosophers; Ranke and Niebuhr, the historians; Heine, the poet; and Beethoven and Wagner, the composers, — all reflect the influence of this nationalistic zeal, described by the German writers Schlegel and Herder.

Pronounced interest in German history was another evidence of the popular desire for unity. Documents dealing with the early history of the German people *Leading Exponents of Revolutionary Ideals* were carefully collected, and such historians as Theodor Mommsen (1817–1903) and Leopold von Ranke (1795–1886) began to write history in a scientific way. The use of contemporary material in the search for truth was emphasized by these fathers of historical writing. Moreover, the past, they believed, could be truly interpreted through an impartial study of all facts. Later other historians — Heinrich von Treitschke (1834–1896), for example — used facts to justify and to glorify a united German state.

One of the outstanding exponents of the absolute state was the German philosopher Georg Wilhelm Friedrich Hegel (1770–1831). In his *Philosophy of History* he extolled the national state to such an extent that it became the ultimate source of social authority, the arbiter of social life, the immortal God. World unity, he believed, would be attained through it. Although he opposed political liberalism and advocated the absolute form of government, nevertheless his emphasis upon a unified German state and the rise of a "people" helped to encourage the national movement.

The influence of revolutionary ideals was evident in German literature. Of the many writers who fought reaction in their books, Heinrich Heine (1797–1856) was preëminent. His highest ambition was to help build a greater and consolidated Germany, regardless of the interdiction of his works in his own country and the oppression he suffered because he was a Jew. Yet "he counted his poetic gifts little beside his fervor for liberty." He wished to be remembered not so much for his songs, which gave their deathless impulse to such composers as Franz, Schubert, and particularly Schumann, as for his struggles toward democracy. These endeavors and his hatred of complacent customs found expression in all his essays no less than in his verses. Like Anatole France he was bitterly cynical and skeptical. Unfortunately, in laying bare the weaknesses of his generation he caused many influential Germans to believe that he was a destructive critic, who favored the overthrow of everything that was sacred in the established order. For example, he wrote:

> Aye, you must have lost your senses,
> Thus to speak before the masses,
> Thus to dare to talk of preachers
> And of potentates and princes.
>
> Friend, you're doomed, so it appears:
> For the princes have long arms,
> And the preachers have long tongues,
> And the masses have long ears.

He represented that opposition to the state in political and social life which, in Germany, was to bring about important changes.

The national ideal also inspired German composers of the nineteenth century. Influenced by romanticism and by the unrest existing in Germany during the latter part of his life, Ludwig van Beethoven (1770–1827) in his music rejected the conventional emphasis upon a standard form and adopted new forms in order to transmit individual, self-conscious feeling. This revolutionary change enabled the German composers to express their inner thoughts. Therefore we see in some of Beethoven's musical compositions, and in the operas of Richard Wagner (1813–1883), a manifestation of German nationalism. Based on the German legends of medieval times, most of Wagner's operas reflect the composer's desire to emphasize, as he says, "the Folk as the community of all who feel a common and collective want." The music itself, with its heavy, massive chords, also pictures the powerful German nation which came into existence before his death.

German nationalism resulted in the rise of one leader who differed from his contemporaries. He was Friedrich Jahn (1778–1852). Favoring physical development as a means of bringing about the rise of a German state, he was largely responsible for the emphasis upon gymnastic exercises in the schools. He also became an ardent advocate of German unity under Hohenzollern rule. In stirring lectures he summed up the national spirit which made possible not only the rise of

Prussia but also the creation of the German empire. "God save the king and preserve the house of Hohenzollern," he said in one of his most famous addresses; "protect our country; increase the German element; purify our national character from aping of things French and foreign; make Prussia a shining pattern for the German union; out of the union call forth the new emperor; and grant graciously and speedily the one thing of pressing need, — a wise constitution."

The formation of a *Zollverein*, or customs union, was one of the most notable achievements of the Prussian government *The Zollverein* during the restless years preceding the revolution of 1848. Most of the German states had had their own tariff frontiers; therefore an article sent from Paris to Berlin in passing through various countries was assessed many duties, which increased its price. Trade and industry could not develop under these circumstances. The customs union, by abolishing these numerous duties, not only lowered the price of a manufactured article to the purchaser but also stimulated the growth of trade and industry and made possible the rise of a small but wealthy middle class, grateful for the economic unity brought about by the government.

Consequently the Prussian authorities enlarged the *Zollverein*, manipulating the tariffs so as to favor states within the union and injure those outside it. Once in the union, the business men who benefited became ardent supporters of the government. Thus, while Metternich was antagonizing business men by secret police, rules, and regulations, the Prussian government won their support. By 1834 the *Zollverein* included most of the German states except Austria, Hanover, Oldenburg, and three Hanse towns. Once this economic web enveloped the member states, it was drawn in such a way as to bring them closer and closer to Prussia. That kingdom, having demonstrated the value of economic unity under her direction, was now in a position to lead the movement for political unity.

Between 1815 and 1848 the opposition to liberalism in the various German states only served to increase the strength of the nationalistic and constitutional movements. After the battle of Jena many Germans had been promised constitutions by their rulers, once they had expelled the hated French conqueror. Now that he was overthrown they asked their kings to carry out these promises. But the monarchs, believing that the constitutional *Development of Liberal Movements* and nationalistic movements would not merely limit their authority but also deprive them of their crowns, opposed both union and liberty.

Opposition to these rulers soon arose from an unexpected source. The younger generation of Germans organized a students' league, called the *Burschenschaft*, at the University of Jena, and the movement spread to other universities. Professors and students soon began to write pamphlets, to engage in discussions, and to foment demonstrations. Adopting the black, red, and gold flag, they instigated a determined attempt to create a liberal and united German nation.

A new fight for freedom had begun. This movement reached its height when, on October 18, 1817, members of the *Burschenschaft* from various universities celebrated at a castle known as the Wartburg the anniversary of Luther's theses and also the battle of Leipzig. At this gathering enthusiastic speakers urged their listeners to help create the German union, which Luther had advocated and which the overthrow of Napoleon had made possible. During the evening, when patriotism ran high, the young Germans threw various emblems of tyranny into the fire and announced the future creation of a constitutional German nation. After the festival a reactionary journalist, August von Kotzebue, regarded as an agent secretly serving Russia, was murdered by a student patriot. A sympathetic minister described this act as that of "a pure pious youth," and as "a beautiful sign of the times." The princes, however, considered the assassination a most dangerous act. Many believed that it marked the beginning of a revolution. Some of them now agreed to establish the constitutions they had promised, but most of them preferred

> To promise, pause, prepare, postpone,
> And end by letting things alone;
> In short, to earn the people's pay
> By doing nothing every day.

Metternich and his supporters decided to act. In his opinion the Wartburg festival and the Kotzebue assassination were manifestations of a movement to destroy the forces of law and order and to repeat the horrors of the French Revolution. Feeble attempts to establish constitutions were put down in Bavaria, in Württemberg, in Saxe-Weimar, and in other small states. At Carlsbad, a place in Bohemia "where sick people go to drink water and to revive their livers," Metternich in 1819 forced the Diet of the German Confederation to indorse decrees regulating the press, intimidating universities, and curbing public opinion in other ways. In Prussia, ardent advocates of German unity and of constitutionalism were arrested and the nationalistic writings of certain patriots were suppressed. Metternich could only delay the march of progress. Liberalism was forced underground for a while, but by 1848 the spread of the revolutionary movement culminated in uprisings throughout Europe.

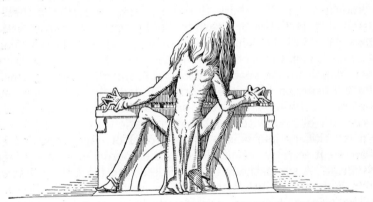

FRANZ LISZT, *Hungarian composer and pianist in the age of romanticism, as he appeared to a caricaturist in 1836*

CHAPTER V

The Crisis: 1848

THE revolutionary movement reached a crisis in 1848. Uprisings which occurred in most European nations at that time were of special significance, since they marked a definite stage in the development and expansion of the middle-class phase of Western civilization. Conservative landowners still dominated political and social life, especially in Austria and Italy. Yet even in these states appeared many signs of impending changes. Among these were emphasis upon the right of the common man to participate in government, opposition to social inequalities and economic restrictions, belief in the need for secular education by means of public schools, insistence upon religious toleration, and the growing recognition of the principle of national self-determination.

The uprising in France in 1848 was a spectacular example of bourgeois opposition to reactionary government. As we have already seen, the middle classes over-threw the autocratic Charles X in 1830 and replaced him with their own candidate, the *Fall of the July Monarchy* citizen king, Louis Philippe. The latter's government catered to the interests of the wealthy bourgeoisie by encouraging economic development and maintaining peace. Opposed not merely by the legitimists, Bonapartists, and other defenders of the old régime, but also by republicans (consisting of many middle-class men and intellectuals who believed that the unrestricted individualism of a republic meant real prosperity and happiness), the position of the July Monarch became precarious. To add to his difficulties the exponents of a newer revolution, the socialists, joined the republicans in agitating for a democracy because they regarded a popularly controlled state as a step toward a government which might reorganize economic life and society in the interests of the workers. The immediate acquisition of the ballot seemed vital to the ultimate realization of such an idea.

In 1847 Louis Philippe's reactionary government, headed by Guizot and supported only by plutocratic elements of the middle classes, encountered the opposition of all other elements. At first a few moderate reformers tried to avoid revolution by demanding that the deputies to the chamber be elected by the people rather than selected by Guizot.

A typical conservative, Guizot claimed that this opposition was the work of a few rascals, and refused to countenance proposed changes. Meanwhile reform banquets took place all over the country. At those held in Paris great enthusiasm was aroused, and at one, all individuals who could, raised their glasses, drank "confusion" to the king, and called for the overthrow of Guizot. On Washington's birthday, February 22, 1848, matters came to a head. The government decided to demonstrate its authority by forbidding the holding of a huge banquet in Paris that evening. Riots led by students and workers the next morning resulted in the killing of twenty-three persons and the wounding of thirty when the royal guards in front of Guizot's house fired on the mob.

These disorders meant revolution. The majority of the citizen soldiers joined the insurgents. Again the turbulent crowds gathered in the narrow streets of Paris, shouting "Down with Guizot!" and "Long Live Reform!" On the evening of February 23 Paris was brilliantly illuminated, for the stubborn minister had finally given way. The revolutionists did not stop here. They now determined to overthrow the monarchy. Another minor massacre served to arouse the enthusiastic hatred of the people. Inspired by the tocsins sounded from the various towers of the city, they engaged in riots, crying, "Long Live the Republic!" On February 24 Louis Philippe abdicated in favor of his grandson, the little count of Paris, and followed his predecessor to England. An assembly, convened to draw up a new constitution, reaffirmed a republic, already proclaimed by the Chamber of Deputies and by the local authorities at the Hôtel de Ville.

The uprising of 1848 was largely confined to Paris. Although the monarch was unpopular throughout France, the men who actually overthrew the government were the Parisian workers, led by a small intelligent group from the middle class. Nevertheless the great majority of the French people gave these insurrections their tacit support, believing that the benefits so gloriously gained through the Great Revolution were at stake.

As in 1789, sharp divisions occurred among the leaders in the new Provisional Government. The socialists had supported the republicans, because they hoped that, once the republic was established, nationalization of property would be effected. *The Attempt to establish a Socialist State* But the republicans felt that things had gone far enough. They proposed to maintain the capitalistic system, and regarded with suspicion the activities of the socialist leader Louis Blanc, though they could not afford to antagonize him. Aware of the unfortunate inequalities brought about by the introduction of machinery into France, the meager wages and unsanitary conditions in factories, and the evils of child labor, Blanc had outlined an economic and social utopia to be gained through the creation of workshops. Let the state, he said, take over industries and factories; then the people through the ballot could rule the state. Once in charge of the government, the workers would assume control of the factories.

The republicans, although they appointed Blanc minister of public works, did not propose to establish socialism. They announced the national guard open to all classes and proceeded to declare for a republic, for universal suffrage, and for the establishment of "National Workshops." For the sake of political expediency they put the unemployed to work on the roads or on other public undertakings. By May 100,000 men, under the direction of a superintendent who was opposed to socialism, were earning forty cents a day destroying roads and then rebuilding them.

Meanwhile the republicans and socialists quarreled over governmental policies. Blanc protested the manner in which the government operated the workshops, saying that the republicans were secretly undermining their existence. Disputes over French foreign policy helped to increase the ill-feeling between the followers of Blanc and the republicans. They quarreled over the advisability of aiding the Poles in their opposition to Russian oppression; the radicals favored intervention, but the moderates opposed this policy, being more interested in domestic matters. Finally a crisis occurred. The abolition of the workshops by the Assembly in June, 1848, resulted in the second phase of the revolution — the conflict between the socialists of Paris and the republicans.

Barricades again appeared across the crooked streets, and bloody encounters took place in various parts of the city. In *The New Revolution* this struggle the socialist cause was doomed. Not only their enemies, the bourgeoisie in Paris, but also their opponents in the provinces of France, including peasants and wealthy landowners who flocked to the capital, were determined to overthrow the new radicals who threatened to destroy the "benefits" of the French Revolution — private property and complete economic as well as political individualism.

Intrusting full authority to General Cavaignac, the republicans successfully suppressed this revolt. On June 26, after four days of desperate fighting, the Assembly, dominated by republicans, again controlled Paris. There were ten thousand casualties and eleven thousand prisoners. The harsh suppression of this revolt created a bitter hatred between the two factions.

The National Constituent Assembly, controlled by the moderates, drew up a vague Declaration of Rights and proceeded to formulate a republican government. *The Second French Republic* Incorporated in this government were a single assembly of 750 representatives, elected by universal suffrage, and a president, elected by the people every four years. The president selected his own cabinet, and the House of Deputies appointed a Council of State, or Senate, over which presided a vice-president. Thus the legislative and executive branches of the administration were separated.

Having created the new government, the Constituent Assembly called an election. The middle classes nominated their leader, General Cavaignac; the socialists named Ledru-Rollin; and the Catholic republicans selected Lamartine to run for the presidency. In addition to these candidates there was a dark horse, Louis Napoleon Bonaparte. Aided by the legend which had grown around the memory of his illustrious uncle, Napoleon I, he promised the people peace, order, plenty, security, and glory. These were the things which most peasants and business men wanted. Glory or power appealed to all, but it was not so much the glory of the future as that of the past which decided the election. In 1848 this man, "with a face like a fish," was elected president of the Second French Republic.

Central Europe at the opening of 1848 was also in a restless state. Everywhere men were disgusted with the older order. A revolutionary spirit was at work, affecting the minds and the activities of thou- *Liberal Ferment in Middle Europe and in Italy* sands in Germany, in Austria, and in Italy. Obviously the policy of repression, anti-national and anti-liberal, had weakened the entire political and social structure in these various countries. Actually there were individuals ready and anxious to lead in a movement which would destroy an old and rotting political and social system which could no longer justify its existence.

The character of the revolutions assumed different forms in the various countries. All of them constituted attempts on the part of the people, usually led by intellectuals and other representatives of the middle classes, to secure national independence or unity and to substitute bourgeois equality for aristocratic privilege.

The liberal movements encountered the determined opposition of the German rulers. These petty sovereigns did not propose to see their authority limited, nor did they welcome attacks upon the confederation *The Revolt in the Germanies* created at Vienna. Sending their representatives to the Diet of the confederation, most of them backed the Hapsburg ruler, who as president tried to maintain at least

a semblance of imperial unity. While working for beneficial
reforms within the various states which composed the confederation, the liberals contemplated the creation of a democratic
German government and the acquisition of personal liberty.

The Germanic Confederation, 1815–1866

Shortly after 1815 it appeared as if the German liberals
would force their sovereigns to establish constitutions. Most
kings or princelets in the confederation promised to grant
constitutions and to appoint liberal ministries. Affecting to
be sanguine over the outlook, monarchs shook hands with
professors, workingmen, and students. When a preliminary
assembly was called in 1848 to make arrangements for the

formation of a national convention which was to establish the new German union, many individuals went so far as to predict the creation of a unified constitutional government.

But these German liberals underestimated the strength of the opposition. They either did not realize that before unity could be attained Hapsburg supremacy must end, or they believed that the revolutionary movement in Austria would destroy Hapsburg power. For a while it seemed as if the old régime in Austria would be easily overthrown. The emperor, Ferdinand I (1835–1848), was virtually an imbecile, it being said of him that he held conversations with horses in preference to human beings. Metternich was becoming aged, and the other advisers were timid and ignorant. By 1848 serfdom, social privilege, injustice, and illiteracy existed as of old, but the obedience of former days was gone. Intellectuals openly attacked this antiquated system, favoring political rights, social equality, and educational development, so that Austria might introduce the Industrial Revolution and prosper.

Even Metternich realized at this time that a change was inevitable. "I am an old practitioner," he said, "and I know how to discriminate between curable and incurable diseases. This one is fatal; here we *Hapsburg and Hohenzollern Reforms* hold on as long as we can, but I despair of the issue." For many years Metternich had defended the autocratic government and what he called "the legitimate revolution." Improvement must come, he had often said, from above. Institutions must grow over a period of time and be cultivated by responsible and intelligent statesmen. With this idea in mind he had favored Austrian participation in the *Zollverein*, the development of industry, and the expansion of transportation,—a program which could not fail to benefit the growing middle classes, whose revolutionary tendencies he dreaded. But his plans for the establishment of an enlightened and efficient governmental system had been frustrated in their inception by the ultraconservatism of the emperor, Francis I, and by the personal opposition of such statesmen as Count Kolowrat, an "aristocratic, ambitious, and a keen reformer, eager for the rights of the middle classes and the amelioration of the peasants' lot." Consequently in 1848 when professors and students participated in conflicts with the imperial soldiers, Metternich, concluding that his period of usefulness was over, fled.

Upon Metternich's departure the panicky emperor decided to turn liberal. He issued an edict in which he promised a popular constitution, freedom of the press, a parliament, and a national guard to his Austrian subjects. Conservatism seemed doomed. At this critical moment the Magyars also arose in revolt, demanding autonomy and a constitution. The Hapsburg ruler, as king of Hungary, again gave way. Granting them a constitution, freedom of the press, and a national guard, he also promised them autonomy in place of complete independence.

While the frightened Ferdinand I was making numerous pledges his neighbor, the Hohenzollern king, was promising similar reforms. By 1848 liberalism was powerful enough to achieve open expression. Mass meetings of workers and students were held in parks and in beer halls, rioting occurred, and demands for liberty and equality finally forced the nervous king to call a provisional diet to discuss a constitution. News of Metternich's downfall inspired the liberals to increase their activities; they were soon practically in control of Berlin.

Frederick William IV (1840–1861) continued to make promises. He conceded a representative constitution and freedom of the press to his subjects; and when the liberals clashed with his soldiers, the terror-stricken Prussian king temporarily allowed the mob to bear arms. Meanwhile he appointed a liberal ministry, announced that Prussia was merged into Germany, adopted the black, red, and gold (the Pan-German colors), addressed the students, and even conversed with the people. His heir, the prince of Prussia, a confirmed reactionary who later became William I, fled to England. But conservatism had not yet reached the end of its tether. Backed by the reactionary junkers, the Prussian king managed to maintain the *status quo* by making one important concession, a constitutional government. Although he refused to accept the scheme drawn up by his assembly, he granted, in 1850, a constitution which, while it provided for certain personal liberties and a bicameral legislature, nevertheless established the class system of voting, by which the loyal, wealthy landowners (junkers) dominated the two houses.

While the Hapsburgs and Hohenzollerns were trying to pacify the liberals in Vienna and Berlin, the Magyars and Slavs, especially the Czechs, decided to strike for freedom. Under their dynamic leader, *The Revolt of the Magyars and Slavs* Louis Kossuth (1802–1894), the Magyars abolished feudalism and established an independent state. Kossuth, however, refused to coöperate with the Slav and Rumanian minorities in Hungary in their revolutionary activities, for, although he desired an independent Hungarian state, he was not concerned with the rights and claims of the Slavs.

At first Ferdinand neglected the situation in Hungary. Confronted by revolutions in Vienna and Prague, he finally capitulated to his Viennese subjects and concentrated upon the Czechs in Bohemia. The *Suppression of Uprisings* latter were very turbulent, demanding a popular diet, equality, and the official use of the Czech language. But Ferdinand soon reëstablished his authority there. The Austrian troops, under the capable General Windischgrätz, by bombarding and capturing the Bohemian capital, Prague, in 1848, managed to end the rebellion. A determined attempt to Germanize the Bohemians followed.

Successful in ending the revolt in Prague, General Windischgrätz now marched to Vienna, determined to crush the uprising. This he did. Thereupon Ferdinand I, who had promised many liberal reforms, abdicated on December 2, 1848, at the request of his reactionary subjects, and was succeeded by his nephew, Francis Joseph I (1848–1916), a lad of eighteen, destined to a long and eventful reign. At first the young emperor was advised by Prince Felix Schwarzenberg, brother-in-law of Windischgrätz, who as a dictator attempted to destroy all traces of liberalism.

Having thwarted the liberal movement in Austria, the conservative supporters of the young Hapsburg ruler turned to

Hungary. Inspired by Kossuth, the Magyars were still struggling for freedom and at the same time were engaged in an earnest effort to prevent the Slavs from obtaining their independence. This selfish policy proved to be a mistake. The Slavs, led by the clever Jellačić, governor of Croatia, succeeded in gaining the favor of the Hapsburg ruler by promising support against the Magyars in the latter's struggle for independence. Therefore when Austria declared war upon the Magyars a Slavic army invaded Hungary.

The uprising was soon crushed. Czar Nicholas I of Russia, convinced that the revolutionary movement had to be checked lest the Poles institute another uprising, sent a Russian army into Hungary. Invaded from three sides by Austrian, Slavic, and Russian forces, the Magyars laid down their arms. Disregarding this surrender, the Austrian general punished the rebels by executing thirteen Magyar leaders and jailing several hundred officers. Atrocities were committed also by the Slavic and Rumanian soldiers, who used this opportunity to express their hatred of the Magyars. By 1849 the reform movement seemed a failure. The Hohenzollerns and Hapsburgs still claimed that they ruled by the "will of God" rather than by that of the nation.

The one hope of the liberals in central Europe was the German parliament at Frankfurt. Inspired by the overthrow of Metternich, liberals from the various German states had met on March 31, 1848, at Frankfurt, to prepare the way for this national German assembly. Most of those men, enthusiastic idealists (like their predecessors who formulated the Declaration of the Rights of Man during the French Revolution), earnestly expressed lofty but impractical sentiments. After wasting much precious time they decided to call a national assembly. On May 18, 1848, representatives to the new German parliament met for the first time. Some five hundred and sixty-eight inexperienced delegates, elected by universal male suffrage, represented the Germans in central Europe.

The Frankfurt Parliament

This national parliament, called to draw up a constitution, was not a representative body, inasmuch as the landed interests, big business, and labor sent few representatives. The assembly was largely under the control of bourgeois intellectuals, professors, lawyers, and literary men, who expressed unctuous but vague ideas. They did, however, decide to select a provisional ruler for the new German government. After a struggle between the Austrian and Prussian factions the Archduke John, a liberal Hapsburg, was appointed "imperial vicar." He was to govern the new German state while the parliament was in session. Opposed by the aristocrats, who favored separate governments, and by the radicals, who protested against a prince as head of the assembly, the archduke exerted little authority.

The delegates at Frankfurt soon found it difficult to agree upon what should constitute the new German state. One group favored a "great Germany" which should include Austria; the other element *Austro-Prussian Rivalry* advocated a "small Germany" which should exclude the Hapsburg state. Representatives from Austria strongly supported the first proposition, believing that it would insure Hapsburg rule in the proposed union, while the Prussian delegates, determined to establish Prussian preponderance, worked ardently for the second plan.

After months of earnest discussion the parliament of Frankfurt, during the latter part of 1848, adopted the idea of a small Germany which should not include Austria. Convinced that the new state should be *Refusal of Crown by Hohenzollern Ruler* purely German, they decided to exclude Austria because that land was inhabited by many non-Germans. Consequently, early in 1849, the parliament authorized the provisional government to enter into diplomatic relations with Austria, thus treating the latter as a foreign power.

The Prussian delegates were very enthusiastic. They approved of the liberal constitution, creating a German nation in which they would be the dominant element. To confirm their hopes the assembly, on March 28, 1849, elected the Hohenzollern ruler, Frederick William IV, German Emperor. But the Prussian king did not share the enthusiasm of the liberal German delegates at Frankfurt. Announcing that he did not propose to become emperor of a "small Germany" which would exclude Austria and which would be weakened because of religious and dynastic antagonisms within, he spurned the offer. Furthermore he stated that he would not accept a crown handed to him by revolutionists rather than by God. His refusal to take the office greatly hastened the disintegration of the Frankfurt assembly.

Although Frederick William rejected the crown offered by revolutionists, he accepted the idea of a German union under
The New German League
his leadership. To achieve it, he believed the consent and the support of the various dynasties were necessary. With this idea in mind he called an assembly, at Berlin, of the rulers, or their representatives, of the most important states, including Austria, Bavaria, Württemberg, Saxony, and Hanover. At this meeting, which occurred in May, 1849, the members were to draw up a constitution creating a German state. The refusal of Austria and Bavaria, however, to participate in the discussions forced Frederick William to create a league of northern German states which counterbalanced the Hapsburg power in the south.

The Austrian dynasty, preoccupied by the uprising in Hungary, was unable to offer much resistance to Prussian activity.
Hapsburg Opposition to the League
By the spring of 1850, however, the revolution having been suppressed in Austria and Hungary, the Hapsburg government, as head of the old German Confederation, called a meeting at Frankfurt to investigate this union, or league, created by Frederick William IV. In response the Prussian ruler assembled his group at Erfurt (March 20, 1850). Thus central Europe was divided into two groups, one dominated by Austria, the other by Prussia.

War now threatened to break out between the two parties. Aware of this possibility, the Prussian king turned to neighboring powers, France and Russia, in order to
The "Humiliation" of Olmütz
ascertain their attitude if a conflict should occur. Louis Napoleon of France conveyed the impression that he would not oppose the formation of a German union under the direction of Prussia, and conse-

quently Frederick William concluded that France would remain neutral. Russia, on the other hand, still appeared loyal to autocratic Austria. For this reason a war with the latter at the time would be inopportune. Consequently the Prussian king temporarily abandoned his plan to establish a German nation. At the famous interview, or "humiliation," of Olmütz (November 29, 1850) Prussia recognized the supremacy in central Europe of the German confederation, created at the Congress of Vienna, and of its president, the Hapsburg ruler, Francis Joseph. The new-born Prussian union was dissolved.

The failure to establish a German nation in central Europe did not prevent the rise of Austria's great rival, Prussia. Prussian leadership, it is true, waned after her king refused the offer of the Frankfurt assembly. Yet she remained a power in central Europe. Austria was not able to destroy the customs union (*Zollverein*), which made possible a remarkable economic development in central Europe. The growing middle classes, benefiting especially by this union and recognizing the value of political unity and the inability of the liberals to achieve this end, later supported a move to create a conservative political state.

Socially and economically liberalism achieved significant changes. By the middle of the nineteenth century, even though autocracy remained, the revolutionary movement had practically destroyed feudalism in Prussia and in other parts of central *Liberal Advances in Central Europe* Europe. Henceforth free land was to become the rule, and the emancipation of the serfs removed social inequalities that hitherto had oppressed the peasants. Although Prussia and Austria were still predominantly agricultural, the growing middle classes by that time were strong enough to play an important rôle in the revolutions. Later they performed more experienced and practical parts in the development of liberalism in their native lands.

One outstanding result of the revolution was the failure of the people to return to such medieval beliefs as the doctrine of divine right. The reactionary movement did not succeed in completely restoring the old political system. Parliamentary

institutions were established in such states as Württemberg
and Bavaria, and even the Prussian king was forced to grant
a constitution. Moreover, nationalism persisted. The Germans, the Czechs, the Magyars, and the Slavs still had visions
of independence and of unity; and the desire for freedom
spread to many other nationalities, including the Jews, who
had suffered much in various parts of central and eastern
Europe. At the same time the middle-class concepts of religious toleration, separation of church and state, and emphasis upon education controlled by the government were
being diffused throughout middle Europe. As in France
before 1789, the old régime in central Europe was falling to
pieces, and the revolutions of 1848 served to hasten the
changes which seemed bound to come.

The uprisings of 1848 were not restricted to central Europe.
Liberalism and thwarted nationalism also provoked a revolution in Italy. Before 1848 the conviction and
Nationalistic Strivings desire that Italy, the home of a great empire,
in Italy should attain unity and centralization had
penetrated the minds of the intellectuals and even the masses.
Mazzini, we have seen, planned a republic which should lead
to the emancipation of common men throughout Europe.
Another leader, Gioberti, believed that this unity could best
be attained under the leadership of the papacy. Prior to 1848
revolution had made little headway in Italy because of the
reactionary influence of Metternich; but practically coincident with his flight from Vienna came the outbreak of new
disorders.

This revolt was largely influenced by the attitude of the
liberal Pope Pius IX. Like many of his countrymen he loved
Pope Pius IX Italy, hated Austria, and desired a united
Italian state. Believing that this could best
be attained under his leadership, he tried to achieve the
great task. As a preliminary step he freed political prisoners. Then he became a middle-class Pope, encouraging material and political advances such as illuminating gas, railways,
and a constitution. Furthermore, he changed his governmental
administration. A council of ministers was appointed to

discuss but not to control the action of the papal government, and the Jews were released from the Ghetto at Rome.

These reform measures inspired the Italians. Metternich was alarmed and had a right to be, for liberalism was revived throughout Italy. In Sicily, Naples, Tuscany, Parma, Milan, Venice, and Savoy the people praised the Pope and planned a united Italy. But Pius soon realized that if a nationalist movement were to continue, he would be deprived of his temporal possessions. Moreover, fearing anticlerical control in a new republic, he withdrew from the liberal cause and "began to dream reaction."

Nevertheless the revolutionary movement continued. Secret societies had increased their membership, and the small but influential middle classes were ardent advocates of national unity. A decisive step in the revolutionary movement was taken when Ferdinand, the cruel king of Naples and Sicily, overcome by fear as to the result of an uprising in Palermo, agreed to a constitution. Other Italian rulers, such as the grand duke of Tuscany, likewise granted reforms.

Charles Albert of Piedmont, king of Sardinia, became the real leader of Italian unity. Sardinia was the least Italian of all Italian states. Charles Albert, the French-speaking king, ruled a people quite different *The House of Savoy* from the Italians in the south. In fact, the position of the House of Savoy, represented by Charles Albert in Italy, corresponded closely to that of the Hohenzollern dynasty in north Germany. The population of Savoy was far more military, more energetic, and more advanced culturally than the other peoples in Italy. With fertile lands and with an increasing middle class this state was in a position to furnish the money and the leaders necessary to attain unity.

The vacillating Charles Albert, his patriotism kindled, wanted to expel the foreigners and to establish Italian unity. At first it appeared as though he would succeed. Louis Philippe had fallen in France, and Metternich had left Vienna. The exponents of the new régime seemed victorious in all parts of Europe. Popular demonstrations broke out in Milan, where students, workmen, journalists, and tradesmen demanded political rights; and Parma, Modena, and Venice rose against the Austrian overlordship.

Austria refused to relinquish her hold in Lombardy, Venetia, and several other small states in Italy without a struggle. Charles Albert now had his opportunity to *The Revolution of* become the leader of Italian opposition to the *1848* Austrians. Nobly he responded to the call, unfurling the tricolor banner of a united Italy and calling upon all Italians to help expel the foe. The Austrians, holding the favorable positions, were able, under their capable leader, Radetzky, to defeat the Italians. Toward the end of the conflict several Italian states — Parma, Modena, Milan, Piacenza, and Venice — voted to merge with Sardinia, but this action came too late.

By July, 1848, the Italian cause was lost. Charles Albert was driven back on Milan after suffering defeat in the famous battle of Custozza, and finally withdrew beyond the frontier. Mazzini announced that the royal war was over and that the people must now have their little conflict. With "God and the people" as his slogan he then raised the republican banner; but he failed to expel the Austrians. Garibaldi, the rough rider of this revolution, withdrew to the mountains, where he planned a guerrilla war. The reactionaries, in the saddle again, restored the old régime. King Ferdinand of Naples destroyed the constitution he had granted his people and reëstablished his brutal despotism, while Austria regained all her Italian lands.

In Sardinia the reaction was not so successful. Defeated again at Novara in March, 1849, Charles Albert, very much discouraged, declared that he had given up everything for the cause of Italy, whereas his allies and even his commanders had deserted him. Then he made his greatest sacrifice. Discovering that the Austrians would not make peace with Sardinia as long as he remained king, he resigned his crown in favor of his son, and then went to Portugal, where he died a few months later.

By this act Charles Albert paved the way for Italian unity. His son, Victor Emmanuel (1849–1878), during the first few days of his reign became the logical leader in the nationalist movement. Urged by Austria to abandon the constitution granted by his father, he refused to do so, declaring himself its determined defender. Thus continuing the work of his predecessor, he remained the leader of freedom for Italy. For many years, however, the Italians were denied unity and liberty. Discipline, unity in leadership, organization, and foreign aid were needed before Italy could be free. Meanwhile in the kingdom of Savoy a leader arose — Count Cavour. This man was able to shape things in such a way as to bring about unification.

By 1848 practically every country had been touched by revolutionary ideas. In England the workers were demanding the right to vote. In Ireland a nationalist group had been organized. In Belgium, the *Significance of Revolutionary Movements* Netherlands, and Denmark the suffrage was widened; while in Switzerland, central Europe, Polish Russia, and the Balkans the nationalist movement was dominant. In the Americas the revolutionary movement was also evident. The struggle between the North and the South in the United States was in the making; while in Hispanic America nationalism and constitutionalism were live issues.

In his poem "At Sunrise in 1848" the English writer Dante Gabriel Rossetti interpreted that year as follows:

> God said, Let there be light! and there was light.
> Then heard we sounds as though the Earth did sing
> And the Earth's angel cried upon the wing:
> We saw priests fall together and turn white:
> And covered in the dust from the sun's sight,
> A king was spied, and yet another king.

The revolutions of 1848, however, were important because they were manifestations on the part of Western peoples of a desire for national unity, control of government, and social equality, — all necessary in order that the capitalistic system might find an environment in which it could flourish. But complete success, the establishment of the middle-class order, was not feasible at that time. Before this transformation was possible the Industrial Revolution had to create, in the revolutionary centers, more numerous bourgeois and working classes. Strengthened in numbers and in wealth, those exponents of the new order, as long as they coöperated, found it comparatively easy to complete the revolutionary movement. But a division between the middle classes and the wage-earners often delayed the progress of liberalism. Opposed to the ideas expressed by the socialists and other so-called radicals, the bourgeoisie, after 1848, often favored certain features of the old régime — the monarchy, for instance — rather than a socialistic or anarchistic order.

National unity, constitutional liberty, and proletarian consciousness, as we have seen, were the three major causes of the revolutions of 1848. In France there was an attempt to obtain a republic, universal suffrage, and socialistic reforms. In Prussia, Austria, and Italy constitutionalism, national unity, and legal equality were the chief objectives. In all these countries, however, the revolutions were important because they were movements in the direction of free will, untrammeled by political, religious, economic, and racial dogmas and traditions. Under middle-class influence men concluded that will rather than reason determined man's action. This belief became a powerful incentive to social growth.

The FLIGHT OF METTERNICH *from Vienna in* 1848
From a contemporary caricature

CHAPTER VI

England, 1815–1848: Decline of the Aristocratic Oligarchy

FROM the French Revolution emanated a wave of salutary reforms which, between 1815 and 1848, washed away numerous abuses and harmful institutions in many countries, notably in France, Germany, and Italy.

But upon one nation, England, the immediate effect was reactionary, despite the fact that she had long needed a complete reorganization of her institutions and policies. Many intellectuals there had favored divers reforms before 1789. At first they welcomed the French Revolution as marking the inauguration of a better age; but when the French radicals deliberately deprived the nobles and clergy of their lands, the landowners of England became frightened. Might not these reforms provoke similar changes in England? Were not the French friendly allies of the Irish? Perhaps they intended not only to free Ireland but also to conquer England. Aroused by these fears, England retreated within the shell of conservatism. Societies supposedly connected with such French clubs as the Jacobins were suppressed, proposed changes were shelved, and England remained the sanctuary of the out-of-date. The Metternich of that island, the large landowner, was in command.

During the Napoleonic wars economic conditions became increasingly bad. Wage-earners were discontented with the long working hours and the extremely low wages. Business reached a standstill as a result of the Continental blockade. The members of the middle classes were suffering, and many of them favored peace at any price. Meanwhile the landowners failed to support the war, as in the past, by the payment of heavy income taxes. When the conflict ended, the government found itself confronted with the largest public debt ever incurred up

England during the Napoleonic Wars

to that time. The problem of finding employment for the re-turned soldiers added to the post-war difficulties. Neverthe-less the conservatives, who had been responsible for the victory over Napoleon and who were well represented by George IV (1820–1830), by Castlereagh (1769–1822), and by the duke of Wellington (1769–1852), managed to remain in power and to maintain the *status quo* for a short period.

Between 1815 and 1832, writes one author, the upper classes in England were "furiously pursuing the fox; the nasty old uncles of Victoria were in the saddle, and the tone of a society that could admire a Byron for his darkly insinuating qualities was anything but Victorian." It was the "vulgar" as con-trasted with its successor, the "proper" age. Sports and amusements were coarse, and the phrase "drunk as a lord" was gaining freighted meaning.

In political and social matters the representatives of the aristocratic class were both selfish and narrow-minded. They opposed self-determination for Ireland, abol-ishing its parliament in 1800. Later they en-couraged the nationalistic revolutions in Eu-rope and South America, in the hope that these uprisings would benefit British trade. In the economic realm they did everything possible to assist the wealthy landowners. In-closure acts enabled aristocrats to drive out the small farm-ers, although the politicians contended that such legislation was designed to improve agriculture. Actually the wealth and the power of the landed nobility increased, while the number of small landowners was reduced.

England under the Aristocrats

In 1815 Parliament passed the Corn Laws, excluding for-eign grain from British ports, unless, as was unlikely, the price of home-grown grain should at any time rise above the high figure of eighty shillings a quarter. Despite the fact that meager harvests caused the price of bread to soar far beyond the pocketbook of the English workers, the landowners saw to it that this law was enforced to the letter, even though the poor were on the verge of starvation. Partly because of this situation there were, in 1821, 2,500,000 "assisted poor" in the country.

During this period the clergy as well as the nobility enjoyed special favors. The Anglican church was the official church of England. Its clergy possessed wealth, special titles, official protection, and state *The Privileged Clergy* endowments. Its courts recorded births, marriages, divorces, wills, and deaths,— the entire cycle of life. In the House of Lords the higher clergy worked hand and glove with the landed aristocracy. Dissenters and Catholics were denied many rights possessed by the Anglicans. Although they enjoyed religious liberty and could participate in political life, Quakers, Baptists, Presbyterians, Methodists, and Catholics were barred from high offices and from taking degrees at Oxford and Cambridge. Special restrictions prevented Catholics and Jews from holding any political or military positions. In Scotland, however, where the state church was Presbyterian, there was a separate system with its own discipline and tithes.

In 1815 the House of Lords was the aristocratic bulwark of England. Through political influence, bribery, and corruption its land-glutted peers controlled the entire governmental machinery, including the House of Commons, the judges, and the various officials. In fact, until 1832 England had "a government of the people, by the landlords, and for the landlords."

Opposition to the established order was ruthlessly suppressed. Over two hundred offenses, including such acts as poaching and shoplifting, were punishable by death. Thousands of convicts spent years *Aristocratic Despotism* in foul holes called prisons, where, managed by brutal keepers, they were herded together regardless of sex, age, or the nature of their crimes. Many of these prisoners were deported to Australia and Tasmania. Whenever revolts occurred, instead of promising reforms the government ordered the rioters shot down.

The year 1819 marked the high tide of reaction in Britain. At that time were passed the famous Six Acts, forbidding military exercise without permission, allowing local justices to issue search warrants for weapons, curtailing freedom of assembly, authorizing the seizure of seditious writings, creating a stamp tax for pamphlets similar to that on newspapers, and threatening agitators with severer punishment. This legislation was the climax of an attempt to stifle political and social progress.

In contrast to domestic conservatism, the British foreign policy was liberal. True, in 1815 Castlereagh and Metternich *Liberal Tendencies* coöperated in the creation of buffer states around France and in the reëstablishment, as far as possible, of the territorial *status quo* in Europe. Nevertheless, when the conservative European powers tried to involve England in the suppression of the revolutionary movements, especially in Hispanic America, she balked.

England was neither as reactionary as autocratic Austria nor as liberal as revolutionary France. It is true that English institutions were held up as models before French reformers and Continentals, but this attitude testified to the political backwardness of eighteenth-century Continental Europe. The king's authority was limited by Parliament, but that body represented only a few English citizens. Voters were controlled by aristocratic property owners, who thus dominated the House of Commons as well as the House of Lords. Rule by an oligarchy rather than an autocracy, however, was at least a step in the direction of democracy.

Furthermore, a certain degree of legal equality had been firmly established in England, whereas it was sadly lacking in many parts of Europe in 1815. English law made no distinction between commoner and nobleman. Positions in the army, navy, government, or church, theoretically at least, were open to all property owners. The system of primogeniture prevailed, however, in the case of landed proprietors, allowing them to leave their huge estates to their eldest sons. Certain political inequalities, such as limited suffrage, endured, but conditions there were less oppressive than in France.

In industry and trade, privilege was less noticeable than elsewhere. The old guilds and favored trading corporations remained; yet there was little oppression of those who carried on industry or trade without belonging to these organizations. Later, when the development of textile and metal industries enabled a few wealthy men to establish the factory system from which they derived greater wealth and power, the guilds became helpless. Their regulations applied only to a small number of England's industries.

The wealthy middle-class men who emerged in the early nineteenth century as a result of the Industrial Revolution were not satisfied with their political status in England. Before long they realized that *Rise of Middle Classes and Workers* they furnished most of the real genius and practically all the formative ideals of the dawning age. They were the builders, and they felt that as such they should rule England. Indeed, it was during this era of the "inspired office boys" that the last golden age of England was born.

Between 1815 and 1832 the ever-increasing number of those who acquired wealth through the manufacture and transportation of goods forced the landowners, little by little, to relinquish the political control which they had selfishly abused. Through a gradual extension of the suffrage the middle class was admitted into partnership in the governing of England and her empire. At the same time the Industrial Revolution, which brought wealth and political influence to this rising class, created a large and constantly growing working and propertyless group of men. Gradually the latter, feeling that they had a right to participate in the government, and demanding that Parliament consider their interests, formed organizations designed to attain these ends.

In 1815 an antiquated system of representation enabled the aristocrats to control the government. The House of Commons consisted of 658 members. Of these, *The System of Representation Prior to the Reform Bill* 489 represented England, 100 Ireland, 45 Scotland, and 24 Wales. Three kinds of constituencies were represented: the counties, the boroughs, and the universities. In England the majority of counties and boroughs had two members, although a few of the latter had only one. Representation had no relation to the size of the population in the county or borough. Large or small, these political units sent the same number of representatives. The king had the right to create new boroughs as towns arose, but seldom exercised such authority. Thus the House of Commons remained the same size, despite the increase of population in certain parts of England. Obviously an increasing inequality in representation constituted an outstanding feature of this political system. Ten agricultural counties in southern England sent 237 representatives to the House of Commons, whereas the thirty other counties, many of which were centers of growing industrial elements and had populations three times as large as the former, were permitted only 252 representatives. The single county of Cornwall in England had almost as many delegates as all Scotland; yet the population of the latter was eight times that of Cornwall.

Restricted suffrage prevented the common man from participating in the election of the two representatives from his borough or county. In the country the voters were chiefly owners of large estates with their dependents. In many counties there were few who could meet the requirement of forty shillings a year income, a prerequisite to voting. Wealthy landowners, therefore, usually controlled the elections in such counties. In one county there were 21 voters out of a population of 14,000. On a certain occasion an election meeting of a county was attended by one individual who declared himself chairman, nominated himself, called the list of voters, and proclaimed himself elected to Parliament.

The influence of the landowning and wealthy classes was even more effective in the boroughs than in the counties. There were several kinds of boroughs: nomination boroughs, "rotten" or close boroughs, and boroughs in which there was a considerable body of voters, where the suffrage was almost democratic. In the nomination boroughs the right to choose the two representatives rested in the hands of one man called the patron. In many cases such places had lost most or all of their inhabitants; yet as geographical areas they were entitled to their two members. One borough had long ago disappeared under the sea; two members represented what was formerly dry land, and the owner of this portion of the bottom of the sea nominated the two delegates.

In the "rotten" or close boroughs either the members were selected by the corporation, consisting of the mayor and aldermen, or the suffrage remained in the hands of the voters, who were generally so few and so poor that the wealthy landowner or patron could bribe or force them to elect his candidate. Under this system the peers in the House of Lords were able to control the election of representatives sitting in the House of Commons. In 1793 one prominent lord had nine representatives, and others had from four to six each. In 1815 a small body of landowning aristocrats had seats both in the House of Lords and in the House of Commons, in the former by virtue of their hereditary privilege, in the latter by means of dummy members, whose selection they controlled.

Local government in England was also directed by the great landowners or magnates. In most European countries taxes were collected by officials representing the state, but in England the local landowner exercised this duty. As a petty despot he ruled over the small farmers, laborers, and factory workers in his district. In the army and navy the English landowners, like Prussian junkers, were the officers; the farmers and workers were the privates and sailors.

Local Government in England

This aristocratic control in the two fundamental branches of government, the collection of taxes, and the departments of war, can easily be explained. In the first place, England was not part of the Continent, and as long as she could rule the British Isles she had no need to fear military attacks. The pressure of centralization, consequently, did not exist. Furthermore, the insular position of England did not necessitate the collection of large amounts of money for military purposes, and at the same time the economic prosperity of that country made it easier for the people to pay taxes. Inasmuch as those who ruled England collected them, it was to their interest to raise the rate, in order that the government should run properly. Even the growing naval expenditures in the nineteenth century did not result in centralization, for the prosperous middle classes, gaining political power, were willing to pay in order to maintain battleships capable of protecting British commerce. Local self-government in England functioned well, because those who conducted it ruled the state. They were in a position to see that their duties as Englishmen coincided with their particular interests as citizens in a local county or borough.

The landowners, nevertheless, were not able to retain their governmental control. During the first half of the nineteenth

Opposition to Aristocratic Control

century the growing middle classes demanded political power, in order that they might protect their economic interests. Like the republicans of 1848 in France, who welcomed the support of the socialists, the middle classes in England, growing in numbers and wealth, but still a minority, gladly accepted the support of the wage-earners. By that time the development of large-scale industry, with consequent unemployment, long hours of labor, disease, decreased need for physically powerful men, and the resultant use of women and children in factories, created unrest among the wage-earners. These workers, supported by unemployed soldiers, at first opposed the introduction of machines and favored the return to the good old days when agriculture was the dominant interest.

Many workingmen believed that the government should protect them, feeling that surely the humanitarian spirit which had fostered the abolition of the slave trade in 1807 would result in better economic and social conditions for the workers. Perhaps these advocates of governmental intervention did not realize that slavery did not exist in England. Therefore the middle classes, having no financial interest in the slave trade, were perfectly willing to accept the view of reformers that this institution was a moral evil. Property owners, however, could not see profits accruing to them through governmental intervention on behalf of the workingman. Consequently the desired social reforms were not adopted.

The wage-earners finally realized that as long as the suffrage was so restricted that the propertied classes ruled the nation, they could hope for little relief. Therefore they began to agitate for the right to send representatives to Parliament, readily joining in all movements and propaganda designed to break down this oligarchical government. At the same time the Catholics and Dissenters were demanding the right to vote and to hold office.

All elements opposed to this landowning and Anglican supremacy soon united to effect the abolition of these religious and political disabilities. The middle-class   *Religious Reforms* dissenters were especially active in this move- ment, and finally, with the aid of moderate Tory landowners, were able to obtain equality for all Protestants by having Parliament, in 1828, abrogate the requirement that office- holders should take the sacrament according to the rites of the Church of England and should make a declaration against the doctrine of transubstantiation. It was only after a pro- longed and acrimonious controversy which almost resulted in civil war that Parliament finally passed the great Catholic Emancipation Act (1829). This law permitted Catholics to sit in either house of Parliament and to hold, with a few exceptions, municipal and national offices. Virtual political equality between Catholics and Protestants was established.

A determined effort also was made to enlarge the suffrage so as to increase the power of those who were not great land- owners, especially the business men. Middle-   *Rise of Bourgeois* class intellectuals proceeded to propagate their   *Reformers* ideas by means of the press. In Manchester, one of the industrial centers of England, John Edward Taylor, a bourgeois reformer who had received considerable fame through his opposition to the suspension of the Habeas Corpus Act, established, in 1821, the *Manchester Guardian*, which became the outstanding middle-class organ of the time. Many other bourgeois newspapers were founded and played an im- portant rôle in "bending public opinion the middle-class way."

As the factories developed and the number of industrial leaders and workers increased, the latter became conscious of power. Agitations occurred in which reformers   *Social Reforms* favored social as well as political changes. In 1833 these leaders forced Parliament to pass factory-reform acts prohibiting employment of children under nine years of age in textile mills and restricting the hours of employment of older children. Subsequent acts extended these factory reforms to other than the textile industries. In the forties laws established a ten-hour day for women and children, and barred boys under ten and women from working in mines.

In addition to these factory reforms Parliament was forced to pass laws designed to ameliorate the barbarous criminal code. In 1823 over one hundred death penalties were abolished, and several years later sanitary conditions in the prisons were greatly improved. Labor also won a distinct victory. In 1825 the law of 1800, which had forbidden labor organizations, was repealed, though workers were not allowed to use violence or to engage in political conspiracies.

The Tories, a group consisting for the most part of a great number of small landlords, bitterly opposed most of these re-

Tory Conservatism forms. Like Metternich, they advocated the *status quo* in politics, society, and religion. Because of the restricted franchise they controlled a majority of the votes and were able to enforce any laws designed to maintain the established church and the supremacy of agriculture. Naturally the opponents of such policies rallied in common opposition to these Tories. Those who advocated the disestablishment of the church and the rights of the middle classes were drawn into the camp of the rival Whig organization.

Until 1815 the Tories were able to retain their superiority without much difficulty. Between 1815 and 1830, however, the Whigs, strengthened by middle-class support and by the tendency of the wage-earners to combine, began to assume an aggressive attitude. Before long this party won substantial political victories.

During the years from 1815 to 1830 the workingmen and certain intellectuals of England became convinced that be-

The Reform Bill of 1832 fore low wages, long hours of labor, and unemployment could be abolished, the wage-earners must receive the ballot. Then they could destroy machinery, the chief cause of their distress. With this end in view they began to agitate for the complete

establishment of universal suffrage. Under the leadership of a peasant's son, William Cobbett, who at that time (1830) was publishing a small newspaper, bourgeois reformers rapidly increased in numbers and power. Public meetings, at which the speakers described the misery and abuse of the working-man in no uncertain terms, stimulated this growing demand for complete political emancipation and social reform. The government tried unsuccessfully to break up these gatherings, both by military force and by passing laws directed against radicals and their writings. During these agitations the manu-facturers supported the workers, because the former desired control of the government. The employers, once in possession of political power, planned to establish complete freedom of trade. In this way they would be able to stabilize wages by reducing the cost of living through the importation of cheap wheat.

Concessions were gradually made by Parliament. Perhaps the revolution of 1830 in France, resulting in the selection of the bourgeois king, Louis Philippe, and the complete fall of the old régime, contributed to the victory of middle-class liberalism in England. Certainly this political change was aided by workingmen who were joining liberal organizations. These wage-earners had in mind economic and social as well as political reforms. They wanted a minimum-wage law and better working conditions. Meanwhile the remarkable in-crease of wealth in England, as a result of the expansion of commerce and industry, tended to strengthen the middle classes, who had become a growing factor in politics. The Whig party welcomed these bourgeois enthusiasts and even listened to the workingmen, counting on their support in the attempt to overthrow the conservative Tories. Victory finally rested on the Whig side. In 1832, despite bitter opposition from the great landowners in the House of Lords, the famous Reform Bill was passed. The passage of this bill marked the end of the old régime in England. It did not, however, make Britain a democratic nation, being in effect only a compro-mise by which the middle classes rose to political power in place of the old aristocratic landlords.

A number of important changes were brought about by the Reform Bill. The privileges of the large landowners were curtailed by abolishing the so-called "rotten" boroughs. Increased representation was now given to the great cities, controlled by the bourgeoisie, hitherto not fairly represented. Voting privilege in the borough was no longer dependent upon the possession of land, but rather on the payment of an annual rent of ten pounds. This requirement automatically excluded any workers whose rent was less.

The Reform Bill of 1832 made the House of Commons a representative but not a democratic body. By admitting to suffrage the wealthier middle classes the number of voters, particularly in the boroughs, was considerably increased, but the laborers and the poorer members of the middle classes still lacked the ballot. Only one out of twenty-two persons in England participated in the elections. Because of this discrimination the great mass of English people did not regard this measure as final, although the conservative Whigs thought they had gone far enough. They were not especially interested in the rights of the poorer classes, even though the latter, by their meetings, riots, and acts of violence, had helped to pass the bill.

Physical and moral decay among the English people as a result of the deplorable social and economic conditions com-
Social Legislation   pelled the Whigs to enact a certain amount of social legislation. In 1833 an antislavery bill abolished slavery throughout the empire. By a poor law (1834) public officials, independent of the local aristocracy, were placed in charge of the destitute. Steps were taken also for the improvement of sanitation and the maintenance of highways. The number of sinecures controlled by the propertied classes was reduced. In fact, the old families in towns lost their privileges, and by 1835 most taxpayers enjoyed civil equality. Although ameliorating conditions, the changes did not obliterate the extreme poverty and suffering which had come in the wake of the industrialization of England.

Granted only a small measure of labor legislation and denied the ballot, the workers proceeded to organize among themselves. They formed a proletarian organization which, although not represented in Parliament, agitated for reforms. Led by a wealthy manufacturer and utopian, Robert Owen (1771–1858), the workers, in 1834, created the Grand National Consolidated Trades Union. Favoring an eight-hour day, with the use of strikes to gain its aims, this organization was important because it signalized the rise of the modern unions which have played and still are playing a significant rôle in the political, social, and economic development of the middle-class order.

Organization of Workers

Backed by the manufacturers, the government declared this union unlawful and deported many of its leaders. Finding the general strike useless against the determined opposition, the workers turned to a radical group, called Chartists, who expressed their whole program in a so-called People's Charter, which was drafted and presented to Parliament in 1848. In this document they proclaimed that the right to vote should be given to every male adult, declaring, "We perform the duties of freemen; we must have the privileges of freemen." They asked that voting be secret, so that every voter might be free from intimidation and from bribery, and they further demanded that property qualifications for membership in the House be abolished and that the members receive salaries, so that even poor men could be elected to Parliament if the people wished. They likewise suggested that members of the House of Commons should be elected for one year instead of for seven. As a whole the charter sought changes which its exponents believed would enable the masses to control the legislature and thus to improve their condition by destroying the new industrial system.

The Chartist Movement

The Chartists were not successful. Mass meetings, demonstrations, and revolutionary threats failed to move the Whigs. At first the government allowed the Chartists to agitate, but by 1848, when these "revolutionaries" planned a general insurrection, the middle classes assumed the rôle of Metternich and as constables maintained the *status quo*.

Adopting a revised plan of campaign, the workers now withdrew from the Chartist organization, deciding to accept the new industrial system, including its ma-

Collective Bargaining of Wage-Earners

chinery. Through their trade unions they tried to arrange separate agreements with their employers, appealing to Parliament for protection but at the same time avoiding entanglement in politics. By this method of collective bargaining they gained many of their demands without resorting to violence or to radical measures.

The success of the unions, however, was largely owing to the remarkable industrial development of England which occurred during the first half of the nineteenth century. Just as the United States after the World War held an advantage over most nations because of her great resources and the disastrous effects of the struggle on the old industrial nations, so England was able after 1815 to dominate the markets of Europe and to profit thereby. Because of this industrial expansion, manufacturers were able to pay high wages. At the same time technical inventions enabled factory owners to make huge profits and to pay generous dividends. Moreover, a great emigration to the United States removed the large unemployed class which might have supported a revolution. These independent emigrants turned their energies to the making of a new English-speaking nation, not realizing perhaps that they were helping to create a powerful state, destined to become England's chief competitor.

In its attitude toward economic and social problems the Whig party adhered to the fundamental policies of the middle classes, so well expressed by the words *laissez*

Abolition of the Corn Laws

faire and compromise. There were times when action was necessary, but the Whigs preferred to temporize rather than to tackle the economic problems which confronted them. In one way the workers were helped by this policy of non-interference in business on the part of the state. The middle classes, for example, in forcing the government to abolish the Corn Laws, won a victory for the wage-earners as well as for themselves.

The Corn Laws, even though the rates had been lowered,

had protected the landowners of England by levying a tax on all imported grain. This legislation was a phase of the mercantile idea that by making England self-sufficing, all would benefit. Manufacturers, however, refused to accept this theory. To them the tariff on grain simply increased the profits of the Tory landlords at the expense of the middle classes and the workers.

Big manufacturers were clever enough to put the controversy on a high moral plane. According to them the tariff on grain led to international wars over trade; *ergo*, in the interest of world peace, the Corn Laws should be abolished. These men, with Manchester as their headquarters, became enthusiastic free traders, led by the idealistic cotton merchant, Robert Cobden, the Quaker, John Bright, and the moderate Tory, Sir Robert Peel. The movement grew rapidly in numbers and influence.

By 1846 the Corn Laws were doomed. England was rapidly becoming an industrial nation and was consequently finding it difficult to raise sufficient food to supply her people. To help solve this problem she had acquired a huge empire capable of furnishing wheat. All she needed was permanent control of the seas to insure a constant supply of grain. By underselling her competitors she then could make sufficient money to buy cheap bread for her workers, to maintain a powerful navy, and to pay huge dividends.

At first the conservative landowners tried to settle the problem by a compromise, but the memorable Irish famine of 1845 prepared the way for the complete abrogation of the Corn Laws. The mainstay of the Irish people was the potato. More than half of the eight million inhabitants depended chiefly upon it for sustenance. In 1845 this crop completely failed; famine resulted, and many thousands perished from starvation. The only way to rescue the population was to repeal the Corn Laws, allowing the importation of food supplies from the Continent to take the place of the blighted potato. Finally, in 1846, after a prolonged controversy, Sir Robert Peel carried the day against bitter opposition. Free Trade was established, and England, enabled to develop her industries, was in a position to become the leading bourgeois state.

With the coming of these reforms the old Tory party disappeared; in its place rose the new bourgeois Toryism, or "Conservatism," as Peel called it. Before long appeared another organization, the Liberal party, consisting for the most part of manufacturers and merchants. The landed aristocrats no longer dominated either faction. Although they retained their social prestige, including titles, they had ceased to wield real political influence.

Rise of Conservative and Liberal Parties

This transition from the dominance of agriculture to that of industry was important not only because it marked the rise of the unprivileged groups but also because of its influence on international affairs. Thenceforth England, a great industrial nation living by means of the exportation of manufactured goods and the importation of grain, had to avoid becoming involved in European disputes, lest her interests as a great trading and colonial power be endangered. Peace and the equilibrium of Europe were necessary if England were to carry on commerce and to maintain her supremacy in world trade. Her commercial and industrial hegemony could be threatened only by a state which could dominate Europe, close European markets to British commerce, compete with England on the high seas, and menace her colonial empire.

British Foreign Policy

Children working in a Rope Factory *in England. From an old engraving.*

PART III. NATIONALISTIC STRIVINGS, 1815-1878

CHAPTER VII

Napoleon III and the Second Empire

FOLLOWING the fall of Napoleon I liberals of all classes were united in bringing about the general acceptance of one idea, nationalism. This phenomenon was due to the fact that peoples for centuries had been conscious of some kind of relationship, based on a common language, a common culture, a common history, and a common economic goal. Before the Industrial Revolution this unity was symbolized by a king, who, ruling by divine right, demanded the loyalty of his subjects, the people. The French Revolution gave a new meaning to nationalism, for just as the words *liberty* and *equality* denoted legal and social equality and the right to participate in the government, so *fraternity* signified the idea of a brotherhood of men, bound together to defend the one thing they had in common, — the country, or fatherland. The king might remain the symbol of this unity, but in the eyes of the nineteenth-century exponent of nationalism the state was the real entity.

NOTE. *The cartoon at the top of the page represents* UNITED GERMANY *from Leuchtkugeln (1848).*

Many advocates of nationalism appeared during the first part of the nineteenth century. Of these Louis Napoleon *Louis Napoleon* (1852–1870), "the nephew of his great uncle" (Napoleon I), was perhaps the most ludicrous. As a presidential candidate in 1848 this genteel, kind-hearted, emotional man emphasized the great work of his illustrious relative, asserting that Napoleon I had been much abused and that he really had been an advocate of the Revolution, standing for equality and national unity.

Louis Napoleon was the son of Napoleon's brother Louis, king of Holland, and Hortense, daughter of the Empress Josephine. As the eldest representative of the Bonaparte family he was well known throughout Europe long before he became president. Living at various times in Switzerland, Italy, England, and America, he had moved in the highest ranks of society, was involved in revolutionary disorders, and firmly believed himself to be another son of destiny.

Thoroughly convinced that he alone could restore law, order, and glory to France, and then spread the revolutionary ideas, especially nationalism, throughout Europe and perhaps the world, Louis Napoleon finally struck out for his native land in 1836. Upon his arrival he planned to raise the imperial flag and to rally all Frenchmen to his cause. He was very soon captured as a rebel and exiled to America, where he lived until he suddenly discovered that Louis Philippe had moved the remains of Napoleon Bonaparte to Paris. Realizing that this act would arouse the Napoleonic supporters, he returned to France, determined to overthrow Louis Philippe. Instead he was arrested and in 1840 was confined in the fortress of Ham on the northern frontier of France. There he played the rôle of a martyr, saw many friends, and did considerable writing. Finally he effected an escape, and the fall of Louis Philippe in 1848 enabled him to return to Paris and become a candidate for the presidency of the Second French Republic.

During his six years of imprisonment at Ham, Louis Napoleon worked out the strategy for a *coup d'état*. His environment both in and out of prison had developed in him a "deep" interest in common men. As one of them he corresponded with Louis Blanc, the socialist, and Proudhon, the anarchist. In 1844 he published a book on the *Extinction of Pauperism*, in which he promised that if ever he were given the opportunity, he would substitute prosperity for pauperism by opening up new fields of industry, by stimulating the cultivation of the land, and by providing work in abundance for all.

By 1848 France had practically forgotten the dark side of the Napoleonic era. Frenchmen had decided, however, that their country was no longer one of the great Continental powers. "What we need," many of them probably declared, "is a man who will restore France to her former place as the outstanding state in Europe. Louis Napoleon will do that, and at the same time he will maintain and extend those great changes brought about by the Revolution." "Why shouldn't I vote for Louis Napoleon?" asked an old peasant who had fought for Napoleon I, "I who had my nose frozen off at Moscow!" The magic of the name "Napoleon" did much to elect this man President of the Second French Republic by a large plurality.

Louis Napoleon possessed administrative ability, but unfortunately his intellect was confused and his will-power weak. His rule was thus destined to be contradictory and ineffective. Although not attractive in appearance, he had pleasant manners and could "keep silent impressively." He was influenced by industrial developments and for this reason favored imperial ventures, contributing to the ultimate completion of an important waterway, the Suez canal. He was not a soldier; yet, like a second-rate Cellini, he wrote on the use of artillery. In international affairs he demonstrated at times a remarkable ability to anticipate the future; he also had some definite political views. To him the days of parliaments were over; through the development of communication the executive government could come into direct touch with the people and need no longer rely upon an assembly. Possibly he felt that he could do what Roman emperors and Napoleon I had failed to do, — maintain a world empire by means of im-

proved communication. Despite Louis Napoleon's interesting beliefs he was not an original thinker. He was merely
trying to justify the past and to carry out his own selfish aims.
He had little new to offer; his few original ideas were acci-
dental and incidental. Bismarck described him as a "great
unrecognized incapacity."

At first Louis Napoleon passed as a loyal defender of the
new republic. Having sworn to support the constitution, he
condemned any attempt by others to alter it.
The Second French Re-
public (1848–1852)
Really an autocrat at heart, he did not have
the slightest intention of becoming a quiet,
conservative, middle-class president. He was convinced that
the French people needed a strong government and that he
was destined to give it to them. Before this aim could be
achieved, however, the constitution had to be changed; Louis
Napoleon made his plans accordingly. He began by trying
to build up a personal following through uniting all of the
conservative elements into a *bloc* which would support him
as the leader of the party of law and order. Many republicans, clericals, and monarchists tended to consolidate in opposition to the socialists, who were attacking private property.
To strengthen his position with the Catholics, he dispatched
an army to Rome to restore the Pope, who had fled because of
republican disorders. Meanwhile the fear of socialism enabled
the conservatives to gain control of the legislative assembly.
By 1849 the republicans possessed little political power.

In 1850 Louis Napoleon felt sufficiently powerful to introduce laws designed to establish his position as the conservative leader. To achieve this end, he decided
An Age of Conserv-
atism
to check radicalism in the schools. Asserting
that "lay teachers had made the principles of
socialism popular in the most distant hamlets," he restored
control of education to the church. By the so-called Falloux
Law clerical supervision over the schools was introduced,
and before long church schools were reëstablished. The middle
classes, fearful of losing their property, willingly permitted the
church, through the schools, to combat the socialists. Next
a law was passed limiting suffrage. Designed to disqualify

the workers, most of whom were socialists, the law declared that in order to vote one must have three years' residence in the district and have his name inscribed on the taxpayers' list. This requirement deprived about three million working-men of the ballot and prevented the formation of a socialist party in the legislative assembly.

United in their opposition to socialism, the conservatives could not agree on an acceptable type of government. Most of them disliked Louis Napoleon. Aware of this enmity, the ambitious president decided   *"A Friend" of the People* to destroy the power of the legislative assembly in order to strengthen his own position. To gain this end, he now turned to the socialists and republicans, saying that the legislative body was controlled by aristocrats and large landowners, and thus was unrepresentative of the people. Posing as the real friend of the common man in his opposition to the legislative assembly, Louis Napoleon planned the creation of an empire by manipulating public opinion and by gaining control of the army and the administration. Finally he asked the legislative assembly to abolish the new electoral law and to introduce complete manhood suffrage. They rejected this request. Whereupon he turned to the people, declaring that the assembly had refused to coöperate with him in an effort to establish real democracy.

Louis Napoleon now tried to have passed through the assembly a law which would enable him to be reëlected president at the end of his four-year term. Un-   *A Coup d'État* successful, he decided to destroy that body. Therefore, like his celebrated uncle, Napoleon I, he planned to seize supreme power through a *coup d'état*. On December 2, 1851, he achieved his end. Urging the people to support him in opposing the alleged attempt of the assembly to abolish democracy, he threw the leaders of that body into jail. Then he occupied the legislative hall with troops and established martial law. Finally he turned to the "dear people," placing before them for popular vote the draft of a new constitution which repealed several reactionary decisions of the legislative assembly, including the limitation of universal suffrage. At the same time he included in the constitution an article extending the term of his office to ten years.

The new president did not deceive the republicans. They knew that he intended to destroy not only the legislative assembly but also the republic. Therefore they opposed his plan and asked the supreme court to indict the president on a charge of high treason. Intellectuals like Victor Hugo and Jules Favre posted placards calling upon the people to revolt against Napoleon, who had made himself an outlaw. Apparently the president's enemies, supported by hundreds of workingmen, planned to stir up an insurrection. He, however, was prepared. Having the army firmly under his thumb, he ordered it to open a systematic fire on the revolutionists, and found excuses to seize republican leaders. More than one hundred thousand were arrested; ten thousand were deported to Algiers; three thousand were interned in France. By these measures he practically annihilated the republican party.

Louis Napoleon could not have succeeded had it not been for the backing of the middle classes, who were still worried about the safety of their property. When the election was held, on December 21, 1851, the majority of voters favored Napoleon's measures, — a ten-year term and universal suffrage. On the other hand, the Legitimists and Orleanists, as well as many intellectuals, realized that Napoleon was ambitious to make himself emperor. They created an opposition which endured until his fall.

The new constitution, which went into effect in 1852, increased the powers of Louis Napoleon and limited those of the assembly. As president he appointed all *The New Constitution* officials, signed all treaties, and had the right to declare war. The legislative assembly was reduced in membership by two thirds and could only discuss laws laid before it by the chief executive, thereby losing all power of initiative. Furthermore, another body was established, the Senate, whose members were appointed for life by the president. This organization was supposed to preserve the constitution, while Napoleon, who held that he was responsible to neither body but to the people, would guide the country. The government, like the consulate, was to be a step leading toward the establishment of an empire. All citizens could vote Yes or No on laws presented to them by the president; but inasmuch as the president chose what laws to lay before them, and practically nominated the representatives selected by the people for the assembly, he in reality was the government.

Louis Napoleon had imperial power even though he lacked the official position of emperor. In 1852, however, he assumed the title, announcing that the empire meant peace and implying that it would also bring glory. The people were asked to vote as to *The Second Empire (1852–1870)* whether or not they wanted an empire. Although the middle classes at first had been alarmed at the rapid rise of Napoleon III, they feared socialism more. Deciding that the new government would not injure their broader interests, they supported it. The peasants, desirous of retaining their property and also dreading a workers' republic or a return to the old régime, added their backing. On December 2, 1852, by a proposal of the Senate, the empire was restored. Louis Napoleon became Napoleon III.

To ardent followers of the emperor another golden age was at hand. The class struggle seemed to have subsided, and many patriotic sentiments were expressed. At first Louis Napoleon tried to increase the power and wealth of the state by adhering to a capitalist-nationalist program. France, he said, by leading in the nationalist movement, was to carry on the work of Napoleon I and to emancipate the oppressed peoples of Europe. As in the days of the first empire, however, this policy led to war and dishonor.

Between 1830 and 1850 the spirit of nationalism had changed. Restless and ruthless competition began to control the relations of states; national patriotism and national loyalty were being made to serve the ends of economic and political expansion; and a national spirit was taking shape and fixing itself as a formative force in great consolidated powers. A national will was to become identified with the concept of the state. "To develop national strength, to become a great power, and if possible a world power, was the main ambition of the concentrated energy of the state."

Moved by such ideas, Napoleon III probably fancied himself a modern Cæsar. As a benevolent despot he attempted to bring material prosperity to all classes in *Benevolent Despotism* France by favoring the establishment of steamer service to America and Asia and by negotiating commercial treaties with Great Britain and Prussia. *Le Crédit Foncier* (a national bank) was established, agricultural societies were multiplied, industrial progress was encouraged, and the capital city of Paris was modernized and beautified.

By means of such improvements, which provided a demand for labor, the emperor endeared himself to many wage-earners. Riding in cabs with engineers, attending meetings of masons, carpenters, and plumbers, drinking their health on all occasions, he acted like many convivial mayors in prominent American cities. Constantly courting popularity, he promised to reduce the cost of living and to supply work for all. He also allowed workers to form coöperative societies for collective buying and selling, to organize labor unions, and to strike. Further, the state was even willing to guarantee voluntary insurance against death and industrial accidents.

Louis Napoleon made his strongest appeal to the financiers and business men. While he was attempting to centralize all political power in his hands, he tried to establish the *laissez faire* policy as far as trade and industry were concerned. Governmental regulation of industry was lessened, the organization of commercial companies was encouraged, a merchant marine was subsidized, and a policy of free trade was instituted. Both industry and commerce were stimulated by the construction of public works. Harbors were improved, swamps were drained, canals were dug, roads were repaired, and railroads were laid throughout the country. This economic development explains why the enriched members of the middle classes remained loyal to Louis Napoleon for many years.

The emperor also endeavored to win the support of the clericals. Handing education over to the church and sending troops to support the Pope in Rome, he posed as the defender of Catholicism. By promoting *Defender of the Church* French imperialism he appealed to both the clergy and the middle classes. Through the conquest of Algeria, completed in 1857, the acquisition of Cochin China and Annam in 1858, commercial concessions in China in 1860, and the erection of a protectorate in Cambodia in revenge for the murder of missionaries in 1863, Louis gave the church an opportunity to save souls and the business man a chance to make money.

Making France prosperous did not satisfy many intellectuals and radicals. They wanted a republic and resented the loss of political liberty brought about by the rise of this Second Empire. As the opposition *Bewildered Despotism* increased, Louis Napoleon established censorship of speech, of the press, and of education, and created a system of espionage to watch the people. At one time Louis had his prefect arrest a woman living in Tours, because she had prophesied that a terrible vine disease was going to break out again. Acts like this served only to increase the hostility of the emperor's enemies and their determination to destroy his autocratic government.

Louis Napoleon tried desperately to remain in power. He endeavored to create a rich and powerful empire which would win the support of the middle classes and of all patriotic Frenchmen who wished to see France again the political, economic, social, and intellectual center of Europe. At the same time he appealed to the exponents of the revolution by posing as the champion of nationalities.

Like the great Louis XIV, Napoleon III intended to make France the outstanding military nation of Europe. His armies looked magnificent; the privates in gaudy uniforms marched to the music of a splendid band led by a huge acrobatic drum major. But it was all pomp and circumstance, parade rather than drill and strategy. The army was lacking in efficient organization and modern equipment, and it was led by "drawing-room generals."

Blissfully unaware of these facts, however, Louis Napoleon thought that he was the war lord of Europe. His first oppor-

The Louis-Napoleonic Wars

tunity to win glory for France by conflict occurred in 1853. At that time quarrels over control of the holy places in Palestine, between Roman Catholic monks and Greek Orthodox churchmen, led to an international crisis. Nicholas I, probably desiring to extend Russian influence in the Turkish Empire and hoping to obtain a seaport and a cultural center through the seizure of Constantinople, took advantage of the controversy to announce a protectorate over all Greek Orthodox Christians in Turkish dominions. Louis Napoleon felt that it was his duty to intervene at this point. He now had an opportunity, by supporting the Sultan against Russia, of making the Levant safe for Christianity and of developing French influence in Turkey. Welcoming the chance of defeating the successor of Alexander I and of avenging the disastrous Moscow campaign of 1812, he announced that he intended to protect all Christians in the Levant. Fortunately for Louis Napoleon, Great Britain and the little Italian kingdom of Sardinia also decided to resist this new Russian aggression in the Near East.

Beginning in 1853, this conflict, called the Crimean War, lasted until 1856 and resulted in the complete defeat of the

The Crimean War

Russians by Turkey and her allies. It is true that France as well as England obtained commercial privileges in Turkey and that Roman Catholic Christians were saved from Greek domination; these rewards, however, did not justify the cost of seventy-five thousand lives and two billion francs. Perhaps Louis Napoleon felt that by having the peace meeting in Paris he proved to all nations that France, and especially Paris, was the international center of the world. At the conference he opposed the harsh terms offered Russia by England, and even went so far as to favor nationalistic movements in the Balkans.

It was apparent to any ordinary man that France lost more than she gained by the conflict, and that no future war should be undertaken without a first mortgage on the opponent's assets. But Napoleon III was no ordinary man, and thus

A *contemporary sketch illustrating the* CONDITION OF EUROPE IN 1859

The two fighting figures in the foreground are France, in the form of Napoleon III, assisting the Italian states against Austria, represented by Francis Joseph. Starting at the left of the picture, we see, watching the conflict, Portugal during a lull between revolutions; Spain looking for an opportunity to force Isabella II to abdicate; England, represented by Lord Palmerston, maintaining neutrality but secretly favoring the cause of the Italian states; Belgium establishing independence under Leopold I; Hanover opposing Prussian dominance in Germany; Denmark holding on to Schleswig and Holstein; Prussia, in the form of William I, planning to escape Austrian dominance; Saxony turning from Prussia to favor Austria; and Russia supporting the new movement for Pan-Slavism. Some of the other objects on the map are the Crimean War, represented by graves; Turkey, "the sick man of Europe"; Greece preparing to revolt against Otto I; Montenegro raising a firebrand while Austria is engaged elsewhere; Garibaldi holding southern Italy for Victor Emmanuel, who is fighting with France against Austria; and between them is the Church straddling Italy and preventing unification under Victor Emmanuel. Between Austria and Napoleon III are three small figures representing Nassau, Frankfurt, and Hesse-Cassel, who are hoping for Austria's victory so that she may later crush Prussia. In France, Marianne is ordering Henry V off her premises.

could not arrive at a simple deduction. Professing to be an idealist, he tried to win glory for France by upholding a noble principle. Thus, although he at first refused to support Sardinia's project to chase the Austrians out of Italy, he soon acquiesced, secretly meeting Cavour in 1858. Obtaining a promise of Savoy and Nice, he agreed to join Sardinia in a war against Austria. He now posed as a champion of Italian nationalism and announced that as a former member of the Carbonari he would fight to free Italy from the autocratic dominance of Austria. Austria, historic obstacle to French expansion, found herself unable to oppose the combined French and "Italian" armies and was quickly defeated.

Louis Napoleon and the Austro-Italian War

Napoleon considered this victory as a personal triumph. Just as he had turned back the Russians in 1856, so had he defeated the Austrians in 1859. In fact, many people regarded him as the master mind of Europe. "Our liberator, our savior, our benefactor," the enthusiastic Italians called him. During the war, when he passed through Milan, his way was strewn with flowers after he had delivered a speech in which he said, "Your dreams of independence will soon be realized if you show yourselves worthy of it." Although many Italians were convinced that he was the greatest man in the world, the clericals were less enthusiastic; they were now hostile toward Napoleon III, fearing the loss by the papacy of temporal power as a result of this attempt to unify Italy.

But suddenly Louis withdrew from the war. Austria had not yet been expelled from Venetia, and Italy was far from being united. Why did Napoleon conclude a separate peace? It is said that he was profoundly affected by the slaughter and horrors of the battlefields; also that he found "glory" too expensive. More probable was the belief that he wished to maintain a balance of power in Italy by allowing the Austrians to remain there, so that the Italians would be forced to continue to seek French support.

Prussia and Russia, moreover, were restless at that time. They did not intend to see Austria destroyed by a successor of her hated enemy, Napoleon the Great. With a strong army ready to fight, Prussia asked England and Russia to mediate and bring about peace. Quickly Louis Napoleon withdrew from the war, winning the bitter hatred of his Italian allies.

The emperor was not discouraged; he actually considered himself the arbiter of Europe. At first he intended to aid the Poles in their struggle for freedom, but when Austria and Russia disapproved and England *The Mexican Debacle* refused to help, Napoleon turned his attention elsewhere. He now dreamed of the creation of an overseas empire. This *was* an idea; French civilization would supplant the Anglo-Saxon and the Spanish in the New World. Glory, converts, wealth, all would accrue to France. Everyone — the bourgeoisie, the clergy, even the workers — would benefit; above all, the empire would make the New World safe for the French.

Mexico furnished the grand opportunity. The Mexicans were engaged in one of their frequent factional squabbles, with one group supporting the republican government and the other furnishing the opposition. To complicate matters, the Mexicans were heavily indebted to France, Spain, and Great Britain. Internal troubles made it difficult for them to pay even the interest on their debts. Therefore, in 1862, the French, English, and Spaniards recognized the legality of international debts and decided to seize the Mexican customs if necessary. Louis Napoleon now saw an opportunity to carry out his idea. He decided that Mexico, like France, needed an emperor. To appear neighborly and to obtain the friendship of Austria (for Russia and England at that time were not sympathetic), Louis Napoleon saw to it that the Mexican crown was offered to the Archduke Maximilian of Austria, brother of Francis Joseph, Austrian emperor.

Maximilian, thirty years of age, was utterly incapable of handling the position. A young, attractive fellow of liberal ideas, handsome, poetical and scientific in a way, living in a beautiful palace overlooking the Adriatic, he should have remained an amateur artist and scientist. One consideration more than any other led to his acceptance of the throne, and this was the ambition of his wife, Carlotta, daughter of Leopold I of Belgium, to be an empress. Encouraged by Louis

Napoleon's promise of military support until 1867, the young man set sail for Mexico in 1864.

The entire project was a good example of Louis Napoleon's mental simplicity. He did not foresee the deadly guerrilla warfare which could be carried on by the Mexicans under Juárez; he had forgotten about his uncles' experience with irregular warriors in Spain; and he ignored the United States, believing that the Civil War would prevent the Americans from opposing European intervention in Mexico. But the Civil War came to an end before Maximilian had established his empire, and the United States soon made it clear that she did not propose to see Mexico become a part of Europe. Meanwhile the Mexicans, by 1867, were making it exceedingly difficult for the emperor to maintain his throne. Carlotta sailed to France to obtain aid from Louis Napoleon, but her pleas were in vain. The unfortunate Maximilian was captured by the Mexicans and on June 19, 1867, was shot.

By 1867 wars had eaten into the financial resources of France. Napoleon's enemies — republicans, clericals, socialists, intellectuals, and monarchists — were *Growing Opposition to Louis Napoleon* rapidly gaining in strength in spite of the emperor's autocratic measures. Hoping to appease his critics, he decided to liberalize the government. By abolishing the censorship of the press, for example, he permitted antagonistic newspapers to appear. This policy seemed equivalent to the signing of his death warrant, for thus he merely gave his enemies a better opportunity of expressing their dissatisfaction.

Opposition to Louis Napoleon was led by a young republican, Léon Gambetta. Of Italian parentage but French by birth, he devoted his unusual oratorical power to a bitter denunciation of the empire. Calling Louis an adventurer who by a *coup d'état* had risen to power and hopelessly involved his country in debts, he maintained that Louis and his followers had destroyed the good things implied by the three watchwords of the French Revolution — Liberty, Equality, and Fraternity. France, he said, could not be free until relieved of the parasite who was ruining the state.

The transition from romanticism to realism in literature helps to explain the widespread dissatisfaction with the emperor. Undoubtedly the romanticists' worship of the past had facilitated the diffusion of the Napoleonic legend and the popularization of another Latin empire. The new tendency to emphasize realities and outward phenomena was an indication of the trend against the "romantic" state. Under Louis Philippe the people, told to practice thrift and get rich, rebelled against a selfish middle-class complacency. During the empire, urged to enjoy themselves, they opposed an autocratic government which brought repression and high taxes.

Superficially France was prosperous. Paris was again the cultural capital of the world. Her streets had been improved, and many public buildings, including the opera house, were being constructed. She was indeed an international tavern. Guests from all parts of the globe were welcomed with magnificence. On the boulevards one could see representatives of all nations — Italians plotting for national unity, Russian princes looking for ballet dancers, American war contractors squandering on clothes and champagne money obtained by chicanery against the Union government, dapper South Americans ostensibly seeking a liberal education in the arts but really securing a knowledge of the gay life of Paris, and Prussians making secret notes in preparation for a war with France. Seldom has there been so much devotion to hearty eating and heavy drinking.

Under the surface, however, there was much unrest. The middle classes, influenced by the materialism of the time and looking for pleasure, found instead increased taxes. The workers, disillusioned by the failure of Napoleon's romantic adventures, were ready to listen to the criticisms of the radical intellectuals. Best known among these was Proudhon, the anarchist, who advocated a collectivist society based on mutualism. According to him, centralized France should be split up into little communes, held together in a loose federation; reason and justice instead of artificial legislation and false monetary standards would lead to a utopia in which government would be reduced to the level of a bureau of

statistics. Blanqui, a Frenchman of Italian origin, also opposed the empire. He favored a violent revolution which
would result in the dictatorship of the proletariat. A militant
minority, the intelligent faction of the workers, was to bring
about this upheaval. These forerunners of Bolshevism were
active during the last days of the Second Empire.

Two wars brought the empire down with a crash. The
first, the Austro-Prussian conflict of 1866, occurred while
Louis Napoleon was engaged in his Mexican
The New German fiasco. Foolishly believing that as arbiter of
Threat Europe he would be able to intervene at the
psychological moment and advance French interests, he stood
aside while the contestants engaged in what he thought was
to be the first phase of a prolonged war. Much to his chagrin
the struggle suddenly ended in a complete victory for Prussia.
Across the Rhine appeared a new rival, the Hohenzollern
dynasty, challenging the French position of leadership in
Europe. This "befuddled incapacity" now strove desperately
to avoid his inevitable fall.

Too late the unlucky Louis Napoleon realized his mistake.
Not until Prussia had won a smashing victory over Austria
did he declare himself in favor of German unity. Although in
reality he opposed this movement, he hypocritically announced
that Prussia's victory was a triumph for the doctrine of
nationality which he had so eagerly championed.

Louis Napoleon tried to bolster his faltering régime by a
diplomatic triumph. In the first place, he asked Berlin to
permit the annexation of Belgium and the purchase of Luxembourg from the king of the Netherlands. Prussia, who herself
had designs in the coveted regions and who was backed by
Great Britain and Russia, refused to accede to Napoleon's
ambition. Therefore the latter had to agree to the independence of Belgium and the neutralization of Luxembourg. Then
Louis Napoleon, aware of the possibility of a war with Prussia,
tried to win the support of Czar Alexander II by calling his
attention to the danger of a Pan-German movement which
might result in the loss of Russian Poland. Alexander, however, spurned Louis Napoleon's friendship. Lulled by Bis-

marck's clever diplomacy, the Czar promised to remain neutral in the event of a conflict between Prussia and France. Louis Napoleon was isolated, for, should a war occur, Austria would not join France for fear that Russia would support Prussia. England, still clinging to her policy of "splendid isolation" and secretly assuring Prussia of neutrality in the event of a defensive war against France, was no help for Napoleon's troubled conscience.

Soon, however, the short-sighted emperor discovered that the effects of his blundering policy, both at home and abroad, could not be avoided by mere words. Confronted by a hostile and powerful Prussia without and by an economic depression within, surrounded by republican, socialist, and intellectual opposition, and weakened by the ravages of an incurable disease, this unfortunate ruler was doomed to topple from his unstable throne. An unsuccessful war, the Franco-German conflict (1870–1871), hastened the end. France should have realized that the Napoleonic legend was but a fairy tale.

A *cartoon of* NAPOLEON III, *from* Punch, 1865.

CHAPTER VIII

Cavour: Architect of a United Italy

THE unification of Italy was one of the outstanding manifestations of the bourgeois nationalist movement in the nineteenth century. For generations that country had been little more than a "geographical expression" — a status legalized at the Congress of Vienna (1815), when a large part of Italy came under Austrian rule. Nevertheless patriots refused to relinquish the hope of Italian unity, a hope shared by many Italians living in the northern and southern parts of the peninsula. Despite linguistic and historic differences they had common interests. To them the greatness of Italy lay in the past; the poems of Dante, the arts of the Renaissance, and the inspiration of Machiavelli, all served to keep alive the belief that Italians were a single and a great people. The creation by Napoleon I of an Italian state, the introduction of liberal ideas, and the common opposition of Italians to the "little corporal" tended to increase their patriotism. Consequently, after Vienna, the Freemasons, Carbonari, and other secret revolutionary societies became active, and great leaders arose, determined to strike for freedom.

Of these Count Camillo di Cavour (1810–1861) was the first to preach the gospel of unity with telling effect. This *Count Cavour* "great 'architect' of United Italy was a singular compound of daring with astuteness; of Machiavellian realism with Liberal idealism; of hot passions with an almost inhuman coldness of intellect. Behind all these qualities, fusing them into a living and sparkling entity, lay the animating and dominating trait in Cavour's many-sided character — patriotism."

The son of a nobleman living in Piedmont and devoted to absolutist ideals, Cavour was at first destined for a military career. While visiting an uncle in Switzerland, however, he imbibed the liberal thoughts of his age. His relative, a disciple of Turgot and Condorcet, taught the young man the middle-class concepts of progress.

These ideas changed his entire life. After a short time in the army as an engineer, he left the service and as a country gentleman claimed to be a bitter foe of absolutism and of clericalism. A gay and affable farmer, he kept a watchful eye on all mechanical inventions, as well as discoveries and innovations in chemistry, that might be of service to him. In 1835 he visited Paris, where he studied and admired the government of Louis Philippe. There he obtained a favorable impression of democracy. "Society is moving fast towards democracy," he proclaimed. "It is impossible to forecast the form that it will take. But fundamentally it cannot be doubted that the reconstruction of aristocratic government as such is impossible. . . . Let us then prepare ourselves, or at least prepare our sons, that they may give it greater consideration than we have done." Then he went to London with Alexis de Tocqueville, the famous French political writer, as a companion. Both were interested in bourgeois problems. Discussing the Reform Bill, ecclesiastical laws, the Irish problem, pauperism, education, prison reform, the labor question, and many other topics, they became thoroughly familiar with the various aspects of the new order.

During his travels in France and England, Cavour sought opportunities for conversing with financiers, industrialists, shipowners, and merchants. These talks revealed to him the importance of economic phenomena in the life of a nation. Influenced by this "materialism," he favored, upon his return, the unification of Italy, the establishment of a constitutional monarchy, and the bourgeois religious arrangement of a free church in a free state.

Cavour was a man of action, and his travels seemed to strengthen that personal quality. Retiring to his farm, however, he became absorbed in books and politics. Influenced by his reading as well as by his travels, he developed into an ardent exponent of liberalism. Convinced of the value of the British middle-class system, he decided that Italy must adopt similar political and economic ideas if she were to become a powerful, united nation. He also believed that if Italy were to imitate such liberal nations as England and France, she would win their sympathy and possibly their support. Apparently he did not realize that the Italian temperament, the historic past, the presence of problems peculiar to Italy (as, for example, the papacy), might make a liberal constitutional monarchy in Italy a failure.

He was successful, however, in his attempt to create this kind of government in Piedmont, which was ruled by the

Bourgeois Reforms in Piedmont

house of Savoy. Through his newspaper, the *Risorgimento*, he urged the establishment of agricultural societies, mechanics' institutes, industrial associations, and banks to aid capital and labor. In 1852, as premier of the Sardinian kingdom, he established a typical middle-class régime. Free trade was encouraged, shipping was subsidized, factories were built, railroads were constructed, education was stimulated, and waste land was put under cultivation. The budget was reorganized and taxes were more equally distributed. The financial as well as the political influence of the church was destroyed, many monasteries were suppressed, the Jesuits were expelled from the country, and an attempt was made to separate church and state so that bourgeois interests could dominate the government without encountering clerical opposition.

Cavour next planned the unification of Italy. The railways, he realized, were to play an important part in accomplishing

Cavour's Plan to unify Italy

this project. Before his eyes arose a vast network of tracks linking together all sections of the peninsula. Such lines would enable the Italians to mingle, to appreciate their common heritage, and to work for unity.

Like Bismarck, his contemporary, Cavour proved that economic development together with clever diplomacy and military power would bring results. Although he realized that the economic prosperity of Piedmont would cause the other Italian states to join in an attempt to make the House of

Savoy the head of an Italian constitutional monarchy, yet he knew that their coöperation alone would not force the Austrians out of Italy.

A powerful European state must help the Italians. So, while he was patronizing secret societies, the Freemasons, the Carbonari, and Young Italy, he was also seeking outside aid. He prepared the way by establishing friendly relations with France and Britain. He considered that they were the two liberal states that would logically furnish support if properly approached. By adopting the English constitutional governmental system in Piedmont, Cavour made a direct appeal to British public opinion. At the same time he hoped that Napoleon III of France might support Italy's attempts to attain freedom. Finally he decided that before he could arouse the interest of these countries and other nations in Europe in Italian aspirations, he would have to make them indebted to Sardinia.

The Crimean War (1853–1856) gave Cavour his opportunity. Italy had no vital interests in the issues between Russia and the allies. The latter, however, needed military aid, and Sardinia obliged them, hoping that by so doing she would be in a position to call the attention of the great powers to her own ambitions. As an enthusiastic Italian soldier put it, "out of the mud [of the trenches] Italy will be made."

Cavour and the Crimean War

At the Congress of Paris in 1856 the conflict was formally terminated. The victors permitted Sardinia to participate at the peace meeting, thus recognizing her as a full-fledged European power. Cavour's "fine Italian hand" had won his first point; he was to gain another. "With the audacity born of success, he arose in the assembly and revealed the grievances of Italy," at the same time stressing especially the flagrant misgovernment in northern and southern Italy which might lead to an international complication at any time. The assembly, however, decided not to arouse the hatred of the Austrians by giving Cavour the support which he desired. He now began his quest for an ally who would help him expel the Austrians.

Cavour turned to France rather than to England, because the latter had traditionally opposed entangling alliances, whereas France wanted Savoy, Nice, and glory at the expense of Austria. Moreover, Emperor Louis Napoleon was still posing as the savior of oppressed nationalities. The two conspirators met at Plombières, as stated before,[1] and the French emperor promised to help Cavour in the "fight for freedom." According to their original arrangements a kingdom under Victor Emmanuel II of Savoy was to be established in northern Italy. Then all Italy was to be united in a confederation over which the Pope should preside. Savoy and Nice were to be handed over to Louis Napoleon, and Victor Emmanuel was to agree to the marriage of his eldest daughter to Napoleon's cousin, Prince Victor Napoleon.

The War against Austria

In 1859 the royal nuptials took place; French and Italian troops fought the Austrians; and the Sardinian kingdom in the North was enlarged through the conquest of Lombardy. A number of small Italian states, including Tuscany, apparently were willing to form a union under the leadership of the House of Savoy in preference to a confederation with the Pope at the head. Louis Napoleon's withdrawal before the Austrians had been completely forced out of Italy, however, prevented complete unification. By the terms of the peace arranged between France and Austria at Zurich, Lombardy was handed over by Austria to Napoleon to pass on to Victor Emmanuel II. France and Austria agreed to support the plan for the formation of an Italian federation under the Pope. Venetia, however, was to remain under Hapsburg control. Austria thus retained a foothold on the Adriatic.

To many Italians this peace marked the failure of the plan to unite Italy. Losing control of himself and threatening suicide, Cavour resigned as prime minister after a violent scene with the more level-headed king. He had been betrayed, he declared, by his friend, Napoleon III. The future looked dark; for, with Austria on one side and France on the other, Italy had two opponents who were determined to thwart her

[1] See page 124.

policies. Despite Cavour's pessimism, Victor Emmanuel II realized that Italy was one step nearer unification.

Cavour had started a movement which progressed even without the minister's masterly guidance. The fame of Mazzini, Cavour, and other great leaders had inspired local patriots to continue the work. Tuscany, Modena, Romagna, and Parma decided to join the kingdom of Victor Emmanuel. The Pope, however, refused to become involved in an international struggle, and thus did not support a scheme which would have made him the head of an Italian confederation.

Cavour finally recovered from his fit of anger and again became prime minister of Sardinia. As soon as he returned to office he took advantage of the sentiment in the small states in favor of merging with *The Plebiscites* Sardinia. In order not to antagonize Louis Napoleon, he adopted the former's favorite method of a plebiscite to determine what territories should join his country. Nice and Savoy decided by elections to unite with France, whereas a number of states in central Italy voted to become a part of what was called the kingdom of Victor Emmanuel II. In his attempt to complete the unification of Italy, Cavour still encountered strong opposition. The plebiscites had brought only a small section of Italy into the union. In 1860 Venetia, Rome, and the kingdom of Naples in the south were still outside; and until they were included within the Italian monarchy, unity would not be attained. Pope Pius IX, however, was bitterly opposed to unification, for he feared that Catholicism would be endangered if the head of this great world faith were to be deprived of his independent position in Rome.

In the Neapolitan and Sicilian kingdom liberalism threatened to lead to anarchy. The masses, uneducated and illiterate, took little interest in the revolutionary movements, whereas the new ruler, Francis II, king of the Two Sicilies, wanted to be a reformer but could not decide what to reform first. Secret societies, especially the unscrupulous Camorra, were more destructive than constructive. These organizations were becoming a menace to law-abiding society. Conspiracies and insurrections were almost continuous.

While plans were being formulated to bring the south into the Italian kingdom, one of the romantic figures of history appeared. This was Garibaldi, the man who, by leading a thousand "red-shirts" into the kingdom of the Sicilies, helped to make it a part of the Italian monarchy.

Garibaldi

Giuseppe Garibaldi (1807–1882) was born in Nice, where he was trained for the navy. Becoming an ardent republican, he conspired at one time with Mazzini to establish a republic. The plot was discovered and he was forced to flee for his life to South America, where in the course of ten years he took part in divers insurrections, displaying great daring as a corsair in the revolted fleet of Brazil. Then he returned to Italy, ready and anxious to join anybody or any cause in an attempt to free his native land. In 1847 he decided to assist Pope Pius IX in this noble purpose. The next year he recruited 3000 volunteers to aid Sardinia in the war with Austria. With the collapse of the Revolution of 1848 Garibaldi, after having been chased around Italy like a wild beast, managed to escape to New York, where he became a candle-maker. He did not return to his beloved Italy until 1854. At this time he purchased the small island of Caprera, settled there, and proceeded to observe the Italian movement. Later he helped Cavour to drive the Austrians out of Lombardy. Then, secretly aided by Cavour, he decided to lead some thousand men into Sicily in order to bring that island and southern Italy into the Italian union.

On May 5, 1860, the expedition of "The Thousand Red-Shirts" embarked from Genoa for Sicily. There the king of Naples had 24,000 troops, and 100,000 more on the mainland. Garibaldi's plan to conquer these regions seemed utter folly, but sheer audacity and good fortune favored the adventurers. Helped by Sicilian insurgents, by volunteers who had flocked from the mainland, and by the incompetency of the Neapolitan leaders, Garibaldi stood master of the island after a campaign of a few weeks.

Conquest of the South

This patriot was so consistently successful that he could not conceive of failure. Consequently he decided to undertake a bolder adventure, the occupation of Naples. Victor Emmanuel, however, advised against this seemingly foolhardy adventure. But Garibaldi refused to stop or listen to advice. Crossing to Naples, this leader of the Argonauts forced King Francis II out of the city and entered amidst the wild enthusiasm of its temperamental inhabitants. In about five months he had conquered a kingdom of eleven million people, an achievement unequaled in modern times.

Garibaldi now decided to push on to Rome. Cavour, however, opposed this plan, realizing that the Eternal City was occupied by a French garrison and that an assault upon it probably would be followed by intervention on the part of Emperor Louis Napoleon. Although Cavour was delighted to see the Bourbon king in Naples overthrown, he did not know what Garibaldi would do next. He questioned the latter's loyalty to Victor Emmanuel and intimated that the leader of the red-shirts was collaborating with the republican idealist, Mazzini; he determined, therefore, to take the military leadership away from Garibaldi. To this end he believed that Victor Emmanuel should intervene at once and then take advantage of the unrest to win over the Papal States.

Pius IX, alarmed at developments, dispatched an army, consisting of French, Irish, and Belgian soldiers, to maintain law and order. This gave Cavour a chance to address a message to the Pope, in which he informed the latter that the king of Sardinia was *The Withdrawal of Garibaldi* sending troops into the provinces, "because he felt himself bound 'in the cause of humanity' to prevent the papal troops from suppressing with violence the popular movements in Umbria." With this excuse the Italian army marched toward Rome and defeated the papal forces. Victor Emmanuel, at the head of the army, now pushed on to Naples, planning to take over Garibaldi's authority as dictator. At first Garibaldi refused to submit, claiming that he had no confidence in Cavour and that the southern kingdom should not be annexed until Rome had been taken. Cavour, however, knew that foreign nations would intervene on behalf of the Pope should the Italian king try to capture the Eternal City.

Temporarily the red-shirts and the king's troops seemed on the point of engaging in a battle over the advisability of taking Rome by force. But Garibaldi, as a true patriot, yielded.

Victor Emmanuel offered him rewards: the Order of the Annunciation, a castle, an endowment, a ducal title. He would have none of them. On 9 November he sailed for his sea-girt crag of Caprera, avoiding all public demonstration, with bloodshot and angry eyes, a flame in his breast, an evil and unbridled tongue; yet great and fine at this moment of his life, for after six months of uncontrolled dictatorship he carried away with him nothing but a sack of flour, a box of red herring, four crowns, a morsel of cheese, and a small crust of bread.[1]

Plebiscites were now taken in the southern kingdom and in the papal territories, and by overwhelming majorities the people declared for annexation to the constitutional monarchy of Victor Emmanuel II.

This successful attempt to conquer a fair-sized kingdom with only a handful of men representing various walks of life, good and bad, was one of the most dramatic events in modern history. In Italy today Garibaldi is a great national hero. His courage and skill, his simplicity and nobility of character, make him the fascinating leader of his age. His political incapacity and his ignorance of the forces which governed international affairs, however, prevented him from becoming a great statesman. He distrusted and hated Cavour, the man who helped him organize his Sicilian expedition. Occasionally he tried to coöperate with Mazzini in an attempt to make the southern kingdom a part of an Italian republic rather than a monarchy. He might have known that a republic would not function in the south and that the clever Cavour, by Machiavellian methods, would succeed in gaining southern Italy for the monarchy.

In February, 1861, the first Italian parliament met in Turin, and in March a new constitutional decree announced that

Establishment of the Italian Kingdom

Victor Emmanuel II had assumed for himself and his successors the title "king of Italy." A new kingdom with a population of about 22,000,000 had arisen within eighteen months and was ready to take its place as one of the great powers of Europe. But

[1] Paléologue, *Cavour*, p. 276.

Venetia still belonged to Austria, and Rome was subject to the Pope, largely because of the protection given by a French garrison maintained by Napoleon III to placate the Catholics.

The Unification of Italy

Eventually these regions also became part of Italy. During the war between Prussia and Austria in 1866 Italy joined the former and freed Venetia, the latter, after a favorable plebiscite, joining the new kingdom. Four years later the Franco-German war, causing the French garrison to be withdrawn from Rome, enabled the Italian government to capture that city (September 20, 1870). Its citizens immediately voted for annexa-

Conquest of Venetia and Rome

tion. Rome now became the political capital of Italy, the Pope losing a temporal power which had endured for over a thousand years. Vainly did he call upon all faithful Catholics to lend him assistance. Most of them, though still recognizing him as their spiritual leader, refused to support his temporal aspirations.

Unfortunately Cavour, largely responsible for the unification of Italy, did not live to see its actual realization. While trying to reconcile the Pope and the Catholic world to the recognition of Rome as the capital of the new kingdom, Cavour suddenly fell sick and died in 1861, in the prime of life. Before his death, however, he had achieved his objective; most of Italy was united under a constitutional monarch.

One phase of Cavour's program, however, proved to be a failure, namely, his attempt to establish a middle-class constitutional monarchy. Nevertheless this does not detract from his reputation as one of the outstanding leaders of the nineteenth century. A man of transcendent talent, indomitable industry, and inextinguishable patriotism, he was able to overcome tremendous difficulties in uniting his beloved country. He lived for Italy and believed that, once united under bourgeois control, she would again become a great and powerful state.

CHAPTER IX

Bismarck: Founder of the German Empire

IN 1848 the thirty-nine independent states in central Europe were loosely combined in a weak confederation. The primary purpose of this union was protection against foreign interference, and the individual rulers of the small member states opposed any stronger form of unity. Moreover, the larger states, Austria and Prussia, intensely jealous of one another, opposed liberalism and thwarted the establishment of a single constitutional German monarchy.

Many Germans realized that before national unity could be attained, the confederation under the presidency of the Hapsburgs would have to be destroyed and the overlordship of the Austrian house in central Europe abolished. But what people was powerful enough to overthrow this medieval dynasty? In answer to this query an ambitious young German junker, Otto von Bismarck, who had attended the ill-fated assembly at Frankfurt, nominated the Prussians; but many refused to consider the Hohenzollern monarchy as the logical leader in German unification. To them the Prussians were part Slavs rather than pure Teutons. Moreover, the predominance of Protestantism in Prussia alienated the support of the southern Catholic states, especially of Bavaria. Disunity under the Catholic Hapsburgs seemed preferable to union under Prussian control.

At the opening of the nineteenth century Prussia was an agrarian state in which the large landowners controlled most of the land, hiring day workers to farm it. The *The Prussian Junkers* sons of these junkers usually entered the service of the state as bureaucrats or as army officers. Favored by exemption from taxation, and with a monopoly of all governmental offices, the junkers resisted fiercely any attempt to change the established order.

141

The heavy cost of military protection paved the way for the diminution of privileges accorded the junkers. Lacking natural frontiers, the Hohenzollern kingdom needed a powerful army for defense. To support this military force, increased taxes were necessary. Inasmuch as the junkers possessed considerable wealth and political influence, the government gradually withdrew some of their tax exemptions and created a bureaucracy more dependent upon the rulers and less representative of these landowners.

Realizing that Prussia must consider the interests of all classes, the administration had introduced important reforms.

Benevolent Despotism The first was the abolition of serfdom (1807), which created peasant proprietors and an important class of day workers who were hired by the landowners to farm their estates. Another reform had made it possible for burghers and Jews to become officers in the army and to hold political positions in the government — places previously monopolized by the junkers. More significant than these changes was the encouragement given by the government to business.

The *Zollverein*, discussed elsewhere,[1] was the most important factor in the economic development of Prussia. By abolishing the numerous tariff walls in central Europe this economic union encouraged the growth of industry, the expansion of commerce, and the rise of the bourgeoisie.

Business men were grateful for the part played by the Prussian government in the economic development of the state. They realized that the administration had removed the social stigma attached to the bourgeois classes and had given them certain local political rights and economic aid. Moreover, the government established a uniform civil code which guaranteed all business men identical treatment throughout the kingdom. Although a minority, the middle classes proved of great service to the Hohenzollerns. Not only did they help to weaken the authority of the junkers, but also, through the economic development of the state, they were able, by paying high taxes, to aid in the support of the army.

[1] See page 76.

Although influential, the bourgeoisie were never sufficiently powerful to dominate the government or to establish a democracy. So great was the authority of the government itself that the best brains of the land competed for official positions. Thus the bureaucracy was not restricted to any particular class.

In determining Prussian political, social, and intellectual policies the church played a subordinate part. The dominant Protestant sect was under the direct control of the government. Consequently there was no clerical check on the all-powerful state, *Religion and Education in Prussia* as was the case in countries where the Roman Catholic church questioned the temporal supremacy of the government. Instead the Lutherans in Germany, like the Greek Orthodox Catholics in Russia, supplied the moral encouragement which enabled the people to endure "the established order." Nevertheless the Prussian government permitted far more intellectual freedom than did the Russian autocracy. Outside of politics many Prussian conservatives were in sympathy with the economic, religious, and social ideas of the eighteenth-century philosophers. In this respect the church, which in Austria strictly supervised new thought, was powerless in Prussia.

A remarkable educational system developed, in which the universities, living in an atmosphere of academic freedom, were able to do much in advancing the sum total of human knowledge and thereby the prestige of Germany. Largely because of this development Germany became a center of music, of science, and of business. No wonder the Germans were content, on the whole, to let "strong" men maintain the political order.

This intellectual freedom was not important at first, for it was limited to the few educated persons who could exchange ideas. The masses were not affected. In time the industrialization of Prussia and the rise of the middle classes were accompanied by an attempt to disseminate education among all groups. This resulted in the growth of a wealthy, powerful, and intelligent Prussian state, capable of bringing most Germans into a union.

Nationalism was a force which made German unity possible. Emphasizing the welfare of the state, Prussia, in the patriotic

Prussian Nationalism

attempt to overthrow Napoleon and to create a great kingdom, enlisted citizens as soldiers, as teachers, as students, and as workers. Prussia did contribute to the downfall of the French emperor. Before she could lead the way in the move to unify the German states, however, a capable leader was needed. But Frederick William IV, the Prussian king, was a stubborn, peculiar, and certainly not an able ruler. As one of his subordinates remarked, "His Majesty's brain works like that of no other mortal." In 1848 he bitterly opposed the liberal movement, leaning heavily upon the junkers, the bureaucracy, and the clergy. He was forced to give the Prussian people a constitution, but he saw to it that the *Landtag*, or legislative assembly, was muzzled and that political liberalism was crushed. Refusing the leadership of the new German state, offered by the liberals at Frankfurt in 1849, he bowed to Austria's overlordship in middle Europe and was apparently willing that Prussia should occupy a subordinate position. Insanity, however, relieved the king of his responsibilities. His successor, William I (1861–1888), acted as regent from 1858 until 1861, when he became king of Prussia.

An ambitious Hohenzollern, the new ruler decided to strengthen the army, which had not grown in proportion to

The Army Bill (1862)

the increase in population. By this method William planned to secure for Prussia a more important position in international affairs, at least so far as middle Europe was concerned. Therefore a bill proposing the enlargement of the army, and extending the service in the reserve from two to four years, was presented to the Prussian legislative body.

According to the constitution the Prussian *Landtag* had a right to consider financial matters. Inasmuch as the army bill involved an increase of taxation, the king had to secure the assent of the body before this proposal could become legal. This constitutional barrier complicated matters, inasmuch as certain groups in the *Landtag* opposed this measure.

The junkers were antagonistic, because as the leading land-owners they would be forced to pay the greater portion of the increased taxes which would result from the proposed military expansion. Many bourgeois liberals also refused to support this policy. In control of the lower house of the *Landtag*, they not only objected to further military expenditure but even went so far as to demand the reduction of service with the colors from three to two years.

Angered by this stubborn opposition and determined not to recognize the supremacy of the constitution created by his predecessor, William I prorogued the lower house of the *Landtag*. The king was sadly disappointed by the ensuing elections, for the liberals returned a larger group than before. Finally facing defeat, the government asked the legislature to grant enough money to maintain the army for one year. It was to be a "temporary arrangement." The king, however, created permanent regiments. In doing this he had the support of the junkers in the House of Lords, the upper branch of the *Landtag*, which had finally decided to accept the increased land tax necessary in order to maintain a larger military force. This change in attitude was probably due to the fact that by 1861 a growing German progressive party in Prussia was advocating the abolition of privileges enjoyed by the landowners, the separation of Church and State, and the reform of the House of Lords.

In 1862 a crisis occurred. The party in control of the lower house demanded that the budget be shown them, so that they might see that the money spent on the army was not drawn from other items. William I opposed the request. Rather than give way to the legislature, he threatened to abdicate. Discouraged at the turn of events, he decided, however, to make a last desperate attempt to force his military bill through parliament. To do this he appointed as his prime minister, in October, 1862, the patriotic and aggressive junker Otto von Bismarck (1815–1898).

This man who rushed upon the stage of European politics was one of the most able, original, and powerful characters of the time. Born in 1815, of an aristocratic junker family, he lived on a large landed estate in Brandenburg, entirely ignorant of the world about him except as he saw it through the con-

Otto von Bismarck

servative eyes of his parents. As a student he was a likable fellow. Constantly in bouts of various kinds, he early exhibited pugnacious capacity, but of the numerous intellectual opportunities for independent thought he failed to take any advantage.

Returning to his father's estate, Bismarck became a typical junker, favoring the *status quo* and a strong Prussia. To him

Early Opposition to Liberalism

real patriotism was unswerving loyalty to his Hohenzollern king; consequently he became an uncompromising foe of all liberals, espe-cially those who advocated a limited constitutional govern-ment. "I look for Prussia's abstinence, before all things, from every shameful union with democracy," he is reported to have stated. As a delegate to the parliament of Frankfurt from Prussia he did his utmost to check the liberal movement. Later, a representative of Prussia at various courts, he studied diplomacy, with one idea in mind, — to establish a strong Germany. He soon discovered that as long as the Hapsburgs dominated central Europe, Prussia could not grow and German unity could not be attained. Therefore he dedicated his life to one thing, namely, the abolition of Austrian influence in the German states.

Possessing intellectual ability and physical strength, Bis-marck had those characteristics which made for success. Al-

Bismarck's Personal Qualities

though not an idealist, he visualized a German empire dominated by Prussia. This new state was not to be a democratic institution. As a junker he believed that the people were incapable of guarding their interests. In reality he had only a faint knowledge of the political life of western Europe, for he knew little of England and had been in France only on a brief diplomatic mission. Nevertheless he was able to rise above the prejudice of his class. He realized, for example, that religious, political, and social questions involved the interests of the state rather than the welfare of one group. More clever, more logical, and more opportunistic than the other junkers, he was an excellent example of the principles of *Realpolitik,* "a policy of opportunism which aims by shrewd calculation of actual forces to secure practical success in politics."

As prime minister Bismarck saw an opportunity to bring about German unity under Prussian leadership. The first steps in that direction were to be the destruction of the German Confederation and the abolition of Austrian influence in the Germanies. Liberalism would then be destroyed through the establishment of a strong German state ruled by Prussia. To attain this end, Machiavellian diplomacy was necessary.

With these aims in mind the new prime minister determined to strengthen the army regardless of opposition. Compromise and coöperation were impossible; one authority, the king, must be supreme. So, when the lower house refused to give provisional assent *The Fight over the Budget* to the military law, Bismarck said that inasmuch as the constitution did not state what was to be done in the event that the crown and legislature failed to agree regarding a budget, the king had the right to make such expenditures, even without the approval of the legislature.

(A) political battle followed. The lower chamber refusing to approve the budget, Bismarck had the House of Lords draw up estimates, and by means of the king's control of the army and the administrative system he collected the taxes. Through manipulated elections he also sent "loyal" representatives to the assembly and at the same time tried to stamp out all liberalism by censorship of the press.

Disregarding bitter criticism which threatened to provoke a civil war, Bismarck made plans to use the army in such ways as to justify his policies. The overthrow of Austrian supremacy in central Europe, he knew, would achieve this end. In his opinion the time was ripe for such an undertaking. England was not interested in European affairs, except as they affected her economic interests. Russia, defeated in the Crimean War and aided by the Prussians in putting down a Polish rebellion, would undoubtedly remain neutral. Italy, desirous of weakening Austria, her traditional oppressor, and being promised Venetia, would actually help Prussia.

Bismarck realized, however, that one must have some sort of pretext for starting a war. It so happened that a series of events gave him his much-desired opportunity. In 1863 King Frederick VII of Denmark, duke of Schleswig and Holstein, died. According to a verdict of the European powers, known as the Protocol of London (1852), the crown went to his relative, Christian IX. The duchies, inhabited mostly by Germans, alleged that under their own law of inheritance the duke of Augustenburg, a German prince, was now their rightful ruler. Believing that the German states would support them, the residents of these provinces saw an opportunity to separate them from Denmark. Nor were they mistaken. Prussia, Austria, and even the little states in the German *Bund*, or Confederation, were aroused and favored intervention in behalf of their brothers in Schleswig-Holstein. At once Bismarck saw an opportunity to use this affair as a means to provoke a war with Austria.

The Schleswig-Holstein Affair (1864)

With this end in view Bismarck persuaded Austria to join Prussia in an attempt to settle the crisis over Schleswig-Holstein. Christian IX now played into Bismarck's hands by incorporating Schleswig, the northern province, with Denmark. Inasmuch as the London Protocol recognized Christian as king of Denmark on condition that he respect the historical autonomy of the duchies, Bismarck urged intervention, claiming that Christian's act had violated this agreement. Austria decided to join Prussia, and an ultimatum was sent to Copenhagen, demanding that Denmark's plan to incorporate Schleswig be withdrawn without delay. Christian foolishly refused to yield, and the German allies declared war upon Denmark in 1864. Denmark was easily brought to her knees and ceded Schleswig-Holstein to the victors.

Trouble now arose over the disposition of the provinces. Prussia wished to annex them, whereas Austria, in order to preserve the German Confederation and her influence, desired to incorporate them in the German *Bund* as a separate state under the duke of Augustenburg. Finally the territories were divided, Austria administering Holstein, and Prussia, Schleswig. But the arrangement did not terminate the Schleswig-Holstein affair.

An Austro-Prussian rupture occurred as a result of the supposed favor shown by Austria to the claims of Frederick of Augustenburg to these provinces. This partiality was regarded by Prussia as an unfriendly act and a sufficient excuse for war, *The Austro-Prussian War (1866)* which had been foreseen and desired for some time. Therefore, when Prussian troops occupied Holstein and thus broke the agreement which gave that region to Austria, the latter demanded the mobilization of the army of the Confederation. On June 16, 1866, Prussia found herself at war with Austria.

Some Prussian leaders did not favor this conflict. King William hesitated, while at one time General von Moltke protested that Prussia was not ready. To strengthen the war party, Bismarck sought and secured an alliance with the new Italian monarchy. Meanwhile he had met Louis Napoleon at Biarritz (1865) and duped that simple monarch by making vague promises of territorial rewards. Several large states in the German Confederation, however, joined Austria. The Schleswig-Holstein affair had thus involved Prussia and Austria in a conflict for the mastery of central Europe.

At the beginning the European powers believed that Austria would win the war. The new Prussian military system was untried; it was thought "that her conscripts would prove to be little more than a national guard," guided by traditions. Concurring in this opinion, Napoleon III of France planned to intervene at the proper time, and, by playing the rôle of peacemaker, to force the contending parties to recognize French supremacy in Belgium and the Rhine country.[1]

Europe soon discovered that it had picked the wrong horse. Austria was unable to offer much opposition, inasmuch as her army was poorly prepared and had to be divided in order to resist an Italian advance. Consequently the Prussians, more quickly mobilized, better armed, and led by more capable generals, were able to converge in three powerful units

[1] See page 128.

upon the Austrians, who were engaged in concentrating their forces near the fortress of Königgrätz in Bohemia. Catching the enemy in a trap at Sadowa, the Prussians completely crushed the Austrian forces on July 3, 1866. This battle marked the end of the so-called Seven Weeks' War. Austria was forced to open peace negotiations, and a truce in July was followed in August of 1866 by the Peace of Prague.

By this treaty Austria ceded her rights in Schleswig-Holstein to Prussia, acquiesced in the dissolution of the German Confederation, and withdrew from German affairs. In addition to these terms Austria also gave Venetia to Italy. Despite these losses she did not suffer greatly. The land cession was not vital, and she was not compelled to pay a large indemnity.

Bismarck was chiefly responsible for the liberal peace terms. Despite the insistence of the king, the generals, and the chauvinistic junkers upon harsh terms, he made a generous settlement. He argued that in the event of a war with another power Austria's support might be needed. Furthermore, with Prussia already supreme in central Europe, he had achieved his principal aim.

Bismarck now proceeded to create the North German Confederation. Twenty-two states joined the new union, accepting the king of Prussia, under the title *The North German Confederation* of president, as the chief executive. Cleverly Bismarck satisfied the local princes, and to a certain extent the liberals, by creating a federal government with two houses, a *Bundesrat* representing the rulers of the participating governments, and a parliament, or *Reichstag*, whose members represented the people and were elected by universal suffrage. To Bismarck's satisfaction this body was at first merely a "discussion group," whereas the upper house, controlled by the Prussian king, who had the largest number of votes, became an instrument of Prussianization.

Although the various states, upon coming into the union, retained a certain degree of autonomy, they gave up their leading sovereign rights, in theory to the *Bundesrat* and *Reichstag*, in fact to the Prussian king, the chief executive.

Powerful not only because he dominated the *Bundesrat* but also because he appointed his own chancellor, the Prussian ruler became the absolute head of the newly founded confederation of 1867. Even though he claimed to rule by the will of God, the success of William I as head of the confederation depended to a large extent upon the personality and ability of his first chancellor. Aware of this fact, the king selected Bismarck, the one man capable of handling matters, as his chief minister.

One circumstance considerably disturbed the newly appointed minister — the failure of the southern German states to enter the union. Bismarck realized that as long as they stayed out, a real German nation was impossible. But how could they be *Bismarck and the Southern States* brought in? The wily Prussian soon solved this problem. First by extending and enlarging the *Zollverein* he tried to show them the economic advantages of union. Next he cleverly posed as the champion of all Germans against France. By denouncing the French attempts to acquire territories near the Rhine, including Belgium and Luxemburg, he did the one thing which would arouse a sense of German nationality. Aware that a war with France would involve the southerners, who also feared that country, Bismarck proceeded to arrange offensive and defensive treaties with them.

To understand how this conflict came about it is necessary to consider again the Second French Empire of Napoleon III. That unfortunate ruler had been unsuccessful in the sixties in his attempt to establish *The Origins of the Franco-German War* an empire in Mexico. Engaged in this foolish undertaking, he had also failed to play a decisive rôle in the war between Prussia and Austria (1866). Consequently the Prussian victory enabled the Hohenzollerns to create a North German Confederation, capable of challenging French ambitions in the Rhineland.

Aware of this menace, Louis Napoleon decided to win the support of his subjects by establishing a more democratic government. This reform served to increase his unpopularity, for his enemies used their freedom to denounce him publicly.

Meanwhile he did his utmost to bring about a coalition of France, Austria, and Italy, and planned a campaign based on the "idea of a great concentric movement against the Prussians." The inability of the three countries to reach a definite agreement, however, frustrated this scheme.

The excuse for war finally presented itself. In the year 1868 a revolution took place in Spain. Queen Isabella, the Bourbon ruler, was expelled, and the revolutionary leaders offered the crown to Leopold of Hohenzollern-Sigmaringen, a young Catholic relative of the Protestant king of Prussia. The prospect of a German prince on the Spanish throne greatly excited French opinion. Many were convinced that it would lead to the establishment of a Hispanic-German empire which would encircle France and threaten its existence.

In his writings Bismarck frankly admitted that he helped to precipitate the Franco-German crisis. He encouraged the candidacy of the Hohenzollerns for the throne of Spain and did little during the critical days of July, 1870, to prevent the outbreak of hostilities. He actually favored the Spanish scheme "as a necessary counterblast" to projected French designs in Belgium and the Rhineland. As Professor Langer states, "With a friendly ruler beyond the Pyrenees, Prussia could count on the French having to leave many thousand men on the Spanish frontier in case of war on the Rhine."

The withdrawal of the Hohenzollern candidacy was a great diplomatic victory for France. French statesmen, however, were not satisfied:

... they insisted on more and demanded that King William of Prussia should write Napoleon an apology as well as promise that the candidacy would never be renewed in the future. Even the most ardent defenders of the French position find it hard to say much in justification of these unreasonable demands. There was no hope whatever that the Prussians would agree to them. On the contrary these demands gave Bismarck exactly the opportunity he wanted to put the French in the wrong and practically force them into war.[1]

On the night of July 13, 1870, the king of Prussia sent Bismarck a telegram informing him of the French attitude.

[1] Langer, *European Alliances and Alignments, 1871–1890*, p. 9.

The message arrived while the astute Bismarck was entertaining the two military war horses, Roon and Moltke, at dinner. After reading it to his guests, Bismarck, with royal approval, prepared a revised copy of the telegram for the press. Determined to precipitate a war, he omitted words and altered the order of sentences in such a way as to change the original meaning of the king's message. Upon reading it the French immediately received the impression that their country had been insulted, while the Germans were angry because of the unreasonable requests made by the French representative. The new version was not a signal for a future discussion of the issue; it was a note of defiance. An intensification of general excitement and of national feeling in both Paris and Berlin was the result. Honor and security, said the French, demanded an immediate war.

At Bismarck's famous dinner Roon and Moltke typified Prussian militarism. Dejected when the telegram was first read, their spirits changed when Bismarck showed them the new version. This dispatch, said Bismarck, would "have the effect of a red cloth upon the Gallic bull." Everybody was happy; felicitations were enthusiastically exchanged. "The old God still lives, and will not let us perish in shame," said old Roon, and even the impassive Moltke felt so gay that he said, "If I only live to lead our armies in such a war, then afterwards the devil may take this old carcass."

The war which followed was one of the most dramatically decisive and most fateful conflicts in the history of Europe. To the victorious Germans it was the most glorious page in their annals; to the French it was the darkest of disasters. From the *The Franco-German War* beginning the advantages in the struggle were with the Prussians. Their first success was achieved when they were joined by the southern German states. Louis Napoleon had hoped that, because of their aversion to Prussia, these would back France; but, as mentioned before, Bismarck had provided for such an emergency by signing offensive and defensive alliances with these powers after the war of 1866. Although obligated to support Prussia, the southern states would have done so even without the agreements, for their national hatred of France caused them to regard Prussia as the leader of the German cause.

On the military side the Germans were superior. The North German Confederation and its allies were able to muster a better-organized army than that of Napoleon even before

The Unification of Germany

the French were under way. Consequently Moltke, the able German leader, assuming the offensive, defeated, in August, 1870, the French armies in Alsace and in Lorraine. The Germans, driving most of the French troops into Metz, where they were now besieged, forced the rest, under MacMahon, back on Châlons. Napoleon III and MacMahon, instead of retreating to Paris and calling upon the people for help, unwisely determined to relieve Metz. Completely defeated at Sedan, and obliged to surrender with his whole army on September 2, the Emperor, after a touching interview with

King William, was sent to Germany as a prisoner of war — an impotent and fallen ruler.

Thus Moltke had managed the campaign with remarkable skill and rapidity. Within a month the Germans, leaving an army to watch Metz, moved on to Paris, planning to dictate terms of peace. They soon discovered that the French capital would not capitulate without a siege. Indignant when they heard of the calamity which had befallen their armies, the citizens of Paris declared France a republic and prepared to oppose the hated Germans. After the last French army at Metz had been defeated, the Germans awaited the surrender of the capital. Forced by hunger, the citizens of Paris finally, on January 28, 1871, agreed to capitulate.

In the definitive treaty of Frankfurt (1871) France agreed to pay one billion dollars and to cede Alsace and a part of Lorraine to the Germans. The outstanding result of the war, however, was the creation of the German Empire. Bismarck's dream had come true; yet at this moment of victory he made two serious mistakes: one was the exaction of a heavy indemnity, and the other was the annexation of two French provinces. At first Bismarck refused to approve the annexation of the larger part of Lorraine, saying, "I do not want too many Frenchmen in our house." But when his generals, believing that "to the victors belong the spoils," insisted, he gave way. Thenceforth the lost provinces became an object of rough coercion. In her humiliation France vowed never to forget, and to wait for the day when she should regain what had been annexed by the enemy. Because of these losses Victor Hugo, the great French writer, at the end of the War of 1870, made a prophecy which is especially interesting to-day in the light of what has happened since 1914.

The day will come when France will rise again invincible, and take back not only Alsace and Lorraine, but the Rhineland with Mainz and Cologne, and in return will give to Germany a republic, so freeing the Germans from their Emperor as an equivalent for the dethronement of Louis Napoleon.

A new Germany arose as a result of this war. Certainly it was not the old divided Fatherland to which the victorious

soldiers returned. The great successes won by the united efforts of north and south had aroused a boundless enthusiasm.;
in all circles the feeling prevailed that the present happy
union must take a constitutional form. Yielding to national
sentiment, the southern German states entered the North
German Confederation. This resulted in a change in title,
for now "German Empire" was the accepted term, and the
Prussian king henceforth asumed the rank of German Kaiser.
. On January 18, 1871, the humiliation of the French and
the completion of German unity were proclaimed to the
world from the Hall of Mirrors in Louis XIV's
The Proclamation of the German Empire beautiful palace at Versailles. Bismarck, the
founder of the German Empire, was raised
to the rank of prince and to the post of chancellor, thus becoming head of the national administration under the Kaiser.
At last Bismarck had achieved the principal aim of his life:
the greater part of Germany was united in an empire in which
Prussia held the predominant position. His policy of force
had apparently been justified; it was a personal success, and
at the same time a victory for Prussianism and for the policy
of opportunism, the *Realpolitik*. The modern Machiavelli
had triumphed.

After 1871 the Prussian state became the center of the new
union. Germany was ruled by the Prussian king, his supporters among the landed aristocracy, and the great host of
officials, high and low, closely knit together in a political machine which controlled the army, the police, and the agencies
of government. As in the time of Frederick the Great, many
Germans now worked for the welfare of one thing only, the
state. Henceforth soldiers, sailors, merchants, teachers,
preachers, farmers, and statesmen had a common ambition,
the creation of a mighty German Empire.

CHAPTER X

Imperial Russia: Infiltration of Liberalism

AT THE opening of the nineteenth century the Russian Empire was firmly established. Geographically Russia was the largest state in Europe, extending over the east-European plains from the Baltic and the Arctic Ocean in the west and north to the Black Sea in the south, and across Asia to the waters of the Pacific. Later annexations and conquests added to her original holdings: Finland, central Poland (in addition to what she had received in the three partitions), Bessarabia, Transcaucasia, trans-Caspian central-Asiatic territories, and the Amur and Maritime provinces in the Far East. By the end of the century she ruled over one sixth of the land surface of the globe.

By 1815 Russia was one of the great European nations. Her old rivals, Sweden and Poland, had been weakened or eliminated. She no longer feared Turkey, and neither in central Asia nor in the Far East did any strong powers at first oppose her advance. During the Napoleonic wars Russia had taken an important part in the economic and military struggles leading to the downfall of the French emperor. At Vienna her Czar, Alexander I, was one of those responsible for the peace settlement. In international affairs Russia wielded considerable power.

But in domestic matters the government's authority was limited, especially in its borderlands. Territorially and ethnographically the composition of the empire was complex. Its center was the old czardom of Moscow, which included the middle, northern, *Problems confronting the Government* and southeastern parts of the European-Russian plain. This region was inhabited by the Great Russian group of the Russians. In the southwest were the Little Russians (Ukrainians), and in the west were the White Russians. Other possessions contained numerous non-Russian groups, such as Finns, Baltic Germans, Letts, Estonians, Lithuanians, Poles, Circassians, Georgians, Armenians, Tatars, other Asiatic peoples, and Jews.

In 1815 the Russian element, a great majority of the 45,000,000 people, dominated all other groups. Nevertheless the government found it difficult to govern these minorities, especially the peoples in the West,— the Poles and the Finns, for example,— who had a higher level of culture than the Russians and received at first a special status within the empire. Later, when the imperial government tried to increase its authority and to acquire these regions, the peoples, deprived of their privileges, became bitter enemies of the existing régime.

Enormous distances, separating one part of the empire from another, handicapped the central government. With few good highways and with little railroad construction until the last part of the nineteenth century, the Czar controlled, often in name only, such far-flung portions of his realm as parts of Siberia.

The size of the empire and the difficulties confronting its government partially explain political and social developments. By 1815 the government was an abso-
The Absolute Government lute monarchy not subject in theory to any limitations. This situation was the natural result of the "exigencies of national defense and imperial expansion." Old assemblies had disappeared, semi-independent nobles had lost their power, and the church had been deprived of its independence.

Like Western despots the Russian rulers displayed benevolent tendencies. Peter the Great tried to introduce reforms, and Catherine II, because of her interest in
The Privileged Nobility arts, letters, and education, merited the title "benevolent despot." The fact that these rulers achieved but limited success may be attributed partly to the influence of the nobility. The latter remained a privileged order, enjoying special economic and social rights, which, embodied in a charter granted to them by the government in 1785, were no

longer justified by service. Freed from personal taxation, compulsory military duties, and corporal punishment, and possessing the right to own serfs and to hold a great share of the land, the nobles were indeed a favored class.

Inasmuch as these privileges were granted by a charter, they could be abrogated by the Czar. Thus the nobles were legally dependent upon the emperor, and only retained their favored positions because the government needed their support. Socially the nobility wielded great influence. Until the latter part of the nineteenth century they constituted the intellectual class and furnished the officials and officers who formed the Russian governing group, or bureaucracy. Moreover, they were autocrats in their communities, possessing practically complete jurisdiction over the serfs and controlling all the important local political offices.

The basis of the Russian economic and social system was serfdom. In 1815 the peasants constituted the great majority of the population of Russia. They paid the taxes, worked the land, and supplied the soldiers, in order that the empire should exist. *The Oppressed Peasants* Aware of their importance, the Russian government, long before the nineteenth century, had attached them to the soil in order to check their migratory tendencies and thus to insure the collection of taxes and the cultivation of lands.

By 1815 the authority of the landlord over the serf was practically unlimited. He had the right to sell, to mortgage, or to give away his serfs; he could exploit their labor without compensation; he could use them either as domestics or as laborers on his land; or he might allow the serfs to work so as to pay him a monetary contribution. Exerting police and legal authority over them, the noble could arrest, try, and punish those who were disobedient. The government did require that the nobleman feed his serfs, and a legal limit was set to the exploitation of serfs' labor. Also it was declared by law that the owner could not require his serfs to work for him more than three days a week, and he was prohibited from mistreating them. It was difficult, however, for the government to enforce these laws.

Between the nobility at the top and the serfs at the bottom were the middle classes, generally consisting of city inhabitants and the clergy. Limited in numbers, *The Bourgeois Minority* they were not influential. Urban life was unimportant in 1815, and the few wealthy merchants and upper clergy were practically joined with the nobility through the possession of exemption from personal taxation, compulsory military service, and corporal punishment. Socially, with the exception of a few of the higher ecclesiastics, they were debarred from the aristocratic circles of the nobility. The parish priest occupied the social position of a peasant.

Up to 1815 Russia had failed to adopt many essential features of Western civilization. This huge empire was largely Byzantine and Oriental in culture. During the *The Eastern Influence* fourteenth and fifteenth centuries, when men *upon Russia* in the West were experiencing a new zest for life which enabled them to paint beautiful pictures and to invent and discover new things, the Russians were under the control of Asiatic nomads called Tatars (1240–1480). During this period Russia knew very little about Western civilization, and Europe was perhaps even less familiar with conditions in Russia. It is true that, later, Peter the Great (1682–1725) cut a window in the wall which separated Russia from the West, but the European influences which poured into Russia were not able to bring about any fundamental changes. Until the nineteenth century the Russians had been little influenced by the important political and social movements that marked the rise of middle-class control in western Europe. They remained essentially Eastern in culture.

One event was largely responsible for the persistence of Eastern influence upon Russia. This was the capture of Constantinople by the Ottoman Turks in 1453 and the disappearance of the Byzantine Empire. From that time the rulers of Russia considered themselves the successors of the Greek emperors and the natural champions of the Greek Orthodox church and Byzantine culture. Assuming the title of "Czar," similar to Cæsar, many of them undoubtedly accepted as true the legend that Moscow was to be the third and last Rome. "The first Rome and the second," it was said, had both fallen through heresies. "The third Rome, Moscow, stands, and a fourth there will not be!"

Western civilization was bound to seep into Russia. To strengthen national defense and to improve the machinery of government, she had to borrow bourgeois technique. In doing this she could not remain *Penetration of Western Culture* culturally isolated. Consequently, when railroads and the factory system were introduced into Russia, they brought in their wake Western ideas, such as constitutional government, civil equality, and personal liberty. Then "enlightenment," which was an important feature in the life of the small group of educated Russians during the latter half of the eighteenth century, was revived. The principle of autocracy, the predominance of the nobility, and the value of serfdom were soon questioned by intelligent Russian intellectuals.

Economic progress after 1815 thus accelerated the introduction of Western ideas as well as of Western practices. Between 1815 and 1855 Russian industry and commerce developed, and capital increased. Landlords, influenced by this progress, tried to increase production on their estates in order to make money, and some even used serfs in factories. But as time went on it became apparent that serfdom was a hindrance to capitalistic development. The productivity of serf labor was low, and a need for free workers existed. Long before the emancipation of the serfs in the sixties, many Russian intellectuals realized that the development of capitalism in Russia had doomed serfdom.

The task of ruling Russia in the nineteenth century was difficult indeed. Alexander I (1801–1825) and Nicholas I (1825–1855) inherited definite political and religious traditions — orthodoxy, autocracy, *Problems confronting Alexander I and Nicholas I* and imperial unity — which they considered it their duty to preserve. At the same time they were confronted by the new tendencies which arose out of the revival of "enlightenment" and the introduction of capitalism. Both rulers tried to accept the developments and yet preserve the old political and social system, but these contradictory factors were practically irreconcilable.

Nevertheless, during the first part of the nineteenth century the governmental machinery was reorganized and an efficient Russian bureaucracy established. Also a systematic code of laws was created in 1832. "Both the codification of laws and the organization of the Russian bureaucracy on a modern basis were principally the work of one man, Michael Speranski (1772–1839), whose administrative genius remains perhaps unequaled in Russian history." Actually these laws were often not enforced or were misconstrued. The lack of an efficient local government and a modern judiciary system made the code an ideal rather than a fact.

The man who ruled Russia during the first quarter of the nineteenth century was the impressionable Czar Alexander I.

The Administration of Alexander I
Influenced by eighteenth-century enlightenment, this autocrat at first displayed liberal tendencies. In the reorganization of Europe in 1814–1815 he simulated the rôle of a sincere reformer. Favoring generous terms to France, insisting that Louis XVIII grant a constitution to his people, encouraging the aspirations of the Germans for a larger political life, he seemed to be the outstanding exponent of nationalism and constitutionalism in Europe. Apparently, when he favored world peace by means of a Holy Alliance which should bind all Christian nations together as brothers, this mystical, colorful personality planned to become a political messiah.

But, as one historian says, poor Alexander had "all the gifts of Heaven except common sense." Lacking will power, he frequently came under the influence of unscrupulous reactionaries, who used him as a tool. It is difficult to reconcile Alexander's plans to recognize the principle of self-determination, to grant a written constitution, and to emancipate the serfs, with his desire to advance the imperial interests of his country through the annexation of a large part of Poland. It is true that in order to win local support he established an independent Polish state, with Warsaw as its capital, granted the Poles a constitution creating a parliament, and promised them liberty of the press and of religion and use of the Polish tongue as the official language, provided that he be king of Poland as well as Czar of Russia. He also treated Finland, acquired from Sweden in 1809, in the same way, joining that country to Russia through a personal union with the Czar, who was given the title of "Grand Duke of Finland." But why did he not give them complete independence? Moreover, why did he fail to grant his Russian subjects the reforms he gave the Poles and the Finns?

According to many historians Alexander I was a hypocrite. Unstable, changeable, and easily discouraged, he shifted from a liberal to a conservative toward the last part of his reign. Perhaps, as certain writers insinuate, Metternich converted this weak ruler to political orthodoxy. Alexander, however, was more sincere and consistent in his policies than he has been pictured. Possibly the opposition to Russian control in Poland and the revolutionary movements in western Europe roused Alexander's fear. Like the enlightened despots of the eighteenth century, he favored liberal reforms, social and intellectual especially, yet his liberalism did not include any notion of self-government. He believed in enlightened despotism, and even though he planned a constitution, he desired one which would not limit his supreme authority.

Autocracy was firmly maintained by Alexander's successor, Nicholas I, who ruled from 1825 to 1855. Ardent defender of the *status quo* in Russia as well as outside her borders, he felt it his duty to combat the *Nicholas I* "spirit of revolution." Greeted by an uprising, called the Decembrist Revolt, when he came to power in 1825, he later witnessed with increasing fear the revolutions which threatened the established order in various parts of Europe. In his opinion the attempt of the intellectuals in the Decembrist Revolt to force the government to grant a constitution was one of the numerous attacks upon law and order.

Like his predecessor, Nicholas I recognized the evils of Russian life, but he believed that by benevolent reforms he could abolish them and yet not change the existing political system. Consequently he tried to improve economic conditions. "Secret committees" and trusted agents were appointed to discuss changes and to investigate conditions. Meanwhile the Czar contemplated the immediate solution of many problems.

Nicholas soon discovered that it was difficult to be a reformer and yet oppose revolution. The situation in Poland convinced him of that fact. Granted more rights by Alexander I than he gave to his Russian subjects, the Polish nobles nevertheless remained dissatisfied. Favoring the reëstablishment of an independent Poland, the upper classes in that land finally succeeded in creating a strained relationship between Poland and the Russian ruler, and a revolution occurred.

The Polish Revolt (1830)

When the Poles rose in rebellion in 1830, Nicholas I decided to break their spirit once and for all. The revolution was suppressed, the constitution granted by Alexander I was abolished, and while the Poles still retained a certain degree of autonomy, their country, during the reign of Nicholas I, was placed under military control.

Thenceforth the new Czar became the bulwark of monarchical authority in Russia. The system of government became one of remorseless repression. A man of great physical strength, a militarist by instinct and by education, Nicholas relied upon army methods in the conduct of government. Criticism of his administration was not tolerated; and a demand for self-government was revolt. Constantly afraid of a revolution, Nicholas proceeded to "freeze" Russia through a brutal police and an elaborate censorship. A liberal was considered a traitor to Russia and severely punished. Thousands were exiled to Siberia merely because they uttered their thoughts. Over one hundred and fifty thousand persons were expelled in twenty years, and many thousands were imprisoned in Russia. Oppression of religious and national groups aggravated the situation.

"Frozen Russia"

Nicholas I was not wholly reactionary. Like Alexander I, he recognized the problem of serfdom. The increasing need for free labor and the growing moral protest against this form of bondage on the part of Russian intellectuals could not help but convince him of the need for eventual liberation. Moreover, the serfs were restless and engaged in several serious outbreaks during his reign. The difficulties involved in their emancipation, however, prevented either Alexander or Nicholas from inaugurating important reforms. The problem included not merely personal freedom for the peasants but also a land settlement in which property belonging to the nobles would be given to the serfs. Rather than risk the opposition of the privileged classes Alexander I had passed laws permitting landlords, if they wished, to liberate their serfs, to sell land to them, or to allow the peasants to pay for the property by services to the owners. Laws were enacted by Nicholas prohibiting either the sale of serfs at public auction or the separation of members of the same family. Attempts were made also to define the punishments which could be inflicted by the landlords upon their serfs. In the Baltic provinces the serfs were made personally free without obtaining any land, whereas in the western provinces the services due the landlords by the serfs were defined by law. Save for these minor changes serfdom remained the same.

Nicholas I and the Problem of Serfdom

The fear that reforms might undermine the political order explains the educational policy of the government. Many responsible leaders recognized the value of education and theoretically favored its spread. During Alexander's reign a ministry of education had been established, and new universities founded. Nicholas I created technical schools, and the number of secondary institutions was increased, although they were few compared to the number in existence today. Fear of radicalism, however, caused Alexander, and especially Nicholas, to create a general system of censorship aimed at ending all opposition to the established order. Henceforth schools and literature were rigidly supervised in an attempt to extinguish the "revolutionary spirit." Education as an aid to economic development was satisfactory until it promoted radical ideas. Universities and public schools were watched and supervised

Education in the Early Nineteenth Century

in order to suppress that which the government feared most of all, freedom of thought.

The authorities failed in their attempt to destroy independent thinking. Indeed, the period of oppression was characterized by the most striking achievements in the fields of art and literature. During these years the national school of Russian music was born with Glinka. Furthermore, Alexander Ivanov finished his "Christ Appearing before the People," perhaps the first important example of modern Russian painting. In literature the reigns of Alexander and Nicholas constitute, according to one writer, "the Golden Age in Russian literary history." The period saw the triumph of poetry and the rise of the novel. Pushkin and Lermontov, great Russian poets, and Gogol, the father of the Russian novel, wrote during the reigns of these two monarchs. These writers were followed by such literary celebrities as Goncharov, Turgenev, Dostoevski, and Tolstoy.

Russian Art and Literature in Early Nineteenth Century

To understand old Russia, one should study her music and literature as well as her history. Her artists and literary men were able to picture conditions in the Fatherland better than contemporary historians. This was due to the fact that the censors found it impossible to suppress symphonies and novels as they did works on history, political science, and economics. Literature and art were two outlets whereby the Russians could express their pent-up emotions. Consequently a group of composers and novelists appeared who astounded the world by their striking originality, moral depth, and artistic technique.

The Significance of Russian Art and Literature

Of the various national schools of music which developed in the nineteenth century the Russian held a conspicuous place. In fact, the relation of music to national life was nowhere more apparent than in this huge empire. Just as the voice of the people was heard in Russia's powerful and somber literature, so there was likewise a tone of struggle in its music, a consciousness of undeveloped strength, and an uncertainty as to what direction should be taken when this strength should at last be set free.

Music

The clash of influences, native and foreign, that caused the turmoil in Russian social and political life was apparent in its music. Numerous compositions, based on the rich store of folk-songs, many of which came down from original Asiatic homes, while others were based on ancient Greek modes, show the influence of the Orient on Russian life and culture. Moreover, they reflect, by means of abrupt interchanges of major and minor tonalities, the dullness and pessimism of the Russian masses.

Perhaps the greatest musical genius that Russia produced in the nineteenth century was Peter Illitch Tschaikowsky (1840–1893). Without a doubt his music was among the most brilliant and individualistic of that time. Its boldness, the varied contrasts, and the strain of passionate melancholy that runs through it have seemed to make it correspond to the general foreign notion of Russian life and character, and hence have given it an interest that is more than personal. Tschaikowsky, like other Russian composers of that century, in his most representative works pictured, by means of musical tones, on the one hand the unrest of the Russian people and on the other hand the possibility of their emancipation.

In Russian literature one finds an even more vivid portrayal of social and economic conditions. Brilliant exponents of realism, the Russian writers were able to bring out the most obscure human frailties. No lit- *Literature* erary contemporaries could equal them in their ability to study the human heart and to describe with marvelous understanding both the noble and the base impulses of men and women. But this realism was not a "mere anatomy of society"; it had a higher background — "a complete subordination of everything to an idealistic aim."

One of the best examples of Russian realism is *Dead Souls*, the most famous work of Nicholas Gogol (1809–1852), who was one of the first of the great realistic Russian novelists. So keen was Gogol's description of serfdom that Pushkin, the Russian poet, said, when he read the manuscript: "God! What a sad country is Russia! Gogol invents nothing: it is the truth, the terrible truth." Ivan Turgenev (1818–1883), in his *A Sportman's Sketches*, also denounces the abuses of serfdom by showing the actual conditions. Turgenev depicts all classes of the Russian people, and in his masterpiece, *Fathers and Sons*, he has created characters who typify the Russians in both their strength and their weakness. In this novel Turgenev has also well described the Nihilist movement.

Of the many brilliant Russian writers Count Leo Tolstoy (1828–1910) was the most outstanding. In *The Cossacks* he discloses his dislike of the artificial life of the city and his desire for the freedom the country offered; in his *War and Peace* he develops his conception of war and history, showing how the destinies of men and women are often determined by external forces over which they have no control; in a number of his writings he indirectly attacks wealth and aristocracy. *Anna Karenina* is considered his masterpiece.

During the reign of Nicholas I occurred a struggle between two groups of intellectuals, the "Westerners" and the Slavo-

"Westerners" and Slavophiles

philes. The former believed that the difference between Russia and western Europe was one of degree only; backward in political and social institutions, Russia needed reform. To the Slavophiles the difference between Russia and western Europe was one of kind, not of degree. In their opinion "Russia's original civilization, in which her Greek-Orthodox religion played an all-important part, was a cherished possession that should be by all means preserved intact." Instead of adopting the Western industrial system, which was "threatened with inevitable decay," they favored the peasant commune, on the basis of which a better economic system, which should satisfy the demands of social justice, could be erected. To this end they desired a benevolent despot, public control of the bureaucracy, a degree of personal liberty, and the abolition of serfdom.

Another group of intellectuals occupied a position midway between the Westerners and the Slavophiles. These were the so-called socialists, who, influenced by the writings of the

French utopianists Saint-Simon and Fourier, and by the German philosopher Hegel, worked out a new scheme of things. Sharing with the Westerners the tendency to criticize Russia's political and social institutions, they distrusted, nevertheless, the European constitutional bourgeois system, and, like the Slavophiles, idealized the peasant commune, "which seemed to them the nucleus of a better social order."

The futility of the attempt on the part of Nicholas I to maintain the old political and social order was revealed during the unsuccessful Crimean War which occurred at the end of his reign (1853–1856). Despite the bravery of her soldiers, Russia, unprepared, was defeated in this conflict.[1] The loss of the war was a shock to her military and political prestige. It was also a serious blow to the political and social system. Revealing the inability of the government to advance Russia's interests in the world, exposing her economic backwardness, the incompetence of her bureaucracy, the corruption of her officials, and the lack of public spirit, the war caused many Russians, conservatives as well as liberal intellectuals, to favor immediate reforms. Even Nicholas I admitted before his death that his régime was a failure. His son and successor inherited a badly run-down empire.

The Crimean War (1853–1856)

The reign of Alexander II (1855–1881) might well be considered a turning point in the history of Russia. During that period there occurred a series of changes which had as their objective the modernization of the empire. Although the Czar was not a liberal, he realized that reforms were impending. Rather than risk a revolution which might force him to accept changes, he decided to subordinate personal inclinations to the welfare of the state. Despite bitter opposition of vested interests, he profoundly changed the life of the people.

The Age of Reform

One of the most important events of Alexander's administration was the abolition of serfdom. Earlier the Czar had expressed the intention of emancipating the serfs on the royal estates, and had tried to induce the landlords to follow his ex-

[1] For additional information on the Crimean War see pages 122, 247–249.

ample. This proved difficult, for the majority of Russian nobles clung to the rights which they had enjoyed under serfdom.

Emancipation of the Serfs (1861-1866)

Finally the government forced an open discussion of emancipation and a land settlement for the liberated serfs. Backed by public opinion and the aid of a few enlightened bureaucrats, the reform was eventually carried through, and between 1861 and 1866 a series of edicts ended Russian serfdom.

The legal phase of the reform, the abolition of human bondage, made the Edict of Emancipation "perhaps the greatest single legislative act in the world's history." Millions of men and women were made citizens, authority over them being transferred from the landowner to the government. Open to criticism, however, was the solution of the land problem. The serfs were generally given the land which they had used for their own support, compensation to the nobles for the loss of this property being made by the government. The peasants were expected to buy this land from the government, paying for it in installments covering a period of forty-nine years. In most cases the amount of land allotted each peasant proved too small and the annual payments too great to meet his needs. Moreover, the fields owned by the peasants were, as a rule, combined into common holdings, the village communes. At intervals the land was redistributed among the heads of the families in the villages. This meant that as the sons grew up the number of peasants eligible to receive holdings increased, whereas the amount of land remained the same. Thus their farms dwindled in size and it became increasingly difficult for the peasants to make a living.

Defects of the Emancipation

Subsequent developments proved that the commune (called *mir*) was an obstacle to agricultural progress. Its advocates had believed that it would insure to the government redemption payments and the collection of taxes, and would prevent the establishment of a rural proletariat. But they were mistaken. The peasants soon discovered that they had less land for their own use than under serfdom, and that they had to pay more than the fields were worth. They became more and more dissatisfied and unrest increased steadily during the next fifty years, and even up to 1914 they seemed to be moving constantly toward starvation. Thousands of the younger generation who had left the farms for the industrial centers were to play important rôles in the upheavals of 1905 and 1917.

A number of important reforms were made necessary as a result of the emancipation of the serfs. With the abolition of serfdom the local judicial and police authority *Other Reforms* exercised by the landlords over their serfs disappeared, and thus a blow was dealt to the despotism of the nobility in the rural districts. The Czar now had to establish an efficient local government to take over the prerogatives of the nobility. Consequently, in 1864, the so-called *zemstvo* institutions were created. Representatives elected by the landowners, the peasant communes, and certain elements of the urban population constituted a *district zemstvo* assembly. They in turn selected a permanent governing body and sent representatives to the *provincial zemstvo*, which elected its own governing board. Both assemblies concerned themselves with the problems of public welfare, whereas general administrative matters and the exercise of police authority remained in the hands of the central government. To carry out their work, which included the maintenance of charitable and educational institutions and highway and agrarian betterments, they were permitted to collect taxes. Consequently the principle of self-government was recognized, and an opportunity was offered to the various social classes to coöperate in improving local conditions, although an unequal franchise enabled the landowners to dominate these bodies.

Reform of the law courts (1864) was nearly as important as the changes in local government. In old Russia the courts seemingly existed in order to perpetuate injustice. Based on class distinction, the administration of the laws had been generally in the hands of corrupt, incompetent, and ill-paid officials, who were subservient to the wealthy property-owners. Hearings were secret, and lawyers for the defense were not available. Justice was very slow and expensive. The reform of 1864 proclaimed the establishment of "laws equally just to all" and abolished class privileges. Courts were independent of the administration, judges were not removable and were paid good salaries, trials were public, and juries were introduced. Russia now possessed a judicial system which could compare favorably with those of other European powers.

By these acts Russia adopted a fundamental principle of bourgeois civilization, the recognition of peasants as citizens. This made possible a large supply of free labor, a necessary element of any industrial system. Favored by this social progress, a rising middle class presaged a new economic order in Russia.

During the early part of his reign Alexander II seemed in process of becoming an enlightened bourgeois ruler. Considerable attention was given to the creation of primary schools and technical education. Universities were given more liberty and more financial support than they had previously enjoyed. Consequently the number of students in these institutions increased rapidly. The press was granted a certain degree of independence, and foreign travel was allowed. Alexander endeavored to treat such subject groups as Jews, Poles, and Finns more liberally. Moreover, plans were formulated to exploit the tremendous natural resources in the empire. A modern Russia seemed to be in the making.

As a result of the emancipation of the serfs the social dominance of the nobles gradually passed away. Deprived of their *Decline of the Nobility* lands and of a free labor supply, obstructed by lack of technical preparation and of money, numerous great landowners simply could not adapt themselves to the new situation. Some became bankrupt; others sold their estates. The transition from the dominance of agriculture to that of industry was under way.

The reforms, however, only served to increase national unrest in Russia. In 1863 the Poles decided that the time *Return of Reaction* was ripe again to strike for freedom. But the foreign aid the Poles counted on was not forthcoming. England, France, and Austria intervened, but only by diplomatic notes, asking Russia to give way to Polish demands. Meanwhile Alexander's armies, with the tacit consent of Prussia, put down the revolt and severely punished the Poles.

A policy of Russification of Poland was adopted. The Russian language was prescribed for the correspondence of officials and the lectures of university professors. Churches, schools, theaters, newspapers, and business concerns also were ordered to use that language only. Anti-clerical legislation deprived the Roman Catholic church in Poland of part of its wealth and limited its authority. Moreover, a law was passed which forced the Polish nobles to transfer part of their lands to the tenants, thus greatly weakening the power of the landowners.

Influenced by the conservatives around him, the Czar finally decided that his reform program threatened to bring about the disruption of his empire. Therefore he determined to restore the past. But it was too late. By that time the revolutionary movement could not be checked. Vainly Alexander tried to extinguish freedom of thought by limiting the independence of newspapers and schools. All individuals suspected of expressing unorthodox political views were arrested. But the Russian people had tasted of liberalism, the forbidden fruit, and wanted more. Consequently the reaction only tended to increase the discontent and to promote a movement among the intelligentsia which before long threatened the very existence of autocracy.

Russian intellectuals of the early nineteenth century were generally romanticists and utopians. Influenced by German writers they approached political and social *Nihilism* matters in a philosophical way. The successors of these intellectuals, however, were different. They had no use for romanticism and metaphysics. To them the world was "not a temple but a workshop." In their opinion science, not art, was the tool of progress. These men were the chief exponents of a movement known as Nihilism, which developed in Russia about the time of the emancipation of the serfs. Nihilism represented primarily the opposition of the younger generation to the existing order. Nothing (*nihil* in Latin) was sacred to these realists unless it could stand the test of scientific investigation. Among the first to favor the emancipation of women, the Nihilists did much to foster the revolutionary movement which developed in Russia.

Nihilism was chiefly a revolt against traditional authority. It aimed at the liberation of the individual from all established conventions. Later, radicalism became more *The Populists* than an individualistic movement. As distinguished from the Nihilists the exponents of another school (Populists) were interested not in the emancipation of the individual but in the solution of social problems. As "uplifters" they decided that it was the duty of the intelligentsia to serve the people, especially the peasants. For centuries the educated classses had been thriving at the expense of the masses; now they should pay the debt by "going to the people" and by leading them along the path of cultural and social progress.

Young men and women, many of the aristocracy, attempted to improve the masses and to arouse them to action. Taking various positions in the villages, these youths developed a remarkable crusading spirit, which, however, lacked a definite objective. Despite tremendous heroism and self-sacrifice the efforts of these social missionaries seemed in vain. The peasants were too ignorant to understand their teachings. Moreover the intelligentsia proved to be just as intolerant and uncompromising in their attitude as the Czar's government had been. Often openly hostile to religion and extremely critical of any idealistic interpretation which was not in accord with their realistic point of view, they won for themselves the bitter opposition of representatives of all classes in Russia. As a result of this radicalism the government arrested, imprisoned, and exiled thousands of these "realists." A determined attempt was made to stamp out this so-called dangerous movement, but the Czar could not silence the thousands of radicals who had left Russia and who in foreign lands continued their attacks.

Among the Russian political writers who, as exiles, helped to promote revolutionary thought, Alexander Herzen (1812– *Revolutionary Writers* 1870) occupies an important place. A profound thinker, he became an influential person in Russian intellectual circles through his journalistic work in Paris and London. His memoirs, *Past Facts and Thoughts*, are valuable historically, for in them he relates the bitter opposition to the existing régime and also to Western bourgeois culture.

For example, in describing Nicholas I, he wrote:

> But there is another — the type of military commander in whom everything social and moral, everything human has died out, and there is left nothing but the passion for domination; the mind is narrow and there is no heart at all; they are the monks of the love of power; force and austere will is manifest in their features. Such were the Emperors of the Prætorian Guard and of the army, whom the turbulent legionaries raised to power for an hour. Among their number I found many heads that recalled Nicholas before he wore a moustache. I understand the necessity for these grim and inflexible guards beside' what is dying in frenzy, but what use are they to what is youthful and growing?

Nikolay Gavrilovich Chernyshevsky (1823–1889) was another literary worker in the cause of Russian freedom. His story *What is to be Done?* written in prison, is a powerful criticism of the economic injustices of the old régime.

Most radical of all the revolutionary intellectuals was Michael Bakunin (1814–1876), the Russian anarchist. To him Utopia was possible only through the overthrow of the state and the triumph of the individual. Anarchy, in his opinion, involved political cataclysms, and violent social upheavals in which religion, the family, and the state were to be destroyed. Undoubtedly his ideas did much to promote the use of terroristic methods by the Nihilists and other radicals to reach their ends.

During the latter part of the reign of Alexander II numerous representatives of the intelligentsia resorted to a policy of terrorism. They decided to bring about by force not merely the downfall of autocracy   *Russian Terrorism* but the complete destruction of the old social system as well. In their opinion Russia had its own peculiar development to foster. Once the old régime was abolished, she should avoid bourgeois capitalism and move directly into the communist stage. Consequently Russian social radicalism in its early development was based on the village commune (the *mir*) rather than upon the factory. It adopted as its objective an immediate social revolution rather than an evolutionary movement in the direction of a socialist state. It believed that violence alone could achieve this end.

The rapid growth of this revolutionary movement only served to strengthen the conservatism of Alexander II. Determined to abandon, or to make harmless, all his liberal reforms, he firmly opposed all attempts to limit autocracy or to extend the principle of self-government. In the late seventies the radicals decided to strike. Several prominent officials were assassinated and a series of attempts were made on the life of the Czar.

Assassination of Alexander II

St. Petersburg and Alexander were thoroughly terrorized. Gladly the Czar favored the League of the Three Emperors (Germany, Austria, and Russia) in 1881, hoping that this would constitute a triangular rampart against revolution. He appointed a dictator, Loris Melikoff. Acting under orders, Melikoff inaugurated a milder government. Political prisoners were released and death sentences commuted. Believing that catering to progressive elements would not weaken the autocracy, Melikoff urged Alexander to win back the popularity the monarch had formerly enjoyed. After much hesitation Alexander approved Melikoff's plan to invite representatives of public bodies to coöperate with the government in working out a program of further changes. In March, 1881, the Czar gave orders for the publication of Melikoff's proposed constitution. But during the same month the hopes of the liberals for immediate reforms vanished with the assassination of Alexander II. This act of violence strengthened the conservatives and made the new Czar, Alexander III, determined to maintain intact the autocratic Russian government.

Nevertheless, by undermining the power of the nobles, the reforms of Alexander II had weakened the old régime. Deprived of serfs and of much land, lacking initiative, special training, and capital, most aristocrats failed to adjust themselves to new conditions. Many became bankrupt, while others, unable to struggle against adverse circumstances, sold their lands.

Significance of Alexander's Reign

The bourgeoisie profited by these changes. The acceleration of industry and commerce made them more wealthy and numerous. Many received political positions in governmental departments. Economic progress also increased the demand for popular education and for teachers, writers, and journalists. The doctor, the engineer, and the professor for the first time became influential members of society. This professional class in turn furnished an intelligentsia "which acquired a definite group consciousness and became the backbone of the opposition to the old régime."

Education advanced rapidly despite frequent government repression. The number of schools increased, and the distribution of students among the various social classes changed considerably. By the end of the nineteenth century the children of the nobility constituted a minority in Russian schools. This spread of education was important inasmuch as it indicated the development of a democratic society. Many intellectuals were convinced that the establishment of constitutional bourgeois government in Russia was imminent.

A RUSSIAN FOLK DANCE. *From an old print.*

CHAPTER XI

The Rise of the Bourgeois System in the Americas

THE opening of the Americas to European expansion constituted an important stage in the extension of Western civilization. From the sixteenth century until the present the New World has served as a frontier of Europe,

Significance of European Expansion "providing a new outlet for energy and commercial enterprise, an expanded food supply, a new home for increasing populations, and a laboratory for social, political, and economic experimentation."

European emigration to America also exerted an important influence upon Europe. The founding of vast empires in North and South America accentuated the great Commercial Revolution in the sixteenth and seventeenth centuries, which in turn contributed to the rise of the capitalistic régime. New markets, increased raw products, and precious metals were all factors in the significant transition from the dominance of agriculture to that of commerce, a change which ushered in the modern era. Struggles between rival European nations for overseas colonies characterized the history of Europe for several centuries, until by the end of the eighteenth all competing states were nearly eliminated from the Americas save Great Britain, Portugal, Spain, and Russia.

New problems soon confronted the imperialistic powers. While England prepared to become a great industrial state,

The American Revolution Spain and Portugal were dissipating the wealth which they had obtained from their empires. Meanwhile the European colonies in America grew up and asserted their individuality. In an astonishingly short time these possessions in South America and in two thirds of North America threw off English, Spanish, and Portuguese control and established a score of independent republics. After freedom had been attained, these new states proceeded during the nineteenth century to struggle for national solidarity, stability, and economic strength, and for an adjustment of relations with each other and with the rest of the world.

Although British rule had not been tyrannical, British colonists were the first to revolt from European control. As Bolton asserts, "the causes were inherent in the situation." In spirit English mercantilist policy was undoubtedly selfish, but in practice it was lightly enforced, and the provincials were in the main self-governing. But the germs of revolution were ever present. England and the colonies had grown apart. Through political experience the Americans had gained strength and were ready to revolt.

It was only after the French and Indian War (1754–1763) that serious trouble developed between England and the thirteen colonies. British colonial policy was becoming increasingly imperialistic, the Stamp Act being but one of many indications of the new attitude on the part of the mother country. Traders in the North and commercial planters in the South, although minorities in the thirteen colonies, opposed British interference because it thwarted their economic interests and prevented their free expansion into the territories over the mountains. Protesting, they adopted slogans and formulated constitutional theories. Disturbed, the English government resorted to coercion, which only served to stimulate colonial resistance. A Revolutionary War (1776–1783) followed, which resulted in freedom for the thirteen colonies and eventually in their unification as the United States of America.

The American Revolution contributed to the breakdown of mercantilism. This anachronistic doctrine was supplanted by a belief in a *laissez faire* policy, which thereafter played an important part in the growth of Western civilization. Henceforth, modifying her imperial policies, Great Britain refused to ignore the rights of her colonies. Partly influenced by the newly popular doctrine of individualism, the Spanish colonies also resented with increasing vigor the restraints and abuses of a moribund mercantile system.

In North America the particularism among the colonies hampered for many years the establishment of a unified nation. The thirteen colonies, each character-

The United States of America

ized by special traits and particular interests, were skeptical as to the desirability of subordinating themselves to one dominant government. The chaotic situation engendered by the Articles of Confederation demonstrated the need of a stronger form of union. Nevertheless it was only after much discussion that the people agreed to adopt a new constitution, creating a national government with authority over an individual comparable to that of his own state. With the inauguration of George Washington as president, in 1789, a new country had definitely embarked upon the stream of history.

A product of a not yet fully developed nationalism, the constitution of the new union neglected to settle the question of states' rights as against the prerogatives

The Constitution

of the national government. Existing side by side, the authority of the individual states and the Federal authority functioned in separate spheres, although each was subject to constitutional restrictions. The states were powerless to make war or to impose customs duties, for such matters were outside their province. On the other hand, the central government was incapable of imposing an income tax or of regulating industry without state permission. Originally there was a sharp differentiation between Federal and state powers, although in recent years the former has tended to encroach on the rights of the latter.

The constitution created an aristocratic republic founded upon a property basis. A bitter struggle occurred, during the first years of the new government, between the Federalists, led by Hamilton, exponent of a strong central government, and the Republicans, led by Jefferson, advocate of states' rights. Not until the twenties and the thirties did "the people" come into power in the United States, through the establishment of white manhood suffrage. Previously dominated by an aristocracy of wealth and talent, the republic passed under the rule of the common man.

It is significant to note that this political shift, starting in 1828, "synchronized with the French revolution of 1830 and the English parliamentary reform of 1832." Then a radical innovation, the American experiment in political democracy aroused great interest in France and England. Many intellectuals there regarded the United States as a model republic and believed that European nations should imitate the Americans and establish similar democratic régimes.

In the newly created republic, however, there were many who believed that true equality and real liberty would not exist in their land until slavery was abolished. They soon discovered that the destruction of such an old institution was indeed difficult to achieve. Although the constitution gave the national government the right to prohibit the importation of Negroes from abroad after 1808, the government had no power to abolish slavery. The controversy between the slave and free states remained, and came out into the open when the Union was enlarged as a result of the acquisition of additional territories.

During the first half of the nineteenth century the United States enjoyed a period of amazing territorial expansion. Originally the control of the thirteen colonies extended to the Allegheny Mountains. At the *The Period of Expansion* close of the Revolution, however, Great Britain yielded to them the territory extending west to the Mississippi River. In 1803 President Jefferson bought from Napoleon I the great expanse of country west of the Mississippi, called Louisiana. Sixteen years later Florida was purchased from Spain, and the latter relinquished claims to the seaboard of Alabama and of Mississippi. Settlers from the various states and from Europe flocked into these regions. In 1845 Texas was annexed, and in 1846 much of the Oregon territory was acquired from Great Britain. In 1848 the present Southwest of the United States, extending from Texas to Oregon, was taken from Mexico by conquest, and the discovery of gold in California resulted in a rapid influx of settlers from the East. The settlement of this great empire in

North America exerted a tremendous influence not only on the development of nationalism and individualism in the United States but also on the solution of an important European question.

By the middle of the nineteenth century many European states were faced by the perplexing problem of providing for a rapidly increasing population, which had re-

European Emigration to the United States sulted from the changes brought about by the Industrial Revolution. This situation neces-

sitated the importation of food from abroad and the deportation of a surplus population. The United States, with its great unsettled lands, offered the immigrants an ideal home. Thousands of them left the old countries for America, thereby enabling the European states partially to solve the critical economic and social problems which rose out of overpopulation and consequent unemployment.

The great Mississippi Valley was especially attractive to oppressed immigrants from other lands. As described by the brilliant French writer, Alexis de Tocqueville, it was the most beautiful home God had granted to mankind; its healthful climate and rich soil were favorable to agricultural development, and this immense region was made accessible by navigation of its great rivers and by the easy construction of railways upon its flat lands. Little did this distinguished French scholar realize that the presence of coal and iron was to make the Middle West an industrial beehive as well as an agricultural empire.

Many reasons explain European emigration to the West. The English settlers found the same language, customs, and similar laws, whereas those from central Europe did not find it difficult to adopt the speech and customs of their new home. Religious freedom, political equality, and economic opportunity attracted the colonists and enabled them to acquire wealth and political influence. After a short residence in the West pioneers were placed on an equal footing with the other inhabitants of the United States. Eventually the territories on which they settled were admitted to the Union on terms of equality with the original members.

Throughout the nineteenth century "rugged individualism" was amply justified. In the United States an absence of governmental restrictions, together with an abundance of natural resources and the existence *The Land of the Self-made Man* of cheap labor, afforded each individual an opportunity to achieve material success by the practice of such bourgeois virtues as thrift, hard work, and personal initiative. Out of this pioneering period emerged the self-made man.

During this era the farmer was the backbone of the nation. Aware of this fact, the government passed laws designed to help him. Accepting the principle that the law of possession in the newly settled land should *The Homestead Act* be on the basis of small peasant proprietorships, the United States permitted the immigrant to purchase public land outright, free of obligations. In 1820 the government, to prevent the growth of large estates, lowered the minimum price of the soil and reduced the minimum quantity which should be sold to any single individual to eighty acres. Even the small purchase price was soon declared no longer necessary. In the years 1830–1840 a settler, by clearing a piece of primeval forest, could claim it as his own and could not be dispossessed by a speculator "on the claim that the speculator had been the first to offer the purchase price for the land." In 1862 the Homestead Act was passed, giving the settler the right, for a small fee, to cultivate a parcel of land for five years; at the expiration of this time the property would belong to him. This liberal land policy arose out of the belief that if the industry and ability of individuals were favored through the easy acquirement of land, the entire country would benefit. The government wanted the poor man to go west to develop small bits of territory, and thereby to increase the prosperity of the nation.

Thousands of industrious European farmers flocked into the Mississippi Valley and became independent cultivators. Agriculture in the United States developed with unheard-of rapidity. Farmers from New England, and Southern poor whites who had only a few slaves or none at all, gladly joined the alien immigrants in taking advantage of the opportunity to obtain more fertile soil and more favorable conditions for life in the Mississippi Valley. Meanwhile a remarkable increase in population was the result of the influx from Europe. Immigration, which between 1821 and 1830 numbered one hundred and forty-three thousand, between 1830 and 1840 totaled about six hundred thousand. Between 1841 and 1850 over seven hundred and thirteen thousand arrived, while in the single year 1847 more than two hundred thousand landed in the United States.

Agricultural Development

These new arrivals soon became loyal citizens. National prejudices and antagonisms of the Old World tended to disappear. In America all, having identical rights, were equal before the law. When the children went to the public schools, they shed most traces of their foreign origins. Immigrants from the British Isles, Germany, and later the Scandinavian lands and other countries were quickly Americanized. They welcomed freedom and opportunity and became loyal citizens of the country that gave them a chance to enjoy these blessings. Little wonder that the United States, as a result of her wise and liberal policy toward these new citizens, rapidly became a wealthy and powerful nation, her domains extending from the Atlantic to the Pacific. She gave the settlers a start by granting them political rights and social equality; as a reward they made her an empire.

During the nineteenth century the United States accelerated the industrial development of European nations by supplying them with needed raw materials and food. Also she became the safety valve for many countries which were confronted by religious, political, and economic problems. In England the hegira of citizens lessened the possibility of an economic crisis and helped that country to become the outstanding commercial, industrial, and imperialistic nation of the nineteenth century. Emigration from Germany relieved the Hohenzollerns of malcontents and enabled them to maintain their autocratic control and to create a great industrial and commercial state.

The United States and Europe

Although the shift of population to the New World reduced European difficulties, it increased social antagonisms in the United States. Emigrants between 1830 and 1860 encountered a serious obstacle to the free settlement of the West,— the slave system in the aristocratic South. Southerners opposed all laws favoring settlements on homesteads. Before the West could really develop, therefore, the system of large land-owners holding privileged positions over their fellow men had to be destroyed. Most reformers in the United States at first believed mistakenly that this could be done without bloodshed.

The textile industry, which was growing rapidly in New England, derived a direct advantage from Southern cotton growers, who furnished considerable raw material. Aware of the importance of the South   *North versus South* as a place to obtain raw products and to sell manufactured goods, the business men of the North opposed every attempt to create an issue which might cause war between these two regions. Nevertheless serious economic issues developed. The North favored free labor and governmental encouragement of infant industries, while the South, since it exported raw materials and imported manufactured goods, advocated slavery and free trade.

By the middle of the nineteenth century slavery had practically been abolished by European countries. Conservatives as well as liberals there had united in opposition to this curse upon humanity. Under these conditions one would expect the antislavery movement in the United States to have had the hearty support of European nations. But such was not the case. In both England and France the ruling classes feared republicanism in the United States, and therefore favored the aristocratic South in its efforts to prolong slavery.

The South was the last stronghold of the landed aristocracy in the United States. This was largely because of the climatic conditions, which enabled the people to develop an agrarian structure. Tobacco, cotton, and rice were cultivated in the South on a large scale, and the planters, owning extensive plantations, found the Negro labor most satisfactory. There were few large cities; consequently the middle classes and wage-earning elements were negligible. The people were divided largely into three major classes: the landowning aristocrats, the poor whites, and the slaves.

In the North the structure of society was different. Commerce, manufacturing, and small-scale cultivation predominated. As a result the business men, the farmers, and the wage-earners were the three chief classes. Slavery could not flourish in the North, because the small farmers and business men found it cheaper to hire free labor than to own and support slaves. Therefore slavery was prohibited and Negroes were given a position of legal equality.

During the latter part of the eighteenth century, slavery was rapidly becoming unprofitable in the South. Had it not been for the invention of the cotton gin (1793) the institution might have been abolished.

The Slave Issue

This machine, which facilitated the separation of the seeds from the cotton wool, augmented the importance of slavery by encouraging the increase of cotton production. Hence ensued the expansion of slavery. Planters now wanted to increase their holdings, while in the northern states of the South, especially Virginia, where the climatic conditions made the cultivation of cotton difficult, Negroes were raised to be sold in the cotton belt.

Opposition to the extension of slavery arose in the North. A contest for control of Congress soon developed between the two sections of the country. This competition was sharpened by the question of the admission of territories as free or slave states. Outvoted in the House of Representatives by the more populous Northern states, the plantation owners hoped to overcome this handicap by retaining control of the Senate, to which each state sent two delegates. To this end the South tried to get the majority of the new states to join its cause.

Because certain elements in the industrial North were indifferent to slavery, the South managed to dominate the Senate until 1820, when a crisis was reached. At that time a bitter dispute occurred over Missouri, the question arising as to whether it should be admitted as a free or a slave state. Finally the Missouri Compromise Bill of 1820 was passed, which forbade slavery north of the 36° 30' line but admitted the territory of Missouri into the Union as a slave state even though it lay north of that line.

This settlement favored the South, not only because the latter was able to retain control of the Senate but also because more land for cotton growing was made available. Unscientific cultivation on large plantations by slaves exhausted the soil; virgin territory was always welcome. The desire for land led to other territorial gains. A war with Mexico, which the Southern states favored, resulted in the acquisition of Texas (as a plantation and slave-owning state) and the addition of California and New Mexico. The annexation of California did not aid the South, for the discovery of gold attracted a large laboring population of free workers to California, who, desirous of being protected against competition, drafted, in 1849, a constitution forbidding slavery.

A typically bourgeois humanitarian agitation against slavery arose in the North. The leader of the movement was William Lloyd Garrison (1805–1879). Establishing, in 1831, an antislavery newspaper known *The Antislavery Movement* as the *Liberator*, and founding at Boston the New England Antislavery Society, he proceeded to organize a movement in favor of emancipation. Yet he represented only a minority in his native state. Business men and manufacturers there, together with other patriotic Americans, feared a dissolution of the Union and economic ruin if Garrison's reckless policy were carried too far. Nevertheless his movement made great progress. In 1840 the Antislavery Society was said to have nearly 200,000 members. Despite the establishment of this organization, however, abolitionists continued to be openly opposed in New England, and did not play so decisive a rôle in precipitating the crisis over slavery as has often been supposed.

Although political leaders tried to arrange a compromise, slavery in the new land acquired from Mexico became a live issue between North and South. By the Compromise of 1850 it was decided that California should be admitted to the Union as a free state, but that in other territories the population itself should be allowed to decide in regard to the status of the Negro. In the District of Columbia the slave trade was prohibited, but the institution was not abolished.

The South, however, did not fear the abolition movement as much as it did the attempt to thwart the expansion of slavery into the territories. As a matter of fact, *The Tariff Question* the issue of slavery did not provoke as great resentment in the South as has been generally supposed. More important, perhaps, was sectional favoritism in such matters as the tariff. The North persisted in placing a high protective tariff on manufactured goods, thus raising the cost of living in the South. On the other hand, the agricultural products of the South were left unprotected. Consequently many Southerners felt that they could not obtain economic justice in the Union.

The antagonism already in existence was aggravated by the Dred Scott decision of 1857, in which the Supreme Court of the United States declared that a slave was not a citizen. But the way was prepared for a definite break when a new political organization, the Republican party, opposing the extension of slavery in the territories and openly committed to a high protective tariff, came into existence.

In 1860 a presidential election was held, and the Republican candidate, Abraham Lincoln (1809–1865), winning all the free states save three of New Jersey's seven *Abraham Lincoln* delegates, was elected. Lincoln was a typical product of the Middle West. His rise in the newly settled country was an extraordinary illustration of the advantage of American equality and of individualism in developing great leaders. The battle against poverty and the struggle for learning often brought out the best in them. One emotion dominated Lincoln at all times — ardent patriotism. He was a devoted adherent of the Union which had given him an opportunity to rise from obscurity ; and, although he hated slavery as a result of his contact with that institution while on trips down the Mississippi, he feared that the abolitionist movement, if carried too far, would cause the South to secede.

When elected, Lincoln resolutely opposed any action which might lead to a civil war and the break-up of the Union. As president he faced a critical situation. Although a Republican majority in Congress supported him in his policies, nevertheless certain Southern states, led by South Carolina, decided that to maintain slavery and free trade they must found a new republic. On December 20, 1860, a convention called for this purpose in South Carolina announced secession of that state from the Union. Six other Southern states followed her example, and in 1861 formed a new political body called the Confederate States of America. Drawing up a constitution, in general modeled after that of the United States, they legalized slavery and forbade the introduction of the protective tariff.

Many Northerners hoped that secession would not lead to war. They knew that the question as to whether or not the states had a right to secede as freely as they had joined had not been decided. They also *The Civil War (1861–1865)* realized that American tradition opposed the use of violence against any community. Lincoln expressed this idea when he declared in 1861 that while the North would not attack the South, the Union was indissoluble. The government, he declared, as long as its property and its right to collect import duties were recognized, would attack no community. But when the Confederates fired upon Fort Sumter, a Federal fort held by the North, the Southerners became the aggressors, because they had attacked government property. Civil war followed.

At first many people believed that the conflict would not last long. Outnumbering the South in man power, and superior in machinery and in the resources important in time of war, the industrial and commercial North seemed capable of easily overcoming the cotton-growing South. To make victory all the more certain, the Union navy obtained control of the sea and blockaded the enemy ports.

The South had certain advantages: superior generals, more efficient military organization, the inner lines, and foreign assistance. As a result the Confederacy was enabled to extend the conflict so long that many persons in the North demanded a compromise settlement, and certain European countries seriously debated the question of intervention. France and England needed cotton in their industries, and suffered as a result of the Northern blockade. Moreover, a victory of the South would have weakened the industrial North, a potential rival of England and France. If the South could have been made a free-trade country, then the North would not have dominated its markets. Opposed to democracy, the European governments sympathized with the aristocratic South and would have welcomed the defeat of the Union.

On the other hand, British statesmen were not unanimous in their support of the slave states. Great Britain at that time was dependent upon wheat imported from the United States. Consequently a number of leaders, including Bright and Cobden, campaigned among the British wage-earners for support of the North. There were also many humanitarians in Great Britain, who, believing that the North was fighting for the common man, opposed any attempt to aid the South. The wage-earners of England especially sympathized with the North. Even though the blockade, which caused a lack of cotton and the closing down of many factories, deprived workers of employment, they refused to support slavery or any institution favoring it.

Dominated by those persons who happened to sympathize with the Confederacy, both England and France endeavored to help the South without actually declaring war. Their antagonism, however, did not prevent the United States from emerging victorious. Nothing but outright intervention could have saved the Confederacy, for the superiority of its adversary was too pronounced. After a long, brave fight against overwhelming odds, the South capitulated in 1865. The Union was preserved.

The defeated states suffered as a result of the transition from slavery to free labor. Most of the Southern gentlemen were bankrupt, and for a long time economic chaos existed. Trouble arose over the question of Negro suffrage. The defeated States were readmitted to the Union on condition

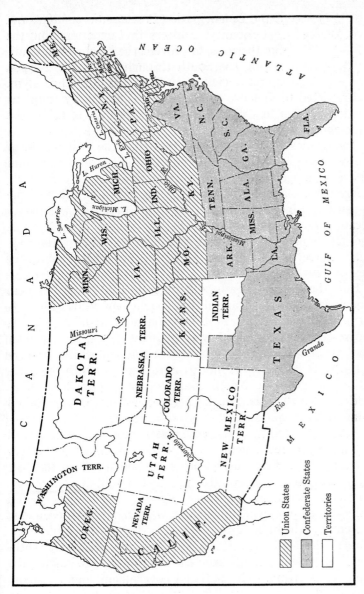

The United States during the Civil War

that they accept the Emancipation Proclamation of 1863 and give Negroes legal equality. Despite this understanding the

The Post-War Situation

Southerners, to prevent the blacks from dominating the South through the ballot, formed secret societies, such as the Ku Klux Klan, and resorted to violence to keep the Negroes away from the elections. Later less violent methods were used to attain the same end.

Today most authorities maintain that the destruction of the slave empire marked the end of an old economic system which no longer paid. This change would have come long before if the slaves had not been reckoned as wealth and the slave-raising industry had not been profitable. It was partly because the Southerner knew that he could sell his Negroes and get money for them that he fought to preserve this system. Slavery, he believed, was his important source of wealth.

But the situation was different in the North. There money was capital,— capital that sought new fields of investment and exploitation. Is it any wonder that the North was progressive and the South was stagnant? Is it any wonder that the sentiments and interests of the democratic farmers of the West lay with the industrial rather than with the plantation states? The North could furnish capital as well as markets, whereas the South offered the West only a limited demand for its products.

After the Civil War the government not only encouraged the westward movement but also developed an aggressive foreign policy. Previously European states believed that the division of the Union would enable them to obtain concessions from the American republic. France had visions of an American empire, while during the war England saw economic supremacy within her grasp. The Northern victory, however, enabled the United States to demand and obtain the withdrawal of French troops from Mexico and thus to sustain the Monroe Doctrine. The national government found it more difficult to arrange a satisfactory settlement with England. As a result of long negotiations the United States was able to receive compensation for the losses suffered through the privateers fitted out in England, but did not secure reparation for the losses resulting from British interference with American commerce. One important outcome of this dispute with England was the settlement of the issue by arbitration. This indicated a new method of solving international disputes.

The maintenance of the Union was the most important result of the Civil War. Henceforth the preëminence of the central government was assured. The sentiment of nationalism had won a tremendous *Significance of the* victory in America as it had in Italy. A unified *Civil War* nation was to develop, powerful enough to dominate its states and to assimilate the various racial groups and nationalities which went to make up the great melting-pot. More important, perhaps, the Civil War vindicated the principle and the example of modern political development,— democracy and its exponent, President Lincoln. In leading the North to victory he justified this form of government, which, through its emphasis upon political liberty and social equality, had made possible his rise.

Thus complete individualism and legal equality, as well as national unity, emerged victorious as a result of the Civil War. Influenced by these factors, the pioneers were able to continue their important work in the Middle West and to make this region the bread-basket of the world. At the same time others in the Far West exploited the great mines there and added to the prosperity of the nation. In the East and slowly in the South, agricultural, commercial, and industrial development also went on at an increasing rate of speed.

The American Revolution and the Civil War were not the only significant bourgeois revolutionary movements in the Western Hemisphere. The former was merely *Revolutionary Move-* the beginning of a series of uprisings, which *ments in Hispanic* resulted in the establishment of over twenty *America* independent states, in South as well as in North America. These nations are today playing an increasingly important part in the development of modern civilization.

In most respects all the uprisings were similar. Like the English colonies the Hispanic-American states obtained independence through outside aid. The people in South America, however, faced more difficulties than those of the United States. Fewer white men, an unfriendly climate, and geographical obstacles made concerted action less feasible. Further, there was a lack of political experience and social solidarity, such as existed in the English settlements. In South America the trade restrictions of Spain, the existence of great landed proprietors, the imposition of heavy taxes on the unprivileged classes, and a conscientiously preserved native or Indian element hindered the rise of an intelligent middle class, capable of bringing about a revolution and the establishment of a stable bourgeois political and economic state.

There were three general classes in Hispanic America: first, the Spaniards, born in Spain, the privileged group; second, the creoles, Spaniards born in the colonies, partly privileged; and, third, the rest of the people, including the Indians, Negroes, and hybrids, or the unprivileged elements. The last group did the work and paid most of the taxes, while the others, especially the Spaniards, owned the lands, held political offices, and enjoyed exemption from heavy taxes.

Class favoritism on behalf of the two privileged groups was a fundamental cause of the revolts. This led, in the eighteenth century, to growing restlessness *Causes of the Revolts* and disrespect for authority. In numerous places the creoles opposed the privileged position of the Spaniards. Many of them as young men visited Europe, especially Paris, drank absinthe, and also assimilated French middle-class ideas, especially the democratic concepts of Rousseau. They became capable agitators who favored the overthrow of Spanish control.

Upon their return to Hispanic America these young intellectuals also did much to create an admiration for French institutions and to spread a belief that French citizens had more sympathy for Hispanic America and Hispanic Americans than the people of any other nationality. No wonder that the French had dreams of the establishment there of satellite states and a Pan-Latin civilization with its capital at Paris! At no time, however, did the Hispanic Americans propose to become political outposts of France. In touch with the English and Anglo-Americans through trade, they became devout advocates of individualism and national self-determination.

Hispanic Americans in the nineteenth century engaged in a struggle not only to obtain freedom from Spain but also to abolish a social order which was based on rigid class distinctions. They demanded the *Aims of the Revolutionists* leveling of the various social groups, especially the reduction of the Spaniards, so that every individual might have the right to achieve distinction, especially wealth. "All are born equal, and if any inequality results, it is due to our achievements on earth." This bourgeois idea was accepted in Hispanic America as well as in the United States. Middle-class virtues, including hard work and thrift, were glorified.

When the uprisings started in Hispanic America, the Spanish King, Charles III (1759–1788), tried to prevent them by introducing many reforms. But these proposed changes did not go far enough, and came too late. Furthermore, external influences played an important part in causing the revolts. Dominated by commercial motives, France and England plotted the liberation of Spain's colonies.

The Spanish-American revolutions passed through various phases. There were first several preliminary movements which did not succeed. Then a general uprising was precipitated, when Napoleon invaded Spain and placed his brother Joseph *The Hispanic-American Wars of Independence* on the throne (1808). The Spaniards and creoles in South America now joined in the opposition to Napoleon, but soon the creoles made the uprisings take the form of a struggle for independence. Dominated by them, the *cabildos*, or municipal councils, became the centers for organized resistance. All classes, including the clergy, were soon involved in the struggle. The majority of the priests joined the revolutionists, whereas a few of the higher clergy, especially bishops, remained loyal to Spain.

"The War of Independence in South America was a great military drama." Consisting of two main movements which started at opposite ends of the continent, encountering one another in Peru, it resulted in the final expulsion of the Spanish rule. In the North, Miranda, the energetic Venezuelan leader, opened the revolt by leading two premature expeditions against the city of Caracas. The *Juntas*, legislative councils, formed during the Napoleonic invasion of Spain to prevent disorders, joined in the struggle for independence; and Miranda, entering Caracas, proclaimed the first republic of Venezuela, which included the seven eastern provinces (1811). This government did not last, for Caracas was reconquered by the Spaniards in 1812, and the arrest of Miranda brought his public career to an end.

Simón Bolívar (1783–1830), the "George Washington" of South America, now appeared on the revolutionary stage.

Simón Bolívar

For fifteen years this brilliant figure struggled to overthrow the Spanish royalists. A second Republic of Venezuela was crushed (1814), but undeterred he headed another at Bogotá (Colombia). For a short time the revolts were stamped out. After Napoleon was overthrown, King Ferdinand VII was restored to the Spanish throne. Spanish veterans, sent to aid the royalists in Hispanic America, won victories everywhere. Despite the formidable opposition Bolívar could not be suppressed. Eventually he set up a Third Venezuelan Republic. Then, aided by British volunteers, he crossed the Andes and defeated the royalists in New Granada (Colombia), recrossed the mountains, and completed the revolution in Venezuela. Assisted by another capable leader, Sucre, he annexed Ecuador and united all his conquests into Greater Colombia (1819). While Bolívar was freeing the north, uprisings also occurred at Buenos Aires, Santiago (Chile), and elsewhere in the South. Led by José de San Martín (1778–1850), Bernardo O'Higgins (1776–1842), and others, the revolutionists threw off the royalist yoke. These patriots, then coöperating with the liberators of the North, made possible the extinction of Spanish power in South America.

Foreign nations contributed to the success of these revolutions.. England sent a few volunteers, especially naval leaders; and, more important, she opposed the attempt of European nations to intervene. *Foreign States and the Revolt* The United States was also sympathetic, and resented European control in the Americas. At first the American government declared itself neutral and declined to recognize the Hispanic-American states until *de facto* governments should be established. Nevertheless unofficial agents were sent. "Filibustering and privateering expeditions were organized in various ports, and President Madison himself encouraged the revolts in Florida." Spain protested, but in most cases, when privateers were tried in courts, the juries failed to convict. Finally, after the United States had seized both Floridas from Spain "for a price," and after a bitter fight in Congress over the question as to whether the Hispanic-American nations should be considered legitimate independent states, recognition was granted to several of them.

By 1821 European nations were worried over the extension of the revolutionary movements in the Americas; but they could not act, because England would not use her navy to enforce their will. Meanwhile Russia, planning the establishment of an empire along the Pacific, precipitated difficulties by assuming an aggressive attitude toward Northwestern America.

The United States opposed European imperialism in the New World. President Monroe and his advisers therefore decided that the time was ripe for a definite declaration by the United States as to its attitude. Consequently, in 1823, he issued his famous dictum denouncing further colonization of America by Europe or the effort to restore monarchy here. Russia soon withdrew all claims below 54° 40', and the allies gave up their plans to reëstablish Spanish rule in America.

Led by Canning and inspired by commercial interests, England soon recognized the Hispanic-American republics. Other nations followed, but Spanish recognition was long delayed. Thus England and the United States were instrumental in keeping Europe out of America and in enabling the Hispanic-American states to win freedom. The next important question involving outside powers, once this end was attained, was to what extent they should aid Spanish-American states to establish orderly and prosperous bourgeois governments. Again the United States stepped in and by means of the Monroe Doctrine discouraged foreign nations, including England, from using loans to the new American states as means by which they could intervene and establish empires.

The difficulties confronting the Hispanic-American nations in their attempts to attain national unity and to create stable governments invited outside interference. After the wars of independence Hispanic America, like the United States, underwent a long struggle for political stability, national solidarity, and economic prosperity. This turbulence resulted from the lack of national cohesion and the need of political experience. Furthermore, racial hatreds, the superiority of the Spaniards over the creoles, and the oppression of the natives, together with the existence of a landed and religious aristocracy, as in Europe, all tended to promote unrest and revolutions. Geographical barriers and sectional and personal ambitions were also factors in fomenting unrest.

In this period of struggle, soiled by cruel and selfish personal ambitions, there were fundamental issues: "centralism versus federalism, conservatism versus liberalism, privilege versus democracy, militarism versus civilian rule, personal ambition versus the commonweal." The struggles between religious, racial, and economic factions, together with strife between nations, led to one-man power in most cases. Bourgeois democracy suffered. But out of the rise and fall of these dictators developed economic and social reforms, necessary before the new political and social system could function in Hispanic America. There was a place for such dictators as Dr. Francia and the Lópezes in Paraguay, Rosas in Argentina, Castro in Venezuela, and Santa Anna and Díaz in Mexico. Some were benevolent; others were selfish and cruel; yet most of them, through their rise to power, were able to prevent chaos and to pave the way

The Age of Dictators

The Americas in 1826

for stable middle-class democracies in Hispanic America. But until the masses have received their rights and have been educated to popular government, and until the landed estates, both secular and religious, have been broken up, that democracy will not function well.

The revolutions of the nineteenth century made possible the creation of eighteen Spanish-American republics, the *Problems confronting* Portuguese-American republic of Brazil, and *the Hispanic-American* the French-American republic of Haiti. In *can States* these twenty states are nearly a hundred million people, consisting of Negroes, Indians, Caucasians, and hybrids. The half-breed today is the typical South American. Indian blood predominates in Mexico, Peru, Ecuador, Paraguay, and Bolivia.

In Hispanic America the racial situation made the introduction of the middle-class phase of Western civilization a formidable task. Moreover, capitalism belongs primarily to temperate climates. In regions of extreme heat, such as certain parts of Hispanic America, the urge to strive and to get ahead is deficient. This condition probably explains the persistence today of the old régime in many parts of Hispanic America. State and church often monopolized the lands and business, exploiting the people. Little wonder that these regions lagged behind Europe and the United States in economic and political progress.

Lacking efficient management and capital to develop their rich natural resources, the Hispanic-American countries often allowed the investment of foreign money in their lands. This policy in turn prevented national progress in Hispanic America, for the foreign investors wanted either their interest or the right to drain the resources from these regions. To achieve these ends they often influenced their governments to interfere in the internal affairs of these countries and to threaten territorial occupation.

"The struggle for nationality in the Spanish American countries during the first half century is typified by the fortunes of Mexico." Disorder and inexperience in this land led to many political developments and numerous dictatorial governments. Mexico suffered foreign invasion and loss of territory to the United States. She found it difficult to establish a democratic government, to deprive the large landowners of their lands, and to establish public schools.

Her political history was especially turbulent. The famous constitution of 1824 embodied the federal principle; but in the next thirty years fifty presidents followed each other rapidly until finally centralists *Mexico's Turbulent History* replaced federalists and "monarchism again raised its head." During years of turmoil Santa Anna and others rose to power only to fall before some new coalition of factions. Finally a new republican constitution (1857) was created, and the colorful Indian leader, Benito Juárez, became president. Under his leadership privilege was attacked and reforms designed to make Mexico a liberal nation were introduced. In the early sixties, when Napoleon III, emperor of France, tried to establish an empire in Mexico, the Mexicans for a few years had to fight foreign invaders.[1] After the French failure the Mexicans continued their attempts to overthrow the old régime and substitute a republic in place of a dictatorship. Recently forceful and energetic leaders, such as Calles, have engaged in what seems to be a successful modernization of Mexico.

Before the American Revolution, Canada was mainly French. There were a few English settlers, but these constituted a distinct minority. During the Revolution, however, many of the loyalists left *Bourgeois Nationalism in Canada* the thirteen colonies and went to Canada. "These United Empire Loyalists were Canada's Pilgrim Fathers." The war of 1812 checked the settlement by Americans who had followed the loyalists to Canada, and there occurred a heavy tide of British immigration. This influx of English people tended to lessen the American influence.

England administered Canada as separate royal provinces. Governors and other high officials were appointed by the crown, and in "upper Canada government was in the hands of a conservative clique known as the 'Family Compact.'"

[1] See pages 125–126.

The people, influenced by liberal ideas which had resulted in a democracy in the United States, became restless. Agitation was followed by revolution, and England wisely sent the astute Lord Durham to investigate the situation. He favored the establishment of a responsible government and the unification of Upper (Ontario district) and Lower (Quebec district) Canada. England accepted his suggestions. By 1849 most of the provinces in that part of Canada settled by white men had achieved responsible government.

While this form of political organization was being obtained, the same half century witnessed the advance of the *Expansion of Canada* British as well as of American influence across the continent into the Pacific Northwest. English fur traders led the way, and in 1825 the Hudson's Bay Company established a western capital at Fort Vancouver. Settlers and railroads followed the traders. During the nineteenth century the great Canadian West became a part of the Dominion of Canada. Before this was to happen, however, another important political change occurred.

Although by 1850 most of the Canadian provinces enjoyed responsible government, they were not satisfied. Influenced by *Establishment of the Dominion* a community of interests, the need of economic coöperation, and fear of annexation by the United States, they demanded a union of all the provinces through the creation of a federation. Many persons in Canada, especially the French Canadians, opposed this plan. Fearing further expansion of the United States in their direction, the Canadians nevertheless decided to unite. In the Quebec Conference (1864) a plan of federation was formulated. Home government was then approved, and by the British North America Act the Dominion of Canada was founded (1867). Although the federation resembled that of the United States, it differed in many respects. Influenced by the fight over states' rights in the United States, the Canadians left many unspecified powers in the hands of the central government. Consequently the dominion became a centralized federation with responsible government. This form of organization was accepted in time by all the provinces. A movement then developed to extend the Dominion from the Atlantic to the Pacific. To facilitate this development, the Hudson's Bay Company relinquished its vast jurisdiction in the West, and Manitoba, British Columbia, Alberta, and Saskatchewan eventually grew to statehood, enabling the federation to stretch from sea to sea.

This sparsely populated dominion was soon welded by transcontinental railroads, and the way was paved for the development of another great center of bourgeois society in the new world. Today, although Canada is tied to England as a part of the British Empire by sentimental and economic bonds, she is practically an independent nation, determined, like the United States and Hispanic-American countries, to play her part in the development of middle-class society.

In general the history of the Western Hemisphere from the discovery of Columbus to the last quarter of the nineteenth century can be divided into two phases: first, *Conclusion* the transplantation of the aristocratic old régime and the planting of colonial societies by Europeans in the New World; and, second, the overthrow of the old order and the creation of a new bourgeois society. By the end of the nineteenth century the middle classes practically dominated the English-speaking countries. In the Spanish sphere of influence, however, the struggle between the old and the new showed no signs of an early termination.

CHAPTER XII

The Spread of Liberalism in Austria-Hungary and the Lesser Powers

MEDIEVAL ideology in the form of a universal Christian state still found expression in modern times in the Austrian empire. The Hapsburgs — rigidly adhering to a nebulous and anachronistic classical ideal, which prescribed one state, one law, and one faith — strove through the nineteenth century to preserve their cosmopolitan patrimony. Austria, a variegated mosaic of diverse peoples with heterogeneous cultural standards and ideals, contained ten nations and numerous sub-national groups. This conglomerate of peoples, permeated by particularistic loyalties, was a living contradiction of the modern principle of nationality. Moreover, the dynasty, in defiance of the liberal trends of the age, tried to immunize the empire to political and social progress. This conscious fostering of cultural backwardness, so as to avoid a dislocation of the old régime, in conjunction with the serious factor of ethnic disunity, only served to weaken the vitality of the state. As a result, despite the mirage of Austrian grandeur during the Metternichian period, a contemporary historian could declare: "Austria is a white sepulchre, an old tree which is rotten within, though it still bears leaves on the outside, but which the first blast of wind will uproot."

During the age of Metternich (1815–1848) Austria experienced a renascence of political power. Napoleon, as mentioned previously,[1] temporarily shattered Hapsburg leadership when he abolished the Holy Roman Empire in 1806. With the fall of the French empire, however, most of the work of Napoleon was undone. Central Europe was again decentralized and the

Reaction under Metternich

---

[1] See page 30.

Hapsburgs enlarged their Austrian domains and also became the titular heads of a new Germanic confederation.

As chancellor of the Austrian empire, Metternich coöperated with his emperor, Francis I (1792–1835), nicknamed by a submissive people "the tiger in the nightgown," in maintaining the absolute monarchy. To this end a highly centralized bureaucratic administration was developed and the police and clergy assisted the state in suppressing every germ of free thought or healthy criticism. Aloof from the currents of political, social, and intellectual progress of the West, Austria was denied reform and became relatively more backward. Conditions became even worse during the reign of the irresponsible Ferdinand I (1835–1848) when clericalism, unenlightened absolutism, and obscurantism reached their height. His rule, even with the assistance of the aging Metternich, was little more than a caricature of Francis's system and has been aptly described as "absolutist monarchy without a monarch."

Temporarily the old order was swept away by the violent uprisings of 1848. Metternich's fear of democracy, which prompted his wife to dub him "the Cassandra of the monarchy," seemed vindicated. Ferdinand, having made liberal promises which he was unable to fulfill, was forced to abdicate in favor of his young nephew, Francis Joseph (1848–1916). Hapsburg power, at one time almost completely extinguished, was reëstablished only through the skill of the imperial generals, Jellačić, Windischgrätz, and Radetzky. Facilitating the restoration of imperial authority were two significant factors. One was the mutual distrust and consequent antagonisms of the subject nationalities and their unwillingness to coöperate against the dynasty. The other was the ignorance of the masses, who were ill-prepared for experimentation in democracy and so fell prey to idealogues and demagogues. Perhaps symbolical of the resignation of the masses was the brilliant Austrian dramatic poet, Franz Grillparzer (1791–1872). His unbalanced temperament, his brooding pessimism, his lack of will power, and his bitter renunciation, seemed to express the thraldom of Metternichian Austria. In his plays, wherein he preached the futility of grandeur and the vanity of worldly greatness, he accurately reflected the defeatism of the people.

The early years of the reign of Francis Joseph, extending from 1848 to 1867, were a significant stage in the dissolution of the Danubian empire — an organic process which lasted until 1918. Relying on the traditional Hapsburg policies of unification, Germanization, and Catholization, the young ruler strove to preserve a patriarchal monarchy in an age of awakening democracy and nationalism. Conceived by Alexander Bach, minister of the interior, Francis Joseph's system of government was an absolutistic centralism, which, with the assistance of bureaucrats, police, spies, and Jesuits, was designed to function with mechanical uniformity. Fundamentally it was a replica of the Metternichian system, in which the administration consisted of "a standing army of soldiers, a sitting army of officials, a kneeling army of priests, and a creeping army of denunciators."

Neo-absolutism of Francis Joseph

Despite the conservatism of this period of neo-absolutism, considerable social and economic progress occurred. Feudalism, in its legal if not in its social implications, was practically destroyed through the principle of civil and legal equality. The serfs were freed, but most of them, in view of the primarily agrarian nature of the empire, remained in an economic thraldom, at the mercy of the great landowners. Nevertheless, as railways, highways, banks, and factories were created, capitalistic economy and the middle-class system made its way, especially in Austria proper and Bohemia. In 1850 an Austro-Hungarian customs union provided for free trade within the Hapsburg domains. Gradually economic improvement bettered conditions, but the unevenness of its diffusion eventually served to emphasize the separatism of the various regions of the empire.

Economic Progress

The quest for diplomatic glory, curiously enough, was largely responsible for the only important political concessions which his subjects secured from Francis Joseph before 1867. Upon his accession, the emperor had turned his back on the

LINGUISTIC
MAP OF EUROPE

Scale of miles

0   100   200   300   400   500   600

constitutional movement (an outgrowth of the revolutions of 1848), had ignored the demands of the subject nationalities, and had preferred a policy of opportunism and day-to-day compromises. An aggressive foreign policy, however, designed to promote *Constitutional Experiments* Austrian prestige, had been temporarily derailed by the defeat at the hands of France and Sardinia in 1859. In the embarrassment of failure, demands for domestic reform could not be disregarded, and so Francis Joseph had to compromise with his formula of divine-right absolutism. In October, 1860, through the creation of a constitution known as the *Diploma,* he repudiated centralism and Germanization, and appealed for support to the feudal nobles of the various countries which he ruled. The failure of this document to attract the loyalty of the Magyars, who still desired the reëstablishment of their constitution of 1848, led to its supersession by the February *Patent* (1861). This instrument revived the old centralist system tempering it with a "show window" of parliamentarianism in the form of unrepresentative provincial diets whose powers were insignificant.

Even more serious than the question of constitutional reform was the ethnic problem. The ruling nationality, the German-speaking Austrians, chiefly concentrated about Vienna and in the Tyrol, and *Problem of the Nationalities* sprinkled through Bohemia and Moravia, constituted only about 20 per cent of the population of the empire. Nevertheless they monopolized the important offices in the government, army, schools, and church. Forming a solid ethnic mass in the valley of the Danube and represented by minorities in the Banat and Transylvania, the Magyars, who were of Asiatic origin, were about equal numerically to the Austrians. Save for a small minority which served as a feudal nobility, they were mostly peasants accustomed to an agrarian economy. Fiercely nationalistic, the Magyars were vehement in expressing their dissatisfaction with Austrian rule.

Slavic-speaking peoples constituted about one half the total population of the empire. They included the Czechs and Slovaks, who were the most numerous ethnic groups in

Bohemia and Moravia. The Czechs, through the exploitation of the coal and iron resources of Bohemia, became industrial rivals of the Austrians. Ardent nationalists and followers of the heretical John Hus (1369–1415), they resented alien rule and disliked the German language. Chiefly peasants, the Slovaks were less capable of offering effective resistence to the dynasty.

Two Slavic peoples, the Poles and the Ruthenians, inhabited Galicia, formerly a part of the old kingdom of Poland. The Poles, chiefly Roman Catholics, were permitted some degree of local autonomy and the use of their language in the schools. Closely akin to the Ukrainians of southern Russia, the Ruthenians were poor and illiterate peasants who were oppressed by their Polish landlords.

In the southwestern part of the empire, the Yugoslavs, consisting of Serbs, Croats, and Slovenes, were the largest ethnic groups. Chiefly herdsmen and peasants, they were unable to make serious headway against Hapsburg power. Nevertheless many of them even in the middle nineteenth century were encouraged to look to Serbia and Montenegro for liberation from their oppressors.

Besides the major groups there were numerous large minorities. In the Trentino and along the eastern coast of the Adriatic were large numbers of Italians. Several million Rumanians resided in Transylvania and the Banat. In addition there were many Jews scattered throughout the cities of the empire. Primarily representative of middle-class society, they were of great economic importance because of their control of a large part of the capital, professions, and business enterprises of the empire. In contrast to the restlessness of the other peoples, the Jews, despite some outbursts of anti-Semitism, generally supported the Hapsburg dynasty.

Paradoxical as it may seem, the multi-national character of the Austrian empire was a source of strength as well as of weakness. Inasmuch as each region of the *Policy of " Divide and Rule "* empire was inhabited by at least one dominant and one minority nationality, it was possible for the government to take advantage of the hatreds which existed between most of the nationalities and to play one off

against another. Each desired the support of the dynasty
and so helped it to combat other groups. Thus by a policy
of "Divide and Rule" the Hapsburgs retained their hegemony. This policy, however, had the disadvantage of promoting particularism and separatism. These embryonic states
(the subject nationalities) one contemporary said were like
"horses absurdly harnessed together" and he warned that
they would "scatter in all directions as soon as the advancing spirit of the times shall weaken and break the bonds."

This policy of "Divide and Rule" was put to a severe test
in 1866. The defeat by Prussia in the Seven Weeks' War,
which glaringly revealed the shortcomings of Hapsburg
militarism and diplomacy, shook the empire to its foundations. With the subject nationalities in a state of discontent
and the Austrian army demoralized, the emperor needed
support. Magyar leaders, particularly Francis Deák, determined to exploit this situation so as to exact concessions as the
price of Magyar loyalty. Negotiations ensued between the
Austrian government and Deák and other Magyar leaders, and
finally in 1867 an Austrian-Magyar compromise was effected.

The *Ausgleich*, as this compromise was called, provided for
a reorganization of the Hapsburg empire. Substituting the
principle of dualism for centralism, it provided
for the creation of the Dual Monarchy. This   *Ausgleich of 1867*
entity was to consist of two states, the Austrian empire and
the kingdom of Hungary. Each was to have its own system
of government, its own language, and its own capital, but the
two were to be linked in a personal union, the Austrian emperor being *ipso facto* apostolic king of Hungary. In addition
to the independent political system which Austria and Hungary possessed, there was to be a supranational dual government. The latter was to consist of the emperor-king as titular
head; three joint ministers of war, finance, and foreign
affairs; and two delegations selected by the Austrian and
Hungarian parliaments. Agreements on tariffs, currency, and
trade between the two partner states and the determination of
the budgets for the army and for foreign affairs were left to the
delegations. Concerning the curious nature of this Hapsburg

compromise between Austrian and Magyar traditionalism,
one scholar observed: "Like an animal form of the tertiary
period, amidst the animal kingdom of the present day, so
the Great Power of Austria-Hungary was a remnant of a previous stage of evolution, of the territorial state of the Middle
Ages."

Unquestionably the creation of the *Ausgleich* was an indication that the empire was weak. It was a device whereby the
Austro-Magyar alliance could partially balance the Slavic
numerical superiority and continue to dominate the subject
peoples by a policy of "Divide and Rule" and thereby preserve the *status quo*. Nevertheless, its creation was a tacit
admission that the imperial bonds of unity — such as dynastic loyalty, the army, the Catholic church, the bureaucracy,
the privileged aristocracy, Jewish capitalism, economic interdependence — were insufficient to arrest the centrifugal or
disuniting forces. The latter — such as ethnic disunity,
Austro-Magyar antagonism, irredentism, and linguistic diversity prevented the development of loyalty to the crown.

During the nineteenth century the small nations of Europe
participated in a common civilization with the greater states,
The Spread of Liberal- being exposed to the same influences and
ism in the Lesser general movements. Most of them overthrew
Powers the restrictions and bondages of the old régime
and adopted capitalistic methods.

Switzerland was an excellent example of bourgeois development. The Treaty of Westphalia (1648), which ended the
Switzerland Thirty Years' War, recognized the independence of the Swiss Confederation. Thenceforth
the newly formed state was no longer a part of the Holy
Roman Empire. Nevertheless the confederation did not
succeed, during the seventeenth and eighteenth centuries, in
increasing to any great extent the national unity of the Swiss
people. Uniting chiefly for defense, it remained a loose union
of semi-independent oligarchic cantons. In many of these
cantons Protestants and Catholics carried on a fierce subter-
ranean struggle long after the religious wars were over. In
addition to other difficulties three languages were spoken —

French, German, and Italian. Unity seemed almost impossible under such unusual conditions.

The French Revolution and the Napoleonic conquest of the confederation stimulated Swiss patriotism. After the emperor's fall the old government was restored, and the powers at Vienna, desirous of creating a buffer state against France, established a confederation of twenty-two free cantons and guaranteed its neutrality.

After 1815, internal problems occupied the attention of the Swiss people. Liberals, attacking the weak government, demanded greater centralization and demo- *Problems confronting* cratic reforms. Shortly after the revolutions *the Swiss People* of 1830 the cantonal constitutions were de- mocratized. Opposing these innovations, seven Catholic can- tons formed a league called the *Sonderbund*. The other cantons declared war on these rebel states and defeated them in 1847. A new constitution was formulated in 1848, and a real democ- racy was established.

Although the cantons retained local rights, the supremacy of the central, or federal, government was recognized. Na- tional legislative and executive powers were *The Swiss Democracy* vested in an assembly of two houses and an executive committee of seven, called the federal council, which was elected by the federal assembly. Although he was no more powerful than the others, one of the seven, entitled the president of the council, presided.

Through the adoption of the referendum and the initiative, first for cantonal legislation and later for federal legislation, the idea of the enlarged town meeting for electing magis- trates and voting laws was carried into the Swiss government. A body of people speaking French, German, and Italian, believing devoutly in either the Protestant or the Catholic faith, and enjoying political equality was indeed a phenomenon in mid-nineteenth-century Europe.

In this period Switzerland experienced a very marked economic and political development. The land became the playground of tourists. Although primarily an agricultural country, she promoted manufacturing to a considerable extent.

Illiteracy was practically exterminated through the establishment of public schools. By the opening of the twentieth century, Switzerland was a democratic country, and her people, especially the middle classes, were better off than their neighbors and brothers across the frontiers.

Belgium, another small country whose neutrality in the nineteenth century became a matter of international concern,

Belgium   was also highly progressive. As stated before,[1] she was united with Holland by the powers at the Congress of Vienna (1815). Objecting to this treatment, the Belgians started a revolution in 1830 and issued a declaration of independence. In the same year they selected a national assembly which met in Brussels and finally chose Prince Leopold of Saxe-Coburg as King Leopold I. Although the Dutch refused to accept this act, the allied powers recognized it. A French army and an English fleet went to the aid of the Belgians, and the Dutch wisely capitulated. The new constitutional monarchy established by the Belgians was moderately liberal. A bicameral parliament was created, of which the lower house was elected directly by the eligible voters, who were few because of a high property qualification.

Independence meant economic prosperity for Belgium under the liberal Leopold I (1831–1865) and the enterprising Leopold II (1865–1909). Situated on the North Sea, the country was able, by means of a network of canals and railways, to connect the entire region with the great seaport at Antwerp and to develop her extensive coal beds. Consequently, by the end of the nineteenth century important industrial and agricultural improvements were making Belgium one of the most densely settled and prosperous areas in Europe.

During this period three important parties struggled for power: the Catholics, the Liberals, and the Socialists. From 1884 to 1914 the Catholic party governed Belgium. Largely through its initiative religious instruction was restored in most of the schools, and political reforms were enacted. By the reign of Albert I (1909–   ), however, the Socialists

[1] See pages 30, 41.

had become a real political force. Joining the Liberals in their opposition to the Catholics, this radical group attacked Catholic control of the schools and the institution of plural voting. In 1913 the Socialists, with their slogan "one man, one vote," attempted a general strike, but the elections of 1914 preserved a comfortable Catholic majority in the Chamber.

As the dominant bourgeois party the Catholic group tried by social legislation to solve economic problems which rose out of the industrial development of the country. An enlightened factory code was passed, trade unions were protected (1898), and a system of old-age pensions was established (1900). These measures were followed by other acts designed to foster or protect Belgium's economic interests. In 1908 the government took over as a colony the huge African territory of the Congo,[1] and in 1909 the army was strengthened and soon fortifications were erected at Antwerp and Liége.

Liberalism affected the Dutch as well as the Belgians. The former received their independence officially in the Treaty of Westphalia (1648). By that time these energetic people, a large part of whose country *The Netherlands* was below sea level and protected by dikes, had developed a huge empire overseas. Through their great sea power they wielded much influence throughout the world. Inasmuch as they were among the first of the modern peoples to appreciate the importance of economic factors in government, they permitted a great middle-class oligarchy to rule and to encourage business enterprises in peace time. During an emergency, such as war, authority was often vested in one ruler, a member of the House of Orange.

The rise of England as a great sea power in the seventeenth century checked the maritime activities of the Dutch. After 1815, although still retaining valuable possessions in the East Indies, Holland was forced to accept Belgium in return for the loss of a considerable portion of her empire in the East, including Cape Colony, in South Africa, and Ceylon.

[1] See pages 408–410.

The king of the Netherlands was William I of the famous House of Orange. During his reign (1813–1840) the state experienced quiet internal developments and played no important rôle in international politics. He did grant a constitution to his people, but he managed to retain most of the authority in his hands. The States-General was restricted to the acceptance or rejection of bills submitted by the government and had no powers of amendment or of origination. The ministry was responsible to the king alone.

His successor, William II (1840–1849), agreed to a new fundamental law in 1848, in which the king was checked by a parliament of two houses. The upper branch was composed of members elected by the legislators of the eleven provinces of the kingdom, while the members of the lower house were chosen directly by an electorate made up of those persons who possessed a given amount of property. The Netherlands established a conservative middle-class federal government similar to those of the United States and Switzerland. Further reforms, such as the extension of the suffrage, did not follow as rapidly in the Netherlands as in many countries. In fact, William III, who ruled from 1849 to 1890, was limited only by a small bourgeois oligarchy. During the reign of Queen Wilhelmina (1890–   ), the suffrage was extended, although the variety of property qualifications remained large. But universal suffrage, demanded by Socialists and Liberals, had not been granted up to 1914.

Despite the loss of important colonies and of Belgium, the Netherlands remained in the nineteenth century a land of hard-working, thrifty people. Still in possession of many important colonies, including Java, Sumatra, part of Borneo, and Celebes in Asia, Dutch Guiana, and various islands in the Americas, the Netherlands, although a small Continental state, is today an important colonial and commercial power.

Near the Netherlands was a tiny independent country called the Grand Duchy of Luxembourg. This region was attached in 1815 as a personal possession to William I, king of the Netherlands. The territory was for geographic or military reasons incorporated in the German *Bund*. When the Confederation disappeared as a result of the Austro-Prussian war of 1866, the question arose as to the future status of Luxembourg. Louis Napoleon III of France coveted it, but William I of Prussia did not propose   *Luxembourg* to allow this region to become a part of France. At a conference of powers held in London in 1867, William III of the Netherlands was confirmed as grand duke of Luxembourg, and its independence was placed under the collective guarantee of the powers assembled.

The three small Scandinavian nations in northern Europe ceased to be states of international importance during the nineteenth century. Despite their political and territorial decline, however, they have   *The Scandinavian States* played a significant rôle in the development of Western civilization. The three nationalities of these north Germanic peoples were the Danes, Swedes, and Norwegians. They were very much alike, speaking similar tongues, professing, for the most part, the same religion (Lutheranism), and promoting similar economic interests, primarily agriculture, commerce, and fishing.

During the Middle Ages Denmark was a formidable Baltic power. Her support of Napoleon and her subsequent cession of Norway to Sweden, however, constituted one of the late stages in her decline. In 1864   *Denmark* she was forced to cede the Schleswig-Holstein provinces to the German Confederation. Consequently she was reduced to a compact agricultural territory, which her citizens have developed to an astonishing extent.

At first liberalism made little headway. Absolutism existed until the revolutionary period of 1848, when Frederick VII issued a constitution (1849), which was revised in 1866 and is still in force. Despite the opposition of the lower house of the Danish legislature, Christian IX, who followed Frederick in 1863, tried to oppose this democratic trend and did so for some time, appointing ministers at his pleasure and insisting on a large army. Economic developments, however, led to democratic concessions. During the nineteenth century the small Danish farmers improved their economic position by intensive dairy farming and by coöperative societies. Gradually public opinion became so powerful that by 1901 it forced the king to accept the parliamentary form of government. Largely because of the scientific development of her agriculture, Denmark, a little nation, enjoyed economic prosperity. She possessed a small empire, owning Iceland, Greenland, and several islands in the West Indies. But she was not over-interested in these possessions, being willing to give Iceland autonomy in 1874 and to sell the West India islands to the United States.

Of the northern countries Sweden has probably played the most important part in modern history. In the seventeenth century she was one of the great powers, threatening to dominate the Baltic Sea and to establish an empire in America. Peter the Great of Russia, however, dragged Sweden from her pedestal and absorbed most of the Swedish conquests along the east shore of the Baltic. In 1809 Alexander I of Russia, by depriving Sweden of Finland, continued the work of Peter the Great.

Sweden

Sweden was partially compensated for these losses as a result of the Napoleonic struggles. Bernadotte, one of Napoleon's marshals, elected to succeed the last of the old royal house (Charles XIII), having supported the allies, received Norway as a reward in 1815. This was a territorial gift of questionable value. The Norwegians resented the transfer from Denmark to Sweden and claimed independence, although they accepted the king of Sweden as their ruler.

In 1818 Bernadotte became king under the title of Charles XIV. He reigned over these two nations, each with its own constitution and administration, until 1844. Although of French origin, the Swedish ruler and his descendants identified themselves with the interests of Sweden and became exceedingly popular.

During the nineteenth century the Swedish people were more conservative than their neighbors because of a powerful aristocratic landowning class set above a large dependent peasantry. Backed by these Swedish junkers, the government was able to oppose liberalism and also to maintain an effective army so as to resist possible Russian encroachments. In 1863 a growing bourgeoisie brought about the abolition of the ancient feudal diet and the establishment of a modern parliament of two houses. Nevertheless high property qualifications kept the property owners in power, and the Swedes did not establish a democracy until 1909. By that time the bourgeoisie and proletariat, the former made wealthy and numerous by the development of mineral resources and water power, were able to deprive the landowning aristocrats of their privileged position.

The Norwegians resented their forced union with Sweden. Living in a country which consisted for the most part of mountains and a narrow coastland, they were largely small farmers, fearless fishermen and *Norway* sailors, and a few industrious merchants. Opposition to foreign control, encouraged by the divergence of their economic interests from those of Sweden, culminated in the peaceful separation of the two Scandinavian states in 1905. A long-repressed desire for equality and freedom had already been partially satisfied by the Norwegian parliament (*Storthing*) when it introduced universal manhood suffrage in 1898. Thenceforth, later reforms, such as woman suffrage, rapidly made Norway one of the most democratic countries in Europe.

In the field of literature rather than in politics and economics, the Scandinavian nations exercised marked influence. Among the important Norwegian writers two, Björnstjerne Björnson (1832–1910) and Henrik *Scandinavian Literature* *and Music* Ibsen (1828–1906), have a sure place in the literary life of Europe. Despite the fact that Björnson was born in the bleak north of Norway, he reveals in such works as *Synnöve Solbakken*, the first of his peasant stories, an optimistic outlook upon life. He was also an intense nationalist. One of his lyrics, "Ja vielsker detta landet" (Yes! we love this our country!), is the national hymn of Norway. Ibsen, however, was the greatest of Scandinavian writers. The most famous of his works are the social dramas, or problem plays, *An Enemy of the People*, *The Pillars of Society*, and *A Doll's House*. In these dramas Ibsen, the pessimist, exposed the smug complacency and hypocrisy of bourgeois society, and described democracy as a means whereby the deceitful governing minority actually created the impression that the masses ruled.

The majority never has right on its side — never, I say! That is one of the social lies that a free, thinking man is bound to rebel against. Who make up the majority in any given country? Is it the wise men or the fools? I think we must agree that the fools are in a terrible, overwhelming majority, all the wide world over. But how in the devil's name can it ever be right for the fools to rule over the wise men?

The Scandinavian nations have also made some noteworthy contributions in the field of music. Northern folk songs are of a peculiar and exquisite charm, and they have tinged more or less all the work of the Scandinavian composers, especially since the European romantic movement threw the attention of the art world back to characteristic national subjects and feelings.

Of the many modern composers one of the most beloved was Edvard Grieg (1843–1907). As a musical miniature painter he has hardly an equal since the great German, Robert Schumann (1810–1856). Cultivating a peculiarly weird and vague kind of harmony and tonality, he adopted the forms and rhythms of popular dances in such a way as to spread an atmosphere of mystery and melancholy. This "serves to bring up associations with gloomy fjords, lonely shores and mountains, with their attendant legends of strange spirits of earth and sea." More than a mere imitation of national strains, Grieg's music is a self-expression of the original artist, a man of the people.

PART IV. THE TRIUMPH OF THE MIDDLE CLASSES

CHAPTER XIII

England's Golden Age: The Mid-Victorian Period, 1848-1878

THE period 1848–1878, a phase of the Victorian era (1837–1901), marked a high point in English cultural progress and a golden age comparable to those of Elizabeth and Augustus. By 1848 the bourgeoisie ruled England. The Technological Revolution, which was rapidly making that country an industrial beehive, enabled them to grow both in numbers and in power. No longer did the squires and their dependents constitute the bulk of the population; in a hundred thriving cities many business men were of more consequence than the great landlords of the shires. Owners of factories, mills, and coal mines ; controllers of warehouses and joint-stock companies; heads of trading houses, broker firms, and banks — they were the products of the new age of iron and

The Supremacy of the Middle Classes

Note. *The picture at the top of the page shows the Prince of Wales (later Edward VII)* Opening a Sluice in the Suez Canal. *From a contemporary wood engraving.*

steam. Some were exceedingly wealthy, and as machinery was improved and production multiplied they became even richer and more influential. But despite the fact that they were blessed with huge incomes and magnificent mansions, these newly rich, many of whom rose from the lower ranks, were looked down upon by high society, which still despised business and middle-class methods of making money.

Business men, dependent for success upon brains rather than upon social position, possessed many socially significant ideas. Of these the most important for England was the doctrine of free trade. This tenet *The Classical Economists* was born toward the close of the preceding century in the work of the French physiocrats and of the English economist Adam Smith, who drew his *laissez faire* theory from his observation of English economic life. Until 1770 the importation of cotton to England had been opposed, lest it should prove fatal to home-grown wool; later the Corn Laws were established to promote the interests of the farming class. Adam Smith maintained that such restrictions were economically fallacious. Competition was the very life of industry and commerce; to hinder competition was to restrict supply and to create high prices. The maximum of effort and of production could be attained only when nations and individuals strained their resources to surpass or to undersell their competitors. These ideas were adopted by disciples of Adam Smith, the men of the "Manchester School" in England, who carried the concept even farther than had the prophet. These advocates of the *laissez faire* doctrine, Thomas Robert Malthus (1766–1834), David Ricardo (1772–1823), and John Stuart Mill (1806–1873), the so-called "classical economists," were the chief exponents of the capitalistic system.

Malthus and Ricardo were especially concerned with the problem of labor in modern society. In his *Essay on the Principle of Population* Malthus set forth the "tendency of population to press upon subsistence." Man, he said, was an animal, physiologically like any other; and the possibilities of his increase in numbers were unlimited. Fortunately disease, war, and famine exerted a limiting effect on the growth of population. Influenced by this Malthusian doctrine Ricardo developed his famous theory of wages. In his opinion wages, by enabling the workers merely to subsist and to perpetuate their race, would check the increase of population. According to Ricardo, labor was no more than an article used for the benefit of society. Apparently he did not believe that employers should treat wage-earners as human beings.

Many English thinkers, conservative as well as radical, questioned the soundness of the *laissez faire* doctrine. As an example of the failure of economic individualism they called attention to the situation in England, where a few persons were extremely wealthy, whereas the majority were very poor. Poverty had increased, even though the bourgeoisie had grown. Many of the latter class admitted that there was something wrong but placed the blame for England's social ills on the corrupt landowning caste who ruled selfishly in their own interests. The workingmen, however, not yet given the vote, soon discovered that they had merely exchanged one set of masters for another. In despair they organized unions and planned the destruction of machinery and factories.

By the time of Victoria's accession to the throne the liberal Whigs had exhausted their ammunition and were satisfied to let well enough alone. While Lord Melbourne was prime minister (1835–1841) little was done to solve the important social and political problems. As a conservative Whig, Melbourne had opposed the Reform Bill of 1832. He thought education was futile and, for the poor, positively dangerous; democracy was a myth. "The whole duty of the government," he said, "was to prevent crime and to preserve contracts." Victoria was a devoted admirer of this amiable but conservative prime minister, because he appealed to her concept of domestic virtue and religious regularity. Always wanting to do the right thing, and resisting even the smug sentimentalism which affected her as it did most of her contemporaries, she could not be forced off the highway of middle-class propriety. Wisely Melbourne arranged to have her surrounded by the wives and sisters of Whigs, so that she should not be exposed to pernicious Tory influences. Consequently she became his devoted follower and relied upon his advice in all earthly matters.

Between 1832 and 1867 an extension of the suffrage was frequently demanded. Wage-earners especially became more aggressive and more powerful as time went on. By 1866, leaders of the two dominant parties, the successors of the Tories and Whigs, — namely, the Conservatives and Liberals, — realized that they must yield at least to the political demands of the wage-earners. Gladstone, Liberal leader of the House of Commons, proposed a moderate extension of suffrage. Many Liberals, however, disappointed because the measure was too moderate, joined the Conservatives in killing it.

The Wage-Earners and the Ballot

With Lord Derby as prime minister the Conservatives now assumed power. Politicians thought that the advance toward political democracy had been checked. But they were deceived. Aroused by the rejection of this bill, the masses held popular demonstrations and demanded the extension of the suffrage. Gladstone, as the fiery apostle of political democracy, furnished the famous battle cry, "You cannot fight against the future; time is on our side." Realizing that reform was inevitable, the Conservatives, led by Disraeli, decided, in 1867, to extend the suffrage and thus to gain the ballots of the new voters. Consequently another Reform Bill was introduced in Parliament. At first it was a typically moderate measure, but Gladstone and his followers in the House of Commons impelled the Conservative government to remodel the bill almost entirely. When it was finally passed, it conformed largely to the ideas of Gladstone, the reformer. As leader of the Conservatives, however, the resourceful Disraeli, who passed the measure, was given the credit.

The Reform Bill, as finally enacted in 1867, ended the political despotism of the middle classes in England. The franchise in boroughs was given to all householders. "Thus, instead of ten-pound householders, all householders, whatever the value of their houses, were admitted; also all lodgers who had occupied for a year lodgings of the value, unfurnished, of ten pounds, or

The Reform Bill of 1867

about a dollar a week." In the counties the suffrage was given to all those who owned property yielding five pounds clear income a year, rather than ten pounds as previously; and to all renters who paid at least twelve pounds, rather than fifty pounds as hitherto. The better class of laborers in the boroughs, and virtually all tenant farmers in the counties, received the ballot. This legislation nearly doubled the number of voters in England.

The passage of this sweeping measure aroused much pessimism among Englishmen. Carlyle pictured a terrible future and called the reform "shooting Niagara." Robert Lowe, who had opposed the act bitterly, shuddered at the prospect of the "uncultured in control." "We must educate our masters," he said. Nevertheless the bill of 1867 actually marked an important step in the political rise of the wage-earning classes. Henceforth the rivalry between the bourgeoisie and the country gentlemen was pushed more and more into the background. As the wage-earners became powerful and active, Liberals and Conservatives were often impelled to unite in opposition to them.

A tendency on the part of workers to organize unions aroused the apprehension of the middle classes. According to the average bourgeois citizen the dominant *laissez faire* policy was the true path of prog-

Social Reforms

ress. To secure a prosperous England, let each man attend to his own business. Under the police protection of the state, although only a few would become wealthy, all would be contented. These beliefs, representing the views of factory owners of that time, were not justifiable in the opinion of the workers. They declared that the state should not be a cold, detached observer of the intolerable miseries of the wage-earners. No man should have the right to hire women and children to work twelve hours a day or to employ men in unsanitary factories at starvation wages.

A number of middle-class liberals sympathized with the workers. The English reformer Robert Owen (1771–1858) tried to help the wage-earners through schools, shorter hours of work, and coöperative stores owned by the workers. Favored by these so-called enlightened owners, a considerable amount of social legislation was enacted. In 1833 the famous Factory Act was passed, which fixed maximum working hours for children under certain ages. This was followed by other beneficial laws, and soon much of Adam Smith's philosophy was discarded as the proletariat slowly forced the antagonistic bourgeois government to interfere in the matter of working conditions and hours of labor in behalf of the laboring classes.

In 1867, however, the wage-earners were not radical. They had accepted the new order. No longer did they fight the machine and the factory; no longer did they look for utopian reforms. Instead their unions tried to exist within the framework of the capitalistic order. Modeled after business enterprises, they had dues, exclusive membership, regulations, and long apprenticeships. Even the workers' coöperative societies underwent a change. The old organizations, urging the reform of all society, were replaced by new consumers' coöperatives, which, being capitalistically owned and operated, conformed to the existing order.

The parliamentary struggles which resulted in social reforms and in the rise of the workingmen to political power *Gladstone and Disraeli* occurred during the ministries of two remarkable English statesmen, William Ewart Gladstone (1809–1898) and Benjamin Disraeli (1804–1881). Son of a wealthy Scotch merchant who had moved from his native land to the city of Liverpool, Gladstone was fortunate enough to inherit a considerable patrimony. On the other hand, Disraeli, whose grandfather, a Jew, had migrated from Italy to England in 1748, began life as a poor, though, to be sure, very clever, young man.

Gladstone was a typical benevolent member of the rising capitalist class. An opportunist as well as a sincere exponent of the doctrines of his fellow countryman Adam Smith, he was wise enough to know that there comes a time when middle-class tolerance and compromise must be discarded in favor of positive rather than negative governmental acts.

This able liberal statesman represented a dominant element of the middle classes — the advocates of free trade. Identified with the movement which had resulted in the abolition of the Corn Laws in 1846, Gladstone seized the opportunity to promote comprehensive industrial, commercial, and intellectual developments, which, in his opinion, had been made possible by such members of the Manchester School as Cobden, Bright, and Mill.

On the other hand, Disraeli became a bourgeois Tory, or Conservative. He was ambitious, eccentric, and common, according to many orthodox Englishmen. The "proper" Liberals consequently did not approve of him. Aware of this antagonism, Disraeli professed at first an opposition to change, a love for the romantic past, an antipathy for the unromantic manufacturers and shopkeepers, and a brotherly interest in the poor workingman. Being politically minded, he joined the Conservative party, despite liberal tendencies.

Counted as an adventurer by many Englishmen, Disraeli, a superb example of opportunism, had managed to rise politically by joining the Conservatives and championing in the sixties the political cause of the workingmen. Although not favoring complete suffrage, he claimed that the House of Commons should represent varieties of classes and interests rather than mere numbers. The vote, he said, should be given to a select aristocracy of laborers.

Disraeli found it difficult at first to make much of an impression in England, save on Queen Victoria, with whom he won great favor by highly diplomatic practices. He tried to gain attention by furthering a pressing political issue. But what question could he utilize for his own benefit? The ballot for workingmen was sponsored and opposed by elements in both parties. Gladstone, moreover, having already jumped into the reform camp, Disraeli found the competition in this sphere exceedingly keen. The cause of protection seemed a possibility, but the remarkable economic progress which attended the repeal of the Corn Laws made the Manchester school far too powerful to be successfully opposed on this score. In the fifties, however, Disraeli indicated that he was soon to find an issue — imperialism. To prepare the way for the adoption of this bourgeois policy, he attacked the

Gladstonian "Little Englanders" of the Manchester School and accused them of furthering pacifism and republicanism instead of a national and truly patriotic program.

After the passage of the Reform Bill of 1867 the Conservatives, instead of being shown gratitude by the newly enfranchised citizens, were swept out of office by the latter, who voted the Liberal ticket in the election of 1868; Gladstone became head of a Liberal ministry. In a few years, however, the Irish question and the contention that the Liberals neglected British foreign interests led to the political fall of Gladstone and Disraeli's return to power.

The Irish question cast a dark shadow upon Britain's golden age. For centuries Irishmen had been oppressed and *The Irish Question* their motherland treated as a conquered country. Deprived of their lands, forced to support the Anglican church, though most of them were ardent Catholics, it is small wonder that they developed an enduring hatred toward England. Lacking unity, however, they were at first helpless to act. In 1800 the English government destroyed the last remnant of Irish independence by merging the Irish parliament with the English legislative body at Westminster.

In the nineteenth century, however, the Irish were able to make some headway against English control. A remarkable leader, Daniel O'Connell (1775–1847), led in a movement which resulted in the passing of the famous Catholic Emancipation Act (1829). This bill gave the Catholics throughout the realm full civil rights. O'Connell, not satisfied with this concession, now urged the repeal of the humiliating Act of Union; but the English government forcibly suppressed this movement. Aroused by this oppression, the Irish formed secret societies which even went so far as to carry on private warfare against the British landlords.

By the sixties conditions had become so grave that Gladstone, as prime minister, decided that he must act to remove some of the most conspicuous evils. In 1869 he had a law passed which disestablished the Anglican church in Ireland. The peasants were thus released from the burdensome tithes which they had had to pay to a hostile religious organization. Henceforth the Catholic church was on an equal footing with the Anglican church in Ireland.

But the trouble did not cease; Gladstone was next faced by a vexatious land problem. At that time most of the land in Ireland was owned by a few landlords, *Land Reform* many of whom were very oppressive. Most of these owners were English who, as absentee landlords, had their estates managed through agents, whose only concern was in exploiting the tenants and in exacting heavy rents from them. The Irish peasants enjoyed no security on their farms, as they could be evicted at the pleasure of the owners. Another evil, overpopulation, caused the increase of rents, inasmuch as the peasants were forced to bid recklessly against each other to get the lands.

A crisis was reached with the famine of 1845, which was followed by wholesale emigration to America. Gladstone tried to save the situation by giving the Irish *The Land Act of 1870* better tenure. In the act of 1870 it was provided that a tenant could not be evicted for any reason except nonpayment of rent, and that he was to receive compensation for any permanent improvement he had made on the land. Also contained in the bill was a clause which would enable the peasants to buy land outright. To help them in this the government agreed to furnish money up to a certain amount, which the peasants could repay by small installments. The Land Act of 1870 did not bring peace to Ireland. Few peasants were able to purchase the land; landlords evaded the law, and the numerous evictions continued. Consequently the bill was a failure. Dissatisfied, the Irish demanded complete repossession of the land.

Gladstone was engaged, in 1868, not only in aiding the oppressed Irish but also in improving the general run of English life by increasing the scope of opportunity for "the common man." The exclusion *Gladstone the Reformer* of Nonconformists from academic privileges was completely abolished. A civil-service bill was passed, creating free competition for positions in almost all departments of the government. But despite these liberal reforms, or because of them, Gladstone's ministry became unpopular. Landowners resented his activities in Ireland, even though he had not tried to deprive them of their privileges, especially their monopoly of land in England. Many high churchmen and Nonconformists also opposed him because of his Education Act. Moreover, the conciliatory attitude of the government in foreign affairs was scornfully branded as tame and submissive.

While Gladstone's Liberal government was becoming unpopular Disraeli's Conservative following was gaining prestige. Expanding the imperial idea, the union of *The Revival of Imperialism* the mother country and her colonies in a closer bond, he claimed that this policy, by aiding commerce and industry and by increasing wages, would benefit both the business men and the wage-earners. In 1874 Gladstone's ministry fell, and Disraeli obtained an opportunity to carry out his ideas.

Before embarking on an imperialistic policy, however, Disraeli very cleverly won the support of the wage-earners. This he did by recognizing unions and their right to indulge in peaceful picketing. Moreover, he had laws passed arranging for better housing conditions. A law which provided for the imprisonment of an employee who broke a contract was modified so that he was liable only to a civil action for damage. In general, improved relations between factory owners and wage-earners ensued.

When Disraeli became prime minister, in 1874, he inherited an imperial policy which was, for the most part, the creation of Lord Palmerston (1784–1865), one of the *Lord Palmerston* greatest of British ministers. A hearty, genial, popular, and somewhat flippant gentleman, much at home in the drawing room, he "cared not a fig for any soul alive." Like George Canning, the British foreign minister in the early twenties, he favored individualism in international relations, so that the cause of liberty and of justice should have a chance, and England should be its champion. He realized that, as a result of the spread of liberalism and the fall of rival empires, England could expand her commerce.

The climax of Palmerston's career was reached in 1855, when he became prime minister. By participating in the Crimean War at that time England helped to check Russian operations in the Near East. In *Great Britain and the Far East* this process Palmerston did his part. Having finished with the Russians, he turned to the Far East and strengthened the British foothold in China. Between 1839 and 1842 England, by means of the Opium War, had forced China to open five ports to trade, and to cede to her the port of Hong Kong. Under Palmerston's direction Britain again came to blows with the Celestial Empire in 1856. During the period 1840–1862 France, Russia, the United States, and Great Britain virtually opened China to peaceful trade and missionary work. The way was prepared for international rivalries over control of the Far East, with Russia and England at first playing the leading rôles.

In 1857 came the Indian mutiny. Stories about the corruption in the British East India Company and its cruelties in India again rose to the surface. Influenced by the situation in India and also by the Russian threat in the Far East, Palmerston introduced a bill to end the East India Company's political dominion and to establish a secretary of state for India, assisted by a council. The plan was finally worked out by Disraeli in 1858.

This imaginative statesman, always fascinated by the East, became more so when he heard about French attempts to create a short highway to the Orient by linking the Mediterranean and Red seas with a *Disraeli and the Suez Canal* canal (later known as the Suez Canal). First efforts in this direction had been made during Palmerston's ministry. Ferdinand de Lesseps, a French engineer, in 1854 secured an agreement with the Khedive of Egypt giving the former the right to organize a company (the Universal Company of the Maritime Canal) to construct a canal. The English, fearing French control of the proposed waterway, opposed it from the first. Palmerston, although pooh-poohing the plan for a canal, succeeded in causing the Sultan to delay granting his sanction to the concession.

Successfully overcoming almost insurmountable obstacles, in the form of financial embarrassments, engineering problems, and unfriendly gestures by the British, De Lesseps completed the canal in 1869 amid the hurrahs of thousands of Frenchmen, who rejoiced that a French dream had come true and that British egotism had been deflated. Disraeli, having doubted the practicability of the project, viewed its successful construction under French leadership as a challenge to Britain's privileged position in the Orient. Soon the greater part of the tonnage passing through the Suez Canal, a direct water highway to India, was British. In 1875, one year after reassuming his position as premier, Disraeli, an opportunist *par excellence*, seized upon a fortunate circumstance, the financial straits of the Khedive of Egypt, to buy up 176,602 out of a total of 400,000 shares in the company operating the Suez Canal. "It is just settled," wrote Disraeli to Victoria in triumph. "You have it, Madam"... "Four millions sterling! and almost immediately. There was only one firm that could do it — Rothschilds. They behaved admirably; advanced the money at a low rate, and the entire interest of the Khedive is now yours, Madam." The English people, except the "petty" Liberals, applauded Disraeli's brilliant stroke. England was now joint owner with France of the Canal; French predominance in Egypt was checked, and the way was prepared for future British aggressions in Egypt.

Disraeli still had his eyes turned toward the east when, as a result of Russian designs in the Balkans and "cruel massacres" of the Christians, a war broke out between the Russians and the Turks (1877). Fearing Russian imperialism in the Near and Far East, he was willing to back the Moslem Turks against the Christian Russians. But his good will did not help the Turkish government, whose armies were easily crushed. Turkey was forced to sign the humiliating Treaty of San Stefano (1878), by which Russia's predominance in the Balkans was definitely established. Consequently Disraeli gladly accepted Bismarck's invitation to the Congress of Berlin (1878), which was really called for the purpose of revising the treaty of San Stefano

Disraeli and the Congress of Berlin

so as to deprive Russia of her newly won influence in the strategically located Balkan Peninsula.

The settlement of the Berlin conference, which will be discussed later,[1] was as complete a victory for the British as it was a defeat for the Russians. A *status quo* favorable to Anglo-Austrian interests was reëstablished. Disraeli, who had attended the Congress, returned to England in very good spirits, satisfied that he had done a difficult job unusually well. He was warmly welcomed by Queen Victoria, the dictatress of Europe, as Disraeli called her. Partially as a result of this diplomatic triumph England was enabled to maintain her Eastern holdings intact, and at the end of the nineteenth century could still boast of the world's greatest empire.

The rise of the middle classes and the revival of imperialism during the mid-Victorian period was accompanied by a remarkable economic (as well as intellectual) *Material Advances* development. Motherland of the Technological and Industrial Revolutions, England truly became the industrial center of the world, leading all rival nations not only in the textile industries but also in almost all others. This increase in production was reflected in an expansion of commerce; the total value of British imports and exports rose from £89,000,000 in 1826 to £879,000,000 in 1900. For the larger and more modern merchant marine necessary for this commerce she built steamships which enabled her to carry over half the world's tonnage of shipping. At the same time she employed the steam engine in mines and on a great network of railways.

Bourgeois inventions kept pace with general material progress. The discovery of magneto-electricity in 1831 by an Englishman, Michael Faraday, made possible *Science and Inventions* the valuable invention and perfection of such everyday conveniences as the electric light, the telegraph, and the telephone. Americans were responsible for all these inventions, Edison for the incandescent light, Morse for the telegraph, and Bell for the telephone. These and many other inventions made the Victorian period an age of convenience.

[1] See pages 252–254.

· Thus, while Germans, Frenchmen, Italians, and Americans were trying to create unified states and democratic governments, Englishmen were developing world markets and acquiring wealth. Consequently, when, between 1870 and 1914, Germany, France, Italy, and the United States, having solved their internal problems, were ready and anxious to become commercial, industrial, and imperialist competitors, England was in a position to offer effective opposition.

During the mid-Victorian period the emphasis upon earthly things helped to make possible an extraordinary development of science. Discoveries in preventive medicine and antiseptic surgery, resulting largely from a study into the causes of infectious diseases, brought the most startling advances in the field of medicine. Largely through the scientific study of medicine in the nineteenth century, scientists extended greatly the knowledge of the causes of diseases. The perfection of certain inventions also aided in the development of medical science. The stethoscope, a French discovery, was adopted in 1819 and enabled physicians to diagnose pulmonary conditions. The clinical thermometer, an English device, allowed doctors to analyze the physical condition of patients with greater accuracy than had been possible before.

The growth of medical science during the Victorian period coincided with a deeper interest in human anatomy and a study of physiology. But these developments were somewhat overshadowed by the work of a Frenchman, Louis Pasteur (1822–1895), who laid the foundation for the great science of bacteriology. By means of his intensive study, in 1855, of the changes brought about by fermentation he discovered bacteria, which are found in earth, water, and air. He concluded that disease is caused by the activities of bacteria introduced into the body. Koch (1843–1910), a German country doctor, announced that bacteria could be grown successfully outside the body. Out of these brilliant researches arose the important science of bacteriology, which has helped to check the spread of many dangerous and infectious diseases by introducing the use of antitoxins and serums.

Much work was done before 1876 in the fields of chemistry,

physics, and geology. During the nineteenth century a new science, organic chemistry, came into existence. Through the development of the atomic theory great headway was made in discovering the composition of matter. In the realm of physics "the most productive of the experimental investigations of the period" were made in the fields of spectrum analysis, electricity, and magnetism. As a result of these researches, scientists not only learned something about the composition of the sun, but were enabled to invent the electric dynamo and other electrical devices. Frankland's researches in the interest of a safe and satisfactory water supply and Sir Charles Lyell's contributions as found in his work *Principles of Geology* indicate the amazing expansion of scientific knowledge during the Victorian Age. The geological research of Lyell (1797–1875) presaged an even more important contribution. When he showed that the present form and appearance of the earth were caused not by a series of catastrophes but rather by the steady and constant operation of geological forces, he really promoted an idea which was applied in the domain of biological science — the theory of evolution.

This theory was not placed upon a scientific basis, however, until the work of Charles Darwin (1809–1882). As a young graduate of Cambridge he sailed on a surveying expedition into southern waters for a five-year cruise. Studying a wide variety of life, he accumulated a vast amount of material for his great work *The Origin of Species*, which he began in 1842 and published in 1859. His treatise proved one of the most important scientific pronouncements of the nineteenth century, not so much because of its conclusions, which were momentous enough, but because it discarded the traditional form of reasoning (deductive analysis, which inferred from the general to the specific) for the more scientific inductive logic (which went from a base of manifold details to an apex of generalization).

Through this process of drawing conclusions from a cumulation of detail Darwin expounded the general theory of evolution, which under his treatment became practically an

The Theory of Evolution

established fact. He argued, first, that the great kingdom of life is governed by unchanging laws, laws that have always been and always will be in operation; secondly, that life has within itself the possibility of constant development from lower to higher, from simple to complex forms, and that through the operation of this power there has developed an almost infinite variety of forms and species, many of which have long been extinct. Thus Darwin was led to his third great conclusion: that nature has selected those species for survival which are best adapted to their environment, or those which have been best able to maintain themselves in the struggle for existence.

These three simple propositions, of unchanging law, orderly development, and selection based on fitness and adaptability, resulted in a complete revolution in scientific theory. Ancient beliefs were abandoned, and the inner structure of every science, including the social sciences, had to be built up on a new foundation. Theology especially felt the shock, for acceptance of the idea of evolution as applied to man seemed to shake the entire account of creation and the fall of man in the Garden of Eden.

In defense of the Darwinian theory there arose many writers, of whom the most able were Thomas Henry Huxley (1825–1895) and Herbert Spencer (1820–1903). Huxley, as a physician on one of His Majesty's ships, was able, like Darwin, to make close observations of marine life; he did much to popularize the theory of evolution through his insistence "that more inductive reasoning was necessary in order to get rid of the large amount of rubbish found in every field of science." Spencer, accepting Darwin's theory, emphasized the process of natural selection and used the striking term "the survival of the fittest." Determined to apply the evolutionary theory to all great fields of life and existence, he published a series of books, which were used by many philosophers and statesmen, to explain not only the struggle for existence but also the conflict of nations and the rise of the superstate.

The middle classes welcomed the evolutionary doctrine.

They began to use it as a justification of the bourgeois theory of *laissez faire*. The principle of free competition, in which the strong rose to the top and the weak fell by the wayside, would result in the rise of self-made men. By their growth they in turn would contribute to the prosperity of the nation and the welfare of all. This belief, in the opinion of many of the bourgeoisie, tallied with the Darwinian concept of the survival of the fittest through natural selection.

Before the exposition of the Darwinian theory Jeremy Bentham (1748–1832) had regarded society in another light. Bentham was keenly concerned with the inequalities of English law. In his *Principles of Morals and Legislation* (1789) he asserted that existing institutions should be judged not for their antiquity but for their utility in promoting "the greatest happiness of the greatest number." Since each individual was actuated by selfish motives, and since the welfare of the majority was the objective, the dominance of the latter was necessary. He believed, therefore, that political democracy was justifiable and desirable.

The emphasis that Darwin and his followers put on orderly progress as the law of life and growth has exerted a profound influence on the study and writing of history. During the first half of the nineteenth century *The Writing of History* English history, for example, was written by such men as Lingard, Macaulay, and Froude. Excellent writers, they approached their subject armed with strong and active prejudices, and so they sometimes interpreted the evidence of contemporary documents in the light of their own political or philosophical opinions. Thus, while these men wrote interesting history in the form of literature, they did not always tell the truth. With the coming of Buckle's and Darwin's books a new school of historical writing appeared, represented by such historians as Stubbs, Green, Freeman, Lecky, and Gardiner. They tried to treat history as a unified development, continuous and orderly, every fragment of which was related to the whole. These English scholars came under the influence of the new German school, which insisted on a detailed study of all the activities of man.

In literature the Victorian period was comparable to the golden age of Elizabeth. It was characterized by abundant good humor and by a moral beauty less *A Golden Age of Literature* harsh than that of the Puritan age and more elevated, if less subtle, than our own. "It was made spacious by the consciousness of scientific discovery, in this sharing a general European movement; and vigorous by a sense of national achievement, also international, although Great Britain and America led in the expression of confident energy, with their Walt Whitman, their Mark Twain, their Thackeray, and their Browning." The renewed sense of personality which entered literature again with Charles Dickens, George Eliot, and George Meredith was another vital trait. Character, indeed, as our fathers used the term, was the quality their writings most eminently possessed.

By the beginning of Queen Victoria's reign Coleridge, Southey, Scott, and Wordsworth had already written their best works, and Shelley, Keats, and Byron, in the sphere of poetry, had made their important contributions. A cloudburst of good literature, however, inundated the British public during the Victorian epoch: Carlyle (1795–1881), the historian and essayist; Tennyson (1809–1892), the poet and ardent patriot; Dickens (1812–1870), whose novels reflect the humor and pathos of everyday life; Disraeli, in his political novels; Elizabeth (1806–1861) and Robert (1812–1889) Browning, in their poems; Thackeray (1811–1863), the novelist and satirist; Ruskin (1819–1900), the inspired critic of art and life; Macaulay (1800–1859), the historian; and Arnold (1822–1888), Pater (1839–1894), and Stevenson (1850–1894), the masters of English prose,— all contributed to the richness of Victorian literature.

The social problems of the day aroused the keen interest of writers. Influenced by the inequalities arising out of the Industrial Revolution, these authors in splendid literary productions demanded a political and social readjustment which would benefit mankind. "For then, laugh not, but listen to this strange tale of mine," wrote William Morris, "all folk that are in England shall be better lodged than swine." Before this age Byron and Shelley, as convinced reformers, argued for Catholic emancipation and for individual freedom. Byron lost his life in trying to help the Greeks in their war for freedom. Even Tennyson, who loved to write of ancient lords and ladies, as well as of England and the empire, had liberal sentiments, believing that the changing world was moving forward to a better and finer day. Mrs. Browning, in her passionate poem *The Cry of the Children,* did much to bring about factory reform. The most effective writer on social conditions, however, was Charles Dickens. In his novels dealing with the lowly in English life he described the horrors of the workhouses, the ludicrous methods of English schools, the endless delays of the courts, and the hapless existence of the unfortunates sent to prison for debts. His *Oliver Twist* attacked the old Poor Laws because they created Bastiles instead of homes for the poor. His novels as a whole became the Bible of contemporary social reformers.

Most of these Victorian writers were not opposed to the Technological and Industrial Revolutions which caused these inequalities. They accepted them as a necessary phase in the economic development of the nation. Their protest was not against these revolutionary changes themselves but against the failure of society to deal properly and adequately with the new conditions. Certain literary artists, however, could see no good in the Industrial Revolution. Carlyle viewed it as a monstrous thing, wholly and hopelessly materialistic, the progress of which was crushing the spiritual instincts of the English people. Ruskin, the great devotee of art, hated it because he was convinced that it alone was responsible for most of the ugliness in English life. He attacked the industrial developments of the age by demanding a "moral code" in commerce as opposed to the "ruthless competition theory of the Manchester School."

One writer in particular opposed the reigning Victorian smugness: Algernon Charles Swinburne (1837–1909), in his poems and ballads, was rebelliously unorthodox. He enjoyed shocking Victorian respectability by emphasizing pagan sensualism. He was a prolific writer, recognized as a superlative stylist, and some of his poems are miracles of beauty. Many, however, are commonplace.

One of the most significant developments of the Victorian period was the so-called Oxford Movement, which took place in the Church of England. The leaders of this *The Oxford Movement* movement came to the conclusion that the church, originating in apostolic times, was not a child of the Protestant Revolt. This belief was reflected in a number of Oxford Tracts, published between 1833 and 1841. In Number Ninety, the last one, Newman, an Episcopal clergyman, argued that the distance from Oxford to Rome was not as great as was generally believed. This aroused a great sensation in England, and Newman and some of his followers, forced to recant or leave the church, selected the latter course and became Roman Catholics.

Various Protestant sects in England, such as the Congregationalists, Presbyterians, Baptists, and Quakers, tended to come closer together and to become more democratic in their church government. Methodism led in this democratic movement, which resulted in lay participation in church control. Out of the Methodist church also appeared the Salvation Army, founded by William Booth, an unattached Methodist preacher. Beginning his work in 1865 by preaching in the slums, he established an organization which spread throughout the East and the West, ministering to the needs of the "down and out."

During the mid-Victorian period the middle classes enjoyed the first sweet fruits of triumph in England. All phases of life were influenced by their ideas. Schol-*Conclusion* ars, philosophers, poets, historians, economists, inventors, and innovators in the various branches of human endeavor expanded under the mellowing influence of doctrines of moderation and compromise, of individualism and egoism, and used their talents to develop and defend this system. Political liberty and equality, universal suffrage, and free education were the high achievements of that age.

By 1914, however, the British government was used by the middle classes to advance their own interests. This break away from individualism was reflected in two highly significant although divergent movements, the development of socialism and the revival of imperialism. Both of these will be discussed in subsequent chapters.

QUEEN VICTORIA *and* DISRAELI

After a drawing in Alan Bott's "This Was England"

CHAPTER XIV

The Near-Eastern Question: Cross Roads of Interests

THE NEAR-EASTERN question is difficult to define. Most scholars consider it to be that problem or series of problems arising out of the governmental decline and territorial disintegration of the Ottoman Empire. In their opinion it was more than the normal problems created by the gradual recession of Turkish power. Rather it was a combination of local and international issues vital to the welfare of certain peoples in Europe, Asia, and Africa.

In 1815 the Ottoman Empire contained a heterogeneous collection of peoples of diverse languages and religions, all strongly attached to their own national ideals and customs. Asiatic Turkey was inhabited chiefly by Moslems (Turks, Arabs, and Kurds) and also by Christians (Armenians and Greeks) and by Jews. In European Turkey, however, the Ottomans constituted but a small part of the population, the majority of the people being Slavic by birth and Christian by faith. These Slavs were split into several national groups.

Nationalities in the Ottoman Empire

With an area of nearly 200,000 square miles, the Balkans were inhabited by several important nationalities, among which the Moslem and Greek Orthodox faiths were dominant. Geographical decentralization and the absence of unifying forces, such as natural barriers separating the Balkans from Europe and from Asia, tended to hinder the development of a single nationality. By facilitating the entrance of alien peoples two of the broad diverging lines of communication which ran across the Balkans, one north toward Russia and the other northwest into central Europe, made national unification difficult.

Although the divers nationalities insisted that their ancestors were ancient peoples, in reality they were for the most

240

part descendants of Slavic tribes who had coalesced with the original inhabitants. The Greeks were probably the most Western in customs and ideas of all the Balkan peoples. Although possessing economic ability, they often used it in corrupt business enterprises. Because of their financial experience they were favored by the Sultan, who appointed them to high offices, made them his tax collectors, and utilized them to oppress the Slavs and Rumanians.

To a limited extent nationalities corresponded to economic groups. Most Rumanians, Serbs, and Bulgarians were peasants, whereas the Ottoman Turks, their conquerors, furnished the aristocrats and the landlords. Commerce was in the hands of the Armenians, Greeks, and Jews, widely scattered peoples who predominated in the middle classes. Greeks could be found in Serbia, Albanians in Greece, Rumanians in Bulgaria. Macedonia was a nationalistic cockpit, with belligerent representatives from most of the Balkan peoples. The desire of the various groups to free their brethren in this region from Turkish rule led later to quarrels and wars. Conflicting national ambitions also frequently involved Russia and Austria, because their territories included regions inhabited by Balkan peoples.

Religious differences stimulated deep hatreds in the Balkans. Most of the inhabitants were Christians, members of the Greek church, similar to the Orthodox faith in Russia. At the head of the church was the patriarch in Constantinople, a Greek, who *Religious Antagonism in the Empire* was appointed by the Sultan. Inasmuch as the Turkish sovereign was head of the rival Moslem religion, his power over the patriarch aroused jealousies and fears among the Balkan Christians.

Turkey in the nineteenth century was an absolute monarchy. The Sultan was not only the temporal ruler but also the caliph, the religious head of the Moslem world. His simple but effective government *The Ottoman Government* consisted of a grand vizier (or prime minister), a *Sheik-ul-Islam* (a religious adviser), and provincial governors appointed by the central government. Uniform laws and a systematized administration, however, were lacking in the Ottoman Empire. Local affairs among the non-Moslems were administered by the religious heads of each unit. Governmental positions, save the most exalted, were open to all, regardless of class or nationality.

Too often has the Turk been misrepresented by hostile Christians. He has been described as a grim-faced man of yellowish and black complexion, with bright, *Characteristics of the Turks* coal-black eyes, a long beard, and a voluminous turban. Clad in undefinable attire, from which projected a hideous scimitar, he has been pictured as the most savage and selfish of human beings, with thirst quenched only by blood, and inclinations for murderous cruelty and the accumulation of wives.

Actually the Turks were a well-fashioned people who, like many Christians, possessed strong passions. Capable, on the one hand, of intense hatred, they could burn with tender and impassioned love. No less honorable and truthful than Europeans, they were hospitable to a fault. Brave, sagacious, and capable of high enthusiasms, they were extremely fond of poetry and fanatically devoted to their religion. Tolerant and in a personal way democratic, easy, indifferent, and almost liberal, they were slow to move; but, when finally roused to action, they could easily shed their inhibitions and become brutal fanatics.

The Turks had traits peculiar to many Orientals. Looking with disdain upon Western civilization and relying upon the Koran for enlightenment, they were for the most part fatalists. Illustrative of their attitude is a commentary written by an early Turkish scribe:

It matters not that the shelter which we call our house is bare, rickety, or in disrepair, for we are naturally dwellers in booths or tents. It matters not that our towns are filthy and unwholesome; that disease and death stalk abroad — the hour will strike when fate ordains, as it would anyway. It matters not that there is plenty today and want tomorrow. Such are the vicissitudes of life. If it rains we are wet, that is all; but if the sun shines, let us enjoy it! When the battle is raging, let us fight too — for Allah wills!

The Turk was not especially interested in the art of government, preferring to enjoy life. In his opinion government existed merely to exact tribute and to obtain the obedience of its subjects. He did not try to devise a scientific system of taxation; instead he permitted corrupt tax officials, mostly middle-class Greeks, to raise more than the traffic would bear, to keep much of what they obtained, and often to use force if the money was not forthcoming. In the nineteenth century the corruption of the Turkish government from the Sultan on down to the local officials was notorious. The history of Ottoman rule in Europe, therefore, was a story of despotism, incompetence, and corruption.

Corruption in the Ottoman Empire

Futile attempts were made to remedy this situation. Mahmud II (1808–1839) tried to reform his administration and to introduce Western customs and institutions, but his efforts were rendered futile by the selfishness and conservatism of the upper classes. Ruling as privileged conquerors, collecting tribute, and refusing to assimilate the peoples they governed, the Turkish autocracy was a cancer which by the opening of the nineteenth century the Balkan nationalities were determined to eradicate.

In 1821 the Greeks rebelled. Desirous of reviving the glorious Greece of ancient times, they fought a long and bitter war against Turkey. The struggle finally ended in 1829, and Greece was later organized as a kingdom with a Bavarian prince, Otto (1832–1862), as "King of the Hellenes." Inasmuch as the new state did not contain all the territory inhabited by Greek-speaking peoples and lacked a stable government, the way was paved for future wars. King Otto proved too much of an autocrat for the so-called liberal Greeks. In 1843 revolutionary insurgents, perhaps with British connivance, forced him to grant a constitution creating a national assembly with an elective chamber and a senate. He did so and managed to retain his throne until 1862, when another military uprising upset him. England again took an interest in the Greeks; and the latter, to gain favor with the British government and to acquire the

The Greek Revolution

Ionian Islands, elected as king Prince Alfred, son of Queen Victoria. He declined the doubtful honor, and then for three months the Greek crown was handed about among the minor princes of European powers until Greece agreed upon Prince George, second son of the heir of the Danish throne. He consented to make the venture as "George I, king of the Hellenes" and ruled until 1913.

The Serbians also engaged in a revolution. Recalling the halcyon days of the fourteenth century, when a powerful and large Serbian state existed, they rose in 1804 *The Serbian Uprising* and, under the enthusiastic leadership of Kara George, a swineherd, expelled the Turks. This revolt subsided in 1813, but the Serbians rebelled again in 1815 under Miloš Obrenović, an energetic fellow who in 1817 instigated the murder of Kara George. He intended to acquire autonomy for Serbia. After long negotiations, aided by strong Russian support, he practically achieved this ambition in 1830, when the Sultan by a decree bestowed upon him the title of "Hereditary Prince" of the Serbians. Thus, after many years of wars and negotiations, Serbia became a principality, tributary to the Sultan but actually self-governing, with a princely house ruling by right of heredity — the house of Obrenović.

But the Serbs were dissatisfied. Peasants were oppressed by landlords, and the country was full of bandits. Two factions, one following the Obrenović family and the other the descendants of Kara George, supported by Austria and Russia respectively, fought for control of the country. By 1867 Serbia was recognized as a semi-independent monarchy, and two years later a constitution was adopted which created a parliament. The Serbians, however, were still not contented, even after their independence was recognized by the powers assembled at the Congress of Berlin (1878). Until they could rescue their brothers in Austria and Turkey, and until they could secure an outlet to the sea, real contentment seemed impossible.

The Rumanians living in the two provinces of Wallachia and Moldavia were affected by the national enthusiasm

which swept the Balkans. They consisted mostly of unenlightened *boyars* (nobles) and of a poor and ignorant peasantry.
Centuries before, the Turks had used the *boyars*
as their agents in the land of the Rumanians,   *Rumanian Unrest*
but when these nobles aided Russia, in 1711, in a war against
the Turks, the latter appointed Greek administrators. This
shift of policy created an unfortunate situation, for these particular Greeks were as unpopular as they were dishonest.
After the Russian invasion, terminated in 1834, the Sultan
tolerated native officials again in order to prevent trouble in
these provinces; but it was too late. Under the leadership of
the sons of rich *boyars*, who had been educated in Western universities, especially in France, a small edition of the revolution
of 1848 took place. Fired by French ideals and their Latin
heritage, these young men stirred up so much trouble that
Russia and Turkey coöperated for once in the congenial task
of suppressing liberalism. But the Rumanians could not be
checked. By 1859–1862 the two principalities of Wallachia
and Moldavia were united under the leadership of the Molda-
vian *boyar* Cuza, who became Alexander I, Prince of Rumania. Thus, after centuries of oblivion the Rumanians, the
self-styled bearers of the old Latin tradition, believed that
they had created another Roman state.

Prince Cuza was not permitted to remain in office long.
Trying to break up the large estates and to help the peasants,
he was overthrown by the *boyars* in 1866, and Charles of
Hohenzollern, a Prussian prince and a cousin of Louis Napoleon, was invited to become prince of Rumania. Despite
Austrian opposition and Bismarck's insinuation that the
position would be merely "a piquant adventure," Charles
descended the Danube in a steamer, disguised as a second-
class passenger, and quietly entered his new dominions.
Becoming Charles I, he proved himself a clear-headed and
moderate ruler. A constitution was established, and by 1875
Rumania was one of the most prosperous of the new Balkan
states.

Influenced also by national sentiments were the Bulgarians.
Recalling the fact that in the Middle Ages they had been a

great and independent people, they finally resolved to be free. Inasmuch as Bulgaria was close to Constantinople, the peasants were at the mercy of Turkish officials as well as of Bulgarian landlords, and the Greek church was under the control of the corrupt patriarch. In 1856, however, the Bulgarians forced the Sultan to permit the official use of their language. In 1870 they secured for themselves a national church and freedom from the patriarch. Despite these concessions the Bulgars, desiring complete liberty, decided to revolt. In the uprising which followed, the Sultan acted so ruthlessly that Russia intervened, and a war ensued between Russia and Turkey, in which Bulgarian independence, as will be shown, became a matter of international concern.

The Bulgarian Revolt

The revolts against the Sultan's authority were not limited to the Balkans. In 1832 Mehemet Ali, the governor of Egypt, desirous of becoming an independent ruler and of establishing a rival Moslem empire, invaded Asia Minor and conquered Syria. Thereupon the Czar supported Turkey, in return for a treaty of Unkiar Skelessi with Turkey which gave Russia the right to station warships in the Straits— a privilege denied other nations.

Mehemet Ali

England and France opposed this Russo-Turkish combination. Finally, when the French, interested in Egypt, decided to back Mehemet Ali against the Sultan, a European war seemed imminent. In 1840 the Sultan determined to reconquer Syria; whereupon France threatened to aid the rebellious governor. England, jealous of French activities, reverted to her traditional policy of maintaining the *status quo* in the Near East and pledged her support to Turkey. Russia, Austria, and Prussia also joined England in sustaining the Sultan, even if, said the energetic Lord Palmerston, they had to chuck Mehemet Ali into the Nile. Rather than risk a war France, under the nervous Louis Philippe, gave way, and Mehemet Ali was forced to surrender his conquests. But he remained hereditary governor of Egypt, a territory which really became independent, although it was technically a fief of the Sultan. In return for this support England, Austria, and Prussia persuaded the Turkish government, in 1841, to disregard the agreement with Russia and to sign a Straits Convention with the European powers which closed the waterways to all foreign warships. This was a direct slap at Russia, who, despite her support of Turkey, was again thwarted in her attempt to secure a "window on the Mediterranean."

But the Straits question was unsettled. It was true that England not only had checked French operations in Africa but also had frustrated Russia's attempt to break through the Straits. Russia, however, was not discouraged. Posing as the "big brother" of all the Slavs, she determined to consolidate her influence in the Balkans. In order to remove possible British opposition, Nicholas I of Russia suggested that Great Britain assist in the dismemberment of the "sick man of Europe." Regarding this proposal as another plan of Russia to strengthen her position in the Near East, the British government declined the invitation.

Russia and the Near East

The nature of Russian expansion accounts for the British refusal. With the Caucasus as a base Russia was in a position to menace Asia Minor and Persia. By 1858 she had expanded to the mouth of the Amur River and was ready to invade Chinese territory. As England viewed the situation, if Russia could break through the Straits the Mediterranean would be in danger of becoming a Russian lake. All roads to Asia would then belong to Russia, and the latter would be able to threaten India, the "jewel of the British Empire."

Russian Expansion

Inspired by this brand of "manifest destiny," Nicholas I decided to disregard British opposition and enhance Russian influence in the Near East. A mighty fortress and naval port was constructed on the Crimean peninsula at Sebastopol, and a Russian fleet was ready to participate in the push toward the Mediterranean.

The Crimean War was the result. An immediate excuse for this conflict arose out of a quarrel between the Roman Catholic and the Greek Orthodox monks over the control of certain shrines. Championing the Greek monks, Russia ordered the Sultan to grant her a protectorate over the Greek Christians in Turkey. The Sultan refused, asserting that this *The Crimean War* would give Russia the right to interfere in Turkey's internal affairs. Thereupon the Czar's armies, in 1853, invaded the Turkish provinces of Moldavia and Wallachia.

England, France, and Sardinia joined Turkey in the war on Russia, while Austria decided upon a policy of friendly neutrality toward the allies. Convinced that Austria would support Russia in return for the aid he had given her in suppressing the Magyar revolt in 1849, Czar Nicholas was shocked when Austria failed "to return this favor." Despite powerful opposition the Russian armies fought bravely in the Crimea. Heavy losses and the unsatisfactory support of the corrupt government, however, weakened the resisting power of the troops, and after a stubborn defense the strongly fortified city of Sebastopol capitulated. Russia then decided that further opposition was useless, and the war came to an end.

The peace settlement was arranged at the Congress of Paris (1856). Attended by representatives of all powers interested in the Near Eastern Question, it was dominated by very practical statesmen. Nevertheless the allies, inspired apparently by humanitarian motives, formulated the famous Declaration of Paris, in which, by defining the rights of neutrals in time of war, they tried to regulate conflicts.

The Treaty of Paris, however, was designed primarily to maintain the *status quo* in the Near East. Russia was forced to destroy her naval shipyards on the Crimean Peninsula, and the Black Sea was neutralized. To minimize the possibility of future wars in the Balkans, the Danube River was declared free to the navigation of all nations, and a commission was to be appointed representing the states bordering upon its shores, to regulate its traffic. Finally Turkey was asked to give Wallachia and Moldavia local autonomy.

Thus ended "one of the most useless wars in history." Russian ambitions in the Near East had been merely checked, while the continued presence of the Turks remained a matter of international concern. A member of the European family of nations, having been invited to attend the Congress of Paris, Turkey emerged from the conflict with increased prestige. Nevertheless she refused to mend her ways; the Sultan made liberal promises, but at the same time he continued to oppress the Christians in his empire.

From 1856 to 1876 English and French interests expanded in the Near East. France obtained the right to safeguard the interests of Roman Catholics in Turkey, while Russia could merely claim the vague privilege *Anglo-French Interests in the Near East* of affording protection for members of the Greek church. Both England and France made loans to the Turkish government. In theory an independent state, actually Turkey was degenerating into a protectorate of Europe, under the special care of England and France.

For many years the European nations had enjoyed the benefits of special treaties, called capitulations. By these arrangements with the Sultan's government their citizens were exempted from the jurisdiction of the Turkish courts, whose laws were based upon the Koran, and were placed under the control of the consular courts of their own state. They were also excused from paying most of the taxes, and their business enterprises were given special concessions and were not subject to Turkish laws. Furthermore, tariff duties were fixed by special treaties. Taking advantage of these arrangements, France and England proposed to bring Turkey under their indirect supervision in order to maintain the *status quo*, to keep out the Russians, and to control commerce with the Ottoman Empire.

The rapid rapprochement which soon followed between France and Russia worried the English. Originating about the time of the Congress of Paris (1856), it was crowned in 1859 by a political agreement of mutual assistance for securing a reëxamination of the treaties of 1815 and 1856. In 1862 Prince Gorchakov of Russia referred to the existence of an "alliance" between France and Russia.

England determined to shatter this friendship. When another revolution occurred in Poland (1863) she suggested joint intervention, knowing that France could not repudiate

her friends the Poles for fear of yielding her influence in
Poland to England. France, giving Poland diplomatic support
by necessity, was forced to relinquish the friendship of Russia.

In the seventies the Balkan situation again occupied the
attention of European statesmen. A crop failure in 1874
The Balkan Massacres made it impossible for the Christian peasants
to pay their taxes, and thereby increased the
persecution which the Christians suffered from the Sultan's
brutal tax collectors. Insurrections were thus precipitated
against the Sultan's government in Bosnia-Herzegovina.
Encouraged by these uprisings, the Bulgarians decided to
strike for freedom by assassinating certain Turkish officials.
In retaliation the fanatical Moslems butchered thousands of
Bulgarians.

In 1876 a new Sultan, Abdul Hamid II, ascended the throne.
Cruel and autocratic, sly and resourceful, this Oriental poten-
tate feigned reform by granting a constitution (suspended in
1878); meanwhile he sent the man responsible for the new
government to North Africa, where the latter was said to
have died conveniently "of a cup of coffee." Despite this
pretended democratization of the empire the persecution of
the Christians continued as the Sultan scoffed at the notion
of intervention by the great powers. Serbia and Montenegro,
however, had already declared war on the Sultan in the summer of 1876, and, like other Christian states in the Balkans,
were making frantic appeals for European aid.

All eyes turned toward Gladstone, head of the British
Liberal party. Demanding the abolition of the unholy alliance between Britain and Turkey, and denouncing "the un-
speakable Turk," he represented a strong public sentiment
when he intimated that it was England's duty to aid the
oppressed Christians. Disraeli, the prime minister, assumed
a less belligerent attitude, for he feared that European
intervention would upset the *status quo*. England therefore
sent a mild warning to the Turks and waited for the affair
"to blow over. "

Russia, however, decided that protests were not sufficient.
As a "Big Brother" she felt called upon to assist the Balkan

Slavs. Public sentiment, therefore, as well as desire for the Straits, led to a Russo-Turkish war in 1877. Before hostilities opened, Alexander II tried to pacify Great Britain by announcing that he did not intend *The Russo-Turkish War (1877)* to annex Constantinople. Assisted by the Rumanians, Russian armies then marched quickly into Bulgaria, where they laid siege to the great fortress of Plevna. After its surrender the Russians poured through the Balkans, captured Adrianople, and were in a position to menace Constantinople. Panic-stricken, the Sultan sued for peace.

The Treaty of San Stefano (1878) between Russia and Turkey marked a significant stage in the evolution of the Near-Eastern question. Serbia, Montenegro, and Rumania were recognized as independent *The Treaty of San Stefano* states, and a new country, Bulgaria, consisting of Bulgaria, Rumelia, and Macedonia, was established. Russia secured parts of both the Dobruja and Armenia, and a war indemnity. In Europe the Sultan retained Constantinople, Eastern Thrace, Thessaly, and Albania. Dissatisfaction, such as had followed previous Balkan agreements, now developed. Coveting parts of Bulgaria, the Greeks and Serbians opposed its unification. England and Austria, as has been mentioned before, also disapproved of this treaty whereby Russia had upset the political equilibrium, had freed many Balkan Christians, and had strengthened her position in the Near East.

Moved by a common fear of Russia's intentions, the great powers therefore refused to recognize the treaty of San Stefano. Maintaining that the Balkan situation was of European concern and that any change in the old settlement arranged at the peace congress of Paris (1856) should be considered by all powers who attended that meeting, they informed Czar Alexander II that the entire question should be submitted to an international conference to be held in Berlin in the summer of 1878. Unwilling to relinquish the fruits of victory, Alexander II at first opposed this plan. By threatening war, however, Disraeli finally forced the recalcitrant Czar to agree to a congress.

Disregarding the Treaty of San Stefano, the great states at Berlin arranged a new settlement. Little attention was paid to national rights, inasmuch as the allies were more interested in strategic frontiers and the balance of power in the Near East; England, for example, strengthened her foothold in that region by taking over the island of Cyprus. Part of the Cyprian revenues were to be given the Turkish government; in return the Sultan glibly promised Britain by a special convention to introduce necessary reforms in the Asiatic provinces. In order that Christians should be protected, military supervision of Bosnia-Herzegovina was taken from Turkey and given to Austria. Disregarding the interests of the Christians, however, the great powers split the newly formed Bulgaria into three parts: the first, Bulgaria proper, was given autonomy under the suzerainty of the Sultan; the second, Eastern Rumelia, was granted more limited autonomy; and the third, Macedonia, was returned to Turkey. The Congress recommended that Turkey give Thessaly and part of Epirus to Greece, which she did in 1881. Russia received the Rumanian strip of Bessarabia and certain Armenian districts on the Black Sea.

The Congress of Berlin (1878)

Having preserved the balance of power in the Balkans, the great states were satisfied. Before the close of the congress, however, they did consider briefly the cause of the trouble — the treatment of Christian subjects in the Balkans. To avoid criticism on that score, they inserted into the treaty a few clauses designed to promote reform in the Turkish government and to safeguard the Christians. But these measures were merely paper reforms, and the Ottoman Empire, whose territorial integrity they guaranteed, regarded them as such.

The Treaty of Berlin did not solve the Near-Eastern question. Emancipated nations were angry because they did not receive the frontiers they desired. Irredentist movements developed in Bulgaria, Serbia, Greece, and Rumania, threatening to precipitate a war at any time. Austria, now a prominent participant in Balkan affairs through her control of Bosnia-Herzegovina, aroused the enmity of her neighbor, Serbia.

Significance of the Treaty of Berlin

The Rise of the Balkan States

Despite the desire of the great powers that the Berlin settlement of 1878 be maintained, the disintegration of the Ottoman Empire continued. During the last quarter of the nineteenth century England and France engaged in a lively struggle for control of the Sultan's lands in north Africa, Egypt being the most prized. Rivals in the Far East, England and Russia also seemed ready to come to blows at any time. These antagonisms enabled Austria and her ally Germany to take advantage of the fact that the other great powers were engaged elsewhere to develop their own interests in the Near East.

By separating the two Bulgarian principalities the Congress of Berlin created another unsatisfactory situation. Grateful to *Bulgaria after the Congress* the Czar for his support at San Stefano, and resentful because of the losses sustained at Berlin, the Bulgarians permitted Russians to hold important positions in the ministry and to organize their military forces. A constitution was established, and Alexander of Battenberg, a young German prince and a relative of the Russian Czar, was made Prince of Bulgaria (1879). When the Russians, however, tended to regard Bulgaria as a vassal, friction developed. By 1883 the Russian ministers were forced to resign, and the king replaced them with Bulgarian leaders. Territorial expansion followed in 1885, when the people of Eastern Rumelia declared for union with Bulgaria, and the ruler, assuming the title "Prince of the two Bulgarias," welcomed them. Certain European powers, especially Serbia, protested this violation of the Congress of Berlin, but international rivalries prevented drastic interference by the great states.

Some Russians, determined to restore their country's prestige in Bulgaria, kidnaped the hostile Prince Alexander and carried him off to Russia. After the Russian party had been firmly established in Bulgaria, he was released. Recalled by his subjects, Alexander, evidently overcome by Russian opposition, finally abdicated in 1886.

The Bulgarian party managed to check Russian influence by submitting to the leadership of a remarkable leader named Stambolov, a strong man of extraordinary intelligence, "whose methods were not those of rosewater." Stambolov succeeded in securing a dictatorship for himself by having the young Prince Ferdinand of Saxe-Coburg elected as the new ruler. For seven years this "Balkan Bismarck" successfully opposed Russian intrigue and Turkish control. Under him Bulgaria increased in wealth, population, and military strength. In 1894 Stambolov fell from power, but his work was finished, for Russian influence was eliminated and Turkish sovereignty was merely theoretical. Two years later the election of Ferdinand as prince was formally recognized by the great powers. Finally, in 1908, the Bulgarians took advantage of a revolution in Turkey to proclaim their complete independence, and their prince then assumed the title of Czar.

By the Congress of Berlin the independence of Rumania had been recognized, on condition that all citizens, including the numerous Jews, should enjoy religious equality. In 1881 Rumania proclaimed herself a kingdom, and her prince assumed the title of *Rumania and Serbia after the Congress* king, "Charles I." Industrial and commercial development followed. The bourgeoisie now demanded that a democratic constitutional government supplant the existing one, which favored the landed classes. In 1907 a peasant movement for more land culminated in an uprising.

Her independence recognized by the Berlin Treaty, Serbia proclaimed herself a kingdom in 1882. A disastrous war with Bulgaria (1885–1886), increasing debts, financial scandals, and the personal immoralities of King Milan (1868–1889), however, tended to discredit the monarchy. Forced to abdicate, the king was succeeded by his young son Alexander, who was murdered in a palace revolution in 1903. His successor, Peter I, found his position very unstable. Nevertheless he was in power when, in 1914, the Austro-Serbian break precipitated an international crisis.

Otto I (1832–1862) was the first monarch to rule over poor, restless, and anarchic Greece. With unsatisfactory boundaries, lacking control of Thessaly (peopled almost entirely by Greeks), and devastated by *Greece* brigandage and a long, bloody war, the outlook of the Greek kingdom was not promising. German aid, unpopular though it was, did much to modernize Greece. Athens became the capital, a university was founded, a police system was organized, and a constitutional government with a bicameral legislature was established.

The desire to enlarge their boundaries and to reach what they considered their natural frontiers was the chief ambition of the Greeks. In 1862 the opposition of the great European powers and the failure of Otto I to defy them resulted in an insurrection and Otto's overthrow. His successor, the Danish prince George I, governed the kingdom to 1913. During his reign Greece received the Ionian Islands from Great Britain (1864), and, aided by British influence, obtained Thessaly from the Turkish Sultan. In 1897 Greece engaged in another war against Turkey. Defeated, she was forced to return parts of Thessaly to Turkey and to renounce her plan to annex the island of Crete. After long negotiations among the European powers Crete was made autonomous under the suzerainty of the Sultan and under the direct authority of Prince George, son of the king of Greece, who remained in control until 1906. In 1913 Crete was incorporated in the kingdom of Greece.

Certain reforms were passed during the reign of George I. In 1864 a new constitution abolished the old senate and left all power in the hands of a single assembly, the *Boule*, the members of which were elected by universal suffrage. Education and economic developments, such as the construction of railroads and canals, were supported by the government. These improvements, however, tremendously increased the national debt and greatly weakened the financial stability of the state during the ensuing period.

By the end of the nineteenth century Macedonia, ruled by the Sultan and inhabited by Serbians, Bulgarians, Greeks, and *Macedonia* Turks inextricably intermingled, was the center of uprisings, massacres, and wars. Here the old strife between Christians and Moslems threatened to cause foreign intervention. In 1908, however, an unexpected event seemed to presage a peaceful union of the various groups under Ottoman rule. In that year the Young Turks, a revolutionary party dominated by the liberal political principles of western Europe, overthrew the despotic, corrupt, and inefficient government of the Sultan, Abdul Hamid II, and planned the creation of a modern liberal constitutional régime. Representatives of all nationalities in the Turkish Empire welcomed this Oriental *coup d'état*. Insurgents and soldiers, Moslems and Christians, Greeks, Serbs, Bulgarians, Albanians, Armenians, Turks, "all joined in jubilant celebrations of the release from intolerable conditions." National and religious hatreds subsided, and Turkish domestic problems seemed at an end.

But this period of brotherly love was short-lived. Becoming ardent nationalists, the Young Turks soon inaugurated a policy of Ottomanization which was as repressive as the old absolutism. This resulted in the liberation of temporarily pent-up hatreds in Macedonia, and in serious international crises and saguinary wars.

CHAPTER XV

Pope Pius IX and the New Régime

EUROPE and the Americas in 1878 were dominantly Christian. In general, Scandinavia, the Netherlands, Germany, England, and the United States were Protestant; Spain, France, Belgium, Austria, Portugal, Italy, and Hispanic America were Roman Catholic; and Russia and most of the Balkan nationalities adhered to versions of the Greek Orthodox faith. The only important non-Christian groups in Europe were the Jews, widely scattered, and the Moslems, living in the southeastern part of that continent.

Inasmuch as the leading Western powers were Christian, Christianity exerted marked influence upon political and economic developments during the early nine-
Christianity and the Middle-Class Régime teenth century. In Protestant Europe and America, especially in England and in the United States, the disciples of Martin Luther and John Calvin were often the leaders in the industrial developments which accompanied the rise of the middle classes. Individualists by religious training, they became ardent exponents of political democracy and the doctrine of *laissez-faire*.

In the Catholic countries of western Europe, especially in France, the bourgeois classes were composed of many free-thinkers and so-called liberal Catholics, that is, Catholics who accepted many liberal ideas but refused to leave the church. Most Catholics, however, supported their religious leader, the Pope, in his frank opposition to the so-called gross materialism of the new order. Led by Pius IX, the Catholic church succeeded Metternich as the most powerful defender of the old régime in Europe. This was not surprising. Many sincere churchmen felt that the French Revolution and the spread of liberalism had illegally deprived the church of its property and temporal power. In its hostility to the new order the

Roman Catholic church had the support of numerous land-owners and peasants.

By 1878 many Catholics and Protestants believed that the materialism of the nineteenth century threatened the existence of Christianity. Although the steam engine, telegraph, and other notable inventions enabled men to create a magnificent civilization, they helped to weaken the spiritual side of life. Aroused by new scientific ideas, some men and women attacked all revealed religion, asserting that it was a ridiculous and superstitious survival of a primitive and ignorant state of society. Science alone, they believed, could reveal the truth. On the other hand, other sincere persons, defending church dogma, maintained that the disappearance of Christianity would lead to gross immoralities and to the destruction of civilization. Most people, nevertheless, willing to neglect or to oppose certain teachings of the church if their political, economic, or social interests could be bettered thereby, still clung to the faith of their fathers.

Protestants did not find it difficult to reconcile their spiritual and temporal interests. An individual's right to be the judge of his own activity rather than to subject himself to dogma enabled the Protestant laymen and churchmen to harmonize their *Protestants and the New Order* religious beliefs with the latest discovery in science or the most recent theory in politics and economics. Consequently numerous Protestants were able to place their interests as socialists, business men, republicans, or nationalists ahead of anything else on earth. Their religion placed no permanent obstacle in the way.

Many Catholics, however, found it difficult to reconcile the new political and social ideas with their religious beliefs and dogmas. Maintaining that their faith was based upon revealed truths which had been delivered by Christ to the Apostles, they op- *Catholics and the New Order* posed the creation of national churches and insisted that the Catholic organization remain a great international institution, and that the Pope must be obeyed in all final judgments on all matters involving religion and morals. Such developments

as republicanism, nationalism, and secular education were
bitterly opposed by many sincere Catholics. To them "modernism" had as its goal the overthrow of the universal Catholic
faith and the establishment of national religions controlled by
business men, more interested in acquiring wealth and enjoying life than gaining a place in the Kingdom of Heaven.

In the early nineteenth century numerous Catholics believed that political liberalism did not seriously concern the
church. Some even went so far as to assert that the church,
having suffered at the hands of certain despotic rulers in the
past, might function better in a democracy than in an absolute
monarchy. Exponents of this view were greatly encouraged
when a liberal Pope ascended the throne in 1846.

A benevolent man of fine character, Pope Pius IX favored
reforms so heartily that many called him "the middle-class

Pope Pius IX   Pope." Wise, honest, and courageous, he soon
                  began to perceive, however, that the spread
of liberalism in Italy meant the downfall of the temporal
power of the church. He believed that, should this happen,
he would no longer be an independent head of a great religion,
and would become instead the subject of the secular ruler of
Italy. Then the church might split into national units
throughout the world, and the unified institution of Christ
would no longer exist. This danger was not the only cause
for his "desertion" of liberalism. Pius IX was aware of the
tendency to emphasize material things. He lived at a time
when the revolutionary teachings of Darwin, the socialism
of Marx, and the great mechanical inventions were taken
as evidences that man was beginning to worship materialism
in place of God. Someone, he believed, must direct the movement to save the spiritual side of life. As head of the universal
church he considered it his duty to lead the faithful.

During the nineteenth century, intellectual attacks, fostered especially by men engaged in a study of the natural

Religion and Science   sciences, struck at the very foundation of
                  Christianity. From the seventeenth century
on through the nineteenth, the rise of rationalistic modes of
thought, the development of historical methodology, and the

study of natural sciences revealed certain inconsistencies, contradictions, and inaccuracies in the teachings and pretensions of the established churches, both Catholic and Protestant. A clash between the church (buttressed by authority and tradition) and modern learning (erected on a foundation of reason and scientific inquiry) seemed inevitable.

Striking discoveries, the implications of which were particularly destructive for established theologies, were made in the field of the natural sciences. Students of geology, biology, zoölogy, paleontology, and of the newer social sciences, such as psychology, archæology, history, anthropology, and comparative religion, acquired much information concerning man and the world in which he lived by adopting so-called scientific methods and by constantly observing, naming, and classifying.

Startling were the discoveries that our ancestors were on this earth many thousands of years ago and that the universe was millions of years old. These revelations tended to show that the history of man as related in the Bible (covering but a fragment of his terrestrial existence) was inadequate.

Scientists, as has been stated before, were largely responsible for the creation of the materialistic age. Unusually successful, some of them became so confident of their ability to solve all earthly problems that they promised to abolish crime and poverty, to prolong life, and even to discover its meaning. The supporters of these "scientific heroes," certain philosophers, adopted the Missourian attitude, and by their particular brand of philosophy, called pragmatism, developed the idea that "the real worth of moral and religious ideas was demonstrable only by their practical effects."

Although at first there was no definite conflict between scientists and churchmen, by the middle of the nineteenth century the way was prepared for a world-wide *Religion and Evolution* struggle between these two groups. Scientists brought forth the famous evolutionary theory, wherein was discredited the historical authenticity of the Bible, which furnished the foundation for both Catholic and Protestant Christianity. Little wonder, then, that Pius IX instituted an attack upon "new thought" as well as materialism, and gave up his liberal ideas. Inasmuch as Catholic doctrines rested on the writings of the church fathers and upon tradition, as well as upon the Bible, members of that faith, however, were not so deeply offended as were the Protestants, who based everything on the Bible. The Protestant phase of the struggle continued to the time of William Jennings Bryan (1860–1925); and although the battle died down considerably, peace was not declared on the scientific-religious front.

On the whole the scientists had the best of the argument. They built up a strong case for organic evolution, even though there were some weak spots in the theory. According to them the Biblical account of the remarkable creation of the universe in six days was demolished. But the enthusiastic partisans of science soon discovered that it would take more than an evolutionary theory to overthrow Christianity.

Inasmuch as Darwinism has been treated elsewhere in this volume,[1] it is not necessary to discuss the theory at this point. It does seem important, however, to emphasize the fact that this belief encouraged the study of all phases of human activity, — political, social, æsthetic, and religious. After the publication of Darwin's works his ideas were discussed and popularized by a number of writers. In 1860, one year after the printing of Darwin's *Origin of Species*, Herbert Spencer began his monumental *Synthetic Philosophy*, of which the last volume appeared thirty-six years later. Therein, as has been mentioned before, he tried, first, to apply the theory of evolution in practically every realm of human thought and, secondly, to bring out the idea of development and progress. When Spencer maintained, however, that behind everything there must be a power which he called the Unknowable, he caused many Christians to shudder. To them Spencer's way of looking at things tended straight toward materialism, atheism, and hell.

Ernest Renan (1832–1892), the able French student of comparative religions, struck a severe blow at orthodox theology. As a result of his textual study of the Bible and his researches in the Near East he concluded that the whole

---

[1] See pages 233–235.

fabric of Christian theology, including the Scriptures, was a compound of myths and fables borrowed from earlier religions. His monumental works on the life of Christ, *Christianity Attacked* whom he called "an incomparable man," not only shocked conservative Catholics but revealed Renan's disenchantment with traditional Christianity. As a professor of Hebrew and a clever writer, Renan became the leader of a group which, seeking "an ideal superior to the ideal of yesterday," was no longer content to be indifferent toward Christianity. Skepticism became an aggressive force, winning thousands of adherents and greatly weakening the Christian church.

Another shock came when a devout follower of the new science, Thomas Huxley, deliberately attacked Christianity. In his *Man's Place in Nature*, published in 1863, wherein he depicted man as a transitional type in the evolution from lower to higher forms, Huxley professed devotion to a modified version of Darwinism. A thoroughgoing materialist, he maintained that cosmic processes bore no relationship to moral ends, holding that the latter were human and not divine in origin. Criticizing the bases of revealed religion, he maintained that he could find no evidence of the existence of God. He therefore repudiated Christianity, declaring that "the exact nature of the teachings and the convictions of Jesus is extremely uncertain."

Many devout persons blamed the new order for these attacks (probably because most of the followers of the scientists, particularly Darwin, were middle-class men, — professors, lawyers, doctors, students, and business men). For example, Gladstone decried the progress of free thought, declaring, "Upon the grounds of what is called evolution God is relieved of the labour of creation, and in the name of unchangeable laws is discharged from governing the world." It was natural, therefore, that Pope Pius, confronted by a wave of skepticism and by political foes, who were attacking the church by threatening to deprive him of the last vestiges of temporal as well as spiritual authority, should have taken a determined stand against the bourgeois program. He believed that only through conservatism in politics could he retain temporal power, — necessary in order that he remain head of an international religion. Skepticism he opposed by asserting that Catholic Christianity was a revealed faith and that through its teaching the phenomena of human life could be adequately explained.

Papal hostility to modernism culminated, in 1864, in the issuance of *Quanta Cura*. In this pronouncement Pius re-

Reactionary Catholicism pudiated many burgeois ideals and reasserted the authority of church over state in matters of faith and morals. Accompanying the encyclical was the famous *Syllabus of Errors*, a collection of eighty propositions dealing with religious and political beliefs which the Pope denounced. Such practices and ideas as Bible societies, religious freedom, secular education, lay control of the church, civil marriages, agnosticism, and free thinking were condemned. To remove any doubt as to his attitude, Pius declared that "the Roman pontiff neither can be nor ought to be reconciled with progress, liberalism, and modern civilization."

Until his death in 1878 Pius IX was the outstanding opponent of the new régime in Western Christendom. Fearful of the dislocative effects of such modern tendencies as democracy, nationalism, and even liberal Catholicism, he endeavored to strengthen the ramparts of the church. Concordats were signed by the Pope in 1851 with Spain and in 1855 with Austria. These devices, besides restoring ancient privileges to the church, raised its prestige among peoples which, although dominantly Catholic, were being influenced by revolutionary ideals. Roman hierarchies were reëstablished in England and the Netherlands, — both strongholds of Protestantism. Loyal clergymen assisted the Pope in his crusade against indifference and laxity by emphasizing spiritual conformity and moral fervor.

The attitude of the Pope toward the new order created considerable consternation among many liberals. Moderates

Criticisms of Pius within the Catholic church feared not only that he was trying to revive spiritual power but that he was aiming at the reëstablishment of the temporal power which the papacy had enjoyed during medieval times.

Numerous Protestants maintained that, far from attacking merely the abuses of liberalism, particularly revolution, he was threatening the very existence of Protestantism. Some enthusiastic nationalists decided that the Pope was about to oppose their plans to unify Germany and Italy and their desires to establish political democracies in France and Spain. Thenceforth his followers were called clericals by their enemies, and were considered by many influential members of the bourgeoisie and their allies, the workingmen, as obstacles to progress. To liberals and radicals the supranational church, with its absolutist and feudal principles, was an anachronism.

Pope Pius was not frightened by these criticisms. Determined to strengthen papal authority and to settle the questions raised by liberalism, he called a gen- *Papal Infallibility* eral council at the Vatican. Meeting in 1869–1870, this assemblage of nearly eight hundred churchmen ratified the dogma of papal infallibility. According to this tenet the Roman pontiff, when he speaks *ex cathedra* (that is, when, as head of the universal church, he defines a belief regarding faith or morals to be held by that body), "is possessed of that infallibility with which the divine Redeemer willed that His Church should be endowed for defining faith or morals; and that therefore such definitions of the Roman pontiff are *per se* immutable and independent of the consent of the Church." In other words, a decision of the Pope in a matter of faith or morals was final.

This doctrine, although it was merely the statement of an idea which had existed for centuries, increased the opposition to the church. Anticlericalism became more pronounced, as Protestants, agnostics, and some members of the Catholic laity denounced the concept. A number of French writers asserted that this doctrine constituted an attack not only upon the liberties of the Gallican, or French national, church, but also upon the authority of an œcumenical council. In Switzerland and southern Germany several thousand Catholics even went so far as to withdraw from the church and to found a sect called the "Old Catholics." Many liberals, alarmed at the reactionary trend of papal policy, alleged that Pius, in disregard of democratic and national tendencies, intended to overthrow the secular state and to reëstablish his universal authority as a temporal as well as a spiritual ruler.

Shortly after the Vatican Council, Rome was seized by troops of the Italian kingdom. In 1861 Cavour had tried to negotiate with the Pope a voluntary renun-

Loss of Temporal Power of Pius

ciation by Pius of his political and temporal sovereignty. Several prominent members of the College of Cardinals approved of this course. Cavour was so encouraged that in February, 1861, he wrote to a friendly cleric who was carrying on the negotiations: "I hope that before Easter you will send me an olive branch, symbol of a perpetual peace between Church and State, between the Papacy and the Italian people. If this comes to pass, the joy of the Catholic world will be greater than that which, nearly nineteen hundred years ago, greeted the entrance into Jerusalem of our Saviour." Suddenly the negotiations ended. Cavour's willing agents were banished from Rome. What had happened? All we know is that from that day Pius IX stubbornly defended his temporal power. "They dispute me this grain of sand under my feet," he exclaimed; "they will not dislodge me from it. This corner of the earth is mine; I received it from Christ; to Him alone will I render it again."

Until 1870 the presence in Rome of French soldiery, lent by Napoleon III, enabled the Pope to retain possession of the Eternal City. With the coming of war between France and the German states, however, the French garrison was withdrawn. Bereft of his chief defenders, Pius IX, with only his papal guards upon whom to rely, could offer but ineffectual resistance to the troops of the recently founded kingdom of Italy. In July, 1871, after the citizenry had voted for union with Italy, Rome was proclaimed the capital. Pius IX protested against this action, refused the sovereignty of the Leonine City, and retired to the Vatican. Rather than renounce his position as head of an international church and acknowledge the temporal supremacy of the Italian king he remained a prisoner there, refusing to step on "foreign" soil or to accept the indemnity offered in payment for the loss of Rome.

Thenceforth Pius IX encouraged the clerical movement by which Catholics throughout the world were urged to work for the restoration of the temporal power of the Pope. Little headway was made at first, because the churchmen were considered bitter enemies of such features of middle-class control as nationalism, secular education, and modern science.

Finally there appeared thinkers who tried to arrange a compromise between science and religion. As a result of their activities many Protestants managed to fit the evolutionary doctrine into their religious scheme of things. *The Religious-Scientific Compromise* They were able to rely upon their private judgment, and thus, by revising their personal opinions of the Bible in the light of this theory, still remain Christian. Moreover, they absorbed Darwinism by recognizing, with reservations, its theories as to the origins of life. Nevertheless they insisted that the church was the great force in determining morals and conduct on this earth and in preparing man for everlasting life in heaven.

The Catholic church also reached the conclusion

that Darwinism was only a hypothesis, which was being confessedly weakened in certain details; that the Darwinian theory, if true, could explain only the evolution of man's material body, not the creation and life of immortal spirits; [and] that the spiritual side of humanity still belonged to the realm of faith and religion as unquestionably as its material side belonged to the province of natural science.[1]

Another development helps one to understand the settlement of the question. This was socialism. In the opinion of many bourgeois churchmen, socialists and anarchists planned to overthrow not only the *Christianity and Socialism* bourgeois political and social order but the spiritual basis of Western culture, — Christianity. Consequently, after 1878, churchmen and middle-class leaders tended to unite. Democracy, constitutionalism, nationalism, and lay education were recognized or at least tolerated by the successors of Pope Pius IX, while many scientists and religious leaders arranged an understanding in which it was tacitly

[1] Hayes, *Political and Social History of Modern Europe*, Vol. II, p. 247.

understood that the earthly field was handed over to the scientists and the spiritual sphere was assigned to the church.

This virtual *entente* did not mean that all the issues between church and state were settled, nor that all church- *The Entente between the* men and scientists were on friendly terms. *Church and the Bour-* Nevertheless the bitter hostility which existed *geoisie* between these groups in 1878 subsided, largely because representatives of both camps were soon engaged in a struggle against common enemies, the representatives of the New Revolution, — the socialists, the anarchists, and other groups. To suppress these radicals, Catholic political organizations, called center parties, and Catholic labor unions were established in many European countries, especially in France and Germany. These organizations set themselves ardently to defend the existing order.

Despite this alliance between the church and the bourgeoisie a certain amount of antagonism continued. Many persons opposed to the Roman Catholic faith still considered the age of Pius IX as important only in so far as it marked the last stand of the citadel of conservatism, the Roman Catholic church, against the modernism of the middle-class régime. Supported by a number of scholars, especially scientists, these critics held that the church was medieval and anachronistic, its pretensions to universal supremacy and papal infallibility absurd.

On the other hand, there were those who could see in the opposition of Pius IX to certain aspects of the new order (as, for example, extreme materialism and rampant nationalism) a resistance to those forces which eventually might bring about the destruction of the new régime. "For," as an influential American cardinal said in an address in 1930, "luxury, to which wealth often leads, is the first step to decadence and degeneracy, personal and national."

Powerful elements within the Protestant and Catholic churches, including the Pope, have not yet capitulated to unrestricted bourgeois individualism. They have recognized the existence of social inequalities and have held individualism partially responsible. Influenced by this belief, they have often favored legislation designed to benefit groups and classes rather than individuals. But, on the whole, both Christian churches continued to support the established order in opposition to the radical forces that would bring about their downfall. Nevertheless they were compelled to shift continually in order to maintain their threatened positions.

Pope Pius IX

CHAPTER XVI

The New Revolution: Rise of the Proletariat

TWO bourgeois movements, the French Revolution and the Industrial Revolution, aided the liberal as well as the material advance of Western society. The new system which resulted had a greatly improved political and social order as its goal. Underlying it was an idealistic philosophy which strove for the breakdown of traditional and artificial distinctions between classes and for a readjustment of social conditions so as to give everyone a fair chance according to his natural abilities. All men, "rich man, poor man, beggar man, thief," benefited.

Liberty, as extolled by Voltaire, became a generally accepted principle of the new order. Men and women were no longer slaves to be bought and sold like horses *The Bourgeois System* or cattle. Provided they paid taxes, rendered military service, and conformed to the law, they were free. Theoretically, at least, men enjoyed civil and legal equality. Class distinctions disappeared in most nations; bankers, workers, lawyers, and thieves — all adopted citizen clothes.

Middle-class equality and freedom were also demonstrated in another way — by the extension of popular and free education. In the nineteenth century, public schools, where the three R's were taught and attempts were made to educate the younger generation for citizenship and for careers other than the church, came into existence. The right of every boy and girl to receive an education was discussed at that time. Practical exponents of "enlightenment" emphasized utilitarian subjects. This emphasis led to the downfall of the classics and the rise of modern languages and the social sciences in universities, colleges, and public schools. Youngsters were trained to make money, to enjoy life, and to maintain the existing order. With all these matters came improvement of school and college buildings, where students were taught by standardized methods.

This progress in the nineteenth century was not shared equally by all classes. Inequalities in the distribution of wealth, and society's failure to provide for the weak and the unfortunate, led to widespread misery among the lower classes. Champions, *The Persistence of Inequality* called reformers, arose to espouse the cause of these "forgotten men." Asserting that economic inequalities were still present, that the introduction of democracy was in reality merely the substitution of property for hereditary privilege, and that wage-slaves had supplanted feudal serfs, they advocated far-reaching political, social, and intellectual changes.

The Industrial Revolution and the resulting problems of low wages, unemployment, irksomeness of labor, and bad conditions of work afforded social reformers an excellent opportunity to favor short cuts to an ideal social order. Influenced by the dreams which the discoveries and inventions stimulated, they contended that by certain changes and readjustments all inequalities would be removed and an earthly millennium attained.

Since the days of Plato's *Republic* through the centuries, at frequent intervals, various plans for human betterment have been advanced. In the early modern period Sir Thomas More's *Utopia* and Tommaso Campanella's *Civitas Solis* were expositions of ideal agrarian societies. It was not until the French Revolution, however, that plans were made for a perfect industrial order. Concluding that plutocrats as well as aristocrats should be destroyed, Saint-Just, a revolutionary leader, envisioned a society in which both wealth and poverty would be eradicated. During the Directory (1795–1799) another idealist, Babeuf (1760–1797), holding that the French Revolution had benefited chiefly the bourgeoisie, organized a Society of Equals for the purpose of bringing about a compulsory equalization of wealth and the abolition of poverty. In 1797 an uprising of these radicals occurred. Babeuf was executed, and his society destroyed.

In the early nineteenth century a number of reformers introduced new panaceas. The fantastic Frenchman Saint-
Saint-Simon
Simon (1760–1825) was much admired by "parlor socialists" and apostles of science. Considered the founder of French utopianism, this wealthy idealist, although unwilling to discard the capitalistic system, proposed that the "great minds," the financiers, the industrial leaders, and the scientists, through inventions, industrial development, and scientific discoveries, should cooperate in a movement to abolish poverty. He believed that confronting the French people was a crisis, which, he wrote, "consists essentially in the change from a feudal and religious system to an industrial and scientific system. . . . France has become a huge factory and the nation a colossal workshop. The real temporal power of today is to be found in the industries, and the spiritual power in the men of science. . . . All social institutions should have as their aim the physical and moral improvement of the most numerous and poorest class." "This was a vision from the heights which," wrote a certain historian, "was far in advance of his time."

Another Frenchman, Charles Fourier (1772–1837), also devised a plan. Instead of a central government, handling the
Fourier and Owen
great business enterprises,— a difficult task,— he proposed that France should be split into small groups of families, called *phalanges* (each of which should contain eighteen hundred members), owning in common the buildings and all implements for the production of the necessities of life. The total product of their work was to be divided so as to give capital four twelfths, labor five twelfths, and talent or management three twelfths. Fourier's plan was international in scope. Visualizing a confederation of phalanges, with the capital at Constantinople, Fourier soon had followers as far west as the United States.

England had a brilliant utopian in the wealthy manufacturer Robert Owen.[1] Aroused by the evidences of poverty, he hoped to regenerate mankind by the formation of cooperative groups which should own and use for their benefit

[1] See pages 223–224.

all the necessary means of production. As manager of a large cotton mill in New Lanark, Scotland, of which he later became the chief proprietor, he paid good wages, improved factory conditions, and transformed the place into a model town. Despite the increased expenditures Owen's factory earned dividends as large as before. Many people visited his place to study at first hand this interesting experiment. Owen, however, did not confine his attention to local reforms. Converted to socialism, he dedicated his life and wealth to this cause. Writing numerous articles and books, appealing to the crowned heads of Europe, and defending his plan before the American House of Representatives, he was indirectly responsible for the establishment of several utopian colonies in the United States and England.

Like their predecessors Plato, Sir Thomas More, and others, these earnest utopianists had visions of a perfect society. Aiming at the creation of an ideal order, they failed to realize that a new state could not be imposed upon an evolutionary society. Sentimentalists and humanitarians for the most part, they suggested reforms which bore little or no relation to reality, and designed panaceas which could in no wise be imposed on human beings possessed of acquisitive instincts.

Certain radicals, often called socialists, did not agree with the method by which the utopianists planned to improve society. Many of these men favored class war- *Socialism* fare as against benevolent reform handed down by the upper groups. They urged workers to take matters into their own hands by organizing political parties and by engaging in general strikes.

Louis Blanc, as has been shown, was the first important Frenchman to favor socialist reforms. His primary object was the establishment of a republic in which the *Louis Blanc* wage-earners, by means of universal male suf- frage, should possess political control. Then the government was to confiscate the factories and to establish national workshops owned by workers. Blanc failed, however, in his attempt to carry out this scheme during the French Revolution of 1848. Nor did the agitations, about that time, of the revolutionary Chartists in England, and of the radical socialists in Berlin, lead to any definite achievements.

From the revolutionary movements of the forties, however, rose the apostle of modern scientific socialism, Karl Marx (1818–1883). During his youth Marx saw Germans trying to unify and liberalize their country, the Industrial Revolution penetrating the Rhineland, and the consequent enrichment of a few and impoverishment of many. Brought up amid the suffering of his fellow men, educated in a German university where freedom of thought, except in politics, was permitted, and conscious of the bitter criticism of the money-making abilities and so-called selfish, unscrupulous characteristics of his fellow Jews, this prophet of the workingman decided to devote his life to the task of revealing social inequalities and of emancipating "the working slaves." He soon aroused the ire of German authorities because of the radical views which he expressed. Forced into exile, he encountered oppression in Paris and in other Continental cities, and finally settled in London, where he studied and wrote until his death.

Karl Marx

As a student Marx had come under the influence of Hegel, the philosophical arbiter of Germany. Accepting Hegel's idea "that each period is characterized by the predominance of a 'world people,' who are possessed of a universal idea which must be given to mankind," Marx asserted that the cause of changes was not in the ideas of God but in material circumstances — climate, soil, inventions, the economic struggles of classes, and similar forces. Therefore, upon the fall of the bourgeoisie, the workingmen were certain to become "the world people."

Influence of Hegel

No one revealed the social and economic inequalities better than Marx. With an enormous amount of detail and logic he described the social conditions in the England of his day. As a correlator of social and economic conditions in Western society during this period Marx was perhaps unequaled. Though of prime importance as a destructive critic of society, especially in his indictment of capitalism, he nevertheless was a great constructive theorist, as evidenced in his analysis of the nature of capital and in his outline of socialism. Writing voluminously on economic history and philosophy, Marx left a strong imprint on almost all the social sciences.

His basic views on political economy were incorporated in a large and influential work, entitled *Das Kapital,* which was left unfinished at his death but was com- *The Views of Marx* pleted by his colleague, Friedrich Engels. Although sometimes called the "workingman's Bible," this book reveals in complex form the cardinal doctrines of socialism as presented by Marx and by Engels. These were more clearly expressed in their other works, especially the *Communist Manifesto.* Nevertheless, in describing the terrible social conditions brought about by the Industrial Revolution *Das Kapital* stands forth as a monumental intellectual contribution.

Marx not only revealed the inequalities of his age, but also, in developing his so-called materialistic interpretation of history, he emphasized many significant fac- *The Class Struggles* tors in human activities which had been neglected by previous historians. With Engels he wrote in the *Communist Manifesto:*

... in every historical epoch, the prevailing mode of economic production and exchange, and the social organization necessarily following from it, form the basis upon which is built up, and from which alone can be explained, the political and intellectual history of that epoch ...

Consequently they maintained:

The history of all hitherto existing society is the history of class struggles.

Freeman and slave, patrician and plebeian, lord and serf, guild-master and journeyman, in a word, oppressor and oppressed, stood in constant opposition to one another, carried on an uninterrupted, now hidden, now open fight, a fight that each time ended, either in a revolutionary re-constitution of society at large, or in the common ruin of the contending classes.

In his writings Marx also asserted that certain events would make inevitable the rise of the proletariat, who would end the hegemony of the capitalistic class by seizing control of the agencies of production and distribution, and consequently of the government. The increasing concentration of wealth under capitalism would in time place all property in the hands of a very few, and as a result the exploited classes would find it comparatively easy to overthrow the established order. The communist prophet did not favor a division of property after the overthrow of the bourgeoisie was effected; he advocated its transfer to the state, which would operate the means of production for the direct profit of the whole people. Contending that the capitalist, as a stockholder drawing dividends, was an idle drone and as useless as a feudal lord in the eighteenth century, he predicted that in time the capitalist ownership would be destroyed and the salaried clerks of great corporations would become the employees of the government.

In justifying his beliefs Marx emphasized the view that labor was the source of all value. Anyone, he asserted, who contributed to the welfare of mankind should *Labor as the Source of All Value* have his share in the total output, whether he were an engineer, farmer, street cleaner, teacher, manager, or artist; but as long as men drew dividends from money invested in machines, workers would not get what they rightfully earned. Under his scheme the state would own all the agencies of production, and private ownership would be confined to food, clothing, furniture, pictures, and books. All would enjoy the available necessities and luxuries. Oppression and poverty would be obliterated. Why should one tenth of the population live in luxury over the labor of the other nine tenths? All should be rewarded or suffer alike. True equality, real democracy, and human welfare, he said, demanded that the workers unite. They had nothing to lose save their chains, and through unity the world was theirs. The time would come when all men would work and no one would become wealthy at the expense of his neighbor. Then, when all had an opportunity to express the best that was in them, poverty would disappear and individuals would become part of a great army to emancipate themselves from hunger and disease. Thereafter Marx assumed that men would be able to live in harmony and brotherly love.

Marxian philosophy was soon trimmed to the winds. As Marx declared, a society would not rise out of the air; it had to evolve out of the prior economic and political order. Unlike the utopians who created a perfect society in their heads, irrespective of all existing conditions, he envisaged a régime which would naturally replace the capitalistic system. Inevitable as the new order was, he urged the workers to organize along class lines, so that they might be prepared to take the lead when the time was ripe for a revolution. Adherence to his ideas resulted in the formation of socialist parties throughout the world. Many thought that the millennium was at hand when the Bolsheviks established a new order based on Marxian principles in war-torn Russia.

Marx was misunderstood by many of his followers, as well as by his opponents. One of the most common misconceptions was the belief that he, from the beginning, favored violent revolution. In reality, in his early works he merely suggested widespread social reform. Predicting with unusual foresight the centralization of wealth in the hands of a few, he was sure that the overthrow of these few was inevitable.

But later Marx, as a result of his study of the Paris Commune, wrote a treatise in which he advocated the dictatorship of the proletariat. Applying his economic interpretation of history, he held that, just *Marx and the Dictatorship of the Proletariat* as the great French Revolution had destroyed the bulwark of feudalism and paved the way for the rise of the bourgeoisie, who consolidated their gains by the revolutions of 1830 and 1848 in France, so the disturbances of the Commune of Paris (1871) marked the rise of the proletariat against the new repressive bourgeois order. Marx then set forth in this study the belief that a minority, creating a strong government, had to rule during the transition from capitalism to socialism; a dictatorship of the proletariat was an essential prelude to the establishment of true socialism.

Undoubtedly one of the keenest critics of the bourgeois régime, Marx believed that ideas of all kinds were to a large extent determined by the economic interests of the people who held them; each class of persons whose interests were similar constituted within itself an intellectual cosmos with a politics, a metaphysics, and an art of its own. He came to the realization that the romanticism, the idealism, and *Marx, Critic of the Bourgeoisie* the revolt of the early nineteenth century were largely bourgeois movements; that is, the merchants, manufacturers, and financiers were fighting the last vestiges of feudalism. He also believed that the new social system, called capitalism, resulted in large-scale exploitation of the working classes. Machinery and credit had enabled the bourgeoisie to replace the feudal lords as the masters of the state.

That capitalism would eventually destroy itself was an important Marxian premise. The capitalist system was competitive: each manufacturer would always try to undersell the other. As a result there would be a constant stimulus to more efficient methods of production. But the more efficient an industry became, — the faster the machines were able to do the work and the fewer people were needed to tend them, — the more workers would be thrown out of jobs; that is, the more commodities were produced, the fewer people would be able to buy them. To sell at all under these conditions, one would have to undersell his competitors, and that would mean more efficient machinery and fewer workers and fewer people, again, able to buy what was being put out. This situation, Marx noted, produced a crisis about every ten years. The more efficiently goods were manufactured, the more money was needed for the plant and the bigger the plants would become. Thus the industries would keep growing and the companies would keep merging until each industry would become one great unified plant with a centralized control, and the money which kept them going would have to be concentrated in the hands of a few capitalists. At last the contradictions involved in this process would jam the whole system so badly that there would be nothing left to do but to take the money and the big plants away from the owners who were unable to conceive them as means to any other end than making themselves rich with the profits. A class-conscious working group would bring about this change.

Although the practicability of many of Marx's ideas has yet to be demonstrated, this great scholar, who spent a large portion of his life reading dusty volumes in the British Museum, proved the greatest inspiration the working class has ever had in its sad and turbulent history. He still remains the prophet of the laboring groups throughout the world.

Marx lived during a time in which criticism of the existing order flourished. "It is doubtful," wrote one contemporary, "whether any other period of human history has been so contemptuously treated by its poets and thinkers as our own." Especially *Critics of the Bourgeoisie* severe was the French writer Gustave Flaubert (1821–1888). He hated above all else the French bourgeoisie, to which he himself belonged, and whose meanness, timidity, and mediocrity seemed to him to have banished from the world all bravery, generosity, and distinction. Society, he declared, so far from being redeemed by the culture and the idealism which had come out of it, had actually cheapened and invalidated culture in all its branches,— politics, science, and art,— and not only these, but the ordinary human relations, love, friendship, and loyalty to cause, "till the whole civilization has become suspect." These ideas were expressed indirectly in his *Madame Bovary* and *L'Éducation Sentimentale*.

Henry Adams described the opposition to the middle classes which existed in the fifties as follows:

The literary world had revolted against the yoke of coming capitalism — its money lenders, its bank directors, and its railway magnates. Thackeray and Dickens followed Balzac in scratching and biting the unfortunate middle class with savage ill-temper, much as the middle class had scratched and bitten the Church and Court for a hundred years before. The middle class had the power, and held its coal and iron well in hand, but the satirists and idealists seized the press, and as they were agreed that the Second Empire was a disgrace to France and a danger to England, they turned to Germany because at that moment Germany was neither economical nor military, and a hundred years behind western Europe in the simplicity of its standard.[1]

[1] *The Education of Henry Adams: An Autobiography*, pp. 61–62. Houghton Mifflin Company, 1918.

George Bernard Shaw (1856–   ), the Irish playwright, was an outstanding British middle-class critic. One of the founders of the Fabian Society, he "agreed to give up the delightful ease of revolutionary heroics and take to the hard work of practical reform on ordinary parliamentary lines." He and his associates endeavored to make socialism respectable by repudiating the idea of class war and favoring instead the attainment of a new order through education and reform. Hating the hypocrisies and stupidities of the English middle classes, Shaw, although himself a member of the bourgeoisie, became a leading critic of the capitalistic system.

Another form of radicalism — anarchism — challenged the premises of capitalism. Like socialism, it was engendered by the Industrial Revolution and arose out of *Anarchism* more or less systematized theories on the part of middle-class reformers as to how poverty and its attendant ills could be exterminated. But it differed radically from socialism in that it would abolish all government.

Two men chiefly are associated with the early modern development of anarchism: the Frenchman Pierre Joseph Proudhon (1809–1865) and the Russian *Proudhon and Bakunin* Michael Bakunin (1814–1876). Proudhon's ideas were a product of the Industrial Revolution, with its accompanying evils in France, and the opposition of the proletariat to the middle-class régime of Louis Philippe. Losing faith in all government, Proudhon wrote his famous book entitled *What is Property?* in which he defined property as theft, but strangely enough did not favor public property. Every man should have an equal right to use property as his personal possession and to enjoy the full benefit of his labor. Authority in any form was anathema to him. He believed that self-determination, or self-government, was the best means for an orderly society. "No more parties," he said, "no more authority; absolute liberty of man and citizen." Like Rousseau, Proudhon also believed that man was fundamentally good but was corrupted by civilization, and that there was a sense of justice inherent in everyone. Thus if individuals could get rid of "man-made laws" and live together, not limited by supreme authority but only by voluntary yet legally binding force of contract, a perfect social order would be attained. Inherently just, men would then obey contracts, which they knew to be necessary. Wrongdoing would be abolished, and complete individualism would make the world a veritable paradise.

Bakunin outlined a more militant form of anarchism. Living in autocratic Russia and exiled to Siberia because of his ideas, he not only disregarded the past but also became a stanch advocate of terrorism. He said:

> The future social order must, from top to bottom, be made only by the free association and federation of workers, in association first, then in communes, in districts, in nations, and, finally, in a great international and universal federation.

These were essentially the ideas of Proudhon. To them Bakunin added the conception of revolution, or of violence, as the inevitable method by which the old order would be destroyed and the new established.

Another French radical, Louis Auguste Blanqui (1805–1881), seemed to have adopted Bakunin's ideas. In appearance thin and sickly, with red hair and restless eyes surmounted by bushy eyebrows, he was *Blanqui* usually clean, though badly dressed, and resembled an aristocrat turned demagogue. Indeed, he was a cold and violent sectarian blindly obeyed by his lieutenants. As a revolutionary conspirator he fought behind the barricades in the Revolution of 1830, and emerged a bitter enemy of the middle classes. Cool, daring, eloquent, and with a gift of secret organization which might have inspired Lenin, he created a following in Paris which consisted for the most part of handpicked revolutionary workingmen. They were secretly drilled for barricade fighting, preparing for "the day."

Like many Jacobins of the French Revolution, this Frenchman of Italian descent favored a policy of extreme governmental centralization, which was to be made possible by the dictatorship of the proletariat. Not only was a violent revolution necessary, but also it was to be achieved under the guidance of the intelligent faction of the proletariat, a group of disciplined workers, the advance guard of the revolution. Blanqui had the interests of the proletariat at heart. Regarding the evils of bourgeois society as far from rational, he decided that Utopia was possible only if private property were abolished. His program, attacking religion as well as capitalism, was revolution, atheism, and communism.

It is not strange, then, that in the nineteenth century the middle classes and the church were uniting in common opposition to these radicals. For with Marx predicting the rise of the proletariat, with Proudhon advocating the abolition of the centralized political government, with Bakunin favoring violence, and with Blanqui believing in the leadership of an intelligent minority of the proletariat in a revolt to overthrow capitalism and Christianity, the way was being prepared for Lenin and Trotsky. The attack upon Western capitalism — the New Revolution — was in the making.

KARL MARX

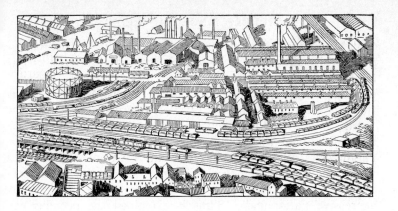

PART V. THE RISE OF INDUSTRIAL POWERS, 1878-1914

Introduction

ALTHOUGH attempts to divide history into distinct periods are more or less arbitrary, there is justification for the selection of 1878 as marking a crucial year in the evolution of a new era. By that time most European nations had assumed the geographical and political forms which they were to retain until the outbreak of the World War. The Dual Monarchy of Austria-Hungary was created in 1867, and in the same year Great Britain, by giving workingmen the ballot, took an important step in the direction of democracy. In 1870 the unification of the Italian constitutional monarchy was attained, and in the following year the German Empire and a provisional republican government in France were established. By 1878 the Balkan states had assumed the forms which, with minor exceptions, they were to retain until the Balkan Wars of 1912–1913.

The extension of the principles of nationalism and of popular control in government between 1815 and 1878 led to far-reaching changes in the New World. A new consciousness

---

of national unity emerged in the United States. Canada, influenced by nationalistic sentiment, secured autonomy within the British Empire. In Hispanic America a series of independent states replaced the moribund Spanish Empire. Even the Far East was affected by Western political ideas. In Japan Westernizing influences led to the establishment of a constitutional monarchy which presaged the spread of a middle-class régime to the conservative Orient. The whole world was succumbing to the inherent superiority of victorious Western capitalism with its attendant industrialism and aggressive nationalism. Thus is explained the peculiar expansiveness of Western bourgeois cultures and the gradual elimination of feudalism and agrarian societies throughout the world.

In 1878 western Europe and the United States, as a result of the introduction of the Industrial Revolution, were experiencing sweeping political and social changes. Of special significance was the entrenchment of the middle classes in positions of political and economic power. These ambitious office men encountered the bitter opposition of the old landed aristocracy. On the other hand, many peasants and artisans, hoping to raise their station in life, adopted the bourgeois philosophy, especially the view that the chief aim of patriotism was to promote prosperity.

Supported by various elements, the bourgeoisie in western Europe were able, by 1878, to overthrow or to subdue their chief opponents, the old nobility, who still struggled to preserve the inequalities and privileges of the old régime. Upon achieving this success the new ruling classes strove to improve and extend their system. Legislation was designed to promote trade, industry, and social betterment. The revival of imperialism, the rise of militarism, the development of free secular education, and the rapid advance of the physical sciences, together with nationalism, now constituted the great dynamics of Western culture.

Bourgeois ascendancy resulted in growing opposition to the Roman Catholic church. Among the middle and lower classes appeared powerful anticlerical groups which were determined to tame that institution and to demolish its pretensions. Exponents of this movement favored the complete separation of church and state and the destruction of ecclesiastical influence in politics, in society, and in education. In the late nineteenth and early twentieth centuries came the culmination of the rationalistic revolt against so-called obscurantism and sacerdotalism.

Middle-class supremacy, however, was challenged by many men, who, by 1878, opposed the *laissez faire* doctrine and favored the rise of the proletariat. According to them an ideal order would not be attained until bourgeois economic and aristocratic social privileges had been obliterated and a dictatorship of the workers established. Toward this utopian end they began to strive.

CHAPTER XVII

Great Britain: Twilight of the Victorian Age

IN 1878 Great Britain was the leading exponent of the middle-class order. Englishmen in those mid-Victorian days were complacent and comfortable, basking in the warmth of an easy existence. The dominating figures, Gladstone and Disraeli in politics, Browning and Tennyson in letters, Ruskin in criticism, and Darwin in science, helped to give Britain political, economic, and intellectual ascendancy.[1] A favorable geographic position, an abundance of iron and coal, and accumulated capital enabled her to become the leading industrial and colonial power. Also contributing to her greatness were a huge empire (including India, Canada, and other valuable possessions), the Suez Canal, and her preponderance of merchant vessels and warships. Able to carry her manufactured goods to the far corners of the earth and to bring back raw materials, money, and food for her industrial population, she was in a position to enjoy the benefits resulting from wealth and power.

Great Britain had advanced far on the road to political democracy. Her king was a figurehead; real executive and

The British Government legislative power rested in the hands of the cabinet chosen by a caucus of the majority party in the House of Commons. This cabinet legislated with the advice and consent of Parliament. Those who could vote or could control the election of representatives to the House of Commons were virtually the rulers. Britain had no written constitution by which to maintain an existing order; the only force which prevented her from becoming too radical was an unwritten constitution based on notable documents, such as Magna Carta and the Bill of Rights, and precedents, customs, and famous laws. In reality the government was

[1] See pages 231–238.

freighted with tradition. This conservatism made reform slow but gave the ship of state stability and security.

It is true that the aristocracy retained considerable authority, since it could delay the passage of legislation through its control of the House of Lords. As conservatives, not outright reactionaries, the aristocrats merely tried to maintain the *status quo.* After the democratic Reform Bill of 1867 and similar legislation in 1868 for Ireland and Scotland, the House of Commons, the real governing body, was selected by an electorate of some two and one half millions. Inasmuch as the better-paid workingman could now share the ballot with the upper and middle classes, democracy was well on the way in England.

The rise of organized parties enabled the voters to express their political views effectively. England had been the first modern state to develop a party system. Between 1870 and 1914 the two leading organizations were the Liberals and the Conservatives. *Political Parties* The Liberals favored individual liberty and free trade, opposed hereditary privilege and the rule of the landed aristocracy, tried to curtail the power of the state church, and urged equality before the law. They also supported Irish home rule and favored extension of the suffrage and improvement of conditions for the workingman. The Conservatives, at first adopting as their slogan "the Crown, the Church, and the Constitution," later accepted certain democratic and social reforms. Ardent imperialists, they generally stood forth as the defenders of law, order, and property. In 1886 a large group of Liberals, opposed to Gladstone's home-rule policy, joined the Conservatives, who thereupon adopted the name "Unionists."

By 1878 England had not solved all important political and social problems. She was not yet a true democracy; all the trappings of aristocracy remained — king, nobles, and clergy. The monarch was merely *Political and Social Problems* a symbol of unity, but the House of Lords could vote legislation which affected landed interests. For national elections the electorate consisted of only a limited number of male voters.

On the economic side the situation was unsatisfactory. Wealth was distributed unequally: 3 per cent were wealthy, 9 per cent comfortable, and 88 per cent poor. Certain evils of the Industrial Revolution persisted, such as unemployment, low wages, long hours, child labor, industrial accidents, and diseases. Seldom were wages sufficient to enable a working-man to save for a rainy day; unemployment and sickness brought hardship to millions; old age stared tragically in the faces of workingmen.

In the mid-Victorian period, however, most liberal leaders believed that social as well as political problems could be solved by abolishing restrictions and by pro- *Gladstone and Bourgeois Individualism* moting individualism. In the sixties Gladstone drew up and had passed a series of budgets by which he shifted the burden of taxation from the poor to the rich by the imposition of income, inheritance, and liquor taxes. He also swept away the import duties on many articles. Both parties believed that Gladstone's free-trade policy would stimulate business and revive general prosperity. The Liberals, further to democratize the country, enacted bills introducing the secret ballot (1872) and the Corrupt Practices Act (1883), which were designed to check bribery. In 1884 Gladstone put through the Representation of the People Act, which increased the electorate from three to five millions, thus making another step toward universal manhood suffrage in Great Britain. The only men remaining unenfranchised in England were servants residing with their employers and sons living with their parents.

Ireland caused Gladstone considerable anguish during his administration. Despite laws which he had passed attempting *Gladstone and Ireland* to provide for religious equality and land reform, the Irish, dissatisfied with the way in which the reforms were carried out, continued to seethe with discontent. In 1880, returning to power after an absence of six years, Gladstone had introduced a bill providing for public regulation of land under the supervision of a Land Commission. The latter had the power to adjust relations between the English Anglican landlords and the Irish Catholic peasants so as to insure a fair rent, fixity of tenure to avoid unreasonable evictions, and free sale by the peasant of his holdings. Enactment of this measure quieted the land problem and prepared the way for a permanent settlement later.

Gladstone, however, was unable to solve the most important phase of the Irish question — self-government. The revolutionary movements of the nineteenth century had encouraged the Irish to demand home rule. In the sixties a radical brotherhood, the Fenians, appeared, demanding the establishment of an independent Ireland. At the same time the home-rule movement, aiming at autonomy of Ireland within the British Empire, gained momentum. The Irish representatives in Parliament, led by the famous Charles Stewart Parnell (1846–1891), soon engaged in an earnest attempt to achieve this end, obstructing legislation by filibustering so that Parliament might listen to reason. Gladstone finally became convinced that nothing less than home rule would satisfy the Irish, and that unless he had their support his government would fall. Therefore he denounced England's traditional attitude toward Ireland and introduced a home-rule bill.

The Protestant Irish, who feared that home rule meant Rome rule, opposed it. They received the enthusiastic support of the dominant landowners in the Con- *The Home-Rule Bill* servative party, who feared that Gladstone's liberal policy toward Ireland might result in the introduction of laws designed to deprive them of their large holdings in England and Scotland. Joined by a group of Liberals led by Joseph Chamberlain (1836–1914), who opposed home rule for Ireland, the Conservatives managed to defeat Gladstone on this issue in 1886 and again in 1893. At the elections held in 1895, with home rule as the issue, the Conservatives won an overwhelming victory. This party governed England for the next decade.

A protracted depression between 1873 and 1888 contributed to the fall of Gladstone. During these years a general decline in prices in agriculture and industry brought ruin to many capitalists, stockholders, and farmers. Unemployment increased so rapidly that during the height of the depression one man out of ten was without work. Imports also decreased, and, what was even more serious, a Royal Commission reported in 1886 that British manufacturing supremacy was being challenged by foreign countries. This state of affairs the complacent Victorians could not ignore.

The Depression of 1873–1888

Numerous inventions in the iron and steel industries help to explain England's industrial troubles. In the eighties science enabled cheap steel to supplant iron as the general article of trade. English iron production received a serious, if temporary, setback. German and American steel industries expanded rapidly, and, to compete, England was forced at great expense to scrap the obsolete machinery in her iron-manufacturing plants.

Manufacturing

British industry suffered when Germany, Holland, and the United States reverted to the gold standard. As a result of this action the total amount of money in use was reduced. Lacking gold mines to replenish the gold supply, England experienced a definite decline in prices, which in turn discouraged business enterprises.

During these years construction in the field of transportation declined. Europe was no longer placing large steel orders to be used in the building of new railroads. A boom in steamship construction had come to an end. Ships were larger in size and fewer in number, and every inch of space in the boats was used to advantage. The revival of shipping competition through the development of merchant marines, by means of subsidies and other governmental aids in France, Germany, and Austria, for example, all contributed to the decline of British shipbuilding and British shipping.

Transportation and Commerce

Nationalism in the seventies and eighties did much to retard British trade. Bismarck, influenced by patriotic motives, became a protectionist and by tariffs practically closed German markets to British goods. Consequently free-trade England suffered a double misfortune : exclusion of her goods from all countries adopting a protective tariff and the flooding of her unprotected markets by cheap products manufactured in other industrial countries.

Agriculture as well as industry suffered during this depression. Free trade enabled foreign countries, especially the United States, to flood British markets with quantities of grain. Agricultural prices fell and *Agriculture* the English farmer, who was paying high rents and had invested considerable capital in the development of his farm lands, was unable to sell his products profitably. Thousands left the farms and went to the cities. Many became small farmers and existed by raising perishable products, such as vegetables, fruits, and even flowers. The large landowner tried to survive by adopting the latest labor-saving devices and by farming on a large scale. Agriculture in England had received what seemed to be a permanent setback.

In 1895 the Conservatives, in power again, decided that the revival of imperialism would end the depression. Therefore they looked overseas for markets, raw materials, and economic opportunities. Gold had *The Revival of Imperialism* been discovered in South Africa. Cecil Rhodes had become a millionaire as a result of the gold and diamond mines he had developed, and the Boers alone stood in the way of complete British exploitation of that region. The imperialist seeds which Disraeli had sown were bearing fruit. England, now conscious of her destiny, was convinced that the British empire was the world's greatest instrument for good. In 1895 the Marquis of Salisbury (1830–1903) became prime minister for the third time. Aided by his nephew, Lord Balfour (1848–1930), and by Joseph Chamberlain, ardent champion of the colonial ideal, he immediately inaugurated an aggressive foreign policy.[1]

The Conservatives, however, were less successful in dealing with domestic problems. At times circumstances impelled them to act. To satisfy the turbulent Irish they were forced to pass land reforms. By the act of 1891 the government set aside 30,000,000 pounds from which the Irish who wished to

[1] For additional information on British imperialism see Chaps. XXIII–XXIV.

buy their lands might borrow. After 1891 two other land-purchasing acts were passed. This legislation enabled the Irish farmer to become a landowner. Usually the purchasing price was a sum equal to the rent of the farm for twenty years. These land acts proved to be a success and removed a sore spot from British politics. The Irish problem, however, was not terminated. Thwarted in their attempts to obtain home rule, many Irish patriots became active in a political society founded by Arthur Griffiths, called Sinn Fein (Gaelic, *ourselves*), which came into existence in 1900 and had as its major aim Irish independence.

The Land Problem in Ireland

At home the achievements of the Conservative government were insignificant. Most of its legislation was considered class legislation designed not to contribute to the welfare of England but to help the Conservative party. Serious economic and social issues were evaded.

The period of liberal government from the fall of the Balfour ministry in 1905 to the outbreak of the World War was an unexciting one. Many Englishmen believed that they were being led by mediocre men. Politicians, in their opinion, were quarreling over trifles. Victorian optimism had vanished and uncertainty, even pessimism, had taken its place. Some bourgeois went so far as to intimate that Great Britain was about to experience an age of decadence and that all ideals had been lost. British workingmen, however, were not of that belief. In their opinion the English laboring man had at last realized his strength.

Liberal Government (1905–1914)

Workers found in the World War an opportunity to complete a development of labor organization that had begun as far back as 1824. In that year the government practically removed the ban on unions. This policy enabled the wage-earners under the leadership of Robert Owen to form, in 1834, the Grand Consolidated Trades Union. By means of the general strike this organization planned to coerce the employers and the government into improving labor conditions. But as long as the government

Rise of Labor

regarded the walkout as an attack upon legal business and a criminal offense, the labor unions in England were powerless. In 1871 and in 1875, however, after considerable agitation by the wage-earners, bills were passed recognizing the legality of the unions, of the strikes, and of collective bargaining. These laws marked the definite establishment of the union as an important factor in British political and social life.

Shortly after this legislation was passed, a national Trade Union Congress composed of representatives of all unions was established, to meet annually to consider the problems of labor as a whole. Unions were now formed rapidly. By the close of the nineteenth century their membership totaled about two million men. Unlike their fellow workers in many European countries, the members of these unions at first were not radicals. Trade unions favored legal, constitutional methods in bringing about reforms, as did their opponents, the manufacturers.

Originally the trade unions did not include the unskilled laborers. Ultimately unsatisfactory working conditions forced these unfortunate men to rally behind leaders. In 1889 they were involved in several strikes. Most important of these was the great dock demonstration for better working conditions and pay. At the head of the strike was the strong and shrewd labor leader, John Burns, who later became a member of Parliament and a cabinet minister.

After the victories of 1889 the unions grew more confident and more radical. In 1892 four labor-union leaders were elected to the House of Commons, including John Burns. Encouraged by this political ad- *Radical Tendencies of* vance, English socialists organized an Inde- *Labor* pendent Labor Party (I. L. P.), the object of which was to obtain "collective ownership of all the means of production, distribution, and exchange."

These radical developments in the labor movement aroused the determined opposition of the employers In their opinion labor unions were legal corporations responsible for damages due to strikes. The House of Lords expressed this point of view in the important Taff Vale decision (1901). In August of the preceding year the workers of the Taff Vale Railway had engaged in a strike. Later the company had brought suit against the workers for damages caused by their walkout. This case was finally appealed to the highest court, the House of Lords, and the latter held that the union was responsible for the illegal deeds of its members acting under its authority.

The Clash between Labor and Capital

The Taff Vale decision was severely condemned by the labor unions. They realized that it threatened the very existence of their organizations. It was true that they could still call strikes; but a walkout, even though it was successful, might result in a suit for damages on the part of the company. Inasmuch as the union funds were limited, the labor organizations were not in a position to pay heavy judgments.

Before the Taff Vale decision a number of union leaders concluded that more could be achieved for their cause through political action than through industrial struggles. Therefore, in 1900 the Independent Labor Party, the socialists, and certain trade-union groups formed a coalition with the purpose of obtaining legislation favorable to organized labor. Out of this alliance arose a new labor party which looked with favor upon such socialistic policies as nationalization of mines, railways, and canals, free education, and old-age pensions. In the election of 1905 the new party won twenty-nine seats. Liberals and Conservatives soon realized that this group must be recognized. Consequently they tried to coöperate with this organization in a common attempt to improve social conditions. In 1906 Parliament passed the Trades Disputes Act, which legalized "peaceful" picketing and practically insured unions against suits for damages as a result of strikes.

Socialistic Tendencies of Labor

The growth of unrest, arising out of a marked increase in the cost of living and the failure of wages to rise as rapidly as prices, enabled the socialists to convert the many conservative English workers to a more radical program. In the late nineteenth century labor unions had tried to standardize working conditions and to increase wages by "bargaining" with employers. Unions had also en-

The Strike Epidemic

deavored to persuade Parliament to enact a minimum wage law in order to establish a satisfactory standard of living. This legislation was obtained by the coal-miners in 1913.

Between 1911 and 1914, however, certain members in the various unions advocated control of industries by unions. An epidemic of strikes was an indirect result of this development. In 1911 and 1912 a crescendo of walkouts among the seamen, the dockers, the railway workers, and agricultural laborers reached a climax in a huge mining dispute involving a million men. In the following year (1913) the miners, the transport workers, and the railwaymen joined forces in a plan to attain their objectives through a general strike. The World War, however, cut short the ambitious project. Labor rallied to the support of the government and did not renew the struggle until the conflict had come to a close.

Despite labor troubles, industry experienced a definite economic recovery between 1890 and 1914. Imperialistic advances, resulting in an influx of gold and an *General Economic* increase of raw materials and economic oppor- *Situation in England* tunities, helped to raise the general price level *(1890–1914)* and thus promoted industrial expansion. British industrial supremacy, however, was never regained. During this period Germany and the United States enjoyed industrial expansion and "good times"; in fact, their industries developed more rapidly than did those of England. By 1900 the United States produced more pig iron, steel, and coal than England. British increase in the exportation of cotton and machinery was not as great as it had been in the past, and the tendency on the part of foreign customers to use local coal deposits and to substitute oil for coal indicated a possible decline in this important trade.

At the opening of the twentieth century England was dependent upon foreign nations for food. Her population was over three quarters urban, unable to live upon necessities raised in England. Therefore Britain had to rely upon her shipping, her investment resources, and her exportations to pay for this imported food. Competition in these fields by foreign states, however, made it very difficult for Great Britain to maintain a satisfactory balance of trade.

To compete with the great industrial combines or cartels of Germany and to end cut-throat competition at home, British *Rise of Big Business* industrialists finally decided to form great combinations. The first of these was the huge Brunner-Monod Salt Union, created in the early nineties. It consisted of about sixty-four competing firms. By 1900 the Coats' Sewing-Cotton organization had been established with a capital of 10,000,000 pounds and a virtual monopoly throughout England. Imitations of the German cartels and the American trusts sprang up in England as the movement in favor of large units of production gained headway. Shipping "rings," whereby steamship companies made monopolistic agreements in which they divided up the trade routes and paid rebates to merchants who used their lines, came into existence. British industrialists were engaged in a desperate attempt to regain their trade supremacy when the World War interrupted for a while their peace-time activities.

The amalgamation of business enterprises and the aggressive activities of labor unions were accompanied by a determined attempt to substitute state-help for *The Liberals as Social Reformers* self-help in economic affairs. Moved by the increasing discontent of the masses, many British leaders finally decided that the doctrine of *laissez faire* would have to give way to a program of social reform. The upshot was control of the government by the Liberals in 1905. Changing conditions had forced the latter into a position in which their chief concern was turned from political freedom and religious toleration to the lot of the lower classes, which they were determined to improve even though the individualism of Adam Smith would have to be thrown overboard.

In 1905 Sir Henry Campbell-Bannerman was asked by King Edward VII to become prime minister. A few days later a new cabinet list, composed of Liberals, was announced. Herbert Henry Asquith became chancellor of the exchequer, Sir Edward Grey was placed in charge of foreign affairs, Lord R. B. Haldane took over the war department, Herbert Gladstone entered the home office, and David Lloyd George became president of the board of trade. With some minor changes this group remained in charge of the administrative functions of the government until May, 1915, when it was succeeded by a coalition ministry.

One man, the clever Welsh attorney and "daredevil" statesman, Lloyd George (1863–   ), stood head and shoulders above his fellow Liberals. Reared in poverty, he developed in early youth a violent opposition to the privileged Anglican or state church and the selfish "ramparts of wealth," the great landowners. Scorn and rage grew in his heart whenever he heard the well-known couplet: *Lloyd George, the Social Reformer*

> God bless the squire and his relations
> And keep us in our proper stations.

Elected to Parliament, he determined to do everything in his power to dethrone these "privileged institutions" and to help the masses. As the champion of a more democratic England, he believed that capitalism was doomed unless the condition of the working classes was ameliorated.

Until 1905 few social reforms involving direct governmental aid had penetrated England. In 1885 Gladstone, the benevolent bourgeois individualist, looked with horror upon "what they call construction,— that is to say, taking into the hands of the state the business of an individual man." Imperialism during the conservative régime (1895–1905) silenced any movement in this direction. Consequently the only relief the masses had received was in the form of legislation against abuses in the industrial system, usually in the form of factory laws. In 1902 this legislation was unified in a single code comprising the chief laws enacted in the nineteenth century and new legislation designed to improve the lot of the workers. This factory legislation and a mine code passed by Parliament in 1906 forbade employment of children under twelve in a factory, regulated hours of work of those from twelve to eighteen, provided for supervision of factory sanitation, and prohibited employment of women and children in the mines. *Labor Legislation*

Factory legislation, however, did not solve the problems of poverty and unemployment. Many humanitarians, especially Lloyd George, felt that these conditions had to be attacked on a broader basis. The poor law, under which poverty was a crime and no provision for sickness or old age a public disgrace, had collapsed. These liberal bourgeois leaders knew that the precariousness of living must be obliterated. But how could this be done? Without hesitating, Lloyd George accepted the leadership and, like Bismarck, fought the spread of socialism by introducing beneficial social legislation.

During the eight years preceding the World War the government tried to give the people security against misfortune. *Social Legislation* Friendless old persons in 1908 were given a small pension at the age of seventy. Those who were sick were aided by an insurance scheme (1909) maintained by contributions of the employer, the employee, and the state. The government was unable, however, to solve the problem of unemployment. A plan was proposed whereby in certain selected trades a fund would be created to support persons temporarily out of work. Many bourgeois leaders felt that this plan would encourage idleness, while certain influential labor leaders were dissatisfied with the contributing feature of this plan, believing that the worker had a "right to maintenance." Consequently unemployment legislation was not passed. By enacting other social reforms, however, the Liberal government did give the masses a feeling of economic certainty which they had hitherto lacked.

There were numerous critics of this social program. To the representatives of socialism and syndicalism these reforms *Criticism of Lloyd George's Policies* were insufficient. Believing that the state should abandon completely the historic *laissez faire* doctrine and engage actively in the solution of labor problems, they demanded, as immediate steps, the nationalization of certain key industries and the initiation of graduated income taxes. The Conservatives, representing the landowners, also denounced the Liberal program, although for other reasons. They claimed that the provisions of the reform acts, especially unemployment insurance, resulted in increased governmental expenditures, which the government met by taxing the landowners rather than the industrial leaders.

Lloyd George, when he introduced his budget bill of 1909, had instituted an attack upon the landed aristocrats and wealthy middle classes. In his opinion these property owners were best able to pay a considerable part of the taxes levied by the government: "The ownership of land," he said, "is not merely an enjoyment, it is a stewardship. . . . Why should I put burdens on the people? I am one of the children of the people." In this budget Lloyd George used all of the old taxes, such as the income and inheritance taxes, and liquor and tobacco duties, and in addition heavier taxes were placed on large incomes and on liquor licenses. A plan for taxing land was introduced whereby the government confiscated a part of the "unearned increment." A tax was imposed on the increase in value of land not due to improvements, upon undeveloped and idle real estate, and upon incomes from mining lands. Those who inherited or were given lands were to pay a special levy, but no taxes were to be imposed upon property used for agricultural purposes.

The Budget Bill of 1909

Opposition to these proposals on the part of the landowners and middle classes rose to such a pitch that many sincere Christians were surprised that Heaven did not strike dead such a wicked man as Lloyd George "before he could accomplish his fell purpose in the ruin of his country." Supported by the masses, this astute reformer succeeded in passing his bill through the House of Commons by a tremendous majority. The House of Lords, however, opposed this unparalleled increase in taxation and claimed that the budget was "something more than a money bill." Therefore, even though the House of Commons had passed the bill, the Lords decided to delay its enactment by refusing to approve it before it had been referred to the people at a special election.

Lloyd George expected to see the Liberals in the election of 1910 swept into office by a large majority. A program designed to abolish poverty by placing the burden upon the rural aristocrats and the middle classes would, he believed, certainly receive the support of the common people. To his surprise, however, neither the Conservatives nor the Liberals were given a majority. Apparently the Liberals could not remain in power without the support of the minority groups, the Irish Nationalists and the representatives of the Labor party. An understanding was reached among the three parties, and the Liberal leader, Asquith, became head of a coalition government.

The Irish, Labor, and Liberal representatives now decided to punish the House of Lords for its resistance to home rule, *The Parliament Act* social legislation, and Lloyd George's budget. The Asquith ministry introduced a bill designed to minimize the political authority of the Lords. Known as the Parliament Act, it provided that (1) the House of Lords was to be definitely deprived of power over money bills; (2) it could delay other legislation by twice rejecting a bill, but one passed three times by the House of Commons in three different sessions was to become a law if two years should have elapsed between the bill's first presentation and its final enactment; and (3) the maximum life of Parliament was to be reduced from seven to five years.

In 1910 Lord Lansdowne, the Unionist leader in the upper house, representing the interests of the Lords, proposed that the matter be discussed in a joint session, and that if it were one of unusual importance, it should be referred to the people. Fearing that they probably would be outvoted, the Liberals refused to agree to this suggestion. Thereupon the prime minister dissolved Parliament. The new election, fought on the issue of "curbing the Lords," returned practically the same relative strength of the parties. Asquith now informed the Conservative leaders that the king might be asked to create a sufficient number of Liberal peers to produce a majority for the measure. Confronted with the prospect of being defeated in this way, the Lords yielded and the bill became law. By the Parliament Act of 1911 the House of Commons received virtually complete power, the nobles merely retaining the right to delay legislation by a limited veto power. England now had in effect a single legislative body.

Having deprived the lords of political authority, the Asquith government attacked another fortress of the old régime, the Anglican church. Conservatives bitterly opposed this governmental policy. Opposition to the state church, they feared, would undermine the established order. Free-thinkers were bad enough, but the Conservatives threw up their hands in horror when the Liberals forced Parliament to repeal that portion of the Coronation Oath which denounced the Catholic religion. Upon becoming king, George V merely recognized the laws which stated that the British rulers had to be Protestants. In 1914 the Anglican church in Wales was disestablished, church and state were separated, Welsh Anglican bishops were deprived of their seats in the House of Lords, and the church lost a considerable part of its property. Bitterly condemning these acts, the Conservatives prepared to resist any further attempts to disestablish the Anglican church.

Religious and Educational Developments

The Conservatives long opposed the education of the masses, believing that it would increase dissatisfaction and radicalism. Under Gladstone, however, the famous Forster Act (1870) established a national system of popular education. This law failed to settle one issue, the relation between schools maintained by the Church of England and other organizations and the elementary public schools created by the government. The national government contributed to both, although the private institutions were forced to rely primarily upon the support of individuals, whereas the public schools received local governmental help in addition to the national subsidy. In 1902 an attempt was made to settle this question. A bill was passed which transferred control of the state schools from local authorities to the county or borough council. Private institutions were to receive government support. The two systems were coördinated in relation to the school population, and both were held to the same standard of work. This act aroused bitter opposition from those who favored secular education. Laws passed between 1876 and 1899 governed other matters, such as compulsory attendance for children under twelve years of age.

In 1906 Lloyd George, supported by Laborites who favored secular education, introduced a bill which recognized only state schools as a part of a national educational system. In these institutions there was to be neither religious instruction nor a religious examination for teachers. The bill was vetoed by the House of Lords. Despite this setback Lloyd George succeeded in passing socialistically colored school legislation. Finding that many pupils were forced to go without a mid-day meal, his government decided to feed them at public cost ; medical inspection of the children was provided gratis.

These reforms, together with the law providing for the care of the unemployed, were a departure from the old prin-ciple of *laissez faire*. To most Conservatives, Lloyd George was simply conforming to the desire of the Laborites and socialists to take much that concerned the Englishman's daily life out of the hands of the people and put it into the hands of the state. In reply to this accusation Lloyd George and his Liberal followers declared that unless the state intervened to aid those who could not help themselves, socialism would supplant capitalism. Expounding the doctrine that if the poor needed assistance, the rich should pay, the Liberals erected in England the framework of state socialism.

When the World War broke out in 1914 the Liberal party was engaged in an earnest attempt to solve the agricultural problem in England. In 1900 less than 12,000 persons owned over two thirds of the land in England, Scotland, and Wales. These owners either leased their lands to renters, or hired laborers to farm for them. In many cases the great landlord could not legally sell his property, but even if he could, he generally held onto his land because it made him the political boss and the social leader of the community. As a local squire he resembled a medieval lord, appointing the Anglican clergyman of the parish and assuming an important rôle in most other local affairs.

The Land Problem in England

The renters and laborers, however, did not prosper under this landowning system. Renters were at the mercy of the landlords in the matter of tenure ; whereas laborers often had to work for meager wages and live in wretched buildings furnished by the landlord. These unfortunates tried to better their conditions by organizing, but the landlords succeeded in frustrating this plan. The only escape seemed to be emigration to the industrial centers of Great Britain. It was partly as a result of this situation that agriculture declined.

Other factors helped to make agriculture an important problem. As stated before, Great Britain by the opening of the twentieth century had become an industrial state dependent upon foreign nations for food. As long as Britain remained the leading industrial and naval power she did not have to concern herself greatly with the grave agricultural situation, for control of the seas and possession of great wealth (in the form of money) enabled her to purchase foodstuffs abroad at advantageous prices. But the sudden rise of Germany, a formidable rival, constituted a serious threat to England's control of the seas. The possibility of being cut off from the source of her food supplies and raw materials, in the event of an unsuccessful war with Germany, loomed as a threatening, although remote, danger.

Influenced by this menace and also by the desire to destroy the economic power of the landed aristocrats, the government determined to improve agricultural conditions. In 1913–1914 Parliament considered proposals to decrease the amount of land used for game preserves, to establish a minimum-wage law for farm laborers, to improve the living conditions of these workers, and to better the situation of tenants with regard to leases and compensation for improvements on the land. The war occurred before these reforms could be put into operation. Heavy taxes, imposed during and after the conflict, upon land, incomes, and industry, removed the necessity for further weakening the aristocratic landowners.

Another important problem was almost solved by a Liberal legislative act when the war postponed its enforcement. Although the Irish question had been ignored, *Home Rule for Ireland* the Liberals had long realized that England would soon be forced to deal with the question. Finally a bill was introduced by the Asquith ministry providing for an Irish parliament composed of a senate appointed by the government and a lower house elected by the people. This new body was to be intrusted with legislation over purely Irish domestic affairs, but it was not to be permitted to establish or favor any particular form of religious worship. Matters of importance to the British Isles, such as military and naval forces, peace and war, and diplomacy and commerce, were reserved to the English Parliament, in which Ireland was to have a representation of forty-two members. These were permitted to vote only on imperial questions.

The announcement that Ireland was to be given home rule was not welcomed by the Protestants of Ulster. Preferring to remain subjects of George V, they began, under the leadership of Sir Edward Carson, to organize military forces against the Irish Nationalists. In 1914 the Nationalists prepared to resist, and it seemed inevitable that the passage of the unwelcome legislation would be followed by civil war. But the outbreak of the world struggle, compelling the government to suspend the bill's enforcement, even though it had been passed by Parliament and signed by the king, resulted in a temporary lull in the Anglo-Irish quarrel.

By 1914 it became evident that England was facing a new era. Hitherto most Englishmen had been devout believers in

England on the Eve of the War

Victorian respectability and progress. Either they advocated Gladstone's "Little England" policy, paying slight attention to the other nations, or they favored Disraeli's imperialistic plan of making the world a hunting preserve for the "Anglo-Saxon peoples." In either case diplomatic isolation was the keynote of England's relations with other powers.

The spread of individualism, in the form of a desire for self-determination among the various peoples and lands of

Attempts to revive Imperialism

the British Empire, caused some disquietude in England. Aroused by the granting of semi-independence to the leading colonies of Great Britain, and convinced that England's insularity would result in the decline of the empire, Rudyard Kipling (1865–   ) and other leaders helped to revive the Disraelian imperialistic spirit. Kipling, by trumpeting in verse the glories of

dominions and by singing of the white man's burden in governing the blacks, tried to interest Englishmen in their overseas
possessions. Calling the attention of the world to the fact that
the British were the "chosen" people, he begged his fellow
citizens to engage again in the greatest crusades, the extension
of British culture and, most important, British control of the
blacks, whites, and yellows of Africa and Asia. No better
example of his imperialistic religion can be found than in the
first stanza of his famous *Recessional* which reads:

> God of our fathers, known of old —
> Lord of our far-flung battle line —
> Beneath whose awful hand we hold
> Dominion over palm and pine —
> Lord God of Hosts, be with us yet,
> Lest we forget — lest we forget!

While Kipling was attacking British splendid isolation and
was trying to revive the imperialistic zeal, other writers were
advocating the development of a humanitarian
mind. These intellectuals constituted the *"Parlor Socialism" in England*
famous Fabian Society, which attempted "to
insinuate, rather than to insist on, socialist ideas."

Among these "parlor socialists" Herbert George Wells
(1866–   ) must be given a prominent place. Since 1895 he
has written constantly and his fame has grown. Romances,
essays of a sociological and religious character, a series of
novels, and last but not least his *The Outline of History* — all
these are to his credit. Most of his works have enjoyed a
tremendous circulation. Like his favorite Utopian, Saint-
Simon, Wells firmly believes that in the course of time the
scientific mind will solve all earthly problems. Always willing
to make predictions, he is certain that the green pastures of
Utopia are directly ahead.

George Bernard Shaw, however, overtops all the Fabian
Socialists and the English dramatists of his day. No one can
help being impressed by his brilliance and versatility, even
though his manners and ideas appear to many crude and
superficial. His most representative plays are usually intended
as tracts to overturn commonly accepted ideas and conven-

tions. A professed socialist before the war and an enthusiastic champion of Russian communism after the conflict, he ridicules such bourgeois moral, social, and religious customs as the family, private property, and Christianity. He opposes classes of any kind — political, economic, or social — and asserts that bourgeois society (which he apparently enjoys) is stupid. In his opinion the emancipation of the individual will be a prelude to Utopia.

Fabian Socialism was one of the numerous by-products of the pessimism which existed in England before the outbreak of the World War. At that time England had lost her favorable balance of trade. She was exporting less of her manufactured goods and was importing more foreign products. What did this mean? Was England no longer the industrial center of the world? How could she support her people? These were a few of the questions raised by many writers at that time. German trade and industry were increasing rapidly. The trade-mark "Made in Germany" had taken the place of British trade symbols in many places throughout the world. It seemed as if Great Britain, the champion of individualism and of free trade, were going to lose her industrial and commercial supremacy to Germany, the outstanding exponent of benevolent despotism in big business.

Despite this severe competition, England's conservative economic captains hesitated to adopt new business and industrial methods. They were especially loath *The Tariff Reform Movement* to renounce old ideas, especially individualism, and to substitute new concepts, such as a protective tariff. An aggressive group of Englishmen, however, believed that drastic changes alone could save England. Led by Joseph Chamberlain, a clear-headed politician and a pushing business man, they proposed that Great Britain should place a tariff on foreign goods and establish free trade among her dominions. This arrangement would enable the British to sell their manufactured goods, and the colonists to market their raw products. The proposal caught the fancy of many Conservatives, and in 1905 it became a battle cry. If adopted, they believed, England would no longer be dependent upon foreign markets, practically closed to her by high protective tariffs. Moreover, she would be in a position to prevent foreign states from dumping their goods in England. Complete prosperity would be restored.

In reply the Liberals, who were free traders, called attention to the fact that England was dependent upon the exportation of manufactured goods and the importation of foodstuffs. If a tariff law were passed, not only would England be forced to pay higher prices for imported food, but also her foreign markets would be destroyed. Her only hope was the establishment of an economic imperial *Zollverein* which should include all possessions within the British Empire. Many Englishmen, however, opposed this plan. In their opinion the empire had brought into existence "great and self-respecting States, modelled on the basis of those free institutions which England has so successfully evolved." Wherever these colonies have proved worthy to control their own affairs England has been willing to grant them virtual independence. Despite this concession England and her colonies have been united by a loyalty to common ideals, rather than by "the artificial bonds of pure self-interest." Any attempt on the part of England to emphasize economic ties would antagonize the colonies and weaken the bonds which held England and her colonies together. Moreover, some of the colonies that had received Dominion status were opposed to this imperial *Zollverein*. Commonwealths, such as Canada, did not propose to remain economic satellites of England. An economic union must encourage the industrialization of all members of the empire, not of England alone.

By 1914 Great Britain was in a critical situation. Confronted by the internal and foreign developments which retarded British economic progress, many Englishmen became exceedingly pessimistic. Some even raised the question, "Will England survive?" Surely this small island, birthplace of the Industrial Revolution, workshop of the world, center of the greatest of empires, would not sink to a position of minor importance. England had always muddled through

The Proposed Imperial Zollverein

in the past by defeating and outdistancing her rivals. Individualism, the key to progress, many still believed, would again enable that nation to overcome her difficulties. Others, however, realizing that the international economic situation had changed vastly within the preceding half-century, were less sanguine about the efficacy of this outworn social concept.

HOME RULE *before the House of Commons*
From a cartoon in *Punch*

CHAPTER XVIII

Liberalism in France, Italy, and the Iberian Peninsula

THE disastrous war with Prussia (1870–1871) offered the restless elements in Paris an opportunity to revolt. Upon the sudden collapse of the Second French Empire they coöperated with the republicans in proclaiming a republic and in creating a provisional government, which met first at Bordeaux and later at Ver- *The Paris Commune* sailles. The people of Paris refused to surrender to the Germans, but after a long siege were finally forced to capitulate (January 28, 1871). After peace was concluded with Germany, the radicals in Paris turned on the National Assembly, in session at Versailles, and denounced it for the acceptance of harsh peace terms whereby Alsace and part of Lorraine were relinquished and a large indemnity was to be paid to Germany. The National Assembly further aroused the ire of many Parisians by abolishing the moratorium on rent and other obligations, declared during the siege of the capital, and by appointing an unpopular commander to the national guard.

A crisis was reached when the Assembly, deciding to dispense with the militia of Paris, the organization responsible for its defense, discontinued the pay of its members. Thousands of men were added to those already out of work. Radical leaders now planned to use this restless mob of unemployed men to overthrow the National Assembly. A central committee was formed by representatives of the national guard, which was concerned not only with the interests of the militia but also with the safety of the republic. Later a newly elected general council of Paris was merged with this central committee to form the government of the commune.

In the new body were radicals of various kinds and degrees. There were Jacobin republicans, advocating another reign of terror and a dictatorship as a prelude to the expulsion of the Germans and the restoration of the republic; followers of Marx, planning a socialist state; and disciples of Proudhon and Bakunin, the anarchists, who hoped to destroy the central government by violence and to establish communes throughout France.

Angry because the rural people had blocked their attempts to overthrow not only Louis Napoleon but also the middle-class order, these radicals of the Paris Com-
Plans of the Radicals   mune actually planned to free the cities from the restraints imposed upon them by the country districts. To achieve this end they decided to subvert the National Assembly. By reducing the authority of the new central government to the barest minimum they planned to make France a federation of autonomous communes, each with complete control of its budget, police magistrates, local taxation, and other governmental matters. The cities would then be in a position to control their own affairs.

Certain radicals in Paris hoped to take advantage of this proposed decentralization by bringing about a despotism of Paris. Country districts, they said, were unfitted to conduct political and financial affairs and should be subordinated to the towns. Since other cities would probably look to her for leadership, Paris would soon dominate France. Upon attaining this goal an intelligent minority in Paris would lead the way in bringing about a complete social revolution.

Most of the delegates elected to the communal government were either nondescript laborers unfamiliar with affairs or indifferent speakers of the professional classes who possessed a few borrowed phrases and little experience in parliamentary methods. Incessant warfare with the provisional government and international dissension deprived them of adequate opportunities for legislation.

In April, 1871, the National Assembly (the provisional government), determined to preserve the authority of the central government by crushing the Commune, began another siege of Paris. Intense personal sufferings among the people followed. After the food supply was exhausted, horses, cats, dogs, and finally rats were eaten. Despite a stubborn defense of two months the communards, on May 28, 1871, were forced to surrender. "Guns, *The Siege of Paris* cartridge boxes and uniforms littered the gutters of the poorer quarters, while in the doorways sat stony-eyed women, waiting chin on hand for the men who would not come back." Elegantly clad Parisians, tittering nervously, could be seen raising the coverings with the tops of their parasols and peering at the faces of the dead.

Frightful vengeance was taken by the bourgeois-peasant party of order. Men, women, and children were shot by the hundreds, many without trial. About fifteen thousand were killed during the two weeks following the downfall of the Commune, and as many more were deported to a "living hell" in the French colonies. "Such was the vengeance of the possessing classes upon the dispossessed, of the old Revolution upon the new, of the provinces upon Paris."

The common belief that the Commune of Paris was primarily an attempt to establish a new social order is not regarded as sound by recent scholarly research. According to one writer, *Significance of the Commune* the Commune was not essentially a socialist movement. At the outset it recruited its adherents from another milieu and, although at the end its strength had simmered down to a revolutionary group pretty thoroughly imbued with socialism, its impetus and *raison d'être* are to be found in causes which lie outside the domain of socialism. The war with Germany, the events of the siege, disgust with a strongly centralized and incompetent government, were of more decisive significance.[1]

Despite this historical reality "a legend of the Commune has been developed in socialist and communist circles which finds the meaning of the revolution in its socialism." This interpretation was more important in the molding of history than the fact itself, inasmuch as "socialism has taken the Commune from the history of France and has made of it a battle cry for the proletariat of the world."

[1] Mason, *The Paris Commune*, p. 370.

After the collapse of the Commune of Paris the National Assembly refused to dissolve itself. Claiming that it was con-
The Provisional Government voked for the purpose of making a constitution, it coöperated for two years with Louis Adolphe Thiers (1797–1877), who had been chosen "Chief of the Executive Power." Under his capable leadership the payment of the enormous indemnity to Germany was completed (1873), and the army was reorganized. The Prussian system of compulsory military service was adopted.

By 1873 many royalists believed the time ripe for a restoration of the monarchy. The monarchists were numerous, but
Royalist Wrangling they were split into three groups: the Legitimists, who upheld the right of the grandson of Charles X, the Count of Chambord; the Orleanists, who favored the claim of the grandson of Louis Philippe, the Count of Paris; and the Bonapartists, who still clung to the fallen Napoleon III or his son. Failing to agree on a candidate, the royalists, after months of wrangling, decided, in May, 1873, to overthrow the republican president Thiers and elect the conservative Marshal MacMahon to the presidency. His election was designed merely to prepare the way for a return of the monarchy.

Legitimists and Orleanists now tried to arrange a compromise settlement. Inasmuch as the Count of Chambord had no heirs, they agreed that he should become king with the understanding that upon his death the crown should pass to the Count of Paris, of the Orleans dynasty. A settlement had been virtually reached when the counts quarreled over whether the "white flag of Henry IV," the ancient Bourbon banner, or the revolutionary tricolor, favored by the house of Orleans, should be adopted. Unable to reach an accord, the royalist factions permitted the republic to continue. Nevertheless they did not renounce their hope of reëstablishing the monarchy. Extending the term of Marshal MacMahon (who had been elected to serve during the pleasure of the Assembly) to seven years, they continued to work for a restoration.

By 1873 the French people, especially the middle classes, were tired of the provisional government. Unable to maintain a strong foreign policy, refusing to make a constitution, and unwilling to relinquish its powers and allow the people to elect a representative body, the Assembly, in 1875, aroused by its increasing unpopularity, passed three organic laws, which collectively formed the constitution. There were provisions for the organization of the government, but the rights of man were not defined.

For several years the monarchists, supported by the clericals, thwarted the efforts of the republicans to seize power. In 1878, however, the latter gained complete control of the government, and a year later they brought about the resignation of Marshal MacMahon. Thereupon the National Assembly elected as president the stanch republican Jules Grévy. Since that time France has been governed by representatives of the middle classes and the peasants.

The constitutional, centralized republic was an attempted compromise between the English parliamentary and American presidential systems. At the head was a president, chosen by the National Legislature for a seven-year term. He had the nominal power of *The Third French Republic* law enforcement, of arranging treaties, of selecting governmental officials, and of making war and peace with the consent of the legislative bodies. He was head of the army and of the navy. But inasmuch as his acts required a ministerial countersignature he was little more than a figurehead. His one real power was that of dissolving or proroguing the Chamber of Deputies.

A ministry composed of a premier and a cabinet was the executive body. The chief minister was dependent upon the dominant party, or group of parties, called a *bloc*, in the Chamber of Deputies. Therefore the actual governing body was this lower house. It consisted of some five hundred representatives, including colonial delegates, elected by popular suffrage for four-year terms. There also was a Senate of three hundred members, elected for nine-year terms, one third being chosen every three years by an indirect election. Having the right to initiate all but fiscal legislation, this assembly served as a check upon the Chamber of Deputies.

Local administration was subordinated to the authority of the central government. France was divided into departments, ruled by prefects, appointed by and representing the national authorities. Local councils existed, but their powers were limited.

In France there were many parties, but no one party could control a majority of the votes in the assembly. Therefore *Political Parties* the chief executive, the premier, relied upon a coalition for support. Inasmuch as it was usually impossible for a political *bloc* to hold together for any length of time, because of the divergence of views, premiers held insecure tenure in office. This rapid change of executives, however, did not signify lack of stability in the French government. Continuity of policy was maintained by means of a highly centralized administration.

There was no party organization as in the United States. Each candidate announced his beliefs and after election joined that party whose platform most closely approximated his views, there being various groups with which he could unite. In the opinion of many Frenchmen this system was superior to the American two-party plan because it represented effectively the different shades of political thought. Of the chief parties the conservatives represented the royalists, who were anti-republican and clerical in policies. Only less conservative was the group known as the *Action libérale*, which endeavored to reconcile Catholicism with conservative republicanism. Somewhat more progressive, representing the upper middle classes, were the Progressist Republicans, usually anticlerical. More extreme in beliefs were the Radicals and the Radical Socialists, who generally favored international peace and drastic social reforms. Most extreme, however, were the Unified Socialists and the Independents. These groups, representing the working classes, favored the complete social and economic transformation of society. Between 1879 and 1914 they made little headway, however, because the governing *blocs* were dominated by the middle classes.

The election of President Grévy was a definite bourgeois triumph. Thenceforth the statesmen and publicists of France were, with few exceptions, lawyers, teachers, or business men, most of them intelligent, well educated, and competent members of the bourgeois class. That such a group of men would devote their efforts to promoting material prosperity was soon demonstrated, for France under their guidance made a greater advance than in any other period. Within two decades the country was recognized again as a power of the first rank in European affairs.

During the early years of the Third French Republic the development of transportation was especially noteworthy. Between 1879 and 1914 thousands of miles of splendid highways were built, several hundred miles of canals were dug, all public dues and private tolls levied upon individuals using certain canals were eliminated, new railways were laid, and all parts of France were reached by efficiently managed governmental or privately owned lines. Water transportation also was improved by deepening harbors and rivers and by encouraging the expansion of the merchant marine.

National Advances

The republican government paid special attention to agriculture. During the decline of the old régime and during the French Revolution the peasants had secured a large number of small holdings. Thereafter they were not only ardent advocates of the system of private property but also earnest opponents of the old aristocratic régime. To insure peasant support the government did everything in its power to aid agricultural development. In 1879 large grants were made to assist the vine-growers, and bounties were repeatedly voted to encourage the culture of silk, flax, and hemp and the breeding of horses. In 1881 a special ministry of agriculture was created. Farmers were permitted, in 1884, to form coöperative societies for collective buying and selling. Under state guarantee mutual loan banks and insurance companies were established (1894) to assist peasants. Agricultural schools were opened and endowed. Tariff protection was given to rural commodities (1885–1892), and taxes were reduced to a minimum. As a result of these measures the amount of agricultural products doubled between 1879 and 1914. Like the industrial and commercial classes the peasants became prosperous, property-owning defenders of the new régime.

In industry development was even more remarkable than in agriculture. Despite the loss of Alsace-Lorraine, which forced France to import one third of her coal supply, she increased its production about threefold between 1871 and 1912. In the making of iron she ranked fourth by 1914. Between 1875 and 1914 the number of machines in factories increased over 300 per cent, while they multiplied themselves tenfold in power. Exports of manufactured goods increased over 25 per cent, even though the chief market for French industries was at home, where industry, like agriculture, was protected by the tariff law of 1892.

France became one of the leading financial and colonial nations of Europe. The thrift and industry of her peasants and business men enabled her to lend billions of dollars to Russia. Business and religious interests as well as historic tradition influenced her to develop a vigorous imperial policy shortly after the Franco-German war. To Algeria were added Tunis, Morocco, and other lands in northern Africa. In the Far East and in the Pacific annexations included Annam and Tongking. Meanwhile the trade of France with her colonies increased from $70,000,000 in 1879 to $400,000,000 in 1914.[1]

This colonial policy strengthened the government. Business men and peasants approved of it because new colonies afforded not only good markets for the sale of the surplus products of their factories and their farms but also excellent fields for the investment of surplus capital in such lucrative enterprises as the development of natural resources and the introduction of internal improvements. The clergy welcomed imperial activity, for it gave them an opportunity to save souls in the heathen lands. Above all, imperialism appealed to the French patriots. Humiliated by the outcome of the Franco-German war, they turned with enthusiasm to the task of reëstablishing a magnificent empire.

[1] For additional information on French imperialism see Chapters XXIII–XXIV.

At the outbreak of the World War, France was a prosperous and wealthy nation, owning not only bonds of foreign governments but also stocks and other securities of foreign private companies. Her wealth was *Social Reforms* more equally distributed than was that of England. Nevertheless poverty existed. Although a minority the proletariat had to work for small wages, huddled in cities and deprived of most of the comforts of life. Many of them bitterly opposed the bourgeois system and favored its overthrow. Their agitation forced the government to act. In 1884 trade unions were recognized, and eight years later a bill was passed creating machinery for an official but voluntary conciliation and arbitration board in cases of collective disputes between employer and employees.

Attempts were made to mollify the workers by means of beneficial social legislation. In 1892 a law was enacted regulating the employment of women, forbidding that of children under thirteen years of age, providing a maximum working day of ten hours, prohibiting manual labor on Sunday except in certain industries, and establishing adequate provisions for the health and safety of persons in factories and for free medical attention. The government in 1893 passed laws designated to protect the health of workers and to provide free medical care for wage-earners and families. Legislation in 1898 forced employers to compensate workers for injuries received during service, and in 1911 a system of old-age pensions was established, embracing all wage-earners not included in previous pension acts. The system was compulsory and contributory, payments to the pension fund being made by the workers, the employers, and the state.

Although the government adopted paternalistic policies, yet, in line with its heritage from the French Revolution, it promoted individualism. Liberty was stressed, and laws guaranteed free speech, free press, and free assembly within certain limitations. The government also passed humanitarian legislation modifying the cruel criminal code and reducing the authority of the father in the family, thus offering better protection to children than was provided by the Napoleonic code. In 1884 divorce was again legalized. Education was especially favored by the republican government. Appealing to the middle classes for support, leading politicians championed secular schools which would give the sons and daughters of France the training necessary for this bourgeois age of "free competition and of the survival of the fittest."

Previously the Catholic church had controlled education. Republicans, however, believed that they had good reasons to abolish this monopoly, inasmuch as the *Educational Develop-* clericals, they asserted, were monarchists, and *ments* thus disloyal to the republic. Between 1881 and 1886 the French public-school system was firmly established. Jules Ferry, the republican minister of education, introduced bills which placed elementary schools in France on a basis similar to that in the United States. By becoming centers of bourgeois republican patriotism the public schools more than proved their worth.

At first clerical educational institutions were not molested. Parents could still send their children to the public, ecclesiastical, or private institutions. This educational program, together with laws directed against "unauthorized" communities of monks and of nuns and the legislation of civil marriage and of divorce, aroused the opposition of the clericals. Despite admonition from the Pope many churchmen supported the monarchists against the republic and thus further weakened the position of the church.

Exponents of a benevolent bourgeois democracy thus encountered strong hostility. To strengthen the position of the government, amendments were passed in 1884 *Opposition to the Re-* which prohibited a change of the fundamental *public* laws creating the republic and abolished senatorial life members and dynasties. Criticism, however, increased. Unstable ministries and corruption involving relatives of a republican president were frequently cited by monarchists and clericals as examples of governmental inefficiency.

In the eighties the opposition to the government came to a head under the leadership of the ambitious but weak General Georges Boulanger (1837–1891). As minister of war (1886) he became one of the most popular men in France because of his jingoistic utterances about a war of "revenge" against Germany. Perhaps he actually believed that *General Boulanger* he was another Napoleon I. His colleagues, however, refused to be impressed by his greatness and thrust him out of the cabinet (1887). Backed now by the monarchists, the Bonapartists, and other enemies of the republic, Boulanger turned on the government and advocated a dictatorship under his leadership.

The resignation of President Grévy, brought about by the disgrace of his son-in-law, who had been proved guilty of trafficking in the decorations of the Legion of Honor, encouraged Boulanger in his attacks upon the republic. But this would-be "man on horseback" was merely a talker and a swaggerer. When the republic was about to prefer charges against him, he fled to Belgium and to England, committing suicide in 1891.

The Boulanger episode weakened the monarchist cause and strengthened the republicans. In order to avoid a military *coup d'état* in the future, the government republicanized the army, retiring the monarchist officers who hitherto had dominated that organization. Aware of the strength of the republic, the Pope asked French Catholics in 1892 to desist from further attacks upon the government and suggested that they work for legislation favorable to the church. Many Catholics refused to heed his admonitions, however, and, continuing to support the monarchists, increased the antagonism between the government and the church.

Another episode demonstrated the power of the republic. In 1894 considerable anti-Semitic sentiment existed in France. Taking advantage of this, monarchists, clericals, and other enemies of the government as- *The Dreyfus Affair* serted that the republic was run by unscrupulous Jewish bankers. The exposure of grave financial scandals in connection with the construction of the Panama Canal, involving Jews and republicans, gave these groups added ammunition. Affairs came to a head when Alfred Dreyfus, a Jewish captain of artillery and a republican, was convicted by court-martial of selling military secrets to the Germans and was sent to penal servitude for life on Devil's Island, off the coast of French Guiana. To the opponents of the government this treachery was absolute proof of an unholy alliance between Jews and republicans.

In 1896 Colonel Picquart, the new head of the intelligence division of the French army, received evidence which convinced him that Dreyfus had been convicted unjustly. An investigation was initiated, and after he and others, including the novelist Zola, had agitated the matter for years, Dreyfus was pardoned and restored to the army (1906). Partially as a result of this affair the monarchists were thoroughly discredited. Republicans and socialists formed a *bloc* which for many years dominated the government.

The wrath of the republic was directed against the "monarchist" church. Angered by the opposition of many clericals,

Separation of Church and State

the government in 1901 passed the Association Act, which provided that no religious order should exist in France without official authorization, and that no member of an unauthorized association should be permitted to teach in any school in France. In 1904 another bill declared that members of religious associations, authorized or unauthorized, should no longer teach in public schools. As a result of this law hundreds of men and women belonging to religious orders were driven out of France, and thousands of church schools were closed.

Through the abrogation of the Concordat of 1801, which had regulated the relations of church and state for more than a century, complete separation of church and state now followed. Under the Separation Law of 1905 the adherents of all creeds were placed on an equal footing and were authorized to form associations of laymen for public worship. The state was relieved of payment of salaries to the clergy, with few exceptions, and churches were turned over to lay associations to be used as long as the organizations lasted.

The Pope and many prominent Catholics objected to this act, especially the part which allowed laymen to participate, by means of associations for public worship, in the management of ecclesiastical affairs. Therefore the church refused to recognize these associations. After a two-year controversy a compromise was finally arranged by the tactful statesman Aristide Briand. A new law of 1907 gave the clergy the right to make arrangements with the local mayors for the use and maintenance of the churches for worship and the privilege of managing their religious affairs as they pleased. These laws were important because they separated church and state, and by so doing insured bourgeois control in secular matters. Moreover, the church was made a private institution. Deprived of much of its property, its state support, and a large part of its educational work, it concentrated upon the spiritual realm, in which it soon showed increasing vigor and determination.

By 1914 the Third French Republic appeared to be a stable government. It had defeated its enemies, and, in control of education, was in a position to promote loyalty *France in 1914* to the republic and to the middle-class system. In the schools French culture was emphasized and alien languages were neglected. Instruction in history was largely concerned with the internal developments of France; foreign affairs received little attention. Children were taught to support the existing order and to work for the glory of the nation. To strengthen its position, the government had democratized the army. The higher ranks were no longer monopolized by the aristocrats. Universal conscription was established, although by 1913 the number of years of military service had been reduced from five (law of 1872) to three (law of 1889) and to two (law of 1905). In 1913, however, the term of military service was increased to three years. While republicanizing the army the government, to ward off invasions, also built powerful forts on the German frontier at Verdun and at Belfort.

Security against a German attack was not the only motive behind these military preparations. Ever since the Franco-German war many Frenchmen had lived for *The Spirit of Revanche* the day when France should obtain "revenge" and regain her lost provinces from Germany. Even though pacifism and socialism were strong forces in France opposed to war, and even though the government seemed to be primarily interested in economic, social, and religious problems, the idea of *revanche* persisted.

In 1914, however, internal problems predominated. The wage-earners were restless. Allowed to organize, they had formed, in 1895, a General Confederation of Labor, including nearly all the unions. In various industrial centers chambers of labor also were established after 1887, where workers could meet and discuss their problems. A national federation of these chambers was organized which in 1902 combined with the General Confederation of Labor. This unification resulted in the popularization of syndicalism, a distinctive feature of the French labor movement. The avowed aim of the syndicalists was a truceless war on capital by means of sabotage and the strike. "We cannot improve the conditions of labor by political action," said the representatives of this movement; "so the logical method is the use of the economic weapon, the strike."

Internal Problems

An epidemic of labor troubles soon broke out. In 1906 a general strike forced the authorities to call out the troops, and in 1910 the government, in order to end a great railway walkout, had to order the men to the colors and then to run the railroads. The failure of this strike caused many wage-earners to desert the syndicalist movement and to join the socialist cause in the hope of winning control of the government and thereby gaining their ends.

By 1914 the socialists had replaced the monarchists as the chief opponents of the bourgeois republic. Their rise is well described in French literature. After the French defeat of 1870 the buoyancy of romanticism declined. A spirit of cynicism swept over France. Guy de Maupassant (1850–1893) wrote his famous stories, in which, with complete frankness, with unusual impartiality, and with convincing realism, he showed the futilities, the follies, and the heroisms of mankind. Then came the so-called naturalistic period in French literature, well represented by Émile Zola (1840–1903), who seemed able to see nothing but the evil and ugliness in the life about him.

Socialism

Unsatisfactory economic and social conditions, however, caused apostles of a new order to appear. In politics Jean Jaurès (1859–1914), the French social philosopher, who advanced in his writings the establishment of a socialist state, became a real power. In literature the radical Anatole France (1844–1924) had few equals. An ironical socialist, he branded injustice of the law to the weak and ignorant. Like Balzac he revealed, in his *Île des Pingouins* (Penguin Island), that intense opposition to the bourgeoisie which has characterized the radical intelligentsia of France. As a spiritual descendant of Renan, France popularized religious themes, which he handled in the satirical manner of Voltaire. Despite his radicalism, France was a true patriot. His love of Paris he eloquently expressed in the following extract from his *Le Crime de Sylvestre Bonnard*:

old and venerable Paris with its towers and spires, all that is my life, it is myself, and I should be nothing without those things which are reflected in me with the thousand shades of my thought, which inspire me and urge me on. That is why I love Paris with a mighty love.

In 1878 Italy was a united nation; and according to her poets, who predicted that she would again become the center of a great civilization surrounding the deep-blue Mediterranean Sea, her future appeared brilliant. Cavour, "'architect' of United Italy," *Constitutionalism in Italy* however, had not been led astray by this classical propaganda. He knew that Italy was materially and intellectually a backward land, but he believed that the obstacles to progress could be overcome by introducing modern ideas and methods.

Of the many problems confronting Italy the most urgent was its lack of wealth. Not only were the people poor, but the country as a whole had limited resources and was backward in agriculture as well as in industry. A heavy debt, incurred by the wars of independence, together with expenditures of money for public improvements, educational developments, imperialistic undertakings, and war preparedness, resulted in the imposition of high taxes upon the Italians. These levies in turn discouraged industrial development and the entrance of foreign capital. As long as this bad financial situation existed a prosperous bourgeois régime could not be established.

Lacking internal cohesion, Italy in 1878 was not ready for democracy. Strong central authority was needed to force the eight former states to lose their identity and *Problems confronting the Government* relinquish their privileges. There was also an important sectional problem, the north versus the south. The former enjoyed a degree of industrial development, its cities being ruled by an intelligent and prosperous middle class, while the latter was still a backward region dominantly agricultural. Much of the land being nonarable and most of it in the hands of a few landowners, the peasants were poor, illiterate, and superstitious. The people as a whole, affected by foreign exploitation in the past and by centuries of bad, corrupt, and cruel government, possessed a contempt for authority. Secret societies, such as the Mafia of Sicily and the Camorra of Naples, resisted the attempts of the new monarchy to maintain law and order and to introduce reforms. Malaria and other diseases, weakening the people physically, only served to increase the difficulties confronting the monarchy.

Italy, as is discussed elsewhere,[1] had a problem peculiar to that country,— the papal question. When Rome was captured (1870), the Italian government, in order to avoid trouble, enacted a "Law of Papal Guarantees," allowing the Pope considerable freedom. Refusing to accept any part of the financial grant, Pius IX shut himself up as a "prisoner" in the Vatican, summoned Catholic princes to coöperate in restoring his temporal power, and positively forbade Italian Catholics to vote or hold offices under the royal government. Later his successors, to check socialism, allowed Catholics to participate in elections.

To help overcome the socialist and Catholic opposition which stood in the way of a strong and united Italy, the government, between 1878 and 1914, tried to foster prosperity by enlightened agricultural and industrial policies. Socialist and Catholic organizations, as well as the government, endeavored to improve agricultural conditions by favoring coöperative

[1] See pages 262–263.

societies and rural banks and by depriving the large land-owners, especially in the south, of their lands, in order to give them to the peasants. In industry Italy, because of lack of coal and iron, made little *Attempts to solve Italy's Problems* headway. She possessed water power, but for its development needed capital, which was lacking. She did succeed, however, in creating a great silk-producing center in Milan. An earnest attempt was made to adjust the un-favorable balance of trade, resulting from the importation of coal and other necessities, by building a great merchant marine. In her endeavor to create a prosperous bourgeois state Italy spent so much money that at various times she was on the verge of bankruptcy.

Two unusual sources of capital,— remittances from Italian emigrants in the United States and in Hispanic America, and profits accruing from tourist trade,— it is often said, kept her from financial ruin. The emigration of Italians to the New World resulted from the unsatisfactory conditions in Italy. Thousands of artisans and peasants left the motherland in order to take advantage of the opportunities offered in the Americas. Having amassed wealth in their new homes, these Italians frequently sent large sums of money to Italy in order to help their less fortunate relatives.

The government also tried to win the support of the work-ers and peasants. Between 1898 and 1910, social-insurance laws were passed providing compensation to workers for injuries, old age, and sickness. But these measures were only partially successful; they did not benefit the peasants, nor did they solve the nation-wide problem of unemployment. Meanwhile the workers tended to listen more and more to radical ideas, and by 1914 many were joining the Socialist and Communist parties.

Numerous Italians criticized the government for its failure to regain "unredeemed Italy." The Hapsburgs still ruled over a great number of Italians living in the Tren-tino region, in Trieste, and in Fiume, thus *"Unredeemed Italy"* maintaining a control of the Adriatic Sea coveted by Italy. The government's failure to complete the unification of Italy, and its inability to create economic prosperity, caused many Italians to become pessimistic.

Cavour had believed that Italy would benefit through the creation of a democratic government. Therefore he established a modern constitutional monarchy in which the king was a figurehead and parliament was the real governing body. The legislature was bicameral, consisting of a semi-aristocratic Senate and a Chamber of Deputies elected by limited suffrage. In the new government the latter was the more important.

As in France, the limited monarchy was centralized. Prefects, advised by local councils, represented parliament in all parts of Italy. The executive power was lodged in the hands of a cabinet appointed by the king but responsible to the Chamber of Deputies. The premier, representing the dominant party or coalition of parties in the Chamber of Deputies, was the head of the cabinet.

The Italian party system also resembled that of France. There were numerous groups in parliament, three or four of

Political Parties

which usually selected the premier. Of these parties, between 1878 and 1914, the most important were the following: the Clericals, representing the interests of the church and of the papacy; the Constitutionalists, supporting the limited monarchy; the Republicans, anticlerical heirs of Mazzini and Garibaldi; and the Radicals (Socialists and Communists), mostly workingmen in northern Italy who favored the strike and the overthrow of the bourgeois government. Within these general groups there were divisions and additional parties.

As a whole the Italians lacked the necessary background of political experience. Consequently they never really understood party government. The existence of numerous political factions did much to weaken the constitutional monarchy. Few premiers were able to retain the support of a coalition of parties (a *bloc*) for any length of time. Without the backing of powerful bourgeois and peasant organizations, they evaded issues and tried to remain in office by weak and corrupt rather than by strong and honest policies. Thus prime ministers rose and fell in rapid succession.

Certain ministers, however, did make conscientious efforts to solve Italy's problems and thus to justify the bourgeois constitutional monarchy. Although resultant high taxes brought about their downfall, the Conservatives at first endeavored to continue Cavour's work by centralizing the government, by nationalizing the railroads, and by establishing universal military service. In 1876 the liberals of the left came into power, promising universal suffrage, lower taxes, and compulsory education. Agostino Depretis (1813–1887), leader of this group, became premier, and with two short interruptions retained this office until 1887.

This bourgeois politician knew little of the internal and foreign problems of his country. "When I see an international question upon the horizon," he once said, "I open my umbrella and wait until it is passed." Although Depretis was elected as a liberal, he adopted conservative policies. Radical or republican meetings were forbidden, newspapers were suspended, labor unions were dissolved, and strikers were sent to prison. It is true that during his administration the suffrage was extended (1882), railways were built, and the army and navy were enlarged. Outside of these few constructive policies, however, his administration was distinguished by corruption rather than by progress.

The more famous Francesco Crispi (1819–1901) became premier upon the death of Depretis in 1887. During his nine years in office Crispi tried to establish bourgeois prosperity in Italy. Imperialism and militarism were stimulated and the alliance with Germany and Austria, arranged during the administration of Depretis, was twice renewed.[1] One of Crispi's first acts was to abrogate a commercial treaty with France. He then encouraged the creation of class economic relations with Germany. Many German bankers and business men took advantage of this situation to expand their interests in Italy. Crispi also tried to extend the suffrage and to promote education. Unfortunately his followers engaged in corrupt bargains with factions in parliament. Patronage, coercion,

[1] For additional information on Italian imperialism see pages 407–408, 417–418.

and bribery, the generally accepted agencies whereby a man could remain in power in southern Italy, soon spread to the north. Even Crispi himself was involved in a bank scandal in Rome. This trouble, together with labor unrest and riots in Sicily and the Italian defeat in Abyssinia (1896), brought about his downfall.

Crispi's overthrow in 1896 and the death of King Humbert in 1900 marked the beginning of new political and social
New Political and Social Policies policies. The next king, Victor Emmanuel III (1900–   ), appeared enlightened, amiable, and democratic. He did not oppose the establishment of a more liberal government in 1903, when Giovanni Giolitti, a professional politician, became premier. Desirous of winning the support of the wage-earners, Giolitti proclaimed the neutrality of the government in all struggles between capital and labor. The workers took advantage of this announcement by instituting a number of strikes. Meanwhile the rapid spread of syndicalist ideas among the wage-earners caused the unions to become more revolutionary. By 1905 Italy seemed on the verge of an upheaval. Aroused by this danger, Pope Pius X gave Catholics permission to vote, thus paving the way for the rise of a bourgeois clerical party.

Endeavoring to solve the economic and social problems which caused the unrest, the government favored industry and workers by means of a protective tariff and social-insurance laws. An act of 1908 made provision for a weekly day of rest for workers, and a law of 1912 nationalized life insurance. Trade unions were legalized, and attempts were made to arbitrate chronic labor disputes. An electoral-reform act, passed the same year, practically established universal manhood suffrage.

Although the Giolitti government at first paid little attention to Italian imperialistic aspirations, many patriots continued to agitate for expansion. Intellectuals, such as Gabriele d'Annunzio (1863–   ), tried to arouse Italian patriotism by recalling the glories of the Roman Empire and the oppression of "brothers" living in "unredeemed Italy."

Finally, influenced by these sentiments, Italy again manifested her "sacred egotism." In a determination to revive the past and to establish a great empire by extending her domain around the Mediterranean and the Adriatic the Italian government reversed its foreign policies. Between 1900 and 1902 Italy had arranged a friendly understanding with her rival, France, concerning their respective interests in North Africa. Plans were revived for the annexation of lands inhabited by Italians around the Adriatic. In 1911–1912 Italy took advantage of a war imposed upon Turkey to seize not only Tripoli, in northern Africa, but also the Dodecanese Islands, in the Ægean. Henceforth she merely awaited a convenient opportunity to withdraw from the Triple Alliance and to regain "unredeemed Italy."

Bourgeois liberalism was not a success in either Portugal or Spain. In Portugal dynastic struggles, attempts to create a parliamentary government, and the dissatisfaction growing out of the loss of her important colony, Brazil, finally resulted in the establishment of a republic (1910). Although the new government resembled that of France, it was in no sense democratic. In spite of the political change, dictators and corruption prevailed.

Industrially and agriculturally backward, Portugal nevertheless was able to cope with political and religious problems. The church was deprived of many priv-ileges, and education was extended. Although *Portugal* numerous citizens opposed militarism and favored a social upheaval, Portugal managed to avoid a widespread revolution. She also retained a considerable portion of her colonial possessions, including holdings in East Africa and islands and ports in various parts of the world. Since trade with them was the most important element in Portugal's economy, her empire was of great value.

In the early nineteenth century, as we have seen,[1] the democratic movement in Spain resolved itself into dynastic struggles. Matters reached a head in 1886, when Queen Isabella was forced to flee and a Hohenzollern was invited to fill the vacant throne. He declined the invitation and the "doubtful

[1] See pages 64–65, 66.

honor" was offered to an Italian prince, who held the position for two years and then abdicated.

From 1873 to 1875 a republican government existed in Spain in name only. To most Spaniards the new liberty meant license, and conditions in Spain went from bad to worse. In 1875 the great majority of Spaniards welcomed the return to authority of the Bourbon monarchy in the person of Alphonso XII. At first he tried to establish a strong government; later he created a liberal constitutional monarchy. Both governments failed to function. Alphonso XII died in 1885 and was succeeded by the posthumous Alphonso XIII. For seventeen years his mother, Maria Christina, governed as queen regent. During her administration liberal and conservative leaders agreed to partition the spoils of office by controlling the elections. Unaware of this arrangement, the people had the pleasure of driving the conservatives out and putting the liberals in, and *vice versa*.

During the regency the Spanish government had many difficult problems to solve. A rebellion occurred in the colony of Cuba. This led to the intervention of the United States and to the Spanish-American War of 1898. Defeated in this conflict, Spain lost the Philippine Islands, Cuba, and Puerto Rico, retaining only scattered remnants of her once great empire. Domestic problems also existed. By the beginning of the twentieth century the religious question became especially important. Inasmuch as Spain had long been the defender and the missionary citadel of the Catholic faith, the church became a wealthy and a powerful institution. The rise of republicanism and socialism in Spain, however, was accompanied by the development of an aggressive anticlerical movement. Partly because of its activities Protestant worship was legalized, and an act was passed prohibiting the establishment of any more religious houses without governmental sanction. Lacking the support of a numerous and powerful middle class, however, the anticlericals failed in their attempt to bring about a complete separation of church and state; but some significant educational and economic reforms were achieved. In

Problems confronting the Government

1909 elementary education was made obligatory; social legislation, such as employers' liability factory laws and state-guaranteed insurance, was passed; and coöperative shops were established.

In trying to retain the few remaining bits of its empire the government lost what little prestige it had gained among the lower classes through its social legislation. In 1912, by agreement with France, Spain added to her few African possessions the northern coast of Morocco and some other regions. The uprisings of the warlike Riffs in Morocco unexpectedly demonstrated her inefficiency in the administration of her colonies. These disorders served only to increase the opposition to the monarchy. By 1914 anti-militarism, anti-imperialism, anti-absolutism, and anti-clericalism were spreading rapidly among the bourgeoisie and the working classes.

Spain, during the nineteenth century, advanced a great deal intellectually and artistically. Many of her writers and painters were among the leading figures of the world. Of the early-nineteenth-century literary lights José de Espronceda (1808–1842), the lyric poet, and José Zorrilla (1817–1893), poet and dramatist, were particularly noteworthy. Their works are fine examples of the early opposition to the artless and cold neo-classic movement of the eighteenth century. Benito Pérez Galdós (1845–1920) was considered one of the leading novelists. Holding aloof from schools and theories, Galdós conceived the novel as the exact reproduction of life in all its phases.

Spanish Culture

By 1914 the attempts to establish an efficient bourgeois system in the Latin countries around the Mediterranean had not been a complete success. Perhaps these failures were due to lack of natural resources, unfavorable climatic conditions, loss of colonies, decline of commerce, the absence of powerful, aggressive, intelligent middle classes, and the need of popular education and of political experience. The classical tradition also helped to explain the limited success of liberalism. Firm believers in the necessity of unity and authority, many of these people found it difficult to accept the bourgeois doctrine of individualism.

Conclusion

CHAPTER XIX

The German Empire: Enlightened Despotism

THE German Empire owed its foundation to diplomacy and war, and its consolidation to efficiency and peace. As chancellor of the new state Bismarck steadily strove to avoid a conflict, so that Germany might become wealthy and prosperous under his paternalistic guidance. His pacific policy did not embrace disarmament, but a peace guaranteed by preparedness. Believing that the existence of Germany would be jeopardized should she ever become too weak to fight France single-handed, he favored throughout his administration the maintenance of a strong army.

Bismarck, determined to nationalize the empire, strove to safeguard German unity. By merging the banks into an imperial financial organization, by adopting a *Bismarck's Objective* uniform system of coinage, by establishing unified law codes and courts, and by creating imperial railways, telegraphs, and telephones, he did much to influence the Germans into submerging local feeling in a common consciousness of national unity. To prevent the dissolution of the empire through the rise of "states' rights," he favored at all times the extension of imperial authority at the expense of particularism.

As chancellor the conservative Bismarck refused to support any policy or to countenance any group which threatened *The Kulturkampf* the security of the state. Although he realized that both Catholics and Protestants had struggled for German unity and fought side by side in opposition to France, he subscribed to an intolerant patriotism which questioned the loyalty of Catholics, Jews, and Socialists. Unconsciously, perhaps, the Roman Catholic Church, under the leadership of the Pope, aroused the bitter opposition of the imperial chancellor. During the Franco-German War a decree

332

of the Vatican Council had affirmed the infallibility of the Pope. As Bismarck interpreted this declaration, the church, under the rule of Pius IX, threatened to become a state within a state. Alarmed, he encouraged the anticlericals and joined them in a conflict which was called the *Kulturkampf*, or battle for civilization. In his opinion the struggle was primarily for political supremacy. The Catholics were representatives of particularism, and Bismarck did not propose to see Catholic Bavarians, Poles, and Alsatians transform the empire into another Holy Roman nonentity.

By influencing the *Reichstag* to pass a law (1872) which expelled the Jesuits he inaugurated the anticlerical campaign. He caused the Prussian *Landtag* to enact the famous May Laws (1873–1875), which, after suppressing numerous religious orders, placed under state control the education, appointment, and dismissal of the Catholic clergy, made civil marriages compulsory, and limited the use of state funds by the Catholic church.

The rise of a new enemy, the red international (socialism), led Bismarck to renounce the fight "for civilization" and to make peace with the church. He realized that to defeat the Pope he might be compelled to resort to force and to govern without parliament, and that such measures would increase the strength of the Socialists. When the moderate Leo XIII succeeded the militant Pius IX in 1878, the way was cleared for a *rapprochement* with the papacy. Alarmed at the growth of socialism, the new Pope hastened to accept Bismarck's overtures of peace. Between 1878 and 1887 nearly all anti-Catholic legislation in Germany was abrogated. However, a Center, or Catholic, party, formed to oppose Bismarck's measures during this period, later became a real force in German politics.

Bismarck and his successors were given intellectual support by three able German economists, Schmoller (1838–1917), List (1789–1846), and Wagner (1835–1917). *Economic Doctrines* Accepting the idea of the supremacy of the state, they maintained that a unified and powerful empire could best be preserved by the establishment of friendly relations among the different social classes, the removal or reduction of injustice, an approach to a more equitable distribution of wealth, and social legislation promoting progress and the moral elevation of the lower and middle classes.

In his work on the mercantile system Schmoller traced the growth of the German state through a policy of governmental regulation and support. List, in *The National System of Political Economy* (1841), preached the gospel of economic nationalism as opposed to the *laissez faire* doctrine. Power, he believed, should be the chief economic aim. "A country can have too many scholars and too few workmen," he said. "To make a great, rich, and mighty nation are needed manufactures, free internal intercourse, foreign trade, shipping, and moral power." Agriculture was insufficient; industry was the key to wealth and culture. Power could best be obtained if a community became self-sufficing, developing its resources to the utmost. Protection, economic exploitation of all resources, regardless of other nations, would, in his opinion, lead to world power. Such was the program he held out for Germany. In harmony with this view another economist, Wagner, held that it was unchristian and inhuman to regard labor as merely a commodity to be bought and sold in the market, and wages as its price. All classes, he said, must coöperate in the creation of a prosperous and powerful German Empire, so that all might benefit.

Economists were not alone in defending Bismarck's paternalistic policies. The great landowners of the conservative party, the Centrists, representing many peasants, and some middle-class National Liberals also supported him. Especially interested in protection for agriculture and industry, however, they were not vitally concerned with Bismarck's social legislation. These groups were rewarded when a law of 1879 established a high tariff on both agricultural and industrial products.

This act marked the beginning of Germany's rise in the economic world. In the decade from 1880 to 1890 a remarkable change occurred. The early nineteenth-century Germany, which had consisted of thrifty workers on the farms and in the handicrafts, suddenly became industrialized. Factories sprang up everywhere, and

Economic Advances

many optimists could see no limit to Germany's prosperity, even though her resources in such basic necessities as coal and iron were sadly limited.

The extraordinary industrial development was facilitated by the indemnity paid Germany by France. It started the ball of industrial progress rolling. Men began to fling money recklessly into all sorts of investments. An era of speculation occurred, and great fortunes were amassed. Eventually, however, the bull market collapsed when the newly constructed factories reached a stage where they were producing more than could be consumed or exported. The bottom fell out of the stock market, and a business depression followed. Wages, stocks, and agricultural prices fell. Soon Germany sought and found markets in which to sell her surplus goods, and a pronounced stimulation of German industries followed. Between 1850 and 1880 German foreign trade increased threefold. The trade-mark "Made in Germany," later found throughout the world, was evidence of this commercial expansion.

Germany's industrial development practically forced Bismarck to modify his colonial policy. Heretofore he had opposed an aggressive imperialism on the ground that it would involve the country in foreign complications. *Colonial Expansion* Colonies, he stated emphatically, were troublemakers; Great Britain might oppose German imperialism, and Germany could not afford to antagonize her friendly neighbor.

Many political and industrial leaders insisted that economic development made colonies necessary. By the eighties German capitalism, they believed, had outgrown its home markets and resources. Germany needed raw materials, opportunities to invest money and to sell goods, and places to which to send her surplus population. Moved by these requirements, certain patriots organized a colonial society, which sent missionaries and explorers to Africa and founded trading posts. By 1884–1885, influenced by Germany's industrial development, Bismarck was committed to the colonial program, and the way was prepared for the rise of an overseas empire.

As established in Germany by Bismarck the political system was intended to unify the country through the concentration of power in the hands of the Hohenzollern emperors. The constitution of 1871 was in the nature of permanent treaties between the North German Confederation and the four South German states. It created a federal union of twenty-six states, in which supreme direction of the military and political affairs of the empire was vested in the king of Prussia, who *ipso facto* was German Emperor.

The Imperial Government

Through special treaties with Baden, Bavaria, and Württemberg the imperial government allowed them to exercise certain powers; but it retained control of matters involving the regulation of corporations, railways, social welfare, industrial relations, defense, foreign affairs, and civil and criminal laws, some of which in the United States were in the hands of the states. The German states, all monarchies with the exception of three city-republics and Alsace-Lorraine, were intrusted with authority to enforce imperial laws.

In the administration of domestic matters the Hohenzollern Kaiser was not dominant. His executive power was slight, as there were only a few federal officials to appoint and he lacked veto power over bills passed by parliament. Possessing greater influence in foreign affairs, he could in the name of the empire declare war and peace, arrange alliances and treaties with foreign states, and appoint and receive ambassadors. He was also commander-in-chief of the army and navy and appointed the chancellor. The latter controlled the cabinet, the other members of which he selected. Subject to the approval of the Kaiser the chancellor, as chairman of the Prussian delegation to the *Bundesrat*, directed the policies of the empire.

The new imperial legislature consisted of two houses: the *Bundesrat*, representing the rulers of the twenty-six states, and the *Reichstag*, representing the people. The *Bundesrat*, consisting of sixty-one members, was dominated by the seventeen delegates from Prussia. They voted as a unit, and, subservient to the king of Prussia, executed his will with respect to all bills, treaties, or appointments considered by this house.

Inasmuch as the *Bundesrat* functioned as arbiter in quarrels between the states, the Prussian ruler was in a position to settle most imperial disputes. He could also reject all constitutional amendments originating in the *Reichstag*, since fourteen votes in the *Bundesrat* sufficed to kill such proposals. Theoretically the *Bundesrat* was entirely in the hands of the reigning princes; practically it was under the control of the emperor.

Of the parliament the *Reichstag* was the more democratic house. Although the initiation of legislation was confined largely to the *Bundesrat*, the former could pass or defeat bills. It had no voice in the selection of the cabinet, which was appointed by the chief executive officer, the imperial chancellor. Actually it was little more than a debating society, whose members, elected by universal male suffrage, could merely express their opinions and pray that their advice be heeded.

The German Empire was not created through the absorption of other states by Prussia; it grew out of the union of all the German states, wherein Prussia enjoyed a dominant position. An outstanding exponent of enlightened despotism, Prussia, as mentioned before, had been able in the eighteenth century to overcome her rivals and to develop her economic resources. After the dissolution of the Napoleonic empire the dominant class was still the junkers, devout upholders of autocracy sustained by a powerful army. Consequently the liberal movement was able to effect few important political changes in Prussia before 1850. A constitution had been adopted, but the junkers controlled the legislative body, the *Landtag*, through the three-class system of voting. The Hohenzollern king remained a despot in Prussia, with power to appoint and to dismiss all cabinet officials and to veto all legislation passed by the *Landtag*. In becoming emperor of Germany he carried over into the enlarged position a great part of the authority he exercised in Prussia. As a powerful Prussian sovereign, usually supported by the conservative junkers, he was able to select and to control the large Prussian delegation to the *Bundesrat* and by it to dominate the imperial government.

The Predominance of Prussia

The proximity of hostile neighbors, the problem of merging twenty-six states into a unified nation, and the Hohenzollern policy of benevolent despotism explain the creation of a strong central government. As chancellor, Bismarck realized that a weak, decentralized German state probably would invite alien (especially French) interference and war. He also recognized the possibility of trouble between the local states and the imperial government. Determined to maintain German unity by means of an autocratic administration, Bismarck revived the paternalistic policies of Frederick the Great. The result was a political organization which was not only remarkably efficient but progressive and sound economically. Laws intended to help all classes were passed; these were executed by carefully trained officials. Extensive social reforms designed to aid all elements and thus to strengthen the prosperous German state were inaugurated.

Reasons for German Autocracy

Although political parties in Germany at first were unimportant, they soon began to participate actively in parliamentary elections and to exert considerable indirect influence in the *Reichstag*. Forming coalitions in order to pass certain laws, most of these organizations had definite religious, class, national, or economic programs. By 1914 they were grouped into five general divisions. On the extreme right were the Conservatives, representative, for the most part, of the Prussian junkers, and the Lutherans, who demanded an autocratic militaristic government, a high protective tariff, and a strong foreign and colonial policy. Next in influence was the Center party, a Catholic organization with great strength among the peasant proprietors of Bavaria, which had as its program the interests of the church, moderate social reforms, and bitter hostility to socialism. To the left of the Centrists were the National Liberals, representative of the industrialists, who opposed socialism and favored militarism, imperialism, and an aggressive foreign policy. Unlike the Conservatives, however, they urged liberal political and social reforms and a low tariff on agricultural products.

Political Parties

Farther to the left were the Progressives, formerly National Liberals, including many professional men, who were more advanced in their views. As constitutional bourgeois monarchists they advocated personal liberty, parliamentary government, secular education, free trade, and a shift of the tax burden to the wealthy through heavy taxes on incomes and inheritance. On the extreme left were the Social Democrats, the party of the wage-earners. Although socialism was their goal, they were willing to coöperate with the Progressive party in obtaining immediate reforms. Unlike the other groups, the Social Democrats maintained a well-organized party, which was characterized by unified control and a well-defined program. They nominated candidates and circulated propaganda in favor of their ideas. Opposed to the sectarian policies of the Conservatives and Centrists were free-thinkers and anticlericals in the National Liberal, Progressive, and Social Democratic parties.

These political groups achieved little, largely because they lacked capable leaders. Most brilliant men in Germany were unwilling to waste their time delivering futile speeches in the *Reichstag*. They preferred to become governmental officials, industrial magnates, or educational experts. Consequently the parties, though mirrors of public opinion, lacked the leadership necessary to dominate national politics.

Many of the middle classes and the workers objected to this enlightened autocracy, but failed to coöperate in common opposition to the government. The bourgeoisie were unwilling to combine with the wage-earners against the state, because they believed *Lack of Opposition to Autocracy* that the proletariat would try to establish socialism under the cloak of democracy. On the other hand, the workers refused to unite with the middle classes, because they feared that to do so would result in the substitution of bourgeois control. In their opinion such a change would not contribute to their economic advancement. This division in the ranks of the opposition to the central government weakened the influence of the liberals and radicals and enabled the autocracy to withstand all attacks.

The loyalty of all classes was promoted by the creation of an imperial army. It consisted of men who, as youths of twenty, were conscripted for one or two years' service and afterwards remained in the reserves

The Army

until the age of forty-five. While in the army they were under the supreme command of the Kaiser and were trained by officers of the conservative junker class. Despite alleged brutal treatment the recruits received an excellent military and physical education and were trained in the ways of obedience and loyalty to the imperial government.

By 1878 the Socialists were open opponents of Bismarck's policies. Avowedly republican, they demanded democracy and social reforms and bitterly condemned the Franco-German War and the annexation

The Socialist Menace

of Alsace-Lorraine. Convinced that these Socialists were traitors and should be treated accordingly, Bismarck sponsored a series of "Exceptional Laws" designed to subdue these public enemies. They were forbidden to form organizations, to hold meetings, or to publish newspapers or books. The police were empowered to expel Socialists from the country in certain cases, and to arrest their leaders upon the slightest provocation.

Bismarck soon discovered that socialism could not be extinguished by force. Under the guise of athletic organizations and secret societies, its champions continued to spread socialist propaganda and to circulate radical newspapers published in Switzerland. By 1890 the Socialists had 1,500,000 members, with 35 representatives in the *Reichstag*. The Exceptional Laws, because of their ineffectiveness, were not renewed at that time.

In his struggle to check socialism the Iron Chancellor displayed an extraordinary grasp of the economic situation in Germany. Soon realizing that the growth of internal dissension was the result of the rapid

Social Reforms

industrialization of Germany, he abandoned force for a new policy of social reform. Thereby he hoped to solve the labor problem and thus to eliminate the necessity for socialism. At first, as an individualist and free-trader, he had adopted the *laissez faire* policy of non-interference by the government in economic matters; but, as a stanch supporter of Hohenzollern policies, he could not depart completely from the economic and social policies peculiar to paternalistic despotism. Inspired finally by the fiery Socialist leader Ferdinand Lassalle, he decided that unregulated capitalism, which through its selfish policies had created a dissatisfied proletariat, must be restrained; the interests of the state demanded a contented working class as well as a vigorous bourgeoisie. Therefore Bismarck was forced to discard entirely the doctrine of *laissez faire*.

To achieve this end and thus, as he is reported to have said, "to kill socialism with kindness," he consented to the passage by parliament of three bills designed to ameliorate conditions among the workers. The first of these was the Sickness Insurance Law of 1883, by which insured workers were given sick benefits, medicines, and medical attention for a period of twenty-six weeks. For the maintenance of this scheme, funds were given by the employers to the extent of one third, and the workers contributed the remaining two thirds. By the Accident Insurance Law of 1884 nearly all the wage-earners were compelled to insure themselves against accident. From funds contributed entirely by the employers, the worker in the event of accident, or his dependents in the case of death, received compensation in the form of a pension. The third of these socialistic experiments, the Old Age and Invalidism Law of 1889, provided for pensions for the workers upon retirement. Contributions to the retirement fund were made by the state, the employer, and the employee.

In enacting this legislation Bismarck had the support of the Conservatives, the National Liberals, and occasionally the Catholic Center. On the other hand, the bourgeois radicals and the Social Democrats disapproved of these laws. The Socialists continued to oppose the government, maintaining that the social reforms were merely sops thrown out to the workers to lull them into inactivity.

In 1888 Bismarck's master and friend, William I, died, and the chancellor's public career came to an end shortly thereafter. Frederick III, who succeeded him, reigned but three months, being replaced by his son, William II. Twenty-eight years of age, energetic and ambitious, the new ruler, despite occasional lapses into melancholia, typified the new spirit of Germany. Inspired with an unbounded confidence in his own prowess, referring to God as "my old Ally," he actually believed that he governed a superior people. His implicit faith in the theory of divine-right monarchy impelled one of his commentators to declare, "Never since the days of Moses and Sinai had the world seen such intimacy between creature and Creator." Substituting for the watchwords *liberty, equality,* and *fraternity* the more materialistic slogans *system, efficiency,* and *discipline,* he willingly accepted the leadership in a crusade to spread German culture throughout the world.

William II

It was not surprising that a willful young emperor and a stubborn old chancellor could not agree. Soon after William II became Kaiser, Bismarck, refusing to subscribe to the emperor's foreign policy, resigned, and the obedient Count von Caprivi replaced him as chancellor. In the words of a contemporary, "The real question was whether the Bismarck or the Hohenzollern dynasty should reign." Germany now appeared to be at the mercy of an inexperienced and rather idealistic ruler. Actually, however, William II did not try to change completely the direction of the ship of state, but, adhering to many of the chancellor's policies, declared: "The course remains unchanged. Full steam ahead."

During the reign of William II, Germany experienced tremendous material progress. Industrial advance through the application of scientific knowledge was especially notable. Iron from Lorraine and Silesia, and coal from Westphalia, Silesia, and the Saar Basin, enabled Germany by 1914 to lead England in the manufacture of iron and steel and to take third place, excelled only by the United States and England, in the production of coal. In the output of machinery Germany surpassed England and enjoyed unquestionable supremacy in the electrical and chemical industries. By 1914 she had a monopoly of the dye industry. In textile manufactures, however, Germany lagged behind her rival, England.

Economic Progress

Scientific methods were not limited to industry. In agriculture scientists and technicians, despite a declining rural population, were able, through the use of fertilizers and farm machinery, to increase production. The greater output of the sugar-beet and potato crops was especially noteworthy.

Paralleling this industrial and agricultural progress was the rise of commerce. Encouraged by subsidies, tax exemptions, and special privileges, German shipbuilders and shippers created a great merchant marine, including all types of vessels from tramp freighters to palatial liners. The opening in 1895 of the Kiel Canal, connecting the Baltic with the North Sea, and the development of river transportation and railways, were instrumental in facilitating the growth of domestic and foreign commerce. By 1914 Germany was second only to England in world trade.

Many are the reasons for Germany's great industrial, agricultural, and commercial growth. One was the emphasis placed upon science and its application to economic activities. In the German labora- *Reasons for Germany's Economic Development* tories scientists were trained to achieve practical results from abstract theories. Thus a modernization of industry was made possible through the studies of chemists, physicists, and metallurgists. Another cause of German progress was the emphasis placed on efficiency in industry. In business, in politics, and in war, men were trained to functions as experts in their particular field. Workers were provided with training in excellent technical schools. Commercial representatives, sent to other countries, gathered data on foreign markets and tried to understand the need and tastes of their customers so as to enable German traders to carry out the motto "We aim to please." A third significant factor in the growth of German economic life was the state. By means of its efficiency, centralization, paternalistic encouragement of business, and development of transportation facilities, the imperial government was to a great extent responsible for the economic prosperity which the German people enjoyed prior to the World War.

Germany's late rise as an industrial power helped her in obtaining a fair share of world trade. Although England had

Large-Scale Business
dominated the world markets, she failed to retain this position of supremacy because the Germans were able to construct more efficient machinery and to adopt more modern business methods than the English. The latter, as stated before, refused to discard their time-worn machinery or to depart from traditional business methods; they relied upon individualism as the sure way to economic prosperity. The Germans, on the other hand, were able to move rapidly, in both agriculture and industry, from the small-scale standards of medieval society to the era of "Big Business" which greeted the approach of the twentieth century. This accommodation to new conditions was due partly to the fact that the government not only encouraged the establishment of large, centralized, well-organized, and efficient military and political institutions, but also carried this policy over into industry. Furthermore, the people, accustomed to tendencies toward consolidation, entertained no suspicions or fears concerning trusts. Hence by 1914 a great part of German economic life, especially in the chemical, coal, iron, and steel industries, was organized into consolidations called cartels. These organizations were associations of firms in which members preserved their separate existence and individuality, but agreed to coöperate with each other in the control of output, prices, and markets. This form of syndicate was advantageous in that it eliminated waste, economized effort, and checked cutthroat competition. On the other hand, it led to the concentration of financial and economic power in the hands of a few big industrialists and bankers, who, by manipulating prices, credit facilities, and production, took advantage of the helplessness of the masses of people. Nevertheless, cartels were spreading rapidly in all fields of production by 1914. The government worked hand and glove with these associations in their attempts to extend their markets abroad and to monopolize those at home.

An excellent geographical position facilitated Germany's commercial expansion. In the center of Europe, she was a natural distributor of foreign goods on the Continent, supplanting less efficient rivals. Her people utilized the Technological, Industrial, and Agricultural revolutions to create an economic centralization as efficient as their political autocracy.

Long before 1914 the Germans had realized, however, that the empire was not self-sufficing in agriculture, and in the event of war might suffer for lack of food. Moreover, they knew that imports as a whole were exceeding exports, as in the case of their *Economic Problems confronting Germany* industrial rival, England. Since Germany's invisible earnings, which partly offset the unfavorable balance of trade, did not equal those derived by England from her empire and her commerce, leading German industrialists were converted to imperialism, believing that colonies would furnish indispensable raw materials as well as outlets for surplus goods and capital. This circumstance helps to explain Germany's economic penetration of the Near East, her eruption into Far-Eastern politics, her creation of a colonial empire in Africa and Oceania, and her aspiration to build a fleet capable of protecting her interests on the high seas.

Upon his accession in 1888, William II, an enthusiastic devotee of the cult of *Weltpolitik*, became the protagonist of German imperialism. Catering not only to his personal inclinations but also to those of *German Imperialism* the industrialists, he at once embarked on a policy of aggressive colonialism. Through a treaty with England in 1890, Germany acquired the island of Heligoland (a potential naval base near the Kiel Canal) and secured British recognition of her control of German East Africa. The Kaiser visited the Near East and facilitated German economic penetration in that part of the world. Calling upon his sailors, in 1898, to fight for the glory of the Fatherland and to avenge the murder of some missionaries in China, he acquired for Germany a foothold in the Far East. Through discovery and purchases German control was also extended over numerous islands in Oceania.

Colonization in the African colonies, some of which had been acquired earlier by Bismarck, had not proved successful, however. German emigrants found it difficult to thrive there because of the heat and malaria, and those who remained were disliked because of their cruel treatment of the natives. The government discovered that these colonies, costly to maintain, were a great liability. To remedy this situation the office of colonial minister was established, to which post Bernhard Dernburg was appointed in 1907. The new minister suggested extensive reforms as a phase of the scientific development of the African possessions.[1]

Germany's rapid commercial development as well as her new imperialistic policy accentuated the need for a powerful navy. William II, abandoning the Bismarckian policy of limited liability through the avoidance of overseas commitments, asserted that Germany, regardless of the feelings of England, must expand her naval power. He declared in 1897, "I will never rest until I have raised my navy to the same standard as that of my army." In 1898 and in 1900 the *Reichstag* appropriated large sums of money for the establishment of a high-seas fleet. Germany's naval activities soon aroused the ire of Great Britain, until now supreme mistress of the seas, who tried to dissuade Germany from the creation of a powerful navy. Chafing under foreign interference, one of the Kaiser's ministers declared, "The times are past when the German left the earth to one of his neighbors, the sea to another, and reserved the sky for himself." William II, British opposition notwithstanding, supported the aggressive policies of his naval chief, Admiral von Tirpitz, the real founder of the German navy.

Establishment of the German Navy

During the reign of William II social progress as well as economic and naval expansion occurred in Germany. The emperor, continuing the policies of Bismarck in social legislation, strengthened the laws passed by the Iron Chancellor. In municipal government achievements were especially noteworthy. Men were trained to hold responsible political offices, a plan nearly identical

Social Advances

[1] For further information concerning German imperialism see pages 411–413, 432, 500–507.

with that of the city managership was adopted, and cities became scientific social centers. Sanitation, water facilities, parks, museums, schools, and hospitals — all under expert management — provided for the physical and intellectual welfare of the people. Most cities had a surprising absence of slums and extreme poverty. Municipal ownership of public utilities was a distinct success, providing the people with light and water at a minimum cost.

From the highest governmental bureaucrat to the lowest city officer, from the general to the private, from the industrial chief to the worker, science, organization, and skill were applied. These factors, together with obedience, efficiency, and discipline, undoubtedly contributed to German power and prosperity.

While historians, statesmen, and philosophers were heaping praise on the German autocracy for its success in improving the standard of living, certain literary men were more intrigued by the significant social and economic problems which they detected. The distinguished novelist Thomas Mann (1875–   ), in his *Buddenbrooks*, wrote an excellent description of the rise of Germany as a great economic state and of the incapacity and helplessness of the individualistic trader of the pre-industrial epoch under modern capitalistic society. Gerhart Hauptmann (1862–   ), with a sense of foreboding, in his play *The Weavers* painted a dark picture of social conditions in Germany, to the great satisfaction of the Socialists. Such critics of the orderly capitalistic society of imperial Germany, however, were, with the exception of the Socialists, not numerous.

Lack of individualism was a weak point in the German armor. The empire was a great machine. Theoretically every person, inspired solely by blind obedience and dependent upon paternalism, was considered part of it. Under this system freedom of political thought and personal initiative were difficult. Nevertheless, long before the outbreak of the war an increasing number of bourgeois liberals, as well as the Socialists, were demanding democratic reforms, especially the creation of a ministry responsible to the representatives of the people.

Absence of individual initiative existed in the realm of literature and history as well as in politics. In Bismarck's time the liberalism of the patriotic historian *Exponents of Despotism* Friedrich Christoph Dahlmann (1785–1860), who pleaded for German unity and a constitutional government, was replaced by the prophet of despotism, Heinrich Gotthard von Treitschke (1834–1896). This eminent Saxon professor, delivering lectures and writing a history of Germany in which he asserted that the state towered above the individuals who composed it, and realized ideals far beyond individual happiness, became the "Bismarck of the chair."

Friedrich von Bernhardi, in his *Germany and the Next War* (1912), and Hans Delbrück (1848–1929), in his works on government, tried earnestly to justify the autocracy of William II. "The vacillations of democracy," proclaimed Delbrück, "weaken any government." A constant policy, subject of course to wise advice, he believed was responsible for the power of Germany. Bernhard von Bülow, imperial chancellor from 1900 to 1909, in his *Imperial Germany*, also defended autocracy by claiming that the lack of frontiers and the presence of enemies on three sides made a centralized government necessary. "The crown," he wrote, "is the cornerstone of Prussia and the keystone of the empire." He admitted that the representatives of the people should advise the emperor. This end could best be achieved, he claims, not by enlarging the sphere of popular rights, but by educating those who have political talent to assist the government.

Autocracy received support from a strange champion — Friedrich Nietzsche (1844–1900). In the last quarter of the nineteenth century the influence of this half-insane genius superseded the waning star of Arthur Schopenhauer (1788–1860). Whereas to the pessimistic Schopenhauer the will to live was the root of all evil, to the optimistic Nietzsche it was the source of all pleasure. In his great works *Thus Spake Zarathustra* and *Beyond Good and Evil*, Nietzsche proclaimed the "will to power" and hailed the coming of the "superman." Christianity, which involved the conception of a God, he denounced for its humility, its renunciation, and its restrictive morals and traditions. As opposed to the "slave morality" of the masses, he advocated a "master morality" for those who, owing to beauty, intellect, and vigor, were born to rule. Thus he justified autocracy, denouncing democracy as the "cult of numbers," and socialism as a "religion of equality." Just as he glorified the ruling classes, whose very power was indicative of their superiority, so did he approve of Germany's ambition, through imperialism and armaments, to become a super-state. The exaltation of the will to power, applicable alike to persons and to the state, was influential in promoting the cult of force as a ruling creed in pre-war Germany.

William II was an adherent of absolute monarchy. Symbolical of his attitude was his declaration "There is only one master in this country and I am he." Turning his back on the liberalism of his father, Frederick III, he opposed democracy and strove *Struggle for Parliamentary Government* to thwart agitation for parliamentary reform. During the chancellorships of Caprivi and Hohenlohe, covering the decade from 1890 to 1900, the Kaiser ruled as a personal despot; but with the appointment of Bülow, in 1900, there was a rather flimsy illusion of parliamentary government. Through favorable combinations in the *Reichstag* Bülow usually secured approval of the imperial, naval, and military policies. Eventually, however, the unpopularity of the heavy expenditures on the colonies caused the Center party and the Social Democrats to form an alliance so as to defeat the colonial budget. Bülow, however, after denouncing the two parties as unpatriotic, dissolved the *Reichstag* and held elections in which a safe majority for his policy was returned. Thereupon he organized a Bülow *bloc*, which supported the administration in the *Reichstag*.

During the reign of William II, despite the emperor's conservatism in politics, a democratic movement developed. The Social Democrats and the Progressives, in their attempts to spread democratic propaganda and to bring about constitutional reforms, won an increasing number of adherents. Ardent advocates of ministerial responsibility, they took advantage of a number of incidents to exert pressure in favor of this important concession to democracy. In 1908 a London newspaper published an account of an interview with the Kaiser, wherein he discussed Anglo-German relations, asserting that he was well disposed toward England and had prepared a plan of campaign against the Boers which he had presented to the British authorities. Such irresponsible talk aroused much unfavorable criticism in Germany. Taking advantage of this reaction, the opposition parties, especially the Social Democrats, secured the passage through the *Reichstag* of a resolution censuring the actions of the emperor.

It was predicted that within a year ministerial responsibility would be established. In 1909, however, because of strained relations with the Kaiser and the defeat of his budget, Bülow, the ablest chancellor after Bismarck, resigned. His successor, the weak Dr. Bethmann-Hollweg, apparently satisfactory to the emperor, now assumed the office, which he did not relinquish until the period of the war. Thenceforth there was little prospect of ministerial responsibility, the new chancellor declaring that inasmuch as his appointment was from the Kaiser he was under no obligations to parliament. Nevertheless, Bethmann-Hollweg soon discovered that the support of political parties as well as that of the emperor was necessary.

At first Bethmann-Hollweg was able to rely upon a coalition of Conservatives and Centrists, the so-called blue-black *bloc*, for backing in governmental legislation. These representatives of the landowning classes were only too willing to support the administration, provided they received something in return. To satisfy them, the state, by levying taxes upon tea, sugar, beer, and other commodities, relieved the producers of part of their tax burden at the expense of the consumers.

One result of the high tariff on foodstuffs which enriched the junker landowners was a rapid rise in the cost of living. Therefore the business interests as well as the *The Junkers versus the Middle Classes* workers opposed this tariff policy. The bourgeoisie now organized to oppose high tariffs on foodstuffs and high taxes, and in the elections of that year (1912) the conservative agricultural groups were badly defeated and the bourgeois and workingmen's parties obtained a majority. The government, confronted by a powerful opposition, was in a difficult position. A crisis occurred when the *Reichstag*, influenced by the arbitrary actions of certain army officers, passed a vote of non-confidence. The weak Bethmann-Hollweg now promised constitutional reforms. At this juncture the Balkan wars (1912–1913) and the possibility of a general European conflict involving Germany caused the people as a whole to rally to the support of the government. In 1913, during this international unrest, reforms were forgotten, the military budget was increased, and the army was enlarged. Leaders of all parties realized that Germany's position as one of the great world powers was in danger. The outbreak of the conflict of 1914 proved this to be the case.

Despite the apparent solidarity of the empire, its boundaries contained several groups of non-Germans. Although the ethnic problem was not nearly so serious as in Austria-Hungary, nevertheless it was disturbing, as there were French and Alsatians in *Treatment of German Minorities* Alsace-Lorraine, Poles in the East, and Danes in Schleswig. The government, through a policy of Germanization which aimed at the eradication of the customs, institutions, and languages of the minorities, tried to transform these peoples into Germans. To facilitate the process of assimilation, German colonists were settled among these groups.

German attempts at assimilation were a failure. The inhabitants of Alsace-Lorraine became more anti-German as a result of oppression, and this served to emphasize the bad feeling between France and Germany. The latter, however, because of the great economic value of the provinces in view of their iron, potash, and textiles, was determined to retain them. In an effort to strengthen its influence the government even went so far as to make Alsace-Lorraine, in 1911, autonomous imperial territory, ruled by a governor appointed by the Kaiser. In German Poland, laws prohibiting the use of the Polish language, expropriating Polish landlords, and regulating the schools only served to intensify the alien nationalism. The Danes, equally indifferent to the appeal of German nationalism, remained Danish in sympathy.

In 1914 William II was the autocratic head of a powerful
and prosperous empire. Consequently, as long as he gave
them peace, security, and at least a moderate
Germany on the Eve of
the Struggle
living, most Germans were perfectly willing to
submit to his overlordship, although they distrusted and questioned his tactless remarks, his medieval
reliance upon God, and his glorification of the army and navy.
Methodical, leisurely, less adventurous than Americans, they
were willing to reach their goal through plodding and thor-
oughness, and were satisfied to place their destiny in the hands
of the few supermen. What personal and political liberties
were to the Englishman, order and obedience were to the
German. Under this talkative successor of Frederick the
Great, therefore, Germany became the land of experts, statistics, regulations, and standardization. She was an empire resembling in strength and massiveness that of ancient Rome.

By 1914 Germany was feared. Jealous rivals and neighbors
found it easy to spread unkindly reports concerning her past
and her intentions. Some even called attention to the fact
that only a short time ago Germany had been in rags, but
now she was wearing expensive clothes. How did she get
these garments? Certain German leaders, however, serenely
confident in the superiority of their *Kultur* and military power,
were convinced that the Germans were the chosen people, the
elect of God, destined to civilize the world. But, warned
others, the aggrandizement of Germany would make war inevitable. This danger was revealed by Bülow when he declared: "In the struggle between nationalities one nation is
the hammer and the other is the anvil; one is the victor and
the other the vanquished. It is a law of life and development
in history that when two national civilizations meet they
fight for supremacy."

CHAPTER XX

Imperial Russia: Decline of an Old Order

THE assassination of Alexander II, in 1881, made a lasting impression on his son, the new Czar, Alexander III (1881–1894). Expressing a firm belief in the infallibility of the principle of autocracy, he retained thenceforth a distrust of all popular movements. Reaction became the dominant motif behind his administration.

Alexander III, upon becoming emperor, inaugurated a twofold policy. As an autocrat he planned to oppose all liberal and revolutionary movements, and at the *Reactionary Rule* same time, as an enlightened despot, he intended to encourage economic progress. His policy was to a large extent influenced by a person who soon was considered the leading exponent of reaction — Constantine Pobiedonostsev (1827–1907). As the tutor of Alexander, Pobiedonostsev had gained a strong hold over the mind of the young man. As Procurator of the Holy Synod he had become one of the most important members of the government. This position he retained during the reign of Alexander III and the first part of Nicholas II's administration.

Pobiedonostsev was an unusual reactionist. In masterly words he pictured the existing order as standing for everything that was good. Separation of church *Pobiedonostsev* and state, national education, freedom of the press, and democracy, he maintained, were evils which would destroy everything that was worth while in the empire. Denouncing liberalism in all of its varied forms he declared that autocratic Russia, the outstanding state not affected by the bourgeois menace, alone had an opportunity to create a perfect social order. Consequently the old formula "Orthodoxy, autocracy, and nationalism" was revived, and conservatism became the order of the day.

To prevent the further introduction of "bourgeois radicalism" the government proceeded to suppress the revolutionary

Tyrannical Policies of Alexander III

movements. Arrests, imprisonment, exile, and death were inflicted upon those accused and convicted of liberal activities. Censorship was strengthened, and freedom of teaching was limited. Laws granting local self-government were changed, and the *zemstvos* were placed in the hands of the nobility.

Orthodoxy in religious matters was favored by the government. The so-called "old believers" and sectarians, groups split off from the Greek Orthodox church, were bitterly persecuted. Although discriminated against, Roman Catholics and Lutherans were tolerated. Nevertheless, "to try to convert a Greek Orthodox into a Roman Catholic or Lutheran," for example, "was a crime punishable under the law. . . . In cases of mixed marriages children automatically became Greek Orthodox irrespective of their parents' wishes."

Influenced by Slavophile ideas, the Czar, by a brutal Russification of such subject peoples as Poles, Finns, German Balts, and Jews, tried to maintain the supremacy of Russian culture. In Poland determined attempts were made to obliterate local and national customs. Deprived of their autonomy after the insurrection of 1863, the Poles were at the mercy of their Russian overlords. The German Balts, even though they had been loyal subjects of Russia for many years, were subjected to discrimination. But the chief victims of this Russification policy were the Jews. Since the beginning of the nineteenth century most Jews had been crowded into restricted areas known as the *Pales*. Alexander increased the severity of these restrictions. Few Jews could leave the *Pale*, and their privilege of attending schools was curtailed. Although the civil rights of the Jews were severely limited, the Hebrews were expected to pay more than their share of the taxes. Russia deliberately repressed those who otherwise might have played an important rôle in the creation of a powerful and prosperous bourgeois empire.

Alexander III believed that he had a mission to perform. Ruling by divine will, he insisted that all legislation should receive his approval and that all public administrators were responsible to him. His council, the governors of the provinces, and his bureaucracy (consisting of aristocrats and bourgeoisie) must therefore carry out his will. To see that they did so, the Czar reorganized the intelligence corps (police force) called the Third Section, responsible alone to him.

The Czar possessed little confidence in his people. He ignored the *zemstvos* and local councils. To satisfy restless nobles and to gain their support, Alexander III made a colossal mistake. While western Europe was coming under the rule of the aggressive and progressive bourgeois classes, Alexander virtually handed over control of local government and of local justice to the nobility. Aristocratic representation in the *zemstvos* was considerably increased, and in 1889 the office of "land captain" was created. These local officials were noblemen appointed by the Czar to rule over the peasants.

Increase of Aristocratic Authority

Many of the aristocrats were decadent and corrupt. Unwilling to work and unable to think, they permitted everything around them, including their estates, to degenerate and decay. Numerous members of the nobility, as local or governmental officials, even went so far as to permit Jews and other oppressed peoples to disobey the laws in return for money payments. This corruption served to undermine the policies of Alexander. His attempt to bring the nobility back into political life proved as futile, further discrediting the government among all classes.

Alexander's reactionary policy was bound to fail. In trying to rule by means of an alliance between the government and the nobles, he was running counter to the whole trend of social evolution. Serfdom had to be destroyed in order that Russia could adopt the capitalistic system and thus be in a position to compete with Western powers. Moreover, when he oppressed the various subject peoples within his empire, he turned his back on the very concept of an empire as a political organization which protected the various peoples and benefited through control of them. Economic progress therefore was destined to modernize the great empire.

During the reign of Alexander III the foundations of the middle-class system were laid in Russia. The abolition of serf-
The Founding of the dom, and therefore the creation of a free labor
Bourgeois System in supply, was the turning point. By the eighties
Russia Russia was ready to develop industries along capitalistic lines. The Industrial Revolution had entered the empire. Railway lines at first were constructed by private concerns with government aid. Later the state took over some of these railroads and built others. By the end of the nineteenth century Russia had constructed the trans-Siberian line and was engaged in more railway construction than any other country in Europe.

Credit facilities were created during the reigns of Alexander III and Nicholas II. Modern banking was introduced and a state bank was organized. By 1897 the gold standard was adopted and Russian currency was stabilized. This in turn promoted commercial and industrial developments within Russia and brought about a marked increase of foreign capital investments.

Construction of railroads and financial reforms greatly stimulated industrial progress in Russia. The discovery of great beds of coal and iron in southern Russia facilitated this development. In central Russia the textile industry showed marked growth. Thus, at the turn of the century, trade and business enterprises were expanding rapidly.

One of the significant results of the Industrial Revolution was the rise in Russian cities of a class-conscious proletariat. As in England, the working conditions of the
Rise of the Class- wage-earners during the early phase of capi-
Conscious Proletariat talistic development in Russia were deplor-
able. Workers in the factories labored long hours in unsanitary shops for meager pay. Formation of unions and the use of strikes by the proletarians were the results of this ruthless exploitation. Moved by this situation and influenced perhaps by German social legislation the government endeavored to improve conditions among the wage-earners. Despite well-intentioned attempts to better the lot of the laboring classes radicalism increased.

The rapid expansion of commerce and industry also resulted in the rise of the middle classes. Through possession of wealth they were soon able to challenge the social supremacy of the landowner. In time the need for lawyers, teachers, doctors, and *The Rise of the Middle Classes* newspaper men to carry on various phases of bourgeois activities enabled individuals to rise through the professions to positions of influence in Russian society. Before the outbreak of the World War a democratic middle class was assuming an increasingly important rôle in Russian affairs.

At first, Russian agriculture was not aided by the introduction of Western ideas and methods. The depression which the farmers of western Europe experienced as a result of their inability to face the growing competition of non-European countries simi- *Improvements in Agriculture* larly affected the Russian landowners. In addition the transfer of land to the serfs in the sixties created a situation wherein the peasants lacked money to purchase and run the farms. The annual redemption payments and high taxes constituted too heavy a burden for the peasants in the *mir*. Consequently many of them were worse off than they had been before their emancipation.

Overpopulation contributed to the unsatisfactory agricultural situation in Russia. "While the rural population was growing very rapidly, there was very little progress in agricultural technique, the land was not used to the best advantage, and the yield of peasant farming remained miserably low." Unfortunately, inasmuch as the factories of Russia could not absorb the excess peasant labor, the latter remained on the farms, which were too small to support them. To the peasant more land was the only solution of the problem. He tried to purchase or lease property from the landlord, but owing to the lack of capital was unable to improve his status to any great degree.

Despite his conservatism Alexander III tried to help the peasants. In 1881 redemption payments were reduced over one fourth, and five years later the poll tax was abolished. A peasant land bank was created in 1882, and peasant migration to Asiatic Russia was encouraged. These relief measures, however, failed to improve conditions. At best they aided but a few peasants. The agrarian crisis persisted, and the demand for "more land" continued up to the time of the Russian Revolution (1917), which obliterated the old régime and inaugurated a new political and social order.

Alexander III succeeded in driving the revolutionary movement underground; but his successor, the young Nicholas II, *Czar Nicholas II* brought it to the surface. Unable to appreciate the significance of the Industrial Revolution, which was creating an ambitious bourgeoisie and a dangerous proletariat, the Czar continued the reactionary policies of his predecessor, even intensifying them in some respects. The new emperor, possessing a scholarly mind and a pleasant personality, as a ruler left much to be desired. Lacking a strong will, unable to get to the heart of political questions, foolishly obstinate, and distrustful, he found it difficult to rule well. Consequently his reign marked the climax of intrigues, personal rivalries, and corruption such as have often preceded the fall of a dynasty.

The revolutionary movement as it developed during the reign of Nicholas II was not exactly the same as the earlier *Russian Socialism* radical development. As a result of the introduction of capitalism and industry, the opponents of the old régime were able to perfect stronger organizations and to work out more definite and inclusive political and social programs.

Marxian Socialism spread rapidly in Russia. Emphasizing the idea of the class struggle and the dictatorship of the proletariat, it was accepted quite generally by the dissatisfied wage-earners. The Russian workers, already influenced by the terroristic methods which arose out of the Nihilist and Populist movements, became the most violent and uncompromising radicals in the world. According to their plans Russia was to abolish the old régime, avoid the bourgeois system, and establish socialism.

Radical parties soon came into existence. The Social-Democratic group, representing the wage-earners, was the leading radical organization. Established in 1889 by disciples of Marx, it tried to get all the workers under its wing by founding local chapters in industrial centers. In 1903 the party split into two factions. One of these groups, led by Plekhanov, was called the Mensheviks, who believed that the first revolution was bound to result in the establishment of a bourgeois society. This new order, however, was to be just a temporary stopping place on the way to socialism. The other group, called the Bolsheviks, maintained that Russia should move directly from the old régime to the communist state. They were led by Nicholas Lenin, a schoolmaster's son whose brother had been executed by Alexander III because of revolutionary activities.

Before the turn of the century the middle classes were organizing with the purpose of advancing their political and social positions. About 1894, to obtain representative and constitutional government, they *Bourgeois Organizations* formed professional groups and tried to organize within the various *zemstvos*. The famous "Union of Liberation" was the combination of these *zemstvos* and professional groups. Led by such men as Struve and Miliukov, outstanding bourgeois intellectuals, this organization was at first the leader in the movements to liberalize the old régime. Later it became the nucleus of the Constitutional Democratic party, also called the Cadets.

Nicholas II should have tried to win over the middle classes. Until 1914 they represented the real educated class in Russia. Instead the Czar practically ignored their demands. Consequently, the sons of the bourgeoisie, in the various universities, proceeded to pave the way for revolution by means of political uprisings and demonstrations.

By 1900 the revolutionary movement had gained momentum. Fortunately for the Czar the various groups were not united. Although the immediate object, the overthrow of the old régime, was the same, the *Revolutionary Russia* factions disagreed as to the method of destruction and also as to the kind of political and social system which was to take its place. Because of these divisions, Nicholas II at first had an admirable opportunity to retain his authority by granting reforms which would satisfy the bourgeoisie, the peasants, and the less radical element in the Social Democratic party. But the weak-willed Czar, influenced by reactionary advisers, hesitated to take drastic action.

The Czar finally decided to act; but he acted in the wrong way. Determined to crush all opposition to the government, he delegated power to Plehve, a confirmed reactionist. The latter immediately proceeded to oppose the liberal bourgeois policies of Count Witte. Backed by the Cadets, Witte, however, was able to withstand these attacks until 1903. At that time Plehve decided to end the liberal propaganda in favor of the extension of the powers of the *zemstvos*, advocated by both the Cadets and Witte, by bringing about the fall of the great bourgeois statesman. Cossacks and spies were turned loose on the people, and groups of thugs were indirectly instructed to attack all Jews. So brutal were these assaults, called pogroms, that the civilized people throughout the world were aroused.

Many revolutionists, who hitherto had blamed the advisers of the Czar rather than Nicholas, decided that the "Little Father" was responsible for the social ills of Russia. Liberal noblemen now joined in the criticism of the government, and a general dissatisfaction with the existing régime gripped all sections of society. "Has the Russian government friends?" asked a former imperial secretary of state. "Most decidedly no. Who can be friends with fools and louts, with robbers and thieves?" By 1905 even monarchists regarded the destruction of the inefficient autocracy as unavoidable, and in anticipation of such an event prepared for consequent changes.

While the revolutionary movement was gaining momentum, Russia became involved in a disastrous war.[1] The struggle was the result of the Russo-Japanese imperialistic rivalry in the Far East. Within a year Japan demonstrated her naval superiority, and the conflict between Japan and Russia came to a dramatic and unexpected end. Russia's defeat did not perturb Nicholas II.

The Russo-Japanese War (1904–1905)

---

[1] See pages 459–462.

All that he wrote in his diary for the day on which Port Arthur fell was, "Had a long stroll, killed one crow, and went for a row on the Gatchina." Similarly Louis XVI of France hunted on the day the Bastille fell (July 14, 1789) and likewise attributed great importance to the killing of harmless game.

The results of the Russo-Japanese War were similar to those of the Crimean struggle. Again the weaknesses of the established order were revealed by the inability of the government to carry on the struggle. Again a humiliating defeat forced the government to embark on a program of reform. Before the war came to a close, however, a real revolution had broken out in Russia.

Radicalism in 1904 was not limited to any particular class or part of Russia. All dissatisfied groups were united in common opposition to the government. At this time bourgeois constitutionalists coöperated *The Revolution of 1905* with extreme socialists in the attack upon autocracy. Nicholas II, frightened by the assassination, on July 28, 1904, of his minister of the interior, Plehve, decided to mollify the opposition. A less repressive policy was inaugurated by the government. Taking advantage of this situation, the *zemstvos* and professional groups proceeded to formulate demands for a constituent assembly and a constitution which would guarantee civil rights. Uniting forces in a so-called "Union of Unions," they agitated openly in favor of these reforms.

The Socialists, however, carried on most of their work underground. Social Revolutionists contributed to the revolutionary cause by assassinating several reactionary officials. Social Democrats, on the other hand, worked among the proletariat in the cities, made converts of them, and encouraged them to resort to numerous strikes. Many intellectuals, especially Jews, who had fled abroad and had been educated in foreign universities, returned to Russia and instituted movements designed to overthrow the old régime.

A crisis was reached when, according to Lenin, "thousands of workers — not Social Democrats, but faithful, loyal people — led by the priest Gapon," marched from all parts of

St. Petersburg "to the centre of the capital, to the square in front of the Winter Palace, in order to submit a petition to the Czar." This petition enumerated the following demands:

Amnesty, civic liberty, normal wages, the land to be gradually transferred to the people, convocation of a Constituent Assembly on the basis of universal and equal suffrage, and it ends with the following words: "Sire, do not refuse aid to Thy people! Throw down the wall that separates Thee from Thy people. Order and swear that our requests will be granted, and Thou wilt make Russia happy; if not, we are ready to die on this very spot. We have only two roads: freedom and happiness, or the grave."

Government troops, not the Czar, however, met this defenseless mob at the entrance to the palace. They fired on the unarmed workers, who on bended knees implored the Cossacks to let them go to the Czar. "On that day, according to police reports, more than 1000 were killed and more than 2000 were wounded. The indignation of the workers was indescribable."

This so-called "Bloody Sunday" intensified the radicalism of the workers. Many wage-earners left the government unions and joined the Socialist party. A series of strikes practically brought industry to a halt. In many parts of Russia peasants, demanding "more land," burned and looted estates and frequently murdered the owners. Life in St. Petersburg was brought to a standstill. Doctors, lawyers, dancers, and cooks refused to work. A similar uprising against the government occurred in Moscow.

Oppressed subject peoples joined in the demonstrations. Poles, Jews, and peoples living in the Baltic provinces and in Transcaucasia all joined the workers in the opposition to the old régime.

This struggle [wrote Lenin] imbued the masses of the Russian people with a new spirit. Only then did the old serf-ridden, backward, patriarchal, pious, and obedient Russia cast off the old Adam. Only then did the Russian people obtain a really democratic and really revolutionary education.

Confronted by this critical situation, the government was constrained to act. Before the strike occurred, Nicholas II had, on August 19, 1905, issued an order convoking a national congress, the Imperial Duma, which was to have deliberative rather than legislative functions. The announcement undoubtedly helped to provoke the general strike, for the people were determined to participate in the government. *The Establishment of the Duma* In this emergency the Czar turned to Witte for advice. The latter "offered his sovereign one of two alternatives: either to establish a military dictatorship or else, if this was not feasible, to grant the people a constitution." With the bulk of his army in the Far East, and not trusting the troops at home, the Czar reluctantly adopted the latter course.

A great majority of the middle classes accepted wholeheartedly this grant made by the frightened Czar in 1905. Many of them actually believed that the revolution was over when, in later manifestos, Nicholas II promised civil liberty and manhood suffrage (although on a class basis), and a Duma with real legislative power. Apparently the Czar planned to establish a democratic constitutional government.

"Russian revolutionary Social-Democracy," however, refused to be satisfied with these concessions. Without hesitation it issued the slogan:

Down with the Advisory Duma! Boycott the Duma! Down with the Czarist government! Continue the revolutionary struggle for the overthrow of the government! Not the Czar, but a provisional revolutionary government must convoke the real popular representative Assembly in Russia!

Groups opposed to the government were divided. Refusing to follow the lead of their allies the Socialists, the bourgeois Constitutional Democratic party now favored less radical policies. Nevertheless they desired to preserve and extend the recently won political concessions. Somewhat more moderate were the Octobrists, who were completely satisfied with the October manifesto and were not desirous of going any farther. A popular reaction against the revolutionary excesses ultimately resulted. Many liberal landowners and bourgeois leaders, opposed to the terrorism of the peasants and the revolutionary activities of the Socialists, threw their support to the government. Backed by these groups as well as by the conservatives and the army, the government by 1907 was able to restore order throughout the country and to suppress the revolutionary movement.

In March, 1906, the elections to the Duma were held. The various liberal groups, with the exception of the Social Revolutionists, who refused to vote, showed great enthusiasm. Consequently they elected a majority of the delegates. Although they disagreed as to what should take its place, nearly every delegate was opposed to autocracy. In the assembly were the moderate bourgeoisie, the Octobrists, favoring a government similar to that in Prussia. The more liberal bourgeois party, the Cadets, championed a democratic constitutional empire. Representatives of the workers (the Social Democratic party) and a group of peasants (called the Labor party) demanded democracy and extensive economic reforms.

The First Duma

Nicholas II believed that the delegates to the Duma would merely offer a few suggestions, listen to his advice, and then adjourn. Much to his disgust, however, the "radicals" demanded additional reforms and consideration of the Polish, Jewish, and land problems. This last suggestion antagonized the nobles. Nicholas now had to support his landowners or the masses. Backing the former, he dismissed the assembly and ordered the election of a new Duma.

About half the members of the Duma decided to oppose the Czar's will. Retiring to Viborg, in Finland, they took an oath similar to the Tennis Court Oath in France in 1789 and issued a manifesto calling upon the people to refuse to pay taxes or to render military service to the government. Their opposition proved to be futile.

Advised by the landowners, who feared the loss of the greater part of their estates if the liberals had their way, the Czar continued his reactionary policies. He changed the electoral law so as to insure control of the Duma by the conservative groups. Moreover, he appointed as his premier Peter Stolypin (1862–1911), a firm defender of the old régime. Immediately the

Stolypin, the Strong Man

latter attempted to put an end to the revolution by the customary repressive methods. During the terrorism which followed, thousands of peasants were exiled to Siberia, hundreds of periodicals were suppressed, and many death sentences were issued. The hanging noose was soon called "Stolypin's necktie."

This "Russian Bismarck" was not a narrow-minded reactionist. Under his leadership the government made an earnest attempt to improve the lot of the peasant. Politically, however, the government remained reactionary.

In March, 1907, the second Duma met. It proved to be more bitter in its opposition to the government than the first body. Revolutionary parties which had refused to vote in the elections of the first Duma sent representatives to the second. Demanding the confiscation of all large estates, the abolition of court martial, and a responsible ministry, the extremists in the Duma finally forced the Czar to dissolve the body. He was now determined to insure the election of those who would support the government. The law was revised in such a way as to give the large landowners preference over the peasants in sending representatives to the electoral colleges. As a result the third Duma, which assembled in 1907, was ruled by the conservatives. Russia, while this assembly existed, was, according to the *Almanach de Gotha*, "a constitutional monarchy under an autocratic Czar." This body survived until 1912, at which time another election was held and the fourth Duma, also conservative, met. It was in existence when the World War began.

Politically the Revolution of 1905 attained limited success. Its exponents, like those in the revolutions of 1848 in central Europe, were actually too weak to achieve important results. Therefore the Revolution of 1905 soon lost most of its gains as a result of a reaction that followed. This reaction was logical. Russia was too large, her peasants were too illiterate and superstitious, and her urban population was too small for a successful revolution.

After 1905, however, reactionary governmental policies failed to check the revolutionary movement.

The semi-repentant Czar failed to check the revolutionary movement. Disappointed in their attempts to establish a democratic constitutional government, the extremists renewed their attacks upon the Czar and his advisers. Stolypin was assassinated (1911), and many others were on the black list of the conspirators when the war began. The landowners, however, remained in the saddle and dominated the imperial government.

Notwithstanding aristocratic opposition the Duma managed to achieve some worth-while reforms. It made citizens of the peasants and extended the general judicial system over the rural population. It also established an educational system which, when the war began, was giving instruction to about one half of the children of school age. Moreover, it exercised real influence upon the conduct of national affairs. The principle of self-government at last had been extended to the field of national administration. In 1914 the parties in the Duma were split into two groups, one consisting of Octobrists, Cadets, and some nationalists, and the other of conservatives. A political struggle between the two factions, which might have resulted in a bourgeois democracy in Russia, was probably prevented by the World War.

Achievements of the Duma

Despite strikes, riots, massacres, and a weak government Russia before the war experienced a marked economic as well as intellectual development. Her manufacture of cast iron doubled between 1900 and 1914, and she greatly increased the production of sugar, alcohol, flour, and tobacco. In 1914 she mined 85 per cent of the coal she used, her forests were just beginning to be exploited, and she had discovered rich oil holdings in the Baku region. Her expansion in the realm of transportation was almost phenomenal. In 1912 she had over 40,000 miles of railroad tracks, including the important Siberian line, 5542 miles in length.

Economic Developments

At first the government, in fostering economic development, maintained a *laissez faire* policy. Lacking business leadership, this individualism led to confusion in many branches of industry. Consequently, after 1870 Russia changed her policy, taking over railroads and extending government control over industry. The leader of this movement was Count Witte. Realizing that Russia could not wait for a powerful bourgeois class to rise by means of "economic individualism," he decided that Russia could become industrialized better and more quickly by governmental aid.

In spite of the backwardness of agriculture considerable progress was made before 1914. Capitalistic farming was introduced on a small scale and resulted in a steady increase in the amount of rural products. The condition of the peasant, however, *Agricultural Improvements* was the chief problem confronting those who wanted to improve agriculture. To the Social Revolutionaries nationalization of land alone would satisfy the desire of the peasants for more property. The Constitutional Democrats, however, planned the distribution of all land belonging to the crown and the monasteries, "and the compulsory alienation of some part of the privately owned land, again for the benefit of the peasants." Compensation by the government was to be given the landlords for the loss of their property.

Refusing to adopt either solution, the state asserted that "if all the land available for agriculture were divided among the peasants the actual increase in their holdings would be comparatively insignificant and thus would fail to bring about a substantial improvement." The government also did not propose to violate the accepted principle of private property. Instead, under Stolypin, it tried to extend peasant ownership by giving the State Land Bank for peasants increased powers in 1905 and by selling large tracts of state and crown lands to the peasants. Numerous private landowners also sold their property. Encouraging peasant migration to the Asiatic provinces in the empire, the government developed an efficient system of expert agricultural assistance in coöperation with the *zemstvos*, which likewise paid great attention to the land problem.

Between 1906 and 1911 Stolypin, by a series of laws, tried to eliminate the commune (*mir*) and to establish individual ownership of land among the peasants. Every member of the commune was given the right to claim his share in the common land of the village as his private property and to obtain it in one compact holding instead of in widely scattered strips. By 1914 about 24 per cent of all the peasant households in European Russia had withdrawn from the communes and were individual proprietors of farms. At that time the peasants owned 75 per cent of the arable land in the country and had been relieved of their redemption payments. Over 30,000 coöperative societies of various descriptions also "helped the peasants to adapt themselves to new economic conditions, taught them self-reliance and group solidarity, and gave them direct material advantages by substantially reducing the part of the middleman." When the war broke out Russian agriculture was on the up grade, and the peasant's standard of living was rising slowly but surely.

Labor conditions also were improving. In 1912 the Duma passed legislation which established health and accident in-
Social Legislation   surance for workers. In 1906 organization of labor unions on a large scale was permitted. In many factories free lodgings, medical services, and educational facilities were provided. At the same time rising wages helped the workers to attain a higher standard of living.

Between 1906 and 1914 considerable cultural progress was made in Russia. In 1908 the scheme of universal educa-
Cultural Progress   tion was first advanced as a practical proposition, and soon the number of students rapidly increased in secondary schools and in universities. "In 1914 the expenses for popular education showed an increase of 628 per cent over the budget of 1894." Governmental censorship diminished, and wide latitude of thought was permitted in universities. Newspaper writers and religious dissenters benefited by this relaxation of governmental supervision. The press was able to express independent views and to influence public opinion. By a law of 1905 religious affiliation was declared a matter of free choice. Even suggestions for the separation of Church and State were advanced. Mean-

while Russian literature, no longer a vehicle of political and social propaganda, tended to emphasize the "quest for beauty."

In 1914 it appeared that Russia was about to evolve into a stable and prosperous bourgeois state. The outbreak of the war, however, interrupted this tendency. All groups, Conservatives, Nationalists, Cadets, Octobrists, Social Revolutionists, and most Socialists, rushed to the defense of Holy Russia and their brother Slavs, the Serbs. Out of this struggle, many believed, would arise a democratic Russian Empire which would liberate all Slavs and would dominate the Straits.

CHAPTER XXI

Austria-Hungary: The Multinational State

THE Dual Monarchy of Austria-Hungary has been described as a "museum of political curiosities." Containing diverse peoples and embracing the geographical area connecting western Europe with the southern and eastern portions of the continent, this polyglot empire was held together by pressure of external forces rather than by internal cohesion. Even after the founding of the Dual Monarchy in 1867, the Hapsburgs for many years managed to resist the triumph of national and liberal principles in their dominions. An anachronism, running counter to nationalistic nineteenth-century tendencies, their empire was a bulwark of conservatism. Its survival was dependent on successful opposition to Western political and social innovations.

After the establishment of the Dual Monarchy, Austria remained an empire under the rule of the conservative Francis Joseph. Although the majority of Austrians, *Austria after 1867* who included the wealthy ruling classes, resided in Austria proper, their far-flung empire of 116,000 square miles described a great arc which nearly surrounded Hungary. It extended from the Dalmatian coast on the Adriatic to the Alps and the Carpathians, thence bending southeast along the line of the latter mountains to the frontiers of Rumania. Of a total population of 30,000,000 less than 40 per cent were Austrians and over 50 per cent were Slavs. Attempts of the rulers to Germanize Austria and Hungary prior to the *Ausgleich* had failed, and ethnic diversity still constituted the most serious problem.

Of the two partners in the Dual Monarchy, Austria was by far the more progressive. Its constitution, adopted soon after the *Ausgleich*, created a parliament composed of an aristocratic upper house of nobles and imperial officials, and a

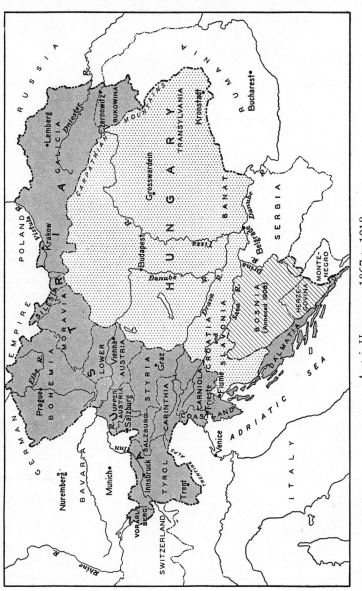

Austria-Hungary — 1867 to 1918

lower chamber which was elected indirectly through a class scheme of voting similar to that in Prussia. In 1907 the five-class system of voting employed theretofore was supplanted by universal direct male suffrage. Nominally responsible to the *Reichsrat*, the cabinet was in reality under the control of the emperor. The multiplicity of political factions, antagonistic to one another and unwilling to coöperate, made it impossible for parliament to assert its control over the cabinet. Moreover, the constitution, endowing the emperor with many powers, enabled him to enact decrees with the force of law while the *Reichsrat* was not in session.

Although Austria enjoyed the forms of liberal government, in practice it remained a highly centralized autocracy under the control of the monarch. The most obvious shortcoming in actual parliamentary rule was the absence of ministerial responsibility. The emperor and his representatives dominated the ministry and controlled the bureaucratic administration. There were frequent demands for democratic political reform, but the government refused to countenance any drastic modifications of the *status quo* until the empire was on the brink of dissolution in 1918.

During the latter part of the nineteenth century, nevertheless, tendencies toward partial democratization encouraged the exponents of the bourgeois order. The middle classes were much stronger in Austria *Reforms in Austria* than elsewhere in the Dual Monarchy, and many of them hoped for real parliamentary government. Shortly after the *Ausgleich* (1867) began to operate, Austria experienced a mild *Kulturkampf*. Although dominantly Catholic, many liberals came to resent the privileged position of the Roman Catholic church. Consequently a number of anticlerical laws were passed. These provided for the secularization of public elementary schools, civil equality of Catholics and non-Catholics, and civil marriages under certain circumstances. Apparently, by the early twentieth century, Austria was undergoing a gradual evolution toward the bourgeois political and social systems of western Europe.

The strivings of the nationalities constituted the most menacing problem to the security of the Austrian Empire. Inasmuch as these groups struggled to realize self-determination, the government was forced either to grant concessions or to adopt a policy of repression. For many years, however, the state was able to remain intact by playing off one group against another. But this policy of *divide et impera* only delayed the final reckoning. The day of judgment was not remote.

Constituting over one half the population of the empire, the Slavs were the most difficult to appease. In Bohemia the struggle between the bourgeois German minority and the Czechs was especially bitter. Desirous of pacifying the latter, the imperial government decided to grant concessions. A Bohemian diet was established, and the Czechs finally were permitted to vote. The University of Prague was divided into German and Czech sections. Aroused lest additional rights be granted to their militant rivals, the Germans even went so far as to threaten to withdraw from Austria and to join Germany. In 1897 matters came to a head when a proposal to grant full equality to the Czech and German languages in Bohemia caused delegates of both nationalities in the *Reichsrat* to change from hurling insults to throwing inkstands at one another; the conflict then spread to the streets, and sanguinary clashes occurred between the rival factions. Fearful of alienating the support of the Germans and Magyars, who despised the Slavs, Francis Joseph renounced his conciliatory policy. Deaf ears were turned toward Czech demands for a triple monarchy, in which the Slavs would have become a third ruling partner. In 1913 the Bohemian diet was abolished and the country was administered directly from Vienna. Thenceforth the Czechs and their neighbors the Slovaks could only struggle to obtain by force what the government had been unwilling to concede: autonomy or complete independence.

The Slavs in Austria

More tractable than the Czechs and Slovaks were the Poles, who were concentrated in Galicia. Before 1918 the hope of a reunited independent Poland seemed remote, inasmuch as it involved the overthrow of three mighty empires — Russia, Germany, and Austria. The Poles, however, received far better treatment from the Austrian Hapsburgs than their kin obtained from the Russians or the Germans. Therefore, although they desired independence, they were loyal to Francis Joseph, who won their fidelity by an earlier grant of autonomy within the empire, together with the privilege of using their own language in the schools. Less fortunate were the four million Ruthenian peasants in Galicia, who were left to the none too gentle mercy of Polish landlords and officials.

In southern Austria the government successfully exploited the situation created by the rivalry between the Yugoslavs and the Italians. Intensely conscious of their nationality, the latter desired to unite with Italy. To counteract this tendency, the Austrians, hoping to submerge the predominantly Italian sections, encouraged the Slavs to settle among them. The government further granted these Yugoslavs economic assistance in order that they might compete successfully against their rivals. Despite such privileges and official encouragement, Slavic discontent was not overcome, nor was *Italia irredenta* obliterated.

The government attempted to unify the empire by a policy of Germanization. It tried to destroy the national institutions, customs, languages, and schools of the subject groups and replace them with Austrian *Attempts to Germanize the Slavs* counterparts. Neither forceful measures nor conciliatory propaganda could achieve these ends. Instead the nationalities, particularly the Slavs, became more and more insistent upon recognition of their own languages, schools, and local institutions. Many of them even demanded the federalization of the empire, in which each group should be accorded autonomy. After 1907 the *Reichsrat* was definitely organized on a national basis, and the federal, or separatist, movement persevered notwithstanding the advantages of imperial economic unity. Agitation and riots continued until the strain of participation in the World War resulted in the collapse of the Dual Monarchy and the emancipation of the Slavs and other peoples.

While the government was attempting to preserve the remnants of the old medieval empire through the suppression of nationalism, the forces of the Industrial Revolution were undermining the old régime. Industry, gradually permeating Austria, transformed the state and brought about important political, social, and economic changes. The introduction of the factory system, the increased use of machinery, railroads, and canals, the growth of maritime commerce, and the modernization of her economic structure led to serious readjustments in social and economic life. Austria and Bohemia became the most highly industrialized sections of the empire. Large cities sprang up; Vienna, the imperial capital, boasted of over two million inhabitants. Agrarian Austria, stronghold of the old régime, was passing away.

Economic Advances in Austria

With the rise of commerce and industry an intelligent and wealthy bourgeoisie developed. Though less numerous, perhaps, than corresponding groups elsewhere, the new capitalistic classes were sufficiently strong to demand improved conditions. Forced to listen to their requests, the government granted a pseudo-liberal constitution, established a public-school system, and initiated a program of social reform. Furthermore, it attempted to win their support by promoting economic prosperity through protective tariffs, commercial treaties, and imperialistic policies in the Balkans.

The industrialization of parts of the Austrian Empire led to the creation of a large proletariat class. Concentrated in the populous cities of the north, the laborers began to agitate for better working and social conditions. In response to their demands the government, during 1884–1885, embarked on a program of social legislation. A ten-hour day was established for workers in the mines, and an eleven-hour day for those in the factories. Sunday labor was prohibited, and the use of women and children in industry was restricted. In 1887–1888 insurance for workers against sickness or accident was made obligatory. Wage-earners were permitted to organize trade unions, the status of which was legally recognized. Notwithstanding these reforms socialism, advancing the idea of a new and more just order, gained thousands of converts among the working classes.

Social Legislation

Although Austria was still predominantly an agricultural state, the existence within it of aggressive bourgeois classes and a restless proletariat, the growing force of socialism, and an active anti-Semitic Christian-Socialist movement, all indicated the rise of problems peculiar to a dominant middle-class régime. Attempting to keep abreast of recent trends, the government adopted intelligent and constructive economic policies. Tendencies toward socialism were visible in the initiation of state ownership of such public utilities as railroads and in enlightened social legislation. By 1914 economic, social, and intellectual progress in Austria was essentially analogous to such developments in bourgeois countries of the West.

Hungary, like Austria, was a multinational state. Occupying the broad, fertile plains of the middle Danube valley, it was dominated by the haughty Magyars. The latter constituted about 50 per cent of a total *Hungary after 1867* population of 20,500,000. The other half of the population consisted of subject nationalities divided as follows: 5,500,000 Slavs, 3,000,000 Rumanians, 2,000,000 Austrians, and 1,000,000 Jews. Lack of ethnic homogeneity afforded Hungary one of her most complex problems.

In contrast to the progressive tendencies in Austria was the backwardness of Hungary. After the establishment of the *Ausgleich* in 1867, Hungary was constituted as a quasi-independent state, the Austrian emperor being *ipso facto* king. Although crowned with special coronation ceremonies at Budapest, the Hungarian capital, his actual power in Hungary was much less than in Austria, as the former country was dominated by an aristocratic oligarchy rather than by an autocratic monarch. A constitution provided for a bicameral legislature consisting of an aristocratic upper house, the Table of Magnates, largely hereditary, and an unrepresentative lower house, the Chamber of Deputies, elected according to a complicated franchise law. By restricting the suffrage to some 1,000,000 men, who were but a small part of the adult males, the parliamentary system insured the ascendancy of the Magyar landowners. Under the control of the conservative Catholic propertied classes political, social, and economic progress was difficult if not impossible.

As late as 1914 the Industrial Revolution had failed to make much progress in Hungary. Ruled in the traditional medieval way, by a few proud, conservative Magyar landlords who oppressed the peasants, the country still remained dominantly feudal in character. The agrarian aristocracy, despising bourgeois innovations and principles, struggled to prevent the introduction of liberalism in politics, in religion, or in education.

Hungary, like her imperial partner, preferred to crush the disruptive force of nationalism rather than to permit a political reorganization of the kingdom. Determined *Subject Nationalities* to preserve their hegemony in Hungary, the *in Hungary* ruling Magyars embarked on a policy of Magyarization. They attempted to suppress the languages and institutions of the subject nationalities and denied them the suffrage. Despite their repressive policies, however, the distinguishing characteristics of the subject nationalities survived. The attempt at forceful Magyarization proved a failure, although it drove over one million emigrants from Hungary between 1896 and 1910. Unable to secure equality or reforms within the Dual Monarchy, the Rumanians and Slavs soon looked abroad, to Rumania and to Serbia, for a solution of their difficulties.

Austro-Hungarian relations constituted one of the fundamental problems confronting the Magyars. One group desired to retain the *Ausgleich*, believing that it secured *Austro-Hungarian* adequate self-government for Hungary and *Relations* that it guaranteed Austrian support should a general Slavic uprising or foreign war occur. Another party, led by Francis Kossuth, son of the famous president of the short-lived Hungarian republic of 1848–1849, favored complete Magyar independence. This group made little headway, however, for whenever its adherents became too active, the Austrian government would threaten to favor the non-Magyar elements in Hungary. Fearing an uprising of the suppressed peoples, the "independents" would quickly subside.

Foreign affairs tended to strengthen the friendly relations

between Austria and Hungary. The Pan-Slav movement, fostered by Russia, threatened to arouse the Slavs in both countries. As their unrest became greater, Austria and Hungary drew closer together in common fear of a Slavic uprising aided by Russian intervention. By 1914 they were willing to disregard their differences and to present a united front to their formidable foe in the North. Like his Hapsburg ancestors, the emperor king Francis Joseph was still the symbol of unity which protected the Dual Monarchy from foreign intervention or internal disintegration.

The personality of the emperor has always been somewhat of an enigma. Ascending the throne in 1848 as a youth of eighteen, this little-understood monarch reigned until 1916, dying at the advanced age *Francis Joseph* of eighty-six. In his later years he seemed a relic of the past; he was a thoroughgoing conservative, whose outstanding trait was opposition to change. He distrusted such new-fangled innovations as automobiles, telephones, enameled English bathtubs, and other modern conveniences. Possessing a strong will, he seemed incapable of original thinking, preferring to cling to traditional practices and ceremonies. Egotistical but conscientious, he led a life of Spartan simplicity and devoted himself to his duty of running the state. He was the living symbol of a decadent conservatism.

In domestic affairs Francis Joseph strove to carry out traditional Hapsburg policies. He desired to preserve dynastic supremacy in the Dual Monarchy and Austrian hegemony in central Europe. Only limited success had rewarded his attempts to maintain the authority of the crown, as he was forced to grant limited constitutional reforms and to forsake a unitary empire for the *Ausgleich*.

The foreign policies of Francis Joseph were unsuccessful. Disastrously defeated by the Prussians in the Seven Weeks' War of 1866, the Austrian government became an unwilling witness of the unification of *Foreign Policies of the* Germany under the leadership of Bismarck. *Emperor* Humiliated, the vexed Hapsburg ruler appointed as his foreign minister the Saxon, Count von Beust (1809–1886), who with the support of his sovereign planned to unite all the southern and middle German states under Austrian leadership in an endeavor to shatter Prussian supremacy.

To achieve this end, Austria, needing the assistance of a powerful ally, turned to France, which was also alarmed at the rapid expansion of Prussian power. When informed of the proposed plan, however, Napoleon III refused to lend his support until Francis Joseph had settled his internal difficulties, especially those concerning the Magyars. The *Ausgleich*, creating the Dual Monarchy, afforded a solution to the Magyar problem. Internal law and order seemed assured with the creation of an Austro-Magyar *bloc* capable of dominating the non-Germanic and non-Magyar elements in Austria and in Hungary. Although the objections of the Slavs, especially the Czechs, could not be silenced, Francis Joseph was confident of success and refused to listen to their demands. With the reëstablishment of internal order he was convinced that the way was prepared for a war of revenge against Prussia and for the restoration of Hapsburg supremacy in central Europe.

The Franco-German clash of 1870 offered Francis Joseph a splendid opportunity to achieve his purpose. But when the Austrian general staff declared that the army was not ready, when the Magyars refused to support an interventionist policy, and when Alexander II of Russia advised the Dual Monarchy to remain out of the conflict, the emperor hesitated. Meanwhile the crushing defeat of the French at Sedan resulted in the fall of the second Napoleonic Empire. His potential ally shattered, and too weak to accomplish his ends unaided, the Austrian emperor saw the last prospect of a renascent Hapsburg hegemony in central Europe vanish when, on January 18, 1871, the German princes assembled in the Hall of Mirrors at Versailles acclaimed the king of Prussia as German emperor. "The lid was nailed on the coffin wherein slumbered the great mid-European empire of Charles V and Ferdinand II."

Chagrined at his failure, Francis Joseph undertook to strengthen his internal position. To placate German and Jewish elements in Austria, he offered liberal political reforms. His appointment of a pro-Czech premier, however, antagonized the Austrians, many of whom, it was rumored, even went so far as to favor union with Germany. Aroused by such reports, he determined to teach his German subjects a lesson *Domestic Policies of Francis Joseph* by promising to have himself crowned king of Bohemia, by issuing an ordinance recognizing the Czech language, and by virtually turning over the civil service in Bohemia and Moravia to the Czechs. The Austro-Germans, aided by the Magyars, however, forced him to restore his German liberal cabinet and to abandon his conciliatory policy toward the Czechs.

The emperor turned to the Magyars for support. Consequently the foreign policy of the Dual Monarchy came, in the seventies, under the control of Count Julius Andrássy (1823–1890), an unusually capable Magyar diplomat. At that time he was a typical cavalier, smart, handsome, and dazzling, "equally irresistible on the sofas of boudoirs and the floor of debate." A man of the world, he had flashes of true insight, and was a peculiar combination of a fiery steppe horseman and a polished Parisian of the boulevards. "He was, above all, a Magyar nobleman. Supremacy of his race (which in the current political jargon really meant his clan) was his Koran." As foreign minister, therefore, he did his utmost to prevent the Slavs in Hungary from rising to power. To him dualism was a dam against the rising floods of discontented nationalities, and had to be preserved.

Andrássy completely reoriented the foreign policy of his predecessor, Beust. Turning his back upon Germany, he faced the east and instituted a policy which followed two convergent lines: to nip in the *Andrássy's Balkan Policy* bud the Slav national movement in the Balkans and to check Russian expansion southward. Andrássy well understood the weak defensive position of Hungary, a state ruled by a small minority of Magyar nobles in the midst of hostile groups of Slavs and Rumanians. Realizing that an offensive course would best serve Magyar interests, he favored an expansionist policy in the Balkans. He claimed that every gain in that region, by diminishing the possibility of Pan-Slavism there, would weaken the opposition in the Dual Monarchy and insure the stability of the established government. The extension of Hapsburg interests in the Near East would strengthen Western influences and check the advance of Russia. Despite declarations that such a course was a civilizing mission, he admitted that Salonica, with its access to Eastern waters, was the final prize.

The Three Emperors' League (1872)[1] seemed contradictory to the *Drang nach Osten* policy of Andrássy. Superficially it appeared that Russia, Germany, and Austria would become close friends, perhaps allies. Actually each of the members distrusted the other two, so that in practice the League was of comparatively slight significance.

Disregarding this friendly combination, Andrássy instituted his Balkan policy by reviving the old hope of Austria-Hungary of acquiring the two Slav provinces Bosnia *Bosnia-Herzegovina* and Herzegovina, owned by the Turks. Military authorities were especially active in promoting the agitation for the acquisition of these districts, so as thereby to gain control of the hinterland of the long and narrow Dalmatian coast. Once in possession of these provinces the Dual Monarchy would be in a position to send armies along the Adriatic or down the Balkans in order to protect Hapsburg interests. Francis Joseph, however, had another reason for desiring these lands. He believed that the addition of the two provinces would make the Slavs so powerful in Hungary that the Magyars and the Germans would become alarmed and therefore consent to the reëstablishment of a centralized autocracy.

Finally Austria-Hungary was given an opportunity of extending her interests in Bosnia and Herzegovina. At the Congress of Berlin, in 1878, she was granted permission to establish military supervision over the provinces, ostensibly to protect the Christians from the "terrible Turks." Regarding this concession as an entering wedge, Andrássy telegraphed to Francis Joseph that the gate to the Orient was at last

[1] See pages 478–479.

open. His optimism was unfounded, however, for all entrances to the Balkans were guarded jealously by hostile peoples, who bitterly resented Hapsburg intrusion.

Especially aroused by the growth of Austro-Hungarian influence in the provinces were the Serbs and Russians. The Serbian government soon concluded that Slav independence could be attained only through the disruption of Austria-Hungary. Moreover, Russia feared that the Dual Monarchy would menace her position in the Balkans. Recalling the opposition of both Germany and Austria at the Congress of Berlin, the Russian government realized that it might be compelled to use force to safeguard its interests in the Balkans. Indeed, one Russian general reflected a popular belief when he remarked, "The road to Berlin leads over Vienna."

By 1879 Francis Joseph, converted to Andrássy's program, assented to the establishment of the Dual Alliance between Germany and Austria-Hungary. At that time he was fully prepared to abandon his hope of revenge against Germany and to support his minister's designs in the Balkans. In domestic matters, however, the ruler followed an anti-German policy. Persevering in his hostility to the German liberals, who had opposed the annexation of Bosnia-Herzegovina, Francis Joseph appointed as his *The Policy of "Divide and Rule"* premier Count Taaffe (1833–1895), who announced a federalist pro-Slav course. Francis Joseph approved of this policy, because he hoped to reëstablish his personal supremacy by securing the support of the Slavs, especially the Czechs.

Certain leaders about Francis Joseph questioned the feasibility of persisting in the policy of "Divide and Rule," and suggested other solutions. His son Rudolph (1857–1889), heir to the throne, felt that the Hapsburg state must be modernized if it were to endure. Declaring Austria backward, he maintained that economic and intellectual advances alone could save her. He advocated opening the window to Western liberalism and urged the establishment of the bourgeois system. Common economic interests, he believed, would then unite all groups in support of the established order.

The conservative Count Taaffe, ruling for Francis Joseph, accurately summed up his own policy when he said, "One must keep all nationalities in a state of well-tempered discontent." Reviving the slogan "Divide and Rule," he pitted Czechs against Germans, Poles against Ruthenians, and Slovenes against Italians. He realized that Francis Joseph feared the Germans more than the people of any other nationality; so, surrounding them with a ring of Slavs and clericals, he reduced the power of the liberal Germans.

General unrest and loss of confidence in the Hapsburgs were the results of Taaffe's administration. The Czechs flirted with Pan-Slavism, the Poles conceived a restored Poland, Croats and Slovenes dreamed of South Slavia, and the unredeemed Italians hoped for union with their brethren in Italy. In Austria the Germans formed a nationalist party which preferred the Prussian Hohenzollerns to the Austrian Hapsburgs and favored union with Germany. Most national groups had at least one thing in common — opposition to the Hapsburgs.

Crown Prince Rudolph was convinced that the Taaffe régime was undermining the empire and that western Europe as a whole was on the decline. "We are living," he declared, "in evil times — graft, theft, rabble in high places, the crudest despotism, hand-to-mouth makeshifts — the State is gliding toward ruin. . . . Verily, old Europe is tottering toward its grave. A great, powerful upheaval must come, a social revolution from which, as after a long illness, a new Europe will blossom forth." In 1888, when the news reached him of William's accession to the German throne, Rudolph prophetically remarked: "William II is unfolding himself. Before long he will start an awful confusion in old Europe; he is just that sort of a person. His mind is limited by the grace of God; he is vigorous and stubborn like a bull, regards himself as the greatest genius — what more do you want? In a few years he will probably land Hohenzollern Germany in the ditch where it belongs."

Gradually the forces of disintegration threatened to disrupt the Hapsburg empire. In 1908 Francis Joseph, by the ill-

timed annexation of Bosnia-Herzegovina and by his impolitic
concessions to the Czechs, had seriously undermined his chief
source of strength, the German-Magyar alli-
ance. Slowly but surely the Austro-Germans   *The Dual Monarchy
were being pushed toward Berlin, while Czechs,   in 1914*
Yugoslavs, and Rumanians were steadily becoming more
insistent in their demands for political and civil equality. The
internal situation in Austria was acute when the coming of
the war interrupted all domestic developments.

By the twentieth century the position of the Magyars in
Hungary was more precarious than that of the Germans in
Austria. Not only did the rapid cultural development of the
Rumanians prove alarming, but, more serious still, the Magyar
peasants began to question the authority of their overlords.
In Bosnia-Herzegovina a most dangerous and unwelcome
south-Slav movement was spreading into Hungary. Proposing to obtain independence and to establish a great Slav state,
these Slav "patriots" were very menacing, since they already
had in Serbia a nucleus for unification and in Russia a patron.
Little wonder, then, that before 1914 many regarded the dissolution of the Dual Monarchy as inevitable.

PERRY acquaints the JAPANESE with the MECHANICAL MARVELS
of bourgeois culture. From a painting by Fortunino Matania

PART VI. IMPERIALISM: DIFFUSION OF WESTERN CIVILIZATION

CHAPTER XXII

The Old and the New Imperialism

TWO waves of imperialism marked the expansion of Europe in modern times. The first, extending from the fifteenth century to the eighteenth, consisted primarily of several competitive colonial movements sponsored by the national states of Europe. The second, starting about 1870, and as yet unabated, affected most of the industrial powers. Whereas the former resulted in large part from dynastic-mercantilistic policies, the latter was a virtually inevitable outgrowth of the capitalistic and industrial system. The inherent superiority of capitalistically organized countries, ruled by the triumphant middle classes, enabled them to surge into backward regions with irresistible force.

Before the fifteenth century Europe was of relatively slight importance in the world. Isolated, agrarian, nearly self-sufficient, unaggressive, and with its political entities poorly

NOTE. *The picture at the top of the page shows the* FIRST RAILWAY TRAIN IN JAPAN. *From an old print.*

organized, this continent was too much concerned with its own affairs to exert great political, economic, or cultural *The Old Imperialism* influence abroad. Gradually, however, the changes effected by the Commercial Revolution, and the emergence of more highly centralized national states in the West, led to expansion and to the political and economic conquest of a large part of the world.

After the great explorations of the fifteenth and sixteenth centuries the newly consolidated national states of western Europe strove to create overseas empires. Portugal, Spain, the Netherlands, France, and Great Britain, fired by religious zealots, explorers, adventurers, traders, and ambitious kings, became important colonizing powers. Also many persons suffering religious oppression in European countries went forth to the New World, where they hoped to enjoy freedom.

The growth of the earlier phase of European imperialism was accompanied by a new economic theory,— mercantilism. *Mercantilism* As colonial powers, especially Spain, became wealthy and powerful, contemporary economists tended to attribute their strength to the success of colonial efforts. These theorists, therefore, favored the development of economic-military states based on absolute monarchy and sustained by the profits of overseas commercial and colonial activities.

Mercantilism was the economic counterpart of absolutism. Its ideal was a highly centralized and consolidated dynastic state, in which the royal government regulated the economic activities of the people. Just as the king was supposedly supreme in political and civil life by virtue of the theory of divine right, so his supremacy in economic spheres was assumed by the mercantile theory. This belief rested on two main assumptions: that business enterprise existed primarily for the benefit of the state, and that precious metals were the chief source of wealth and consequently of economic and political power.

The principal aim of the mercantilist theory was the aggrandizement of the state through the acquisition of wealth. Inasmuch as the various means whereby precious metals might be secured were inadequate to satisfy the needs of a powerful economic-military state, the mercantilists turned to commercial and industrial activities for a solution. They believed that the creation of a favorable balance of trade — an excess of exports — would lead to the accumulation of wealth. With both industry and commerce under governmental regulations, it seemed feasible to manipulate them in such a way as to promote an influx of precious metals.

During the early modern period certain European countries were partially industrialized. Although primarily agrarian, they evolved a capitalistic order, and the old régime began to decay, especially in the western states. Factories, banks, commercial companies, and capitalists appeared as precursors of the Industrial Revolution. Since there was slight opportunity for expansion in agrarian Europe, such phenomena help to explain the economic basis for the earlier imperialism. As industries developed, the desirability of colonies as outlets for surplus manufactured goods and as sources of raw materials became increasingly apparent. For nearly three centuries after the exploration of the Portuguese and Spanish *conquistadores* the more advanced powers of western Europe struggled to acquire overseas possessions.

Under the mercantilist system the colonies themselves were assumed to exist purely for the benefit of the mother country. To maintain such a closed arrangement, vast shipping and sea power were necessary to exploit and protect overseas possessions from smugglers and foreign powers. The mercantilist colony was of the plantation type, intended to supply tropical or semitropical raw products which Europe lacked but desired. By abstaining from manufacturing, the colony would remain a potential market for manufactured goods and avoid becoming a rival of the mother country. All profits accruing from colonial commerce, trade, and exploitation were restricted to the subjects of the colonizing power who had borne the burden of expense.

Although these early modern colonizers struggled valiantly to maintain the "closed door," they were generally unsuccessful. It was impossible to police the seas effectively and

protect the coásts from smugglers and from attacks by buc-
caneers and enemies. Furthermore, as the colonies developed
they became restless under the merciless exploitation of the
monopolistic system. Colonial merchants and officials often
conspired with illegal traders whose goods might be cheaper
or more desirable. Consequently the absolute restrictions
and pure monopoly of the mercantile system were seldom
maintained in practice. Imperfect methods of control and
overrigid mercantile and colonial policies culminated in a
breakdown of the earlier wave of European imperialism.

The eighteenth century, primarily an age of revolt against
the past, witnessed a decisive reaction against the maximum
state control involved in seventeenth-century
Breakdown of Mer- absolutism, paternalism, and mercantilism.
cantilism Doctrines of *laissez faire* and individualism
permeated European society, leading to revolutionary atti-
tudes which eventually undermined the old régime and the
absolute monarchy. Both in Europe and in the colonies the
system of political and economic regulation was criticized and
condemned, and the new revolutionary spirit swept the colonial world, bringing with it a revulsion of feeling against
mercantilism.

Soon the colonial empires began to fall away from their
parent states. The defeat of France in the Seven Years' War
(1756–1763) led to the loss of the bulk of her
Decline of Old Empires colonial empire to England and Spain. Twenty
years later the success of the American Revolution deprived
England of some of her most valuable colonies. By the eighteenth century the Portuguese and the Dutch had already
lost many of their possessions to stronger competitors. The
earlier decline of Portugal and the Netherlands, together with
their political and economic collapse during the Napoleonic
period, effectively prohibited any serious attempts at colonial
rehabilitation. Between 1810 and 1824 Spain lost the greater
part of her overseas possessions, and in 1822 Portugal was
forced to grant complete independence to Brazil.

The blight which seemed to have stricken the great empires
soon led to a revulsion of feeling in Europe against them, and

the belief became widespread that colonies would normally reach an ultimate stage of maturity, when they would separate from the mother countries and become independent. *Opposition to Colonies* Thus the expenses involved in colonization, administration, protection, and colonial wars seemed wasted. The old mercantilist regulations and restrictions tended to disappear as the powers gave up the hopeless task of enforcing impracticable monopolies. Reforms were introduced into the colonies which permitted them considerable political and economic freedom. The older colonial movement as well as mercantilism had broken down, and many statesmen and theorists thenceforth condemned overseas enterprises as fervently as the earlier mercantilists had praised them.

In the late eighteenth and early nineteenth centuries a powerful anti-imperialistic reaction developed. Most European states, involved in the Napoleonic wars, became less interested in colonies. After 1815, alarmed by the specter of revolution and liberalism, Continental statesmen were largely concerned with maintaining the *status quo* and erecting conservative dikes against the seething waves of liberalism and thwarted nationalism. Meanwhile the gradual development of the Industrial Revolution, though ultimately a cause of imperialism, resulted in the rise of many political, social, and economic problems in European states which called for early solutions. Concerned primarily with national and industrial consolidation until the third quarter of the nineteenth century, European states generally were not interested in imperial ventures, which appeared both costly and profitless.

During the nineteenth century the Manchester School in England popularized the newer economic belief of "Hands off." The growth of the idea of individualism as opposed to state interference in business, and the rise in England and elsewhere of liberals to whom repression of colonies was repugnant, further strengthened and justified the doctrine of free trade. Opposition to imperialism was stimulated in England as a result of these beliefs. This was indicated by the speeches and policies of her political leaders, such as Gladstone and other

Little Englanders, and by British reluctance to annex New Zealand, Fiji, or Natal.

Indifference to imperialism also developed in continental Europe. The problems of internal reconstruction and national consolidation retarded the economic advance of the European states and diverted their attention from imperialistic ventures. The motives, therefore, which later inspired a revival of imperialism were not yet ripe. Political and economic liberalism still held sway and delayed by several decades another movement toward colonial expansion.

The second outburst of imperialism came in the third quarter of the nineteenth century. This newer imperialism may *The New Imperialism* be defined as the tendency of modern industrial states, especially since 1870, to seek control of backward, nonindustrial, non-European peoples and countries. Far transcending the older form in virulence and subtlety, it was less concerned with the acquisition of subject peoples and territories than with the control of their raw materials, mineral resources, markets, and economic opportunities.

In contrast to the old type the new imperialism was characterized by the multiplicity of its forms. These varied from outright annexation to protectorates or simply indirect political or economic domination such as spheres of influence. Primarily exploitative, this imperialism aimed at securing economic privileges and advantages for national groups, often to the detriment of foreign competitors and subject peoples.

By 1875 a new world of economic conditions had been evolved as a result of the Industrial Revolution. The growth of the capitalistic system and large-scale business, with giant output and enormous profits, led to a vast accumulation of capital which caused a further growth and expansion of business enterprises. Out of the changed economic order arose the bourgeois classes, more powerful and more wealthy than ever before. During the nineteenth century these groups, especially in England, tending to wrest political hegemony from the landed aristocracy, paved the way for the subordination of the state to business interests.

But the development of capitalism menaced its existence. Inasmuch as this system of production was essentially dynamic and competitive, individual industries and concerns were constantly forced to increase their efficiency by reinvesting in industry a large proportion of the profits. *Capitalism and the New Imperialism* With the increase in efficiency and in labor-saving devices, production was greatly augmented, but a large number of wage-earners were thrown out of work. Thus capitalistic society found itself in a very embarrassing position, there being more goods to be disposed of and fewer people to buy them, and also more capital to invest but fewer productive enterprises to absorb it. The domestic markets being by necessity cluttered with an excess of goods, capitalists, to avert devastating crises, were forced to seek foreign markets which would absorb not only the surplus goods but also the surplus capital which had been accumulated. "The need of a constantly expanding market for its products," wrote Marx and Engels, "chases the bourgeoisie over the whole surface of the globe. It must nestle everywhere, settle everywhere, establish connections everywhere." Imperialism was the result. And this must be said for it: imperialism often preserved capitalism from catastrophe and annihilation.

Owing, therefore, to the large profits from factories, mines, rents, banks, and "big business," under the bourgeois system, a tremendous expansion of capital occurred. Improved means of communication and transportation, especially telegraphs, steamships, and railways, accentuated the spread of capitalism. By making the world relatively smaller these conveniences contributed to the development of profitable trade with distant lands. Vast sums were expended in the creation of these transportation facilities. To safeguard these and other business interests, capitalists soon urged their governments to assume direct or indirect control over remote parts of the earth.

Mercantilism reappeared in a modified version, — economic nationalism. This theory, frequently designated as neomercantilism, by fallaciously assuming the existence of economic solidarity in a country, linked the concept of the national state with a belief in its economic unity. Groups of capitalists for their own benefit influenced their *Economic Nationalism* governments into establishing protective tariffs and regulating economic activities by means of diplomacy, military and naval demonstrations, and even wars. Imbued with a spirit of patriotism and believing such practices identical with the interests of the state, the masses of the people usually supported the government. Nationalism became an important force in stimulating the growth of imperialism. Ardent patriots usually believed a great colonial empire to be a necessary appanage if a state were to maintain its prestige. They thus found aggressive imperialism compatible with their faith in the national destiny, often being willing to make sacrifices and even to fight for expansion. National administrations often became the tools of restricted groups of capitalists, and the belief developed that the nation existed for the benefit of business.

Many neomercantilists, desirous of seeing the national state in control of necessary raw products, food, and markets, made economic self-sufficiency their aim. The economic nationalist, however, abandoning the attempt at direct monopoly and the exclusiveness of the mercantilist, tried to achieve similar ends by tariffs, state subsidies, and methods of discrimination which controlled the markets, raw products, and economic opportunities in the interests of the nationals.

Although the costs of imperialistic ventures, especially wars, were borne by the many, only a few enjoyed the direct profits. Such groups as exporters, importers, shippers, and industrialists dependent on colonial raw products and markets, as well as manufacturers of armaments, uniforms, and materials used in colonial development, benefited greatly. Enormous profits, which were reinvested in other extranational localities, often accrued to financiers and bankers who invested in colonies or industrially backward countries. Colonial administrators and their families, explorers, adventurers, and missionaries were prone, for various reasons, to support foreign interference in backward countries. To promote the acquisition of naval bases and strategic frontiers and the erection of buffer states, military and naval men encouraged imperialism as a mode of defense. Moreover, the need of imperialist powers for large armaments enhanced the prestige of certain men and their personal opportunity for distinction and advancement. Statesmen such as Disraeli, Ferry, Chamberlain, and Theodore Roosevelt, by appealing to the imperialistic and nationalistic enthusiasm of their patriotic countrymen, improved their own political fortunes. However, the people as a whole — especially the wage-earning classes — received but indirect and often only theoretical rewards. Usually they were assured that their work, their wages, in fact their entire standard of living, depended upon the maintenance of foreign, including colonial, trade.

Despite these vague rewards the general public supported imperialism. The national pride of the sincere patriot led him to favor the acquisition of strategic naval bases, colonial markets, and the control of raw products. He was especially desirous of *Imperialism and Patriotism* seeing his country possess lands containing materials essential to war or to future prosperity. Surplus population, often in reality economic underdevelopment, led to much emigration from European states and perturbed the patriot, who became alarmed at the steady loss of nationals. This drain provided another justification for colonial expansion, since overseas possessions would presumably afford havens for emigrants. Finally, jealous of the prestige of his country, the ardent patriot was usually willing to support his state in any aggression for some actual or fancied insult to the flag or national honor; hence the complex of national superiority was carried over into the field of imperialism. Failing to comprehend that international rivalries, tariff wars, or actual hostilities might exert detrimental effects on the national state, he often backed incompetent and aggressive leaders in policies which proved more disastrous than beneficial.

To justify rampant imperialism, altruistic rationalizations appeared desirable, to obscure the real motives, often selfish in character. Kipling devised his concept of the "white

man's burden" to assuage uneasy consciences; he made it
appear as if the benefits to the natives far surpassed the profits
accruing to the mother country. In France it was the *mission civilisatrice*, and in Germany the spread of *Kultur*, which
provided the requisite humanitarian urge. American pride
in sanitary and hygienic achievements often sufficed to silence
popular criticism of "dollar diplomacy."

The religious motive was a powerful incentive contributing
to imperialism. Many pious Christians, both Catholic and
Protestant, hoped to see the true faith carried
Imperialism and Reli- to the heathen, and formed societies and spon-
gion sored periodicals for such purposes. Thou-
sands of missionaries preached the gospel in remote sections
of Asia, Africa, and the islands of the Pacific. Besides receiving religious instruction the natives were acquainted with
European hygiene, sanitation, medicine, and clothing. Believing that the extension of European control would result in
the propagation of the faith and the spread of Western civilization, many sincere Christians espoused the cause of imperialism. Often the precursors of this movement, the missionaries engendered a popular interest in backward countries
and by their activities demonstrated to traders and adventurers the unexploited potentialities and opportunities.

Not always beneficial, however, was the influence of imperialism on the missionary movement. Unscrupulous governmental agents often hoisted the flag while the prostrate natives
were being guided in prayer by the imported representatives
of God. At other times they discouraged missionary activities
in certain localities for fear of arousing religious unrest and
political discontent. Frequently the humanitarian work of
clergymen engaged in teaching Christian virtues was undone
by rapacious governmental officials, traders, and adventurers,
who often debased and exploited the natives. Forced labor,
the spread of social diseases, and the sale of firearms and
liquor were among the evils which undermined native character and ruined primitive societies. Imperialism in many cases
resulted in "the black man's burden"; for while the work was
done by the natives, the profits went to the foreigners.

The Reverend John G. Paton, a pious cleric, described exceedingly well the unsatisfactory relations between missionaries and traders. As a young student in a divinity hall in Scotland he heard the "wailing of the perishing heathen in the South Sea Islands." Responding to what he regarded as a divine call, he went to the New Hebrides Islands in the fifties. After encountering many obstacles in his attempt to convert the cannibals, the missionary met real trouble when an unscrupulous English sea captain deliberately wrecked his boat near the island in order to collect insurance for the company. Leaving adequate food supplies on board, he and his men waded ashore, where they were entertained by the missionaries and the natives. During the night the crew were discovered while attempting to rob their hosts, and only with the utmost difficulty did the Reverend Mr. Paton prevent a massacre of the "Christian thieves" by the indignant natives. "Glad were we," he wrote, "when a vessel called and carried away these white heathen savages."

In a world in which economic interdependence was the reality and national self-sufficiency apparently an unattainable ideal, overseas markets, raw materials, and economic opportunities had to be obtained. *"Inevitability" of Expansion* Without noncapitalistic territories to absorb surpluses in goods and wealth, industrial countries might have found themselves with serious problems of unemployment, low wages, and poverty.

Capitalism, in its ruthless conquest of the world, tended to obliterate rival systems. Wherever it penetrated, less efficient societies were forced to give way. Marx and Engels, as early as 1848, realized this fact when they wrote:

The bourgeoisie, by the rapid improvement of all instruments of production, by the immensely facilitated means of communication, draws all, even the most barbarian, nations into civilization. The cheap prices of its commodities are the heavy artillery with which it batters down all Chinese walls, with which it forces the barbarians' intensely obstinate hatred of foreigners to capitulate. It compels all nations, on pain of extinction, to adopt the bourgeois mode of production . . . to introduce what it calls civilization . . . that is, to become bourgeois themselves. In a word, it creates a world after its own image.

In many respects the partial adoption of European culture proved beneficial to the inhabitants of backward regions.

Effects of Imperialism on Backward Peoples

Improved facilities for hygiene, sanitation, agriculture, transportation, and communication were introduced, and better standards of living evolved. Many barbaric practices, such as human sacrifice, infanticide, cannibalism, mutilations, and slavery, were abolished or at least restricted by enlightened foreign authorities. New ideas penetrated, some backward peoples being stirred by the same dynamic factors which revolutionized nineteenth-century Europe — nationalism, liberalism, and industrialism. Consequently natives have often been placed in a difficult position, for contacts with an enlightened civilization caused them to lose faith in primitive customs. Indeed, many found themselves in a dilemma, incapable of assimilation into Western civilization and too advanced to subscribe to the traditional beliefs and practices of their own cultures.

Westernization of native peoples had, and probably will continue to have, a revolutionary effect on the world. The adoption of European political and social standards may conceivably lead to widespread uprisings against foreign rule and the establishment of independent national states. If these countries, free from alien political and economic bondage, then develop their own vast natural and labor resources, they may establish overseas capitalistic systems against which European competition will be ineffective. It remains to be seen what would happen should capitalism triumph in all parts of the world.

CHAPTER XXIII

The Partition of Africa

IN THE latter part of the nineteenth century Africa, a continent characterized by its lack of capitalistic development, felt the shock of the new imperialism. Said to consist of forbidding wastes and impenetrable jungles, it was reported to be a continent of climatic extremes, cultural and ethnic contrasts, barbarous savages, and fabulous mystery. It was until recent times a land virtually unknown. In the eighteenth century Jonathan Swift satirized the Europeans' dearth of knowledge of Darkest Africa when he wrote:

> Geographers, in Afric maps,
> With savage pictures fill their gaps,
> And o'er unhabitable downs
> Place elephants for want of towns.

The inhospitable physical nature of Africa was largely responsible for much of the earlier ignorance concerning the continent. Scarcity of good harbors on the long, regular coast lines was one of the greatest barriers. Flanking the hot, swampy, disease-infected coasts were mountain ranges which cut them off from the healthier interior plateau. Vast desert wastes stretched across the northern portion of the continent, while dense jungles covered the central section. In the south a tableland, barren and rainless, was nearly as desolate as the northern deserts. Waterfalls and rapids made unnavigable, until recently, the four great rivers which drained the interior.

An enormous continent of some 11,262,000 square miles, Africa lacked anything approaching geographical homogeneity. The northern coasts, Morocco, Algeria, Tunis, *Geographical Features* Tripoli, and the Nile Valley, inhabited by Caucasian peoples and contiguous to the Mediterranean littoral, had participated in or had been marginal to the higher

397

cultures of Europe and the Near East for thousands of years. Geographically and economically they were a part of the Mediterranean world and had little in common with the tropical jungle lands of the blacks.

To the south lay the gigantic Sahara. Millions of square miles of barren desert extended across the continent from the Atlantic to the Red Sea. From north to south this desert belt attained a depth of several thousand miles. The enormous waste land, dotted here and there with oases and cut by scattered caravan routes, was almost unoccupied except for war-like tribesmen who participated in or preyed upon the caravan trade. Cultural contacts between the northern littoral and the tropics were effectively minimized by the desert buffer.

Below the Sahara was Darkest Africa,— the Sudan and the tropics, — inhabited chiefly by various types of Negro peoples living in the jungles. There were to be found cannibals, big game, ivory and wild rubber, and primitive cultures. It was the black man's land, infested with tropical diseases deadly to the whites; here natural and primitive forces resisted the inroads of civilization. Although penetrated by great rivers, the mass of central Africa remained virtually inaccessible to Europeans until the nineteenth century.

The southern part of the continent was inhospitable. Deserts and waste lands isolated the tropical jungles from the more temperate regions of South Africa. The climate and environment, however, were less hostile to the white man, and European settlements were able to flourish for more than a century.

Africa escaped complete partition during the early imperialistic movement. Beginning with the seizure, in 1415, of the Moroccan port of Ceuta by the Portuguese, the European powers, including Great Britain, Spain, the Netherlands, and France, during the early modern period concentrated chiefly on the slave trade and the control of way stations for their commerce with the Far East. To achieve these ends they desired merely to control strategic points and harbors where their ships could be repaired or their supplies replenished. By the eighteenth century, however, the naval and maritime power of England

The Old Imperialism in Africa

enabled her to best her rivals and thenceforth to dominate the Oriental trade. Owing to the abolition movement of the eighteenth and nineteenth centuries there was a rapid decline of the slave traffic and a consequent loss of profits from African ventures. A general let-down of interest in Africa followed, practically simultaneous with the decline of the older colonial movement.

Despite decreased attention to the economic potentialities of Africa a period of discovery ensued in which explorers, adventurers, missionaries, and traders contributed to the opening of the Dark Continent. *The Period of Discovery* From 1770 to 1772 James Bruce made the first of a long line of notable journeys into unexplored regions when he traversed Abyssinia and Sennar and reached the source of the Blue Nile. In 1795, under the auspices of the African Association founded in England in 1788, Mungo Park explored the region from Gambia to the Upper Niger. Ten years later he passed near Timbuktu and descended the Niger as far as Bussa, where he lost his life.

The epoch-making expedition of Mungo Park in 1795 was the prelude to other explorations. During the next century French, Portuguese, British, and German explorers penetrated most of the regions theretofore unknown. A scientific expedition in southeast Africa was conducted by the Portuguese explorer Dr. Francisco José de Lacerda up the Zambezi River to Tete and thence to the vicinity of Lake Mweru. The first recorded crossing of the continent by Europeans was made between 1802 and 1811, by two half-caste Portuguese, who penetrated to the interior from Angola on the west coast and descended the Zambezi River to the east coast. In 1823 three Englishmen left Tripoli, crossed the Sahara, and penetrated to Lake Chad. Two expeditions reached Timbuktu during this same period.

Perhaps the most famous of the early African explorers was the Scottish missionary David Livingstone (1813–1873). He believed that the suppression of the horrible slave trade and the spread of Christianity and Western civilization could best be facilitated in Africa by opening the continent to the white man. Therefore he devoted the greater part of his life to exploring the vast unknown interior. Proceeding north of the Orange River in 1849, he traversed the Kalahari Desert and reached Lake Ngami. Between 1851 and 1856 he crossed the continent from west to east, exploring the little-known regions of the upper and lower Zambezi and discovering the Victoria Falls. This journey aroused so much public interest that he presented an account of it to the Royal Geographical Society and published his *Missionary Travels and Researches in South Africa*. The last fifteen years of his life he devoted to the exploration of East Africa, investigating the region east of the upper Congo River between the Zambezi and the headwaters of the Nile. After his death in the African interior, in 1873, native followers brought his body to Zanzibar, whence it was taken to London, there to be enshrined in Westminster Abbey. Livingstone had done much for Africa and its primitive inhabitants. Besides exploring a third of the vast continent he aroused the civilized world to the iniquities of the slave trade and by his writings stimulated missionary activities.

Inspired by his example, explorers and adventurers from every land desired to carry on the work of exploration so ably forwarded, and helped to dispel the general ignorance concerning the interior. In 1858 an English expedition reached Tanganyika and Lake Victoria Nyanza, and four years later an English expedition descended the Nile into Egypt. Lake Albert Nyanza was discovered in 1864 by Sir Samuel Baker. Between 1860 and 1875 Morocco, the Sahara, and the Sudan were penetrated by German explorers.

Popular interest in Africa during this period was stimulated by a Welshman, Henry Morton Stanley (1841–1904). After an early life of adventure he became a reporter for the New York *Herald*. In 1871 public alarm for the safety of Livingstone, from whom no word had been received for some time, prompted the owner of the newspaper to commission Stanley to go in search of the missing missionary. Eight months after leaving Zanzibar he located Livingstone, deep in the interior, and supplied him with food and medicines. In 1872 he published a picturesque account of his exploit, entitled *How I*

Found Livingstone. The following year he served in Ashanti as a war correspondent to report the progress of the conflict being waged there between the British and the natives. The three years from 1874 to 1877 Stanley spent in crossing Africa, and he reached the Atlantic Ocean by descending the Congo River to its mouth. He published an account of this expedition, called *Through the Dark Continent.* World-wide interest had at last been aroused in Africa, and the age of exploration was on the verge of being superseded by that of occupation.

In 1875 very little of Africa was under European control. Great Britain, France, Portugal, and Turkey were the only powers retaining important possessions. Of an estimated total of some 700,000 square *Africa in 1875* miles claimed, effective British control was extended over but 250,000. Included therein were the former Dutch settlements in Cape Colony and Natal, and posts in Lagos, Sierra Leone, the Gold Coast, the Niger Delta, and Gambia. The French held about 170,000 square miles, embracing Algeria, a colony in the valley of the Senegal River, and small footholds at Obok on the Red Sea, at Gabun near the mouth of the Congo, and on the Guinea and Ivory coasts. A few scattered islands and coastal settlements, totaling some 40,000 square miles, were all that remained of the once extensive colonial empire of Portugal. Spain still retained scattered remnants embracing about 1000 square miles. A coaling station at Assab on the Red Sea was held by an Italian steamship company. Tunis, Egypt, and the Egyptian Sudan were under Turkish suzerainty, although they actually enjoyed considerable freedom. Tripoli, however, was administered as a Turkish colony after 1834.

Thus most of Africa was independent of Europe. Morocco, Abyssinia, Zanzibar, and Liberia were sovereign states; the tiny Boer republics, the Orange Free State and the Transvaal, settled by Dutch immigrants, were also independent. Generally the European colonies were of the enclave type; that is, they embraced the coastal sections but left the adjoining hinterland under native rule. Therefore the larger part of Africa was still under the control of Negro-Bantu peoples.

Sporadic attempts by local chieftains to create larger native federations had not been very successful, so that most of the interior remained politically decentralized in a welter of tiny entities. Apart from the Sahara about half the continent was controlled by natives who had not yet been seriously affected by Christian or Moslem influences.

In the seventies conditions were ripe for a rebirth of imperialism. The causes for this movement, as discussed in the last chapter, are to be found in the altered

Revival of Imperialism in Africa

economic situation in Europe. Africa, with its rich natural resources and large primitive population, loomed as a fruitful field for imperialistic exploitation. The opening of the Congo in 1877, therefore, ushered in a new age. Explorations and missionary activities, which had stirred the popular fancy, began to dwindle in importance as the era of occupation developed. Struggles for railway routes, river basins, raw materials, and native markets led to the seizure by the great powers of most of Africa. Before its partition only one tenth was under European control. After the capitalistic powers had seized all they could get, only two states remained independent.

In the nineteenth century North Africa consisted of a number of countries governed by practically independent

North Africa

monarchs. Inhabited by Moslem populations, these states usually paid lip service to their overlord, the Sultan of Turkey, who was also the caliph. In practice, however, the local dynasts generally did as they pleased. Depending on piracy for revenue, the more westerly of these powers — Tunis, Tripoli, Algeria, and Morocco — kept alive the anti-Christian crusade traditions and came to be known as the Barbary States.

A controversy with one of these Barbary States, Algeria, led to the first permanent French acquisition on the north

Establishment of the French Empire in Africa

coast of Africa and the inception of the dream of a great Mediterranean-Congo empire. Disputes over alleged piratical depredations on the part of the Algerians culminated in an insult to the French representative at Algiers in 1827. Anticipating, perhaps,

that spectacular success abroad would divert the French mind
from internal difficulties and shed new glory on the declining
prestige of the Bourbon dynasty, Charles X of France determined to punish the insolent offenders and to force them to
abandon their attacks on French commerce. In 1830 he dispatched an expedition which occupied Algiers and other ports.
Succeeding French governments expanded their new acquisitions by the gradual conquest of the hinterland. It was not
until 1847, however, that the French succeeded in securing
the military submission of the fierce Berbers led by Abd-el-
Kader, a genius of guerrilla warfare.

As imperialism became more popular during the Third
French Republic statesmen and expansionists began to rely
more and more upon Algeria as the keystone of a new French
overseas empire. Originally seized and pacified as a matter of
political expediency, the new conquest became indispensable
as the base of operations for further expansion. Therefore a
policy of pacification and assimilation was adopted. Marshal
Lyautey did remarkable work in reconciling the Berbers to
French control. Civil rule replaced military government,
and concessions were granted to the natives. Algeria later
became identified with France as an integral part of the state,
her inhabitants being recognized as French citizens and enjoying representation in the Chamber of Deputies. Great
economic development followed; agriculture was encouraged; financial resources were made available; and immigrants were welcomed to the new France beyond the seas.

Since much of Algeria consisted of barren desert lands, its
indefinite frontiers were difficult to police. Native uprisings
and border raids by the seminomadic Berbers of the Sahara,
Tunis, or Morocco kept the new provinces in a state of unrest.
Determined to maintain order and safeguard the frontiers,
the French were forced to engage in perennial guerrilla warfare. Gradually enticed beyond the political boundaries of
Algeria, they began to penetrate the Sahara and to press
eastward toward Tunis.

This policy of defensive expansion led in 1881 to the virtual
annexation of Tunis, long regarded by the Italians as a logical

field for expansion. The French occupation came to Italians as a violent shock. Too weak to contest the issue by force of arms, Italy soothed her ruffled feelings by joining with Austria and Germany in the anti-French Triple Alliance. Meanwhile France reorganized Tunis as a protectorate under a regency, actually under her direct control. With the western Algerian frontiers now safeguarded, France proceeded to round out her northern acquisitions by pressing into the desert to the south and into the sultanate of Morocco to the west.

While France was engaged in creating an empire in northwest Africa, Great Britain was gaining a dominant position in the extreme northeastern section of the *The Struggle for Egypt and the Suez Canal* continent, especially in Egypt. This home of ancient civilization was strategically located near the main trade routes connecting Europe with Asia. Napoleon I recognized its importance when he occupied it in 1798, hoping thereby to cut off England from India and the East. His expedition proving a failure, the English replaced the French and remained until 1803.

In the ensuing decades Egypt staged a spectacular political recovery. By force and cunning an Albanian adventurer, Mehemet Ali (1769–1849), became pasha and secured practical independence from his nominal suzerain, the Sultan of Turkey.[1] He established a centralized despotism and promoted economic advance by improving irrigation and crops and by developing ports and factories. Building modern fleets and armies, he initiated an imperialist policy. Temporarily parts of Arabia, Palestine, and Syria came under his control. In 1821 his forces, in quest of gold and slaves, overran the Egyptian Sudan.

The successors of Mehemet Ali were less capable. Expending enormous sums of money on courts, fêtes, and vast projects, the incompetent Ismail attempted to create a very fantastic imitation of Western civilization. A grandiose imperial policy led to the partial conquest of Somaliland, and he dreamed of an empire extending from the Mediterranean to the Indian Ocean. Despite burdensome taxes sufficient

[1] See page 246.

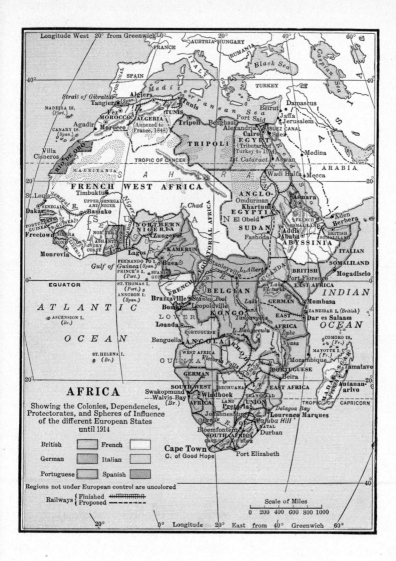

AFRICA

Showing the Colonies, Dependencies,
Protectorates, and Spheres of Influence
of the different European States
until 1914

British   French
German   Italian
Portuguese   Spanish

Regions not under European control are uncolored

Railways { Finished
           Proposed

Scale of Miles
0   200 400 600 800 1000

revenue was not available to carry out the aims of the ambitious pasha. Consequently he contracted loans from French and English financiers at high rates of interest, and by the seventies found himself faced with bankruptcy.

Among the most notable of Ismail's achievements was the promotion of the Suez Canal. This great artificial waterway, constructed by the French engineer Ferdinand de Lesseps at enormous expense, connected the Mediterranean with the Red Sea. Its commercial and naval significance, especially to a maritime power such as Great Britain, could scarcely be exaggerated. Opened in 1869, it linked Europe with the Orient by a short all-water route.

In 1875 Ismail found his finances so uncertain that he was forced to sell his Suez Canal stock. Although the tradition of French influence in Egyptian affairs was strong and her financial and economic interests were great, France was compelled to forego the opportunity of purchasing the stock. The defeat of 1870–1871 had temporarily crippled her, and the celebrated war scare of 1875 made unfeasible the outlay of extensive capital in overseas investments. As is related elsewhere, Great Britain gladly purchased the stock.[1]

Despite the sale of these shares Egypt did not prosper. In 1877 the finances of the extravagant Khedive were in such a precarious condition that England and France established a joint control over them. Because of dissatisfaction with foreign domination a nationalist revolt broke out in 1882 which threatened to annihilate all foreigners. Failing to overcome the influence of French anti-imperialists who opposed a joint Anglo-French invasion of Egypt to crush the revolt, Great Britain was forced to go in alone. The English, unembarrassed by an ally, quickly smothered the uprising and established a temporary military administration which was to rule Egypt only until such time as a stable Egyptian civil government could be developed. Despite French protests, however, the English remained, and the protectorate which they proclaimed in 1914 merely provided official recognition of a state of affairs which had existed for some time.

[1] See pages 229–230.

After 1882 control of the strategic Suez Canal and the Egyptian hinterland became of paramount importance to
Anglo-French Rivalry in the Sudan
Great Britain. Thenceforth she was determined to maintain her ascendancy in the Nile Basin and the Red Sea in order to protect the all-important route to the East. Eventually Egypt became the keystone of the British Empire, a vital link in the route to India, a terminus in the Cape-to-Cairo railway projected somewhat later, the scene of great financial investments, and a source of valuable raw products, notably cotton. The English promoted the prosperity of the country through the modernization of agriculture, of urban economic life, of transportation, and of communication.

British concern at the growth and expansion of French Northwest Africa, and French chagrin at the successful British intrusion into Egypt, led to a terrific Anglo-French rivalry for control of Somaliland and the Sudan to the south of Egypt. Prior to 1904 this competition for the Sudan was but one of the many Anglo-French clashes which occurred throughout the world. Hoping to establish a transcontinental empire, France attempted to drive a wedge across Africa from Algeria to the French enclave colony of Somaliland on the Red Sea. The latter, which had been secured in 1862 by Napoleon III, constituted an important key to the lower Red Sea and the Gulf of Aden, and would have served as the terminus for a trans-African route from Algeria. Accordingly French expeditions began to penetrate the Sahara, and by an agreement with England, in 1890, their possession of the vast desert was confirmed.

In 1898 Captain Marchand headed a French expedition which crossed the desert and reached Fashoda, a point on the upper Nile, in the Sudan. Alarmed, since a French wedge in the Sudan would have isolated Egypt from the rest of Africa, thus spiking the Cape-to-Cairo project, the English dispatched Lord Kitchener with a superior force. He arrived at Fashoda some two months later. A serious crisis arose, and the two great states stood on the brink of war. The skillful diplomacy of the shrewd foreign minister, Delcassé, helped to avert hostilities, and the French gave way in the Sudan, allowing England to retain the upper Nile valley.

Although the rivalry between France and England for the domination of northern Africa had culminated in the Fashoda incident, the pacific policies of Delcassé had borne their fruit; shortly thereafter an Anglo-French rapprochement resulted. By liquidating and compromising all conflicting interests throughout the world the celebrated *entente cordiale* of 1904 — an understanding rather than a formal alliance — reduced Anglo-French friction to a minimum and constituted a potential guarantee of stronger coöperation. In this general agreement the two powers settled their African rivalry, England giving France a free hand in northwestern Africa and France recognizing the preëminence of British interests in Egypt and the Sudan. Thus, after years of bickering, the two world powers were enabled to curb their antagonism without recourse to war. Thenceforth Anglo-French solidarity was an important factor in promoting the imperial growth of both powers.

While the English were consolidating their position in Egypt and the French were engaged in driving their transcontinental wedge through to the Sudan the Italians were attempting to carve out an *Italy in Africa* empire on the Red Sea and the Indian Ocean. Seeking to dominate eastern Africa, the ambitious Italians had established enclaves in Eritrea (1882) and Somaliland (1889). They then attempted to exert pressure on the native kingdom of Abyssinia from two directions. After some success they nearly converted this independent state into an Italian protectorate. Native opposition led by Menelik, aided by French arms and advice, checked the Italians, who suffered a decisive defeat at Adowa, March 1, 1896. This reverse, the only serious repulse suffered by an imperial state in Africa at the hands of the natives, led to the fall of Crispi, the imperialistic foreign minister at Rome. Italian imperialism temporarily abated, with two worthless enclaves as the only positive achievement. The repulse of Italy was soothing to both the French and the English, inasmuch as Italian success, by driving a counterwedge into the French advance and cutting across the potential Cape-to-Cairo route, would obviously have frustrated their aims.

In 1906 a tripartite agreement by France, England, and Italy guaranteed the integrity and independence of Abyssinia. This eliminated the prospect of conquest by any of the three competitors. England had meanwhile occupied the British Somaliland in the Gulf of Aden as additional security for the control of the exit from the Red Sea, a strategic point on the India route. Thus by 1904 the bulk of northern Africa had been virtually partitioned between France and England, with Italy merely securing insignificant sections along the east coast. Only Morocco, Tripoli, and Abyssinia had successfully evaded European rule. French encroachments in Morocco pointed to future penetration, while Italian designs on Tripoli were secretly encouraged by the great powers.

Whereas the struggle for the north was mainly between France and England, with Italy but a poor third, the contest for central Africa was characterized by keen competition among a number of aggressive powers. Before 1880 the European states held scattered enclave colonies along the west coast of Africa, remnants of the old slave trade. The British retained footholds in Gambia, Sierra Leone, the Gold Coast, Nigeria, and Cape Colony in the extreme south; the French possessed posts in Senegal and on the Guinea and Ivory coasts and laid claim to the island of Madagascar; and the Portuguese still held title to settlements in Guinea and the west of Angola, south of the Congo River. Rio de Oro, adjoining western Morocco, and Rio Muni, near the equator, belonged to Spain. All these establishments were restricted to the coast, the hinterland remaining neglected until the eighties.

The Struggle for Control of Central Africa

The story of the occupation of central Africa was closely associated with the achievements of Leopold II of Belgium (1865–1909), founder of the Congo Free State. His interest was so stimulated by the glowing accounts of the notable explorations in Africa that he invited leading explorers, geographers, and unofficial delegates of the

The Congo Free State

European states to a conference at Brussels in September, 1876. From this meeting there emerged the "International Association for the Exploration and Civilization of Africa." This consisted of an international committee, assisted by national committees, which unofficially represented the various states at the conference. Its alleged purposes were the development of bases in Africa for the opening of the interior and the Christianizing and civilizing of the natives.

Leopold and his associates determined to launch their venture in the Congo Basin. They had heard of the populous districts of the Congo, with their valuable natural resources, particularly wild rubber, ivory, palm products, and tropical woods. Through the Belgian branch a "Committee for the Study of the Upper Congo" was created. In 1879 Stanley was sent to Africa as its agent and laid the practical foundations for the Congo scheme of Leopold and his associates. During the next five years the explorer negotiated treaties with the native rulers, established trading stations along the river, built a road fifty-two miles long around the cataracts that barred continuous navigation, and transported by land, piecemeal, several small steamers to the river above the falls.

While Stanley was thus engaged in the Congo the Belgian king was endeavoring to reconcile Europe to his project. Its success was endangered by the extensive explorations of the Frenchman Pierre de Brazza in the Upper Congo and by the revival of old Portuguese claims. A territorial compromise in 1884 allayed the opposition of France. Through political influence and intrigue Leopold secured, in 1884, general recognition of the association as an independent sovereign state, and successfully evaded Portuguese claims. Entirely aside from his position as king of Belgium he assumed the rôle of sovereign of the Congo Free State. By treaties with neighboring colonial powers he gained complete control of nearly a million square miles of one of the most fertile regions in Africa.

Pretending that his interest in the Congo was primarily humanitarian, Leopold soon established an administration and began to develop the vast central-African hinterland of the Congo Basin. Little real progress was made, the natives being neither converted nor civilized, but actually subjected to cruel forced labor. Desirous of exploiting the vast supplies of wild rubber, his organization employed brutal overseers, who compelled the natives to bring out the rubber on pain of beatings, mutilation, or death. From 1885 to 1908 enormous profits accrued to Leopold and his associates. Attempts were made to bar outsiders who might have divulged the nature of Leopold's supposedly disinterested humanitarian activities. Nevertheless reports of extreme cruelty began to trickle out, and in 1903 and 1904 two British citizens, Roger Casement and Edmund Deville Morel, revealed the true conditions to the general public in Europe and America. When their reports were confirmed by a "Nonpartisan Commission of Inquiry" in 1905, public indignation became so great that Leopold was forced, in 1908, to cede the Congo Free State to Belgium, in return for a handsome indemnity.

The scandal of Leopold's régime led to an immediate and thoroughgoing reform in what became the Belgian Congo. Ruthless mismanagement and the destructive methods of Leopold's system had resulted in an enormous decline of population and practically exhausted the supply of wild rubber. Thereafter the chief value of the Congo lay in its mineral resources, particularly copper, gold, and diamonds, in addition to ivory and palm products. The success and efficiency of the reformed Belgian administration, however, was in great contrast to the earlier exploitation. From 1908 the Congo Basin began to undergo a slow process of recovery from the earlier evils of European imperialism.

When the potentialities of the Congo Basin first became apparent, a number of great powers established or revived claims to sections of Africa. Realizing the danger of rivalries and clashes, they held a conference at Berlin in 1884–1885. Here, by the "General Act," signed February 26, 1885, a set of legal and diplomatic rules for the impending partition of Africa was prepared. The chief provisions were the following: (1) the maintenance of free trade and the open door in the Congo Basin; (2) the

The Berlin Conference

abolition of slavery and the slave traffic; (3) the neutralization of the Congo Free State about to be organized; (4) international freedom of navigation on the Congo and Niger rivers; (5) future occupation of African territory to be announced to powers in advance; and (6) occupation to be effective, not merely a paper declaration. The rules of the game defined, the powers were now ready to compete for the remainder of the continent.

The partition of the west coast of Africa and its hinterland was quickly consummated. Priority of exploration, based on the activities of explorers, missionaries, and traders, usually furnished the excuse for effective occupation. The rights of native peoples were generally disregarded or nullified through treaties entered into by their rulers.

A triangular struggle involving Great Britain, Germany, and France, in which France won the lion's share, decided the fate of most of West Africa north of the Congo. A vast area just above the Free *The Partition of West and Northwest Africa* State, explored by Brazza, was acquired as the French Congo. The French initiated a great drive into the interior of the Sahara and the Sudan from their enclaves on the Ivory, Guinea, and West coasts. This push resulted in the occupation of most of the Senegal and Niger river basins, occurring at about the same time as a drive south from Algeria and Tunis, which led to French control of the greater portion of the Sahara and the western Sudan.

The British and Germans were less successful in northwest Africa. The former enlarged their holdings on the Guinea coast and extended their colony of Nigeria toward Lake Chad in 1884. After 1859 private German commercial companies had posts in the Cameroons and Togoland. It was chiefly the German explorer, Dr. Gustav Nachtigal, commissioned by Bismarck, who concluded treaties with the native rulers and laid the foundation for the two German colonies established there in 1884. The native republic of Liberia, farther north, was left unmolested.

French, British, and Germans engaged in a struggle for the control of the district around Lake Chad, an important junction for caravan routes in the interior. In this conflict Great Britain and Germany each gained a share, but France secured the greater portion of the region. By an agreement with England, August 5, 1890, France acknowledged the British position in the region between the Niger River and Lake Chad. In return French claims to the Sahara and to the gigantic island of Madagascar off the southeast coast of Africa were recognized by the British government. A Franco-German convention of March 15, 1894, recognized French control of the central Sudan and a strip of territory connecting it with her possessions in the Congo. A later Anglo-French convention of June 14, 1898, partitioned the region around the west end of the lake.

The Division of the Interior

By the close of the century France possessed a magnificent north-African empire. Extending from the Mediterranean and from the Atlantic to the east Sudan, it gave France control of the bulk of northwest Africa. Only a series of British, German, Portuguese, and Spanish enclaves, and the independent states of Liberia and Morocco, prevented her from controlling the entire northwestern mass of the continent. This vast empire of over four million square miles was won by the energy of French explorers, missionaries, traders, colonial officials, and soldiers. France again became a leading colonial power.

Great Britain, Germany, and Portugal shared the west coast below the Congo. The Portuguese, reviving claims to neglected districts, pushed into the interior and created the large colony of Angola. Sandwiched between the latter and the British possessions about Cape Colony was a barren area which the British and Portuguese had neglected to acquire. In 1883 Adolph Lüderitz, a Bremen tobacco merchant, purchased part of this area from the natives. He planned to exploit its commercial opportunities and mineral resources. The following year, after some negotiations with the British government whereby Great Britain retained control of the strategic Walfish Bay, Germany annexed the entire region from Angola to South Africa. By 1890 the whole west coast of the continent, with the exceptions of Morocco and Liberia, had succumbed to European rule.

The east coast suffered a similar fate. Neglected claims of Portugal to Mozambique were revived, and the Portuguese occupied a rather extensive section in south-east Africa. Their hopes of establishing a *Partition of the East Coast* transcontinental empire in South Africa extending from Mozambique to Angola were thwarted by the British, who linked their possessions in South Africa with Lake Tanganyika, thus driving a wedge between the Portuguese possessions. A delimitation of the British and Portuguese frontiers was effected by an agreement of June 11, 1891.

Above Mozambique but below Somaliland and Abyssinia was the enormous sultanate of Zanzibar. Hitherto under the rule of a sultan, Zanzibar after 1884 was the scene of a struggle between British and German private interests. Karl Peters eventually succeeded in winning much of the land for Germany; Sir Harry Johnston and William MacKinnon performed a like service for England. Finally, in 1890, the two powers agreed to a compromise in the famous Anglo-German treaty of that year. In the partition of Zanzibar Germany secured the southern part, which subsequently became German East Africa, an undeveloped region with great potentialities. The British received the northern section, British East Africa, or Kenya. They also retained the strategic islands of Zanzibar and Pemba just off the coast. In addition to settling conflicting British and German claims in east, west, and southwest Africa the treaty provided for the cession of the island of Heligoland from Great Britain to Germany.

Directly north of German East Africa the British secured Uganda, a buffer strip of land lying between British East Africa and the White Nile. By holding Germany at arm's length England thus provided protection for her Egyptian acquisitions. Nevertheless the German East African wedge, which cut straight across from the Indian Ocean to the Congo Free State, was disappointing to many British imperialists.

Although British ambitions had been partially checked by the French in northwestern Africa and by Germany in east Africa and on the west coast, in the extreme south British imperialism was unquestionably triumphant. English

interests in South Africa dated largely from the occupation
of the Dutch colonies there in 1806 and their subsequent
Triumph of British annexation in 1815. The Boers, or Dutch colo-
Imperialism in South nists, smarting under alien rule which seemed
Africa to favor the native blacks, determined to
leave, and in 1836 moved north in the so-called Great Trek
under Retief, Potgieter, Pretorius, and other leaders, establishing a short-lived independent republic in Natal (1838) and
more permanent ones in the Orange Free State (1836) and
the Transvaal (1838). Until 1877 these two republics managed
to maintain their existence, with occasional difficulties. In
that year, however, the imperialist Disraeli interfered and
annexed the Transvaal, thus provoking the first Boer War,
which culminated in a British defeat in 1881. The return
of the liberal Gladstone now brought a slackening in British
aggressiveness, and the independence of the Boer republics
was again recognized. Seemingly British imperialism had
received a decisive setback.

During the next two decades popular sentiment in England
became so overwhelmingly imperialistic that both Liberals
and Conservatives found it expedient to further the cause of
expansion. At this time Cecil Rhodes, the diamond king and
empire builder in South Africa, agitated for the British occupation of the entire southern section of Africa, anticipating
the possibility of a Cape-to-Cairo railway. This project
depended on the establishment of British rule over the thousands of miles of territory intervening between the northern
and southern extremities of Africa. Primarily owing to his
efforts a British protectorate was established in 1885 over
Bechuanaland, to the north of Cape Colony. Organizing the
British South Africa Company for the penetration of regions
still farther north, Rhodes secured the valuable Lobengula
concession and was chiefly responsible for the extension of
British rule to Lake Tanganyika over the region now known
as Rhodesia.

During the nineties, however, the British did not yet
dominate all of South Africa. Two Boer countries, the Orange
Free State and the Transvaal, still retained their independ-

ence, although the discovery of valuable gold mines somewhat earlier had led to a great influx of foreigners, especially Britons. Even though these outsiders, or Uitlanders as they were called, owned two thirds of the land and 90 per cent of the personal property, paying 95 per cent of the taxes, yet they were barred from participation in political life and subjected to heavy assessments and economic restrictions. Irritated and annoyed at such treatment, the Uitlanders became restless and clamored for reform. Since these demands proved ineffectual, the more daring of them began to advocate an attack on the Boer authorities. Secretly aided and encouraged by Cecil Rhodes and led by Dr. Jameson, some of them attempted, in 1895, a *coup d'état* against the Boer government. The famous Jameson raid proved a fiasco, but its results were most significant, for the Boers became more suspicious and arbitrary, whereas the Uitlanders hoped for eventual British intervention on their behalf.

From that time the Boer government became more repressive and the Uitlanders more restless. The latter finally appealed to Great Britain for aid. Accepting the recommendations of Sir Alfred Milner, *The Boer War* the British government determined to lend its assistance. Alarmed at the prospect of British intervention, President Kruger instigated long-delayed reforms; but it was too late. Despite the criticisms of Hobson, Hobhouse, Lloyd George, and other anti-imperialists, England in 1899 embarked on the Boer War.

The British encountered surprising difficulty in crushing the tiny Boer states. Directed by daring leaders, the Dutch waged a most successful guerrilla warfare against the English, who were compelled to put over half a million men in the field. It was only after three years of desperate struggle that the Boers succumbed. England was subjected to the moral censure and hostility of the leading powers, particularly Russia, France, and Germany. None of them intervened, however, and by 1902 British arms were victorious and the whole of South Africa was brought under the sway of imperial Britain.

Three years after the close of the war the Liberals, many of whom had opposed the conflict, replaced the Conservatives in control of the British government. Less inflexible and more conciliatory than their predecessors, they enjoyed conspicuous success in reorganizing the enormous conquests in South Africa. Liberal concessions were granted in order to win the loyalty and support of the defeated Boers. In 1908–1909 a constitutional convention was held in South Africa, which provided for a South African self-governing federation. A federal union of the Transvaal, Orange Free State, Natal, and Cape Colony was formed in which liberal home rule and constitutional government were established in 1910. Although many of the Boers were dissatisfied, others submitted to the inevitable and determined to win autonomy by parliamentary measures. Such notable Boer fighters as Generals Smuts and Botha soon became political leaders in the newly formed union and built up a strong Anglo-Boer nation which remained loyal to England during the World War, thus vindicating the generous British policy of conciliation.

The Union of South Africa

After the establishment of the union, economic development paralleled political advance. Although gold and diamonds were the chief sources of wealth, live-stock and wool industries developed rapidly. Certain obstacles to prosperity, however, persisted. One concerned the blacks, who greatly outnumbered the whites, and another resulted from the need of a competent labor supply. Neither of these was satisfactorily solved. Chinese coolies were imported in 1905–1906 and Indians in 1911, but experiments in alien labor led to social complications, and the color problem remained an outstanding one.

By 1902 Europe dominated all of Africa with the exceptions of Liberia, Abyssinia, and the two Mediterranean regions Tripoli and Morocco. Before 1914 the latter two had also succumbed. The French policy of peaceful penetration into Morocco had been going on for several years, until the outbreak of civil war in 1902 afforded the French an adequate pretext for

Western Imperialism in Morocco and Tripoli

more effective interference. Pretending that their policy was dictated by a most disinterested motive, a sincere desire to reëstablish order and security, the French were in a fair way to absorb the declining sultanate and add it to their vast collection of colonial acquisitions. As will be related presently, French attempts to secure Morocco were contested by Germany and resulted in a series of crises which exercised Europe from 1905 to 1911.

Finally, upon the French advance to Fez in 1911, a German gunboat was dispatched to Agadir in Morocco, and the saber was rattled so loudly that a war seemed imminent. Reluctantly France was forced to buy off German opposition by the cession of a large strip of the French Congo, which was added to the Cameroons. Thenceforth the imperial German government lost interest in the affairs of the Moroccan sultan. By this time Fez and the interior of Morocco were occupied by France. The Moslem population, however, resented the loss of its independence, and France required many years before she could effectively pacify her newly acquired territory. Spain, meanwhile, found the problem of controlling Spanish Morocco much too difficult, and that district accordingly remained in a state of disorder for some time.

Disappointed over her failure to get Tunis, snatched up by France in 1881, and her imperial policy a fiasco in East Africa and Abyssinia, Italy had set her heart upon wrenching Tripoli from the feeble grasp of Turkey. For this purpose special provisions, recognizing the preëminence of Italian interests there, had been added to the renewal of the Triple Alliance with Austria and Germany. Later, when Italy began to be detached from the Central Powers, she entered into secret agreements with France, Russia, and England which virtually secured their approval of Italian designs on Tripoli. Thus Italy was very careful to pave the way for the acquisition of that region and to safeguard herself from the hostility of any of the major powers.

In 1911, when Turkey was disorganized as a result of the Young Turk Revolution, Italian statesmen finally felt that the time had come to launch a decisive blow for Tripoli.

After an unprovoked ultimatum to the Porte on a trumped-up charge the Italian government declared war. This was followed by the military occupation of Tripoli, which proceeded rapidly in the face of weak resistance. Italy partially quenched her thirst for imperial glory, but her acquisition proved to be a white elephant. The expenses of the conquest, of Moslem uprisings, and of colonial administration were not adequately offset by the colony, which was largely desert country with but a sparse population.

In 1914 the assumed benefits of imperialism had not materialized in Africa. This was due partly to the failure to
Africa in 1914　invest sufficient capital for adequate development. Furthermore, the problem of securing labor often led to devices verging on slavery or forced labor of the natives. The so-called culture systems of the Germans and the Congo Free State, the imposition of poll and hut taxes, and the expropriation of the natives' lands were methods of forcing the black to work for a living. Meanwhile raw materials and colonial markets failed to develop to the extent expected. In many cases the expenses of occupation, colonial administration, and international feuds more than offset the profits resulting from the imperial ventures.

The outbreak of the World War saw the liquidation of Africa nearly complete. Only two states, Abyssinia and Liberia, remained free of European rule. A protégé of the United States, founded by American abolitionists in 1847, Liberia enjoyed nominal independence. Of the competing imperial powers Great Britain and France had won the laurels. They had secured the most populous areas, with valuable markets and raw materials, as well as the most strategic sections, with important commercial and naval bases. But Belgium and Portugal also had gained valuable colonial empires, and other countries had secured lesser possessions.

Italy and Germany were both unsuccessful in Africa. A meager collection of unimportant acquisitions left Italy dissatisfied, and Germany, with but a few colonies, was still struggling for a "place in the sun." In 1914 the latter collaborated with Great Britain in preparing a draft treaty which provided for the partition of Portugal's colonies. The coming of the war, however, terminated this abortive scheme, and Portugal was able to retain her possessions.

DIGGING FOR DIAMONDS *at Kimberley*

From a wood engraving published in 1872

CHAPTER XXIV

The Exploitation of Asia and Oceania

EARLY in the nineteenth century great Asia, the largest of the continents, with its enormous area and teeming millions, excited the cupidity of Western capitalists and traders, who desired to tap its fabled wealth and resources. For centuries the ancient civilizations and the power, mystery, and vastness of the continent had impressed and fascinated the Westerners. Comparatively few Europeans had penetrated its hidden recesses, however, until the industrial and military developments of the capitalistic age enabled Westerners forcibly to enter the reluctant East.

Ancient civilizations had formerly flourished in Asia. At a time when Europe was still in a primitive state, China, *Ancient Civilizations* India, and the Tigris-Euphrates valley had been the centers of great cultures. The ancient Near East remained intimately associated with the Mediterranean, giving birth to classical civilization. During medieval days this culture merged with Teutonic society to form Western civilization, the diffusion of which led to a transformation of the world in the nineteenth and twentieth centuries.

Whereas the Near East remained in close touch with Europe, India and China rapidly tended to lose contact with the West and to become more or less exclusive and self-sufficient. What traffic and travel survived between East and West were extremely restricted and were subject to the arduous difficulties of climates, distances, geographical barriers, and hostile peoples. Moreover, the interjection of the Moslem world between Christian Europe and the East after the seventh century tended to minimize the reciprocal influences.

By the fifteenth century the East and West were tending to draw together again. After 1498 the Portuguese established trade depots on the western coast of India, entered

China in 1516, and about 1542 reached Japan. Jealous of the prosperity and dominant position of Portugal in the Eastern trade, the Spanish, Dutch, French, and English obtained holdings in the Orient. *Early European Contacts with Asia* Anglo-French rivalry in India during the eighteenth century marked the climax of the early struggle for the Pacific world, with its myriads of islands and its millions of inhabitants.

While the Western powers were competing against one another in these regions Russia was building an extensive empire in northern Asia. The conquest of vast regions of Siberia, extending from the Ural *Russia in Northern Asia* Mountains to the Pacific and from central Asia to the Arctic Ocean, was a phase of her eastward movement. She was the only European state engaged in true colonization in Asia, that is, in the transfer of her people and institutions. Seeking better lands and greater opportunities, many Russians drifted into Siberia, especially after the sixteenth century. Daring explorers, adventurers, and traders drove farther and farther into the confines of Asia, finally reaching the shores of the Pacific. Control of the Aleutian Islands and Alaska gave Russia a bridgehead to the New World and enabled her to loom as a great power in the Pacific.

The subsequent decline of the older colonial movement left the European powers with scattered remnants of empire. Portugal retained the ports of Goa, Daman, and Diu in India, Macao in China, and a part *Decline of the Old Colonial Movement* of the eastern end of the Island of Timor as evidences of her vanished greatness. After the decline of the Netherlands her once extensive empire fell into neglect. In 1798 the bankrupt Dutch East India Company, formerly the chief instrument of Dutch imperialism in the East, was dissolved. Spain still possessed numerous groups of islands, of which the most important were the Philippines. Insular possessions in the Pacific and a few ports in India comprised the chief remains of the French empire in the East. Great Britain and Russia were more fortunate. The former retained, after 1763, a dominant position in India and an extensive island empire in the Pacific and Indian oceans, while Russia preserved unimpaired her vast domain from the Baltic to Alaska.

The breakdown, in the eighteenth century, of the first wave of European imperialism left most of Asia free from foreign control. With the exception of Russian Siberia, only the fringes of the great continent had been touched. Until the nineteenth century Asia was dominated by independent Oriental states. Practically unaffected by the movements which led to the rise of middle-class civilization in the West, they pursued their own courses and policies. The Renaissance, the Reformation, the Commercial Revolution, the French Revolution, and the Economic Revolution found little echo in the East.

In the nineteenth century the sweeping industrial transformation of western Europe had far-reaching effects on *The New Imperialism* remote Asia. Business men were soon prone to tap the resources of Asia and to exploit its economic opportunities. Faced with expansion or destruction, the capitalist countries of western Europe embarked on the second wave of imperialism. Desirous of penetrating Asia, within a few short years they shattered its seclusion and subjected the greater part of the continent to European political or economic control.

The Chinese Empire, because of its vast population, natural resources, and political disorganization, was a fertile field for *Early European Contacts with China* European imperialism. It had an area exceeding that of Europe, with a population of some three hundred millions, most of whom were crowded into the two great river valleys of the Yangtze and the Hwang. The unpopular Manchu dynasty (1644–1912) could do little more than control the central portions of the empire. China's enormous size and the backwardness of transportation and communication rendered a centralized, uniform administration impossible. The outlying regions, such as Manchuria, Mongolia, Tibet, and Sinkiang, were sparsely settled frontier districts which enjoyed virtual independence.

China possessed political and cultural hegemony in the Far East. The great unifying factor was its civilization. Proud of its antiquity, its glitter and magnificence, its achievements in art, literature, philosophy, and other fields, the Chinese resented foreign intrusions or innovations. Opposition to change was characteristic of the Celestial Empire, whose customs and traditions were supposedly eternal, having existed since times immemorial. Other peoples of the Orient imitated the civilization of China. Siam, Burma, and Indo-China were practically its vassals. Its culture was considered superior and its might irresistible. Little did the proud Chinese realize that this material backwardness would lead to their undoing at the hands of the despised Occidental peoples.

Opposition to Western civilization had prompted China to resort to a policy of "splendid isolation." At first the alien traders and missionaries, who came in increasing numbers after the sixteenth century, were welcomed. From ancient times there had existed trade connections between China and Europe, but these dwindled to a minimum during the Middle Ages. China and Russia were continuously accessible to one another, although both were remote from nations of the West. After the Crusades European interest in the Far East revived and was especially stimulated by the tales of Marco Polo (1254–1324), and the accounts of travelers, missionaries, and merchants. The first Western trading station in China was established by the Portuguese at Macao in 1557. British and Dutch traders appeared somewhat later, while Russians began to penetrate China from Siberia. Hated as "foreign devils," the aliens were heavily taxed and were there only on sufferance.

Constant bickering among competing Christian sects and between rival traders led to a change of policy on the part of the Chinese authorities. In 1724 foreign religious activities were suppressed, and aliens were barred from China. With the exception of the Russians the rather limited stream of foreign trade was confined, in 1757, to the port of Canton. Despite the arbitrary methods of Chinese customs and port officials the enormous profits in the exchange of tea and silk for opium and specie proved ample compensation for such annoyance.

The first decisive blow to Chinese seclusion came with the Opium War (1839–1842). Aware of the demoralizing effects of opium, the Chinese government forbade its importation. Through smuggling and bribery of officials the East India Company was able to continue its lucrative traffic and by 1839 was selling annually some 30,000 chests. After long wrangling the quarrel finally culminated in a war which lasted until 1842. To the surprise of the Chinese the British gained a decisive victory and imposed upon them the Treaty of Nanking. This provided (1) for the opening of five "treaty ports" (Canton, Amoy, Ningpo, Foochow, and Shanghai) to foreign trade; (2) for the cession to Great Britain of the island of Hong Kong, near Canton; and (3) for an indemnity of $21,000,000. Subject to certain restrictions the opium traffic was permitted to continue. Other powers interested in the Oriental trade — the United States, France, Prussia, Belgium, and the Netherlands — soon gained identical trading privileges in the treaty ports by arranging separate agreements with China.

The New Invasion of China

The next important step in the destruction of Chinese seclusion was the second Chinese war (1857–1860). In this conflict, following the capture of a British vessel by pirates and the death of a French missionary, Great Britain and France united their efforts to defeat the sleeping giant of the East. Tientsin and Peking were seized and the emperor's summer palace was burned. By the treaties of Tientsin (1860) the following arrangements were made: (1) six additional ports were opened; (2) foreign ministers were permitted to reside at Peking, the imperial capital; (3) aliens were allowed to trade along the Yangtze River; (4) protection of missionaries was guaranteed; (5) England secured a foothold on the mainland near Hong Kong; and (6) a large indemnity was levied upon the defeated empire.

Not only was China forcibly opened by the Western powers, but during the next few years her independence was undermined. Permanent legations were established by Great Britain, France, and Russia in 1861, and by the United States the following year. Control of the Chinese tariff was regulated by special treaties with foreign powers. By the privileges of extraterritoriality, foreigners were exempted from the jurisdiction of Chinese courts and were placed under the judicial control of representatives of their own nations. Domestic discontent with the Manchu dynasty for its inability to cope with the intruder provoked the Taiping Rebellion (1853–1864). This devastating flare-up was a protest against the concessions to foreigners. Finally, after frightful destruction to property and life, the government was able to put it down with foreign assistance, especially that of a British officer, General "Chinese" Gordon.

Shortly after the treaties of Tientsin (1860) the powers engaged in a partial partition of China. The Chinese borderlands passed under foreign control, and many ports were leased for long periods. In 1860 *Partial Partition of China* the coast south of the Amur River, to the northeast of China proper, was annexed by Russia. In the extreme south, the French appropriated Cambodia in 1863, adding Annam and Tongking in 1885. Burma, adjoining India, was partially seized in 1826 and completely annexed by the British in 1886. Even Japan was sufficiently Europeanized to assist in the partition of her neighbor. As a result of her victory in the Sino-Japanese War (1894–1895), by the treaty of Shimonoseki Japan secured (1) recognition of the independence of Korea, (2) cession of the island of Formosa and the Liaotung Peninsula, and (3) an indemnity and certain commercial privileges. Owing to pressure by Germany, France, and Russia the treaty was revised. Shortly thereafter Germany procured Kiaochow, and Russia gained control of the strategic Liaotung Peninsula through a lease for twenty-five years of Port Arthur and the neighboring harbor of Talienwan. To strengthen her influence in the south, the French procured Kwangchow. Not to be outdone by her rivals and especially apprehensive of the Russian possession of Port Arthur, Great Britain demanded and secured, in 1898, the port of Wei-

haiwei, across the Yellow Sea from Port Arthur. Control of
these harbors was valuable not only for commercial purposes
but also for strategic reasons, inasmuch as a future war would
probably necessitate the use of naval bases in the Far East.

The next stage in the penetration of China, coming in the
last decade of the nineteenth century, was its economic par-
Economic Penetration of China   tition by foreign states. Much as gangsters
subdivide a modern American city for exploi-
tation, the powers proceeded to carve the
Celestial Empire into spheres of influence,— an economic
rather than a political partition, since territorial division
would have been both dangerous and costly. In the spheres
of influence the nationals of the imperial power usually enjoyed a monopoly of the concessions involving railways,
factories, mineral resources, and other economic opportunities. In the north, Russia was influential in outer Mongolia
and held concessions in Manchuria and the Liaotung Peninsula, and was prepared to contest the expansion of Japanese
interests in Korea. The Germans held special concessions in
Shantung. The British dominated the extensive valley of the
Yangtze River, while the French concentrated their attention
on the three southern provinces which adjoined their possessions in Indo-China. The struggle for these advantages was
indeed a "battle of concessions," in which China was the
stake. Foreign capitalists, aided by diplomats and occasional
demonstrations of force, secured a strangle hold on the economic life of China.

As the virtual staking out of China by the great powers
seemed to presage ultimate partition, grave concern was
The Open-Door Policy   felt in the United States. Since the American
government had taken no share of the Chinese
spoils, it was feared that the intense exploitation of foreign
spheres of influence would lead to discrimination against other
nationals and result in the annihilation of American business
interests. Moved by these dangers, Secretary of State John
Hay, in 1899, sent to the competing powers his famous circular note advocating the maintenance of the "open door" in
the rival spheres of influence. In this celebrated document he

recommended that the powers agree (1) not to interfere with treaty ports or vested interests within their spheres, (2) to allow the application of the Chinese treaty tariffs to ports within a sphere of influence without discrimination against any nationality, and (3) to maintain equality of harbor and railway dues for all nationals.

Designed to secure fair and equal treatment for all, the maintenance of the open door would have reduced the special privileges and advantages enjoyed by certain national interests. Rather than admit their imperialistic designs, however, the great powers eventually accepted the proposal in principle, — France, Germany, England, and Japan contingent upon general approval; Italy unreservedly, since she had no special position in China; Russia after raising objections concerning the equality of harbor and railway dues. Despite the somewhat vague nature of international approval Hay announced the general adoption of the open-door policy and in 1900 declared it in operation.

By this time new social and economic forces were slowly transforming China. The conservative Chinese despised the middle-class civilization of the West, but they were unable to prevent its penetration. To *Changes in China* enrich themselves, foreign capitalists were exploiting neglected economic opportunities. Steam navigation was introduced in 1863, the first permanent railway was built in 1887, iron works were in operation after 1890, and imports and exports increased several fold between 1842 and 1900. A few Chinese, some of whom traveled and studied in Western countries, began to master foreign languages, science, and institutions. A distinct minority, they advocated change and the partial adoption of certain features of the bourgeois system.

The reaction of China to foreign aggression was reflected in the growth of two parties in governmental circles. Both desired to save their country from the ravages of imperialism, but they disagreed as to methods. The conservatives of northern China *Opposition to Foreign Aggression* hoped for the preservation of their ancient civilization and an alliance with Russia as a safeguard. The southern party preferred to follow the Japanese example and modernize China by the introduction of reform and Western methods.

Temporarily the reform party of the south gained the ascendancy. In 1898 the young emperor, Kwangsu, issued a series of decrees designed to modernize the government and to promote the growth of a bourgeois society. Corrupt and superfluous governmental officials were dismissed, an attempt was made to balance the budget, educational reforms were introduced, and schools copied after European models were established. Railway and mining development by the Chinese was also encouraged.

Westernizing tendencies on the part of Kwangsu provoked the opposition of the conservative faction. A palace revolution followed. The old dowager empress, *The Boxer Rebellion* Tzu-Hsi, emerged from her retirement on the Mount of Ten Thousand Ages. Returning to Peking in 1898, she seized control of the government and imprisoned the young emperor. The reform measures were nullified and the leaders of the party punished or driven into exile. A violent reaction now set in. A secret Society of the Harmonious Fists, popularly known as the Boxers, urged the complete expulsion of foreigners and their works from China. Sympathizing with the desire to expel the "foreign devils," the dowager empress secretly encouraged this society. The hostility of the masses to alien teachers, missionaries, and traders was reflected in the enthusiastic support which the Chinese gave. From 1898 to 1900 a strong antiforeign movement was demonstrated by frequent local outbreaks and riots which cost the lives of some two hundred and fifty aliens. Many fled to the legations at Peking, where for several months they were besieged by mobs goaded to fury by the Boxers.

The British, French, German, Japanese, and American governments, alarmed at the plight of the many foreigners who had taken refuge in the legations, promptly dispatched an international army to their relief. Brushing aside the ineffectual opposition of the Boxers, the foreign troops rescued the legations and sacked the famous Forbidden City at Peking, and vigorously crushed the Boxer Rebellion. The invaders insisted on the execution of guilty officials, levied an indemnity of $325,000,000, and demanded the suppression of all anti-foreign societies. Thus the only serious attempt to resist alien encroachments was a complete failure, and the powers retained intact, until the World War, their privileged positions on the Chinese coasts and borderlands.

With the revolt a failure, the reform movement could not be delayed. Although she had strongly resisted Western innovations and influence, the dowager em- *Reforms in China* press now welcomed them; the army was reorganized along European lines in 1906, educational facilities were improved, and a commission was appointed to study constitutional methods of government. A program was developed for the gradual liberalization of the Chinese administration; but the strong-willed empress died in 1908 and was followed by a weak regent, whose vacillating policies permitted the reform movement to get out of hand, so that in 1911 a revolution resulted.

Beginning in the Yangtze valley, the revolt spread into the southern provinces, and soon a wave of liberalism swept over the empire. The army finally became disaffected and was won over to the revolutionary cause. In February, 1912, the ancient monarchy was terminated and replaced by a republic, with the able Chinese leader Yuan Shih-k'ai as its first president. The disquieting effects of foreign penetration and exploitation, the disturbances resulting from the spread of liberalism and Western ideas in China, and the cultural differences between northern and southern China led to the further disintegration of the great state. From relative stability China passed to the horrors and turmoil of civil strife, from which she had not yet emerged with the coming of the war in 1914.

In dramatic contrast to the plight of China at the outbreak of the conflict was the influential position occupied by Japan. As will be described in the next chapter, the *Rise of Japan* island empire, by becoming modernized, managed to escape the bitter humiliation and ravages of European imperialism. Taking over middle-class civilization,— constitutional practices, industrialism, and militarism,— Japan joined the pack, became the hunter rather than the prey, and created an imposing empire. A victorious war with China (1894–1895) was evidence that a new world power had arisen in the Far East. An alliance with Great Britain in 1902, designed to check Russian imperialism in Asia, testified to Japan's growing importance.

Southeast of Asia and extending thousands of miles out into the Pacific were myriads of islands. They varied in size *The Rush for Islands* from the continent of Australia and the giant islands of Borneo, Java, Sumatra, New Guinea, and New Zealand to tiny coral reefs. Some of the larger, especially Australia, the Philippines, and the East Indies, contained extensive populations, natural resources, and raw materials. Although many of the smaller were of no particular importance in themselves, they were valuable as potential naval bases and as cable and whaling stations.

In the middle of the nineteenth century several European powers retained remnants of empires in Oceania. After the decline of the older colonial movement in the eighteenth century these had been neglected. With the rebirth of imperialism, however, states revived claims and seized unoccupied islands. In the late nineteenth and earlier twentieth centuries a complete partition of Oceania was effected, and Great Britain, France, Germany, Japan, the Netherlands, and the United States created important insular empires.

During the nineteenth century Great Britain acquired the most extensive colonial possession in the Pacific. In 1770 *Australia and New Zealand* Captain Cook visited Australia, and in 1788 an English penal colony was founded there at Botany Bay. The origin of sheep-raising in Australia dates back to 1805, when the first sheep were imported. Attracted by the rich farming and grazing lands, free settlers came in increasing numbers during the nineteenth century. The discovery of gold in 1850 gave Australia a new importance and provoked an influx of additional settlers. Six colonies rapidly developed, one on the island of Tasmania and the remainder on the mainland. In 1900 the six self-governing colonies were combined into a federal union with a constitution and parliamentary government, and were given dominion status.

The dominion of New Zealand occupies an archipelago over a thousand miles to the east of Australia. English missionaries, who began to go there in 1814, were followed by settlers who depended on sheep-raising. In 1840 the islands were annexed by the British government. The discovery of gold in 1853 resulted in a large influx of immigrants, causing the population to rise from 60,000 to 350,000 by 1878. From 1860 to 1870, wars with the Maori tribes, arising out of disputes over land, temporarily interfered with the peaceful growth of the islands. In 1856 the settlements were organized into six provinces, each with its own legislature. Twenty years later, however, they were combined into a self-governing unitary colony. In 1907 New Zealand received dominion status in the British Empire.

Colonization of Australia and New Zealand led to the growth of two English-speaking democracies in the South Pacific. Amazing replicas of middle-class civilization resulted, characterized by their unusual social progress. In Australia the labor parties developed early and promoted progressive political and social legislation. In New Zealand, especially after 1890, state socialism was very pronounced. The government acquired ownership of railways, telegraphs, telephones, express lines, savings banks, insurance companies, and certain coal mines. Factory laws were introduced to safeguard the labor of children and women, disputes between labor and capital were subjected to compulsory arbitration by the state, a Labor Department was created which tried to reduce unemployment and combat poverty, and a system of old-age pensions was established. In an effort to maintain existing standards of living, immigration was curtailed both in Australia and in New Zealand.

Less important than the two dominions were the other British possessions in Oceania. Thousands of islands of all sizes scattered throughout the Pacific were acquired. Some were useful as commercial and naval stations, but many were

worthless. It was only in the seventies that the British seriously undertook to expand their acquisitions. The Fiji group
was annexed in 1874. A few years later a
*Other British Islands
in the Pacific*
British North Borneo Company was organized. Despite Dutch protests the northern
part of Borneo was cleared of pirates and converted into
an English colony. In 1886 a threefold partition of New
Guinea (Papua) was made, England securing the southeastern portion, Germany the northeastern, and the Netherlands the western half. These annexations gave the British
the largest of the Oceanian empires.

Second to the British as a colonial power in Oceania were
the Dutch. They controlled most of the East Indies, which
formed a sort of connecting link between Asia
*The Dutch Empire in
the East*
and Australia. After many years of inertia
the Dutch, in the late nineteenth century, were
reawakened to the value of these populous islands with their
plantation products, especially rubber. Abusive systems of
forced labor, similar to that of Leopold in the Congo, were
temporarily revived and then abandoned. Subsequent humane reforms, leading to social and economic progress, made
these enormous islands among the most valuable of colonial
possessions.

Late in the nineteenth century Germany undertook to
construct a great insular empire in the Pacific. German
colonial expansion, of which William II was
*German Imperialism in
the Pacific*
a strong advocate, was closely allied with the
expansion of her economic and naval interests.
In addition to the Marshall Islands and the northeastern portion of New Guinea, procured in 1886, the Germans purchased
several island groups from Spain in 1899. In return for
$4,200,000 the Caroline, Pelew, and Mariana (or Ladrone)
groups (except Guam) were ceded to Germany. Valuable chiefly
as whaling and cable stations, many produced considerable
quantities of copra and phosphates. In 1899 the two larger
islands of the Samoan group were acquired by a treaty with the
United States, but the easternmost, containing the important
harbor of Pago-Pago, went to the American nation.

Chiefly confined to the south Pacific, French acquisitions were not extensive. New Caledonia was annexed in 1853 after the murder of a French survey party. Until 1896 it was used as a penal colony, the capital of which was appropriately named Criminopolis. Partially on the basis of earlier explorations Tahiti, the Marquesas, the Society Islands, and other islands were obtained during the nineteenth century. Although such possessions served her commercial and naval purposes, France's Pacific interests were distinctly inferior to those of Great Britain, the Netherlands, and the United States.

French Imperialism in the Pacific

The rise of two new world powers, the United States and Japan, further complicated the tangled problems of the Pacific. By the purchase of Alaska from the Czar's government in 1867 the United States secured an important position in the north Pacific. The war against Spain, in 1898, provoked a great flare-up of American imperialism in Oceania. It resulted in the cession to the United States of the Philippines and Guam, an important naval and cable station in the mid-Pacific. An earlier joint protectorate with Great Britain and Germany over the Samoan group was terminated by their partition in 1899. Meanwhile the United States acquired a number of miscellaneous islands, and in 1898 annexed Hawaii. The rapid expansion of American colonial and commercial interests in Oceania made that country one of the most important Pacific powers.

American and Japanese Imperialism in the Pacific

Prior to 1914 Japanese imperialism in Oceania was not particularly successful. The empire itself consisted of groups of islands extending from near the peninsula of Kamchatka, in Russian Siberia, to Formosa, not far from the Philippines. Regarding expansion as imperative, the Japanese would have liked to increase their holdings on the Asiatic shores and on the islands of the Pacific. All available lands were already occupied by other powers, however, and barriers were erected against Oriental immigration, especially by the United States, Australia, New Zealand, and Canada. Japanese imperialism in Oceania was definitely checked for the time being.

The Middle East from Persia to Indo-China also passed under European control. In contrast to the Far East and
The Middle East
Oceania, where a number of powers shared the spoils, British imperialism was singularly triumphant in this part of the world. Russian expansion in central Asia and French acquisitions in Indo-China were dwarfed by the magnitude of British success in the greatest of all imperial ventures,— India.

India was almost a continent in itself in size, with a population exceeding three hundred millions. Like China this
The "Jewel of the British Empire"
enormous peninsula was the scene of a deteriorated higher civilization of great antiquity. Successive inroads of alien invaders had engulfed the earlier inhabitants and partially accounted for the ethnic and cultural diversity. The people were also split by religious cleavages, particularly between Hindus and Moslems, and by a rigid caste system, the restrictions of which decentralized the inhabitants into isolated groups. Political solidarity had disappeared with the breakdown of the decadent Mogul empire in the eighteenth century.

The nineteenth century witnessed the consolidation of British power within India, and expansion into adjoining regions. Prior to this period British control over India was relatively slight, being limited to a few coastal districts under the East India Company. With the approval of the home government and supported by armies and fleets, the company organized a civil administration and functioned as a state. The inefficiency and corruption of company rule, however, led to the Regulating Act of 1773, whereby a council of four members, nominated by Parliament, was established at Calcutta to maintain a check on the governor-general, representative of the India Company. Further reforms were introduced in 1784 by the Government of India Act. This legislation created at London, for the supervision of Indian affairs, a board of control with a cabinet member at its head. Henceforth the governor-general and the higher officials in India were to be nominated by the British ministry. This act remained in effect until 1858.

A century of expansion followed the defeat of the French in the Seven Years' War (1756–1763). Free of foreign interference and taking advantage of the decay of the Mogul empire, as a result of which most of India was decentralized into political entities of various types and sizes ruled by native princes, the British were able to extend their influence in India. Friction with these local sovereigns often provoked conflicts and additional British annexations. By 1858 a number of great empire builders, from Robert Clive (1725–1774) to Lord Dalhousie (1812–1860), had established British rule over nearly three quarters of the Indian population.

Rapid British expansion and an influx of many Western innovations and reforms now followed. The introduction of steamships, harbor improvements, telegraphs, better roads, railway projects, a postal system, competitive civil services, public aid to schools, and agricultural innovations were evidences of the British attempt to spread the benefits of middle-class civilization. Coal and iron deposits were investigated, and British investors were attracted by the economic potentialities of India.

Opposition was aroused by Lord Dalhousie's zeal to annex and Westernize backward and misgoverned native states. The suppression of certain barbarous customs and interference with native religious beliefs and traditions aroused special resentment. *Opposition to British Expansion* Like the Boxer uprising in China, therefore, the Sepoy Rebellion (1857–1859) was a protest against foreign interference and exploitation. In 1857 there were fewer than 40,000 British soldiers and over 250,000 sepoys, or native troops, in the employ of the Company. Oriental opposition to Western innovations was aggravated by annoyances arising out of native military service. Despite religious objections to sea travel the Hindu sepoys were forced into overseas service. The enforced use of greased cartridges offended both Moslems and Hindus. On May 10, 1857, the mutiny of a native cavalry regiment initiated the uprising. Hastening to the ancient imperial capital at Delhi, the rebellious troops offered their services to the Mogul. The revolt against the British

became general in the Ganges provinces and central India.
Native dynasts, resentful of foreign intrusions on their hereditary rights, supported the insurrection, as did the populace
in many places.

At first the Mogul was triumphant. European residents
and British troops were massacred or besieged, and native
rule was reëstablished over many provinces. But the home
government soon rushed reënforcements, and Delhi, Cawn-
pore, and Lucknow were retaken. By the summer of 1858 the
rebellion was checked, but it was not completely crushed until
the following April. A terrible vengeance ensued as thousands of mutineers were shot from the mouths of cannon
and the aged Mogul was exiled to Rangoon.

The Indian mutiny led to political reforms. In 1858 the
rule of the Company was abolished by the Better Government of India Act, and its remaining powers
Political Reforms in India were assumed by the state. Thenceforth India
was ruled as a crown colony, with supreme
control vested in the Secretary of State for India, a cabinet
member, assisted by a small council in London. In India the
actual administration was conducted by a viceroy, a representative of the crown, who was selected by the cabinet. He
was aided by executive and legislative councils. The central
government was located at Calcutta until 1912, when it was
removed to Delhi. Subordinate to the central authorities
were provincial administrations under governors assisted by
nominated councils or chief commissioners who dispensed
with councils. In addition there were over six hundred native
states not under British administration, whose dynasts were
dependent on English protection and supervision. British
India, however, embraced some three fifths of the area, with
seven ninths of the population. In the main this political system continued in force for the next half century; the only
important change was the proclamation of Queen Victoria
as Empress of India in 1877.

Between 1858 and 1914, however, the spread of Western
ideas among the more intelligent educated classes led to a
nationalist movement which aimed at the creation of a demo-

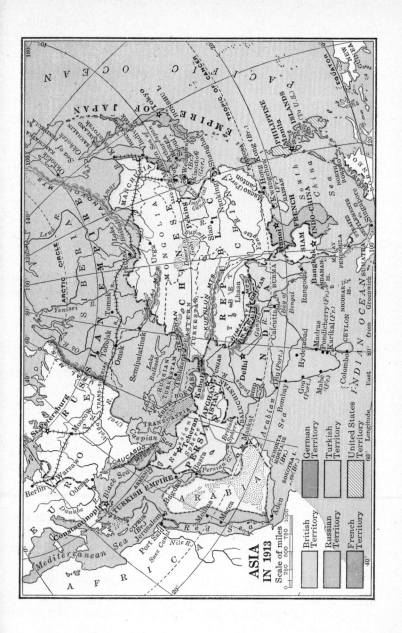

ASIA
IN 1913

Scale of miles
0 250 500 750 1000

British Territory
German Territory
Russian Territory
Turkish Territory
French Territory
United States Territory

cratic representative administration. The British, provided they could retain direction of the government, were willing to make concessions to native sentiment. In 1907 two Indians were appointed on the Coun- *The Nationalist Movement* cil of the Secretary of State and one on the Executive Council of the viceroy. In 1909, by the Indian Councils Act, provision was made for the election of twenty-five of the sixty-eight members of the viceroy's Legislative Council. In six of the nine provinces of India the local assemblies were to contain majorities of nonofficial members. Some of these were to be elected and others appointed. In the remaining three provinces unrepresentative governments under chief commissioners were continued.

Notwithstanding these concessions native opposition to British rule persisted. The Indian Councils Act was denounced as unfair, since it did not afford the natives adequate representation or a real voice in political affairs. By 1910 the criticism became so widespread that the government curtailed the freedom of the press, established a censorship of mails, and forbade seditious meetings. The agitation for constitutional reform continued, and native congresses were held. Conspiracies, assassinations, and riots disturbed the land. An informal revolution seemed to be in progress after 1910. The absence of national solidarity, however, and particularly the unwillingness of the Moslems and Hindus to coöperate with one another, weakened the cause of the nationalists and enabled the British, with a centralized bureaucracy backed up by armed forces, to dominate this vast empire.

Despite native unrest the material progress of India between 1858 and 1914 was amazing. The establishment of railways, canals, extensive irrigation, good *Progress in India* roads, and modern communications linked the country together. Millet, pulse, and sugar cane were grown for consumption, and great quantities of coffee, tea, rice, wheat, opium, jute, and cotton were produced for export. Artistic native goods greatly esteemed by foreigners were manufactured, such as fine fabrics, gold, ivory, and trinkets. Vast quantities of British manufactured goods, especially cotton and iron goods, were imported into India. Enjoying almost a monopoly of India's foreign trade, the British were accused by certain natives of discouraging local manufacturers in order to favor English producers. The economic life of that land was almost completely monopolized and exploited by British capitalists for their own ends.

Great benefits were conferred upon India by British rule. The law was codified, infanticide and the suicide of widows were abolished, sanitary and hygienic improvements were introduced, famines were reduced to a minimum, local wars and internal disorders were suppressed, and most of the land made peaceful. Although in 1912–1913 only 6 per cent of the population were literate, educational facilities were extended despite native opposition. Regardless of their political autocracy and of their exploitative economic policies the British laid the foundations for a progressive middle-class civilization in the Middle East.

During much of the nineteenth and twentieth centuries the desire to hold India exerted a decisive influence on British foreign policy. Before the outbreak of the *India and British Foreign Policy* World War the British were confronted by two challenges to their supremacy there. One came from French expansion in Indo-China to the east, and the other from the Russian advance in central Asia. To forestall these threatened attacks the British resorted to defensive expansion and occupied the borderlands around India. Their policies, designed to keep their potential adversaries at arm's length, were successful, since they forced the Russians and French to accept compromises which left India secure from the menace of foreign conquest.

East of India and below China the enormous peninsula of Indo-China jutted far to the south, separating the Bay of Bengal from the China Sea. Here were located, *Indo-China* in the early nineteenth century, the kingdoms of Burma, Siam, Cambodia, and Annam, which included Cochin-China and Tongking. All enjoyed independence, although China claimed Burma, Siam, and Annam as vassals. Farther to the south were the tiny native sultanates of the

Malay states, and on the extreme tip of the peninsula was the British crown colony of the Straits Settlements, convenient for naval and commercial purposes, as it included Singapore and the control of the strategic straits of Malacca.

In this part of Asia, France elected to build an empire. A victorious war waged upon the king of Annam by Napoleon III resulted in the acquisition, in 1862, of three provinces of Cochin-China at the mouth of the *Anglo-French Rivalry* Mekong River. In the following year the neighboring kingdom of Cambodia was converted into a protectorate under French control. In 1867 the three remaining provinces of Cochin-China were annexed. Continued French aggressions against Annam and Tongking provoked a war, in 1883, with their suzerain, China. Although her suzerainty over Annam and Tongking was recognized, China was finally forced to acquiesce in the establishment of a French protectorate. By this time France controlled nearly half of the great peninsula.

Additional pressure to the north and west menaced the territorial integrity of China and Siam. The extension of French interests into southern China led to the creation of a sphere of influence including the port of Kwangchow, acquired in 1898. A French thrust to the west threatened the security of Siam and seemed to presage an advance toward Upper Burma and India.

The British were alarmed. They determined to forestall the French by occupying all Burma as a buffer to hold their rivals at arm's length. In 1826 they had seized a slice of Burma, and in 1852 they secured all of the lower portion. Fearful of a further French aggression, the British, in 1884, waged a third war upon the arrogant Burmese king and in 1886 annexed all upper Burma. After 1885 the British and French watched one another with growing suspicion, and the two powers were brought to the verge of war in 1893 because of the French contention that Siam had no claim to territory on the left bank of the Mekong. Three years later they negotiated a temporary agreement whereby the Mekong River was accepted as the line of demarcation between the

spheres of the two powers. It was not until the general
Anglo-French colonial liquidation of 1904 that the rivals
agreed to preserve Siam as an independent buffer state, with
the Mekong River as a permanent boundary. The French
retained their extensive possessions in Indo-China, but the
British defensive expansion in Burma protected India from
the too close proximity of a powerful neighbor.

Russia, having already built a great empire in northern
Asia from the Urals to the Pacific, in the early nineteenth
century extended her influence over much of
Anglo-Russian Rivalry Turkestan. Control of the khanates of Bok-
hara, in 1868, and Khiva, in 1873, carried Russian rule to the
borders of Afghanistan. Alarmed, the British established a
protectorate over Baluchistan in 1876, and annexed that
barren region seven years later. In 1878, suspicious of the
friendly attitude of the emir of Afghanistan toward the Russians, the British waged war against him. The peace settlement left the country independent, but the control of the
great mountain chain of India's northwestern frontier passed
into British hands.

The culmination of the Anglo-Russian rivalry for the control of the Middle East and the approaches to India came in
Persia and central Asia. This region, which included Afghanistan, Baluchistan, and Tibet, was not a fertile field for European imperialism. Most of Persia was a sparsely populated
desert; Afghanistan and Baluchistan, though more thickly
populated, were very mountainous and inaccessible, whereas
Tibet was a bleak plateau in the most remote confines of
central Asia, lying between India and China. Nevertheless
it was in these out-of-the-way regions that the clash of Russian and English interests was to unfold one of the grimmest
of imperial rivalries.

The conflict became even keener as Russian interests began to press farther south and penetrated Persia, Afghanistan,
and Tibet. Establishment of a Russian bank in Persia was
the beginning of a game of financial diplomacy which soon
held that country in a vise. Enormous loans at exorbitant
rates of interest to the shah, the ruler of Persia, were guaran-

teed by Persian customs and revenues. Thus was presaged the loss of Persian independence, with the ultimate possibility of Russian military intervention to protect Russian investments. The economic life of the land passed under foreign control as Russian and British capitalists competed against one another in a lusty battle for railway, mining, and other concessions.

Early in the twentieth century serious tension developed over Tibet. This state, a vassal of China, was ruled by the Dalai Lama, the supposed reincarnation of Buddha, who lived in the sacred city of Lhasa. *The Crisis in Tibet* Lying between Tibet and India, the native states of Bhutan and Nepal had already been closely attached to the British Empire. Tibet retained its seclusion until 1901,when disturbing rumors reached British ears. Reports of a secret draft, whereby Russia was to assume the suzerainty of Tibet, so alarmed Lord Curzon, viceroy of India, that he resolved on a determined course of action. An armed mission under the command of Colonel Younghusband was dispatched from India, and penetrated to Lhasa on August 3, 1904, encountering little opposition. Upon his arrival Colonel Younghusband discovered that the Dalai Lama had fled, but other officials were forced to conclude a treaty, in which it was stipulated that no other foreign power was to receive territorial or economic concessions in Tibet, and an indemnity was to be paid to England. Thus Tibet was snatched from the grasp of Russia and became indirectly attached to the British Empire.

The British victory in Tibet and the earlier timely occupation of Baluchistan and intervention in Afghanistan had weakened Russian influence and strengthened English prestige and interests in the Middle East. Moreover, the defeat of Russia in the war with Japan (1904–1905) struck a severe blow at the Czar's interests in the Far East. Forced to relinquish her designs on Korea, southern Manchuria, and the Liaotung Peninsula, Russia lost one of the great pincers by which she had hoped to dominate Asia. Nevertheless she was still a formidable power.

Another crisis, however, was impending in Persia. Nationalist opposition to foreign economic domination and misrule forced the Shah, in 1906, to grant a constitution and call a parliament. A period of disorder followed this experiment in political democracy, and the lives and property of foreigners were jeopardized.

The Crisis in Persia

While Persia was in a state of turmoil the two competing countries, Russia and Great Britain, began to take alarm at the tremendous expansion of German interests in the Near East. After 1900 Germany became the most influential of the great countries in the Ottoman Empire. By the rapid construction of the Berlin-to-Bagdad railway she was on the point of securing the shortest and quickest route to the Orient. Both England and Russia were menaced by this late comer, and, encouraged by their joint friend, France, decided to liquidate their rival interests and to effect a compromise. By the treaty of August 31, 1907, Persia was divided into spheres of influence. The northern zone, consisting of about one half the country, was left to Russia; the southeastern part was reserved for England; while the intervening district was to be a neutral strip, — a sort of no-man's land undisturbed by the two competitors. Russia gained most in Persia, but she failed to secure the approaches to India. Great Britain persuaded the Czar's government to recognize the fact that Afghanistan lay outside the sphere of Russian interests. Tibet remained an independent neutralized buffer state, both powers agreeing to negotiate only through her suzerain China and to relinquish all attempts to secure special concessions there. Thus the Russian steam roller was stayed in Persia, Afghanistan, and Tibet, and India was no longer menaced by Russian aggressions.

The Anglo-Russian agreement of 1907, however, did not settle the Persian difficulties. Outraged at the political and economic plight of their country, Persian nationalists engineered a revolution in 1908–1909, and overthrew the discredited Shah. He took refuge in the Russian legation and later escaped to Russia, where he was used as a pawn by the Czar's government. The victorious nationalists set up a new Shah and with the aid of an American financial expert, Morgan Shuster, appointed in 1911, attempted to rehabilitate Persia by adopting Western methods and institutions. Russia and England, desirous of preserving their privileged positions, balked the reforming efforts of the new régime, and finally some Persian leaders in Russian employ effected a *coup d'état*, took charge of the government, dismissed Shuster, and dissolved the Majlis, or national assembly. From 1911 to 1914 Persia was ruled by a clique of unscrupulous politicians who were willing tools of the partitioning powers. Banditry and turmoil flourished, conditions went from bad to worse, and Persia ceased to exist as an independent nation. Nevertheless, the period of stress and foreign control was a significant one; for it unified the Persian spirit and gave birth to a strong nationalist movement.

By 1914 most of Asia save Japan and Siam had been subjected to the domination of Western powers. Lacking modern techniques and methods, the Oriental states were unable to cope with Western industrialism and militarism. Nevertheless, the stimulation of national and liberal ideals and the introduction of Western social and economic institutions were bound to result in significant changes. The penetration of the East by the Occidental powers planted the seeds for the eventual modernization of Asia.

The first IMPERIAL RECEPTION OF FOREIGN LADIES *in China*

After a sketch in Alan Bott's *This Was England*

CHAPTER XXV

The Young Capitalistic Powers: The United States and Japan

D URING the nineteenth century two non-European states became great powers — the United States and Japan. As has been related in an earlier chapter, middle-class civilization, firmly established in the United States, resulted in the creation of a powerful commercial and industrial nation. By the end of the century the development of capitalism had been so marked that the new state was impelled to seek economic outlets. Consequently, like the older capitalistic powers and for the same reason,— economic necessity,—she turned to noncapitalistic countries as fields for exploitation. Meanwhile Japan, through an amazing transformation which modified her political, social, economic, and cultural life, also developed into a leading exponent of capitalism and imperialism. The rise of these world powers added two more national sagas to the history of bourgeois expansion.

The triumph of the North in the Civil War (1861–1865) was followed by the strengthening of the bonds of union. *The Colossus of the New World* Despite disorders after the conflict, resulting from resentment of high-handed actions by Northern officials and the sudden freeing of the slaves, law and order were reëstablished in the South. During the reconstruction period the schism between the two sections of the country was partially healed, and a more united nation developed. In 1870 the Southern states were readmitted to the Union, and two years later the Confederate leaders' political and civil rights were restored. For the next half century the solid South expressed such opposition to the North as survived by adhesion to the Democratic party.

A partial solution of the complicated slave problem tended to unify the nation. A series of constitutional amendments defined the status of slaves. Slavery was abolished by the Thirteenth Amendment (1865), citizenship for the slaves was established by the Fourteenth (1868), and their right to vote was affirmed by the Fifteenth (1870). Dissatisfied with conditions in the South after the war, many Negroes went to the North or to the West, where they contributed to the industrial growth of the nation. Actual social equality or democracy for the blacks was a myth, but those who migrated found greater opportunities awaiting them.

While the government was endeavoring to solve the postwar problems, settlers and immigrants were moving into the fertile regions of the Middle and Far West. Agricultural, horticultural, and stock-raising *Economic Progress* activities were soon carried on in regions which had recently been unoccupied. Cities sprang into existence and became thriving industrial and commercial centers. Transportation was improved by the building of roads, railways, and canals. The first transcontinental railroad was completed in 1869. Natural resources were developed, oil wells were exploited, and the lumbering industry was expanded. Moreover, the desire of Northern business men to invest led to an influx of capital and to further development.

The nation as a whole entered into a period of unparalleled economic progress. Agriculture became more important as the area under cultivation increased several fold. Remarkable industrial progress followed, with the development of iron and coal mines, textile mills, and factories. Roads and railways, telegraphs and telephones, linked closely the remotest sections of the country. As a consequence of this economic growth larger business corporations appeared, and banks and insurance companies multiplied in number. There was also tremendous commercial expansion as markets developed and production increased.

By the late nineteenth century the United States reached the era of "Big Business." After 1880, although production increased, the number of independent mills, mines, and factories declined, dropping 30 per cent within a decade. Great trusts, or combines, developed, which tried to squeeze out

Big Business

the small *entrepreneurs* and create monopolies. Trusts appeared in such services as railroads, steamship lines, mines, oil, steel mills, express, textiles, and foods. In 1899 there were three hundred and fifty trusts, with capital amounting to over \$3,000,000,000; in 1905 there were over a thousand, with a total capital of some \$30,000,000,000. Ineffectual attempts were made by the Sherman Anti-Trust Act of 1890 and by later legislation to check the growth of these great combines.

A significant result of this intense industrial growth and consolidation was imperialism. Increased profits had led to

Expansion of the United States

shorter hours and better wages for working-men, and had also resulted in the accumulation of capital. The enormous output created a surplus of goods which could not be consumed in domestic markets. Furthermore, the need of certain raw materials which the United States lacked became more imperative as production increased. Toward the end of the century, therefore, if the capitalistic system in the United States were to avoid a crisis due to overproduction and glutted markets, expansion was necessary.

Outlets for the United States were secured in two main regions. One, the first to develop, was in the backward Hispanic-American countries, which afforded great opportunities for economic penetration; the other, especially important after 1898, was concerned with the Pacific and the Far East. Both of these developments grew out of the earlier industrial background which made them necessary.

As described elsewhere,[1] the development of independent states followed the ruin of the colonial empires in Hispanic

The United States and Hispanic America

America. The backwardness of these countries may be attributed to various causes, particularly the following: (1) scarcity of energetic European peoples, (2) survival of a system of large plantations under clerical and lay landlords, (3) lack of capital to develop

[1] See pages 193–201.

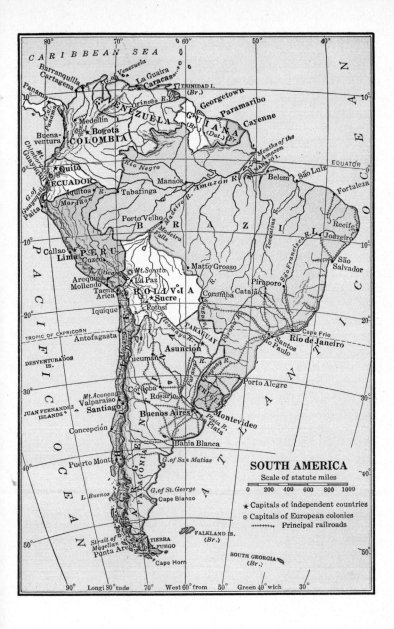

SOUTH AMERICA

Scale of statute miles

0   200   400   600   800   1000

★ Capitals of independent countries
◎ Capitals of European colonies
+++++++ Principal railroads

extensive resources, (4) political instability, (5) deficient education among the masses, and (6) exploitation by foreign interests. Argentina, Brazil, and Chile were much more advanced than other Hispanic-American nations, but even they had not established a firm basis for a bourgeois order.

To aid these states, James G. Blaine, the American Secretary of State, had attempted in 1881 to create a "Concert of the Americas" through a Pan-American Union. With the United States acting as mediator in their disputes, it was hoped that those countries would develop harmonious relations and greater political, economic, and social stability. Consequently a Pan-American Congress met in 1889, and a bureau, the later Pan-American Union, was established and came to serve as a sort of clearing house for Hispanic-American problems. This organization, together with the Monroe Doctrine,[1] tended to establish a benevolent American despotism which emphasized the solidarity and exclusiveness of the Americas in their relations with European powers.

Fearful that the European states would seize these regions, the United States had enunciated the Monroe Doctrine in 1823. Although European powers occasionally meddled in Hispanic America, the American *European Penetration of Hispanic America* government had never been compelled to enforce the Monroe Doctrine. On several occasions, however, especially after the revival of European imperialism, American contentions were called in question by European states. For example, only vigorous threats of war prompted France to withdraw her support from Maximilian's Mexican venture, which terminated in 1867. Later, in 1895, when a dispute over the boundary between Venezuela and British Guiana threatened to lead to war, the United States asserted its prerogative to intervene in any controversy which threatened the peace of the New World. In demanding that Great Britain submit to arbitration, Richard T. Olney, American Secretary of State, declared, "the United States is practically sovereign on this continent, and its fiat is law upon the subjects to which it confines its interposition." Temporarily

[1] See pages 197, 198.

there was danger of an Anglo-American conflict, but Great Britain eventually consented to arbitration. During 1902–1903 the integrity of Venezuela was again menaced when European creditor states blockaded that country for failing to pay its debts. A war was narrowly averted as the powers submitted to American arbitration.

Hispanic-American countries continued to attract the attention of foreign states. Despite the inability of the latter to extend their political sway in the New World, they embarked on a vigorous policy of economic exploitation. Great Britain and Germany were particularly successful in winning trade and markets and in placing investments. It was estimated that by 1913 Great Britain had expended $5,000,000,000 and Germany $2,000,000,000 in these countries.

European powers, especially Germany, were not content with mere economic penetration. They desired to go farther and to make territorial acquisitions in disregard of the Monroe Doctrine. A German publicist, in 1896, declared: "We need a fleet capable not only of coping with the miserable forces of South American states, but powerful enough, if need should arise, to cause America [the United States] to think twice before making any attempt to apply the Monroe Doctrine in South America." In the following year, when Spanish-American relations were severely strained, William II attempted to organize a grand European coalition to chastise the United States and to uphold the "monarchical principle." Austria seemed sympathetic toward his scheme, but Great Britain refused to give it serious consideration, and it soon collapsed.

An important period in the development of American foreign policy was introduced by the Spanish-American War of 1898. A long-drawn-out revolution in Cuba had jeopardized American business interests there, and the alleged mistreatment of the civilian population by the Spanish authorities had aggravated the situation. Finally the blowing up of the battleship *Maine* on February 15, 1898, with a loss of two hundred and sixty lives, precipitated an American declaration of war. After a

The Spanish-American War

short conflict the Spanish forces were completely defeated on land and sea, and the struggle was terminated on December 10, 1898. To the chagrin of Germany the United States, with the approval of Great Britain, forced Spain in a peace treaty to relinquish all claims to Cuba, and to cede Puerto Rico in the Caribbean, and Guam and the Philippines in the Pacific.

The war with Spain was a great incentive to American imperialism in the Caribbean Sea. Having barred Europe from further aggressions in the New World, the American government proceeded to secure *The United States and the Caribbean* political and economic domination in that region. In 1901 the United States, by the Platt Amendment, reaffirmed the independence of Cuba, but at the same time virtually made that country a protectorate. By conquest, lease, purchase, and intervention the United States soon dominated the Caribbean area. The desirability of controlling the trade routes and approaches to the Panama Canal (completed in 1914), together with the possibility of exploiting the raw products, markets, and economic opportunities of middle America, motivated the American government in its efforts to maintain stable conditions in this part of the world. Attempts to preserve order and to afford protection against foreign powers gradually resulted in the extension of American control over much of this region.

Protection of American interests in the Caribbean was associated with attempts to take over the Isthmus of Panama. The construction of an interoceanic canal *The Isthmus of Panama* across this narrow strip of land, either in Nicaragua or in Panama, had been foreseen. In view of the importance of such a project, however, many persons, even before it was built, questioned the desirability of leaving it under the control of a single state, and felt that it should be neutral or international. Therefore, by the Clayton-Bulwer Treaty of 1850, Great Britain and the United States agreed that if a canal were built, it should be neutralized, unfortified, and internationalized, with equal rights for all.

In 1878, however, a French company, headed by Ferdinand de Lesseps, engineer of the Suez Canal, stepped in and obtained a concession from Colombia to dig a waterway connecting the Pacific and the Atlantic. After nearly a decade, characterized by corruption, inefficiency, and scandal, in which some $260,000,000 was expended, the project was dropped. Later, French rights were purchased by the United States for $40,000,000. The way was also prepared for the digging of the canal when, in 1901, by the Hay-Pauncefote treaty, which abrogated the Clayton-Bulwer settlement, Great Britain gave the United States right of way to build a canal on condition that it be open to all nations without discriminations or inequalities of tolls.

A serious obstacle, however, jeopardized the success of the American plan to build a waterway across the isthmus. Colombia refused to lease the strip of land necessary for its construction. But in November, 1903, a "fortuitous" revolution against the Colombian government resulted in the independence of Panama. Immediately accorded recognition by President Theodore Roosevelt, the new republic granted a perpetual lease on a ten-mile strip. Work on the canal was soon begun, and it was opened to traffic in 1914.

During the period after 1898 the United States established a virtual hegemony in the Caribbean. American business *Supremacy of the* interests achieved economic penetration in *United States in* neighboring countries, purchasing Nicaraguan *Middle America* bonds and acquiring plantations in Cuba and Costa Rica. Within a few years industrial and agricultural investments increased several fold. Between 1899 and 1925, investments in Mexico rose from $185,000,000 to nearly $1,319,000,000. Thus "dollar diplomacy," backed by an aggressive interpretation of the Monroe Doctrine and the use of the "big stick" in the guise of threats and occasional naval demonstrations, was effective in extending American economic control over Middle America.

Although Cuba, Puerto Rico, and the Canal Zone formed the basis for American imperialism in the Caribbean, there was a tendency to expansion over neighboring regions. Financial control was established over Santo Domingo in 1905, and the landing of marines to quell civil disturbances there led to an

American military régime after 1916. Nicaragua and Haiti were also brought under American sway. The former granted the United States the exclusive right to build a canal through Nicaragua and the use of a naval base on Fonseca Bay — reminiscent of foreign naval bases in China. Customs revenues were collected under American supervision, reducing Nicaragua to the position of a mere protectorate. Subsequent internal disorders further involved the United States in Nicaraguan domestic affairs. A treaty with Haiti placed that country's customs administration under American supervision, and marines were stationed there until 1924. The purchase of the strategically located Virgin Islands, formerly the Danish West Indies, in 1917, was another step toward establishing American naval and imperial hegemony. In short, the Caribbean was practically converted into an American lake and was one of the most important fields of American imperialism.

Mexico and South America were also affected by American expansion. Prior to 1914 money, goods, and men from the United States penetrated these regions. Concessions were sought and often obtained from corrupt governments. The frequent overthrow of these unstable régimes, however, often led to the cancellation of grants and the repudiation of foreign loans. Controversies followed, and many Hispanic Americans became convinced that North Americans were more concerned with the accumulation of profits than with the welfare of these countries.

Originally developed as a protective policy, the Monroe Doctrine had gradually evolved until it became the corner stone of American foreign relations. With increased emphasis appeared new responsi- *The Monroe Doctrine* bilities and greater opportunities. As American commerce and industry expanded, capitalists became imperialistically minded, and demanded that their government exert influence to win concessions and markets in Hispanic America. By virtue of the Monroe Doctrine the United States claimed the sole privilege of intervening in the affairs of her neighbors. Consequently that country had an advantage over European rivals, for that diplomatic device could be invoked not only to protect the states of Central and South America but also to obtain concessions and special advantages for North Americans.

Active participation of the United States in imperial ventures had both good and bad features. Material benefits, such as sanitary and hygienic improvements, greater political, social, and economic stability in neighboring countries, the introduction of the institutions and ideals of the middle classes, were commendable. On the other hand, the Hispanic-American states, becoming increasingly suspicious, believed that their sovereignty was being menaced. American imperialism, it was said, was not consistent with the professed principles of democracy, national self-determination, and traditional isolation. Consequently many Hispanic Americans and Europeans came to view the attitude of the United States as hypocritical, and the Monroe Doctrine, with its bourgeois altruism and its modern interpretations, met considerable adverse criticism both at home and abroad.

With respect to the Pacific and the Far East the United States reversed its earlier policy of isolation. The trend of *The United States in* American public opinion becoming generally *the Pacific and the* imperialistic at this time, President McKin- *Far East* ley's administration was supported in its decision to annex the Philippines in 1898. The United States stated that American rule was only to be temporary and that the inhabitants of the archipelago in the Far East were to be trained in the art of self-government until such time as they might be granted independence. To this end the Organic Act of 1902 provided for a governor and executive council, both appointed, and a representative lower house. By 1901 a native insurrection led by Aguinaldo was suppressed. In establishing order, rectifying Spanish abuses, introducing sanitary and hygienic reforms, and educating the natives the United States performed valuable services.

Despite material benefits the Philippine natives became impatient of the American régime and demanded independence, but for many years the American government turned a deaf ear to all such requests; certain business interests in the

United States would have been adversely affected by the independence of the Islands. Philippine trade with the United States was classed as coastwise traffic and therefore exempt from duties. Thus foreign competition was seriously handicapped, and in effect the American policy amounted to the closed door with discrimination against foreigners. These economic privileges, together with the value of the Philippines as a naval base and apprehension lest Japan seize them, constituted the chief reasons for American reluctance to grant the Philippine demands for national self-determination.

Another valuable Pacific possession, the Hawaiian Islands, was acquired by the United States. The development by Americans of sugar interests in the Hawaiian Islands led, after 1850, to special privileges for Americans, notably naval rights in Pearl Harbor. When in 1893 the native queen, Liliuokalani, tried to promulgate a new constitution which abrogated American privileges, the American residents effected a *coup d'état*, terminated the native monarchy, organized a provisional government, and requested union with the United States. Finally, in July, 1898, the Islands were duly annexed in spite of protests from the Japanese government. They prospered enormously under American control, although foreign elements virtually swamped the dwindling native population. Useful as a way station to the Far East, the Islands constituted one of the most important naval bases for the protection of the Pacific coast.

The United States made other territorial annexations in the Pacific, obtaining the important naval base of Guam from Spain in 1898, and Samoa in 1899 through an agreement with Germany and England. Other smaller and relatively less valuable islands were secured in the Pacific, which, together with Alaska and the Aleutian Islands, purchased in 1867, afford the United States a veritable network of naval stations extending well across the vast Pacific and forming an effective bridge to the Far East.

During the administrations of Presidents Roosevelt (1901–1909), Taft (1909–1913), and Wilson (1913–1921) the United States began to participate in world politics. Defending

China's integrity after the Boxer uprising of 1900, advocating the open door in the Far East, permitting American loans to China, supporting Japan against Russia in 1904–1905, and opposing Germany in the Venezuelan and Moroccan crises, the United States indeed had emerged from its isolation. By 1914 the hermit state of the Western Hemisphere had become a great nation concerned with world politics and the European balance of power.

While the Colossus of the Americas was gradually emerging from international obscurity and isolation in the nineteenth century, Japan, the island kingdom of the East, *Awakening of Japan* was enveloped in a feudal régime such as characterized Europe in the fourteenth century. Located on a chain of islands off the east coast of Asia and isolated from other peoples, Japan had for many years existed in a state of almost total seclusion. Earlier relations with the mainland had given Japan a culture based primarily upon that of China. Incidental contacts with European sailors, traders, and missionaries in the sixteenth and seventeenth centuries had not proved salutary, so that in 1636 foreigners were generally excluded and Japanese were forbidden to leave their country.

A subsequent period of hibernation resulted in the full development of Japanese feudalism. As the authority of the emperor became negligible the prestige and *The Old Régime* power of the nobles (*daimios*) and warriors (*samurai*) increased. Real power passed into the hands of the great families. Of these the Tokugawa family was among the most influential, for its members retained the hereditary office of shogun from 1600 to 1867. Virtual mayor of the palace, the shogun was the representative of the emperor, but in practice completely usurped his functions and prerogatives. Japan remained a feudal and an isolated kingdom until the middle of the nineteenth century.

The destruction of Japanese seclusion came with dramatic suddenness. In 1853–1854 Commodore Perry appeared with a fleet and forced the island kingdom to grant special trading privileges to Americans, and to open certain ports. Other foreign powers followed suit, and the shogun was forced to accord their nationals similar treatment. Distrust of Japanese judicial methods led foreign nations to demand extraterritoriality for their citizens. Thus not only was Japan's long isolation shattered, but her actual sovereignty was infringed upon by those capitalistic nations which sought to extend their trade.

The End of Japanese Isolation

This opening of the island kingdom came as a terrific shock to the Japanese. Contacts with merchants and traders who represented Western civilization had disquieting effects on the people, who still held to their antique notions of chivalry and self-sufficiency. The impending collapse of old Japan, with its anachronistic institutions, and the coming of the ruthless materialism and exploitative methods of Western bourgeois civilization, threatened to disrupt the nation. As in China and Korea, a conflict developed between the progressive party, favoring Westernization, and the conservatives and exclusionists, who preferred to retain the old order. There were sporadic antiforeign outbursts which provoked occasional retaliation by the great powers. Eventually the downfall of the exclusionists led to the Westernizing of Japan.

An era of *Meiji*, or enlightenment, now began as steps were taken toward national consolidation and modernization of the state. In 1867 the shogun was deprived of his extensive influence, and the emperor Mutsuhito, aged fifteen, was brought from seclusion and his power reëstablished. This restoration of the monarchy and the abolition of the shogunate was a decisive victory for the progressives, for the emperor allowed the government to remain in the hands of a small group of patriotic nobles who determined to combat European imperialism by adopting the bourgeois system. Furthermore, foreign legations were established, and alien traders and travelers were welcomed. The death knell of the old régime had been sounded. This rapid modernization of Japan led to the early foundation of typically middle-class political, social, and economic institutions. Telegraphs were established in 1869, and the construction of railways was begun in 1870.

The Modernization of Japan

The industrialization of Japan was quickly consummated, although abundance of natural resources was lacking. Rapidly the factory system of production replaced the old hand manufacturing as steam power was introduced and textile mills were founded. Shipyards were established and vessels were built for foreign trade. As a result Japanese products were soon able to compete successfully in the markets of Europe and America. Western industrial and commercial methods had completely undermined the earlier feudal society and had led to the foundation of a typical modern industrial nation dominated by economic interests.

The breakdown of seclusion and the growing industrialism substantially modified Japanese social conditions and necessitated institutional changes. Simultaneously with the readjustments in Japanese foreign relations and economic life there occurred a complete social transformation of the hermit kingdom. Feudalism was abolished in 1871 and was soon followed by the suppression of serfdom. In the same year a national school system was founded and education became free and compulsory for all children. Several imperial universities were established at Tokyo and elsewhere.

Advancements in the political sphere were not so rapid. After 1877 demands began to be made for liberal concessions. Marquis Ito, as head of a commission, was sent to Europe to study governmental systems, and as a result of his investigations a constitution was promulgated in 1889. This instrument gave the emperor extensive executive power and an absolute veto over legislation. The legislative branch of the government consisted of an aristocratic House of Peers, reminiscent of feudal Japan, and a House of Representatives with rather restricted powers selected on the basis of a very limited suffrage. Although the new Japanese government fell short of Western standards of democracy and liberalism, it was at least a constitutional one and represented a distinct advance over the archaic shogunate.

Other changes were introduced. Japan reorganized her judicial and legal system with the aid of French advisers, while American experts helped to establish a postal service, and Germans prepared commercial laws and modernized the system of local administration. In 1871 the feudal army was supplanted by universal military service patterned after the German model. Drilled in European methods and equipped with European arms, the new army ended the military privileges of the warrior noble class, the *samurai*. Under English guidance a respectable navy was built, and Japan soon emerged as a leading sea power in the Far East.

Industrialized, modernized, and militarized, Japan was soon able to adopt an aggressive foreign policy. National and industrial consolidation led to the disappearance of the humiliating privileges previously *Japanese Imperialism*
granted to foreigners, and the new state soon imitated her Western teachers by embarking on imperial ventures. Rapid industrial expansion led to constant demands by Japanese capitalists for overseas markets and economic opportunities. By the nineties the nation was convinced of the need for imperial expansion both as a solution of the problem of surplus population and as a defensive measure through the acquisition of strategic bases.

The attention of the Nipponese government was early focused on Korea, over which China claimed suzerainty. A conflict of interests between China and Japan culminated in war in 1894–1895, with an overwhelming victory for Japan. As is related elsewhere,[1] the terms of the treaty of Shimonoseki (1895) were highly favorable to the Japanese. Although the Sino-Japanese war was an amazing victory for a relatively small power over a supposedly invincible adversary, it was the superiority of Western technique which enabled Japan to emerge as the strongest of Asiatic powers.

Decisive as the victory had been, Japan was not allowed to retain her extensive conquests. The cession of the Liaotung peninsula was very obnoxious to certain European powers, and accordingly Germany, France, and Russia presented a joint note to Tokyo demanding that the Japanese government relinquish all rights on the mainland. Rather than risk an unequal war against such a formidable array, and the prob-

[1] See page 425.

able loss of her other conquests, Japan consented to give up the Liaotung Peninsula and to accept $23,700,000 additional indemnity as a substitute. She was resentful, however, of this interference, especially when the great powers seized China's leading ports and prompted the enunciation of Hay's open-door policy.[1]

The Battle of Concessions and the international conflict of interests in China prepared the stage for the clash between

Russian Expansion in the Far East

Russia and Japan. Russia's attention, while occasionally concentrated on the Near East, usually vacillated between Constantinople and the Far East according to the degree of success which Russia enjoyed in either sector. As early as the sixteenth century she had been moving toward the Pacific, and almost all of Siberia had been acquired by the middle of the nineteenth century. An impetus was given to further expansion in the Far East after the defeat of Russia's ambitions in the Russo-Turkish War and the disappointing Congress of Berlin (1878). Thereafter Russia concentrated again on the Orient. Through the construction of the trans-Siberian railway, Siberia and the Far East were made more accessible to penetration by Russian interests. Under an agreement with China in 1896, the Czar's government obtained the right to lay part of the railroad across northern Manchuria, thus considerably shortening the transcontinental route. The Chinese Eastern, as this line through Manchuria was called, became an instrument of Russian economic influence in that region.

At the end of the century the chief objects of Russian interest in this part of Asia were Manchuria, the Liaotung Peninsula, and Korea. The Japanese success against China in 1894–1895 had alarmed Russian imperialists, but the diplomatic intervention of the great powers had partially nullified Japan's gains. Russia therefore proceeded to intrench herself in northeastern China by the extension of her interests. A Russo-Chinese bank, largely financed by French capital, was established in 1895, and Russia later managed to secure a concession for the construction of a railroad linking

[1] See pages 425–427.

Port Arthur (leased in 1898) with the Chinese Eastern Railway. The significance of this line lay in the fact that it virtually delivered Manchuria into the hands of Russian militarists and traders, and marked a distinct advance of Russian interests on the Pacific slope.

During the Boxer Rebellion (1900) Russia took the opportunity to send a strong force into Manchuria to protect Russian interests. When these troops remained there, *Anglo-Japanese Opposition to the Russian Advance* Japan became apprehensive, for the Russian advance into China threatened to checkmate the designs of Japanese expansionists. Great Britain also, fearing an impending conflict for the mastery of the Far East, viewed with increasing suspicion the consolidation of Russian interests in Manchuria.

In 1902 Great Britain and Japan entered into an alliance in which each agreed to maintain benevolent neutrality if the other should become involved in a war with a third state. By this agreement the independence of China and Korea was recognized, and the two powers declared themselves to be uninfluenced by imperial aims in either state. The terms also provided for five years' duration, and marked the first alliance in recent times between an Asiatic and a western-European power on terms of equality. Thenceforth Great Britain felt reassured as to the thwarting of Russia, and Japan proceeded with increased confidence in the evolution of her imperial policies on the Asiatic mainland.

Although the Russian penetration of Manchuria appeared to menace Japanese interests in Asia, it was Russia's aggressive attitude in Korean affairs which actually *Rivalry over Korea* precipitated a crisis and culminated in the Russo-Japanese War. Unstable conditions in Korea had resulted in the flight of her king, in 1896, to the Russian legation for protection, and there he lived with a few of his ministers for over a year. The Korean sovereign came under the influence of his hosts, who persuaded him to replace Japanese officials with Russians. Lumber concessions on the Yalu River were extended to a Russian merchant. To the dismay of the ambitious Japanese, to all outward appearances Korea,

like Manchuria, was going to be swallowed up by the vora-
cious Russian bear.

The lease of Port Arthur seemed another step toward
cementing Russian control in this part of the world. Despite
indignant public opinion, thoughtful Japanese statesmen were
desirous of arranging a compromise with Russia. Willing to
recognize Manchuria as outside the sphere of Japanese interests, they hoped by this concession to secure Russia's
renunciation of special interests in Korea and a recognition
of Japan's privileged position there. Russia refused to strike
such a bargain; consequently, in the Nishi-Rosen convention
of 1898, the two rivals recognized the complete independence
of Korea and agreed to respect one another's interests. Temporarily the Russian avalanche seemed to have been halted,
and the Japanese hoped to consolidate their interests in Korea
and dominate the theoretically sovereign peninsula by peaceful penetration. Having forced China out of Korea in 1895,
the Japanese did not intend to be shoved aside from their
allegedly legitimate field of imperial enterprise.

Although Japanese foreign policies were well formulated
and were calculated to conciliate other powers, Russian affairs,
under the incompetent direction of men like
The Russo-Japanese War Lamsdorff and Alexiev, became uncertain
and vacillating. Despite the settlement with
Japan, Russian troops, in the summer of 1903, still remained
in Manchuria and menaced Korea. Determined to preserve
the latter for Japanese exploitation, the Tokyo government
engaged in a long exchange of diplomatic notes with Russia,
but failed to achieve an agreement. Finally, on February 3
and 4, 1904, two impressive councils, held before the throne
in Tokyo, determined the Japanese course of action. Two
notes were sent to St. Petersburg: one announced the cessation of the hitherto futile negotiations, and the other severed
diplomatic relations.

Confronted with the possibility of war, the vacillating
Czar Nicholas II found himself in a dilemma. German diplomats encouraged both the Russians and the Japanese,
hoping to get the Czar's government hopelessly embroiled in

Far Eastern difficulties. France refused to aid her ally, Russia, in an extra-European war, while Great Britain and the United States were pro-Japanese in sympathy, if not actively hostile. Disregarding the conciliatory advice of his more far-seeing ministers, Nicholas determined to place his reliance on the sword as a solution for the tangled Korean issue.

In embarking on a serious war Japan was really better prepared than her adversary. In addition to the political, social, and economic backwardness of Russia, her enormous army was incapably led, poorly equipped, inefficiently organized, and lacking in morale. The first-line troops were generally kept at home, and it was the reserves who were sent to the front to be slaughtered. Added to the weakness of the army was the corruption and graft in official circles. Russia was indeed a colossus with feet of clay, her backwardness offsetting her greatness in size and numbers.

In contrast to Russia's weakness were the national and industrial solidarity of Japan, her splendidly trained army, her valiant modern navy, and her high morale and national patriotism. Japan's proximity to the Asiatic battleground also facilitated her transport of troops and supplies, whereas the Russians had to rely on the Vladivostok railway or the longer and less certain sea routes. Familiarity with conditions, protection against cold, disease, and famine, enhanced Japanese prospects of victory in a conflict in this sector.

Disregarding the formality of a declaration of war, the Japanese assailed Port Arthur immediately upon the diplomatic break, and captured the great Russian stronghold after a long siege. The major portion of the war was subsequently fought in Manchuria, and the Japanese victory at the sanguinary battle of Mukden, February 25 to March 10, 1905, proved the most decisive engagement and virtually crushed Russia's military power in the Far East. On May 27, 1905, the destruction of the Russian Baltic fleet practically forced Russia out of the conflict. Threatened with a revolution at home, with its military and naval forces in the Far East destroyed, the Russian government finally accepted President Roosevelt's offer of mediation.

Envoys of the two powers met at Portsmouth, New Hampshire, and, after considerable wrangling, managed to work out peace terms. The Russian emissaries had been instructed to play for time and reject a permanent settlement, whereas the delegates of the victorious Japanese, forgetful of their nation's dwindling financial and military resources, hoped to gain more by prolonging the war. Supposedly because of pressure by Roosevelt and the English, the two combatants finally agreed to the following terms: (1) recognition by Russia of the preëminence of Japanese interests in Korea, (2) cession by Russia of the southern half of the island of Sakhalin to Japan, (3) evacuation of Manchuria by both parties within eighteen months, (4) transfer to Japan of the Russian lease of Port Arthur and the Liaotung Peninsula, (5) surrender by Russia to Japan of the southern section of the railway between Port Arthur and Harbin, and (6) the grant to the Japanese of fishing rights along the shores of the Bering Sea. Signed on September 5, 1905, the treaty of Portsmouth, although praised in the United States and in Europe, was bitterly denounced in Japan for its failure to secure more adequate rewards for her sacrifices.

The Peace Settlement

Nevertheless, Japan proceeded to reap the spoils of victory. A Japanese protectorate over Korea was established, with the Marquis Ito, an experienced statesman, as resident general. Unwillingness of the Korean government to coöperate with the Japanese in establishing reforms resulted in the forced abdication, in 1907, of the Korean emperor in favor of the crown prince. The new régime proved no better, and the assassination of Ito in October, 1909, by a crazed Korean, prompted the Japanese to terminate Korean independence and proclaim the annexation of the country. By a treaty concluded in August, 1910, the emperor of Korea ceded his rights of sovereignty to Japan. Extraterritoriality was abolished, and thenceforth Korea was ruled as an integral part of the Japanese Empire.

Japan in Korea and Manchuria

Japanese control of Korea resulted in great material advance. Internal improvements such as roads, railways, factories, schools, and increased foreign trade, however, did not thoroughly compensate the Koreans for their loss of independence. Although sporadic outbreaks and protests against Japanese domination were rigidly suppressed, discontent persisted down to the outbreak of the World War.

The Japanese penetration of southern Manchuria also resulted in great economic progress. The South Manchurian railway opened up new markets and resources. Many Japanese settled there, and by 1914 southern Manchuria had been converted into a Japanese sphere of influence. Japan's political and economic position in Manchuria, however, was consolidated without actually violating the territorial integrity of China, which, together with the policy of the open door, had been acknowledged in principle by the statesmen of the island empire.

Thus by 1914 Japan had built up a large empire for herself, comprising a long chain of islands from Formosa to Sakhalin, as well as Korea and a sphere of influence in southern Manchuria. By virtue of the renewals and revisions of the Anglo-Japanese alliance in 1905 and in 1911, Japan was practically an indirect member of the Triple Entente comprising France, England, and Russia. Therefore when the war came she was able to seize the German leasehold in Shantung and to menace the sovereignty of China. Many Japanese now felt that the time was ripe for their country to become the "Big Brother" of the east.

The rise of the two great extra-European powers, the United States and Japan, had a profound effect upon world politics. European states were no longer in a position to settle arbitrarily the affairs of Hispanic America and the Far East; they had to take heed of two new formidable competitors. Capitalistically organized, these two nations also were in a position to struggle for the *El Dorado* of economic opportunities which the backward regions of the world supposedly offered.

The PROCLAMATION OF THE GERMAN EMPIRE *at Versailles in 1871*

PART VII. INTERNATIONAL ANARCHY

CHAPTER XXVI

Internationalism before the World War

SINCE ancient times men have not only talked about "peace on earth, good will toward men" but have struggled to realize such ideals. The Roman Empire was at certain stages a great force in the promotion of peace. Early Christian fathers denounced the brutal destruction of human life, and during the Middle Ages the Christian church, through the Truce of God and the Peace of God, made noble but largely ineffectual attempts to diminish warfare. Although the Holy Roman Empire attempted to revive the concept of a universal state capable of reëstablishing the *Pax Romana*, the Protestant revolt and the ensuing religious wars of the sixteenth century shattered the ideal of a peace maintained by a universal church and state.

During the later Middle Ages certain factors, such as the rise of cities, the growth of the bourgeoisie, and the creation of strong monarchies, led to a decline of the almost incessant

---

NOTE. *The illustration on this page suggests the* DIFFICULTIES OF THE HAGUE CONFERENCES. *From a cartoon in Punch.*

feudal strife. Although less numerous, wars became more destructive in effect and international in scope. For the most part these conflicts were between rival monarchs rather than between feudal lords.

Opposition to war was pronounced during the early modern period. Influenced by pacifist ideas, many men devised schemes for the prevention of conflicts. The

Opposition to War in Modern Times

celebrated Borgia Pope, Alexander VI (1492-1503), envisaged a warless world wherein there would be a confederation of friendly states under the leadership of the papacy. Vittoria, a Spaniard, hoped to accomplish a similar end by making Philip II of Spain the head of a European league.

Of these early projects the most famous was the so-called Great Design, attributed to Henry IV of France or to his minister Sully. By this scheme the French ruler planned to create, under his supervision, a confederation of European states which would weaken the Holy Roman Empire. It was asserted that the preservation of peace would be insured through a restoration of the balance of power in Europe. In reality, however, this pseudo-peace project was designed to create a powerful league capable of overthrowing Hapsburg supremacy and of establishing France as the leading state in Europe.

In the seventeenth century more practical steps were taken for the restriction of armed struggles. By the Treaty of Westphalia, which brought the Thirty Years' War to a close in 1648, the signatory powers, including France, Sweden, and the Empire, recognized the existence of a family of nations. In that settlement an attempt was made to solve European territorial and religious problems in such a way as to avoid future conflicts. During this same period Hugo Grotius (1583-1645), often called "the Father of International Law," expressed in his works a profound appreciation of the evils of war and a sincere desire to reduce its savagery and frequency. He laid the foundation upon which rest the modern rules regulating the preparation of treaties and alliances, the conduct of war, and the making of peace.

Despite these attempts to limit or to abolish conflicts, the dynastic struggles broadened out in the eighteenth century into great commercial and colonial wars. Influenced by these clashes, notable figures of that period, such as Voltaire, Montesquieu, and Rousseau in France, Pitt the Younger in England, Lessing and Kant in Germany, and Benjamin Franklin in America, expressed pacific ideals. Certain economists, especially Adam Smith, in condemning the selfish mercantilist system, maintained that the general acceptance of the *laissez faire* doctrine would lead to the substitution of non-belligerent economic rivalry for destructive commercial and colonial conflicts.

The revolutionary movement of the eighteenth century also advanced the cause of peace. Many idealists believed that the revolt of the thirteen colonies, by weakening the principle of autocracy and by strengthening the cause of liberty, marked a definite step not only toward the emancipation of mankind but also toward the establishment of world peace. They assumed that the replacement of irresponsible government by popular rule would mark the dawn of a new era of enlightenment, in which wars would be obsolete. Supposedly good, and corrupt only because of faulty political systems, the people of the various nations would then remain at peace with one another.

During the French Revolution the bourgeois Girondins, filled with crusading ardor, planned to abolish conflicts by spreading the principles of revolution. Favoring the establishment of semi-aristocratic republics throughout Europe, they hoped that these states would ultimately form a confederation characterized by free trade and harmonious relations. Later Napoleon Bonaparte revived the classical concept of world empire, but the attempt to realize this archaic ideal provoked years of frightful warfare instead of a new *pax Romana*.

While Alexander I was sponsoring the Holy Alliance in 1815,[1] Great Britain, Prussia, and Austria agreed to join with Russia in maintaining a concert of Europe through the

[1] See pages 45-46.

continuation of the Quadruple Alliance, which had overthrown Napoleon. This arrangement was chiefly the achievement of *The Concert of Europe* Metternich, who believed that by preserving the conservative coalition and by holding periodic conferences the great powers could act as an international police force for the retention of their conquests and the maintenance of the *status quo*. Accepting the notion that the victorious nations were interdependent and must therefore coöperate to maintain peace and the Vienna settlement, the allies found themselves in agreement with the suggestions of the Austrian chancellor.

The members of the Quadruple Alliance, as has been stated, soon disagreed as to its purpose and functions.[1] Metternich sincerely believed that it was designed to preserve the established political and social order. Great Britain, on the other hand, held that it should merely prevent the restoration of Napoleon and enforce the Vienna settlement for twenty years. She refused to carry out the desires of her allies to suppress the revolutions in Hispanic America. The revolutionary movements of the nineteenth century, the establishment of newly independent states, and the rise of additional world powers in Germany, Italy, the United States, and Japan upset the international harmony of the concert of Europe. Two groups of nations finally appeared which established a precarious balance of power.

Despite the breakdown of the Metternichian system of alliances the idea persisted of a concert of Europe which should maintain peace. At the Congress of *Attempts to maintain Peace* Paris, which brought the Crimean War to a close in 1856, and at the Congress of Berlin in 1878, the powers readjusted the situation in the Near East so as to reduce the danger of future Russian aggression there. By the Declaration of Paris (1856) they defined the status of neutrals, condemned privateering, and established rules for blockades. In 1864 the leading states, by signing at Geneva a convention which included provisions for the treatment of wounded soldiers and for the neutrality of official staffs of

_____
[1] See pages 45–51.

ambulances and their equipment, tried to regulate and to humanize warfare. The wounded were no longer to be retained as prisoners, and the equipment was not to be regarded as prizes of war. For the execution of the regulations an International Red Cross Society was organized, with its headquarters at Geneva and with branches in most countries.

In western Europe the bourgeois system contained elements which predisposed people in favor of peace. The Technological Revolution not only initiated new methods of conducting war by means of dreadnaughts, submarines, airplanes, and machine guns, but *Bourgeois Tendencies toward Peace* also promoted pacifism by bringing diverse localities together through the significant developments in transportation and communication. Expansion of foreign trade, increase of foreign travel, and international undertakings also made people interested in and dependent upon each other; at the same time the rapid spread of science, popular education,— in fact, the spread of the bourgeois system itself,— reflected in similar standards of clothing, food, architecture, and politics, were tendencies, many believed, in the direction of a cultural, social, and political unity.

Establishment of numerous international organizations appeared to presage a movement toward permanent coöperation among nations. Thirty countries formed the Universal Telegraph Union in 1875, twenty- *International Organizations* three adopted the metric system of weights and measures in 1875, sixty adhered to the Universal Postal Union in 1878, and five joined the Latin Monetary Union in 1865, for the regulation of an interchangeable coinage for Latin countries. Certain optimists even asserted that the creation of international patent and copyright laws was a step in the direction of world peace.

The universal character of social, intellectual, and scientific interests was shown in the formation of international congresses of socialists, scientists, and Christian churches. International Rotary Clubs, Boy Scouts, and other similar organizations all indicated, so the pacifists believed, the trend toward world unity. Before 1914, international meetings of economists, of socialists, of historians, and of scientists, the exchange of professors, and international sports were also considered forces in favor of the growth of an "international mind" and the frustration of the god of war.

Inspired by these signs men revived and devised arguments against armed combat. Sponsoring this intellectual attack was the famous Peace Society, founded in *Pacifism* England (1816) and established in the United States (1828), in Geneva (1828), and in Paris (1841). By 1914 there were one hundred and sixty similar organizations with many branches. Peace congresses were held, beginning in 1843, and after 1889 they became annual occurrences.

Philanthropists throughout the world supported this movement. The Swedish chemist and engineer Alfred Bernhard Nobel made a fortune by his invention of dynamite, and then established a prize to be awarded at stated times to the person who had performed the greatest service toward the promotion of peace. Andrew Carnegie, the steel baron, devoted a large part of his fortune to the pacifist movement. Other men gave freely and nobly of their time, their ability, and their money to spread the gospel of peace.

Before 1914 a host of pacifists, in books and in speeches, denounced war as a relic of barbarism. They declared that it was immoral, anti-Christian, and dangerous to bourgeois culture and progress. One of these writers, Norman Angell, asserting in his work *The Great Illusion* that war was out of date, built up a strong case for the futility of all conflicts.

By 1914 many believed that in arbitration an important substitute for force had been discovered. The United States and England had settled by arbitration the *Arbitration* *Alabama* case (1871–1872), the Bering Sea controversy (1892), and the Alaskan boundary dispute (1903). Other nations also resorted to arbitration: Germany and Spain settled colonial differences (1886); Great Britain, Germany, and the United States composed their difficulties in Samoa (1899); Argentina and Chile submitted their longstanding disputes to arbitration (1902); and France and Germany peacefully adjusted Moroccan differences (1905–1911).

According to the pacifists, however, militarism constituted the chief obstacle in the way of permanent peace. The reduction of armies and navies, they felt, would produce conditions in which all disputes could be settled without resort to war. These opponents of preparedness maintained that the growing burden of taxation and the withdrawal of able-bodied men from productive work placed heavy burdens upon the various nations. War seemed the chief justification for military expenditures; therefore states were predisposed to fight.

Opposition to Militarism

Pacifists determined to abolish militarism. To this end they ardently supported the limitation of armaments by international agreements and by an international court of arbitration. Inspired by the inauguration of Pan-American conferences, certain European statesmen proposed a similar organization which should include all nations. Such a league, they believed, would be able to cut armaments, reduce taxes, and promote the cause of peace.

In August, 1898, Czar Nicholas II of Russia, alarmed at Austria's military development, decided to imitate the idealistic Alexander I in urging the creation of a league to prevent war. Acting upon this idea, he addressed a circular letter to all the independent states of Europe and Asia and to the United States and Mexico, inviting them to send representatives to the Hague the following year, prepared to discuss and work for international peace. In January, 1899, the Czar announced that the object of the meeting was to limit armaments for a fixed period, and thereby to relieve the financial budgets of all countries. Known as the First Hague Conference, this meeting was attended by representatives of twenty-six states, mostly European. Although it failed to achieve its aims, it did indicate an existing hostility to unbridled militarism.

The Hague Conferences

At this conference, inasmuch as Germany opposed drastic military reductions and Great Britain turned deaf ears toward suggestions of naval disarmament, the pacifists had to content themselves with minor gains and achievements "in principle." The delegates voted to establish at the Hague a regular tribunal which should adjudicate international disputes sent to it. It was also decided to draw up a systematic codification of the laws and customs of war and to apply the principles of the Geneva Conference of 1864. Naval warfare was discussed, and certain powers promised to abstain from the use of poisonous gases and "dumdum" bullets. It was furthermore agreed that projectiles and explosives should not be launched from balloons. With the coming of the World War, however, when the states of Europe were engaged in a life-and-death struggle for their very existence, all these rules were disregarded.

In 1907, at the suggestion of President Roosevelt and at the invitation of Czar Nicholas II, a Second Hague Conference was held, with forty-four states represented, including nineteen American nations. Again the delegates failed to agree upon a plan to limit armaments, although humane laws designed to regulate maritime and naval war were passed. An international prize court was created, and conventions were adopted requiring a formal declaration of war before the opening of hostilities, and restricting the employment of force for the recovery of foreign debts. The conference further recommended that a third assembly be called.

To many pacifists the ultimate creation of a great international state was but a matter of time. With its capital at the Hague, with its regular congresses, with its statutes and codes, and with a permanent court of arbitration, this organization would make war unnecessary. "The United States and Switzerland are successful federal states," said these enthusiasts. "Why should not an international federation function?"

Militarists, however, scoffed at the idealism of the pacifists. They believed that the latter were too trustful of human *Opposition to Pacifism* goodness and that a certain degree of preparedness was essential. In their opinion, nationalism and imperialism, which stimulated hatred between peoples, militated against international understandings. Grave territorial problems existed, they said, in the nineteenth century, which apparently could not be settled by arbitration. As long as Germany retained Alsace-Lorraine, war was imminent between France and Germany. Before the world conflict Germany would not contemplate their surrender or the arbitration of this dispute. She had won the provinces in a trial at arms and apparently would relinquish them only in the same manner. The desires of the various nationalities and other dissatisfied minorities in the Dual Monarchy and the Ottoman Empire, militarists maintained, were bound to lead to conflicts. Independence for these groups meant the dissolution of the two empires and a struggle for territories among the emancipated peoples which would involve foreign intervention. Attempts had been made by the concert of Europe to prevent or to end conflicts by maintaining the *status quo*. This, however, became increasingly difficult. Despite all plans to end wars the desire to be free, the quarrels over territorial boundaries, the imperialistic rivalries which involved peoples in all parts of the world, were actual forces leading to conflicts which abstract pacifist theories could not prevent.

It is not surprising, therefore, that the major powers placed increasing trust in their armies and navies. Citizens in all countries were constantly influenced by the ideas of national security and the talk of "coming war," stressed by powder manufacturers and military officials. Therefore Germany, Austria-Hungary, France, Japan, Russia, Italy, Great Britain, and the United States maintained strong military or naval forces in order to guard their national welfare.

Militarists were not the only advocates of preparedness. Numerous philosophers, scientists, poets, historians, and sociologists justified it. Certain thinkers took over the theory of evolution advanced and popularized by Darwin, Huxley, and Spencer. *Intellectual Exponents of Militarism* Emphasizing the concept of "the survival of the fittest," they asserted that it applied to nations as well as to individuals. Inspired by these "scientists," many believed that the life of states was a struggle for existence. War thus became a biological necessity. Moreover, it became a cult, — a religion of the brave. Said a German cavalry general in 1912:

War is the father of all things. The sages of antiquity long before Darwin recognized this. The struggle for existence is, in the life of Nature, the basis of all healthy development. All existing things show themselves to be the result of contesting forces. So in the life of man the struggle is not merely the destructive, but the life-giving, principle. . . . War gives a biologically just decision. . . . The knowledge, therefore, that war depends on biological laws leads to the conclusion that every attempt to exclude it from international relations must be demonstrably untenable. But it is not only a biological law, but a moral obligation, and, as such, an indispensable factor in civilization.

Thus modern science, with the manifold and unquestionable blessings which it had conferred upon the world, was employed by certain persons as a forceful argument against pacifism. Even though many intellectuals held that war destroyed those biologically fit, the military experts asserted that it was but a phase of the evolution of the species. "Peace was the great illusion; war the great solution."

Exponents of preparedness refused to admit its aggressive tendencies, often asserting that it was essential for security. The French looked to the army for safety; to *Preparedness: Arguments Pro and Con* the British the navy constituted security. Even the Germans professed to believe that the army and navy were forms of peace insurance. "Preparedness," said a prominent American general before 1914, "is the best insurance against war." Unfortunately, replied the pacifist, each nation's armament was regarded by her neighbors as aggressive rather than defensive in purpose. The French army law of 1913, for example, was passed largely because Germany was considering military increases. On the other hand, the French military expansion in 1913 was viewed by the Germans as indicative of French plans for war and good reason for additional German preparations. Thus armaments tended to breed hostility and suspicion.

Between 1870 and 1914 the desire for increased military strength was partially responsible for the creation of the *Growth of Armaments* Triple Alliance and the Triple Entente. Statesmen of the great powers, aroused by the militaristic activities of their rivals, concluded that it was impossible for one nation to maintain sufficient armaments to protect itself against any conceivable alliance of other powers. Consequently coalitions were formed, and by 1914 the leading European nations found themselves divided into two groups, or "armed camps." These coalitions merely increased the menace of war, for each nation was now in danger of being involved in the quarrels of its allies.

Armaments in themselves constituted an obstacle to conciliation or arbitration. The possession of a large and powerful army and navy was a constant temptation to aggressive diplomacy. Influenced by her military strength, Germany was often arbitrary and uncompromising in her relations with other countries. Indeed, some of her statesmen believed that by her merely "rattling the saber" other states would be intimidated and so permit settlement of issues favorably to the Fatherland. The possession of a strong army also enabled a nation to use mobilization as a threat in diplomatic disputes. In the Bosnian crisis of 1908–1909 the Austrian and Serbian governments mobilized their armies as threats to one another. Both Austria and Russia considered mobilization during the Balkan Wars of 1913, to guard their interests. In the critical days of July, 1914, the psychological effects of mobilization were especially important. Certain writers assert that, inasmuch as military authorities had generally agreed that mobilization meant war, Russian military preparations in 1914 were responsible for precipitating the world conflict.

The press also was an agency which played an important rôle in promoting international friction and jingoism. For the prosecution of a war in a bourgeois age the loyal support of all classes was vital. *The Press and War* Therefore the issues, true or alleged, were brought to public attention by journalists. Since the newspapers derived profits from spreading news, the clever editor tried to print those things which would result in the greatest circulation. The more striking the news, the more popular was the paper. Of the subjects which interested people and thus increased circulation, war was among the first, creating both a supply and a demand for news. The Crimean struggle brought phenomenal prosperity and prestige to *The Times* in London. During the Franco-German War the circulation of the *Daily Telegraph* rose from 50,000 to 150,000, and while the Anglo-Boer conflict was in progress in South Africa the circulation of the *Daily Mail* doubled, rising to a million. Although not all newspapers had favored conflicts, increased circulation and resultant profits due to war predisposed editors to emphasize national hatreds and international controversies. And in 1912, for example, Russia expended large sums of money to influence French public opinion in her favor, subsidizing newspapers which supported the military bill of 1913.

German, English, and French newspapers played an especially important part in the formation of friendly or of hostile sentiments during the early twentieth century. By a continual policy of criticism and misrepresentation, often false and malicious, on the part of the German and the English press, the confidence and good will which had existed between the two countries for decades was undermined. On the other hand, French papers coöperated vigorously with the British in bringing about cordial relations between their respective governments, and mediated with solicitous care between England and Russia, whereas the German press, ineffectual abroad, did much to create a situation in which Germany, virtually isolated, was involved in a war against a large part of the world.

By 1914, despite the rapid spread of pacifism throughout the world in the nineteenth and twentieth centuries, peace remained an ideal and war the reality. The emphasis upon nationalism and the war cult proved infinitely stronger than the doctrinaire arguments and pious hopes of well-intentioned idealists. The one agency capable of preventing a world conflict and of maintaining the *status quo* — the concert of Europe — had declined. Within it two coalitions had arisen, and by 1914 they preserved a precarious equilibrium in Europe. This armed peace could not endure, and the international anarchy which resulted from their rivalry led to the World War.

CHAPTER XXVII

The Precarious Equilibrium

A NEW volume of history was opened when, on January 18, 1871, the triumph of the Germans over the French was celebrated by the proclamation of the German Empire in the Palace of Versailles. Under the leadership of Bismarck Germany rapidly became a great and powerful state, while the impoverished Third French Republic declined temporarily to the position of a second-rate power.

But even in the hour of victory the Germans lacked peace of mind. They could see the day of reckoning ahead. Old Moltke struck a pessimistic note by declaring, "What we gained by arms in half a century we must protect by arms for the next fifty years, if it is not to be torn from us again." Bismarck himself did not disregard the danger of another war. Failing in his opposition to the annexation of Lorraine, he devised an elaborate system of alliances which should insure peace and defend the recently attained German ascendancy. He realized that the quarrel with France could not be terminated permanently save at a price which Germany was unwilling to pay. Understanding that the everlasting hatred of a patriotic people would be directed toward his newly created empire, he felt that Germany should arrange alliances and avoid antagonisms.

At first Bismarck did not attempt to conclude agreements with the great powers. Prussia's old rival, Austria, was too weak and still somewhat hostile. Great Britain was so preoccupied with domestic problems as to neglect foreign affairs. Russia's external policies were under the direction of Gorchakov, who not only was a Germanophobe but had an intense personal dislike for Bismarck.

Certain political changes, however, enabled Bismarck to arrange an informal league composed of Germany, Austria, and Russia. In the early seventies Count Beust, the Austrian foreign minister, who delayed a rapprochement with Germany, was dismissed and replaced by Count Andrássy, the Magyar leader. This appointment, as mentioned previously, led to a shift in Austrian diplomacy. To strengthen her position in the Balkans Austria abandoned her hostility and assumed a conciliatory attitude toward Germany. Czar Alexander II was in a mood to welcome a friendly agreement, since he was confronted by the opposition of the Nihilists at home and by the need of outside support in his Near Eastern activities. Bismarck, desirous of insuring peace on Germany's eastern and southern frontiers in the event of another Franco-German war, welcomed an opportunity of establishing friendly relations with both Austria and Russia.

Since Russian determination to dominate the Balkans clashed with Austrian aspirations, a mutual understanding between the two powers was difficult to arrange. Despite this obstacle Bismarck, by bringing about the meeting of the three emperors, made possible the establishment of an informal league (1872) in which Russia tacitly agreed to cease encouraging unrest among the Slavs in the Dual Monarchy in exchange for Austria's promise to preserve a disinterested attitude toward the Russian Poles.

The Three Emperors' League

In certain respects the Three Emperors' League was the successor of the Quadruple Alliance. No written agreement existed, there being an informal understanding to the effect that these states would coöperate in checking the spread of revolutionary doctrines, in maintaining the monarchical system, and in opposing socialism. Thus, by aligning the conservative nations against the revolutionary movement which emanated from France, Bismarck tried to build up opposition to that country.[1]

Many Germans believed that their country had something more tangible to fear than liberalism; she must destroy or

[1] In 1873 — to the satisfaction of Germany — Austria and Russia even decided to discuss common action in the event that a third power should threaten the peace of Europe.

render powerless her chief enemy, France. By 1875 it looked as though war alone could achieve this end. The republic had made a remarkable recovery, paying the heavy indemnity levied by Germany, establishing what seemed a stable republican government, and strengthening her army. At that time France and Great Britain were keen rivals in Egypt. Aware of this antagonism, jingoistic elements in Germany and in England proceeded to stir up much ill feeling. A Russian minister, jealous of Bismarck, helped to create a real war scare by circulating reports that Bismarck wanted a free hand against France so that he could start another war. These remarks were not true. The German chancellor was willing to frighten France, but rather than risk another conflict he preferred to isolate that nation through the creation of a hostile coalition.

Bismarck feared that the Three Emperors' League would be disrupted by Balkan troubles. In 1875 uprisings and massacres of Christians by the Turks in the Balkans threatened to result in Russian intervention and an Austro-Russian conflict. At that time Bismarck frankly informed the Czar's ministers that he would not allow either Russia or Austria to suffer a decisive defeat in a war over the Balkans. He promised neutrality only on the condition that both powers guarantee the Treaty of Frankfurt, which had ended the Franco-German War. A European conflict was avoided when Austria and Russia, by a secret convention in 1876, agreed that if Turkey were ever partitioned, Austria should receive the Bosnian provinces and Russia should obtain Bessarabia. Autonomy, as a prelude to independence, would be granted Bulgaria and Rumelia.

In 1877 Russia decisively defeated the Turks and imposed upon them the Treaty of San Stefano. In this settlement Russia, as stated before, strengthened her *The Congress of Berlin* influence in the Balkans, and thus aroused the fear of both Great Britain and the Dual Monarchy.[1] Bismarck, also fearing Russian influence in the Near East, favored the partition of the moribund Ottoman Empire with

[1] See pages 251, 252.

awards of Bulgaria to Russia, Bosnia-Herzegovina to Austria, Egypt to Great Britain, and territories in North Africa to France and to Italy. But England and Austria opposed Russian control of Bulgaria, Italy and Russia objected to Austrian rule in Bosnia-Herzegovina, and France was not willing to relinquish her rights in Egypt to England. Convinced that he could not satisfy everyone, Bismarck decided to assume the rôle of an "honest broker" and to support the views of the English and the Austrians in the new congress which met at Berlin in 1878 to consider the Near Eastern situation in the light of the war between Russia and Turkey.

Posing as a mediator, Bismarck presided at this conference, trying to deal fairly with all parties. He felt that he could afford to participate in a movement designed to check Russian aspirations in the Balkans, believing that French republicanism would prevent an alliance between Russia and the republic. He was also of the opinion that France could be placated by encouraging her imperialistic aspirations in North Africa. Salisbury of England supported this view, and, like Bismarck, disregarded Italian designs in that part of the world.

Even though she had received Bessarabia and certain provinces in the Caucasus region, Russia resented keenly the loss of influence which she would have exerted in the Balkans had the Treaty of San Stefano been accepted. Considering the congress little more than an anti-Russian coalition, Russia accepted the Berlin settlements with a sulky air. What could she do? She was practically alone in the world. Germany, the nation she had aided during the Franco-German War by influencing the Dual Monarchy to stay out of the conflict, was indifferent to her interests in the Near East. France, inasmuch as she was facing internal difficulties and was favored by the English, the Austrians, and the Germans in her desire to secure Tunis, was not now so anxious to make friends with Russia. Therefore a Franco-Russian alliance was not consummated at this time.

Bismarck, rather perturbed about the Russian attitude after the congress, decided to create definite agreements. At first he tried to arrange an alliance with England. But Salisbury, still clinging to the traditional policy of "splendid isolation," was lukewarm to the proposal. The iron chancellor then turned to his neighbor Austria-Hungary, who, grateful for German support at the Berlin Congress, and seeking added strength for her Balkan policy, was more than willing to ally herself with Germany. Consequently an Austro-German alliance was concluded in 1879. It provided that, should either Austria or Germany be attacked by Russia, they were bound to lend each other aid and not to conclude peace save by joint agreement; should one of them be attacked by another power, the ally would observe an attitude of benevolent neutrality; if the attacking power, moreover, were supported by Russia, the obligation of armed help would arise, and the war would be waged jointly until the conclusion of peace.

The Austro-German Alliance

This Dual Alliance was purely defensive. Bismarck was assured of an ally should France, supported by Russia, inaugurate a war of revenge. But Bismarck had to abandon hopes of bringing the Austro-Germans into the empire, and Austria was forced to relinquish her ambition of dominating middle Europe. Bismarck realized that by this alliance he ran the risk of war, inasmuch as Germany could easily become embroiled in an Austro-Russian dispute over the Balkans. Conscious of this danger, he warned Austria to avoid undue aggressiveness in this region.

The iron chancellor was not content with a single insurance policy. Unable to reach an agreement with Great Britain, he decided to maintain friendly relations at least, and by so doing to convey the impression that an alliance between the two states was possible at any time. Russia, England's rival in the Orient, would, he believed, reach an understanding with Germany and the Dual Monarchy rather than permit an Anglo-German friendship to materialize into an alliance. In 1881 Bismarck's policy was rewarded. The Three Emperors' League was revived, and its members agreed to remain neutral should either one of them be attacked by a fourth power. Thus Germany was assured of Russian neutrality in

The Alliance of the Three Emperors

the event of being assailed by France. Russia and Austria also promised to coöperate in the solution of any problems arising out of the Near East.

About the time when the Three Emperors were arranging their alliance France was developing her imperial interests. Influenced by visions of an African empire, *The Triple Alliance* she acquired Tunis in 1881, with Bismarck's blessing, for he hoped that this expansion in Africa would make the French forget Alsace-Lorraine, the Rhine, and *revanche*. Italy, however, vigorously opposed the French occupation of Tunis; she had planned an empire which should include this seat of ancient Carthage. Not prepared to contest France, however, Italy turned to Germany for support. But Bismarck refused to agree to an alliance which should exclude the Dual Monarchy. Aware of *Italia irredenta* and of Austro-Italian rivalry in the Balkans, he was not overenthusiastic toward the prospect of an alliance with Italy. Tempted by the opportunity to strengthen the opposition to French *revanche*, however, he was willing to admit Italy into a combination which should contain Austria.

Italy, not so much out of love for Germany as out of hatred for France, agreed to include her arch-enemy Austria in this unnatural alliance. In 1882 a secret league was formed, in which Germany and Austria promised to aid Italy if she were attacked by France, and Italy agreed to help Germany if the latter were assailed. If any one member were menaced by two or more powers, the other two would likewise give their ally full support. Each state, also, was to remain neutral if one of the others were attacked by a fourth power. Thus the Dual Alliance became the Triple Alliance. Although its duration was fixed at five years, it was renewed four times, being in force at the outbreak of the World War.

Lacking agreements with Russia, Great Britain, and France, Bismarck very cleverly took advantage of their rivalries to advance Germany's interests. He gladly encouraged the discord between Russia and England in Asia in order to prevent an alliance of these nations against Germany; a convert to imperial expansion, he advanced Germany's colonial ambitions in Africa by playing off one power against another. Thus he was able to acquire for Germany, despite her lack of sea power, southwest Africa, the Cameroons, East Africa, and other possessions. By encouraging Russian activities in the Far East he also decreased the pressure in the Near East, preventing a crisis there which might have broken up the Triple Alliance by causing Russia and Italy to war upon Austria.

Encouraged by Germany's support, the Dual Monarchy tried to strengthen its influence in the Near East at the expense of Russia. In 1881 Serbia and Austria signed an alliance by which the former practically became a vassal of the latter. The importance of this agreement was demonstrated when Austria, disregarding Russia's disapproval, backed Serbia in the Serbo-Bulgarian War (1885). In 1883 Austria also arranged a protective alliance with Rumania, directed against Russia. Even though it was in a sense a violation of the spirit of the Three Emperors' League, Germany underwrote this Austro-Rumanian agreement. She did so because she believed that these treaties, strengthening the influence of the Dual Monarchy in the Balkans, would establish a balance of power in the Near East.

Bismarck, however, continued to fear a conflict between Russia and Austria rising out of their intrigues in the Balkans. After 1881 Serbia, backed by Austria, tried to prevent Bulgaria and Eastern Rumelia from uniting to form the Bulgarian monarchy. Angered by the part the Dual Monarchy played in this affair, Russia announced her intention of not renewing the agreement that bound her to the Three Emperors' League, which ended in 1887. Bismarck realized at once that Russia, if she carried through her threat, would be in an admirable position to arrange an alliance with France and to weaken Austrian influence in the Balkans.

To prevent this possibility the chancellor welcomed negotiations which resulted in the famous Reinsurance Treaty between Russia and Germany (1887). By its terms each contracting party agreed to main- *The Reinsurance Treaty* tain a friendly neutrality if the other became involved in a war with a third party. This clause, however, was not to

apply in a conflict resulting from either a Russian attack
upon Austria or a German attack upon France. Germany
recognized Russia's historical rights in the Balkans and her
claim to a preponderant and decisive influence in Bulgaria.
The principle of the *clôture* of the Straits was to be maintained,
and a secret protocol stated that Germany would help Russia
establish a legal government in Bulgaria as well as lend support in any measure that the Czar might find it necessary to
take to guard the "Key to his Empire." On the surface it
appeared that Germany, in this treaty, which was to last three
years, had made important concessions to Russia and had
almost betrayed the interests of Austria-Hungary in the
Near East. But Bismarck knew what he was doing; he
assured Austria that the Reinsurance Treaty was in no way
directed against her, and that its underlying purpose was
merely the maintenance of the *status quo*.

Bismarck also encouraged the First Mediterranean Agreement, concluded on February 12, 1887, by Great Britain and
Italy and joined by Austria in March. Its

The Mediterranean Agreements aim was to preserve the existing territorial
situation in the Mediterranean and Black
Sea areas. By this arrangement Russian aspirations in the
Near East were checked and the way seemed prepared for
British participation in the Triple Alliance, inasmuch as Italy
gained tacit British support in her North African policy. To
maintain the *status quo*, Germany promised to support Italy
against French aggression in North Africa, and steps were
taken to bring Spain into the Mediterranean League. In
December, 1887, the Second Mediterranean Agreement was
signed. It bound England, Austria, Italy, and Spain to oppose any disturbance in the Near East and to defend the independence of Turkey. It also prevented the Sultan from
ceding the Straits or his rights in Bulgaria to any other power.
Russia seemed effectively checked in her desire to control the
Straits and thereby to dominate the Near East.

In 1889 Austria, Italy, Great Britain, Rumania, Serbia,
Spain, and, indirectly, Turkey, as well as Russia, were included by various treaties in Bismarck's scheme to isolate

France and to prevent a war. The hegemony of Germany was a reality; Bismarck was the master diplomat of Europe. No modern statesman had ever constructed so formidable and imposing a system to preserve peace and to insure the growth of his country. But even with these safeguards Bismarck was not fully satisfied. He now attempted to arrange a definite Anglo-German alliance. The Iron Chancellor's career, however, came to an end in 1890, when he was forced to resign before he could arrange this last guarantee of the *status quo*.

There are those who believe that if Bismarck could have remained in office he would have been able to make Germany a world power without antagonizing Europe. *Bismarck's Diplomacy* But this achievement was improbable. By permitting the annexation of Alsace-Lorraine, by levying the huge indemnity on France, and by proclaiming the German Empire in Versailles he had accentuated the hatred between the French and the Germans. In establishing the Austro-German alliance he had created a situation wherein Germany might at any time be involved in an Austro-Russian dispute over the Balkans. Moreover, the agreement with Austria obligated Germany to support the Hapsburgs in sustaining their anachronistic empire, and as a result to oppose a definite trend of the period, namely, that toward national self-determination. It might even be said that this engineer of the German Empire laid the foundation for future war.

Bismarck's system of alliances, because of the shifting interests of the powers, could not remain intact. With thousands of her people living under Austrian rule Italy could not be expected to remain true to an agreement which would prevent her from striving to liberate them. Also, Bismarck's reliance upon militarism and upon adroit diplomacy was sure to arouse Germany's rivals. Russia was veering toward France even before the fall of Bismarck. A coalition of enemies, brought together through common fear of a powerful state, was the logical outcome of the chancellor's policies and presaged the end of German hegemony.

Although an ardent exponent of the *Weltpolitik* idea, the young emperor, William II, left the direction of affairs in the hands of his advisers in the foreign office, especially in those of Baron Friedrich von Holstein (1837–1909). At first a col-

The "New Course"   laborator of Bismarck, he later opposed the latter's policies secretly but none the less vigorously. Holstein, according to available evidence, seems to have exerted tremendous influence upon German diplomacy until his retirement in 1906. Refusing to sign many governmental documents, wrecking the careers of numerous diplomats by the exposure of questionable episodes in their private lives, working long hours, avoiding the public eye by stealing quietly home near midnight and arriving at his office in the early morning, this unusual and influential German official was the great unknown of his day.

Holstein, it is believed, was largely responsible for the disagreement between William II and Bismarck over relations with Russia which led to the latter's resignation. It is also said that Holstein brought about the dropping of Bismarck's Reinsurance Treaty. Opposed to Russia as well as to Bismarck, Holstein, backed by certain military officers, succeeded in convincing the government that Germany had to choose between an alliance with Russia and the Triple Alliance. The two together were incongruous. Conflicting interests in the Balkans, in his opinion, were bound to lead to a war, and it was Germany's duty and self-interest to support her ally, the more so because the latter had the backing of England and Italy. Holstein had his way, and the Reinsurance Treaty with Russia, upon its expiration in 1890, was allowed to lapse despite Russian willingness to renew the agreement revised to suit Germany's desires.

The government of William II, upon discontinuing the Russian friendship, drew closer to Great Britain. In 1890 Germany concluded with the latter power the famous Heligoland Treaty, by which she obtained the island of Heligoland off the Weser and Elbe rivers in return for certain important concessions in Africa. This agreement was followed by the Kaiser's visit to England, repeated during ensuing years. Impressed by these evidences of friendly relations, many European newspapers predicted that Great Britain would eventually join the Triple Alliance. Was not England, by participation in the Mediterranean Agreement, a virtual ally? Had not the Germans and the English together fought the French at Waterloo? Was not the Emperor's mother an Englishwoman?

Optimistic as was the tone of these questions, Great Britain was actually in no hurry to consummate with Germany an alliance which would practically assure the latter's complete ascendancy on the Continent. She preferred to maintain an equilibrium in Europe and a policy of "splendid isolation"; by so doing she would be free to act in any European crisis which deeply affected her interests.

Russia, left out in the cold by Germany in 1890, and France, long confronted by a group of hostile powers under Germany's leadership, were both seeking a strong friend. Knowledge that the Kaiser was supporting Ferdinand of Coburg, a German, for the Bulgarian throne, and sending officers to train Turkish troops, capped the climax of Russian resentment against Germany, which had been aroused by the latter's support of Austria at the Congress of Berlin and by the failure to renew the Reinsurance Treaty. After 1885 French opposition to Germany was considerably increased. Georges Clemenceau (1841–1929), a republican patriot who had witnessed the French humiliation of 1870 and had vowed never to forget, succeeded in overthrowing the French minister Ferry, who was coöperating with Bismarck in colonial matters. This political change marked the revival of the idea of *revanche*, well expressed by Raymond Poincaré (1860–   ), the able French statesman, in a speech before a group of university students:

When I descended from my metaphysical clouds, I could not see for my generation any reason for existing unless it were for the hope of recovering our lost provinces.

Russia and France, therefore, with a common fear of the rising German *bloc* of powers, drew closer together. In 1891 an agreement was arranged between the two states, providing for mutual coöperation in all questions which endangered the maintenance of general peace and for counsel as to military and naval measures if war should threaten. Regarding this understanding as inadequate, French military authorities desired a more definite arrangement — one which would anticipate a hostile move by the central powers. At first Russia hesitated, still hoping to improve her relations with Germany; but in 1892 she yielded, and the two states formed an entente. The following year a military convention was concluded in which both powers agreed to mobilize simultaneously should the Triple Alliance or one of its members begin to gather its military forces. Rather than submit the negotiations to public discussion, France and Russia made these arrangements in the form of secret military conventions. Technically this agreement was not an alliance, inasmuch as it was not approved by the French Chamber of Deputies, as provided by law. Actually, however, it proved to be a military alliance.

The Franco-Russian Alliance

Although Russia desired French support against Great Britain in the Near and the Far East, the French government insisted that the alliance be purely European in scope. Russia yielded the point, and the two states, in the Dual Alliance of 1894, agreed that "if France is attacked by Germany, or by Italy supported by Germany, Russia shall employ all her available forces to attack Germany. If Russia is attacked by Germany, or by Austria supported by Germany, France shall employ all her available forces to fight Germany." By this alliance German hegemony in Europe was ended, and in its place was substituted an equilibrium of Europe, maintained by two groups, the Triple Alliance and the Dual Alliance.

The Dual Alliance of 1894, originally defensive in purpose, was not transformed into an offensive coalition until the opening of the twentieth century. From the beginning, however, the terms provided for joint mobilization as soon as Germany called her soldiers to the colors. Although unaware at first of the exact nature of this agreement, Germany, cognizant of its existence, was much perturbed.

During the time that the various alliances were being established in Europe, British colonial interests ran counter to those of France and Russia, and to a less degree to those of Germany. France, besides planning the establishment of a great empire in North Africa from the Mediterranean to the Red Sea, directly opposed British imperial policies in Egypt, Burma, Siam, and Newfoundland. Russia, through her expansion in Middle Asia, competed with England for economic supremacy in this region and constituted a threat to Britain's dominion in India. Germany's ambitions, together with those of France and Russia, in the Far East (especially in China) worried British imperialists.

British leaders, in 1895, desirous of improving Anglo-German relations, decided to end one of the chief causes of international friction, the Near Eastern Question, by suggesting to Germany that the Ottoman Empire be partitioned. This "friendly" *Anglo-German Relations* proposition, vaguely stated, provided that England should receive Egypt; Italy, Tripoli; Austria, Salonica; and Russia, Constantinople. Germany was suspicious of this offer. Several of her statesmen doubted the sincerity of Salisbury, the English prime minister, who appeared to be responsible for this project. Certain Germans of high rank even went so far as to intimate that Salisbury made this suggestion merely for the purpose of encouraging the powers interested in the Near East to express their views, so that Great Britain might modify her course accordingly. William II apparently feared that England was planning to provoke a war which would convulse all Europe and would yield the British handsome dividends. Although Germany refused to fall in with the British scheme, she agreed to Russian acquisition of the Straits should Turkey be partitioned. Her interest in Russia's plan to gain this strategic holding was based on the belief that, once in possession of the Straits, the Czar's government would be willing to dispense with France as an ally.

The nineties saw the rise of considerable anti-German sentiment in England, which, although it arose for the most part out of the colonial, commercial, and naval rivalry of the two countries, was intensified by a number of unfortunate incidents. In 1894, when England sought to conclude an agreement with the Congo Free State which would enable her to construct a railroad from Cape Colony to Egypt, Germany, by exerting influence on the Free State, effectively blocked the way. In 1896 William II tactlessly sent a telegram to Paul Kruger, president of the Transvaal, congratulating him on having successfully repulsed the Jameson raid without foreign assistance. Also, two years later, Germany embarked on a "big navy" program and insisted upon executing her ambitious policy to the fullest extent, all British beseechings and discouragements notwithstanding.

Several British statesmen decided that their country, having too many enemies and too few friends, should abandon her traditional policy of isolation and seek *British Abandonment of* allies. The rivalry of foreign powers in the *"Splendid Isolation"* Far East, the clash with France over the occupation of Fashoda by French troops, the outbreak of the Boer War, and especially the fear that the Dual and Triple Alliances might combine against England,— all these developments undoubtedly influenced England in adopting this new course. Attempts were made, therefore, to establish closer relations with Russia and Germany. First Great Britain suggested that Russia and England coöperate in the division of Turkey and China into spheres of influence. The Russian ministers, paying little attention to these proposals, ordered the occupation of Port Arthur. Russia was moving closer to the Celestial Empire.

Joseph Chamberlain, the British Secretary of State for the Colonies, unable to interest Russia, discussed with the German ambassador the possibility of a defensive alliance between the two countries, but his proposals were opposed by German diplomats. The German foreign office believed that the British Parliament would never ratify a treaty, and that such an agreement might involve Germany in Anglo-Russian rivalries in Asia and in Anglo-French disputes in Africa. Bülow of the German foreign office therefore instructed his ambassador at London to arrange a colonial agreement without concluding a definite alliance. Chamberlain's negotiations with Germany merely resulted in a treaty (1898) which provided for a subsequent division of the Portuguese colonies in Africa between Great Britain and Germany, and another (1898) designed to end their conflicting interests in China.

While Germany was negotiating with Great Britain the Triple Alliance was crumbling under her feet. Largely because of the vexatious problem of *Italia irredenta* in Austria, and of the Austro-German failure to support her African policy, Italy was *The Franco-Italian Understanding* from the beginning a discontented ally. It was true that in the renewals of the alliance Italy's allies had recognized her interests in Tripoli, but she was not satisfied. Although Germany promised support in the event of war, the Italians feared that they could not rely upon this guarantee because Germany would not want to antagonize Turkey, France, and Great Britain. Italy, moreover, viewed with alarm the Austro-German penetration of Turkey, for her Near Eastern aspirations apparently were receiving little consideration.

French diplomats, in 1900, probably aware of Italy's dissatisfaction and quick to see an opportunity to weaken the Triple Alliance by resuming friendly relations with Italy, broken off when France annexed Tunis (1881), desired to arrange an understanding with their neighbor. At that time France had designs on Morocco. To extend her interests there, she knew that she must have Italian as well as Spanish and English approval. After a secret exchange of letters, France and Italy arranged to recognize each other's aspirations in Morocco and Tripoli respectively, and Italy also agreed to acquiesce in the French protectorate over Tunis in return for certain political and commercial privileges.

In 1902 France and Italy signed a secret agreement which provided that Italy was to remain neutral if France were attacked by another power or if France declared war as a result of a direct provocation. France made a reciprocal pledge. This treaty actually destroyed the Triple Alliance, for Germany could no longer count on the support of Italy in the event of a war with France.

While France was winning Italy's affections, England was acquiring a friend in the Far East. By 1902 the presence of the Russians in Port Arthur and the establishment of a German holding in Kiaochow had caused the British at Weihaiwei to notify London that, unless something were done, England's holdings in China and India would be threat-

The Anglo-Japanese Alliance

ened and a Russo-German combination might dominate the Far East. In Japan, a nation whose interests were also challenged by the Russian advance, the British diplomats saw a potential ally. After preliminary negotiations Great Britain and Japan therefore arranged an alliance in which each was to support the other if it were attacked by two or more states, and each was to remain neutral if the other were attacked by one power. England thus agreed to remain neutral if Japan should fight Russia, but to support Japan if Germany or France backed Russia.

Determined to continue a policy of winning friends, Great Britain welcomed an opportunity to settle her difficulties with France. The two powers had been tradi-

The Entente Cordiale

tional enemies for centuries. The Hundred Years' War, colonial conflicts, the American Revolution, the French Revolution, and the Napoleonic era had all served to strengthen the unfriendly feelings between these nations. In the latter part of the nineteenth century the revival of imperialism found England and France still suspicious rivals, France, as noted previously, resenting the British activities in Egypt and regarding the Fashoda affair (1898) as another humiliation. Both competed for concessions in middle Asia, engaged in boundary disputes in western and central Africa, and quarreled over fishing rights in Newfoundland and over the frontier of Siam. In addition to these troubles there was tension over Morocco, where both the British and the French had important interests. Great Britain also disapproved of the French alliance with Russia, England's rival in Asia. Other minor factors contributed to Anglo-French antagonism. The British disliked French Catholicism and considered the French fickle, unreliable, immoral, and decadent. Many Englishmen gladly subscribed to the fallacious notion that the Teutonic peoples were superior to the so-called Celts and Latins.

France was not unwilling to discuss the proposed entente. Some of her best minds believed that France could not create a great colonial empire and at the same time regain her lost provinces and predominance in Europe unless she had British support. They also concluded that since the Franco-Russian and the Anglo-Japanese alliances might at any time involve England and France in a war, Germany would be in a position to exact important concessions from either nation in return for her support or benevolent neutrality. Rather than permit such a situation to arise, the French preferred to arrange a settlement with Great Britain. As foreign minister, Théophile Delcassé (1852–1923) therefore instituted a movement toward an understanding with Great Britain, who, after having decided to terminate her policy of splendid isolation, forgot her traditional antagonisms with France.

As a result of the discussions which followed, a treaty known as the *Entente Cordiale* was signed in April, 1904, by France and England, providing for the arbitration of questions of juridical nature but not involving "national honor" and "vital interests." Negotiations were next undertaken designed to end the rivalries between France and Great Britain over Newfoundland, western Africa, the New Hebrides, Siam, Madagascar, Egypt, and Morocco. In 1904 all these disputes were finally settled by concessions on both sides. France and Great Britain disclaimed any intention of altering the status of Egypt and of Morocco. France merely consented to recognize the position of England in Egypt, and England in return declared France to be the preponderant power in Morocco, although it was understood that British commercial treaties with Morocco would be respected by the French. To this agreement were appended secret articles not published until 1911, which provided for the liquidation of Morocco and of Egypt in their respective hands.

The *Entente Cordiale* was not an alliance and contemplated no action against potential enemies. It was merely an understanding over colonial affairs. Nevertheless it did cause England and France to rely upon each other in the event of trouble with Germany. Also France, feeling certain of British support, embarked on an aggressive policy in Morocco, ignoring Germany and thus paving the way for an international crisis.

By 1904 the Anglo-Japanese Alliance and the *Entente Cordiale* were openly hostile to German and Russian interests in the Far East. Great Britain, France, and Japan, already strongly entrenched in the Orient, opposed the Russo-German advance, especially when Russia occupied the Liaotung Peninsula and made Port Arthur a great seaport across from Japan, and when the Germans secured part of Shantung.

William II had ambitions. He hoped to revive the Three Emperors' League by supporting Russian expansion in the Far East and Austrian interests in the Near East. Germany, backed by these two nations, would become a world power, the arbiter of all imperial problems and the protector of Christians and white men against the heathen and the "yellow menace." Inspired by this dream, he telegraphed to the Czar in 1898, when Russian sailors marched into Port Arthur, as follows:

German Ambitions

> Please accept my congratulations on the arrival of your squadron at Port Arthur. Russia and Germany at the entrance of the Yellow Sea may be taken as represented by St. George and St. Michael shielding the Holy Cross in the Far East and guarding the gates of the continent of Europe.

To achieve the imperial supremacy she desired, Germany was convinced by 1905 that she must prevent the threatened isolation of the Central Powers. The revival of the Three Emperors' League and the merging of the Triple and Dual alliances, the Kaiser thought, was a means of avoiding encirclement. Russia, England's bitter rival in Middle Asia, could still be enticed into an alliance against the latter, provided France were included. If this scheme should prove successful, the Dual and Triple alliances would then be merged into one big league of the five Continental powers. Thus Japan and Great Britain would be isolated.

William II, during the Russo-Japanese war, prepared the way for the combination. Exchanging many letters with his "dear cousin Nicky," he tried earnestly to win the confidence of that bewildered ruler. In 1905 occurred the famous Björkö conference. Meeting the Czar in northern waters, the Kaiser made a desperate attempt to arrange an alliance. Perhaps

William II thought that he was another Napoleon I and that Nicholas II was another Alexander I. At least he is said to have assured "Nicky" that the Russian ruler was "Admiral of the Pacific," while he, William, was "Admiral of the Atlantic." He even intimated that together they might rule the world.

The meeting of these two monarchs was interesting even though it was not important. After several conversations William II succeeded in influencing Nicholas II into signing a treaty which provided that, *The Björkö Episode* should either Russia or Germany be attacked by a European power, the other would lend her support. According to the verbal arrangements France was to be brought into this pact. This agreement was signed by William and Nicholas on July 24, 1905, a day which the Kaiser predicted would be recognized as a turning point in the history of Europe.

To William's dismay, however, both his ministers and the Russian diplomats threw cold water on the scheme. Bülow, the German chancellor, threatened to resign because the Kaiser had modified the draft sent him from the foreign office, while the Czar's minister, Lamsdorff, who could hardly believe his ears when news of the agreement was brought to him, finally got Nicholas II to see that France could not be forced into such a combination. Consequently Nicholas II informed the Kaiser of his inability to go through with the project. The Kaiser's personal attempt to unite the Triple and Dual alliances and to insure German supremacy had failed.

Germany's rivals were successful in their plans to settle their respective colonial problems. Following the *Entente Cordiale* came the institution of negotiations designed to bring about a settlement of all *Formation of the Triple Entente* Anglo-Russian difficulties in Asia. France, emphasizing at all times the common suspicions of Germany, did everything in her power to bring her ally and her friend together. She did so not only because she wanted to isolate the Central Powers but also because she desired to bolster up the Czar, who owed France considerable money and was finding it difficult to cope with the revolutionary movement at home. The Russo-Japanese War marked the real turning point in Anglo-Russian relations. Checked in the Far East, Russia was less dangerous than before. At the same time, being outside the Triple Alliance and bound to France only by military agreements, she felt the need of more friends.

Isvolski, a capable Russian diplomat, was one of the most active men of affairs in Russia desiring an entente with England. During the Russo-Japanese War, as an obscure minister to Denmark, he came under English influence and became an ardent advocate of an Anglo-Russian rapprochement. Among the many arguments which he soon advanced in favor of it were the following : that the alliance with France alone was not enough to maintain a balance of power with the Triple Alliance; that a settlement with England would presage an agreement with Japan by which Manchuria would be divided for exploitation; and that an understanding with England would enable Russia to obtain something in middle Asia and would at the same time strengthen her position in the Near East. The latter was his chief reason for an Anglo-Russian entente. Checked in the Far East, Russia, he asserted, had an admirable opportunity to return to her first love, the Near East. Here she could count on French and English support because of their fear of Austro-German ambitions and activities in this region.

By 1906 the stage was set for the rapprochement between England and Russia. Statesmen on both sides, including Isvolski, who was now Russian foreign minister, had concluded that distinct advantages would be gained by both Great Britain and Russia through a settlement of their disputes in middle Asia and the acceptance of a general understanding with regard to all their imperial rivalries. In August, 1907, the two countries agreed upon a convention in which they liquidated their conflicting interests in Asia. The German government was thunderstruck when the news arrived. Its significance was soon made apparent even to the most guileless of Germans. Russia and Britain were now friends and would oppose in common any attempt on the part of the Central Powers to disturb their respective positions as great world states. What had been considered impossible had happened. The Triple Entente, comprising Great Britain, France, and Russia, was established. Germany and Austria, not France, were now isolated.

Russia meanwhile had reached an understanding with Japan also, signing an agreement in July, a month before the Anglo-Russian settlement. By the terms of the Russo-Japanese pact both states promised to maintain the existing situation in the Far East, the territorial integrity of China, and the principle of the open door. There were also secret clauses in which Japan and Russia defined their spheres of influence in Manchuria. Likewise Japan signed an agreement with France regarding their mutual interests in the Far East.

The Central Powers realized by 1907 that they were in a difficult position. The members of the Triple Entente had settled their territorial disputes and were united in a desire to maintain the *status quo* and to prevent further Austro-German expansion. To many Austrians and Germans the Triple Entente was a hostile iron ring designed to break the Triple Alliance, to end the Dual Monarchy, and so to destroy German hegemony. The fact that France and Russia were united by an alliance essentially military in character, and the rumor (which was true) that Great Britain, France, and Russia had supplemented their agreements concerning colonial matters by various military and naval conventions, made a bitter pill for any patriotic German to swallow.

Desperately Germany tried to weaken the opposition. Several years before Russia arranged the Triple Entente with Great Britain certain German officials had claimed that Germany could maintain her position as one of the leading world powers by *Germany and the United States* disrupting the *Entente Cordiale* and by bringing the United States into an alliance with Germany and China, designed to maintain China's territorial integrity and to oppose the Anglo-Japanese *bloc* in the Orient. William II and his chancellor, Bülow, believed that they would encounter little trouble in arranging such a pact. The United States was outside the *Entente Cordiale* and, like Germany, was trying to defend her interests in China. Consequently Germany and the United States had at least one interest in common. Both were blocked in their Far-Eastern policies by the Japanese and British coalition, a combination which might some day close China to the Germans and the Americans.

At the conclusion of the Russo-Japanese War (1905), therefore, Germany made a determined attempt to establish friendly relations with the United States. The trouble between Japan and the United States over immigration (1906–1907) enabled William II to emphasize his idea of the "yellow peril." Germany and the United States, he said, must unite in opposition to Japan and Japan's unscrupulous partner, Great Britain. Furthermore, Japan, aided by her friends, Great Britain and France, was planning to gain control of the Pacific Ocean and of China. Bülow, William's chancellor, announced, therefore, that Germany was willing to go hand in hand with the United States in maintaining China's territorial integrity. William himself suggested that China try to arrange a convention with the United States.

President Roosevelt, however, refused to consider an alliance which would force the United States into direct opposition to Great Britain, Japan, and France. Therefore he rejected the Kaiser's suggestions, saying that the time was not yet ripe. But the Germans were persistent. According to Speck-Sternburg, their ambassador at Washington, Kiaochau, the German holding in China, would offer the American navy a strategic base in the event of war with Japan. If the conflict were fought on American soil, he said, the United States would find German soldiers useful, since Japan would probably land her forces in Mexico or Canada.

The United States, however, found other friends in the Pacific. In 1908 the American fleet made a memorable tour of the world. Visiting Australia, it received an enthusiastic greeting, "exceeding in fact the welcome extended to the Prince of Wales when he went to open the Commonwealth Parliament." England, said one writer, was astonished and a bit nonplused. But the premier of New Zealand partially accounted for this attitude by declaring openly, "Australia looks to America as her natural ally in the coming struggle against Japanese domination."

At this critical moment a very clever and enterprising Japanese diplomat, Baron Takahira, arrived in the United States as Japan's ambassador. Immediately he proceeded to create good feeling by emphasizing an "unwritten alliance between the two countries." Moreover, he openly stated that the Anglo-Japanese alliance was not directed against the United States. He therefore suggested a Japanese-American understanding, which had been discussed even before his arrival. On November 30, 1908, the famous Root-Takahira agreement was arranged, in which the United States and Japan promised to maintain the *status quo* in the Pacific and to preserve by all peaceful means at their disposal the independence and integrity of China and the principle of equal opportunity for commerce and industry of all nations in that empire. In return the United States recognized the position of Japan in Korea.

The American-Japanese Agreement

This agreement was very significant. By arranging a settlement with Japan the United States had refused to join Germany in an alliance opposed to the *Entente Cordiale* and Japan. Thenceforth the American republic identified its Far-Eastern interests with those of Great Britain and Japan.

The SERBIAN COCK, *backed by the* RUSSIAN BEAR, *defying the* AUSTRIAN EAGLE
After a cartoon from " Mr. Punch's History of England "

CHAPTER XXVIII

The Drift toward War

THE accession of William II to the throne presaged a rising interest of Germany in the Near East. Inspired by the concept of *Weltpolitik*, many Germans, including the young Kaiser, pictured this region as a German bridge to world power. Aiming at the establishment of a *Mittel-Europa* extending from the Baltic to the Persian Gulf, Germany developed a "friendly" interest in Turkey,— the prelude to a German-Turkish entente. Royal visits there marked the beginning of a close relationship between the two empires. In 1889 the German emperor and empress went to Constantinople, the Ottoman capital, where they were entertained by Abdul Hamid II in sumptuous fashion. Bismarck, disapproving of this trip because he did not wish to antagonize Russia, assured the latter that the Kaiser's main purpose in visiting the East was a desire to see ancient Athens. After the visit, however, a commercial treaty was concluded (1890), the Deutsche Bank founded a branch at Constantinople, and German capitalists, traders, and artisans invested or settled in the Turkish Empire.

In 1898 William II made his second "pilgrimage." In the absence of the discreet Bismarck the affair was well advertised rather than hushed up. Then took place the enthusiastic reception at Constantinople, the triumphant entry into Jerusalem through a breach in the wall made by the infidels, the dedication of a Lutheran church at Jerusalem, the hoisting of the imperial standard on Mount Zion, the gift of hallowed land to the Roman Catholic church, and finally the visit to the grave of Saladin at Damascus, with a typical William Hohenzollern speech in which the Moslems were assured of the German emperor's eternal friendship. These events were so ridiculous

Germany and the Near East

500

that they passed off lightly. It is said that the French were highly amused and that the English chuckled, for they knew that the visit would make the Russians very angry.

By 1898 Abdul Hamid II and the Kaiser were ready to mix business with pleasure. Deprived of Tunis by the French, of Egypt by the British, of Crete by the Greeks (aided and abetted by European powers), the Sultan concluded that he could rely only on Germany. France, Great Britain, Russia, and Austria, — all these nations had robbed Turkey; Germany alone seemed trustworthy.

Turkey was especially in need of a friend. Greeks, Serbs, Bulgars, and other national groups in Macedonia were turbulent, and the Albanians in the Balkans and the Arabs and Armenians in Asia Minor were ready to revolt. During 1894–1896 Abdul Hamid initiated attempts to reëstablish law and order by several well-executed massacres. These brutal episodes again aroused the Christians in Europe and provoked sharp warnings from Great Britain and Russia. The failure of the powers to do more than remonstrate did not surprise the Sultan, however, for he knew that the various Christian states were too jealous of one another to intervene.

Germany, desirous of strengthening her relations with the Turkish government, refused even to express an official opinion. After the Kaiser's second visit she received her reward, obtaining the concession of a railway through Asia Minor. In 1888 a line connecting central Europe and Constantinople had been completed. At that time a group of German capitalists obtained a valuable concession of the right to construct and administer a railroad from a port across the Bosporus from the Turkish capital into Angora. This project, completed by 1893, was the beginning of a plan to construct a line to Bagdad.

By 1902 a German-controlled railroad had been built across the Balkans, reaching Asia Minor, and was ready to be extended to the Persian Gulf and the Red Sea. In 1903 Abdul Hamid granted the German company permission to continue its line to Bagdad and thence to a point on the Persian Gulf. Turkey also accorded the company mining concessions within a twenty-kilometer zone on each side of the railway, and the right to develop its interests at Bagdad and Basra and to navigate the rivers of Asiatic Turkey in the service of the railroad. Plans were made to extend the line to the south as far as the Red Sea.

The Berlin-to-Bagdad railway aroused great enthusiasm in Turkey and in Germany. Believing that the road would be a means of reorganizing and consolidating his empire, Abdul Hamid was particularly delighted. To the Germans this project constituted the first step in the creation of a huge economic empire which would include the Near East. Rich in oils, in cottons, and in agricultural products, this region offered Germany the raw materials she needed. Moreover, the development of this ancient land would result in the establishment of a rich market for German manufactures. "What greater inducements could have been offered to German imperialists, living in an imperialist world? Turkey was destined to fall within the economic orbit of an industrialized Germany." Consequently German merchants, investors, and missionaries rushed into the Ottoman Empire.

By 1903 the British, French, and Russians were alarmed at the progress of German interests in the Near East. Al-

International Rivalry in the Near East

though a few British and French capitalists accepted German invitations to invest money in the railway and to share in its profits, the French and British governments were distinctly hostile to the idea. The latter realized that Germany would soon control a short highway to the East. Should the Kaiser secure a naval base on the Persian Gulf, he would then be in a position to assume an active rôle in Persian affairs and might even threaten British interests in India.

Great Britain resolved to check this German menace. The sheik of Kuweit, on the Persian Gulf, whom the British had under their "special protection" and with whom they had "special agreements," announced that he would not permit the railroad to cross his country. Meanwhile the British government frankly stated that it would not permit any foreign power to establish a naval base or a fortified port on the Persian Gulf. France and Russia joined Great Britain in opposing the Berlin-to-Bagdad railway. Temporarily it appeared that the project would become an international issue.

By 1905 the discovery of oil and other minerals in Asia Minor had increased the importance of that region and led to a scramble for economic concessions. Controlling churches, hospitals, schools, and public buildings in that part of the Turkish Empire, Germany and Austria-Hungary also obtained the major railway concessions, especially those in Anatolia and Mesopotamia. The French built lines in Syria, the English wandered up and down Mesopotamia, and the Russians were ready to enter Turkish Armenia.

A number of treaties tended to allay the bitter international rivalry in Asia Minor. In 1910 William II and Nicholas II met at Potsdam, where they agreed that, in return for Russian recognition of German rights in the Bagdad railway, Germany should recognize Russian interests in Persia. In 1913–1914 Great Britain arranged an agreement with Turkey, settling their disputes in Arabia and Mesopotamia and along the Persian Gulf. Then France entered into an agreement, in February, 1914, with Germany, in which the latter recognized the French spheres of influence in Syria and eastern Anatolia in return for reciprocal recognition of German interests along the Anatolian and Bagdad railroads. A similar settlement between England and Germany was reached in June, 1914, with respect to their spheres of influence in Asia Minor and Mesopotamia. Presumably prompted from behind the scenes by capitalists of the two countries, the diplomats negotiated a treaty by which British interests in Mesopotamia were safeguarded, to compensate Great Britain for recognizing German control of the eastern section of the Berlin-to-Bagdad railroad. To placate the British, Germany also promised not to extend her railway to the Persian Gulf. Diplomatic conversations and corresponding conventions between Great Britain, Russia, and France accompanied these treaties, which practically divided Asia Minor into spheres of influence. Before some of the agreements became operative, however, they were abruptly terminated by the outbreak of the World War.

This conflict arose out of the failure of the Triple Alliance and the Triple Entente to maintain a precarious European equilibrium. Between 1908 and 1914 the increase of armaments, the Anglo-German naval rivalry, the absorption of lands in North Africa and middle Asia by Western powers, the antagonism of nationalities and minorities in Asia Minor, in the Balkans, and in the Dual Monarchy, together with the knowledge that control of the Balkans by any one Western state might overturn the balance of power in Europe, all tended to increase the danger of war. Many European diplomats were aware of this situation. As Great Britain and France secured the Turkish borderlands in North Africa, and as the Central Powers increased their economic influence in the Balkans and in Asia Minor, European statesmen realized that intervention in the Balkans by a single nation from either group might embroil the Triple Alliance and the Triple Entente. This danger of war was clearly demonstrated by a number of international crises in North Africa and in the Balkans.

Among the earlier of these critical events was a series of international misunderstandings which grew out of conditions in Morocco after 1904. In the eighties *International Rivalry in Morocco* that country, formerly a part of the Ottoman Empire, was recognized by the powers as an independent sultanate. A backward region, it became the scene of conflicting French, Spanish, British, and German economic interests. By 1900 Germany had intimated that she was interested in the Atlantic coast of Morocco and would oppose penetration there by other powers. Interpreting this pronouncement as a notice of Germany's intention to establish a German coaling station on the Atlantic, the British, becoming alarmed, were willing to see Morocco pass under the control of a friendly foreign power. France was soon considered as a likely candidate. In 1902 this nation had her eyes definitely fixed upon Morocco. During the next two years she arranged a secret agreement with Italy in which she recognized Italian aspirations in Tripoli in return for Italian backing in Morocco. To win Spanish support she planned a division of this region with Spain, but the latter suggested that Great Britain and Germany be consulted. Delcassé, the French foreign minister, accepted the first part of this recommendation, and in 1904 France and Great Britain arranged the *Entente Cordiale*, discussed elsewhere, which adjusted their colonial differences.[1]

France thus had agreements over Morocco with all the powers interested in that region save Germany. Asserting that the latter "has no concern in Morocco," she did not bother to consult Germany. Delcassé might have thought that the latter power, aware that France had British support, would let the matter drop. More likely, perhaps, he feared that Germany would ask for concessions which he should be disinclined to grant.

Bülow and Holstein, the German ministers, believed that their government should have been considered. As one of the signatory powers of the Madrid agreement which dealt with Morocco, the legal position of Germany was unimpeachable. Despite the Kaiser's indifference his ministers promoted and were prepared to defend German economic interests in Morocco. By 1905 the government resolved to assert its right to be consulted in this matter of "international concern" and to force the European nations, especially France, to recognize the policy of the open door in Morocco. As the first step William II was to visit Tangier. Personally he opposed this plan, declaring that "in Tangier the devil is already loose." Nevertheless his ministers insisted that he go, and so "he abandoned himself to the waves, the wind, and the Moroccans." By his visit Germany proclaimed her interest in this region and her right to participate in all discussions involving its welfare.

To force the hand of France, Germany agitated for an international conference to settle the whole problem, and called upon the United States to support her in establishing the open door in Morocco. President Roosevelt gave Germany his moral support and tried to arrange an understanding between Great Britain and Germany. His efforts were unavailing, however; Great Britain, accusing him of being pro-

[1] See pages 492–493.

German, rejected his plan. France now consented to deal directly with Germany; but the latter, not trusting the French government, declined to take part in any negotiations.

Finally, in 1906, convinced of their ability to control the situation, France and Great Britain consented to attend an international congress at Algeciras. Germany *The Algeciras Congress* assumed that in a serious emergency England, France, and Russia would not coöperate, and by not so co-operating would weaken the solidarity of the Triple Entente. She was mistaken, however; for Great Britain, Spain, and Italy backed France, and even the American and Russian delegates sympathized with French claims. Consequently Germany, outvoted, had to content herself with a "theoretical" victory. The policy of the open door was accepted in principle, but the political predominance of France in Morocco became a reality.

Germany, however, refused to consider the question settled. In 1908 another serious disturbance made Morocco a scene of international friction. A number of Germans had deserted the French foreign legion at Casablanca, and the imperial government proceeded to intervene on their behalf. France, however, supported by Russia and Great Britain, took a firm stand. Again Germany was thwarted, and on this occasion she agreed to refer the matter to arbitration by the International Court at the Hague. In a convention which she signed with France in 1909, however, she did manage to secure equality of commercial rights.

A provocative challenge to the French in the form of the dispatch to Agadir of a small German gunboat, the *Panther*, on July 1, 1911, reopened the entire question. *The Agadir Affair* Although it was announced that the government sent the ship merely to render assistance to German subjects in case of need, and to protect German interests during native uprisings, in reality the act signified that Germany was planning to wring concessions from France. Whatever the reasons, the arrival of the German boat at Agadir caused a good deal of apprehension both in France and in England, the former considering it as a thrust at her position in Morocco, and the latter fearing the establishment of a German naval base on the Atlantic.

Germany soon discovered that she would have either to be involved in a war or to negotiate a compromise. She took the latter course and effected an agreement with France. In return for territorial concessions in the Congo, which German diplomats hoped would appease the chauvinistic elements at home, the Kaiser's government recognized France's preëminent position in Morocco. This settlement ended the Moroccan affair. Both the diplomatic recovery of France and the strength of the *Entente Cordiale* were demonstrated. Germany now realized that until she had a powerful navy she could neither advance her interests overseas nor shatter the solidarity of the hostile Anglo-French *bloc*.

While these successive Moroccan crises were menacing the peace of the world the possibility of war in the Balkans alarmed the European nations. Relations among the small powers there had never been *Intrigues and Disturbances in the Balkans* effectively stabilized. On several occasions after 1878, alliances of the Balkan states had been proposed. Greece, purportedly backed by Great Britain, tried to arrange an alliance with Serbia and Bulgaria directed against the Turks. At times Russia favored a Slavic coalition to include Bulgaria and Serbia and designed to liberate the Slavs in Austria-Hungary. These plans failed to materialize, however, for jealousies among the Balkan states prevented their consummation.

Disturbances in Turkey had complicated the Near-Eastern situation. In 1908 a revolution by the Young Turks resulted in the establishment of a constitution, followed a few months later by the overthrow of Abdul Hamid II. Ardent Turkish nationalists, but at the same time pseudo-liberals, they equaled the cruelty of Abdul Hamid in their attempts to Turkify the subject peoples in the Balkans. Resulting massacres and disorders not only afforded the Dual Monarchy an excellent opportunity to annex Bosnia-Herzegovina but also kindled the desire of the Balkan states to expel the troublesome Turks from Europe.

By this time Russia had begun to revive her aggressive policies in the Near East. Checked in the Orient, and having

The Annexation of Bosnia-Herzegovina by Austria

established friendly relations with England and France, the Russian government determined to take advantage of the rivalry between the Central Powers and the *Entente Cordiale*. As a preliminary step Isvolski, the foreign minister, planned to obtain for Russia the right, which had been prohibited by the earlier treaties, of sending warships through the Straits. To this end he approached the Austrian minister, Aehrenthal, in 1908, with the proposal that if the Dual Monarchy would support Russia on the Straits question, Russia would ignore her brother Slavs in the Balkans and allow Austria to incorporate Bosnia-Herzegovina outright. At Buchlau the astute Aehrenthal accepted this proposition and proclaimed the annexation of the two provinces before Isvolski could obtain permission from the other great powers, especially England, for the opening of the Straits. Opposed to Isvolski's plans, England advised the Turks to fortify the passage and to resist Russian pressure.

Isvolski soon realized that Aehrenthal had stolen a march on him. The only way left by which he could yet thwart the Austrian diplomat was to insist upon the calling of another European conference to consider these proposed changes of the treaty of 1878. Then Austria as well as Russia would be forced to coöperate or submit to the will of the other nations. But Austria-Hungary refused even to consider this proposal. She was in Bosnia-Herzegovina, and there she proposed to stay. At this juncture Germany came to the aid of Austria and suggested that the powers should individually grant their approval of the Austrian action instead of engaging in a drawn-out conference for this purpose.

Isvolski's prestige suffered as a result of the affair. The Slavs denounced him for allowing Austria-Hungary to occupy the two provinces in return for her support in his Straits plan. Feeling very bitter toward Austria, the resentful Isvolski awaited his day of *revanche*. After resigning as foreign minister, in 1910 he was appointed Russian ambassador to France. There he had an opportunity of effectively expressing his hatred of the Dual Monarchy. Coöperating with the energetic French statesman Poincaré, he used his influence to make the Franco-Russian alliance an aggressive coalition. One of its primary aims soon came to be the weakening of the position of the Central Powers in the Balkans.

In 1908, developments in that peninsula tended to increase the danger of an international war. Before the annexation of Bosnia-Herzegovina, Bulgaria, under a German ruler, Ferdinand I, proclaimed herself independent of Turkey. Austria and Russia *Increasing Tension in the Near East* thereupon developed a profound interest in this country. In view of the bitter opposition of the Serbians, who were incensed at the annexation of Bosnia-Herzegovina, the Dual Monarchy would have welcomed closer relations with Bulgaria. But at first Russia succeeded in gaining Bulgaria's affections. The Central Powers seemed to have earned the united opposition of the leading Balkan states, including Turkey, by the annexation of the provinces.

Ottoman antagonism did not endure. As ardent nationalists the Young Turks instituted a number of reforms which would generate the spirit of patriotism. They attempted to Ottomanize the various minorities and nationalities in the empire, who preferred to retain their own customs, languages, and laws. To achieve this end they looked for outside help, especially financial, and requested aid in Great Britain and France. Unable to float the desired loans, and unsuccessful in their efforts to Ottomanize their subject peoples, the Young Turks imitated Abdul Hamid II not only in their resort to force and violence but also in their reliance on the Central Powers for financial aid. Germany again became Turkey's close friend and adviser.

After 1908 Serbia was bitterly opposed both to Austrian imperialism and to Turkish nationalism. Frustrated by the Austrian annexation of Bosnia-Herzegovina in the hope of establishing a Yugoslav union, *The Turko-Italian War* shut off from the sea and economically dependent upon trade with the Dual Monarchy, the Serbs desired to emancipate their brother Slavs in Turkey and

Austria and to obtain an outlet to the Adriatic or the Ægean. In 1911 a Turko-Italian war over Tripoli afforded Serbia and other ambitious Balkan states a splendid opportunity for despoiling Turkey.

The four Balkan powers,— Serbia, Greece, Bulgaria, and Montenegro,— encouraged by the Turkish military weakness demonstrated in the war with Italy, and covetous of territorial rewards, formed a coalition against the Turks. Realizing that a local struggle in the Balkans might provoke a general war by involving either Austria or Russia, the Triple Alliance and the Triple Entente feared a conflict at this time. Disregarding the warnings of the great powers, however, the Balkan states sent to the Turkish government an ultimatum in which they demanded autonomy for Macedonia. Upon the Turkish refusal to acquiesce they declared war in 1912.

Thus began the first Balkan conflict. Attacked on all sides, Turkey was not able to muster effective opposition. The Montenegrins invaded Albania ; the Serbs, *The Balkan Wars* northern Macedonia; the Bulgarians, Thrace ; and the Greeks, southern Macedonia. The Bulgarians, proving themselves capable fighters, won most of the important victories. In 1913 the Turks were forced to sue for peace, and the European states, welcoming a cessation of hostilities, promoted a peace conference at London. Compelled to cede all of her European territory except Constantinople and adjacent regions, Turkey became primarily an Asiatic power.

As was to be expected, the Balkan states quarreled over the division of the spoils. Bulgaria claimed all of Macedonia, as assigned to her in 1877 by the Treaty of San Stefano. Opposed to this demand, Greece asked for a share which would include Salonica. Serbia, deprived of her conquests in Albania by Austrian influence and seeking to reach the Ægean, also demanded territory in Macedonia. Although not one of the belligerents, Rumania wanted territorial compensation south of the Dobruja which would give her an outlet to the Black Sea.

Bulgaria received the major share of the spoils, but her

triumph was short-lived. Jealous of her success, Serbia, Rumania, Greece, Montenegro, and Turkey assailed Bulgaria in a second Balkan war in 1913. After brief resistance Bulgaria capitulated and signed the Treaty of Bucharest. Thereby she lost nearly all the territory she had won from Turkey, save part of Macedonia and western Thrace. Greece now obtained southern Macedonia, including Salonica; Montenegro got half of Novi Pazar; Rumania received the coveted Bulgarian territory south of the Dobruja; and Serbia obtained a large part of Macedonia and half of Novi Pazar. By the treaty of Constantinople with Bulgaria, Turkey recovered Adrianople and eastern Thrace.

The second Balkan conflict had significant consequences. Smarting from the losses which she had suffered, Bulgaria turned to Austria-Hungary for support. Serbia, on the other hand, because Austria had thwarted her ambition to secure an outlet to the Adriatic Sea through Albania, hated the Dual Monarchy more than ever. Russia continued to advance her interests in the Balkans, principally by encouraging the Serbs to spread propaganda among the Slavs in the Dual Monarchy. Russia and Serbia hoped that this policy would lead to a successful uprising of the Slavs in the Dual Monarchy and in the Balkans.

In 1913 the Central Powers were aware of Russian opposition. By that time the Turks had decided to reorganize the civil administration. The English were to help develop the navy, and the Germans were to reorganize the army. General Liman von Sanders, sent by the German government to direct the military reforms, was placed in charge of the first Turkish corps at Constantinople. The Russian foreign office, alarmed and fearful of a German-Turk alliance, protested against the appointment of a German officer to a Turkish position. To avoid complications, Von Sanders gave up his command of the Turkish army corps at Constantinople to become inspector of the Turkish army. Although the transfer ended an embarrassing situation, it did not decrease Russian suspicion of the Central Powers.

Europe, in 1914, was in a state of international anarchy.

Through the defection of Italy the Triple Alliance was rapidly being transformed into a Dual Alliance. As a result Germany was more dependent upon the Dual Monarchy *International Anarchy in 1914* than she had been in the past. On the other hand, Austria-Hungary feared lest her ally succumb to British blandishments. Encouraged by Russia and indirectly supported by France, Serbia was becoming more aggressive and hostile in her attitude toward the Hapsburgs. Meanwhile Rumania had practically withdrawn from the orbit of the Triple Alliance. Austria, therefore, could see in the Balkans, with the possible exception of Bulgaria, only enemies who were determined upon her ruin. Desperate, she was ready to seize the first opportunity of suppressing this opposition.

Germany had tried to settle international difficulties in such a way as to placate the Entente powers. Rivalries in Asia Minor had virtually been ended by a number of agreements. Even though the naval question had not been settled, a friendly understanding between Great Britain and Germany was being considered. England had sent Lord Haldane to Berlin in 1912 to discuss the matter, but the German government had insisted that a definite promise of British neutrality should accompany any proposed naval holiday. Refusing to enter into such an agreement, Sir Edward Grey, the British foreign minister, declared that England was willing to promise not to attack Germany or to join any hostile combination. Beyond this Great Britain would not go. Under no circumstances, he added, would England promise to remain neutral should Germany become involved in war. He did not propose to sacrifice the friendship of France unless Germany had something positive to offer. Consequently Germany and England were inclined to be unfriendly, the former feeling that the latter was blocking her colonial aspirations, and England intimating that Germany was constructing a fleet in order to destroy British naval supremacy. Yet the interests of the two countries were not irreconcilable. In fact, England and Germany were on better terms between 1912 and 1914 than they had been for some time.

In 1914 the Dual Monarchy was determined to maintain the *status quo* at home and in the Balkans. This policy might have been feasible between 1878 and 1903, the time in which a friendly dynasty ruled Serbia and that country was in the Austrian sphere of influence. It might also have been successful even as late as 1905, when Russia was preoccupied in the Far East. But after this period, with the Serbs desirous of expanding and with Russia developing increased ambitions in the Near East, the preservation of the empire was possible only if a triple monarchy were set up with the Slavs as a partner, and if the Serbs were placated in the Balkans. The Austrian government refused to do either. In fact, it intensified the hatred of Serbia by annexing Bosnia-Herzegovina in 1908.

As the incompatibility between Austrian imperialism and Serbian nationalism became increasingly apparent, many leaders on both sides came to believe that war was inevitable. A number of Austrian officials *Austro-Serb Antagonism* were of the opinion that Russia, as soon as she had regained the strength she had lost in the conflict with Japan, would support Serbia and force a war on the Dual Monarchy. To anticipate such a conflict, they believed that Austria should arrange a settlement with Serbia before Russia was ready. Delay seemed dangerous; for Germany was adjusting her rivalries in Asia Minor with England, Russia, and France, and might later refuse to help her ally. Certain leaders in Russia and France, fearing an entente between Great Britain and Germany, favored a war with Germany before England became committed to the other side.

By 1914 Count Berchtold, Austrian foreign minister, firmly believed that a showdown was inevitable between the Dual Monarchy and Serbia. In his opinion the Bal- *Count Berchtold* kan wars (1912–1913) had only tended to increase the antagonism between the two countries. Serbia, having failed to obtain territory which would enable her to reach the sea, was more determined than ever to oppose the state which was threatening her very existence. Nevertheless, to avoid war and as a prelude to an eventual readjustment of the Balkan situation, Berchtold sought to arrange new alliances. Believing that Germany had left Austria in the lurch by refusing to allow that country to intervene on behalf of Bulgaria, Berchtold even turned to Russia for support. That power, however, preferring to back Serbia, spurned his overtures.

For a long time Russia had hesitated between a Western policy, which would have resulted in the division of the Balkans into spheres of influence, and a Slavo-phile program, which would have led to the conquest of Constantinople and the union of the southern Slavs under Russian protection. Until the Russo-Turkish war of 1877–1878 the Western tendency was uppermost, and Russia, outwardly at least, expressed no plan to obtain Constantinople. In 1896, however, the cabinet of Nicholas II considered seizing the Bosporus; but the hesitant Czar, faced with complications in the Orient and with internal problems, demurred. Therefore, in 1903, Russia signed the Mürzsteg treaty with Austria, whereby Austria and Russia agreed to coöperate in securing reforms in Macedonia. After the failure of her policies in the Orient, however, Russia concentrated her attention on the Near East. The Slavophile policy again rose to the surface as Russia, becoming imbued with a desire to conquer Constantinople, planned ostensibly to "start a crusade against corrupt Western ideas."

Russia's Near-Eastern Policies

After 1910 the Austrophobe Isvolski, the Russian ambassador in Paris, and the vacillating Sazonov, the Russian foreign minister, were willing to risk a war to obtain Constantinople. To this end Isvolski endeavored to strengthen the alliance with France so as to reassure the Czar of support by his ally. It was fortunate for the Russian diplomats that in 1912 Poincaré was placed in charge of French foreign affairs. An energetic realist and nationalist, he did all in his power to encourage the *revanche* movement in France. Believing that Franco-German antagonism over Alsace-Lorraine could only be settled by war, he, like Isvolski, helped to consolidate the Franco-Russian alliance.

The Balkanized Dual Alliance

Sazonov and Poincaré took the first step in this direction by defining the scope of the alliance. According to the agreement Russia would give France military help in vital questions only, but she could not promise assistance in extra-European disputes. France, on the other hand, would not coöperate with Russia unless Germany were implicated in the conflict. Knowing that any Balkan disturbance which led to Austrian intervention would involve Germany, Russia accepted this arrangement. Therefore French support of Russia was assured, and since both powers were willing to be drawn into a war to prevent further aggrandizement by the Central Powers in this region, the Russo-French alliance became "Balkanized."

Public opinion, however, had to be considered. Poincaré felt that the French people should be "tuned up" to the idea of embarking on a war over a Balkan issue. Consequently, as stated before, part of the money borrowed by Russia from France was used to influence the French press in popularizing the Russo-French accord. To strengthen this union Delcassé was sent, in 1913, to Russia to work out additional coöperative schemes regarded as necessary in the event of war. General Joffre also visited Russia, where he suggested military reforms and the building of strategic railroads through Russian Poland.

Great Britain, although her military and naval preparations were defensive, was not entirely committed to the Franco-Russian program. At the opening of *Great Britain and the* the twentieth century she had been hostile *Franco-Russian Pro-* toward Germany because of the growth of the *gram* latter's naval power. By 1914, however, the British, realizing that their persistent opposition to the German naval program might lead to war, practically decided to abandon further resistance. Moreover, the center of rivalry had shifted to the Near East, where Great Britain feared Russian as well as German intrigue. Rather than allow either nation to dominate that region she preferred to retain the *status quo* there.

Although Great Britain desired peace, she could not ignore the possibility of war. Therefore, with the tacit approval of the government, military and naval officials entered into arrangements designed to strengthen the British position. They agreed, for example, on the locations of the British, French, and Russian fleets in the event of war. Technically these commitments did not bind Great Britain, but they made it very difficult for her to avoid being drawn into a conflict over the maintenance of the equilibrium. At the same time England, lacking a definite pact, was unable to control either Russian or French foreign policies. Instead Grey, as long as British interests were not menaced, allowed Russia and France to do what they pleased. Although he announced that England would not take part in an offensive war against Germany, Russia and France believed that a conflict between Austria and a Balkan power would probably involve Russia and Germany and ultimately England. Therefore France and Russia relied on British support.

The military and naval arrangements were but a link in a great diplomatic chain which eventually involved all the leading states in a complicated and dangerous set-up. Should a conflict occur, Serbia felt that she could rely on Russian support. Russia was assured of French backing and was also convinced that, if Germany were involved, Great Britain would intervene to preserve the balance of power. Furthermore, it was generally presumed that if Germany entered the struggle she would violate the neutrality of Belgium. The menace of a strong power in this strategic region would virtually force England to take a hand.

Great Britain was not the only state which had placed its future in the hands of aggressive friends. Germany also found *Austro-German Relations* herself led astray by her friend and ally, Austria. At first Germany had the upper hand and prevented a war between European powers over the Near East. By 1914, however, as the Triple Alliance crumbled, Austrian support seemed essential to Germany. Aware of her importance, the Dual Monarchy tended to become more independent and more aggressive in her foreign policies. She knew that Germany could no longer say "Watch your step."

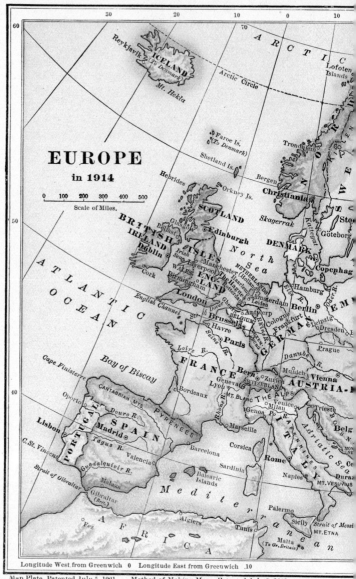

EUROPE

in 1914

0 100 200 300 400 500
Scale of Miles.

OCEAN

Tundras

Arctic Circle

White Sea

Archangel

Dwina R.

Lake Onega

Lake Ladoga

St.Petersburg

VALDAI HILLS

Nizhni Novgorod

Moscow

RUSSIA

Saratov

Kiev

Dnieper R.

Dniester R.

Pruth R.

Odessa

Bucharest

MTS.

Adrianople

TURKEY

Bosporus

Constantinople

Dardanelles

Smyrna

Crete

Cyprus

(To Gr. Britain)

TURKEY IN ASIA

A S I A

Ob R.

Ural Mountains

Petchora R.

Perm

Kama R.

Kazan

Volga R.

Oreuburg

Ural R.

Volga R.

Don R.

Sea of Azov

Crimea

Sevastopol

Black Sea

CAUCASUS MTS.

MT. ELBRUS

Tiflis

Trans-Caucasia

Astrakhan

Caspian Sea

Baku

Trebizond

Erzerum

MT. ARARAT

S I B E R I A

Tobolsk

A S I A

Aral Sea

Comparative Area.

OHIO

41,040 Square Miles.

40   50   60   70   80

60

50

40

30   40   50

70

Black Sea

On June 28, 1914, occurred the tragedy which actually precipitated the World War. On that day the Archduke Francis Ferdinand, the heir to the Hapsburg throne, and his wife were assassinated at Sara- *The Crime at Sarajevo* jevo, Bosnia. As a result of the new complications in Austro-Serb relations economic rivalries, national hatreds, competition in armaments, greeds, fears, groupings of powers, jealousies of rulers, and stupidities of statesmen, hitherto moving under the surface, now clashed openly.

Even though the world was shocked at this brutal attack upon two defenseless persons, the powers were too concerned with their own problems to take an active part in this affair. In Austria, however, public feeling ran high. To many of her leaders this assassination marked the failure of her attempt to maintain the balance of power in the Balkans by means of an alliance. Regarding the outrage as a climax, Austria redoubled her efforts to punish Serbia, whom she considered responsible for the subversive Slav attack on the Dual Monarchy.

Berchtold, convinced of Serbia's guilt, determined to settle this Balkan problem "once and for all." Believing that, since Russia had been "bluffed out" of helping her protégé in the Bosnian crisis in 1909, she could be disregarded in 1914, he decided to strike. He was mistaken, however, for the earlier rebuff had made Russian diplomats determined that they would not "back down" a second time. He soon decided that he would not immediately rush into a conflict with Serbia. In this decision he was influenced by Count Tisza, the old Magyar statesman, who, fearing that a war with Serbia could not be localized, felt that a harsh note would serve Austria's purpose well enough. Berchtold therefore determined merely to send a stern communication to Serbia, and to announce at the same time that the Dual Monarchy had no intention of annexing territories in the Balkans.

Although assured of German support, Berchtold delayed sending the note. Perhaps he wanted President Poincaré, then about to leave Russia, to be at sea when "the fireworks started." According to some writers Berchtold's delay was a mistake, because it gave the neutral nations an opportunity to recover from their intense indignation at this murder. Consequently, when the note was sent, they were more concerned with their own interests than with seeing the guilty brought to justice, and less sympathetic toward Austria. The failure to settle with the Serbs at once also gave Poincaré an opportunity to emphasize the fact that Russia could count upon French support in the event of war.

While waiting to send the note the Austrian government had ordered an investigation of the assassination. Although the evidence was limited, enough was secured *Serbia and the Assassination* to involve Serbia in the affair. Since the war, however, research has proved that in 1914 there was considerable Slav propaganda in Serbia against Austria. One organization, a black-hand society, was especially active. Its members were scattered throughout Serbia and Austria, and many Serbian government officials were either members or supporters of this "Society of Union and Death." In 1914 its organizer and moving spirit was none other than Colonel Dimitrejevitch, chief of the Intelligence Department of the Serbian General Staff. It was he who helped to organize the plot in Belgrade and provided three Bosnian youths with the bombs and Browning revolvers used at Sarajevo.

Investigation has discovered a political motive for the assassination. Dimitrejevitch had heard of the proposed visit of the Austrian archduke to Bosnia and was convinced that an attack was being planned on Serbia. A murder alone could prevent it. As a matter of fact, Francis Ferdinand really visited the province to call on his people and to witness the military maneuvers, which, tactlessly enough, were held there on a Slav patriotic holiday. Serbian officials did little to prevent the three young "patriots" from entering Bosnia. Apparently aware of the plot, they ordered the arrest of these conspirators only when it was too late. Perhaps in connivance with the boys, the frontier officials allowed them to enter Bosnia from Serbia. At all events the Serbian government failed officially to notify Austria of the plot. A half-hearted warning was sent, but it was not sufficiently specific. Seemingly the

Serb officials, cognizant of the plot to murder the archduke, made no earnest attempts to prevent its consummation.

Berchtold waited until July 23 before he sent the note to Serbia. On July 5 Germany, although suggesting that Italy be consulted, practically gave him a free hand, — the celebrated blank check. Aware that a *The Austrian Note to Serbia* general war might result from an Austro-Serb conflict, the Kaiser nevertheless apparently believed that the affair could be localized. Poincaré of France and the Russian diplomats disagreed, for they were determined that this affair should not be settled by the Central Powers alone. Realizing that this crisis gave the Triple Entente an opportunity to function as the arbiter of Europe, Poincaré told Russia to back Serbia, promising French support should complications ensue.

Although the contents of the Austrian note to Serbia were not divulged before it was sent, the diplomats of most European states were able to surmise its nature. The demands made by the Dual Monarchy were more drastic than was generally expected. The most important of them were the following: (1) that the Serbian government officially condemn the anti-Austrian propaganda by its citizens; (2) that it suppress all publications and societies which incited hatred and contempt of the Dual Monarchy; (3) that all anti-Austrian teachers and books be eliminated from the public schools; (4) that all officials implicated in the anti-Austrian propaganda be dismissed; (5) that two Serbian citizens, named in the ultimatum, be arrested at once; (6) that Serbia accept the collaboration of Austrian officials in the suppression of anti-Austrian propaganda within her borders; and (7) that Serbia accept the help of Austrian officials in the investigation of those implicated in the Sarajevo crime. A forty-eight-hour limit was attached to the ultimatum.

The Entente powers at once suggested that the Dual Monarchy extend the time limit, but Austria bluntly rejected their request. To many it seemed as though Berchtold, by rushing matters, was deliberately antagonizing both Serbia and Russia so as to prepare the way for a general European conflict. Playing a lone hand, he disregarded Germany's suggestion that before imposing drastic terms upon Serbia he consult Italy and offer her "a fat bite" in the Trentino region. Instead he ignored Italy's unsolicited warning that Austria must not threaten the independence of Serbia. Certainly Austrian officials must have realized the possibility of war when they sent the ultimatum.

Serbia, agreeing to most of the Austrian demands, submitted her reply before the time limit expired. Those pro-

The Serbian Reply   visions dealing with the participation of Austro-Hungarian officials in the suppression of anti-Austrian propaganda and in the investigation of the crime she rejected on the ground that, if accepted, they would constitute a violation of her rights as a sovereign state. Nevertheless, in the event that Austria should consider her reply unsatisfactory, she asserted her willingness to refer the whole matter to the Hague International Tribunal or to a decision of the great powers.

The Serbian reply was conciliatory and seemed to lay the basis for negotiations. When William II was informed of its contents, he declared that it removed "every reason for war." Desirous, however, of a complete humiliation of their hated neighbor, the Austro-Hungarian officials declared the answer unsatisfactory and severed relations with Belgrade. Great crowds, delighted with the news of the break with Serbia, paraded the streets of Vienna, "singing songs till the wee small hours of the morning."

Alarmed at the bellicose trend of events, Russia determined to prevent the complete humiliation of Serbia. Al-

Russia's Attitude   though not fully prepared for war, Russia felt that she could not afford to permit Austria-Hungary to aggrandize herself in the Balkans at the expense of Serbia. Therefore the government, protesting its pacific intentions, ordered a partial mobilization of the Russian armies along the Austrian frontier and secretly prepared for the war which seemed imminent.

The Russian military preparations between July 24 and July 28 alarmed Germany. Her strategists realized that Germany's chief advantage in the event of a war on two fronts, against Russia and France, was her preparedness. They had worked out a plan based on the assumption of tardiness in Russian mobilization. This scheme provided for a speedy invasion and defeat of France and then an attack on Russia. By proceeding with mobilization, however, Russia was upsetting this plan. Alarmed, William II feared that a terrible war was looming. Austria-Hungary had gone farther than he had expected, and the military preparations might easily precipitate a crisis from which the diplomats would not be able successfully to extricate their countries. William, however, took no steps to curb Austria until July 28, when it was too late, inasmuch as Berchtold had already persuaded the old emperor, Francis Joseph, to declare war on Serbia. On the next day the struggle opened with the bombardment of Belgrade.

At last the Kaiser decided to act. First he proposed that Austria agree to allow Serbia to carry out her promises, pending which Austria should occupy certain Serbian territory. Berchtold, resentful of the interference, refused to listen to the German *Intervention of Germany* emperor. Meanwhile, at the suggestion of Germany, Sazonov of Russia, on July 26, had attempted to get Austria-Hungary to discuss a revision of the ultimatum so as to enable the Dual Monarchy to obtain her chief demands and at the same time to make the terms acceptable to Serbia. Berchtold evaded this suggestion until after July 28; then he rejected the plan on the ground that war had already been declared. Convinced that Austria desired to conquer Serbia, the Russian authorities proceeded with their preparations in anticipation of a general conflict.

Sazonov, aware that Germany was supporting Austria, believed that he might impel Germany to hold back Austria if he let it be known that Russia intended to back Serbia to the bitter end. Therefore, on July 29, he took a dangerous step when he approved the order for general Russian mobilization against Germany as well as against the Dual Monarchy. France telegraphed her approval of his policy and promised support.

Before July 28 England, recognizing the possibility of a general conflict, tried to mediate in the interest of peace. Grey and other British diplomats at first believed that the matter was purely an Austro-Serb affair, but they soon realized that the dispute could not be localized. Therefore, to avoid misunderstandings, they urged direct conversations between Vienna and St. Petersburg. Poincaré vetoed the suggestion, however, for he wanted the Entente to present "a solid front." Thereby he hoped that the Central Powers would be forced to submit the case to the Triple Entente as a whole.

Intervention of Great Britain

Grey then made other proposals. He suggested that Germany, Italy, France, and Great Britain mediate between Austria and Russia; but when France, in opposition to this plan, stated that mediation between the two principals, Serbia and Austria, was the only suitable course, Grey, on July 26, suggested that the four powers instruct their ambassadors in London to meet in conference with him for the purpose of seeking a solution. Germany, distrusting Italy, declared that she could not participate without Austria's approval. This consent the latter refused to give, and Grey's scheme came to naught. Despite the declaration of war by Austria against Serbia, July 28, Grey, on the following day, recommended mediation, suggesting to Germany that Austria occupy Belgrade, or other towns, as pledges until a settlement satisfactory to her was arranged. Germany, informing her ally that in the event of a refusal Great Britain would join the opposition, strongly urged the acceptance of the proposal.

Berchtold, however, held to his opinion that Austria-Hungary could not back down unless Russia stopped her mobilization and Serbia unreservedly accepted the demands. On July 31 the Austrian government officially adopted his point of view. Therefore Francis Joseph, having proclaimed mobilization against Russia, informed William II that his decisions had been made with full reliance both on German support and on the justice of God.

Meanwhile Russia was preparing for general mobilization. The pacific Nicholas II opposed war, which he feared might precipitate a revolution in Russia; but he was too weak to take a determined stand against his more bellicose advisers and his French ally, who seemed to favor an aggressive course. On July 29, therefore, he *Russian Mobilization* signed an order for general mobilization and then sent a telegram to his "dear cousin Willy" (William II) urging the latter to come to his rescue. In reply the Kaiser asked Nicholas to delay mobilization. Complying with this request, the Czar countermanded his earlier order, much to the chagrin of the chauvinistic Russian military leaders.

On the afternoon of July 30, however, Sazonov again interviewed the Czar and secured another order for general mobilization, which was definitely issued in the evening. On the following day (July 31) Isvolski informed his government that France, in expectation of war, desired that both powers should concentrate their forces against Germany. Henceforth there was seemingly little prospect of avoiding the long-feared conflagration; the Rubicon was crossed.

Until July 31 Bethmann-Hollweg, the German chancellor, had tried to avoid war by carrying on negotiations designed to halt Russian preparations. But the Russian *Declarations of War* decision of the day before, to engage in a general mobilization, forced the hand of Germany. Leadership passed from the civil chancellor to Moltke, head of the military machine, and the German government issued a proclamation of the imminent danger of war. Germany then presented an ultimatum to Russia, demanding the cessation within twelve hours of all measures against Germany and the Dual Monarchy. As no answer was forthcoming, at 7 P. M. on August 1 Germany declared war on Russia. Two days later, unable to extract a tangible guarantee of French neutrality, she also declared war on France. The latter, perhaps to convey the impression that she was about to engage in a defensive struggle, announced the withdrawal of her troops to a distance of ten kilometers back from the frontier.

The expansion of the conflict involved Great Britain and her interests. It was well understood that England could not afford to permit Germany to win a war which would probably result in the latter's supremacy not only in Europe but also in the Near East. Nevertheless, when the struggle opened, Great Britain was not formally committed to either side.

Germany, hopeful of keeping England out of the conflict, tried, on July 29, and again on August 3, to get Great Britain to state the terms on which she would remain out of the war. All replies from Grey, who was unwilling to bind himself, were vague. To the great relief of France, however, on August 2 Grey at last promised to support France should a German fleet attack her coasts or shipping.

During these critical days Grey was apparently in an embarrassing position. He had practically pledged England to the Franco-Russian side but had failed to gain the approval of Parliament. The foreign minister needed a great moral issue which would influence that body and the people into joining the Allied cause. A German invasion of Belgium, Grey hoped, would furnish this altruistic pretext. For some time it had been generally understood that in the event of a European war Germany, because of strong fortifications on the eastern frontier of France, would probably strike at France through Belgium. In fact, Franco-British military arrangements had been made in anticipation of such an eventuality. Consequently Grey must have been certain that this invasion would take place when, on August 3, 1914, he informed Parliament that England's hands were not tied by a treaty. He did remind Parliament, however, that obligations of honor and of interest must be regarded, and he left it to every Englishman to decide as to the honorable and wise thing to do.

Despite British warnings, on August 4 German troops had crossed the Belgian frontier. Although promised independence and an indemnity, Belgium refused Germany permission to move her soldiers across the country and prepared to resist the invaders. The moral issue involving British interests, so vital to Grey, had at last presented itself. Germany had violated the neutrality of Belgium and had challenged a cardinal principle of British foreign policy, namely, the preservation of the independence of the Low Countries. Bitterly denouncing Germany for her invasion of Belgium, whose neutrality had been guaranteed by the great powers in 1839, the British government, on the night of August 4–5, declared war on Germany.

The conflict now became European in scope. On August 6 Austria-Hungary declared war on Russia. Montenegro joined Serbia on the following day in opposing the Dual Monarchy, and two days later the two South-Slavic powers proclaimed the existence *Expansion of the Conflict* of a state of war between themselves and Germany. During the next three days France and Great Britain declared war on Austria. As was expected, Italy, Rumania, and Bulgaria, uncertain as to the ultimate winners, announced their neutrality, on the ground that they were under no obligations to support either side. On September 4 Russia, France, and Great Britain transformed their entente into a wartime alliance by signing the Pact of London, whereby each promised not to conclude separate peace terms.

Meanwhile Japan espoused the Allied cause. The Japanese agreed to destroy German power in the Far East in order to relieve the British from danger in that part of the world. Japan was willing to do this in order to lessen by one the number of powers competing with her in the exploitation of China. On August 15 she demanded that Germany withdraw her warships and surrender her leased territory in Shantung. Upon the refusal of the Kaiser's government to comply, Japan, on August 23, declared war on Germany, and proceeded to carry out these demands by force.

Shortly thereafter Turkey joined the Central Powers. At first she had announced her intention of remaining neutral. Her friendship for Germany and her fear of Russian designs on her territories, however, made it difficult for her to remain out of the conflict. At the outbreak of the war, despite the protests of the Allies, she had allowed two German cruisers to take refuge in the harbor at Constantinople. Furthermore, by closing the Straits to commerce, she severed Russia's communication with the Mediterranean. On October 29, when one of the German cruisers, masquerading as a Turkish ship, shelled Russian towns on the Black Sea, and three Turkish torpedo boats raided the port of Odessa, Russia determined upon war. Between November 3 and November 5 Russia, England, and France declared war on Turkey. Consequently, when New Year's Day (1915) was celebrated, Germany, Austria-Hungary, and Turkey found themselves opposed by Russia, France, Great Britain, Japan, Belgium, Serbia, and Montenegro. At last the long-feared world conflict was a reality.

Scholars interested in the study of the origins of the war were fortunate in having available, soon after the conflict, documents which under normal circumstances would have remained under lock and key in the archives of the interested nations. In order to discredit the capitalistic and monarchical governments which they considered responsible for the conflict, the post-war governments in Germany and Austria and the Bolsheviks in Russia gladly opened their archives. These documents soon convinced most investigators that the red, yellow, and other colored governmental publications, issued early in the war, failed to throw much light on the real reasons for that conflict. They were merely propaganda in which the powers had tried to justify their participation by printing only those documents which ennobled their own acts and damned those of their enemies.

The War Guilt

To the discomfiture of those who had subscribed to the theory that good was wholly on one side and evil on the other, these documents demonstrated that war guilt could not be fastened on any one nation. Evidence caused most scholars to conclude that Serbia, Russia, France, and even Great Britain, as well as Germany and Austria-Hungary, should share the blame. A dispute arose among historians, however, as to the extent to which certain nations and individuals were responsible for the war. While some scholars maintained that Germany and Austria-Hungary were chiefly guilty, others asserted that Russia and France were the principal culprits.

There were those, however, who preferred to place the blame for the war not upon nations or individuals but upon certain underlying defects in Western civilization. To many, militarism, imperialism, and nationalism caused the war. Although German militarism seemed provocative, France, Russia, Great Britain, and the other countries also possessed large armies or navies. But to most patriots of these powers their countries' military and naval forces existed merely to maintain peace and security. And it is true that, although excessive preparedness impelled the nations toward the war, nevertheless it was not responsible for the conflicts of interests or the diplomatic events which culminated in the catastrophe of 1914.

Many contended that the world conflict was one of economic necessity. Western capitalism, bringing about an ever-increasing supply of goods and capital, forced nations to compete for markets and for places in which to invest money. Great Britain and *The War as an Economic Necessity* Germany, for example, were engaged in a bitter industrial, commercial, and colonial struggle prior to the war. On the other hand, some writers maintained that business men in both nations, aware of the harm done to trade by a conflict, were unwilling to risk war. Grey of England well understood the terrible economic and social consequences of a conflict; for, in July, 1914, he said, "Whatever the issue, one thing certain is that it will end in ruining industry, commerce, and the power of capital." Admittedly, secret economic ambitions played a large part in the political aims that dominated the situation in 1914. Certain nations anticipated benefits to be derived from the liquidation of Austria-Hungary and of Turkey. The fact that Great Britain and Germany were dependent upon other countries for food and markets created a feeling of insecurity. Consequently these nations, like their neighbors, tended to rely more and more upon military and naval guarantees.

Although most of the conflicting economic interests, including colonial rivalries, could have been adjusted, their very existence, by reviving questions of prestige and of national sentiment, made nations unfriendly. Taking advantage of growing fear and suspicion, rival governments promoted patriotic propaganda which influenced their citizens in approving of war. Unless they could be elevated to a moral plane, however, economic interests in themselves were perhaps insufficient to precipitate a general conflict.

The war resulted not from preconceived plans but from a complex of disturbing factors. Europe was a collection of nations many of which had very old traditions *Conclusion* that were as hard as steel. Military and naval rivalries, Russia's drive on the Straits, the idea of *revanche* in France, irredentism everywhere, but especially among the Slavs and the Italians, and trade rivalry, all predisposed European nations toward war and made it increasingly difficult for the Triple Alliance and the Triple Entente to maintain the equilibrium of Europe.

All these factors were realities. No diplomat, king, or citizen had invented them or could direct their influence in such a way as to prevent war and to maintain peace. Nevertheless most statesmen, although fearing a war which they regarded as inevitable, endeavored to guard the interests of their countries. They did not deliberately plan a conflict, but rather than relinquish a single advantage for their states they permitted the world to drift toward the catastrophe.

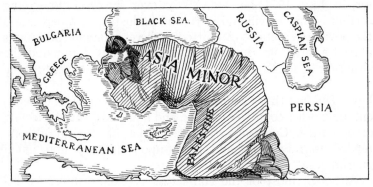

THE NEAR EASTERN PROBLEM IN 1914

From a cartoon in *Punch*

CHAPTER XXIX

The World War, 1914–1916: The Deadlock

THE World War was different from all other struggles. Previous conflicts were won or lost on the basis of armies and generals, of campaigns and strategy. In the World War the importance of military tactics was only slight; battles and campaigns were successful through the sheer force of overwhelming man power as well as the superiority of modern equipment and resources.

The New War

During the conflict the sovereignty of the state became a grim reality. Private enterprises had to give way to the business of war. Vast loans, domestic and foreign, were floated to conduct this undertaking. Industrial factories were transformed into munition plants; sciences and arts were enlisted in the work of discovering effective methods for wholesale killings. Artists, newspaper writers, religious leaders, and teachers were used to uphold patriotic beliefs and to reveal the alleged wickedness of the enemy. The World War was a struggle involving men, women, and children. Nothing was too sacred to be used if it could contribute to ultimate victory.

At first even the military leaders generally believed that the struggle would consist of marches, sieges, strategy, and battles. They assumed that it would be another war of movement, with combats merely fought on a larger scale,— more men, heavier guns, and greater losses. Soon, however, they discovered that the manner of warfare was to be very different. Within a month after the outbreak of hostilities, armies on the Western Front were fighting and living in trenches which extended across northern France from the English Channel to Switzerland.

Although trenches were not entirely new, they were now used much more extensively than ever before. They were no

529

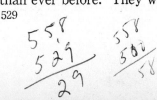

longer hastily-prepared temporary protections, to be vacated when a fort was taken and the enemy expelled or captured. In the new conflict, trenches were continuous fortresses of steel, concrete, and barbed wire, in some places over two hundred miles in length and over a mile in width. Often stronger and more effective than chains of forts, they supplied a continuous network of lines, sometimes with four or five parallel lines linked by interlacings. They were dug far below the surface of the earth, secure from the heaviest artillery. In previous conflicts a series of forts might be taken by siege, but in the World War it was practically impossible to capture an entire line of trenches so as to outflank the enemy. Instead, by bombardment, sapping, and assault, attempts were made to break definite sections of the front in order to force the entire line to give way. This method of attack was very difficult, however, for the enemy generally had time to transfer reserve troops and guns to the threatened sector and to build secondary trenches, so as to prevent a collapse of the front. It was only after the exhaustion of German resources, due largely to the Allied blockade, that the war front of the Central Powers finally gave way before the offensives of their adversaries.

This trench deadlock caused men on both sides to search for ways and means by which they could obtain advantages over their opponents. No single general was able to devise strategy and to strike a blow capable of immediately terminating the war. Victory, if it were to come, would be from coöperation and coördination of all forces. Men of science, not generals, became the leaders. In October, 1914, for example, the Germans fired shrapnel containing poison fumes against the English. In April, 1915, they instituted a gas attack, something new as a device of warfare, along four or five miles, and were able to make a deep breach in the Allied lines. Soon gas was used not only to make the trenches and dugouts untenable but also to prevent the movements of troops and supplies. Moreover, it was dropped by bombing planes on towns behind the enemy lines, in efforts to demoralize the civilian population. Counter measures were devised for protection from gas attacks. Masks were invented for this purpose, but odorless gas was then developed, which often could not be detected until it was too late.

The extensive use of the airplane and the hydroplane was the outstanding technical development of the World War. Theretofore flying had been largely in an experimental stage, but during the conflict both sides depended upon airplanes for reconnaissance along the battle front. Airplanes and Zeppelins were effective military weapons for fighting, bombing, gassing, observation, photography, and locating distances for gunners.

Science made other important contributions to military and naval warfare. The tank, or armored car, introduced by the British in September, 1916, was valuable because of its ability to advance despite all obstacles and to spread death and destruction in its path. Dubbed a "mechanical toy" by the conservative Lord Kitchener, it was not used extensively until the late phases of the war, when the Allies had sufficient tanks on the Western Front to institute a tremendous attack upon the German lines and shatter their entrenchments. The wireless telegraph and telephone greatly facilitated the effective conduct and coördination of war activities. Armies, cities, and nations were enabled to communicate with one another notwithstanding breaches in the telegraph wires and cables. France and Russia exchanged messages by wireless code across the Central Powers.

Old weapons were very much improved during the World War. The Germans used long-range guns with considerable effect during the early stage of the struggle, and before the armistice they were making cannons (the Big Bertha, for example) capable of projecting shells about seventy-five miles.

Technology changed naval as well as military warfare. Germany's use of the submarine in attacking British commerce marked a distinct phase in the evolution of modern fighting. Certain naval authorities maintain that if Germany had possessed enough submarines at the beginning of the conflict, she might have destroyed Britain's sea power, brought that nation "to her knees," and won a complete victory. Before the end of the war, however, the Allies, by means of mines, nets, depth bombs, and speedy destroyers, were able to decrease considerably the effectiveness of the submarines.

Mechanical and chemical inventions practically revolutionized modern warfare. Generals still maintained discipline and planned and executed attacks in orthodox fashion, but the men who made victories possible were the civilian scientists and bourgeois industrialists, who developed new techniques and provided adequate supplies of goods and munitions.

The conflict, however, did not diminish the importance of man power as the final determining factor. The larger and more numerous devices for killing made the number of men required for military service greater than ever before, and those who could not bear arms were essential for the production of war materials and food supplies. Universal service by conscription, which mobilized men for the front, was extended to include the conscription of man power in the factories which produced goods necessary for carrying on the war.

Women played a more active part in this conflict than ever before. They functioned as nurses and Red Cross workers; they entered naval and war offices in various capacities, ranging from clerks to boiler-cleaners. Before the end of the struggle, in England especially, many women were making munitions and gas masks. It may be asserted with little exaggeration that they participated in all phases of the war. In short, this conflict was a clash between nations, not states represented merely by armies. Each nation was fused into a compact, mobilized whole, straining every nerve, using every science and art, summoning all powers of ingenuity, enduring cruel military discipline, to achieve one end — triumph over the enemy. The "nation-in-arms" was a reality.

The men, however, who were chiefly involved in the outbreak of the war and the enlargement of its scope were the diplomats. Having failed to prevent the awful catastrophe, they strove to bring it to a victorious conclusion. They tried to achieve this end by enticing neutrals in on their side.

Italy, as was to be expected, announced her neutrality at the beginning of the conflict. In her opinion she had not been recognized as a member of the Triple Alliance, for the Dual Monarchy had not consulted her during the negotiations between Germany and Austria-Hungary which finally culminated in the declaration of war. *Spread of the Conflict* Italy also asserted that the conflict was not defensive in character, and that consequently she was not bound to support her allies. Then occurred a contest for Italy's support. The Dual Monarchy, urged by Germany, offered to cede to Italy sections of Austrian territories inhabited by Italians, but Italy desired additional towns and lands around the Adriatic Sea, occupied for the most part by Slavs. Austria refused to give up these territories, for they constituted her one outlet to the sea. The Allies found no difficulty in promising Austrian territory to Italy. By a secret treaty signed in London early in 1915 they assigned Italy the Trentino and the Tyrol up to the Brenner Pass, Trieste, Istria, northern Dalmatia, and adjoining islands. Italy was also to get Valona and the Dodecanese Islands, which she already occupied. She was promised the right to conduct the foreign affairs of Albania, and to share in the partition of Turkey, should this occur. The Allies, neglecting the interests of their associate, Serbia, granted Italy supremacy in the Adriatic. Thus, promised more by the Entente than by Austria, and anticipating an Allied victory, Italy, on May 24, 1915, declared war upon Austria-Hungary.

In the struggle to bring Bulgaria into the conflict the Central Powers were successful, because Bulgaria wanted Serbian Macedonia, which obviously the Allies could not give her. The Central Powers easily assured her this territory, and so Bulgaria entered the war, on October 12, 1915.

Rumania also was the center of diplomatic bargaining. The Central Powers promised Rumania territory in Bessarabia, but the Entente offered more — Bukowina, Transylvania, and the Banat of Temesvár — at the expense of Austria-Hungary. Despite this generous promise Rumania hesitated; she wanted to pick the winner. After a successful Russian offensive on the Eastern Front, however, she declared war on her former ally, Austria-Hungary, on August 27, 1916.

Greece was in a quandary at the opening of hostilities. Sharply divided into parties, one pro-Ally, the other pro-German, with a neutral group in between, the Greeks found it difficult to join either side. Although officially Greece pursued a policy of armed neutrality, temporarily the government under King Constantine leaned toward the Central Powers. The Entente nations, needing Greek territory in order to establish a battle front in the Balkans for the purpose of aiding Serbia, landed troops at Salonica in violation of Greek neutrality. They then literally forced Greece to adhere to the Allied cause. The Greek postal and telegraph systems were seized, the diplomatic representatives of the Central Powers were expelled from Greece, newspapers were censored, and the navy was commandeered. The Greek government protested. But uprisings, encouraged perhaps by the Allies, led to a revolution and the overthrow of the government, after which the pro-Ally Greek minister Venizelos took charge of the country, and the pro-German king was forced to abdicate. In the fall of 1917 Greece officially joined the Allied cause.

By this time all Europe save Spain, Switzerland, Holland, and the Scandinavian countries had become involved in the struggle. Little Portugal, long a satellite of Great Britain, had joined the Allies in 1916.

As will be shown in the next chapter, the diplomats of the Allied countries did not confine their activities to bringing

War Aims neutral countries into the war or to keeping unfriendly states out. They also planned beforehand the division of the spoils. The Central Powers were just as hungry for additional territories as were the Allies. In their case, however, Germany was all-powerful, so that, with the exception of the promises which Austria made Turkey and Bulgaria, practically no bargaining occurred. Undoubtedly Germany and Austria would have rectified their frontiers and advanced their colonial interests if they had won the war. The terms imposed upon Russia at Brest-Litovsk in 1918, and upon Rumania about the same time by the Treaty of Bucharest, in which these countries were stripped of valuable territories and placed under heavy economic burdens, suggest what the Central Powers might have done if they had been victorious. Powerful interests on both sides looked forward to victory as a means to definite ends — territorial aggrandizements and economic rewards.

An accurate account of the military events of the World War is not possible at this time. Although numerous works have been written on the subject, many phases of the most important campaigns and maneuvers are still matters of considerable controversy. French, English, German, and American writers have found it difficult to agree upon vital points. Therefore an exhaustive treatment of the military developments, involving as it does that moot question, Who was most responsible for the Allied victory? will not be undertaken.

In the first year none of the plans made by the German military leaders for a short and a glorious war succeeded. Years before, they had formulated the famous *The Schlieffen Plan* Schlieffen Plan, by which they intended to carry on a brief but decisive conflict in France and then turn to Russia in the east and put that nation out of the struggle. Anticipating a war in which the enemy would probably outnumber the Central Powers in man power and in resources, the military leaders of Germany determined to defeat their opponents before the latter could overwhelm the Fatherland by sheer weight of numbers and guns. The Kaiser's strategists knew that the enemy would probably possess naval superiority. This advantage would enable the latter to employ their own resources, to use those of neutral nations, and to blockade Germany.

Even in 1914 German military leaders were aware of the fact that time was on the side of the Allies. For this reason France should be overwhelmed without delay. Because the short frontier between France and Germany was strongly fortified by a line of French fortresses from Verdun down to Belfort, the Germans decided that an attack at this point would prevent a rapid advance. Therefore they accepted the Schlieffen Plan of a march across Luxembourg and Belgium. Inasmuch as the main railways and roads from Berlin to Paris ran across the level territory in these neutral countries, and as the French fortifications on this part of the frontier were feeble compared with those at Metz, Toul, and Verdun, the plan offered the advantage of a quick invasion of France, the conquest of her industrial region in the north, and the envelopment of her forces by a wide encircling movement of seven or eight German armies, with Luxembourg as the pivot.

The British, French, and Russian military authorities were probably aware of this proposed strategy. Certainly, antici-
The Allied Plans　　pating a German invasion of Belgium, they had a general plan for meeting it. According to this scheme the Germans were to be lured deeper and deeper into Belgium and France, while the Russians were to mobilize rapidly and to sweep with full strength into Austrian Galicia. At a given time counter attacks were to be launched in the west and east, catching the Germans at a fatal distance from their base of supplies. Obsessed with the will to win, French military authorities added one new feature to this general plan: they intended to attack the enemy in the Vosges region, in order to regain the "lost provinces," and then to outflank the German armies as they marched through Belgium and northern France.

Little Belgium offered unexpected resistance. Eighteen days were required by the Germans to cross Belgium and
The German Invasion　　reach the French frontier. The fortified city of Liége and the reputedly impregnable fortress of Namur resisted the Germans and delayed their advance. But the huge guns used by the Germans demonstrated the fact that these strongholds, hitherto considered indestructible, could be shot to pieces. As their armies crossed Belgium, however, a small British expeditionary force and the French troops were prepared to meet the German advance.

From the outset the French, led by General Joffre, had endeavored to carry out their plan of marching into Alsace-Lorraine. Partially successful, they nevertheless failed to break the German line and to attain the real objective. By August 23 the Germans had captured Namur and were ready to enter France. It was now too late for the British and

French to offer effective opposition. Lacking sufficient troops, the French failed in an attempted offensive in southeastern Belgium, and, unable to hold the Germans at Charleroi and Mons, the French and English, abandoning the industrial center of France, began a strategic retreat.

In the course of three weeks the Germans had accomplished the initial phase of their plan, the invasion of Belgium, and were now ready to rush down upon Paris and envelop that city and the Allied forces. The French government moved from Paris to Bordeaux. It was evident that one of the great crises in the history of Europe was at hand. By September 1 the German authorities revealed their aims. Lacking sufficient soldiers to march on both sides of Paris (they had concentrated most of their troops on the left half of the line and also had just sent several divisions to the Eastern Front from their weakened right wing), they decided to march east of the capital and to destroy the French field troops. Meanwhile, on August 25, General Joffre had ordered all Allied armies to join forces and to resist when directed.

Gallieni, the newly appointed military governor of Paris, however, was among the first to appreciate fully the significance of the German decision to swing around east of Paris. Aware that the right flank and *The First Battle of the Marne* rear of General Kluck's army would be exposed as it passed the French capital, Gallieni planned to use a French army, near Paris, "to strike Kluck and with him the whole advancing line of German armies behind their right shoulder blade." Joffre gave him permission to do this, and also, on September 5, ordered the French and British troops "to attack and repel the enemy. Any troops," he said, "which can no longer advance will at all costs hold the ground they have won, and allow themselves to be slain where they stand rather than give way." Thus the famous order of the day was sent out. On September 6 occurred the electrifying "right about turn," with half a million bayonets and five thousand cannon suddenly turned on the invading hosts. The battle of the Marne, the greatest in history up to that time, had begun.

Two colossal armies faced each other along a line of two hundred miles, extending from Paris to the Swiss frontier. Although outnumbering the French and British forces, the German troops, wearied by their rapid marches, were not so effective as they had been. Moreover, the German plan of attack was practically nullified because of the failure to concentrate sufficient troops on the right wing. The battle was won by the Allies when the French struck the right flank of the German army passing east of Paris. Kluck, in trying to shake off the French, drew his army back and lost contact with General Bülow's troops on his left. The latter, having been ordered to form a flank guard against a possible attack from Paris, thereupon had his army pivot, his right going back, his left forward, so that he could face Paris. As a result a gap thirty miles wide was opened between the two German armies. Unaware of the situation, the British forces marched into the opening and, like the Germans, being exposed to enemy cross fire, were in a difficult position.

Meanwhile the aged Moltke, general in charge of all the German forces, received reports far from the scene of battle at his headquarters in Luxembourg. The Germans had been held in the center by General Foch at the head of a French army. On their right the Germans were outflanked. Too old to be near the battle front, lacking confidence in himself, in reality merely the shadow of a great name,— nephew of a brilliant general,— Moltke became panicky. Deciding, on September 9, to order a general retreat, he wrote to his wife, "The fighting east of Paris has not gone in our favor, and we shall have to pay for the damage we have done." By September 12 "weary, war-ravaged troops were in a loose, desperate combat; then all of a sudden one side [the Germans] sustained the impression that it was the weaker, and that it had the worst of it." The battle was over, and the main German army fell back to a strong position on the river Aisne, where they had prepared trenches for their infantry and concrete foundations for their big guns. From this position the Allies were unable to dislodge them in the first battle of the Aisne.

The war was not lost by the Germans in the battle of the

Marne. "But never after that," wrote a patriotic English
statesman, "could their proud militarism receive such a justification." A German victory in the battle of the Marne could
have ended the war in six weeks, and then Germany might
have retained its supremacy for many generations, handing down the legend of invincible military force. With the

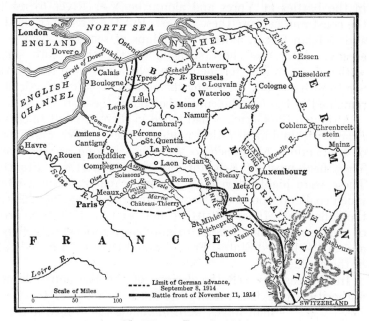

The Western Front in 1914

repulse at the Marne, Germany could no longer win a quick
and decisive triumph.

After this battle the Germans retreated to the Aisne River
and there entrenched, resisting every attack of the Allies.
Even though they had failed to achieve their objective, the
Germans had conquered the richest industrial districts of
France and Belgium. The capture on October 10 of Antwerp,
the great Belgian seaport, and of Ghent, an important coast
city, further strengthened their cause. Complete success, however, evaded the Teutons as the Allies launched counter-attacks.

Although the French and British lacked the heavy guns and shells that were necessary to expel the Germans from the Aisne region, the Allies were able to extend their line northward just in time to prevent the Germans from occupying the channel ports, Calais, Boulogne, and Dunkirk, the gateway to England. In October of 1914, the Germans tried desperately in the battles at Ypres and along the Yser River to reach the coast and capture these places. But the French, English, and Belgian forces, aided by warships at sea, held back the enemy. After this short struggle for the coast both sides settled down in long fortified lines, which ran from the North Sea to Switzerland. "Digging themselves in" they practically remained in the trenches until the end of the war.

Although the Germans had failed in their attempt to crush France within a month, they made conquests which were later of tremendous assistance to them in carrying on the war. They held most of Belgium and part of northern France. These were highly developed regions, capable of furnishing much coal and iron to the Central Powers. What they gained the Allies lost. Indeed, if it had not been for British control of the seas, enabling France to purchase supplies in England and in the United States, France would have been forced out of the conflict.

In the east as well the designs of the German military authorities were frustrated. Inasmuch as most of the German forces were marching on France and invading Belgium, the Russians decided to invade Germany and by so doing relieve the enormous pressure on France. Completing a surprisingly rapid mobilization, Russian armies were pouring into East Prussia even before the German troops had reached the French frontier via Belgium. Russia was confident; victory seemed to be within her grasp.

The Eastern Front, 1914

But Russia's hope for a complete triumph on the Eastern Front was soon destroyed. Before the Russian army was able to march very far the incapable German general Prittwitz was replaced by an old retired military leader, Hindenburg, and, under him, another general, Ludendorff, who had displayed marked ability during the invasion of Belgium. Meanwhile two Russian armies were invading East Prussia, one from the east, via Vilna, the other from the south, via Warsaw. Curiously enough the two forces failed to coöperate. While the one from the east was plunging ahead the Germans converged upon the Russian army from the south. In the famous battle of Tannenberg (August 26–31) which followed, practically two thirds of the Russian army was annihilated or captured. Even more disastrous to Russia than the sacrifice of men was the tremendous loss of equipment. This German victory was one of the most decisive of the entire conflict. The results were that the other Russian army was expelled from East Prussia, and the Germans, having gained the upper hand, inaugurated great assaults on the Eastern Front.

At the same time that the Czar's armies were invading East Prussia other Russian forces were attacking the Austrians in Galicia. By the end of August considerable success had crowned their efforts in that region. Powerful Austrian outposts had been captured, and Lemberg, the capital of Galicia, was about to be besieged. The city was soon taken, and the Russians, having chased the Austrians into the Carpathian Mountains, menaced the important city of Cracow. Once they were in possession of that strategic stronghold, direct roads would enable the Russians to march toward Vienna and Berlin. Also it appeared that the Russians might enter Rumania south of Galicia, force that country into the conflict, and then invade Hungary via Transylvania. By the fall of 1914 Russia threatened to bring about the dissolution of the Dual Monarchy.

The Russian advance in Galicia checked the Austrian pressure in Serbia. Encouraged by this aid, the Serbs and Montenegrins then instituted an attack which resulted in the expulsion of the Austrians from Serbian soil. The Serbs, however, failed in their attempts to invade the Dual Monarchy and to liberate the Slavs.

On the water the Allies were completely successful. The dominant British navy was soon able to sweep all German commerce from the seas. German submarines at first attacked

British warships, but did little damage. Daring raids, however, were made by German cruisers, caught in foreign waters

Naval and Colonial Phases of the War

when the war broke out. For a brief time they did considerable damage to Allied shipping, but they were finally sunk or interned. True, England lost a few engagements, in particular one with a small group of German ships off the coast of Chile (November 1, 1914). By the spring of 1915, however, practically all German war vessels had been driven off the seas, and the British grand fleet was blockading the German battle squadron in its own home waters near the Kiel Canal. Thenceforth the British and German high-seas fleets avoided a naval conflict, fearing that defeat would be disastrous to their respective causes.

Germany lost most of her colonies at the beginning of the war. Her possessions in the Far East were taken over by Japan, November 10, 1914, and her islands in the Pacific were captured by Japanese or British colonial forces. In Africa the German colonies offered futile opposition to the Allies. It is interesting to note that German East Africa, however, was not surrendered until November 14, 1918, three days after the signing of the armistice.

The German military authorities, failing to defeat France in 1914, decided to abandon the Schlieffen Plan and to concentrate in 1915 on the Eastern Front. Here they hoped to expel the Russians from Galicia and Russian Poland, and, if possible, to force them out of the war.

Early in 1915 the British and the French undertook an offensive in the Near East. They realized that Russia, separated from them, was to be subjected to considerable pressure by the Central Powers on the Eastern Front and by Turkey along the Caucasus, and they feared that a Moslem holy war might inflame India and Egypt. Consequently they decided to go to Russia's rescue. The point of their attack was the Dardanelles. Once the Straits and Constantinople were in their hands, Russia would be relieved of Turkish pressure and would be able to communicate with her allies and exchange her wheat for much-needed military supplies. Furthermore, in control of Constantinople, the Allies also could terminate the danger of attack upon the Suez Canal and Egypt, as well as upon India, — entirely feasible if the Central Powers and Turkey could have stirred up a religious uprising in these regions. The Allies would then be able to establish a battle front in the Balkans which would threaten Austria and cause the neutral Balkan states, Greece, Rumania, and Bulgaria, either to remain neutral or to join the Allied cause. Great Britain especially was desirous of occupying Constantinople. She knew that Russia planned to obtain permanent possession of this city, and she proposed to frustrate this design by placing Constantinople under Allied control.

Many English and French officials questioned the advisability of the Dardanelles campaign. In their opinion it was too hazardous an undertaking, inasmuch as the Allies needed all available men on the Western Front. Moreover, the German fleet *The Dardanelles Campaign* was still a menace. England could ill afford to send a large part of her naval forces to the Near East.

Those in favor of the campaign, however, dominated the situation. A squadron of British and French battleships, sent in February, 1915, to the Dardanelles, bombarded the forts at the entrance of the Straits. After checking the gunfire the fleet entered the narrow channel. The Allied forces were thereby enabled to fire upon the forts at the narrows, farther up the Straits, at long range, and soon had victory within their grasp. The guns along the Straits and the big Krupp cannons in the forts, it is claimed, were either silenced or were ineffective for lack of munitions. Mine-sweepers had cleared the Straits of most of the mines. But at this time the British admiral in command committed what proved to be a fatal error; he ordered the ships to withdraw from the Straits.

This action on the part of Admiral de Robeck, the Allied commander, in what appeared to be the moment of victory, is nevertheless explicable. By March 18 a Turkish steamer succeeded in placing, unnoticed, about twenty mines lengthwise along the Asiatic shore instead of across the Straits.

Unaware of these mines, a number of Allied ships struck them and were destroyed. According to Winston Churchill, the British statesman and writer, these unexpected and unexplainable disasters affected the morale of the Allies, especially of Admiral de Robeck, and the fleet was recalled. On the other hand, some writers maintain that the large German guns on the land and floating mines in the Straits inflicted so much damage on the Allied ships that further advance was impossible. At all events the Allies gave up this attack, although it is said that victory was within their reach if they had advanced the next day.

The Allies, however, refused to renounce their plans to aid Russia and to control the Straits. They next resorted to a land attack. Gathering an inexperienced army composed of Australian, New Zealand, Indian, and French colonial troops, they inaugurated, on April 25, 1915, their attempt to capture the narrow Gallipoli Peninsula at the opening of the Straits. But the Turks, directed by the skillful German general Liman von Sanders, had strengthened the fortifications on the peninsula. So, after making three costly attempts to occupy this region, the Allies withdrew their troops and moved them over to Salonica in Greek territory, in order to establish a battle front in the Balkans.

This unsuccessful campaign only served to increase the influence of the Central Powers in the Balkans by bringing Bulgaria into the war on their side. Moreover, it promoted unrest in Russia. Unable to assist their Allies in the Dardanelles campaign, overwhelmed by a combined Austro-German assault on the Eastern Front, and handicapped by diminishing supplies and an ineffective government at home, many Russians lost hope and predicted the complete collapse of their country.

The declaration of war, in May, 1915, by Italy against Austria-Hungary, encouraged the Allies. But although it *Italy and the Allies* did relieve French fear of an Italian attack, the entrance of Italy failed to change to any great extent the general course of the war. She sent no troops to Gallipoli and but a few, later, to France, asserting that she needed her soldiers to guard the Austro-Italian frontier. Here she made little headway, for the Austrians, taking advantage of the narrow passes, which made an Italian invasion difficult, were able to hold the Italians back without concentrating a large number of troops on this frontier. Consequently Italy's intervention in the war did not greatly concern the Central Powers.

In 1915 conditions in the east seemed to be turning in favor of the Central Powers. In the early spring, although the Russian military situation appeared bright on the surface (it seemed that the Russian forces would capture Cracow and invade Prussia, *The Eastern Front, 1915* Austria, and Hungary), the diminishing supplies of munitions and other war materials and the inability of the Russian government to replenish them, owing to corruption and inadequate production and transportation, weakened the Russian armies. The Central Powers, on the other hand, had generous quantities of heavy guns, rifles, and war materials. Thousands of experienced troops also had been transferred to the east from the Western Front. Consequently by April, 1915, a combined Austro-German force of at least 2,000,000 men and 1500 guns was placed under the command of the able German General Mackensen, who was to expel the Russians from Galicia. This achieved, the Germans and Austrians planned to turn on the dangerous salient held by the Russians in Poland and force them into the interior of Russia.

On May 1, 1915, the Germans were ready to deliver the decisive blow. A tremendous concentration of men and guns had been made by the Germans and Austrians along the section of the line near Cracow. After a terrific bombardment — the like of which had never been seen and which almost annihilated the Russians and completely destroyed their trenches for many miles — fresh shock troops were sent ahead to take possession of the shattered parts of the Russian front. Thus the enemy was forced to retreat in order to reëstablish a continuous battle line. Hastily the Russians abandoned nearly all of Galicia, including the great fortresses which they had captured after so much effort.

Having achieved the first part of the Eastern campaign, the Austro-German forces now turned on Russian Poland. From the north and the south Teutonic armies converged upon the

The Eastern Front in 1915

famous city of Moscow. The outlying Polish fortresses were taken; then Warsaw; then the second-line fortresses; and finally Brest Litovsk, the center of the Russian system of defense. When the retreat came to an end the Russian armies had been forced into the interior of Russia. With winter approaching, the Central Powers refused to follow Napoleon I's example of invading Russia. Instead they halted their advance in a line extending from Riga to Rumania. Apparently the Germans had not accomplished their objective — the complete destruction of the Russian armies. Under the able leadership of Grand Duke Nicholas, one of the outstanding military commanders of the World War, Russia was saved this humiliation. The Russians, however, were practically eliminated from the struggle. But if ample guns, food, and munitions had been available they might later have been an important factor in the winning of the war.

By the fall of 1915 the Central Powers were in a position to attack on other frontiers. The capture of Brest Litovsk and Vilna in August and September of 1915 had definitely ended the Russian pressure on *The Conquest of Serbia* the east. Therefore they decided to "steam-roller" Serbia and then concentrate on the Western Front. By conquering this Balkan state the Central Powers felt that they would remove the Slav danger in the Balkans, insure the safety of the Dardanelles, isolate Russia completely, enable the Turks to act in Asia Minor, keep Rumania from joining the Allies, and finally increase their own supply of foodstuffs and copper. Most important was their realization that defeating Serbia would enable them, by bringing Bulgaria in on their side, to dominate the Balkans.

Bulgaria by that time had concluded that the Central Powers were bound to win the war. Therefore on September 6 Bulgaria, having been promised Macedonia and certain other territories, signed a military agreement in which she promised to strike the Serbians on the eastern frontier, while the Austro-German armies, under the command of Mackensen, crossed the Danube into Serbia. The latter country, outnumbered in men and materials and attacked on two frontiers, was unable to offer much opposition. Soon the remnants of the Serbian army, consisting of scattered bands, fled into Montenegro and Albania. Expelled from these countries by the enemy, the Serbians finally found refuge on the Greek island of Corfu. Later they were transferred to the Allied battle front at Salonica, where they remained during the war.

The Allies failed to anticipate developments in the Balkans. At first they were of the opinion that Bulgaria would not join the Central Powers. Greece, they believed, because of an alliance with Serbia (1913), would aid the latter. But the pro-German Constantine of Greece, holding that the treaty with Serbia applied only to a purely Balkan conflict, refused to enter the struggle. Unsuccessful in their attempts to capture Constantinople, the Allies finally violated the neutrality of Greece and landed two divisions at Salonica. This inadequate force was joined by the Allied troops from Gallipoli.

From the beginning of the war the German authorities considered the navy merely an adjunct of the army. Intending to win the conflict on land, and fearing the superior naval forces of the Allies, they did not deem an offensive by a German battle fleet advisable. Plans were made, however, to weaken the Allied navy by submarine attacks, and if these proved sufficiently effective in destroying Allied battleships, then to hazard a naval engagement.

A Naval Phase of the War, 1915

The Allies, on the other hand, used their naval preponderance to prevent the importation of contraband of war by the Central Powers. According to England the general character of modern war had greatly changed the distinction between contraband and non-contraband goods. Practically all seaborne commodities served the nation in war, inasmuch as increases in foodstuffs or supplies for the civilian population released other things for military use. Therefore, Great Britain seized all neutral vessels thought to be carrying goods to the Central Powers. The United States, the leading neutral engaged in maritime trade, challenged the right of England to stop the transportation to Germany of non-contraband goods and foodstuffs. In the opinion of many Americans the commerce of the United States had not been ordered around so unceremoniously since the Napoleonic era. England, however, called America's attention to the fact that she had never signed the Declaration of London (1909) which defined contraband of war and refused to recognize the legality of American objections to this policy.

Germany, convinced that Great Britain was determined on an illegal blockade of the Central Powers which would starve them into submission, decided to retaliate by the unrestricted use of the submarine against all vessels excepting only neutrals when they could be recognized. Germany knew that the most vital communications of the Allies were by sea. If they were cut, France, deprived of much-needed troops and materials from her allies, and England, unable to import food and supplies for her population, would capitulate. Germany now claimed that she was fighting for her very existence against a foe who was determined to destroy the German people by a cruel and illegal method — starvation. She believed that she had a moral right to end this hideous war by the use of the submarine.

Early in February, 1915, Germany announced that the waters around Great Britain should be considered a war zone, in which her submarines would sink all enemy merchant vessels and might even destroy some neutral boats. The United States, as was expected, objected to this policy. In reply Germany stated that she would adhere to this unrestricted use of the submarine as long as England persisted in her illegal attempt to starve the Central Powers. England announced that she intended to stop all overseas trade with Germany. Moreover, she planned in the future to search all neutral vessels and to confiscate all contraband goods. As a result of these policies the neutrals had no more rights on the seas than they had during the struggle between Great Britain and Napoleon I, and anti-British as well as anti-German feeling developed in the United States.

On May 7, 1915, the British liner *Lusitania* was torpedoed and sunk with a loss of over a thousand lives, including one hundred and fourteen Americans. Aroused by this disaster, pro-Ally sympathizers in the United States soon cited this illegal act as proof *Sinking of the Lusitania* of German ruthlessness and lawlessness. As a result public opinion, disregarding the fact that Americans had been warned not to sail on the ship and that the *Lusitania* carried munitions, became very antagonistic toward the Central Powers.

In a note sent to Germany, the United States expressed its disapproval of this unfortunate affair and warned Germany "not to let it happen again." Inasmuch as Germany was not desirous of bringing the United States into the conflict, and since the unrestricted submarine campaign had not greatly hindered British war operations, German submarines were ordered not to attack liners; and after the sinking of the *Sussex* in 1916, in which additional American lives were lost, Germany promised not to torpedo merchant ships unless she warned and rescued the passengers and crews.

Having given up her submarine offensive, Germany, in the fall of 1915, decided to end the war by a powerful attack upon the Western Front. At that time the Central Powers seemed to be in a position to complete the work started in 1914. Russia, temporarily at least, was out of the war; Serbia had been crushed; and the Central Powers were dominant in the Near East. In fact, the capture by the Turks of a British force under General Townshend at Kut-el-Amara (April 29, 1915) was interpreted as marking the first step in the abolition of Allied influence in the East. It appeared as if the Turks, backed by the Central Powers, would be able to start a general uprising in the Orient against Allied, especially British, control. All that remained, asserted certain German leaders, was to defeat decisively the Allied forces in the west, and then a German peace could be dictated. Moreover, the German people, straining their resources to the utmost, were growing dissatisfied. Informed of numerous Teutonic victories, they wondered why, despite these triumphs, the war continued. Influenced by these factors, their military leaders decided to strike a decisive blow.

The Western Front, 1915–1916

During the winter of 1915–1916 the German authorities discussed the possible fronts on which the great offensive could be launched. It was not difficult for them to decide upon the western line as the logical place to attack. France must be defeated before England could throw her great reserve power into the war. An attack upon the Austro-Italian front, or on the Russian line, would not enable them to accomplish this objective. Moreover, Italy and Russia were not dangerous opponents. Once France was defeated, they could be easily subdued. But what point was the most desirable for this purpose? A drive against the British in the north was a possibility, but its final objectives — control of the Channel ports and expulsion of the English from the Continent — would neither necessarily end the war nor even put England out of it. Consequently this plan was excluded.

The French line in the west was finally selected by the German military strategists. Defeat France, they said, and the Allied cause will collapse. Unable to withstand the German forces, the British army would be helpless and a Teutonic triumph would result.

To achieve this end, the German military authorities were of the opinion that there was no necessity for aiming at important distant objectives, such as Paris. The immediate aim should be to force a battle in a sector that France would defend at all costs. Belfort and Verdun answered this requirement, for the pride of the French nation would be touched, and Frenchmen would lose their last drop of blood rather than surrender these forts, "felt by them to be the flesh of their flesh." If Germany could capture Verdun then, in the opinion of her leaders, French patriots would lose hope of regaining the lost provinces — Alsace-Lorraine — and would consent to terms of peace.

In December of 1915 the decision to attack Verdun was made, and in January and February of 1916, Germany massed every available man and gun on a twenty-mile line opposite the city. Convinced that a massing of guns around the French defenses would bring victory, the German military leaders, according to the French general Pétain, the able defender of Verdun, planned that they would "open an immense breach in our lines; and that, in taking full advantage of a success of this nature against a French army cut into two separated sections, the Imperial Armies would have every prospect of pushing on to a brilliant victory."

The British and the French were aware of German plans to assume the offensive. They arranged to rush troops to any threatened sector, the English agreeing to take over part of the French line west of Paris in order to enable French soldiers to be transferred to the sector east of that city if the Germans attacked at that point.

On February 21, 1916, an unprecedented German bombardment heralded the beginning of a supreme attempt on the part of General von Falkenhayn to break through the Western Front. "For twelve and a half hours guns of every calibre poured 100,000 shells per hour on a front of six miles. History had never seen so furious a fire. It blotted out the French first lines, it shattered the communication trenches, it tore the woods into splinters, and altered the very shape of the hills." German scouts now proceeded to investigate the amount of damage wrought by their artillery. Then the German gunners shifted their range so as to create a shield of fire behind the enemy trenches, while the German infantry occupied what remained of the first-line trenches with little opposition.

The Teutons expected to be in Verdun in four days. The French, they believed, could not stand the heavy gunfire and then resist the massed infantry as it advanced. But the Germans soon discovered that they were mistaken. Moving forward to attack Fort Douaumont, one of the keys of the defense of many forts, they were met by French reënforcements brought up by General Pétain and determined to make good the watchword "They [the Germans] shall not pass." One line after another of Germans marched up the hill leading to the fort, only to be swept down by French gunfire. Finally the Kaiser's troops reached Fort Douaumont, a heap of ruins, and later Fort Vaux.

During March, April, and May the battle continued, first at one place, then at another. Both sides fought bravely with bulldog tenacity. In June, when the Germans penetrated to within four miles of the city, even General Joffre doubted the ability of the French to hold Verdun. According to Pétain, Verdun probably would have fallen if the Germans had attacked on all sides at this time. But they limited the area of the assault, and the French, exhausted as they were, were able to strike back wherever they were attacked. By June 30 the tide of battle had definitely turned. The French had recovered the lost ground and thus had deprived the Germans of their advantage. On July 1, the Teutons were suddenly confronted by a tremendous British drive on the Somme. Now on the defensive the Germans were forced to receive rather than to deliver sledge-hammer blows. Concentrating their troops on this new battle area, they gave up their attempt to capture Verdun. Fierce fighting, however, continued on that sector until the fall of 1916. At that time the most terrific battle in history was actually ended.

A victory for the French was the result. The Germans had failed to achieve their objectives. Verdun had not fallen, nor had the French front been shattered, nor had French man power been exhausted. Furthermore, their plan to inveigle the British into an ill-timed advance had worked to their own disadvantage. The Germans had gained a few square miles of territory, but it did not compensate them for their frightful losses. Indeed, Germany was "bled white" as a result of this battle. General Ludendorff, describing the situation at that time, said, "On the Western Front we were completely exhausted." But the French, suffering tremendous losses, had won an expensive victory.

During the sanguinary battle of Verdun, the North Sea was the scene of unquestionably the greatest naval conflict of the war. Having given up the use of the *The Battle of Jutland* submarine against merchant vessels, the German naval authorities decided to revert to their original plan of weakening the British forces so as to give the German fleet a chance of victory should a battle occur. With this idea in mind a German scouting force was ordered to maneuver off the coast of Norway in the hope of luring out a British squadron. Should the Germans succeed in accomplishing this purpose, then the German battle fleet, under Vice-Admiral Scheer, would rush forward and annihilate the British forces.

To the surprise of the German authorities the British fleet, perhaps aware of the enemy plans, had been ordered to concentrate in the North Sea. Consequently the German fleet, instead of meeting a British squadron, encountered the British high-seas forces on May 31, 1916. To complicate matters, the British succeeded in placing their warships between the German fleet and its home base, but were apparently afraid to launch an attack. Refusing to fight it out, the German fleet managed to escape during the night through an unguarded section of the British line and returned to Heligoland. Although the Germans inflicted the greater damage in this engagement, the important result was that British control of the seas was never again seriously challenged.

This battle of Jutland, as well as that of Verdun, did much to nerve Great Britain for mightier efforts. During the early part of the war she had tried to increase her army by voluntary enlistments, hoping that her allies would be able to bear the brunt of the attack on land while she guarded the seas. By the spring of 1916 it was apparent that she would be forced to send more troops to the Western Front than she could obtain by voluntary enlistments. Therefore she adopted, in January, 1916, a system of universal military service which included all able-bodied men between the ages of eighteen and forty-five (later extended to fifty-one, with restricted service for those up to fifty-five).

Shortly after this important step had been taken the British and French began, east and west of Amiens, their long-talked-of drive, the battle of the Somme, which lasted from July to November, 1916. Here the new military invention, the tank, made its first appearance and did effective work in breaking barbed-wire entanglements and crushing German intrenchments. The French also used the famous sixteen-inch mortars for hurling shells. As at Verdun, the loss of life on both sides was tremendous. Although the Allies were successful in reaching the plateau held by the Germans and in hurling them down the other side, they were not able to break the enemy line. Indeed, they gained only a few miles of territory after a frightful expenditure of lives. By fall the heavy rains made the battle field impassable, so the struggle came to an end with

The Battle of the Somme

both sides greatly weakened. The battles of Verdun and the Somme had not broken the deadlock on the Western Front.

A similar situation existed on the Italian battle line. In May, 1916, the Italians were suddenly hurled back by a great Austrian drive. By August they not only had lost the little ground they had gained, but also had been forced to evacuate some of their own territory. Fortunately the Russians, despite the loss of Poland, attacked Austria at this critical moment and thus relieved Austrian pressure on Italy. To defend her eastern frontier the Dual Monarchy had to give up, for the time being, its plan to shatter the Italian front.

The Italian Front, 1916

The temporary successes of the Allies, especially the Russian gains in the southeast, encouraged Rumania, in August, 1916, to enter the war on the Allied side. Rumanian troops now invaded Transylvania, which their government had long considered a part of Rumania. But Germany sent Generals Falkenhayn and Mackensen to lead the Austrian soldiers against this new enemy. Assisted by the Bulgarians, they attacked Rumania from the west and from the south, and captured Bucharest, in December of 1916. About two thirds of Rumania was soon in the possession of her enemies, who could now supplement their supplies from her rich stores of grain and oil.

The Conquest of Rumania

Meanwhile the German failure at Verdun had resulted in important changes. Marshal Hindenburg, assisted by General Ludendorff as quartermaster-general, was placed in direct charge of the Western Front. These men had succeeded in leading the Central Powers to victory in the east. Now they were expected to turn the tide of battle in the west, break the deadlock, and win the war.

Many Germans, however, realized that a complete victory was impossible. In their opinion Germany would gain more through a negotiated settlement than through a continuation of the war. Therefore they planned to welcome any attempt on the part of President Wilson to arrange a peace meeting. Wilson had considered mediation almost from the beginning of the conflict. In the

Peace Proposals

winter of 1915 he had sent his adviser, Colonel Edward Mandell House, to Europe to make peace proposals. Wilson, at that time, advocated peace terms favorable to the Allies. The restoration of Alsace-Lorraine to France, the establishment of an independent Poland, the acquisition of Constantinople by Russia, and a League of Nations were a few of the things he favored. Moreover, through House he conveyed the idea that Germany had better accept these terms; otherwise the United States might join the Allied cause.

In 1916 William II of Germany frankly asked Wilson to bring about peace negotiations. Meanwhile Colonel House made another trip to England and to France and proposed a conference to discuss peace terms. This "peace talk," however, stirred up considerable resentment in England. By that time the Allies were determined to continue the war until Germany had been "knocked out." Blind to everything except a fierce hatred of Germany, they rejected Wilson's and the Kaiser's attempts to "save Europe from ruin."

By the fall of 1916 the Central Powers were determined to do everything possible to bring about a peace conference. Inasmuch as they had conquered a considerable part of Europe and had not suffered a real defeat, they believed that their peace proposals would prove that they were not defeated but honestly desired to end the war. Moreover, if the Allies rejected their proposals, the Germans and Austrians would realize that they were fighting an enemy bent upon their very ruin.

On December 12, 1916, Germany sent notes to the Allied governments suggesting a discussion of peace and stating that the Central Powers did not intend to destroy their opponents and would welcome a settlement which would create a lasting peace. If the Allies refused to accept this offer of conciliation, the war would continue. In such an event the Central Powers would not consider themselves responsible for the terrible bloodshed which would follow.

In this communication Germany neglected to state definite peace terms. As a matter of fact, she could not do so; for if she did and the terms were harsh, the enemy would reject them, asserting that Germany planned to conquer the world. This declaration would strengthen the morale of the Allies. If the terms were lenient, the German people would question the loudly heralded success of the Central Powers and would become discouraged.

The Allies refused to accept the invitation without a clear understanding with the Central Powers that the only terms upon which it would be possible for peace to be proclaimed were "complete restitution, full reparation, effectual guarantees." These sentiments were embodied in an official note to Germany which was presented on December 30 in the names of all the countries on the Allied side.

Upon receipt of this reply the Central Powers sent a note to neutral governments stating that they had made a sincere attempt to terminate this conflict and to prepare the way for peace and that the Allies had refused to take this road and therefore were responsible for the continuation of the struggle. William II took advantage of the situation to revive the crusading spirit in Central Europe. Germany's enemies, he claimed, had refused to join in a common attempt "to bring a new light into the affairs of the world." With God's help, he insisted, all Germans must force their foes to accept "the hand of understanding," he had offered them.

CONTRIBUTION of the UNITED STATES to the WAR: A German Caricature

CHAPTER XXX

The Allied Triumph, 1917-1918

THE Allied response to President Wilson's invitation of December 20, 1916, in which the Central Powers and the Entente were requested to state their peace terms, brought little comfort to Germany. Whereas the latter merely proposed an immediate meeting of delegates from all belligerent states at a neutral place, the Allies definitely stated their war aims. These involved the following: (1) the restoration of Belgium, Serbia, and Montenegro, with compensations due them; (2) the evacuation of the invaded territories in France, Russia, and Rumania, with just reparation; (3) the restitution of the regions formerly torn from the Allies by force or against the wishes of their inhabitants; (4) the liberation of the Italians, Slavs, Rumanians, Czechs, and Slovaks from foreign control; (5) the emancipation of the populations subject to the tyranny of the Turks; and (6) the expulsion from Europe of the Ottoman Empire as decidedly detrimental to Western civilization. Acceptance of these terms would have been the equivalent of a German surrender. Therefore the Central Powers preferred to continue the struggle and, by means of a gigantic attack upon the Western Front, possibly to dictate a peace.

For some time German naval authorities had been urging the resumption of unrestricted submarine warfare as the only way by which the Allies could be forced to ac-
Resumption of Submarine Warfare
cept peace. Bethmann-Hollweg and Hindenburg, however, had opposed this policy. By the end of December, Hindenburg decided that in order to win the war Germany must resort to submarine warfare. Hollweg still believed that peace negotiations would result in peace. The refusal of the Allies to consider the German peace offers finally enabled the war group to dominate the situation.

Both General Hindenburg and General Ludendorff, in welcoming the resumption of submarine warfare, stated that unless this were done Germany would not be able to hold the Western Front. They accepted the views of the admiralty that England would suffer such severe losses as a result of submarine attacks that she would cry for peace in a few months, and that the United States, even if she entered the war, was so unprepared that the struggle would be over before she was ready. Germany, on January 31, 1917, announced that, beginning the next day, all sea traffic within certain zones adjoining Great Britain, France, and Italy, and in the eastern Mediterranean, would, "without further notice, be prevented by all weapons." Vessels, neutral or belligerent, were to be sunk by German submarines. Special permission was granted for a weekly sailing in each direction between Great Britain and the United States of one American passenger steamship carrying mail, subject to the observation of a number of strict rules. In adopting this policy Germany was hopeful that it would "result in a speedy termination of the war and in the restoration of peace which the Government of the United States has so much at heart."

Unfortunately for the Central Powers the United States did not appreciate this kind of "peace movement." American exasperation, inflamed by active Allied propaganda, had been increasing steadily for some months. By January, 1917, the preponderance of American sentiment was on the side of the Allies.

Importance of Propaganda

Highly organized agencies for influencing public opinion were characteristic of the World War. In previous conflicts attempts had been made to influence neutrals, as well as the enemy, by means of handbills, promises of rewards, and other methods. Peculiar conditions, however, favored a much more extensive use of propaganda during the world conflict. The existence of democracy impelled governments to justify themselves before their peoples and their neighbors. The mere declaration of war by the government, as in the days of absolutism, did not suffice. Printing-presses, photographs, post cards, motion pictures, and airplanes dropping leaflets —

all of these enabled the clever manipulators of public opinion to "educate" the people quickly and thoroughly.

All warring countries recognized the importance of propaganda. In August, 1914, Great Britain established a small bureau to send out pamphlets. Later such work was carried on by divisions within the home office, the foreign office, and the war department. Toward the close of the conflict there was a Minister of Information, with Lord Northcliffe as "director of propaganda in enemy countries." In Germany similar attention was given propaganda, the headquarters of the army having a press service which censored all information, including that sent out by civilian propaganda branches. France also had a "press house." On the whole the Allies surpassed the Central Powers in the unscrupulous business of spreading "official information" useful in winning the war.

Certain definite objectives were to be gained by the powers from spreading propaganda. In the first place, they desired to consolidate the fighting spirit and the national pride of their own people by creating a hatred for their adversaries. Secondly, they hoped to demoralize the enemy by stirring up a revolutionary spirit among their peoples and their armies. Thirdly, they tried to win allies by tempting or frightening neutrals into entering the conflict against the foe. Fourthly, they endeavored to keep neutrals from joining the enemy. Governments, individuals, and private societies worked to achieve such ends.

As the war continued, both contestants drew up long lists of "atrocities" asserted to have been committed by the other side. According to the Germans the Central Powers were encircled by savage foes who were committing terrible offenses, worse than the normal violence of war, in order to win victory. Germany, they claimed, had tried earnestly to maintain peace. On the other hand, the Allies sent stories from the battle front in which the Germans were accused of mutilating civilians and even of dropping poisoned candy from airplanes for children of the Allied countries. To question such tales during the war was to suffer the charge of treason. Subsequently nearly all of these atrocities were proved to be fictitious.

Propaganda was not limited to atrocities and personalities. As the war continued it included a great variety of ideas and of mental stereotypes. At first cartoons published in the United States pictured Germania as a fair lady humbled by the Kaiser. By 1915 she was depicted as a nation of barbarians and the Kaiser as a ruler of cruel, savage Huns. At the beginning of the war the struggle was described as an attempt to overthrow an ambitious dynasty; before the Armistice was signed the people in Allied countries were told that they were fighting militarism, imperialism, and autocracy in order to "make the world safe for democracy."

Attempts were made by both sides to enlist the services of God. The Kaiser repeatedly asked his subjects and his clergy to pray to God "for his help" and "for our gallant army." A French propagandist asserted that France was engaged in her perennial crusade for civilization. The conflict, he believed, was between Catholic France and Protestant Germany. When Turkey joined the Central Powers, numerous "patriots" on the side of the Allies insisted that the war was between Christianity and the followers of Mohammed. Yet France and Great Britain were enrolling in their armies thousands of Moslems recruited from their colonies.

Ill-informed persons actually asserted that the war was a racial struggle. Certain Frenchmen believed that it was a conflict between the Latins and Slavs, on the one side, and the Teutons, on the other, whereas many Germans considered it a war of Germanic culture against Slavic barbarism. Each nation insisted, in obvious disregard of reality, that it was fighting to save its particular brand of "culture." Germans, Frenchmen, Italians, Englishmen, and Russians maintained that civilization was the issue. Obviously they failed to take into account the fact that the English spoke a Teutonic language, and that thousands of Magyars and Slavs were enrolled in the armies of the Central Powers. Moreover, no attempt was made to arrive at an understanding as to what was meant by the term *civilization*, although superpatriots were determined to save it.

From the beginning the Allies emphasized the theme that

England and France were fighting a war for democracy and
for the liberation of oppressed peoples. The Germans, not to
be outdone, also assumed a "liberal" spirit, denouncing the
unenlightened autocracy in Russia and offering liberty to
Ireland and to India. Actually the Allies as well as the Germans found it difficult to justify the war on moral grounds.

During the first year of the struggle the United States was
officially neutral. Sentiment among the people, however, was

*Propaganda in the
United States*

divided, inasmuch as there were in America representatives of all the states engaged
in the conflict. Consequently this powerful
and wealthy country became the battleground for national
groups and foreign propagandists. At the beginning of the
conflict German propaganda was especially apparent. A determined attempt was made to convince Americans that Germany had all the right on her side and that the United States
should therefore remain out of the war and lend neither financial nor other material aid to the Entente. In influencing
American public opinion, Entente propagandists, as already
mentioned, were more active, clever, and successful than their
rivals. British control of the seas and of the cables enabled
the Allies to interpret the war for the Americans. British
propaganda also succeeded in utilizing the friendly services
not only of newspapers but of influential people in every pro-
fession in the United States. These persons did much to prepare the minds of Americans for participation in the war on
the Allied side.

By 1917 it had become apparent to many American citizens that a German victory would injure their political and

*Reasons for American
Intervention*

economic interests. In the Far East the United
States was indirectly committed to the Allies
through an agreement with Japan (1908).
Moreover, German activities in Hispanic America, previous
to 1914, convinced these men that in the event of a German
victory not only would American interests in the Far East
suffer, but also her predominant position in the Americas
would be questioned. It was even said that Germany would
ignore the Monroe Doctrine and would establish her hegem-

ony in South America. To avoid such a danger, many influential Americans decided that the United States should help maintain the equilibrium of power in Europe by joining the Allies.

Economic interests also aided in drawing the United States into the conflict on the Allied side. During the war, despite German disapproval, she sold munitions and other goods to the Allies. Her international banking houses also lent considerable money to them. By 1917 the situation, however, had become so critical that American bankers found it difficult to sell Allied bonds in the United States. To give the Allies the support which they required, the United States had to participate in the war. Conscious of this circumstance, leading industrialists and bankers became ardent advocates of war. The press, sensitive to their ideas, immediately inaugurated a bitter newspaper campaign against the Central Powers. Subsequently American intervention enabled the government to use its credit to float loans (Liberty bonds) and to lend the proceeds to the Allies.

President Wilson seemed unwilling to rush headlong into war. Even after the belligerents had failed to state their aims, as he had suggested, and to agree to peace negotiations, he was willing to discuss the *American Intervention* problems involved in a settlement. On January 22, 1917, he delivered an address in which he said that peace must, among other things, provide for equality of right for both great and small nations, security for subject peoples, direct outlet to the sea for every nation, freedom of the seas, and limitation of armaments. He also declared:

No peace can last, or ought to last, which does not recognize and accept the principle that governments derive all their just powers from the consent of the governed, and that no right anywhere exists to hand people about from sovereignty to sovereignty as if they were property.

All hope of a peaceful settlement through negotiations ended on February 1, 1917, when Germany opened her unrestricted submarine warfare. President Wilson responded on

February 3 by breaking off diplomatic relations with the German government. Count von Bernstorff, Germany's ambassador to the United States, accused of permitting a German spy system to flourish in America, was sent home. By this time an increasing number of citizens were criticizing President Wilson for being too patient. The sinking of American ships by the Germans had served to increase their anger, and they insisted upon war. American newspapers published an account of a German attempt to arrange an alliance with Mexico. Without questioning its authenticity many patriots decided that this was the culminating insult.

At last President Wilson decided to act. At a special session of Congress, April 2, 1917, he read a memorable address in which he said that Germany had to all intents and purposes declared war on the United States.

A steadfast concert for peace can never be maintained except by a partnership of democratic nations. No autocratic government could be trusted to keep faith within it or observe its covenants. . . . The world must be made safe for democracy. Its peace must be planted upon the trusted foundations of political liberty. We have no selfish ends to serve. We desire no conquest, no dominion. We seek no indemnities for ourselves, no material compensation for the sacrifices we shall freely make. We are but one of the champions of the rights of mankind. We shall be satisfied when those rights have been made as secure as the faith and the freedom of the nation can make them.

He then proposed that the United States join the Allies.

War fever rose quickly. Both houses of Congress approved, by a large majority, the proposed resolution that the United States carry on war against Germany. Provisions were made for borrowing vast sums by issuing Liberty bonds. Taxes were increased and many new ones added. In May, 1917, a "selective draft" was introduced, and all able-bodied men between twenty-one and thirty-one were declared liable to military service. Preparations were made for training great bodies of troops, so as to help break the deadlock on the Western Front. Energetic measures were also taken to build ships to replace those destroyed by German submarines.

One influential American, however, refused to sanction intervention at this time. Determined to maintain strict neutrality, William Jennings Bryan, Secretary of State, had, during the conflict, opposed many presidential policies which, in his opinion, favored the Allies. When he saw that American participation was inevitable, he resigned and retired from public life.

While the United States was preparing to enter the war, Russia experienced a stupendous political and social upheaval. By March, 1917, that country was no longer able to compete with the type of warfare waged by the highly industrialized Germany. *Russian Withdrawal from the War* Moreover, the corruption, weakness, inefficiency, and, to a certain degree, the treason of the Russian government created a very critical situation. Discouraged by the losses suffered in the trenches on the Eastern Front, angry because of the blunders of the government (which by 1916 had become practically paralyzed), and desperate as a result of the breakdown of transportation and the scarcity of food, the Russian citizens and soldiers in Petrograd finally revolted, and a provisional government was established. The new leaders, as will be shown, tried to continue the war.[1] Late in 1917, however, the Bolsheviks overturned the provisional government and called for a general peace conference. In December the Bolshevist government opened peace negotiations with the Central Powers, and on March 3, 1918, finally signed a treaty of peace at Brest-Litovsk.

During 1917 the intervention of the United States and the threatened withdrawal of Russia created a situation wherein both sides had to declare their war aims. Previously considerable bargaining had taken place, but no definite statement had been *The War Aims of 1917* drawn up on either side as to the ultimate purpose of the conflict. The Bolsheviks, however, by proclaiming that the war was an imperialist quarrel over trade and colonies, and by publishing secret treaties that tended to prove that territorial bargains had been arranged between warring powers, had

[1] See page 632.

forced the belligerents to act. As spokesman for the Allies President Wilson advanced the idea that the purpose of the conflict was to make the world safe "for every peace-loving nation which, like our own, wishes to live its own life, determine its own institutions, be assured of justice and fair dealing by the other peoples of the world as against force and selfish aggression."

This statement of the war aims of the United States greatly raised the morale of the Allies. The masses again felt that they were engaged in a crusade, and the impression spread around the world that the Allies were indeed fighting for right against might. At the same time France and Great Britain, even though they benefited by President Wilson's attempt to place the war issues on a high level, were also embarrassed by his statements. Consumed by selfish ambitions in 1916, these countries were not especially desirous of American intervention. After Verdun and the Russian collapse, however, Great Britain and France, realizing that they needed additional support, welcomed American assistance and tacitly allowed President Wilson to place the war on a high plane.

The progress of the struggle had created new territorial problems. By December of 1917 the Central Powers had gained military possession of Belgium, Luxembourg, northeastern France, Poland, Lithuania, Courland, Serbia, Montenegro, and Rumania. Great Britain had captured Jerusalem and Bagdad. Most of the German colonial possessions in Africa, the Pacific, and the Far East were in the hands of the Allies. Questions naturally arose concerning the reconstruction of Europe which would follow once the war was ended. The Central Powers were not committed to any definite program, while the Allies, if victorious, were undecided as to the particular form the new map of Europe should take and to what extent the Germans should pay for the damages inflicted upon Belgium and northeastern France.

Secret treaties arranged between the Allies during the conflict were incompatible with the war aims advanced by President Wilson. Anglo-French agreements had provided for the partition of the German colonies in Africa, and Anglo-French and Russian understandings had awarded Constantinople to Russia and had divided Persia. The Allies, in the Treaty of London, had promised Italy important regions around the Adriatic, including Trieste and *Secret Treaties during the War* Pola, whereas the Russians, the French, and the English had virtually partitioned Asiatic Turkey, and Russia and Japan had reached a settlement regarding Germany's interests in the Far East.

In addition to these arrangements other Allied agreements provided for the partition of Austria-Hungary. One of the most important of these wartime bargains was the Franco-Russian accord, in which France was to obtain Alsace-Lorraine and to control the Saar Basin and the left bank of the Rhine. Russia was to enlarge her frontiers at the expense of the Central Powers. Great Britain, however, refused to become a party to this agreement, as she did not want any one nation to dominate Europe and thus to endanger her position.

These treaties insured very generous rewards for the leading Allied states. But they did not square with Wilson's statement that the Allies were fighting to make the world safe for democracy, to obtain justice for small nations, to check imperialism, and to end wars. Whereas his aims were published, the Allied agreements were kept secret. As a result neutral states, aroused by his idealism, were inclined to favor the Allies. Cuba, Panama, China, Brazil, Siam, Liberia, and Greece joined the Allied cause in 1917, and were followed by the Central American countries in 1918.

On January 8, 1918, President Wilson, in his famous Fourteen Points, summarized his war aims. These were the following: (1) abolition of secret diplomacy *The Fourteen Points* and treaties; (2) freedom of the seas; (3) removal of economic barriers; (4) reduction of armaments; (5) adjustment of colonial claims in the interest of people concerned; (6) aid to Russia to rehabilitate her national life; (7) restoration of Belgium; (8) evacuation of France and the return of Alsace-Lorraine; (9) readjustment of Italy's frontiers; (10) autonomy for subject nationalities in Austria-Hungary; (11) restoration of the Balkan states; (12) self-

government for non-Turkish nationalities and the freedom of
the Dardanelles for all ships; (13) an independent Poland;
and (14) a League of Nations. This program, designed to promote democracy, nationalism, and a world commonwealth,
was heartily and uncritically approved by many people, and
made clearer than any previous declaration the war aims of the
United States. The Allies, however, did not unreservedly
accept these terms as an expression of their war aims.

Wilson's demand for the absolute freedom of commerce in
time of war encountered the uncompromising opposition of
Lloyd George. Later, in defiance of Wilson's threat "to build
up the strongest navy our resources permit," the English
prime minister declared, "Great Britain would spend her last
guinea to keep a navy superior to that of the United States
or any other Power." During the peace conference Wilson,
preoccupied with other problems and perhaps trusting to the
League of Nations to effect a settlement, did not seriously
raise the issue.

The Central Powers reacted rather favorably to the Fourteen Points and to conciliatory war aims as expressed by Lloyd
George. They accepted many of the demands and conditions,
but stated definitely that Germany would retain a large part
of Alsace-Lorraine and that the frontiers of Russia, Italy, and
the Balkan states were to be determined by local agreements.
The Belgium problem and the occupation of northern France
were to be left to the peace conference.

These discussions failed to check the war activities of either
side in 1917. Once in the conflict, the United States, determined to place troops on the Western Front in
American War Prepa-
rations
the minimum amount of time, proceeded to
draft a law mobilizing about five million men,
to build boats, and to manufacture huge quantities of war
supplies. President Wilson appointed "dictators" and administrative boards to organize the country for the prosecution of
the war. As in other nations this "war-time state socialism"
worked very well. Personal liberty was curtailed, but immense quantities of goods, [ships, munitions, and materials
of all sorts were sent to the needy Allies. Money was mobi-

lized as well as men. By issuing Liberty bonds the United States raised $21,000,000,000 to carry on the war and to lend to the Allies. As a result of these effective measures, in addition to the successful guarding of ocean lanes through which the transports could be conducted by American as well as British warships, large American forces under the command of General Pershing were, by the spring of 1918, in France, ready for action.

At that time the submarine policy of Germany was breaking down. Although terribly injurious at first, destroying many British merchant vessels, it had now lost much of its effectiveness. Science had come to the aid of the Allies. Increased manufacture of ships, improved weapons of defense, submarine chasers, patrol boats, aircraft, and an efficient system of convoys and the use of camouflage, all eventually made the submarine a less powerful weapon and forced the Germans to stake everything on their great military machine in the West.

In March, 1917, the Germans decided to shorten their lines on the Western Front from Noyon on the south to Arras on the north. As they withdrew they devas- *The War in 1917* tated the land so completely that the English and the French found it impossible to utilize most of the territory which the Germans had held so long. The Allies made desperate attempts to break the German lines while the latter were establishing their new defenses. But the Hindenburg Line was so well fortified that despite these attacks, which resulted in a tremendous loss of life among the Entente powers, it held with few exceptions throughout the year.

The British did make some progress in forcing the enemy back on the Belgian coast. Zeebrugge, the base from which the German submarines made their departure to prey upon English commerce, was the objective of a British drive. Attempts to take St. Quentin, the important mining town of Lens, and the city of Cambrai failed. Nevertheless the terrible slaughter continued, tens of thousands being killed or wounded every week.

In the summer of 1917 war weariness affected the leading

nations engaged in the struggle. During the three years of the conflict over four million lives had been lost and many other millions had been wounded or permanently disabled. Furthermore, menacing prospects of national bankruptcy, together with future burdens of taxation for every belligerent power, lowered the public morale in almost all of the nations involved in the struggle.

Defeatism in 1917

To many people the continuation of the struggle seemed futile. Numerous Germans could see that, despite the victories and conquests won by the Central Powers over Russia, Serbia, and Rumania, the "war map" was no index of the relative strength of the two groups, for it did not take into account control of the seas and of the world's chief resources and materials. They felt that a further attempt to defeat the Entente was not worth the price. On the other hand, many men in the Allied countries realized that even though they had succeeded in gaining superiority in man power and in materials and were able to assume the offensive, the Central Powers had a strong military machine, which, as a result of the collapse of Russia, could be concentrated on the Western Front. Men shuddered when they thought of the terrible offensive the Germans were about to inaugurate in the west, and many decided that further resistance was useless. In all countries involved in the war the masses, discouraged and tired, prayed earnestly for peace.

The effect of this so-called "defeatism" was first evident in Russia, helping to precipitate a revolution there. It also existed in the Central Powers. During 1917 the submarine campaign failed to live up to expectations. Many German and Austrian leaders therefore realized that the strength of the Central Powers was waning and urged peace negotiations, involving concessions, to end the war. Austria was the first to feel the effects of this defeatist movement. Confronted by the unrest of the Poles, Czechs, and Yugoslavs in his kingdom, Emperor Charles, who succeeded Francis Joseph in November, 1916, decided to enter into peace negotiations with France. Despite the protests of Germany, he promised to give territory on the Adriatic to Serbia, the Trentino to Italy, and Constantinople to Russia.

Opposition to the continuation of the war developed in the German Empire. Erzberger, leader of the Catholic Center party, aware of the critical situation in Austria and Emperor Charles's attempt to obtain peace, said frankly that Germany had lost the war. On July 19, 1917, the German *Reichstag* passed a resolution asking "for a peace of reconciliation with no annexations and no indemnities." Bethmann-Hollweg went even farther than the *Reichstag* and stated that he would favor the restoration of Alsace-Lorraine to France in order to obtain peace. But by 1917 the German government was in the hands of her generals. Bethmann-Hollweg was forced to resign and the Kaiser had to submit to a military dictatorship.

War weariness was also felt in the Allied countries. In 1917 the submarine campaign, even though it failed to attain its objective, did help to bring about a food shortage in England. This situation tended to promote extreme pessimism among many English people. In France mutinies occurred in the army. In Italy a strong defeatist movement resulted in uprisings in Turin and insubordination in the army. Influenced by this defeatism prominent men — for example, Joseph Caillaux of France and Lord Lansdowne of England — came out in favor of a revision of war aims. Offer Germany more moderate terms, they said, and the peace party there will end the war. Both men believed that the prolongation of the conflict would bring ruin to the civilized world. One leader, however, refused to be moved by this "policy of despair" — Georges Clemenceau. Fanatical patriotism caused this bitter foe of Germany to insist that before peace could be attained Germany must be defeated. At the head of the war party he helped to re-create belief in victory and to revive patriotism.

At a time when defeatism seemed to be on the increase in the Allied countries the Central Powers arranged to attack the Italian forces. On October 24 they struck that part of the line called the Julian front, broke through, captured 100,000 prisoners, and reduced the rest of the Italian army on the sector to a fugi-

The Attack on the Italian Front

tive rabble. For a time the entire Italian line threatened to give way. If it had, the Central Powers would have been in a position to march into Italy and then into southern France. French and British reënforcements, together with fresh Italian troops, were rushed to the front in November and December and helped to check this Teuton advance. Resistance to the invasion had cost Italy 800,000 men, but it had roused her fighting spirit. Moreover, out of it came a movement for a unified command. Early in November the premiers of France, Great Britain, and Italy met at Rapallo, and from their conference arose the Supreme War Council of Versailles. "Henceforth, in theory at any rate, there was but one front between the North Sea and the Adriatic, a single exchequer, and a single granary."

During the winter of 1917 the stage was set for the final German drive on the Western Front. At that time the British were rapidly losing their confidence, the French had not recovered from the extreme pessimism which had affected most of the Allies the preceding year, and the Americans were still a negligible factor in the drama. These conditions, together with the withdrawal of Russia, gave the Germans an admirable opportunity to break through the Western Front and to achieve at least a compromise peace.

The Last German Offensives

Germany's military leaders believed that further peace negotiations would simply enable the enemy to increase the strength of their armies. As patriots and soldiers they sincerely felt that Germany must strike quickly and not surrender until all her resources had been exhausted. And what an opportunity presented itself in 1918! One-half million men and many heavy guns could be transferred from the east and flung into the western scale. Moreover, the vast battering ram of artillery was now to be supplanted by a novel attack called infiltration, in which the Teutonic troops would literally sift into the Allied lines. Germany could not afford to neglect this opportunity to crush the Allies on the Western Front and by so doing to win the war.

Consequently plans were formulated for a great German offensive. The military authorities, headed by Ludendorff, decided to institute a drive upon the St. Quentin sector, the weak spot of the Allied line, in the spring of 1918. At this point the British and French armies joined; and inasmuch as the English tended to strengthen their forces near the coast, and the French near Paris, this section of the line was especially weak. Behind the Allied trenches was a railroad center, Amiens. If this place could be captured, the main transportation lines

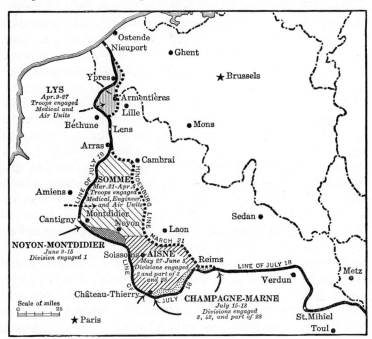

The German Offensives of 1918
Courtesy of the United States War Department

between Paris and London would be cut. Meanwhile the British armies would be rolled back to the coast, while the Germans, attacking along other sections of the line, would envelop the French forces and put them out of the conflict.

After some minor attacks on the Champagne and Ypres fronts the Germans, on March 21, 1918, threw over five hundred thousand men against the Allied line between Arras and La Fère. Outnumbered by the Germans and losing contact with the French on their right, the British, fighting desperately to save the strategic city of Amiens, had to give way. Temporarily the Germans succeeded in breaking through the line, but the collapse of the German transport system prevented them from taking advantage of the breach. On the twenty-sixth the gap was closed, and although the British continued to retreat, the line was not broken again. One explanation for the British withdrawal, which almost proved to be a disaster, was General Pétain's refusal at first to send sufficient troops to aid the British in resisting the enemy. He was resolved to concentrate his troops for the defense of Paris, even though he would have to break contact with the British by so doing. Clemenceau, the French premier, however, opposed this plan, so that the French line held and the German attack was checked after the Allies had retreated some thirty-five miles and had suffered heavy casualties.

This German offensive led to important results. It galvanized the Allies and the United States into action. Many who felt in their hearts that the war was won now realized that victory might be snatched from them unless they cooperated and hastened preparations. A defeat coming before the United States could exert her weight might prolong the conflict and prevent a complete Allied victory. Consequently the British, the French, and the Americans were keyed up to almost superhuman efforts. Men were trained rapidly and then sent to France in British and American ships to complete their military education. Urged on by the vehement appeals of Lloyd George and Clemenceau for help before it should be too late, the United States succeeded in sending nearly 700,000 troops to Europe between May 1 and July 31, 1918. This number was well over twice as many as were sent in the preceding year.

On April 28 the first American regular army division, composed of soldiers who had received intensive training in active parts of the battle line, began real fighting on the Picardy front. A month before (March 28) the Allied leaders — Pétain, Foch, Haig, Clemenceau, and others — had met and agreed to recognize General Foch, considered one of the outstanding generals, as the leader of all forces on the Western Front. In the following month he was given supreme control by being appointed commander in chief of the Allied armies. "In the midst of the advancing cannonades, throbbing ceaselessly in the ears of the leaders assembled, Napoleon's spirit incarnate in Foch received the august mission which he relinquished only when it had been gloriously fulfilled."

William II dismissed his reactionary cabinet and appointed a liberal ministry, with Prince Max of Baden as chancellor. This new ministry sent a note to President Wilson, asking for an armistice in order that a treaty of peace based on the Fourteen Points might be arranged. A similar appeal was sent from Austria. Meanwhile the Allies continued to advance, breaking through the Hindenburg line and forcing the Germans practically out of France and Belgium.

On April 9 the Germans, trying to break through to the Channel ports, opened a second attack upon the British left wing, between La Bassée and Armentières. The British troops, however, checked the Germans and succeeded in preventing them from attaining their objective. Even though the Germans had suffered over half a million casualties in these two attacks, Ludendorff continued his "peace drive." By the end of May he had replaced three fourths of his losses in man power with youths and with men returned from the hospitals. On May 27 he delivered his third great blow, this time against the French line between Soissons and Reims. Capturing Soissons, the Germans bent the French line until, by May 31, they had created a triangular salient which extended to the Marne River and had Soissons, Reims, and Château-Thierry as its three corners. At this time the fresh American troops began to play a decisive rôle in the battle. Thrown into the struggle at the southern extremity of the salient near Château-Thierry, they helped to check the German advance.

By the midsummer of 1918 the German forces were in a dangerous position. They had created two salients, one near Amiens, the other reaching south to Château-Thierry. Unless they converted them into one, the enemy might envelop the

German troops in either salient and greatly weaken the German position. Aware of this danger, the Teutons instituted, between June 9 and June 15, a fourth attack on a twenty-two-mile front reaching from Montdidier to Noyon. Reënforced by the American first division, the French checked the attack of the Germans after the latter had advanced only six miles.

While the Germans were trying to break the deadlock in the west the Austrians opened a similar offensive against the

The Last Austrian Drive

Italians on the Piave River. Nature favored the Italians this time; for on June 17, after more than 100,000 Austrian troops had succeeded in crossing the shallow stream, the sudden flooding of the river turned it into a raging torrent which swept away ten of the fourteen bridges. Meanwhile the Italians, reënforced, advanced and soon occupied the west bank of the Piave. In this struggle the Dual Monarchy suffered over 150,000 casualties. It was her last great effort. Broken in spirit, faced by grave economic problems and by nationalist uprisings, Austria practically withdrew from the war.

In July, 1918, the Germans made a final desperate attempt to break through the Western Front. At that time they de-

Turn in the Tide of Battle

cided to strike the French line east and west of Reims, capture the city, split the French front (cutting the vital railways from Paris to Nancy), and then roll the French armies back, enveloping them and capturing Paris. The great attack opened on July 14. After a four-hour bombardment the German troops advanced and succeeded in crossing the Marne between Château-Thierry and Dormans. But at this point their advance ceased. On the southeast part of the salient, which extended to Château-Thierry, Italian troops blocked the way, while on the southwest American troops not only checked their advance but forced them to retreat across the Marne. The German assault east of Reims was also repulsed by French and American troops, and the capture of the city prevented. Again the Germans had failed to gain their objectives.

At this time the entrance of the Americans into the World War was rapidly changing the tide in favor of the Allies.

Previously only American money and supplies had sustained the flagging Allied forces on the battle fronts. Now American enthusiasm and American men, led by General Pershing, were also thrown onto the scales. These elements were decisive and made possible the complete triumph of the Allied cause.

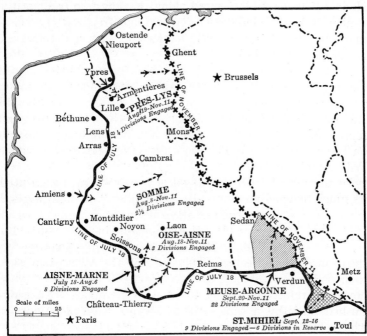

The Allied Offensives of 1918
Courtesy of the United States War Department

During July the offensive changed hands. Foch was in a position to undertake a general advance. With 85,000 American troops engaged in the second battle of the *The Allied Offensive* Marne, their forces increased during the months of July and August until over a million Americans were in the field when the war came to an end on November 11, 1918. Within a short time the Marne and Amiens salients were completely wiped out. Château-Thierry was regained on July 21, and other places were recaptured. Then the Allies crossed the Somme, with the Germans in rapid retreat. The Germans exhausted their reserves in their July attack, and their resistance collapsed. Within six weeks over 150,000 German prisoners, 2000 big guns, and 14,000 machine guns were captured by the Allies. On August 8 a powerful allied advance was instituted along the southern front of the Amiens˗salient. General Ludendorff now realized that Germany had lost the war, and therefore he suggested the opening of peace negotiations.

Austria was about to surrender. On August 30 she warned Germany of her intention of taking independent action by suggesting a conference of all belligerents. On September 15 Austria asked all nations involved in the conflict to send representatives to a "confidential and nonbinding discussion on basic principles." This appeal was ignored by President Wilson and the Allies.

In the fall of 1918 the Allied army at Salonica instituted its much-delayed advance. By September 25 it had invaded Bulgaria, and the Bulgarian government asked *Capitulation of Bulgaria and Turkey* for an armistice at once, which was signed a few days later (September 30). According to the terms of the agreement Bulgaria gave the Allies permission to cross her territory in order to attack Turkey. The Turks, however, refused to wait for this contemplated invasion. Pushed back by a rapid Allied advance in Asia Minor, in which Damascus, Beirut, and Aleppo had been captured, and fearing the loss of Mosul, the oil region in Mesopotamia, and Adrianople in Thrace, the Turks sued for an armistice and withdrew from the war on October 31.

Austria-Hungary was now in a difficult position. She not only had to hold back the Italians but also had to prepare for an invasion of the Allied army in the Balkans. *Surrender of the Dual Monarchy* To increase the difficulties, Rumania had abrogated the treaty she had signed with the Central Powers and was preparing to join the Serbs and the Allies in this invasion. Internal troubles added to the problems confronting the Dual Monarchy. Magyars, Czechoslovaks, Yugoslavs, German Austrians, and Poles were demanding independence. The Hapsburg ruler could do but one thing, — capitulate. This he did, signing an armistice with the Allies on November 3, 1918.

Germany was left to fight a large part of the world alone. In September the Germans were forced back to the Hindenburg Line, having suffered a million and a half casualties. The Allies continued their attacks. *The German Collapse* Between September 12 and September 16 the American first army, under the personal command of General Pershing, undertook its first major operation, wiping out the St. Mihiel salient. On September 28 General Ludendorff again admitted that the war was lost. During the early part of October peace negotiations were instituted.

The Americans inaugurated their greatest offensive between the Argonne Forest and the river Meuse. Over a million troops, advancing through tangled woods and underbrush, pushed the German line back until they reached the outskirts of Sedan. By cutting the Sedan-Mézières railroad at this point they now made the German line untenable, and the Allies occupied Sedan itself.

By November the Germans realized that they would have to capitulate. The collapse of Austria-Hungary and the fact that the Allied armies could now cross this country to attack Germany from the south made the continuation of war impracticable. Moreover, the flight of the Kaiser to Holland, the mutiny in the navy, the proclamation of a republic in Bavaria, and the creation of a socialist ministry under Friedrich Ebert — all these events presaged an impending revolution in Germany. To avoid an invasion of Germany and a radical revolution, peace had to be made.

On November 5 President Wilson informed Germany that Marshal Foch was empowered to conclude an armistice. Determined to disarm the enemy completely, the French general presented the following *The Armistice, 1918* severe terms: (1) the evacuation of Belgium, France, and Luxembourg within two weeks; (2) the evacuation of all territory west of the Rhine within one month; (3) Entente occupation of the west bank of the Rhine and the chief crossings; (4) renunciation of the German treaties with Russia and Rumania; (5) the surrender of German submarines and warships, together with 5000 locomotives, 5000 motor lorries, and 150,000 railway cars; and (6) continuance of the economic blockade. Unable to offer further effective resistance, the German government accepted these terms, and at 11 A. M., November 11, 1918, the armistice was signed and the World War came to an end.[1]

[1] Of the sixty-five million men mobilized, over eight millions either were killed in action or died of wounds; the total cost of the conflict was estimated at over $186,000,000,000,— just about the wealth of the United States in 1918.

The Place where the ARMISTICE was SIGNED

PART VIII. THE AFTERMATH: BOURGEOIS CONSERVATISM AND THE NEW REVOLUTION

CHAPTER XXXI

The Conference of Paris and the Peace Settlements

DESPITE the withdrawal of her allies and the reverses at the front Germany could have prolonged the struggle. With slight hope of victory, however, there seemed better prospects for favorable peace terms if an armistice were arranged before the military situation became worse. Therefore the German government surrendered on the basis of the Fourteen Points.

Serious obstacles stood in the way of the impartial settlement demanded by a war-weary world. The peace program of the American president, vaguely expressed and indefinite as to specific arrangements, *Obstacles to an Impartial Settlement* neglected the special desires and practical needs of the victorious states. Although the Allies had accepted in principle some of the famous Fourteen Points,

NOTE. *The picture on this page shows the* SIGNING OF THE TREATY OF VERSAILLES. *After a painting by Sir Philip Orpen, R.A.*

their interests frequently clashed with the higher aims expressed therein. Apparently not impressed by Wilson's idealism, Clemenceau of France observed that though God needed only ten commandments, Wilson required no less than fourteen. War-time idealism was thus succeeded by a spirit of cynicism and revenge which ushered in a "hard-boiled" era.

Conflicting national aspirations proved difficult to reconcile. War-time propaganda, intensifying public opinion, often led to excessive demands by the victorious powers. Attacks of opposition parties in many countries forced responsible diplomats to make unreasonable claims. The rights of other nations, and especially of the hated enemies, were usually disregarded by ardent nationalists, who desired to promote the welfare of their own countries. Although the theory of national self-determination was recognized in principle, in practice it gave way before the interests of the great states.

Imperialism was another obstacle to a just peace. Unknown to many idealists and the general public the post-war division of spoils, as stated before, had been anticipated during the conflict by secret negotiations, which provided for the distribution of the German colonies in Asia, Africa, and the Pacific; the partition of the Ottoman and Hapsburg empires; and the partial dismemberment of Germany.[1] These earlier obligations had to be satisfied before the victors could proceed to the arrangement of an enduring settlement.

Militarism, especially the armed might of the Allies, was detrimental to the exercise of moderation in dealing with the vanquished. The higher military authorities, regarded by the public as national heroes and oracles, wielded enormous influence. Constantly advancing the shopworn concept of security, they demanded the establishment of strategic frontiers. Marshal Foch favored the Rhine for France, and Italian militarists insisted on the Brenner Pass as security against future Austro-German aggression. Taking advantage of the armistices, which provided for temporary occupation of frontier regions, the Allies and their protégés planned to retain permanent possession of these territories.

[1] See pages 566–567.

The waves of idealism and pacificism radiated by President Wilson and others were partially counteracted by the wartime propaganda. Perhaps necessary to sustain the public morale, the deliberate falsification of facts and misrepresentation of enemy motives made forgiveness difficult. Germany was popularly regarded in the Allied countries as the malicious instigator of the war and the perpetrator of frightful atrocities; many clamored for the punishment of Germany and her "war criminals." The press, popular demagogues, and the public demanded that Germany defray the expenses of the conflict, and some even proposed that indemnities be levied upon the enemy so as to relieve burdensome taxation in Allied countries. Despite socialist opposition the thesis of Germany's war guilt and her obligation to make reparation for the actual destruction in France and Belgium was generally accepted. The estimates as to the defeated nation's capacity to pay often reached grandiose proportions, certain naïve Frenchmen and Englishmen being under the delusion that one hundred billions or more would not be excessive.

During the months immediately following the cessation of hostilities political conditions in Germany were precarious. The unstable republican government but recently established in that country faced the danger of a *coup d'état*, being menaced both by the royalists on the extreme right and the radicals on the left. The unexpected collapse of the imperial administration, the sudden blasting of German hopes of victory, the privations, famines, and suffering resulting from the Allied blockade, and the weaknesses of the new régime left Germany an easy prey for extremists. There was a grave possibility, recognized by the Allies, that Bolshevism might sweep Germany and overturn the new republic. Hence they considered the promises of the German government unreliable.

Disorders in eastern Europe were also menacing. Petty conflicts, such as those between the Poles and the Ukrainians, the Poles and the Czechs, the Rumanians and the Magyars, threatened to precipitate greater conflicts. General chaos in the Russian borderlands and in south-central Europe seemed to presage the spread from Russia of the dreaded Bolshevism.

Therefore the Allies hastened to sustain their protégés and the newly founded states in an effort to restabilize central and eastern Europe so as to build a bulwark of capitalism against the forces of the new revolution.

If war-torn Europe was to be saved from chaos and disorder, an early settlement of its problems and ills was vital. Nevertheless, some two months elapsed before the opening of the Paris peace conference and the beginning of the great work of reconstruction and rehabilitation. It took several weeks before the victorious nations could restore order in their domestic politics, assemble their peace delegations, and transport them to the French capital. Premier Lloyd George determined to secure a national vote of confidence from the British electorate. His campaign on the basis of "Make Germany pay and hang the Kaiser too" proved triumphant at the polls on December 14, and he went to Paris with the support of the nation. By the middle of January, 1919, most of the delegates, official and otherwise, had assembled.

At Paris were gathered the hosts of diplomats, experts, and secretaries who constituted the delegations of thirty-two *Composition and Organization of the Peace Conference* Allied and associated powers. Included in their number were some of the world's most distinguished men. Heading the American delegation was President Woodrow Wilson, arch-idealist and exponent of world tranquillity, who had sought a "peace without victory." Less idealistic were Premier Lloyd George of Great Britain, a clever opportunist; Premier Clemenceau, "the Tiger of France," an ardent nationalist; and Premier Orlando of Italy, ineffectual but determined. Becoming the "Big Four" of the conference, these men were largely responsible for the final peace terms. Assisting them were technical experts, advisers, secretaries, committees, and commissions, who transformed the ideas and plans of their chiefs into an actual settlement. In addition there was a multitude of miscellaneous unofficial delegates (scholars, lawyers, journalists, business men, and propagandists, representing diverse subject nationalities, minorities, labor, business interests, and other groups), who hoped to secure concessions or advantages for the interests which they represented. Paris was indeed the center of the world in the winter and spring of 1918–1919.

Few assemblages have been called upon to solve such a bewildering array of detailed, technical, and complicated problems. Strangely enough, however, although every conceivable group which hoped to profit at the conference was represented, the delegates of the enemy and neutral powers were barred. The "enduring peace" was to be a dictated rather than a negotiated settlement.

With the gathering in Paris of the heterogeneous array of diplomats, preliminary steps had to be taken to organize the vast congress. On January 12, 1919, at an informal meeting of the two ranking delegates from the United States, Great Britain, France, and Italy, it was agreed that plenary sessions of the conference should consist of the plenipotentiaries of all powers which had declared war against or severed relations with Germany. In accordance with its size each state was allowed from one to five members, the great powers each having the maximum number of representatives. While in theory the approval of the plenary session was required for all decisions, in practice the influence of this body was insignificant. Meeting only six times during the course of the preparation of the German treaty, the plenary session did not receive the full text until the day before its presentation to the Germans. Even then its formal approval was not secured by vote.

In the initial stages of the conference the Council of Ten was the most important single organ. Partly an outgrowth of the Supreme Inter-Allied War Council, it consisted of two representatives from each of the five major powers,— the United States, Great Britain, France, Italy, and Japan. Its functions were (1) to determine what matters should be referred to the general conference and (2) to consider, in a preliminary fashion at least, those questions which it deemed sufficiently involved or important to merit special attention. Thus the Council of Ten arrogated to itself the real direction of policies and affairs for the first two months of the conference.

The great states dominated the machinery of the assembly. They monopolized the membership of the Council of Ten and sent delegates to all commissions and committees. Lesser states were to be represented only in matters which directly concerned them. At the secret meetings of the Council of Ten they could appear to present their cases.

On January 18, 1919, the forty-eighth anniversary of the proclamation of the German Empire at the palace of Versailles, President Poincaré opened the congress in the French ministry of foreign affairs. Premier Clemenceau was elected president, and despite some protests the arrangements previously made for its organization were approved. Dissatisfaction felt by the lesser powers concerning the domination of the principal states was unavailing.

After two months of dalliance, however, the Council of Ten had produced little to justify its virtual dictatorship. Not much more than the provisions for German military, naval, and air disarmament had been determined. Slight progress had been made with the complicated territorial, economic, and financial terms. A multitude of special commissions of experts whose findings were subsequently incorporated into the treaty had been created to hurdle many of these highly complex problems.

Conditions in Europe, however, called for a speedy settlement. There was serious danger of minor wars resulting from conflicting aspirations. Chaotic situations in central and eastern Europe seemed to invite the spread of Bolshevism. To expedite matters, therefore, and to reëstablish stability and order, the Big Four superseded the Council of Ten. On March 25 Wilson, Clemenceau, Lloyd George, and Orlando ceased attending the sessions of the Council of Ten, and thenceforth met informally. The council degenerated into a superior commission, and the Big Four, with the assistance of various committees, worked out the remainder of the peace settlement.

The great personalities dominating the conference frequently found themselves in disagreement. So heated became some of the controversies that on one occasion, during a dispute between the English and French representatives, Clemenceau, it is said, losing control of himself, jumped up from his chair and "reached for Lloyd George's throat"; but fortunately Wilson was able to separate the two. The latter, whom Clemenceau called a "benevolent wolf," attempted to maintain peace within and without the council. In both respects he achieved only moderate success.

Lloyd George and Clemenceau were too clever for their American adversary. The actual practice of secret diplomacy freed them from the unwelcome glare of publicity. By a series of compromises they managed to construct a treaty which, while seeming to accord with the idealism expressed during the war, more than adequately safeguarded the special interests of their own powers. Therefore the peace treaties represented a curious intermixture of quixotic idealism and *Realpolitik.*

Of the earlier problems which concerned the conference, the projected League of Nations, discussed in the next chapter, was the most significant. Realizing the almost *Drafting of the Covenant for the League of Nations* universal demand for some form of international organization to prevent war, President Wilson and many idealists urged that provision for such a body be incorporated into the peace treaty. Practical diplomats, alarmed at the European situation, believed that an immediate peace was imperative, and felt that the drafting of a covenant for the proposed League of Nations should be postponed. After some preliminary skirmishing, however, the idealists gained their point. On January 25 the second plenary session voted for the inclusion of the League Covenant as an integral part of the treaty.

Another problem seriously disturbed the serenity of the conference. This was the matter of French security. Fearful of German revenge, French militarists and *French Security* nationalists, who saw only "barbarism and confusion east of the Rhine," had worked out a definite program. In flagrant disregard of the principle of national self-determination their plans were concerned only with the safeguarding of French interests against a Germany already demoralized and disarmed. French military control of the

Rhine was considered vital. Clemenceau, of whom it has been written, "He had one illusion — France; and one disillusion — mankind, including Frenchmen," demanded that Germany's western frontier be fixed at the Rhine and that she be deprived of all territory west of the river. He then proposed to create a neutral and autonomous buffer state from the ten thousand square miles of territory lying west of the Rhine. In 1917 Russia's consent to such a scheme had been secured, it being further specified that the new state be occupied by French troops until Germany had fulfilled the final peace terms. Furthermore, Marshal Foch and others demanded that the French be allowed to occupy the Rhine bridges as guarantees that Germany would live up to her treaty obligations.

The opposition of Lloyd George and Wilson to the scheme for an independent buffer state between France and Germany led to a crisis of many weeks' duration. Finally the French gave way and Clemenceau relinquished his project. An inter-Allied military occupation of this area for at least fifteen years, however, was designed to guarantee the German execution of the treaty terms. The left bank of the Rhine and a strip fifty kilometers in width on the right bank were demilitarized. In addition Lloyd George and Wilson agreed to a security pact which provided Anglo-American aid in the event of unprovoked aggression by Germany.

A serious crisis resulted from French pretensions to the Saar Basin. Since it contained very rich and highly concentrated coal beds, this relatively small section of the left bank was of great economic importance. In 1913 the Saar Basin was estimated to hold seventeen billion tons of coal,—an amount greater than the known reserve supply of all France and equal to about 22 per cent of the German reserve. With a population of 650,000, chiefly German, this region had highly developed industries which were closely connected with those of Lorraine. Clemenceau, egged on by certain persons, demanded full ownership of all the mines and territorial sovereignty over the part of this basin which had previously been ruled by France.

The Germans had deliberately destroyed French coal mines in 1918. Therefore the Allied diplomats, although opposing political annexation of the entire district, approved of the demand for the acquisition of these mines by the French. Consequently they were ceded to France, the Saar Basin being included in the French customs union even though it remained under German sovereignty. For fifteen years the region was to be ruled by a commission under the League of Nations, at the expiration of which period the people who resided there at the time the Treaty of Versailles was signed were to hold a plebiscite. Then they would be allowed to unite with Germany or with France, or to remain under League control. In the event of reunion with the first-named the mines were to be purchased by Germany.

Possibilities of further weakening Germany intrigued the French. They desired to reduce greatly her territorial extent. It was hoped that the post-war German political organization would be so weakened as to frustrate her recovery. While the Allies were to remain armed, the principle of naval, air, and land disarmament was to be applied to Germany. The ruin of the latter's economic fabric was sought by the alienation of her important natural resources, by the levying of a huge indemnity, and by the practice of discrimination against all German goods.

This French program also called for readjustments in the east. France hoped to create alliances with such states as Poland and Czechoslovakia, which presumably would share the French fear of German revenge and future aggression. French chauvinists already envisaged the establishment of a military hegemony in Europe and the isolation of Germany, surrounded by a ring of hostile states.

Reparation was the most perplexing problem confronting the diplomats. Originally the British and French wanted to force Germany to pay for all damages and war costs. They disagreed with the American delegates, who said that the demands which *Preliminary Reparations Settlement* might be made on the Germans were limited by the pre-armistice agreements. The dispute was referred to the Big

Four, and Wilson persuaded his colleagues to agree that the reparations should cover only actual damage done, the cost of the war being excluded. In the case of Belgium, however, an exception was made, Germany being expected to defray this country's war costs as well as damages. It proved very difficult to define precisely what was meant by the term *damages*. There was general agreement as to ten distinct types of damage to be covered, but there was some dispute as to whether war pensions and separation allowances should be added. Finally the approval of the Big Four provided for their inclusion.

Fixing the amount, the schedule, and the method of reparation payments was no easy task. Although the American delegates urged the setting of a definite and reasonable sum, the Allies were loath to present official appraisals as to the amount of damage which they had suffered. Wilson, although advised of the inconsistency between the inclusion of pensions and the spirit of the Fourteen Points, supported the Anglo-French position, declaring: "Logic! Logic! I don't give a damn for logic. I am going to include pensions." Allied estimates as to the total to be demanded from Germany varied from $10,000,000,000 to $120,000,000,000. Some of the Allied statesmen feared that it would be unwise to set a definite figure, since their war-inflamed peoples were making preposterous demands. Therefore a provisional settlement was arranged. Germany was required to pay in gold or its equivalent the sum of $5,000,000,000 by May, 1921. A reparation commission was empowered to determine at a later date the total amount to be collected, and to arrange the schedule of payments.

The problem of recreating a "united and independent Poland" proved very perplexing. Opinions varied widely *Creation of Poland* as to what should constitute the extent of the revived state. Mindful of the enormous size of the former kingdom, Polish nationalists, supported by the French, demanded far-flung boundaries. The Allies had promised the Poles all territory inhabited by them and also "a free and secure access to the sea." To recognize Polish territorial claims without infringing on the rights of other nationalities who inhabited the disputed areas was difficult. With Germans, Poles, Czechs, Russians, and Lithuanians hopelessly intermixed, it was impossible to draw the boundaries along national lines without creating islands of isolated ethnic groups.

A special commission was appointed to deal with the extraordinarily complicated Polish question. In March it recommended that a corridor be constructed in German territory from Poland proper to the city of Danzig on the Baltic. This strip of land would provide the new country with an outlet to the sea, but had the disadvantage of separating East Prussia from Germany. Also, many districts in the proposed corridor, especially the city of Danzig, were overwhelmingly German.

The persistent opposition of Lloyd George compelled a modification of the commission's scheme. Although Poland secured her corridor providing access to the Baltic, she did not obtain complete sovereignty over the entire territory. The important Marienwerder district, dominantly German in population, on the east bank of the Vistula River, was not ceded to Poland. Instead a plebiscite was to be held to ascertain its ultimate disposition, and it later voted to remain with Germany.

Danzig, with its environs, was established as a free city under the protection of the League of Nations. Its chief executive was to be a high commissioner appointed by the League. The Allies, however, arranged a treaty between Poland and Danzig by which the latter was to be included in the Polish customs union. Free use of all waterways and docks, and Polish administration of the means of communication between Poland and the Free City, were designed to facilitate Polish commerce. The conduct of the foreign relations of Danzig was in Polish hands. In addition Poland and Germany were expected to conclude a reciprocal treaty granting one another adequate facilities for transportation and communication across the corridor and German territory lying between Poland and Danzig.

A number of other disputes concerned with Polish territorial aspirations proved difficult to solve. The desire of the Poles to reëstablish the "historic" nation caused them to lay claim to districts not dominantly Polish. A bitter disagreement over the German-Polish frontier in Upper Silesia could not be settled satisfactorily; consequently the Treaty of Versailles provided for a plebiscite in order to determine the people's wishes. As will be shown later, the problem was temporarily solved on a compromise basis with the partition of the region, after the whole matter had been submitted to the League of Nations.[1] Disputes between Poland and Lithuania over the cities of Vilna and Memel were also settled subsequently, although in a more arbitrary manner.[2]

The Italian delegation precipitated a crisis which nearly broke up the conference. Hoping to make the Adriatic an Italian lake, Orlando and his colleagues demanded greater territorial cessions than those stipulated by the secret Treaty of London of April 26, 1915. The latter had provided for the acquisition by Italy of the districts at the head of the Adriatic and part of the eastern shores, including Trieste and Pola. Farther south the Croatian and Dalmatian coasts, including the ports of Fiume, Spalato, and Ragusa, were to go to Croatia, Serbia, and Montenegro.

Struggle over Italian Claims

Flushed with victory, however, the Italian people were dissatisfied with their share of the spoils. Their entrance into the war had been largely due to a determination to weaken Austria-Hungary and to secure mastery of the Adriatic. The consolidation of the Serbs, Montenegrins, Croats, and Slovenes into the kingdom of Yugoslavia, however, created a powerful state to the northeast of Italy, which, if it acquired the Croatian and Dalmatian coasts, would become a formidable menace to Italian aspirations in the Adriatic. The immediate crisis centered around the city of Fiume, the cession of which was requested by the Italian diplomats. Wilson, opposing the execution of the secret Treaty of London, rejected their claims. Italy, never having agreed to accept Wilson's peace program, continued to demand Fiume.

[1] See pages 615–616.   [2] See page 615.

Both the Yugoslavs and the Italians believed that they had legitimate rights to the Adriatic city. Italy's claims, dictated largely by public opinion at home, rested on the contention that Fiume contained many more Italians than Yugoslavs. The Italians also argued that Dalmatia, isolated from Yugoslavia by mountain barriers, was geographically in close contact with the Italian peninsula, and that a similarity in climate, vegetation, commercial activities, and culture seemed to link Dalmatia with Italy rather than with the Balkans. The Italian delegates frankly claimed that the possession of the strategic Dalmatian coast was vital to the defense of Italy. On the other hand, the Yugoslavs pointed out that less than 10 per cent of the population of Dalmatia was Italian. Even in the city of Fiume, if the suburbs were counted, the Yugoslavs enjoyed numerical superiority. The Yugoslav arguments, however, were not concerned purely with the principle of national self-determination. Fiume was the logical outlet to the sea. Therefore to give that city and Dalmatia to Italy would place the latter in a strategic position to menace the newly united kingdom and at the same time to exploit its economic weakness.

The impasse concerning a solution of the Dalmatian frontier continued, although the conference, after a long deadlock, allowed Italy, by annexing the Brenner Pass, to establish an almost impregnable frontier in the Tyrol. For geographical and strategic reasons her northeastern frontier was pushed to the top of the mountain ranges, and 300,000 Yugoslavs came under Italian rule.

As Wilson showed no sign of relenting on the Adriatic issue, Orlando and Sonnino returned to Rome on April 24, 1919. Finding themselves sustained by public opinion there, and fearful that their absence might cause Italian interests to suffer, they came back to the conference on May 9, Orlando resuming his place in the Council of Four. The fall of the Italian ministry on June 18, however, caused the final withdrawal of Orlando and Sonnino, and their replacement by Nitti and Tittoni. Therefore the solution of the Dalmatian problem was left to Italy and Yugoslavia to work out by direct negotiations.

There were many difficulties involved in the disposition of Germany's overseas empire. During the war, by a series of secret treaties, her possessions had been prac-

Division of German Colonies tically partitioned among the great powers, the British Empire, France, and Japan being scheduled to receive the bulk of them. When the problem of their disposal first came up in January, the great states desired to annex them outright. Wilson, however, supported by Lloyd George, favored a novel plan of trusteeship, which had been worked out separately and individually both by General Smuts and by Colonel House. Despite the opposition of Australia, New Zealand, and the South African Union the mandate system was accepted and applied to the former German colonies and the non-Turkish sections of the Ottoman Empire. Its underlying principle was trusteeship; that is, the state which held the mandates was obligated to develop and administer the colonies as wards of the League. The policy of the open door was to be maintained, and the powers were expected to promote the welfare of the mandates and to present an annual report to the League.

Inasmuch as the regions to be converted into mandates varied widely, three main classes were designated: A, B, and C. Included in class A were the former Turkish possessions of Syria, Palestine, Iraq, and Transjordan. In these regions the people were sufficiently well advanced to look forward to independence after preliminary tutelage in administration. The six class-B mandates were in central Africa and were intrusted to Great Britain, France, and Belgium. Rather backward districts, it was assumed that they would need considerable supervision for many years. The class-C mandates went to Japan, Australia, New Zealand, Great Britain, and the Union of South Africa. They included the former German Southwest Africa and the islands of the Pacific which,

owing to the sparseness of their population or their small size, or their remoteness from the centers of civilization, or their geographical contiguity to the territory of the Mandatory, and other circumstances, can be best administered under the laws of the Mandatory as integral portions of its territory.

In all cases, however, the welfare of the native populations was to be the prime consideration, and the League was to be the guardian of their interests and was to supervise the mandatory powers.

Trouble arose, at the conference, over the question of Shantung. During the war the Japanese had conquered the German concession on Kiaochow Bay, and China had been forced to acquiesce in its transfer. In 1917 the Allies had promised Japan the German holdings in Shantung and all German islands north of the equator. The participation of China in the war, however, created a difficult situation. Backed by Wilson, China demanded that the German concessions in Shantung be returned directly to her and not handed over to Japan.

The Shantung crisis became acute. In possession of the German sphere since 1914, the Japanese refused to evacuate it. When the withdrawal of the Italian delegation produced a strained situation, the Japanese threatened to do likewise unless their demands were granted. Fearing a breach, Clemenceau and Lloyd George recognized their pledges of 1917, and Wilson also agreed to Japanese demands rather than risk the failure of the League Covenant. By April 30 the Japanese claims to the German concessions were accepted. The Mikado's government, however, promised to return the Shantung district to China, retaining only the economic privileges which the Germans had held, and the right to maintain a settlement at Tsingtau. In 1922 the Japanese fulfilled their pledge.

Finally the preliminary draft of the Treaty of Versailles was completed. On April 29 the German delegates, headed by foreign minister Count Brockdorff-Rantzau, arrived at Versailles. They were isolated from *Signing of the Treaty of Versailles* the other delegations and allowed to communicate only with their own country. They received the draft on May 7. Given only three weeks to consider the terms, and denied all opportunity for oral discussions with other delegations, the German representatives were nevertheless permitted to offer written observations. Accordingly the Germans presented 443 pages of counter proposals which reached the

Big Four on May 29. After consideration by ten inter-Allied commissions of experts the Germans received a reply. The terms remained substantially the same, with the exception of a few minor concessions, particularly with regard to the Polish frontier.

Permitted five days to sign the treaty or resume hostilities, the Germans, deprived of all powers of resistance by the terms of the armistice, had no choice but to accept. The unwillingness of the Scheidemann government to consummate the treaty led to its resignation, and the succeeding ministry, including Gustav Bauer as chancellor and Hermann Müller as foreign minister, proved less obdurate. In view of the ministerial crisis in Germany the Big Four granted two additional days, extending the time limit to 7 P.M., June 23; but at 5.20 P.M. on the last day the press and the display of flags from the hotels informed the people of Paris that the Germans had consented to sign.

With an almost medieval regard for symbolism the Allies arranged the final ceremony in the Hall of Mirrors at Versailles. Here, on June 28, the fifth anniversary of the assassination of the Archduke Francis Ferdinand, in the identical room in which the German Empire had been proclaimed in 1871, the signing of the treaty occurred. After the German plenipotentiaries, Müller and Bell, had attached their signatures upon the invitation of Clemenceau, the other delegations followed in the alphabetical order of their countries, Wilson signing first for *Amérique du Nord*. Only China, protesting against the loss of Shantung, did not sign. Meanwhile the guns boomed, the people outside cheered, and the fountains of Versailles played for the first time since the outbreak of the war.

Although the signing of the Treaty of Versailles did not conclude the work of the peace conference, this historic document was its greatest achievement. Written in two languages, French and English, and comprising some 440 articles in fifteen parts, it was indeed an unusual pact. Germany was deprived of some 25,000 square miles of Continental territory as well as of her

Territorial Clauses of the Treaty

vast colonial empire. Alsace-Lorraine was returned to France. The German-Belgian frontier was subjected to slight re-adjustments,— small districts near Moresnet, Malmédy, and Eupen going to Belgium. Plebiscites allegedly unfair in procedure secured the latter two for Belgium, whose strategic and economic strength was thus enhanced.

The Treaty of Versailles declared that the "frontier between Germany and Denmark shall be fixed in conformity with the wishes of the population." Northern Schleswig had been torn from Denmark by the Prussians in 1864. The promise that the people should be permitted to express their preference for union with Prussia or Denmark had never been carried out. The settlement of 1919 provided for two plebiscite zones, and at the elections held in the following year the northern section voted for reunion with Denmark, whereas the south remained with Germany.

In the east Germany suffered severe losses. Recognizing the independence of Poland, she was forced to relinquish the large sections of the old Polish kingdom which she had acquired. In East Prussia she had to submit to plebiscites in Allenstein and Marienwerder, but both voted to remain with the Fatherland. The loss of the Polish corridor and the Baltic ports of Danzig and Memel left East Prussia isolated from the main body of the German nation. After a plebiscite most of industrial upper Silesia was lost to Poland, and a part of it went to Czechoslovakia. Thus Germany's eastern frontier was badly haggled and seriously weakened.

Outside of Europe, Germany surrendered all her possessions. She was forced to renounce her colonies, which were subsequently distributed among her victorious opponents in the form of mandates. In addition Germany was compelled to relinquish all property and treaty rights in China, Siam, Liberia, Morocco, Egypt, Turkey, and Bulgaria. The loss of her overseas possessions, together with the cancellation of her treaty privileges in the countries named above, placed her at a serious disadvantage in competing against other capitalistic states.

In addition to the foregoing terms there were a number of

other political clauses. Germany was forced to consent to the abrogation of the treaties of 1839, which established the neutrality of Belgium. The grand duchy of Luxembourg was withdrawn from the German customs union, its special neutrality terminated, and German railway privileges therein canceled. Coal mines in the Saar Basin were ceded to France, and for fifteen years territorial sovereignty over that region was intrusted to the League; at the expiration of this period a plebiscite was to be held. Renouncing all hope of an Austro-German union without the previous consent of the Council of the League of Nations, Germany was also compelled to recognize the independence of Austria. The treaties of Bucharest and Brest-Litovsk with Rumania and Russia respectively were both nullified, and Germany agreed to recognize all treaties entered into between the Allies and the former Russian provinces which had since become independent.

The settlement also contained provisions for the effective disarmament of Germany. Universal military service was abolished, her army was reduced to 100,000 men, and all military and naval air forces were forbidden. To prevent evasions through frequent changes in the personnel, it was stipulated that all officers must enlist for twenty-five consecutive years and men for twelve. The numbers of customs officials, coast guards, and police guards were limited, and these groups were not permitted to assemble for military purposes. Educational institutions and all types of associations were forbidden to engage in military activities.

Not only was Germany's army reduced, but its use was restricted. The left bank of the Rhine and the right bank to a depth of fifty kilometers were demilitarized, Germany being allowed no fortifications, no armed forces, and no military maneuvers therein. Her southern and eastern frontiers were limited to fortifications already in existence. Heligoland and the Baltic zone were also demilitarized. In addition to these general provisions drastic limitation of the manufacture of arms, munitions, and other war materials was entailed by the treaty; import and export of all war goods were prohibited; and poison gases could be neither manufactured nor imported.

Limited to six small battleships of 10,000 tons, with six light cruisers, twelve destroyers, and twelve torpedo boats, the once proud German navy was reduced to impotence. The maintenance of submarines, either naval or commercial, was prohibited, and those still in existence had to be surrendered to the Allies or destroyed. Subject to the same restrictions as the army, the naval personnel was limited to 15,000; men in the mercantile marine were not allowed to receive naval training.

To make sure that Germany lived up to the disarmament requirements, a number of inter-Allied commissions of control were established, and agents were sent throughout Germany. The expense of maintaining these supervising commissions and their work was to be borne by the Germans. As an additional guarantee the Allies were to occupy the left bank of the Rhine and three bridgeheads for fifteen years.

The obligation to pay reparations was imposed upon Germany by Article 231 of the peace treaty, which stated, "The Allied and Associated Governments affirm and Germany accepts the responsibility of Ger- *Economic Clauses* many and her allies for causing all the loss and damage to which the Allied and Associated Governments and their nationals have been subjected as a consequence of the war imposed upon them by the aggression of Germany and her allies." Germany was therefore forced to undertake the payment of reparations for all damages done to civilians and to their property. Included therein were the military pensions which the victorious governments paid. Germany also had to reimburse Belgium for all the loans which she had secured during the war, with 5 per cent interest.

The Reparation Commission, created by the treaty, was to inform Germany on or before May 1, 1921, of the total amount due. By that date Germany, as stated before, was to hand over the equivalent of $5,000,000,000 in money and goods. Among the commodities to be given to the Allies as partial repayments for shipping destroyed in the war were all German merchant ships of over 1600 tons gross, one half of those from 1000 to 1600 tons, and one fourth of her steam trawlers and other fishing boats. Also, the Reparation Commission was empowered to require the construction of ships in German yards for the Allies; the total gross tonnage over a five-year period was not to exceed 200,000 a year.

Upon Allied demands Germany could be required to devote her economic resources to the rehabilitation of formerly occupied areas in Allied countries. Deliveries in coal and its derivatives had to be made over a period of ten years. Belgium was to receive 8,000,000 tons; France, 7,000,000; Italy, 4,500,000 to 8,500,000; and Luxembourg was to obtain such amounts as the Reparation Commission designated. France also secured additional coal shipments, as well as benzol, coal tar, and sulphate of ammonia. The Reparation Commission was empowered to credit to Germany's account any other deliveries of goods. Machinery, live stock, tools, equipment, and natural products were consequently to be turned over to the Allies as part payments. Should Germany fail to make proper restoration and restitution, or not make her financial payment, the Reparation Commission could offer recommendations as to the proper course to be taken.

Protection of their commercial interests in Germany was secured for the nationals of Allied countries. Germany was obligated to accord her late enemies most-favored-nation treatment in regard to the application of tariffs and customs duties and in internal transportation. There was to be no discrimination against citizens of the Allied countries. Property confiscated during the war was to be returned, and Allied trade-marks and copyrights were to receive the full protection of German law.

Steps were taken to insure the freedom of international communications and transportation. The river highways — the Rhine, Elbe, Oder, Niemen, and Danube — were placed under international commissions. This procedure was designed to afford landlocked powers adequate outlet for their goods. Czechoslovakia was allotted free zones in the harbors of Hamburg and Stettin. The Kiel Canal was to be opened free to all commercial vessels and warships of powers not engaged in war with Germany. Within that country there was to be free transit of mail, passengers, and commerce, and identical treatment for German and Allied ships in inland waterways and for German and Allied aircraft flying over German soil.

There were several articles primarily concerned with technical and miscellaneous matters. Provision was made for the treatment of prisoners of war and for graves; Germany was to adhere to the international *Minor Provisions* labor office and its legislation; the ex-Kaiser was to be tried before a special tribunal on the ground of having committed "a supreme offense against international morality and the sanctity of treaties"; but his flight prevented the execution of this article, and the Allies dropped the matter when their request for his extradition was rejected by the Netherlands. Meanwhile the so-called "war criminals" allegedly guilty of "atrocities" were to be tried by Allied military tribunals. Later the Allies permitted Germany to deal with them, a few being tried but most of them escaping with nominal penalties. Although she was as yet ineligible for membership, Germany's adhesion to the League was also required.

The Treaty of Versailles dealt Germany a staggering blow. In Europe she was deprived of 25,000 square miles and 6,000,000 inhabitants. Her loss of raw materials and mineral resources was serious, *General Consequences* involving 65 per cent of her iron, 45 per cent *for Germany* of her coal, 72 per cent of her zinc, and 57 per cent of her lead. From 12 to 15 per cent of her agricultural products and 10 per cent of her manufactures were also lost as a result of the territorial readjustments. Abroad she relinquished her entire colonial empire, with an area of over 1,000,000 square miles and a population of 12,000,000. Her foreign concessions and privileges were also gone. The German merchant marine shrank from 5,500,000 tons to a paltry 400,000. To aggravate her economic reverses, the imposition of reparations virtually placed her in a position of financial bondage. Furthermore, the destruction of her great military and naval machines reduced her prestige and hampered her recovery in world politics.

Austria and Hungary were compelled to accept settlements similar to that of Versailles with Germany. On June 2, 1919, the Treaty of St. Germain was presented to the Austrians. Allowed to make written observations, the Austrian delegates contended that their country, "German Austria," was not an enemy power but one of the succession states of the now disintegrated Hapsburg monarchy. Preferring to regard Austria as the former partner of the Dual Monarchy, the Allies refused to sanction this interpretation. The Austrians were required to omit "German" from their title and to pay reparations, and an Austro-German union was specifically forbidden. On September 10, 1919, the Austrians signed the treaty, and subsequently ratified it.

Settlements with Austria and Hungary

The settlement of Trianon with Hungary was delayed. In March, 1919, the weakness of the Karolyi government, which had replaced that of the vanquished Hapsburgs, led to a revolt. The Communist régime under Bela Kun, which replaced it, lasted until August. A Rumanian invasion then led to the flight of Bela Kun and the collapse of the Communist state. After a period of looting, the invaders withdrew, but it was not until November that a government was established in Hungary which the Allies would recognize. After they had consented to the substitution of the term "Hungary" for "Hungarian Republic," the treaty was accepted and signed, June 4, 1920, and subsequently ratified. Although a return of the Hapsburgs was forbidden, the way was open for an ultimate restoration of a monarchy.

Even though the break-up of Austria-Hungary had not been anticipated in the original war aims of the Allies, the territorial terms of the two treaties provided for the disintegration of the Hapsburg monarchy. Intensification of nationalism among the various subject peoples of the pre-war state led to their virtual independence when the Dual Monarchy collapsed at the end of the conflict. As a result three new countries appeared,— Austria, Hungary, and Czechoslovakia ; Galicia went to the newly formed Polish republic ; the Yugoslav provinces and Dalmatia joined Serbia and Montenegro to form Yugoslavia; Rumania received Transylvania, Bukowina, and most of the Banat of Temesvár; the Trentino, southern Tyrol, Trieste, Istria, and some islands went to Italy; and Hungary was deprived of a slice of her western section, which was given to Austria. Several plebiscites were scheduled in order to determine the need for rectifications of frontiers. The treaties, however, were silent concerning the disposition of Fiume and the Dalmatian coast, over which Italy and Yugoslavia were at odds.

In executing the estate of the Hapsburgs the Allies only partially observed the principle of national self-determination. The *Anschluss*, or Austro-German union, was strictly forbidden by Article eighty-eight of the Treaty of St. Germain. For economic and strategic motives Czechoslovakia was constituted so as to include 3,000,000 Germans, 700,000 Magyars, and 400,000 Ruthenians in a total population of 13,000,000. In the Polish heritage there were 3,000,000 Ruthenians. Rumania found herself with 1,500,000 Magyars. For strategic purposes Italy was granted the Brenner Pass, with 250,000 German inhabitants. In short, the peace settlement, in attempting to solve the problem of conflicting national, economic, strategic, and historical interests, created many new minorities. It was impossible to placate all interests and at the same time to create an ideal peace.

Like Germany, Austria and Hungary were disarmed. The Austrian army was reduced to 30,000, and the Hungarian to 35,000. Neither state might maintain naval or air forces. Other terms were similar to those of the treaty with Germany, providing for limitations on munitions, reductions of armaments, and supervision by the Allies. The states surrounding the alleged culprits, fearing Austrian or Magyar revenge, remained armed to the teeth.

The economic provisions of the treaty were also similar to those of Versailles. Measures were designed to insure the freedom of international transportation and communication; the Danube remained internationalized from source to mouth; the defeated states were not allowed to practice discrimination against Allied nationals; Austria and Hungary were required to pay reparations, whereas the succession states assumed only their portions of the pre-war debt. In the treaty, labor and economic clauses and agreements concerning the League of Nations were similar to those in the German settlement.

Since the substitution of a number of jealous and highly competitive small states for Austria-Hungary led to economic as well as political decentralization, the effects of the treaties of St. Germain and Trianon on south-central Europe were not altogether happy. Before the war the old polyglot multinational empire was beneficial to the extent of providing economic unity and thereby facilitating commerce. Politically the treaties brought about the "Balkanization" of south-central Europe, with the possibility of ultimately leading to an aggravated international situation.

The Treaty of Neuilly terminated the war with Bulgaria. Prepared at Paris by the Allied delegates, it was signed November 27, 1919, and ratified the following *Settlement with* year. Bulgaria suffered severe territorial losses. *Bulgaria* Her claims to the Dobruja and part of Macedonia were rejected, and she was forced to cede western Thrace to Greece and to make three tiny frontier cessions to Yugoslavia for strategic purposes. Bulgaria thus lost her direct outlet to the Ægean. The Allies tried to compensate her by making special but unsatisfactory arrangements for the handling of her goods at Salonica. She was required to pay $450,000,000 as reparations over a period of thirty-seven years, beginning January 1, 1921. Her military forces were limited to 20,000, subject to restrictions similar to those in the other treaties. The general provisions were identical with the terms of the other peace settlements.

Most highly characteristic of the imperialist aims of the Allied Powers was the treaty imposed upon Turkey. Drafted by the delegates at Paris and by the Council *Treaty Arrangements* of Ambassadors, this document was signed at *with Turkey* Sèvres on August 10, 1920. Of the defeated powers, however, Turkey had the unique distinction of being the only one which refused to ratify a treaty dictated by the Allies.

EUROPE

AFTER
THE WORLD WAR

Scale of Statute Miles

0   100   200   300   400   500

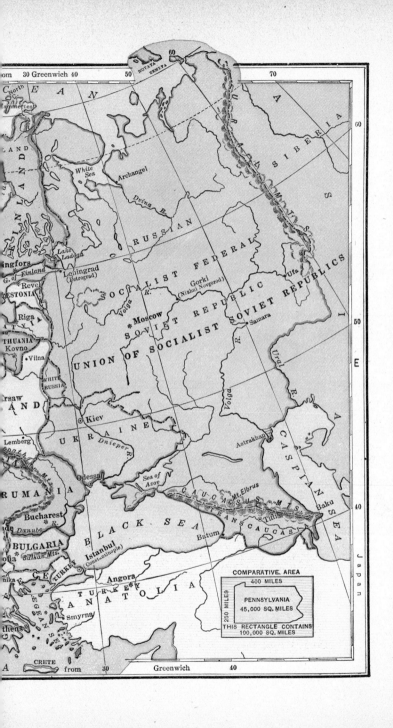

Before the end of the war the Allies had anticipated the partition of Turkey. Russia was to get European Turkey to the Enos-Midia line, including the long-desired Constantinople; Imbros and Tenedos; the Asiatic side of the Bosporus and all the islands of the Sea of Marmara; and the provinces of Erzerum, Trebizond, Van, Bitlis, and part of Kurdistan. England's share was to be southern Mesopotamia and Bagdad, besides the Levantine ports of Haifa and Acre. France was to receive Syria, the vilayet of Adana, and the hinterland. Italy was promised the Dodecanese Islands and the district stretching from Smyrna to Adalia, with the adjoining hinterland as far as Konia. Arabia and Palestine were to be constituted as independent states.

The terms of the notorious secret treaties were never carried out. Russia's renunciation of her share by the Bolsheviks, and the establishment of the mandate system as a substitute for annexation, dislocated the earlier bargains. Meanwhile the rivalries of the great powers and their uncertainty as to the disposition of Constantinople and the status of the Straits led to indecision. Attempting to take things into their own hands, the Greeks occupied Smyrna and western Thrace and demanded a share in the spoils. Inasmuch as the earlier schemes were all thrown out of gear, the Treaty of Sèvres had to be modified so as to adjust the imperial ambitions of the great powers with the new conditions brought about by the Russian withdrawal, the rise of the Greeks, and Wilsonian idealism as manifested in the mandate system.

Foremost among the paper achievements of the now defunct Treaty of Sèvres, however, was the dismemberment of the Ottoman Empire. In general the non-Turkish elements were to be severed from Turkey and to be placed under foreign control. British mandates were established in Palestine and Mesopotamia, including Mosul, while Syria was converted into a French mandate. To Italy went the Dodecanese Islands and Rhodes, a plebiscite being promised in the latter after five years. The Greeks secured the remaining Ægean islands, western Thrace up to the Chatalja lines, and Smyrna, the last being subject to a plebiscite in five years. In addition Turkey was required to renounce her claims to a number of former possessions long since under foreign control. Thus was legalized the earlier acquisition by the European powers of Egypt, Tripoli, Tunis, Morocco, and Cyprus.

Certain subject nationalities were to be liberated from Turkish rule. An independent Armenia, whose boundaries were to be designated by President Wilson, was to be constructed from the old provinces of Erzerum, Trebizond, Van, and Bitlis. Kurdistan was to be permitted to develop autonomous government or become independent of Turkey if a plebiscite so determined. In accordance with certain obligations incurred during the war the independence of the Arabs of the Hejaz was also recognized.

Turkey, stripped of a large portion of her vast empire, was suffered to remain under economic bondage. Her government was forced to confirm all pre-war concessions to the Allied Powers, the older debts were recognized, and Turkey was to pay war costs. An inter-Allied commission was to supervise Turkish finances and was empowered to veto all new foreign loans or concessions. Means were taken to insure freedom of transportation and communication, which included the internationalization of the Straits. The capitulations were reëstablished, and the Turks promised future reform of their judicial and penal systems.

As a supplement to the Treaty of Sèvres, France, Italy, and Great Britain signed a tripartite agreement on August 10, 1920. This provided for coöperation of the three great powers in their Near-Eastern policies. They agreed to share the control of the Bagdad and Anatolian railways. Furthermore, the signatory powers recognized the preëminence of French interests in Kurdistan and Cilicia, and of Italian interests in southern Anatolia, including the Heraclea coal basin. Apparently the remnants of Turkey were to be converted into spheres of influence, reminiscent of those in China.

By the settlement of Sèvres, Turkey was reduced to a minor power. Her empire gone, there was left only eastern Thrace up to the Chatalja lines, Constantinople, and the remote Anatolian uplands. Foreign economic control seriously undermined her independence. While the Sultan's government consented to the political disintegration and foreign economic bondage of the Ottoman Empire, loyal Turks in remote Anatolia refused to accept the settlement as final. Soon they revolted, overthrew the Sultan's government, set up one of their own, and liberated their country. The Sèvres arrangements never became effective and were eventually superseded by the Treaty of Lausanne (1923).

In addition to the settlements with the five defeated powers,— Germany, Austria, Hungary, Bulgaria, and Turkey,— "minorities treaties" were prepared. The mixture of national groups in Europe apparently made inevitable the creation of minorities, especially in the Balkans and the succession states. In view of the danger from dissatisfied or oppressed groups the powers virtually required Poland, Czechoslovakia, Rumania, Yugoslavia, and Greece to sign treaties. By guaranteeing minorities civil and political equality, liberty of public and private worship, and freedom in the use of their own languages and schools, these agreements were designed to protect religious and national groups. All disputes involving minorities were to be referred to the Permanent Court of International Justice, and the League stood as the guarantor of their freedom from persecution.

Protection for National Minorities

Although the American delegation had played a prominent rôle in the preparation of the peace treaties, the United States Senate, supported by public opinion, refused to ratify them. The Covenant of the League and the Shantung settlement were particularly objectionable to the United States. Therefore, resolving to effect a separate peace, Congress, by a joint resolution of both houses, to which the President affixed his signature, declared the war terminated on July 2, 1921. The subsequent American treaty with Germany conformed to that of Versailles in many respects. It adhered to the arrangements made by the Paris peace conference concerning the following: disposition of German colonies; military, naval, and air clauses; treatment of prisoners and graves; financial and economic clauses,

The United States and the Peace Settlements

including reparations; articles concerning aviation, ports, waterways, and railways; the army of occupation; and many miscellaneous matters. The United States was not bound by the following: the League of Nations Covenant, the territorial changes in Europe, the transfer of German concessions in the Far East, and the labor clauses. American settlements with Austria and Hungary were generally similar. As the United States had never formally been at war with Bulgaria or Turkey, it was unnecessary to arrange treaties of peace with those states.

Collectively the settlements presented a curious compound of idealism and practical politics. Liberal principles were partially applied, and national self-determination
Judgment of the Peace Settlements was adopted with regard to the territory of the defeated states, save in Asia and Africa. Numerous exceptions were based on economic, strategic, and historical grounds, and national self-determination was not applied to the victorious and neutral powers. Nevertheless, despite certain defects, the post-war map of Europe was an approach to one based on nationality. It marked a distinct advance over the map of 1914, and the total population of subject nationalities was decreased. The economic freedom desired by idealists was not achieved. Although the principles of freedom of transit and nondiscrimination against foreigners were imposed upon the losers, they were not applied to winners or neutrals. In effect, the peace settlement was designed to cripple the economic power of Germany, and the thesis of her war guilt and the levying of reparations were not in accord with the more enlightened ideals of fair play.

Certain liberal views, however, were partially applied. The victorious and neutral states adopted disarmament in principle at least, while the defeated powers were disarmed in practice. Definite attempts were made to improve international labor conditions and to protect minorities. Furthermore, the Covenant of the League of Nations as an example of international coöperation seemed to presage a better era in world politics.

Nevertheless there was widespread dissatisfaction. The

defeated states resented the harsh treatment which they received and particularly objected to the thesis of German war guilt, expressed in Article 231 of the Treaty of Versailles. Liberals in the United States and Great Britain believed the treaty to be overly severe, especially in view of the earlier-expressed idealism. Representing the triumph of bourgeois self-interest and practical politics, its compromises with idealism were usually detrimental to the latter. Far harsher terms might have been imposed upon the Central Powers, however, had it not been for the restraining effects of Anglo-French rivalry, of Bolshevism, and of Wilsonian idealism.

The treaties exerted a profound effect upon world politics. By the practical elimination of several great states the equilibrium of Europe was temporarily upset. Germany had ceased to count as a formidable state, Austria-Hungary had disintegrated, Bolshevist Russia was ostracized by the capitalist powers, and the United States maintained a policy of isolation. Even before the treaties were signed, discord among the victors rent the Allied solidarity, and many observers said that France was again aiming at the military and diplomatic hegemony of Europe.

CHAPTER XXXII

The League of Nations: In Quest of an Ideal

THE League of Nations was established in response to a widespread demand for a universal and everlasting peace. Partly because of the horror and grief aroused by the devastating effects of the World War, the hope prevailed throughout much of the civilized world that, through the development of international law and machinery for its enforcement, another such catastrophe could be averted. Consequently, during and after the conflict, President Wilson and others formulated various plans for an assembly of nations. On January 25, 1919, the plenary session of the Paris conference, influenced by these idealists, approved the inclusion, as an integral part of the peace treaty, of an international Covenant. For the preparation of the latter a commission under the chairmanship of the American president was appointed. Within a few weeks it prepared a preliminary draft which represented a composite of the plans of Wilson, Sir Robert Cecil, General Smuts, and others.

Considerable opposition greeted the proposed Covenant of the League. In the United States apprehension was felt lest it restrict American foreign policy, especially *The Acceptance of the Covenant* in regard to the Monroe Doctrine. This fear was partially allayed, however, when Wilson, on April 10, procured the commission's approval of an amendment to the Covenant, guaranteeing the legality of arbitration pacts and such regional understandings as the Monroe Doctrine. Largely because of the pressure of prominent Republican senators in the United States other modifications were adopted. Provision was made for the withdrawal of a member state, and domestic matters were excluded from the jurisdiction of the League. Less successful in attempting to secure a revision of the Covenant were the Japanese, who urged the inclusion of "the principle of the equality of nations and the just treatment of their nationals." Fear on the part of the British and the Australians that such a statement might justify unrestricted Oriental immigration contributed to the ultimate rejection of the Nipponese proposal. Finally, on April 28, 1919, the revised Covenant was submitted to and approved by the plenary session.

Designed to provide for an association of nations, the Covenant formally came into effect on January 10, 1920. All sovereign states and self-governing dominions, provided they were approved by the League Assembly and furnished effective guarantees of their willingness to observe their international obligations, were eligible to membership. Russia and the defeated powers were excluded temporarily. Except the United States most of the other powers joined. Germany became a member in 1926. The Bolshevist government, regarding the League as an organization of bourgeois countries, denounced it as a capitalistic weapon for the extirpation of communism. Vigorous campaigns, beginning in 1919, for American adhesion had little success. Several powers, the most notable of which were Japan and Germany, subsequently took advantage of the clause permitting withdrawal upon two years' notice. Consequently, at no time did the League enjoy full world membership, and the absence of several major powers greatly undermined its prestige.

The Covenant was the constitution of the League of Nations. With the approval of the Council and a majority of the Assembly, amendments could be added. In *The Covenant* effect it was a mutual treaty accepted voluntarily by the signatory powers, and although it laid down general principles for the solution of any problem which might arise, it also allowed elasticity in interpretation and method of treatment. The regular machinery for the operation of the League consisted of three organs: an Assembly, a Council, and a Secretariat.

The Assembly, which met annually in Geneva, represented

all member states equally. Although delegations consisted of from one to three members, no country could cast more than one vote. Regular officers were chosen for each session, and for practical purposes the Assembly was divided into six standing committees. These dealt with constitutional questions, technical organizations, budget and administration, political affairs, social matters, and armaments. Special committees were appointed for individual cases. Empowered to deal with all matters affecting world peace or lying within the League's sphere, the Assembly, lacking lawmaking power, really constituted a forum where the states might deliberate and discuss international questions. The Assembly also admitted states to League membership, selected the non-permanent members of the Council, helped to choose judges for the Permanent Court of International Justice, and controlled the budget.

The Council, representing the great powers, was the executive body of the League. Until 1922 it contained four non-permanent and four permanent members, the latter being France, Great Britain, Italy, and Japan. In that year two non-permanent members were added, and in 1926 Germany was given a permanent representative and the temporary states were increased to nine. New rules were also adopted whereby the terms of the latter were fixed at three years and provision was made for the retirement of three of them annually. Although the scope of the Council's work was identical with that of the Assembly, its duties were more specific. It was expected to afford mediation in all international disputes, to protect member states from foreign aggression, to promote disarmament, and to supervise the mandates. Decisions of the Council were ordinarily to be unanimous.

The Secretariat, consisting of a secretary-general and a large staff of assistants, was designed to gather information and make it available. It contained some five hundred experts, gathered from forty countries. Within a short time of its establishment it became a sort of international clearing house for authentic information, and its research afforded the League a sound body of data upon which to base its decisions.

special commissions,
diction, undertook t
Impatient with th
pointed at its result
solutions. Particular
ern Europe, where s
several conflicts. A
oped between Swede
which, despite the S
were ruled by Finlan
the Baltic states, b
Council in July, 19
Council reported tha
but insisted on local
continued demilitariz
recommendations of t
armed conflict.

Lithuania became i
Friction with Poland
seizure of the city by
of the League to settl
1922 the Council w
Lithuanian protests
Lithuania was more si
mer German seaport
city had not been dete
anians were fearful l
made into a free city
1923. After protests h
dors the matter was fin
appointed a commissi
into a report which wa
by March 15, 1924. T
some local autonomy
recognized Lithuanian
One of the most co
was called upon to so
Polish claims in Upper

In addition to the regular organs of the League there were a number of closely related organizations. These included technical groups concerned with problems of international health, finance and economics, communications and transit, and sundry other affairs. Among the most important of these bodies was the International Labor Organization.

The International Labor Organization

This association, consisting of a General Conference, a Governing Body, and an International Labor Office, represented the interests of states, labor, and capital. It maintained contacts with various states and labor groups throughout the world, gathered data, and enunciated general principles for the improvement of labor conditions. It also drafted numerous recommendations and conventions, the force of whose influence was felt even in far-off Asia.

Another autonomous agency of the League was the Permanent Court of International Justice, which came into being in 1921. Commonly designated as the World Court, it is not to be confused with the older Hague Court of Arbitration. A tribunal of law and not of arbitration, the decisions of the World Court were to be determined upon the basis of established principles of international law and existing treaties. Its jurisdiction was of two types: voluntary and compulsory. Disputing states could voluntarily submit a case to the court. Certain countries, however, accepted a more rigid arrangement whereby they were obligated to recognize the jurisdiction of the Court in all disputes involving questions of international law and the interpretation of treaties.

The Permanent Court of International Justice

Designed to promote a new age in international relations, the League of Nations had as its primary object the preservation of peace. By Article 10 of the Covenant member states agreed to respect and preserve the independence and territorial integrity of the signatory powers. All circumstances which threatened to disturb international peace could be referred to the League by any country. Member states, obligated to accept arbitration or judicial settlement, were bound by a League decision, which could be

The Covenant and Peace

rendered ↑
the Coun(
cluding al
were the
    Penalti(
in defianc
expected
offender, (
coercion,
precise fo
fronted w
drastic me
cerned, th
    In its e
frequently

The League in A

(in 1922)
assistance,
Persecuted
subject pe
procured e
as the Fre
provided a
wise migh
rivalries.
    From it
serious pol
war readju
conference
many unso
garian and
territorial
status of S
dates had
schedule o
the Suprer
representa

of Versailles a plebiscite under Allied supervision had been held there on March 20, 1921. Because the Germans polled a decisive majority of the votes, they insisted on retaining the entire province, whereas Poland demanded those districts having Polish majorities. Polish irregulars, hoping to settle the issue by force, overran much of the area, and it was with considerable difficulty that British troops finally restored order. The Inter-Allied commission, which had conducted the plebiscite, split into factions when the pro-Polish French refused to accept an Anglo-Italian proposal for a division of the region. Unable to break the deadlock, the Supreme Council, on August 12, 1921, referred the case to the League.

A solution was devised by that organization. In conformity with the recommendations of the League's committee of investigation, Upper Silesia was partitioned, Germany receiving the greater area and population, while Poland secured most of the economic resources, which included coal, iron, zinc, and lead mines. To minimize the disturbing effects of the partition upon the social and economic life of Upper Silesia, a German-Polish convention, recommended by the Council, was signed on May 15, 1922. This agreement provided for a special régime for fifteen years, during which certain utilities, such as railways, water power, electricity, and postal and monetary systems, should be regulated to the advantage of the several sections of Silesia. An Upper Silesian Mixed Commission, to supervise the execution of the convention, and an Arbitral Tribunal, to settle private disputes, were also created. On July 9, 1922, Allied troops were withdrawn and a knotty problem was temporarily solved.

In 1921 the Albanian question was thrust upon the League's attention. The boundaries of the little Balkan state had been delimited in 1913–1914, but both during and *The Problem of* after the war parts of her territory had been *Albania* occupied by Greek, Italian, and Yugoslav troops. Consequently Albanian patriots, fearing for their country's independence, applied for and secured the admission of Albania into the League in 1920. While the Council of Ambassadors was preparing to delimit her frontiers Albania nearly fell a prey to the Yugoslavs. In 1921 the latter introduced money, arms, and munitions into Albania in an effort to promote a revolution. After the suppression of the uprising by the Albanians Yugoslavia dispatched an army into the coveted country. Realizing the acute danger of war should the imperialistic Italians resent this Yugoslav aggression, England appealed to the League on November 7. In view of the tenseness of the situation the Council of Ambassadors hastened to recognize the Albanian frontier of 1913–1914, along with minor border rectifications in favor of Yugoslavia. Pending a final delimitation of the frontiers a temporary neutral zone along the northern border of Albania was designated. From this area the troops of Albania were required to withdraw. These arrangements, acquiesced in by Albania, were accepted by Yugoslavia upon the League threat of an economic blockade.

Serious difficulties in the Near East afforded the League another opportunity of demonstrating its effectiveness. The conference at Lausanne (1922–1923), which met to settle the Turkish problems after the discard of the Treaty of Sèvres, had recom *Complications in Western Asia* mended that the frontier between Turkey and Iraq be settled by direct Anglo-Turkish negotiations. Friction over the disposition of the important Mosul oil district had caused a deadlock, and on August 6, 1924, the matter was referred to the League. To avoid an outbreak of hostilities, the Council laid down the "Brussels Line" which was to function as a provisional frontier while the League studied the issue. An international commission, appointed to investigate the situation, presented its report to the Council in September, 1925. This document recommended that the Turkish request for a plebiscite be rejected and that, for economic reasons, the Mosul region be united with the British mandate of Iraq. The latter provision, however, was contingent upon the continuation of the mandate for twenty-five years and upon the grant of special consideration to the Kurd inhabitants. In accordance with these recommendations, on January 13, 1926, a treaty was arranged between Great Britain and Iraq which guaranteed the maintenance of the mandatory régime for twenty-five years, or until Iraq should be admitted to the League. The League's final decision, which involved the recognition of the "Brussels Line" as a permanent frontier, was given on March 11. Both powers accepted the solution.

Among the most serious cases referred to the League was the Italo-Greek controversy of 1923. To delimit the frontier between Albania and Greece the Council of *The Italo-Greek* Ambassadors had created a commission under *Dispute* the chairmanship of an Italian. On August 27 this man and his four companions were murdered on Greek soil. Mussolini's government promptly dispatched an ultimatum to Greece. Sending a conciliatory reply, the Greek government accepted all the demands except those concerning Italian participation in the inquiry and the payment of an indemnity of 50,000,000 lire. On August 31 Italy responded to the Greek reply by seizing the island of Corfu after a naval bombardment.

Greece thereupon appealed to the League. Mussolini denied the competence of the latter to deal with the matter, claiming that the affair could best be settled without outside interference. Although the League coöperated, the Council of Ambassadors was responsible for the settlement. A Greek investigation, conducted under the supervision of an inter-Allied commission, reported that the guilty parties had not been apprehended. On September 26 the Council of Ambassadors, supported by the League, virtually required Greece to pay the indemnity demanded by Rome, and on the following day the Italians evacuated Corfu.

Another potential war in the Balkans was averted in 1925, owing to the prompt action of the League. A Greco-Bulgar border incident, wherein several soldiers were *The Greco-Bulgar* killed, caused a Greek army to invade Bul-*Argument* garia on the ground that a major Bulgarian offensive was contemplated. On October 22 Bulgaria appealed to the League for help. The latter demanded the immediate cessation of hostilities and sent neutral observers to the affected areas. Within a week the Greek army had been withdrawn and a League commission was at work studying the case. As a result of its report of November 28 the Council declared both states innocent of aggressive designs, but required Greece to indemnify Bulgaria for the invasion. The decision of the Council was accepted by the two contestants.

Until 1931 the League was relatively successful in settling the more serious disputes which arose. During 1931-1933 the events growing out of the Sino-Japanese controversy, however, tended to diminish public confidence in the League as a guarantor of international rights and obligations. Allegedly a victim of Japanese imperialism and militarism, China's appeals to the international organization aroused sympathy but no active assistance. The League, despite Japanese opposition, on December 10, 1931, appointed the Lytton Commission to study the Sino-Japanese difficulties in Manchuria. On February 24, 1933, its findings, which denounced Japanese aggression as premeditated, and criticized the nature of Chinese rule in Manchuria, were adopted by the League. Thereupon Japan withdrew from that organization, and the latter considered the advisability of invoking sanctions. Apparently the League, without the coöperation of all the great powers, including Russia and the United States, was powerless.[1]

The League: Success or Failure?

The lack of "teeth" in the League, and the selfish interests of the leading states, impaired its prestige as an international arbiter. In practice the threat of resort to sanctions was generally ineffectual in dealings with great powers. The interests of the latter concerning problems of war debts, reparations, security, armaments, and treaty revision, proved so contradictory as to make real coöperation in major issues ineffective. Still emphasizing the theory of national sovereignty, states feared to enter into obligations which would impair their freedom of action. They preferred paper pacts and agreements "in principle."

To many persons efforts to preserve the peace were vain. Capitalistic states had to expand, and by so doing they clashed with other powers, thus making imperialistic wars likely.

[1] For an account of the Sino-Japanese controversy see pages 793-801.

Therefore the League represented an attempt at checking forces which were beyond the control even of the aggressor countries. Moreover, the pre-war system of competitive national states survived, and the plan to control it through parliamentary methods in the League was not a success.

Despite its decline as an international arbiter the League justified its existence by other achievements. It coöperated in a program of disarmament[1] which, though not a conspicuous success, took certain steps toward the reduction of armaments. The League was concerned with the restriction of slavery and of traffic in opium and white slaves. Through periodicals, reports, and books it enlightened millions of people concerning world problems. It also aided in the promotion of the Red Cross and of war against disease; it improved labor conditions and assisted refugees and prisoners of war. As a forum of world opinion it afforded the benefits of publicity and parliamentary methods in international affairs. Through security pacts it promoted some measure of international solidarity and world opinion. An immediate triumph of the international ideal, however, was improbable in view of conflicts of interests and the persistence of tradition.

[1] See pages 739–740.

UNCLE SAM *and the* LEAGUE OF NATIONS

Germany: "He can go in, and won't. I want to go in, and can't"

After a cartoon in *Amsterdammer*, 1921

CHAPTER XXXIII

Bolshevist Russia: The New Revolution

A STRONG tendency on the part of Russia to become a great capitalist nation was thwarted by the advent of the World War. Rural life was seriously dislocated by the mobilization of millions of young men most of whom were drawn from the country districts, by the extensive requisitions of cattle and horses for military purposes, and by the depletion of farm implements resulting from the enemy blockade, which cut off imports and caused domestic factories to be devoted to the manufacture of war materials. The breakdown of the transportation system and the depreciation of the currency made it difficult for the peasant to dispose of his crops at a profit. Therefore, despite the great demand for agricultural produce, the sowing areas had decreased seriously by 1916.

Russia during the War

Industrial life also suffered. Industry was not prepared for war-time requirements, so that a national economic collapse was almost inevitable. Most of the factories devoted to the production of war materials lacked sufficient fuel, cotton, and other raw materials. Conscription in 1914 crippled production by depriving these concerns of 40 per cent of their skilled workers.

The World War put a terrific strain on the proletarians, who were compelled to labor long hours overtime. Their holidays were curtailed; working conditions were unsatisfactory; wages were low and prices high. Consequently the industrial workers, whose numbers the war had increased, became restless. Strikes and riots occurred as the wage-earners developed a bitter antagonism toward the autocratic government, which consistently supported the oppressive factory owners.

The position of the administration was not an enviable one. Involved in a gigantic war, it found itself seriously menaced by financial difficulties. The prohibition of the liquor traffic, the breakdown of foreign and domestic trade, the decline of railway revenues, and the enormous expenses of the struggle led to a large annual treasury deficit. Because of this situation the administration resorted to foreign loans and to the establishment of an income tax (1916). But these measures proved ineffectual. Russia was confronted with economic and financial chaos.

In 1914 most of Russia had supported the government. But as defeat followed defeat and the suffering at home became intense the Czar was forced to call the Duma, in August, 1915. Leader of a *bloc* of Octobrists and Constitutional Democrats, Paul Miliukov urged responsible ministerial government, administrative reforms, the punishment of military inefficiency, and a vigorous prosecution of the war. The Czar, vexed at the liberal demands, prorogued the Duma. Reactionary policies now led to serious riots and strikes. Boris Stürmer, an ultraconservative later suspected of pro-Germanism, became premier. Meanwhile the mystic Gregory Rasputin, reputed ex-monk and charlatan, developed a fatal influence over the imperial family. With the Czar spending much of his time at the front, and the Czarina under the monk's guidance, the government became increasingly repressive. Official spies were everywhere, and executions and imprisonment were frequent.

Patriotic Russians who suspected the government of Germanophilism tried to save their country. Rasputin was assassinated in 1916. His follower, the hated Protopopov, proved little better. Suffering from disordered nerves, he retailed the latest news from heaven, telling how the deceased Rasputin went from saint to saint praising the virtues of the Romanovs. Plots were arranged to murder the Czar, and the high command even planned to arrest the Czarina. Meanwhile corruption, inefficiency, and treason continued to flourish in a government no longer able to command the support of the nation.

The disintegration of the army had already begun. As defeats, famines, and depression increased, many soldiers, especially the 10,000,000 idle reserves behind the front, began to succumb to revolutionary propaganda. Insubordination was frequent, and excessive brutality merely aggravated the discontent. According to Kerensky, subsequent minister of war, upwards of 1,200,000 desertions had occurred before January 1, 1917. Most of the remaining troops were disaffected and ripe for revolt.

Agricultural Russia was not the ideal state for a Marxian revolution. According to the law of capitalistic development as advanced by Karl Marx, uprisings would occur as a consequence of a series of economic crises in the most highly industrialized nations. *The End of the Old Régime* But in Russia the revolution resulted from no such development, for capitalism had barely scratched the surface of her economy. It took place because this semi-agricultural, semi-industrial state, lacking a powerful middle class, was the weakest link in the capitalistic chain.

The revolution occurred suddenly, in the early spring of 1917. On March 8, starving people demanding food appeared on the streets of Petrograd. Between 80,000 and 90,000 workers went on a strike and joined the disorderly masses. Soon revolutionary placards and red flags appeared, and there was frequent rioting. The police forces, numbering 28,000, maintained fair order during most of the day, but in the evening bakery shops were looted. Fraternization began between the turbulent crowds and the soldiers of the garrison. As the disorders became more serious the Petrograd authorities lost their grip on the situation. A mutinying company of the garrison, which had refused to fire on the people, had to be disarmed by the élite Preobrazhensky regiment. Rodzianko, president of the Duma, advised the Czar, then at the front, of the gravity of the crisis. To relieve the tension, the military governor of the city ordered the strikers to return to work. Premier Golitzin attempted, unsuccessfully, to prorogue the Duma.

Efforts to stem the revolutionary tide were ineffectual. Refusing to be dissolved, the Duma appointed a temporary emergency committee which it invested with vast powers to deal with the situation. The strikers declined to resume work and established the Soviet of Workmen's and Soldiers' Deputies, which proceeded to organize the masses and to win over the soldiers to the revolutionary cause. On the twelfth 25,000 soldiers had joined the revolutionists, including the famous Preobrazhensky regiment, which had mutinied and shot some of its officers. With the workers and soldiers in control of Petrograd the Czarist officials and bureaucrats relinquished their authority, and many of them were arrested. Telegrams to the front met with little response until Nicholas II finally wired the war minister that he was returning with troops to quell the disturbances.

On March 13 the revolutionists organized a provisional government. Already appointed by the bourgeois Duma, the committee assumed executive functions. Meanwhile the Petrograd Soviet, representing the soldiers and workers, created a temporary executive committee which attempted to exercise supreme administrative functions. After some hesitation the two centers of revolution amalgamated their efforts, and a joint ministry was created. The new provisional government consisted entirely of bourgeois ministers drawn from the Octobrists and Constitutional Democrats, with the exception of Alexander Kerensky, who came from the radical left. Although certain extremists felt some misgivings as to the advisability of coöperation with the bourgeois Duma, the Petrograd Soviet approved of the government by an overwhelming majority.

Nicholas II's attempt to reach Petrograd being frustrated by workmen, who pulled up the railway tracks, he dispatched General Ivanov to the capital with an army. When the General arrived, however, most of his troops deserted to the revolutionary cause. Nevertheless, by belated promises of responsible ministerial government and reform the Czar hoped to stem the tide of revolution. But reliance on stanch regiments and strategically placed machine guns was of no avail; Nicholas II's authority was at an end. His cause now was hopeless, and, deserted by his troops, the Czar bowed to the public demands for his abdication and, on March 15, resigned for himself and his son, requesting that the succession pass to his brother. The demands of the Petrograd Soviet for a republic prompted the Grand Duke Michael to surrender all claims to authority. Supreme power was vested in the provisional government until a constituent assembly could be called to pave the way toward a better political future.

The bourgeois stage of the revolution now began. Drawn chiefly from the Octobrists and the Cadets, save for the more radical Kerensky, the ministry in- cluded Prince Lvov as premier and Paul *The Bourgeois Gov-* Miliukov as foreign minister. It was repre- *ernment* sentative of the middle classes — industrialists, landowners, and professional groups. In contrast to the radicals, who wanted sweeping changes, the moderate ministry desired to establish in Russia a characteristically bourgeois system such as existed in western Europe. Furthermore, it was determined to prosecute the war to a victorious conclusion in co-operation with the Allies. The overthrow of the inefficient autocracy and the coming of a liberal government were hailed with enthusiasm in Allied countries, who now felt that Russian support would be more effective.

This provisional government immediately tried to liberalize Russia. Freedom of speech, the press, and assembly were recognized. A general amnesty was proclaimed for all political offenders, and 80,000 exiles returned. Arbitrary arrests, long-delayed trials, and capital punishment were abolished, and labor unions and strikes were legalized. The government abandoned its policy of forcible Russification of minorities and subject nationalities. Finland was permitted to reëstablish her constitution, and Poland was guaranteed independence.

Serious problems, however, menaced the security of the provisional government. To keep a hopelessly shattered Russia in the war was extremely difficult. Her economic structure in a state of collapse, her political and administrative machine ruined, and her army largely dissolved, she was in no condition to carry on hostilities. Meanwhile the sufferings and discouragement of the masses of people caused them to lose faith in a government which persevered in the futile struggle against the Central Powers. As the revolutionary tendencies among the masses became more pronounced the government found itself impotent and forced to rely on moral prestige rather than on coercive measures.

At the beginning of the Revolution six major parties struggled for power. Representing the bureaucrats and the great landowners, the Monarchists and Octobrists *Major Parties in Russia* favored a constitutional monarchy. These groups soon gave way to the Constitutional Democrats, popularly called the Cadets. Favoring the middle classes and vested interests, working for a democratic, parliamentary constitutional monarchy, and urging the handing over of the land to the peasants, with adequate compensation to property owners, this party at first dominated the provisional government and tried to continue the aggressive military and foreign policies of the Czar. As the menace of radicalism became greater the Cadets tended to become conservatives, thereby losing the support of the masses. Three radical parties — the Menshevist Social Democrats, the Bolshevist Social Democrats, and the Social Revolutionaries — now threatened to take over the government. A communist state was their objective.

Communism includes "those systems and movements which aim at communalizing the means of production, justify *Communism in Russia* their pursuit of this end by a scientific analysis of the capitalist system of economy, and in their efforts to reach it, count principally on the support of the masses of industrial workmen, the proletariat and the numerous classes of lower clerks, etc." There were a variety of forms of communism, but most of them rested more or less on the doctrines of Marx and Engels as expounded in the *Communist Manifesto*. Interested primarily in the cause of the workers, these schemes aimed at a general leveling of society through a class war which was necessary to shatter the bourgeois hegemony in capitalistic countries. Then readjustment of society would occur through the following means: (1) the communalizing of the means of production so as to increase the total output and consumption, (2) a broader and more equitable distribution of goods, and (3) reorganization of social classes and all creative achievement.

Russia, as will be seen, became the parade ground of communism. The type there differed from the earlier forms, although Leninism, named after the Bolshevist leader Lenin, sprang from the *Communist Manifesto*. Discarding the evolutionary notion that a capitalistic transitional stage was a prerequisite to the class war, Leninism assumed that a world revolution was feasible in all countries, regardless of the stage of their economic development. It asserted that, other methods failing, revolution was the road to success, and that a militant minority was required to represent the generally unenlightened, nonhomogeneous proletariat. Therefore the Communist party was to function as an advance guard or as a committee of intelligent workers to overcome the bourgeois threats of police repression or unemployment. Asserting that "the phrases of democracy bear no relationship to present realities," it undertook to rescue the propertyless man from the bourgeois dictatorship characteristic of capitalistic society. In order to resist a counter-revolution, therefore, there would have to be a temporary Communist dictatorship.

To the Communists the state was an organ for the exploitation and repression of other classes by the dominant one. They hoped to emancipate all society by gaining control of the government and by substituting the administration of things for that of persons. Class distinctions would be obliterated as the state as a special class organ gave way to the machinery of a homogeneous Communist society. Anticipating such changes, Engels had declared years before, "The machine of the State is put into the museum of antiquities, alongside of the spinning wheel and the bronze axe."

After the March uprising of 1917 the champions of the new revolution became increasingly popular in Russia. For years the Socialists had advocated comprehensive reform programs and had dared to defy the Czarist autocracy. Restless malcontents of all classes had joined them, so that their numbers had increased greatly. Nevertheless, beyond their doctrinaire

Bolsheviks and Mensheviks

principles the Socialist groups, when the March Revolution came, still lacked unity and a well-defined program of action. At first divergent views contributed to the chaos among the Socialists. Later they were agitated by such problems as the attitude of Russia toward the war and her allies, the nature of the new state power, and the political and social aims of the revolution.

The Bolsheviks and the Mensheviks, however, had long been in general agreement as to aims. Both accepted Marxian tenets, such as the following: the materialistic interpretation of history, the theory of surplus value, the law of the concentration of capital, the inevitability of the class struggle, the eventual triumph and dictatorship of the proletariat, the socialization of the means of production and distribution, and the collectivist theory of the supremacy of the state. But the two divisions of the Social Democrats disagreed as to methods; the Mensheviks favored a gradual evolutionary process toward the realization of their aims, whereas the Bolsheviks were not averse to the use of force. As early as the party convention of 1903 the two groups had virtually split. Later the Bolsheviks, under the direction of the exiled Lenin, proclaimed themselves a distinct party and broke forever with all other groups and subgroups. The old central committee of the Social Democrat party was deposed, and Zinoviev declared, "We are the party. We have raised the standard of the Bolshevik party. Who is not with us is against us!"

The Social Revolutionaries constituted a third important radical party. More numerous among the peasants than in the ranks of the factory workers, they were exponents of agrarian reforms and advocates of violence. Led by radical intellectuals, they sought the destruction of the existing political and social order and desired, above all, the conversion of private property into "the property of the whole people."

At first none of the above-named groups were able to obtain control of the government. The suddenness of the March Revolution caught them unprepared. Largely through their advantageous position in the Duma the Octobrists and Cadets dominated the first provisional government. Meanwhile the opposition parties, particularly the three Socialist groups, took stock of their aims and planned to win over public opinion and to determine the course of the revolution. Taking advantage of the liberal policy of the government in permitting political freedom, they prepared the way for the overthrow of the bourgeois administration.

The soviets became the cells, or the nuclei, of the new revolution. These were composed of local groups of soldiers, workers, and peasants, who aimed at a social revolution which should overthrow the bourgeoisie and bring about a division of the land without compensation to the owners, the socialization of the factories, the cessation of the war, and a peace "without annexations and indemnities." Controlled by the Social Revolutionaries and the Mensheviks, both virtually unrepresented in the provisional government, the soviets became restless. Soon they denounced the bourgeois provisional government for its dilatory methods in dealing with the land problem, its imperialist policy, and its delay in calling a constituent assembly.

In April, 1917, an all-Russian Congress of Soviets convened in Petrograd. Nearly five hundred delegates, representing soviets of soldiers, workers, and peasants, were gathered in a national assembly. Whereas the provisional government was chiefly bourgeois, this congress represented the masses. Clashing with the ministry's policies, it denounced imperialism and the continued participation in the war.

The determination on the part of the bourgeois ministers in the provisional government to continue hostilities finally led to a crisis. Meetings of protest were held in the large cities, and workers and rioters demanded withdrawal from the World War and *Menshevik-Bourgeois Alliance* shouted, "Down with Miliukov!" Finally the obnoxious administration resigned, and the Mensheviks, hitherto opposed to coöperation with the bourgeoisie, reversed their earlier policy and demanded more representation in the government.

The new ministry marked a distinct shift to the left. Although Prince Lvov remained as premier, Kerensky now became minister of war, in a cabinet which included three Social

Revolutionaries and three Mensheviks. On May 19 the reorganized government repudiated imperialism and indicated its desire to effect "a peace without annexations or indemnities," based on the principle of national self-determination. The provisional régime represented a compromise between the bourgeoisie and the more radical soviets. Nevertheless it was weakened by the reorganization, for it now alienated the support of the conservatives without winning over the radicals. By the late spring and summer the Bolsheviks were menacing the government. Fear of them was partly responsible for the abandonment by the Mensheviks of their noncoöperation policy. Mensheviks and moderate Social Revolutionaries preferred to support the bourgeois government rather than to permit the Bolsheviks to gain power.

Playing no great rôle in the earlier stages of the revolution, the Bolsheviks became more active after the return from exile of Lenin on April 16, 1917. This remarkable leader, whose real name was Vladimir Ilyitch Ulianov (1870–1924), possessed will power and energy. As a youth he received a good education and became a lawyer, but later he took part in subversive revolutionary activities which led to his exile. While abroad he developed the policies and tactics of the Bolsheviks and became their real leader. In contrast to the orthodox Marxian Mensheviks, who desired the interpolation of a bourgeois democracy between semifeudal Russia and a socialist régime, Lenin and the Bolsheviks desired to dispense with the intermediate capitalistic stage and proceed directly to the creation of a communist régime.

Rise of the Bolshevist Leaders

Lenin, upon returning to Russia, began to build a strong party about himself. Political intriguers, self-seeking opportunists, sincere idealists, and disaffected proletarians soon attached themselves to him. Crude but masterful, he placed great stress on party discipline and solidarity, and urged a complete social upheaval. Influenced by his radical ideas, the group of energetic Bolsheviks of which he was the leader eagerly awaited their opportunity to seize power.

Second in importance to Lenin among the Bolsheviks was

Leon Trotsky (1879–   ). This adventurer, after years of exile, also returned to Russia in 1917. Despite his amazing conceit this obscure Jew was a very capable military leader and organizer. As director of the Red armies, during a period when the Bolsheviks were threatened with disaster, he greatly strengthened their morale by such grandiose assertions as "We may have to go, but when we do, we shall bang the door so that the whole world will tremble."

In addition to Lenin and Trotsky there were other capable leaders. Zinoviev, who later organized the Third International and labored for a world revolution, was unscrupulous but clever and energetic. Bukharin, Krasin, Chicherin, Stalin, and others since famous, were also associated with the early Bolshevist movement.

Endeavoring to win over the dissatisfied workers, soldiers, sailors, peasants, the unemployed, and political extremists, the Bolsheviks made reckless promises of peace, bread, and land. A simple program, designed *Bolshevist Plans* to please the dissatisfied classes, was devised. First the Bolsheviks planned to negotiate a just peace, so as to relieve Russia from her present plight. Then the factories were to be turned over to the workers, the lands were to be confiscated and distributed among the peasants, and the government was to assume control of the means of production and distribution. Thus by civil war was the socialization of Russia to be effected.

A new government based on the soviet was devised by the Bolsheviks. Propertied classes were to be excluded from participation in politics, a dictatorship of the proletariat was to be established, and subject nationalities were to be permitted the right of self-determination. An opportunist, Lenin believed that the end justified any means. Therefore he placed the blame for Russia's ills on the provisional government and tried to lure all classes into support of his plan for the new revolution, a proletarian uprising against the bourgeoisie and the old régime.

The Bolsheviks planned to come into power through the soviets. To achieve this end they supported the movement to vest all political authority in these local councils, and set out to gain control of them. At first they met with but limited success, for when the All-Russian Congress of Soviets assembled at Petrograd, in June, 1917, the Mensheviks were still in control and continued to support the coalition administration.

Meanwhile the provisional government was faltering. The failure to make peace, the shortage of food, and the delay in calling a constituent assembly reacted unfavorably upon the general public. Existing problems were too baffling for the government to solve, and consequently it was unable to hold public support. Lenin exploited the situation to the utmost in trying to undermine the strength of the authorities.

Fall of the Provisional Government

Despite the critical social and economic situation in Russia, Kerensky, the Menshevist head of the provisional government, concentrated on the war. He hoped that a successful offensive against the Austro-Germans would increase the prestige of his administration and revive the morale at home. Late in June, therefore, the last great Russian drive was launched against the Central Powers. After some initial successes the Russians suffered another defeat. Discipline and organization virtually disappeared as mutinies, desertions, and Bolshevist propaganda dissolved the military machine. Kerensky's provisional government was practically doomed.

While the ministry struggled to sustain the military front the Bolsheviks sowed dissension at home. On July 16, 1917, they made their first serious attempt to gain political control of Petrograd. Armed workmen and disloyal troops milled through the streets of Petrograd carrying red flags and revolutionary placards; Trotsky and Zinoviev made inciting speeches which were applauded by the mobs. Kerensky, however, sent 60,000 loyal troops from the front, who crushed the Petrograd uprising after two days of street fighting. Thus the first attempt to overthrow the provisional government proved abortive, and Lenin determined to work more slowly thereafter and to win over the mass of the army.

The Bolshevist uprising caused another ministerial crisis. Alarmed at the trend of events, Premier Lvov and two Cadet ministers resigned, and Kerensky formed a nonpartisan national government consisting of Cadets and Socialists. Desirous of making the new government a strong one, Kerensky adopted vigorous measures. Censorship of the press and of speech, arbitrary arrests, capital punishments, and courts-martial were revived. *The Kerensky Government* Unsuccessful attempts were made to arrest the Bolshevist leaders, and temporarily Kerensky succeeded in reinvesting the provisional government with a mantle of power.

Scarcely were the Bolsheviks and their demands for a dictatorship of the proletariat silenced when the authority of the government was challenged by the conservatives and reactionaries under the leadership of Kornilov. Fearing that Petrograd was under Bolshevist control, he dispatched troops from the front and sent an ultimatum to Kerensky. He demanded the proclamation of martial law in the capital, the resignation of the provisional government, and the surrender of Kerensky. Hastily endowed with dictatorial powers, the latter won over Kornilov's army to the governmental cause and effected the arrest of the rebellious general. The revolt was crushed, but many people, influenced by Bolshevist propaganda, suspected Kerensky of complicity in the affair. For the first time the Bolsheviks gained control of the Petrograd soviet; public confidence in the provisional government rapidly evaporated.

Kerensky struggled frantically to prevent the collapse of his régime. To counteract the Bolshevist control of the Petrograd soviet, the Mensheviks transferred the seat of radical authority from the soviets to the All-Russian Executive Committee, dominated by the Mensheviks. Meanwhile the provisional government was powerless to check the dissolution of the army or to halt the German advances. Martial law also failed to stop the confiscations of land and the increasing shortage of food. In view of the terrible conditions Kerensky postponed the elections of the constituent assembly from September 30 to November 25. This incident greatly accelerated the rise of the Bolsheviks. Many questioned Kerensky's loyalty to the revolution, believing him counter-revolutionary and opposed to reforms. Inasmuch as the masses of Russian people were more anxious to bring about the overthrow of the landlords than of the Austro-Germans, disaffected peasants, workers, and soldiers, holding the government responsible for all their difficulties, flocked to the Bolshevist standards.

The Bolsheviks mustered their forces. In September Trotsky formed a military-revolutionary committee and prepared the Petrograd garrison for another uprising. The Petrograd Soviet elected him as its president on October 8, and two weeks later declined to pass a vote of confidence in the provisional government. Later in October, Trotsky, by the authorization of the Petrograd Soviet, became chairman of a war-revolutionary committee which maintained direct contact with all military and naval units in Russia. The stage was set for the November Revolution when Lenin procured the unanimous approval of the Bolshevist central committee for an armed insurrection. On November 6, Bolshevist troops seized public buildings and strategic points in Petrograd. The following morning the overthrow of the provisional government was proclaimed, and its authority was transferred to the war-revolutionary committee. With the exception of Kerensky, whose flight was successful, the deposed ministers were arrested and imprisoned. On November 8 the newly assembled All-Russian Congress of Soviets approved of the Bolshevist *coup d'état* and formally assumed the burden of government. The same day that the provisional administration was overthrown the All-Russian Congress established a Soviet of the People's Commissars, of which Lenin was chairman and Trotsky commissar for foreign affairs. Shouts of "Long live the Revolution of the workers, soldiers, and peasants!" greeted the new régime.

The November Revolution

Russia thus passed under the dictatorship of the Bolsheviks. All opponents were ruthlessly suppressed, and the " Red Terror " sprang into being. Counter-revolutionary activities were crushed. From Petrograd, the head of a highly centralized administrative system, the Bolsheviks were able to dominate the agricultural mass of Russia, which was isolated, disorganized, and powerless to resist an energetic government that controlled the political and economic sinews of the country. Perhaps as early as October, 1917, Lenin foresaw such a situation, for he then inquired: "Will the Bolsheviks be able to retain power? The state is an organ or machine for the domination of one class over the others. One hundred and thirty thousand landlords have been able to rule over Russia. Cannot 240,000 members of the Bolshevist Party now do the same?"

In power, and determined to stay there by suppressing counter-revolutionary movements, the Bolsheviks proceeded to fulfill their promises. Immediate steps were taken to transfer the land from the great proprietors to the peasants and to dissolve the municipal council of Petrograd, which was opposed to withdrawal from the war. On November 25, elections to a Constituent Assembly were held on the basis of universal adult suffrage. When the elections returned a Socialist Revolutionary majority, the Bolsheviks, realizing that they constituted a minority party in Russia at large, determined to thwart the Assembly, postponing its meeting from December to January. Finally, on January 18, 1918, the Assembly convened in Petrograd, and the majority, the Social Revolutionaries, attempted to crush the Bolsheviks. Enraged, the latter proclaimed the Constituent Assembly a counter-revolutionary body and dissolved it by force. Thenceforth the Bolshevist party constituted the Russian government and proceeded to consolidate its position by exterminating the bourgeoisie and other enemies.

While Russia was torn with revolutionary strife her vast empire disintegrated. The March Revolution had been a signal for a movement toward autonomy on the part of the many subject nationalities. *Disintegration of the Russian Empire* Inspired by the former Bolshevist assertions of the right of national self-determination and by the successful *coup d'état* on November 6, some of the subject nationalities proclaimed their independence. The Baltic provinces (Finland, Estonia, Latvia, and Lithuania) and the Ukraine and Moldavia (Bessarabia) in southern Russia set up autonomous governments. A Siberian Confederation was proclaimed at

Tomsk; the Transcaucasian Federal Republic declared for autonomy and then for independence. On November 24 Lenin authorized the subject nationalities to establish independent states, but hesitated to grant them recognition unless they were dominated by Bolshevist elements.

Confronted by domestic problems the Bolsheviks determined to withdraw from the war. In November they notified

Russian Withdrawal from the War

foreign diplomats that they intended to conclude a separate peace. Meanwhile the Central Powers, anxious to release their troops on the Eastern Front and to secure access to Russian resources, were desirous of getting Russia out of the conflict. Armistice negotiations were therefore opened at Brest-Litovsk. At the meeting the German attitude was uncompromising; despite Russian protests the Germans insisted on the cession of the Baltic provinces and of Poland. Because of Russian obstinacy the conference broke up, although it extended the armistice to February 12. Two days before the end of the armistice Trotsky informed the Germans that Russia was withdrawing from the war, but he would not sign the peace treaty. The German armies now resumed their advance, and consequently Lenin and Trotsky capitulated. More drastic peace terms with a forty-eight-hour time limit were now imposed, and the Russian delegates were forced to sign.

On March 3 peace was concluded between Russia and the Central Powers by the Treaty of Brest-Litovsk. The terms were as follows: (1) renunciation by Russia of Poland, Courland, and Lithuania, their future status to be determined by Austria and Germany; (2) evacuation by Russia of Finland, the Åland Islands, Estonia, and Livonia: (3) Russian evacuation of the Ukraine and recognition of the latter's treaty with the Central Powers; (4) cession to Turkey of Batum, Kars, and Ardahan; and (5) termination of Bolshevist propaganda in territories of the Central Powers or of those concerned in the treaty. In August, 1918, Russia was forced to sign supplementary treaties with the following provisions: (1) six billion gold marks indemnity to Germany; (2) the grant to Germany of most-favored-nation treatment in Russia; and (3) free export of rough and hewn timber without restrictions. The peace terms were harsh and thrust Russia back from western Europe; she was again isolated and cut off from the more advanced West. Nevertheless Russia secured that greatest of boons, peace.

The hydra-headed counter-revolution, however, threatened to destroy the Bolsheviks. Many people in Russia disapproved of the ruthless methods and radical doctrines of the Bolsheviks, and therefore *Anti-Bolshevist Movements* supported the ousted aristocrats and bourgeoisie in counter-revolutionary activities. Numerous anti-Bolshevist movements sprang up during 1918–1919, and the Bolsheviks were compelled soon to defend their newly won power. "White" leaders, with conservative or moderate tendencies, set up independent rival governments, created armies to defend them, and tried to raise the countryside to their support. A "North-Russian Provisional Government" was established in the neighborhood of Archangel and Murmansk, and furnished one nucleus for an anti-Bolshevist campaign. In the independent Baltic provinces General Yudenitch prepared a White army to crush the Bolsheviks, while in southern Russia the former Czarist generals Kornilov, Alexiev, and Denikin created a "Government of the Volunteer Army" and prepared to contest the Soviet régime. In remote Siberia and eastern Russia anti-Bolshevist forces seized the trans-Siberian Railway. At Omsk was established an independent government, first under a directorate and later under the control of Admiral Kolchak. As these White armies, supported by the Allies, prepared for a simultaneous advance against the Bolsheviks in 1919, the Soviet government seemed doomed.

Vexed because the Bolsheviks had withdrawn from the war, the Allies were bitterly opposed to them, for the Central Powers were thereby enabled to release the eastern armies for service in the west and to replenish dwindling supplies by securing access to the vast resources of Russia. Moreover, in quitting the conflict the Bolsheviks had denounced the imperialist aims of the Allies, had called for an international revolution of all workers in capitalist countries, and had repudiated the enormous debts to their former partners incurred by the Czarist government. Aroused, the Allies attempted not only to thwart German interests in Russia but also to destroy the Bolshevist régime. Allied expeditions were sent to occupy Murmansk and Archangel, in northern Russia, and Vladivostok, the eastern terminus of the trans-Siberian Railway. The French seized the port of Odessa on the Black Sea, and the British occupied the republics in Transcaucasia. By the end of the year 1918 the Allies were maintaining an effective blockade of Bolshevist Russia, and they lent their support to the counter-revolutionary movements which developed in 1918–1919.

The adherents of the new revolution in Russia were not discouraged. Two instruments — the *Cheka* (a superior police and spy organization for the purpose of terrifying opponents of the new régime) and the Red army — were organized to quell the counter-revolutionary movement. Both instigated a Red Terror which resulted in thousands of arrests, imprisonments, exiles, and executions. Among those executed were the former Czar and his family, on July 16, 1918, because of fear that they might become the nuclei for new plots.

In 1919 the Whites made a supreme effort to shatter Bolshevist power, and failed. By the end of 1920, with the exception of the Japanese in Siberia, all Russia was cleared of Allied and White armies. The most decisive factor in the failure of the counter-revolution in Russia was the attitude of the peasants. To them the reactionary generals, with their White Terror, stood for the old régime — the landlords, oppression, the loss of their recently acquired land, and the return of Czarist practices which they abhorred. Therefore the mass of Russian peasants preferred to support, at least passively, the Bolsheviks, who seemed to symbolize a new freedom.

While the counter-revolutionaries, supported by the Allies, were attempting to dislodge the Bolsheviks, the latter were engaged in an effort to establish a new régime. In the summer of 1918 they created a new political system. The fifth All-Russian Congress of Soviets met at that time and adopted the constitution which created the Russian Socialist Federated Soviet Republic (R.S.F.S.R.). Henceforth the governmental structure rested on the urban and rural soviets, which were under the control of the workers.

The New Order

Therefore, without regard to sex, only productive workers and their housekeepers, soldiers, and sailors, who had attained the age of eighteen years, were entitled to participate in politics. Certain classes were debarred from the suffrage: namely, (1) persons who hired labor for profit; (2) persons with income apart from that derived from their own labor; (3) private merchants, brokers, and traders; (4) all monks and clergymen; (5) former Czarist police, agents, and spies; (6) members of the dethroned dynasty; and (7) criminals, lunatics, and persons under guardianship. Thus the bourgeoisie, the old landowners, and the Czarist bureaucrats were denied the right to participate in the government. An estimated 8 per cent of the adults in rural districts and a slightly higher proportion in urban communities were disqualified from the suffrage.

Rural soviets controlled local government but were very indirectly represented in the higher administration. Those persons who were entitled to vote met in the village and elected one deputy from the soviet for each one hundred inhabitants. Village soviets in a given district sent delegates to a district congress, and the latter in turn sent representatives to a county congress. All county assemblies in a certain region sent delegates to regional and also to provincial assemblies, the latter sending representatives to the All-Russian Congress of Soviets and the Union Congress of Soviets.

Deputies from urban soviets were selected on an occupational basis, usually in the ratio of one delegate to each thousand inhabitants. Independent vocations and large factories chose delegates to the city soviet, and the latter in turn sent representatives to sit with the rural delegates in both regional and provincial congresses. Urban and rural soviets were also represented in the All-Russian Congress of Soviets. Rural delegates were designated in the provincial congresses in the ratio of one to 125,000 inhabitants, whereas urban representatives were selected directly in a ratio of one to 25,000 inhabitants. Thus urban districts, since they were strongholds of communism, were given relatively greater political recognition by the Bolsheviks. The All-Russian Congress of Soviets was the body in which supreme power in the Russian Socialist Federated Soviet Republic (R. S. F. S. R.) was theoretically vested. It was originally designed to meet semiannually, but it met only once a year after 1921.

The All-Russian Central Executive Committee, controlling the legislative and executive functions of government, was the dominant organ in the state. It met four times yearly, convoked the All-Russian Congress, appointed the Council of the People's Commissars, and, when not in session, was represented by a præsidium. The Council of Commissars, responsible to the Central Executive Committee or its representative, the præsidium, was the executive of the state. It numbered seventeen members, and its functions were analogous to those of a cabinet in a parliamentary government.

This political pattern, described above, for Russia proper was the original basis of the Soviet government. With the collapse of the White régimes, however, the Bolsheviks began to spread propaganda which led to the reintegration of all the old empire with the exception of Poland and the Baltic provinces. In 1922 the independent governments which had been set up in the recovered districts were persuaded to enter voluntarily into a Union of Socialist Soviet Republics (U. S. S. R.). This new arrangement became effective July 6, 1923. Henceforth each state possessed a political structure identical with that of the R. S. F. S. R.

The political machinery of the U. S. S. R., consisting of a Union Congress of Soviets, a Union Central Executive Committee, and a Union Council of Commissars, was very similar to that of the R. S. F. S. R. The U. S. S. R., barring local government, had virtual monopoly of power. It controlled foreign affairs, foreign and domestic commerce, internal transportation and communications, and the armed forces of the Union. Furthermore, the exploitation of the land and natural resources and the control of labor legislation, education, and

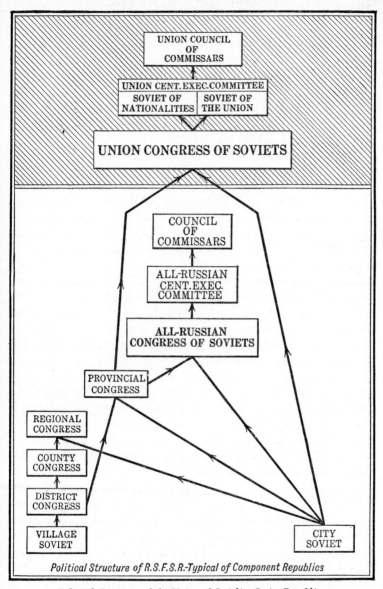

Political Structure of R.S.F.S.R.-Typical of Component Republics

Political Structure of the Union of Socialist Soviet Republics
From F. L. Benns's *Europe Since 1914.* Courtesy of F. S. Crofts & Co., N.Y.

public health were included in its functions. The Union could abrogate any decision in the constituent republics which infringed on its authority.

Dominant in the soviet system of the government was the Communist party. By indirect representation in rural dis-

The Communist Party tricts, by occupational representation, by the disfranchisement of so-called nonworkers, and by the union of governmental functions the Bolsheviks succeeded in creating a government which could be controlled by this relatively small group.

The Communist party consisted of some 38,000 local organizations called cells. The latter selected representatives to an annual party congress, which in turn chose a central executive committee. This organ was all-powerful in the administration and designated a political bureau of nine members, who determined the party policies. After Lenin's death (1924) Stalin dominated this bureau. In 1926–1927, however, an open revolt against Stalin's program and authority was instigated by Trotsky and Zinoviev. Their attempt proving unsuccessful, they were dropped from the party and exiled.

With little more than a million members, the Communists became the only recognized party in the new régime. Its members were rigidly disciplined and had to conform to party decisions or be expelled. The avowed purposes of the Communist party, which controlled the governmental machinery, were to maintain an oligarchy and to discourage democratic tendencies. It promoted propaganda in education and maintained a strict censorship of the press, speech, and the drama. Over two million boys and youths, varying in age from ten to twenty-three, were included in the Pioneers and the League of Communist Youth, organizations designed to inculcate communistic principles. An able police force, the *Cheka*, crushed counter-revolutionary activities until 1922, when it was replaced by the G. P. U., which endeavored to suppress political and economic counter-revolution, espionage, and banditism. All opposition was destroyed by systematic repression.

Intrusted with the task of establishing a new order, the

Communist party remained the ruling group in Russia. To achieve its aims, it took over the government.

The undisguised and deliberate use of the State institutions as an instrument in the class struggle is fully in accord with the Marxian doctrine of the State, namely, that it is a class organization; in this case it is the organization of the ruling proletarian class. This conception of the State permeates all forms of social and economic life in the Soviet Union.[1]

The Bolsheviks, however, believed that the state would be a class organization only until the "parasitical" groups, such as the bourgeoisie and the *kulaks* (capitalist farmers), were wiped out. Then a classless state would be attained.

Bolshevist experiments in economic life were far more revolutionary than the political reforms. Attempting at first to establish pure communism, the Bolsheviks desired to nationalize the land, forests, natural *Economic Experiments* resources, and all means of production, transportation, trade, banking, and insurance. Such services were to belong to the state, which was controlled by the soviets of workers. Profits were to go to the proletariat, and the surplus to the state. Thus the bourgeois system of landlords, capitalists, and wage-earners would be supplanted by a new classless society.

In 1917 the Bolsheviks proclaimed the nationalization of land and the establishment of workers' control over industries. This accelerated the disintegration of Russian economic life, for the workers soon discovered that the factories could not run without expert management and capital. By June, 1918, the situation was so chaotic that the government undertook to ameliorate industrial conditions by establishing a system of centralized supervision. A Supreme Economic Council was empowered to coördinate industries and to see that all factories were supplied with the needed materials and food or wages for the workers. As production fell off alarmingly, attempts were made to "militarize" labor. Also, a policy of nationalization brought Russia's economic structure under state control.

[1] *Guidebook to the Soviet Union*, pages xxxiii–xxxiv. International Publishers, 1928.

One of the chief problems confronting the Bolsheviks, after their rise to power, was the collapse of agriculture. As has been said elsewhere, it began during the war and was hastened by the policy of so-called "war communism." Permitted to seize over 96 per cent of the land of Russia, the peasants opposed the government's policy of nationalization. They refused to surrender their surplus produce or to accept worthless paper money from the state. Furthermore, the disparity between the prices of industrial goods and those of farm products — called the "scissors" — was such that the peasants hoarded their grain. The government, meanwhile, had adopted the ration system and was under obligation to supply the urban workers with food. To combat the peasants' obstinacy, poorer farmers were appointed to confiscate grain from the richer peasants, the *kulaks*. This policy was a failure and was abandoned in 1918. Then the "Food Army" of armed city workers and soldiers was authorized to seize the grain. Despite frequent uprisings a supply was secured.

The peasants now began a policy of passive resistance. They raised only enough grain for themselves, and there was no surplus to seize. In 1920 the sowing area was 71 per cent of the 1913 harvest, and the 1921 harvest amounted to but 42 per cent of the average harvests for the four years preceding the war. Because of this decline, and because of a terrible drought which resulted in the famine of 1921, both the farmers and the starving city workers were discouraged and revolts were frequent.

As a result of these conditions the government was forced to abandon pure communism and resorted in 1921 to the New Economic Policy (NEP). Although under this

The New Economic Policy (1921-1928) program the Communists retained control of the government, finance, large-scale industry, foreign trade, and the transport system, they permitted a certain degree of compromise with capitalism. These new policies involved (1) the abandonment of a forced requisition of the peasants' goods in favor of a fixed tax; (2) the existence of some retail trade subject to restrictions as well as competition from the state-owned stores and consumers' coöperatives which were encouraged by the government; (3) the denationalization of factories with less than twenty employees and their restoration to private capitalists; (4) graduated wage scales and a modified system of food rations; (5) the abolition of compulsory membership of workers in trade unions; (6) state trusts to control the means of production and distribution; (7) the reëstablishment of a money economy with an intricate state banking system, with the chervonetz nominally stabilized at $5.15; and (8) the grant of economic concessions to foreign capitalists, whose investments were guaranteed against nationalization. The last provision was designed to attract foreign capital and technical skill, so vital for the modernization of Russia. Owing to the NEP, Russia's economic life became a curious composite of capitalism, state socialism, and communism.

This new policy marked a shift in tactics and was designed especially to encourage the peasantry and to augment production. The policy of requisitioning grain from the farmer was abolished, and he was required to pay a tax commensurate with his ability. By means of this change the farmer's incentive to work and to secure profits was reëstablished, and he dropped his passive resistance. Also, the government, while insisting on its ownership of the land, allowed the peasantry to remain in undisturbed possession of that which they cultivated. The renting of land, with certain limitations, was permitted after 1925. Some peasants became wealthy; others, poor. Therefore in 1928 the government adopted a tax system whereby the former (the *kulaks*) paid a heavier tax, while the latter were exempt. Those peasants who were between the two extremes paid a light tax.

The government, determined to revive agrarian life in Russia, adopted a number of measures designed to increase agricultural production. These took the form of official encouragement of mechanization of farming, scientific cultivation, use of better seeds and fertilizers, reclamation and settlement of unoccupied lands, elimination of disparity between industrial and agricultural prices, raising of crops for industries, agricultural banks and societies, and state and collective farms. As a result of these measures, by 1926 the area sown equaled that of 1913. Particularly important was the promotion of state and collective farms. The former were managed and operated by a department of the government and later were organized into trusts. Collectives were developed, especially after 1930, sometimes through governmental coercion but more often by the voluntary accord of the peasants, who lacked agricultural implements. These organizations consisted of poor and middle peasants who were organized into groups called "artels" for the purpose of increasing production through the elimination of individual competition and of profit-seeking. Owing to coöperation in working, buying, and selling, these collectives, encouraged by the state, often proved very efficient.

Russia began to recover after the adoption of the New Economic Policy. Her currency was restabilized and the national finances were put in order. State industries reached pre-war standards as to quantities by 1926–1927. In the fall of 1928, to further accelerate the Russian economic recovery, Stalin and his associates, through the celebrated Five-Year Plan, launched a drive to industrialize Russia. This project was designed to promote economic development so that within five years Russia could supply her domestic needs and acquire a surplus for export. Its authors hoped to increase vastly the output of iron ore, coal, steel, petroleum, electric power, and grain. They planned for the construction of huge factories and for the manufacture of agricultural machinery, tractors, and automobiles. The government, through the improvement of railways and highways, the development of better housing conditions and technical schools, the reduction of illiteracy, and the introduction of music, drama, and books into all villages, hoped to effect a cultural transformation of Russian life. It was estimated that a total of some $35,000,000,000 would be needed for such stupendous achievements as were designed. The plan called for an early expenditure of $7,800,000,000 in industrial development, $4,800,000,000 in transportation facilities, and $1,550,000,000 in electrification.

The Five-Year Plan

To finance this gigantic undertaking the state relied chiefly on increased taxes, on the profits from the state trusts which controlled most of Russian industry, and on domestic loan issues. As phases of a general economy program, governmental expenses were curtailed, the use of luxuries was banned, and a ration system for most foodstuffs was reëstablished. It was further hoped that a decrease of expenses in carrying out the vast project could be effected by reducing production costs one third and by doubling the productivity of labor.

In many respects the Five-Year Plan was a remarkable success. The production of oil, agricultural machinery, autos, tractors, peat, sugar, and coal, for example, far surpassed the original schedule. Progress in electrification, railway construction, the iron, steel, and textile industries, and the building of great dams and giant industrial plants exceeded the expectations of the authors of the plan. Collectivization of the farms, which was supposed to equal 20 per cent of the total cultivation in 1933, had actually attained 60 per cent two years ahead of time. Owing to agricultural improvements the increase in wheat production was so great that Russia was in a position to flood the markets of the world by 1931. Collectivization in domestic trade also progressed, for by 1932 the consumers' coöperatives, with 55,000,000 members, controlled 160,000 stores and left but 5½ per cent of the retail trade in private hands. Furthermore, during a period of world depression, when millions were unemployed, Russia suffered from shortage of labor — a significant fact which could not be ignored by the adherents of capitalism.

Complete success, however, was not realized under the Five-Year Plan. The scheduled reduction of production costs and the increase of the productivity of labor were not maintained. Moreover, the lack of technicians and skilled workers, the absence of effective discipline in the factories, and the tremendous speed at which the government was trying to modernize Russian industry resulted in numerous accidents and a neglect of quality in manufactures. These factors, together with the backwardness of transportation facilities (which handicapped distribution) and the inadequacy of food supplies, threw the whole scheme out of balance. A decline in the standard of living, and the hardships undergone by the masses, impelled the government to make certain adjustments in its policies, such as the recognition of the principle of wage inequality for skilled workers, the restoration of factory discipline, a relaxation of the discriminations against non-communist workers and *kulaks*, and attempts to increase the food rations. Despite these problems, which were aggravated by the absence of liquid capital and foreign credit and the difficulty of securing favorable trade treaties abroad, Soviet Russia, by 1933, had made stupendous progress toward large-scale industrialism.

Before the completion of the First Five-Year Plan, Stalin issued a challenge to the capitalistic world by the announcement of a Second Five-Year Plan in January, 1933. Claiming success for the earlier project, which was 94 per cent complete after four years and three months, he asserted that the aim of the second would be "to change the country from one with the technique of the Middle Ages to one of contemporary technique — to make the nation independent of the whims of capitalism." He declared that the production of war materials, food supplies, and manufactured goods was to be increased so as to safeguard the future of the Bolshevist régime. Furthermore, he snubbed the advocates of a return to private farming by flatly declaring that collectivization in agriculture would be continued.

Among the most striking changes effected by the Bolsheviks were those in education and religion. Education was *Education and Religion in Soviet Russia* strictly secularized and communized. The schools were designed to create intelligent skilled workers, to promote "an intellectual revolution," and to win over the younger generation to the communist principles. At the same time a tremendous offensive against "ignorance and superstition" was launched. Religion was dealt a severe blow by the state. The property of the old church was confiscated by the government, education was removed from its hands, and religious instruction could not be given to persons under eighteen. Atheism became practically a state dogma, and extremists regarded religion as a manifestation of counter-revolution.

Soviet Russia found it difficult to establish friendly relations with foreign powers. Vexed with the Allies because of their support of the Whites from 1918 to 1920, the Bolsheviks retaliated by circulat- *Russia in International Affairs* ing propaganda in those countries designed to create a number of revolutions against capitalist powers. Through the Third International, under the leadership of Zinoviev, the Bolsheviks spread the doctrines of the new revolution, hoping to cause uprisings of workers in the western European states. Their attempts proved futile, for, with the exception of the communist régime of Bela Kun in Hungary (1919) and the disorders in post-war Germany and Italy, workers of other countries seemed deaf to the Bolshevist appeals. A need for foreign capital caused the Bolsheviks to abandon their "world-revolution" propaganda and to court the friendship of the capitalistic states. Until 1921 only the four Baltic countries — Lithuania, Latvia, Finland, and Estonia — recognized Russia. In that year, however, Great Britain and Russia entered into a provisional trade treaty, and similar arrangements were concluded with Germany, Austria, Italy, and Norway.

The repudiation of debts was one of the greatest obstacles to Russia's resuming her position in the family of nations. At the Genoa Conference of April, 1922, thirty-four powers, including Russia, attempted to solve this problem. Her creditors made the following demands: (1) Russian recognition of repudiated debts, (2) compensation for nationalized property belonging to foreigners, and (3) protection for all commercial and other types of contracts in Russia. The Soviet representatives, however, required complete cancellation of war debts, the grant of credits to Russia, and a moratorium on such foreign debts as Russia agreed to pay. No definite settlement was reached either at Genoa or later at another conference at the Hague.

During the next few years Russia's international position improved. Germany granted her *de jure* recognition by the

Treaty of Rapallo (April, 1922), and commercial and industrial agreements with Germany, Czechoslovakia, and Denmark soon followed. In 1924 Russia, fearful of a hostile coalition of foreign powers, began a drive for *de jure* acceptance. The rise of Ramsay MacDonald's Labor party to power brought British recognition on February 1. Practically all the other major governments, with the exception of the United States, followed suit the same year. A number of non-aggression pacts were signed with Turkey, Germany, Afghanistan, Lithuania, Persia, Finland, Poland, France, and Italy between 1925 and 1933. Moreover, by virtue of the so-called Litvinov Protocol of March, 1929, Russia induced most of the states on her European borders to agree to put the Kellogg-Briand Pact for the outlawry of war into immediate operation.

Russia, represented by the "rotund bespectacled" Maxim Litvinov, played a surprisingly important rôle at the World Economic Conference at London in 1933. While other delegates disputed over currency stabilization and various economic issues the Soviet commissar of foreign affairs did much to smooth the way for American recognition, completed negotiations for purchasing cotton from the United States, and agreed to release the two British engineers imprisoned at Moscow in exchange for revocation of the retaliatory embargo on Russian goods. His efforts were rewarded on November 17, 1933, when the United States finally recognized Soviet Russia.

As a result of Litvinov's clever diplomatic negotiations a non-aggression agreement was signed by Russia, Rumania, Czechoslovakia, Yugoslavia, and Turkey. Moreover, a pact with the same text but limited to Russia's immediate neighbors was signed by Afghanistan, Estonia, Latvia, Persia, Poland, Rumania, and Turkey. Thus Litvinov, taking advantage of central European and French fears of Hitlerism, obtained the support of Czechoslovakia, Rumania, and Yugoslavia, as well as France, in his plan to maintain the territorial integrity of Soviet Russia.

Despite this gradual rapprochement with the capitalist powers, however, Russia did not utterly discard her world-revolutionary program. From 1923 to 1927 the Bolsheviks encouraged communist uprisings in Germany, Bulgaria, Estonia, Latvia, and Finland. During the general strike in England in 1926 Bolshevist activities and intrigues were apparent, and diplomatic relations between England and Russia were broken off. Meanwhile, abhorring capitalism and its offspring, imperialism, the Bolsheviks were responsible for spreading much anti-imperialistic and anti-capitalistic propaganda in Asia. By arousing in the peoples of the East, especially in China and central Asia, a desire for national self-determination, they played a significant rôle in bringing on the "Revolt of Asia."

The new revolution, regardless of its ultimate success or failure, was one of the notable experiments in history. In 1933, through a new Five-Year Plan and other devices, the Bolsheviks were still trying to create a model communist régime which would inspire other countries to imitate their example. Some people believed that Russian communism would gradually be modified until it approximated the bourgeois system; many, however, asserted that it would eventually lead to the overthrow of capitalism.

WHICH WAY does the Wind Blow?

After a cartoon in the Philadelphia *Inquirer*, 1917

CHAPTER XXXIV

Fascism in Italy: The New Cæsarism

AT THE conclusion of the war the constitutional monarchy in Italy was an obvious failure. Noted for its weak, inefficient, and corrupt policies, the parliamentary system had never been a conspicuous success. The war strained Italy's resources to the utmost; and when the conflict ended, there was an enormous deficit, which amounted to over twelve billions of lire in 1919–1920, over eighteen billions in 1920–1921, and over seventeen billions in 1921–1922. Fearing lest industry suffer and the capitalists and trade unions become hostile, the government did not dare to reduce its expenditures. Fiscal reforms designed to produce greater revenue proved inadequate. The national finances were further demoralized by the steady depreciation of currency, which fell to less than one third of its face value shortly after the conflict.

Cheap money was accompanied by a tremendous rise in the cost of living, which caused much suffering among the unemployed. Discharged soldiers, unable to secure work and food, became especially restless. Confronted by a serious situation, the government sold food below cost and granted subsidies to the sufferers. Such measures, however, afforded only temporary relief.

A spirit of unrest pervaded the nation. Agrarian and industrial disturbances gave radicals an opportunity of spreading their doctrines. Preaching the gospel of *Radicalism in Italy* Bolshevism,— strikes, the seizure of factories and lands, and the establishment of a dictatorship of the proletariat,— they made converts of many peasants, workers, and other disaffected groups. As a result, in the parliamentary elections of November, 1919, the Socialists won one hundred and fifty-six seats in the Chamber of Deputies. They were thus enabled to obstruct the government's attempts to stem the revolutionary tide through constructive legislation. By 1920 the Socialists controlled thousands of the communes, and probably one third of Italy was in sympathy with their aims.

These radicals utilized the strike as their chief weapon. Hoping to bring about a dictatorship of the proletariat by means of a revolution, they sought to promote internal disorders. Walkouts became frequent in all occupations. The very existence of the nation was at stake; for often strikes would occur in the vital services, such as the light and food supplies in the cities, the railways, tramways, and postal and telegraphic communications. These attempts to paralyze the country through strikes resulted in the loss of 19,000,000 working days in 1919 and over 16,000,000 in 1920.

The subversive revolutionary movement also spread to the rural districts. Most of the land was owned by a small number of persons. Peasants, tenants, and ex-service men committed outrages in trying forcibly to seize estates. Although little was actually taken, the property-owning classes were alarmed, for they knew that the supine government was impotent to protect them. In the city and in rural communities the established order was on trial for its life.

While the constitutional monarchy and the capitalist system seemed to be crumbling, popular discontent was further aroused by the government's unsuccessful foreign policies. Stirred by memories of ancient *Italy's Unpopular Foreign Policies* Rome, ardent nationalists had hoped to see Italy emerge from the war with vast imperial acquisitions. But her diplomats at the Peace Conference in Paris failed woefully to live up to expectations. Italy's alleged "vital interests" in the Adriatic, Africa, and the Near East had not been adequately safeguarded.

Seizure of Fiume by Gabriele d'Annunzio, the Italian nationalist poet-aviator, precipitated a crisis which greatly discredited the government. The Peace Conference had not awarded this Dalmatian port to Italy, nor had it delimited the Yugoslav frontier in Dalmatia. National sentiment was therefore inflamed. In September, 1919, D'Annunzio, with a group of followers, seized the city. The government, however, refusing to countenance this illegal act, entered into the Treaty of Rapallo, in November, 1920, with Yugoslavia, whereby the independence of the Free State of Fiume was recognized. With the exception of Zara the whole Dalmatian coast to the south of Fiume was surrendered to Yugoslavia. In the following month Italian troops were utilized to expel the militant poet and his legionnaires. Popular indignation with the government's weak surrender expressed itself in violent denunciations of its policies.

Lack of success in Albania further damaged the government's popularity. Occupation of this strip of the Balkan coast, opposite the heel of Italy, had long been contemplated as a phase of the conversion of the Adriatic into an Italian lake. During the war Italian troops occupied part of Albania, and a tripartite treaty was planned which would have partitioned the country between Greece, Yugoslavia, and Italy. The latter was to retain the strategic port of Valona, which controlled the Strait of Otranto. The scheme was never consummated, and the close of the war found Italian troops still occupying Albania despite the opposition of its dissatisfied inhabitants, who in a guerrilla conflict nearly expelled the invaders. Alarmed by conditions at home, Premier Giolitti ingloriously relinquished Italian designs and in 1920 recognized the independence of Albania. The Italians retained only the island of Saseno, from which they hoped to dominate Valona and the Strait of Otranto. The Italian Adriatic policy had failed as miserably in Albania as in Dalmatia.

Italian colonial policies were not very successful. Chiefly through national pride, the pressure of a rapidly increasing population, and the need for additional economic opportunities, imperialism had become a fundamental factor in foreign policy. But by 1914 Italy had managed to secure only such unimportant colonies as Tripoli (Libya), Eritrea, and Somaliland. By the secret treaty of London (1915), however, Italy was promised territorial rewards in Africa and in the Near East.

Italy's Colonial Ambitions

The Paris Peace Conference did not satisfy the desires of

Italian imperialists. Their country failed to procure a share of the enemy colonies in Africa, and cessions of territory from England and France to enlarge her colonies in Libya and Somaliland were of slight value. Italian patriots had hoped to create an empire on the ruins of the Ottoman state, and with that idea in mind had kept troops on the Dodecanese Islands since 1911. Italian railway concessions in Adalia and the hope of procuring control of coal mines and of the city of Smyrna in Asia Minor also caused the government to send troops and battleships to the Near East. But the Treaty of Sèvres handed Smyrna and its hinterland over to Greece, and the subsequent recovery of Turkey resulted in the Italians' being forced to relinquish all rights in Adalia save commercial concessions.

As these imperialist policies of the constitutional government became more unsuccessful its prestige decreased proportionately. In August and September, 1920, the revolutionary movement precipitated a crisis. *Unrest in Italy* The struggle between the employers and the industrial workers had reached an impasse. Some 600 factories, with approximately 500,000 employees, had been seized by the workers. Powerless to intervene, the central government seemed destined to be replaced by a dictatorship of the proletariat. The wage-earners soon discovered, however, that control of the factories without expert management and without access to foreign markets and raw materials was futile. Heeding the moderates, the workers returned the factories to their owners. Meanwhile the trade unions accepted the government's proposal to initiate a bill providing for the creation of factory councils. In January, 1921, the majority of workers began to swing away from radicalism. Although aware of the government's inability to better conditions, conservative and moderate classes everywhere rallied to its support in opposition to the Socialists, who were now divided, a split having created a moderate group who continued to be called Socialists and a revolutionary faction who were thenceforth called Communists. Consequently the forces in favor of a stronger central government were strengthened.

The rise of the dictator Mussolini and the Fascist party was the result of this situation. Benito Mussolini, born in 1883,

Benito Mussolini

the son of a village blacksmith, received a fair education and became a teacher. Later he went to Switzerland, where his interest in socialism involved him in semi-revolutionary activities which caused his expulsion by the Swiss government. An ardent radical, he was temporarily imprisoned in Italy in 1908 for his part in socialist and agrarian disorders. Then the Austrian government expelled him from Trent for spreading irredentist propaganda. In 1912 he became editor of *Avanti*, the official organ of the Italian Socialist party. As such he earned the reputation of being a revolutionary agitator and an energetic journalist.

During the war Mussolini experienced an unusual conversion. As a Socialist he first favored Italian abstention from the capitalistic struggle and urged the workers to prepare for a social revolution. In October, 1914, however, he reversed his policies and, deciding that the welfare of Italy could best be secured by advancing Italian national ambitions rather than by establishing socialism, he became an advocate of intervention. Repudiated by his party and compelled to resign the editorship of *Avanti*, he established a daily paper in Milan, *Il Popolo d'Italia*, in which he urged Italian participation on the Allied side and stressed the nationalist ambitions of Italy. From 1915 until he was wounded in 1917 he served as a private on the Isonzo front. Procuring exemption from further military service, he returned to his daily paper and utilized his journalistic talents to sustain the Italian morale during the depressing days of 1917–1918.

After the war he organized a group known as the *Fascio di Combattimento*. This band of one hundred and fifty followers,

Creation of the Fascisti

founded in March, 1919, was composed chiefly of ex-service men, nationalists, interventionists, and former members of the syndicalist wing of the Socialist party. For their emblem they adopted the *fasces* of the Roman lictors, signifying their close union ; hence their name *Fascisti*. Their avowed purposes were the crushing of the Bolshevist and socialist movements and a vigorous foreign policy.

The program of the Fascisti was at first a combination of republicanism and nationalism. Their chief aims were (1) a national constituent assembly, abolition of the Senate, reduction of the age limit for electors and deputies, woman's suffrage, and proportional representation; (2) a legal eight-hour day, minimum-wage laws, national occupational councils, and participation of workers in control of industry; (3) creation of a national militia for defense, and nationalization of factories producing arms and munitions; (4) a heavy tax on capital, sequestration of 85 per cent of all war profits, seizure of property of religious organizations, and abolition of episcopal revenues; and (5) recovery of Fiume and Dalmatia, and the restoration of Italian national prestige.

At first, owing largely to Mussolini's reputation as a radical and to the demagogic methods of his followers, the Fascisti encountered strong opposition. In 1919 the two Fascist candidates for the Chamber, polling less than five thousand votes between them, were both defeated. In the socialist disorders of 1919–1920 the Fascists played no great rôle. Speeches, pamphlets, and demonstrations, however, spread the ideas of the Fascisti, and their alliance with D'Annunzio's Nationalists increased their popularity. With the collapse of the factory-seizure movement in 1920, Fascisti branches, composed of employers, landlords, and ex-army officers, appeared in northern and central Italy and prepared to combat radicalism. *Squadristi* of veterans, youths, and patriots, armed with cudgels, some guns, and castor oil, soon attacked Communists. During 1920–1921 there were almost daily clashes between the Fascisti and the radicals. Both sides displayed great bravery, but the Fascist "Black Shirts" finally won, killing many Communists and destroying their printing presses. Secretly aided by the Giolitti government and most of the conservatives and liberals, the Fascists were regarded as the champions of law and order. In 1920, peasants, workers, and entire labor unions also flocked to the support of the Black Shirts. Fascism became a national force.

By 1921 radicalism was definitely on the decline. In the elections of May the Socialist representation was greatly reduced, while thirty-five Fascisti, including Mussolini and ten Nationalists, were elected to the Chamber of Deputies. The Fascist movement was soon transformed into a national society. In November, 1921, a congress of all Fascist organizations was held in Rome, and after a review of their achievements a party was formally created and a platform devised. During the next few months the new organization was greatly strengthened, and public opposition was won over by the general belief that Fascism had saved the country from Bolshevism.

The program of the Fascist party provided rules for both political and moral conduct. Great emphasis was placed on nationalism: "The nation is not merely the

The Platform of the Fascist Party

sum total of living individuals, nor the instrument of parties for their own ends, but an organism comprising the unlimited series of generations of which individuals are merely transient elements; it is the synthesis of all the material and nonmaterial values of the race."

Concerning Fascist ideology Mussolini declared:

Our conception of the nation is synthetic, not analytic. One who marches in step with others is not thereby diminished ... he is multiplied by all those who move shoulder to shoulder with him. Here, as in Russia, we are advocates of the collective significance of life, and we wish to develop this at the cost of individualism. That does not mean that we go so far as to think of individuals as mere figures upon a slate, but that we think of them chiefly in relation to the part they have to play in the general life of the community. Herein may be recognized a very remarkable advance in national psychology, for it has been made by one of the Mediterranean peoples, who have hitherto been considered unfitted for anything of the kind. A sense of the collectivity of life is the new spell that is working among us.

The Fascisti stressed obedience rather than liberty. In 1923 Mussolini declared: "Liberty is today no longer the chaste and austere virgin for whom the generations of the first half of the last century fought and died. For the gallant, restless, and bitter youth who face the dawn of a new history there are other words that exercise a far greater fascination,

and these words are: order, hierarchy, and discipline."
Therefore, in repudiation of democratic rule of the majority, the Fascisti believed in the necessity for a dictatorship of the enlightened few who would serve in the interests of all classes and individuals who collectively constituted the nation.

Cæsarism was also extended to the economic sphere. Although Mussolini accepted the bourgeois principle of individualism and the system of profits, he did so with reservations. He realized that clashes of economic groups and classes would threaten the public repose. Therefore, through a system of coöperation with capital and labor, he endeavored to make the state the arbiter in economic life. As producers, individuals were to be supervised by technical councils; trade unions were to be encouraged, but not permitted to disregard the inequality of individual abilities. Legal recognition was to be granted to the authority and responsibilities of both workers' and employers' organizations. No strikes detrimental to public welfare, however, were to be tolerated. Although the state reserved the right to intervene in all class conflicts, the usefulness and legality of private property were recognized.

In 1921–1922 Fascism rapidly gained strength, and the constitutional government steadily lost ground. During the fall of 1922 Premier Facta had persistently declined to form a new cabinet including five Fascisti or to dissolve the Chamber and hold *The Fascist March on Rome* new elections. Suddenly Mussolini decided to act. Determined to secure control of the government, thousands of the Fascisti held a great congress in Naples. The premier now offered concessions, but it was too late. Some two hundred thousand Black Shirts began a march upon Rome. In northern and central Italy local government and public services and utilities were already in the hands of the Fascisti. As they approached the Eternal City the king refused to sign Facta's decree for a state of siege. Bowing to the inevitable, Victor Emmanuel III requested Mussolini to form a new ministry, and on October 30 the latter created a coalition government in which the Fascisti were predominant. Henceforth the Fa-

scisti became the bulwark of the monarchy, which they determined to reorganize and to bring into conformity with their
doctrines.

As a prelude to the reorganization of the state, Mussolini
received from the Chamber of Deputies dictatorial powers
which were to last until the end of 1923. Later
Reorganization of
Government his authority was extended, and in 1927 he
stated that his position would probably be
maintained for ten or fifteen years longer. Free of parliamentary control, he was directly responsible to the king, — a
figurehead who constituted little check on the omnipotent
Fascist leader. Mussolini was now made the permanent
head of the armed resources of the nation — the army, navy,
and air forces — and was empowered to issue governmental
decrees with the force of law; his ministers became little
more than secretaries. At one time he personally held nine
portfolios in the cabinet, although on September 12, 1929,
he resigned all but the premiership and the ministry of the
interior. Moreover, he possessed the ultimate decision in all
matters which came before either house of parliament.

Shortly after Mussolini became dictator the centralized
national and provincial administration of Italy passed under
Fascist control. This was accomplished by the removal and
replacement of all prefects and subprefects who were not
loyal adherents of the new cause. Later a law was enacted
which legalized the dismissal of all civil servants whose political convictions differed from those of the new Cæsar. "Better
no helpers than poor ones" constituted Mussolini's explanation of these changes. Parliament was also modified. An
electoral reform bill, the Acerbo law, was passed, which provided that the single party receiving the greatest number of
votes in the parliamentary elections should secure two thirds
of the delegates. The remaining seats were to be distributed
to other parties in proportion to the votes which they received.
This scheme blasted any possibility of opposition by a strong
minority and assured the majority party of sufficient strength
to control the government without resort to a coalition.
Ministerial stability was thus made certain. The general

parliamentary elections of April, 1924, in which the Fascists occasionally resorted to intimidation and force, resulted in a sweeping victory for them.

Steps were taken to insure Fascist control of municipal governments, consisting of mayors and town councils under popular control. An act of November, 1925, suppressed these governmental agencies in all municipalities with populations of less than five thousand. Officials called *podestàs*, appointed by the central authorities at Rome, thenceforth administered these small municipalities. In 1926 *podestàs* took charge of all towns and cities except Rome, which was already under the rule of a governor appointed by the state. Communal and provincial as well as municipal elections were suspended.

Despite these changes the Fascisti did not feel secure. Rejecting liberal principles in favor of the concept of the national state and its welfare, they next tried to stifle all opposition. A strict censorship of *Strong Government* the press, of speech, of assembly, and of education was established. All organizations, societies, groups, and individuals who dared to oppose the will of the state were ruthlessly crushed. Military tribunals were created to try those accused of plotting against the Fascist dictatorship. As a result many were exiled, while others were imprisoned. Unsympathetic Italians abroad were deprived of citizenship and property.

Inextricably bound up with the remodeled government was the Fascist party. In the form of a rigid pyramidal hierarchy, it contained some ten thousand *The Fascist Party* *Fasci* (local units) as a base, with *Il Duce* (Mussolini, the leader) at the apex. The Fascist Grand Council, which initiated, coördinated, and directed all party activities, presided over by Mussolini, was composed of the premier as chairman, certain cabinet members, the general secretary, as well as certain central and local officials of the party. *Il Duce*, having the privilege of adding anyone to the Grand Council who had been of special service to Fascism or to the nation, always controlled that body. As head of the government and chairman of the Grand Council he united and synchronized the policies of the government and the party.

In addition to this body a National Directorate, wielding executive power, and a National Council, exercising political and administrative control of the Fascist party with disciplinary authority, were created. There were also a General Secretariat and a secretary-general of the Fascisti (nominated by the National Council), provincial secretaries, councils, directorates, and local *Fasci* (the cells of the Fascist system). The organization as a whole constituted a centralized institution in which the high officials exercised autocratic power in the party and in the state.

A number of auxiliary organizations were also created, to foster and to protect Fascist principles. Desirous of winning over the youth of the land to Fascism, Mussolini established two boys' organizations: the *Balilla*, open to boys from eight to fourteen years of age; and the *Avanguardia*, open to youths of from fourteen to eighteen. Both groups received premilitary training. In 1926 the ranks of the Fascist party were closed to all but the graduates of the *Avanguardisti*, which contributed annually some forty thousand new members to the party. There were also Fascist organizations for women and for young girls which stimulated loyalty to party ideals.

Fascism was militaristic as well as nationalistic. In 1923 the Black Shirts were disbanded and replaced by a Voluntary Militia largely recruited from their own ranks.

The Voluntary Militia This organization, open to all duly qualified citizens from seventeen to fifty years of age, constituted an inexpensive military machine devoted to the maintenance of the public safety and internal order. Its members took the oath of allegiance to the king, and its officers were selected from the national army. The permanent unit of the militia consisted of a small group of officers, most of whom were in civil life and received no pay. If the state called them out to deal with an emergency, they received a daily allowance. The militia had charge of the premilitary training of the *Avanguardisti* and, numbering some three hundred thousand, constituted a powerful weapon for the suppression of all opposition.

The Fascist party played a unique rôle in Italian political

life. In the earlier stages its actions and policies were comparable to those of an extralegal party in any parliamentary state. In 1928, however, Fascism was legalized. An electoral reform act in that year empowered the Fascist Grand Council to draw up the list of candidates for the Chamber of Deputies upon whom the electorate was to vote. Legislation later in the year authorized it to nominate candidates for the premiership and other high positions in the state, and entitled it to be heard on all constitutional questions affecting the organization of the government. The relations of church and state and questions concerning the disposition of national territories fell within its province. Its members became inviolate,— subject neither to arrest nor to police restrictions. In fact, the Fascist Grand Council became an integral part of the political machinery of the state.

Fascist doctrine was called a "state of mind"; for it was not concerned purely with a party but dealt with all national institutions. Holding that the citizen existed *The Fascist Doctrine* for society, the Fascisti rejected liberalism, democracy, and socialism. They asserted, however, that individualism should not be abolished but merely subordinated to the state. In other words, the individual was free to conduct his personal affairs only as long as they did not run counter to the national welfare. Underlying this idea, claimed the Fascists, was the desire to eliminate class struggles and to provide justice for all. Opponents of Fascism, however, regarded this altruism as a cloak to hide the crimes and violence which had been committed in its name.

The Fascist aim was to create an autocratic, not a democratic, government. To this end the Fascists undertook to destroy any class or clique which opposed this *Fascist Policies* purpose. They restored discipline in every state department and in every aspect of life, they created a powerful and efficient bureaucracy, they stabilized national finances, and they rehabilitated the state. They initiated vast educational reforms also. Admitting that freedom in the ordinary sense of the term had been destroyed, the Fascists claimed that by the restoration of central authority they had created a real opportunity for the people to work and to produce for the common good. Frequently Mussolini asserted that the people wanted, not liberty, but railways, houses, bridges, roads, drains, water, light, and other economic improvements. Therefore, embarking on an extensive scheme of economic reform, the Fascist state undertook to improve the agricultural and industrial life of the nation. Intervening in the struggle between labor and capital, it attempted to regulate labor conflicts peacefully. Mussolini tried to reinvigorate the economic structure as well as the political machinery.

To achieve this regeneration the Fascists catered to labor. Contending that the latter was the basis of human welfare and progress, the Fascists thus seriously modi-
The Fascists and Labor fied the bourgeois system in Italy. Fascist trade unions were established as rivals of extant Socialistic organizations. In 1923 a general Federation of Fascist Syndical Corporations was founded; and as the numbers of their members greatly increased, in October, 1925, the Italian Industrial Employers' Federation recognized these Fascist syndicates as the only representatives of their employees.

On April 3, 1926, the Fascists reorganized Italian labor. The law of Legal Discipline of Collective Labor Relations created in Italy six national confederations of employers and seven of employees under the direct control of the state. These organizations had extensive authority and could engage in collective agreements concerning hours, wages, and conditions of labor. Contracts were binding on all workmen in a given industry. The syndicates also had authority over workers and could extract an annual contribution from nonmembers as well as from members. In addition to the syndicates, workers' unions could exist, but, lacking legal recognition, they had no voice in the settlement of industrial disagreements.

Above the syndicates of employers and employees were the seven corporations existing in the textile, chemical, metallurgical, and mechanical industries, and in commerce, the chemical trade, and agriculture. Their function was to promote production and prosperity by adjusting differences between labor and capital, by the maintenance of employment offices, and by the control of apprenticeship. These corporations brought together the employers' and employees' syndicates and were organized into a department of state under the minister of corporations. The latter nominated and could remove the head of any corporation.

All labor was under the control of the syndicates and corporations. Strikes and lockouts were illegal, and disputes had to be taken to them or to a labor court from which there was no appeal. In 1927 the Charter of Labor, issued by the government, laid down a series of principles and regulations by which industrial life was to be controlled. Labor was described as a social duty to the state, and it was stipulated that capital must share the profits with labor. Furthermore, the state foresaw the need of improved working conditions and provided for the present and future needs of the wage-earners by the creation of various types of insurance against old age, illness, and unemployment.

The electoral reform law of 1928 linked the syndicalist system more closely with the Fascist party. The membership of the Chamber of Deputies was reduced from 560 to 400, and the right to nominate members was given to the syndicates of employers and workers. Syndicates were to propose a list of 800 candidates and submit it to the Fascist Grand Council. The latter selected a list of 400 and held a national plebiscite. Thus the voters either accepted or rejected the approved candidates as a whole. If the list failed to secure a majority at the national election, a second election was held, all organizations with a membership of over 5000 submitting lists of candidates. In 1929 the first election under the new electoral law gave an overwhelming victory to the Fascisti, who controlled the state, the electoral machinery, and the syndicates. The political system, in theory, rested more on an occupational than on a territorial basis. Another step toward a guild state was taken when, in November, 1933, the legislative power of the Chamber of Deputies was transferred to the National Council of Corporations.

In justification of the government's direction of industry Mussolini said :

The Fascist State directs and controls the *entrepreneurs*, whether it be in our fisheries or in our heavy industry in the Val d'Aosta. There the State actually owns the mines and carries on transport, for the railways are state property. So are many of the factories. All the same, this is not state Socialism, for we do not want to establish a monopoly in which the State does everything. We term it state intervention. It is all specified and defined in the *Carta del Lavoro* [Charter of Labor]. If anything fails to work properly, the State intervenes.

After their seizure of power the Fascisti were confronted with many difficult problems. Among the most serious was that of finance. They found the budget hopelessly unbalanced and the national currency badly deflated. By the drastic reorganization and modernization of the fiscal system, the dismissal of superfluous employees, and the increase of taxation the deficits were gradually decreased. In 1926–1928 the lire was restabilized on a gold basis at a ratio of nineteen to the dollar, small foreign debts were paid, and debt settlements were arranged with the United States and England. By 1933 Italian finances were again in order.

Fascist Achievements and Problems

Italy's economic situation was the most difficult problem with which the Fascisti had to contend. The two fundamental elements therein were overpopulation and lack of natural resources. With a total of 41,000,000 inhabitants and with a density of 323 per square mile the pressure of population in Italy was very serious. Despite this condition Mussolini aimed at 60,000,000 by 1950. "Otherwise," he said, "we cannot make an empire; we shall become a colony." Hitherto millions had gone to the Americas, but with the United States Immigration Act of 1924 that avenue of escape was partially closed. Meanwhile overseas colonies offered no solution, since those of Italy were scarcely suitable for large-scale colonization. A dense population, nevertheless, continued to be the chief incentive for Italian imperialism; the Fascists hoped to secure additional colonies which would accommodate surplus inhabitants and thus, by keeping them under the Italian flag, preserve the nationals for their mother country.

Hopelessly inadequate was the supply of natural resources. Coal and iron, generally absent, had to be imported. The increase of water power in northern Italy was promising, but the maximum development of hydroelectric energy would hardly furnish a solution for the problem. Agricultural products were also insufficient, so that foodstuffs had to be imported. A favorable balance of trade, greatly to be desired, was possible only through an increase in exports.

Restoration of internal peace, order, and security, however, did much to revive Italian economic prosperity. The syndicalist system and efficient central authority reduced strikes, disorders, and much waste in industry. Manufacturing was stimulated, although the reliance upon foreign capital and imported coal, increasing the cost of production, forced Italian goods to compete against alien commodities at a disadvantage in foreign markets. To overcome this handicap, high tariffs were raised and wages were necessarily lowered, despite the fact that the cost of living remained high. By 1929 Italy was leading in hydroelectric development and in the production of rayon and silk. Shipbuilding was stimulated, and in 1926 Italy was the second-largest builder of boats in the world. A large merchant marine assisted by state subsidies was also developed, and Italy soon dominated the trade of the eastern Mediterranean. After the war, tourist travel increased, but this again was offset by the decline in remittances from Italian emigrants abroad. In general, Italy's economic outlook was not brilliant.

Remarkable progress occurred, nevertheless, in the material and spiritual life of Italy. To engender prosperity, a vast project of public works was begun in 1922 which involved programs of reforestation, the draining of marshes and reclamation of waste lands, the improvement of railways, the building of highways, the development of air lines and radio service, and the modernization of agriculture. To the latter end increased agrarian production was stimulated by prizes, the establishment of agricultural banks, and the introduction of modern methods of farming. Attempts were made to break up the large estates in southern Italy. Moreover, between 1927 and 1931, the Mafia, or Black Hand Society, was suppressed in Sicily.

Education was promoted through the construction of more schools, the stricter enforcement of laws requiring attendance up to fourteen, and the introduction of newer pedagogic methods imparted by Fascist texts and loyal teachers. As a result of these efforts adult illiteracy, which in 1911 totaled 40 per cent, had declined to 25 per cent by 1931. But perhaps the greatest achievement of the Fascists was the creation of a national discipline. In the words of the philosopher Gentile :

Fascism means to take life seriously. Life is toil, effort, sacrifice, hard work; a life in which we know very well that there is neither matter nor time for amusement. Before us there always stands an ideal to be realized, an ideal which gives us no respite. We have no time to lose. Even in our sleep we must give account of the talents entrusted to us.

A new irredentist problem confronted post-war Italy. Before the conflict there were many "unredeemed" sections under foreign (especially Austrian) control. After the war these territories were secured from the defunct Dual Monarchy. Unfortunately, however, large German and Slav minorities lived in these lands acquired by Italy. They refused to submit to their new lords. Attempts to assimilate, or Italianize, them by forcible and repressive measures merely increased the friction. Nevertheless the Fascist government persisted without success in its attempt to stifle their minority characteristics and to convert them into good patriots. Protests from Austrian and German officials were unavailing.

Another vexatious problem was the Roman question. After the seizure of the Eternal City in 1870, the Pope had shut himself up as a voluntary prisoner in the Vatican and refused to recognize the Italian kingdom. As over 97 per cent of the Italians professed to be Catholic, the hostility between the Vatican and the state was very distressing. Mussolini felt it incumbent upon him to bring about a rapprochement between church and state. Religious instruction and crucifixes were reëstablished in the schools, chaplains reappeared in the army, and the salaries of the clergy were increased. Although the Catholic Boy Scouts were forced to become part of the Fascist *Balilla*, the priests were permitted to devote one hour a week to the religious instruction of all boys therein. Freemasonry was abolished.

On February 11, 1929, the Fascist leader achieved a great triumph,— church and state were reconciled. The Pope, through his secretary of state, and Mussolini signed a treaty, a concordat, and a financial convention in the Lateran palace, all of which established the future relations of the two powers. By this treaty Italy recognized the sovereignty of the Pope over the state of the Vatican City, which consisted of some 100 acres, with less than 500 inhabitants. In all respects the Vatican City was an independent sovereign state, making its own laws, conducting its own foreign relations, and determining its own domestic policies. By the concordat the Roman Catholic church was regarded as the state church of Italy, and the Italian government undertook to enforce canon law among Catholics, and recognized marriages performed by priests. Religious education was compulsory in both elementary and secondary schools, but there was to be no ecclesiastical surveillance of schools or of curricula. Although bishops were to be selected by the church, the state could protest their appointments on political grounds. Furthermore, the Pope's person was declared sacred and inviolable, and ordained priests were released from military duties. By a financial convention the Pope agreed to accept 750,000,000 lire in cash and 1,000,000,000 lire in government bonds at 5 per cent as a recompense for the fall of Rome and his loss of temporal power. As a result of these settlements the Roman question was terminated.

The foreign policies of Mussolini were chiefly concerned with realizing Italy's imperial ambitions and with establishing her position as a great power. In both respects he met with only limited success. *Foreign Policies* Nevertheless the position of Italy in Europe was stronger than at any other epoch throughout the modern period.

A great strengthening of Italy's position in the eastern end of the Mediterranean occurred. After the Turkish rejection of the Treaty of Sèvres, Mussolini's predecessors repudiated the Italo-Greek Treaty of 1920, whereby the Dodecanese Islands were handed over to Greece. The Fascist dictator sustained this action, and by the Treaty of Lausanne, between Turkey and the Allies, in 1923, Italian ownership of the archipelago was recognized. Save as naval and commercial bases for penetration into Anatolia the islands were of little value. Nevertheless the Italians constructed the fortified naval base of Leros.

Italy's relations with Yugoslavia, another eastern neighbor, were disturbed by Italian imperialism in Albania and in the Adriatic. The Treaty of Rapallo, of 1920, made Fiume an independent city, but the arrangement proved unsatisfactory to both parties, inasmuch as the city's trade dwindled and the economic life of the hinterland was upset. Mussolini opened direct negotiations with Yugoslavia and finally secured a readjustment by the Treaty of Rome (1924). Fiume was partitioned; the city proper was given to Italy, while Port Baros and a fifty-year lease on one of the three basins of the Fiume harbor were granted to Yugoslavia. Under Italian rule Fiume never regained its pre-war prosperity, despite the fact that Mussolini attempted to stimulate business by concluding, in 1927, a treaty with Hungary, which made Fiume a free port for her trade.

With the settlement of the Fiume controversy by the Treaty of Rome, Italy and Yugoslavia, in 1924, signed a pact of friendship. Both powers agreed to coöperate and to assist one another in the event of an unprovoked attack by another power. They also promised to maintain intact the peace settlements of Saint-Germain, Trianon, and Neuilly. In 1925 a convention provided for friendly relations and commercial advantages for Italians; but, being unpopular in Yugoslavia, it failed of ratification until 1928.

A number of treaties of conciliation and arbitration were entered into with Czechoslovakia, Rumania, Hungary, Turkey, Greece, Yugoslavia, Spain, and Austria between 1924 and 1930. In 1926, by the Treaty of Tirana, the Italians appeared to have won control of Albania. A practical protectorate in the process of development was cemented by loans and by the sending of military advisers to assist in reorganizing the Albanian army. Yugoslavia, resentful, signed an agreement with France in 1927, Italy retaliating by entering into a twenty-year alliance with Albania. Although the two Adriatic rivals denied hostile intentions, their pact of friendship, which lapsed in 1929, was not renewed, and the two powers remained somewhat estranged.

Mussolini also conducted a vigorous Mediterranean policy, especially with regard to the internationalized African port of Tangier. In 1920 Great Britain, France, and Spain initiated negotiations for a new international régime for this city. Mussolini's subsequent demands for Italian participation were opposed by the French. In 1923, therefore, he refused to accept an inferior position for Italy in the administration of this city. In 1926 he tried to steal a march on France by negotiating a pact of conciliation and neutrality with Spain. Then, when the Franco-Spanish negotiations concerning Tangier were under way in 1927, three Italian warships were dispatched to that city. By 1928, however, France became conciliatory, and the final arrangements for Tangier's international régime gave Italy full recognition.

Many critics held Mussolini's diplomatic saber-rattling to be dangerous. His theatrical gestures, inflammatory speeches concerning Italian imperialism, and high-handed policies antagonized foreign powers, especially France and Yugoslavia. There was danger, they claimed, that an overwrought Italian populace, led by a less capable successor, might precipitate a European war. In reply to this criticism *Il Duce* asserted that his policies were pacific, as witnessed by his numerous treaties of arbitration and conciliation, Italy's adhesion to the pacts of Locarno and Paris, and her willingness to disarm.

Furthermore, Mussolini, in explaining his policies, declared :

There are half a dozen different kinds of imperialism. There is really no need for all the blazons of empire. Indeed, they are dangerous. The more widely empire is diffused, the more does it forfeit its organic energy. All the same, the tendency toward imperialism is one of the elementary trends of human nature, an expression of the will to power. Nowadays we see the imperialism of the dollar; there is also a religious imperialism, and an artistic imperialism as well. In any case, these are tokens of the human vital energy. So long as man lives, he is an imperialist. When he is dead, for him imperialism is over.

Fascist Italy, to support her national and imperial interests, maintained heavy armaments at great expense. With her long coast line, her dependence on foreign products and markets, and her imperial policies, Italy needed a strong navy. As a result a heated naval competition developed between France and Italy. The latter demanded parity; the former, superiority. Unable to agree, they refused to adhere to the London Disarmament Pact of 1930.

Italy was aligned with the revisionist powers in post-war European politics. In favor of modifying the treaties of Paris and opposed to the Continental hegemony of France, Italy found herself in sympathy with Great Britain, Germany, Austria, Hungary, and Bulgaria. Therefore Mussolini recommended the scaling down or abolition of both war debts and reparations. In supporting the liberal policies of the revisionist powers, however, he found himself often in direct opposition to France and to France's allies. In fact, Franco-Italian relations were strained as a result of their naval and colonial as well as their diplomatic antagonisms.

In the spring of 1933 Mussolini displayed a willingness to coöperate with France. At that time political and economic discontent threatened to engulf the world in war. Therefore the Italian dictator presented his plan for the stabilization of Europe. This project provided for a four-power dictatorship consisting of Great Britain, France, Germany, and Italy. These states, "in a spirit of mutual understanding and solidarity of reciprocal interests," were to police the small powers. His scheme also envisaged a revision of the peace treaties, the rearming of the defeated states, and a joint policy of the proposed "Big Four" in western Europe for ten years. Despite Anglo-German support, opposition on the part of France and her allies to a scheme which would virtually have superseded the League of Nations and supplanted the French system of alliances caused a delay in the acceptance of the Mussolini plan. French antagonism, however, was eventually overcome by amending the original draft so as to provide that any revision of the peace treaties and existing boundaries must be in accordance with the Covenant. Thus reassured, France acquiesced in the plan, which was signed in July of 1933 by representatives of the four great powers. The serious attention which Mussolini's proposal had aroused among the great states was material evidence of the increasing prestige of Fascist Italy.

The NEW CÆSAR

After a cartoon in *Punch*

CHAPTER XXXV

The German Republic: An Experiment in Democracy

IN 1914 most Germans, convinced that the war was a struggle to preserve the Fatherland, loyally supported the
imperial government. But when the quick victory promised by the German military chiefs was not forthcoming, and

Opposition to the Government

the hardships and privations of the people increased as a result of the diminishing supply of
foodstuffs and raw materials, opposition to
the government's war policy developed. In 1916 the Social
Democratic party was split when their parliamentary leader,
Haase, denounced the continuation of the war. As head of the
newly formed Independent Social Democratic Party he assailed the war and anathematized the Social Democrats as
nationalists and imperialists. During the years 1917–1918
the Spartacists, radicals from the Independent left wing led
by Karl Liebknecht and Rosa Luxemburg, bitterly attacked
the government and favored the adoption of obstructionist
tactics to end the struggle. In the summer of 1917 an anti-
government *bloc*, including Socialists, Centrists, Progressives,
and some National Liberals, was organized in the *Reichstag*.
As a result of its demands for responsible parliamentary government, electoral reforms, and peace without annexations or
indemnities, Chancellor Bethmann-Hollweg resigned. He was
succeeded by Dr. George Michaelis, who three months later
was replaced by Count Hertling. The latter promised electoral
changes and the instigation of peace negotiations.

In the winter of 1917–1918 Bolshevism began to penetrate
Germany. Won over to the revolutionary movement, the
Spartacists and the Independents sought to create councils of
workers and soldiers similar to the Russian soviets. The industrial disorders which followed were suppressed. Spartacists
and Independent Socialists then resorted to violent measures.

Late in September, National Liberals, Centrists, and Social Democrats, realizing that the war was lost, endeavored to save the floundering state by coöperating on a reform program and by securing peace. The *The Overthrow of* military dictatorship of General Headquarters *Aristocracy* was destroyed, and the liberal Prince Max of Baden became chancellor on October 2, 1918. A coalition cabinet, including for the first time two Socialists, Scheidemann and Bauer, was established, and the empire was now hastily converted into a constitutional monarchy. Within a few days a democratic parliamentary government based on ministerial responsibility was created; freedom of speech, assembly, and the press was guaranteed and an immediate cessation of the war planned. Many hoped that these measures would avert a violent revolution.

These reforms, however, were too late. Antimonarchical propaganda caused Scheidemann, on October 29, to advise the Kaiser to renounce the throne. In the same month a naval mutiny heralded the coming of the revolution. A decisive crisis was reached when, on October 28, the naval officers, believing that the terms of the armistice would probably include the surrender of the German navy, ordered the fleet to engage the British in a last desperate battle. The sailors, however, realizing that peace negotiations were going on, refused to sacrifice themselves. The mutiny spread throughout northern Germany. During the first week of November, sailors, soldiers, and workers revolted, formed councils, and demanded the abdication of the Kaiser, the termination of martial law, the establishment of universal suffrage, and the release of those imprisoned in a 1917 mutiny. A socialist revolution followed in Bavaria, and a provisional council, representing soldiers, workers, and peasants, with Kurt Eisner, an Independent Socialist, as chairman, proclaimed, on November 8, a Bavarian democratic socialist republic. Later in the day the chief German cities succumbed to the revolutionary fervor, and the uprisings became general.

On November 7, Social Democratic leaders, aroused by the diffusion of the revolutionary movement and the discontent which existed in their party, delivered an ultimatum to the chancellor. This called for the renunciation of the throne by the Kaiser and the crown prince, greater representation for Social Democrats in the government, permission for the Independents openly to hold their meetings, and a reorganization and democratization of the Prussian government. Unless these demands were accepted by the state, Scheidemann and Ebert, the Social Democratic leaders, stated that a revolution was certain to result.

William II at first refused to abdicate. But after making certain that the army was no longer loyal, on November 9 he renounced his position as emperor, and a provisional government was established. That same night he fled to Holland by special train, and on November 28 signed a formal and complete renunciation of the throne.

The Imperial government gave way to a provisional régime. Ebert and Scheidemann, heading a deputation of Majority *Proclamation of the German Republic* Socialists, forced Prince Max to hand over the chancellorship to Ebert, and on November 9 Scheidemann proclaimed the German Republic. By this time all the local dynasts had been deposed and republican governments had taken their places. With the Conservatives and Monarchists discredited, three important parties, however, soon engaged in a struggle for control of the newly founded republic.

Led by Ebert, Scheidemann, and others, the Majority Socialists were the least radical of the three parties. They were *Major Radical Parties* opposed to Bolshevism and regarded the introduction of the soviet system as a purely temporary expedient. They favored evolutionary socialism, advocating nationalization of the most vital industries with adequate indemnities to the factory owners. The Majority Socialists also wished to convoke a constituent assembly at the earliest opportunity in order to establish a middle-class democracy. The Independent Socialists were more extreme. They represented a group midway between the evolutionary doctrines of the Majority Socialists and the Bolshevist communism of the Spartacists. They believed that, before a constituent assembly was called, a socialist régime should be established. More radical were the Spartacists, or Communists, led by Karl Liebknecht and Rosa Luxemburg. Adherents of Bolshevism, they combated middle-class democracy at every turn. Seeking to establish a communist state under the dictatorship of the proletariat, they therefore struggled to prevent the calling of a national assembly and were willing to resort to terrorist methods to attain their ends.

The Imperial government under Prince Max fell and was followed, on November 9, 1918, by a provisional one composed of Majority Socialists and Independents. A joint council of six People's Commissars was formed, each party being represented equally. *Opposition to Provisional Government* In contrast to the Communists, who declined Ebert's invitation to participate, the Independents were willing to coöperate with the Majority Socialists, fearing that a Bolshevist régime would throw Germany into a state of anarchy. But in certain matters the two parties diverged. They disagreed as to how soon the national assembly should be called; in military policies the Independents wished to reduce drastically the fighting machine, whereas the Majority Socialists regarded it as a weapon against the radicals and thus opposed any plan to weaken it.

By November, councils, or soviets, of soldiers and wage-earners had been organized and had seized control of local governmental machinery throughout Germany. These groups, especially the Berlin council of workers and soldiers, also approved the People's Commissars, who were acting temporarily as the supreme authority of the nation. On December 16 there was held in Berlin a congress of all the councils, which rejected radicalism and supported the moderate policies of the Majority Socialists.

The Spartacists were disappointed at their failure to dominate the Berlin Congress of Councils, especially when the latter scheduled the election to the national assembly for January 19, 1919. Regarding this act as a counter-revolutionary move, the Spartacists later incited a revolt among sailors stationed in Berlin. Through the utilization of veteran imperial troops the government successfully suppressed the uprising. Denouncing this high-handed policy, the Independents resigned from the government on December 28, 1918. The central committee of the councils of workers and soldiers approved of the administration's policy, however, and two of their members entered Ebert's ministry. Henceforth the Majority Socialists remained in complete control of the provisional government, and a steady shift to the right reduced the Bolshevist menace.

Realizing that the middle-class régime was gaining ground everywhere, the Spartacists decided to stake all on a *coup d'état*. They determined to seize the government by violent methods, to prevent the elections to the national assembly, and to continue the revolution to more radical extremes. During January 5–6, 1919, over a hundred thousand armed Spartacists and Independents struggled for the control of Berlin, but were finally crushed by the governmental forces under the ruthless Gustav Noske. Over a thousand casualties and the assassination of Karl Liebknecht and Rosa Luxemburg were the results of this uprising.

Increasing opposition to radicalism led to the rise of conservative and moderate parties. Discarding their old *Rise of Conservative* platforms, the Conservatives and Monarchists *and Moderate Par-* tried to readjust themselves to the new order *ties* by favoring democracy. The old Conservative party was supplanted by the German Nationalists. Consisting of conservatives, militarists, pan-Germans, and junkers, the new organization, representing the right and for the most part monarchical in sentiment, struggled to maintain private property and inheritance. Slightly less conservative was the German People's party, led by Gustav Stresemann. Successor of the right wing of the old National Liberals, it supported the big-business interests and bitterly opposed socialism and communism. The former Center (Catholic) party was converted into the Christian People's party, ably led by Matthias Erzberger. Opposed to radicalism, it favored a democratic bourgeois republic. Middle-class in nature was the German Democratic party, composed of former Progressives and the left wing of the old National Liberals. It desired not only the establishment of a republic but also the partial socialization of industry.

The Majority Socialists, retaining the name and platform of the Social Democrats, were the strongest single party. Success in maintaining order during the early stages of the revolution had greatly enhanced their prestige, especially when they supported a democratic parliamentary republic with a program of gradual evolutionary socialism. Because of these policies, however, they were denounced by the Independents and were called traitors to Socialism.

All parties, with the exception of the Spartacists, who declined to participate, took part in the national elections of January 19. Over 30,500,000 men and women went to the polls. In the triangular struggle for votes between conservative reactionaries, moderate liberals, and radical revolutionaries the middle group won a decisive victory, the distribution of seats being as follows: Majority Socialists, 163; Center party, 88; Democrats, 75; Nationalists, 42; Independent Socialists, 22; People's party, 21; and minor groups, 10.

Despite the vehement protests of the central committee of workers' and soldiers' councils and the Independents, the national constituent assembly was convened *The National Constitutional Assembly, 1919* at Weimar on February 6. No single party was strong enough to control the national assembly. The rule of the Majority Socialists gave way to a moderate coalition of Majority Socialists, Centrists, and Democrats. This marked a distinct shift to the right. Friedrich Ebert was elected first president of the German Republic on February 11, and on March 4 a constitutional committee of twenty-eight members, selected on the basis of proportional representation, was established. For some three months it deliberated on a model constitution drawn up by Hugo Preuss, a noted legal authority; this model was finally adopted with modifications on July 31, 1919.

Meanwhile the provisional government of the Weimar Assembly was compelled to face some difficult problems. A

starving population had to be fed, and the national economic
system needed to be reëstablished. Dissatisfied with the

*Problems confronting
the Assembly*

policies of the national assembly, the Spartacists had incited sporadic uprisings throughout
Germany. Over twelve hundred persons were
killed and millions of dollars of damage done by a revolt in
Berlin, which was suppressed by Noske. On February 21
Kurt Eisner, the premier of Bavaria, was assassinated by a
junker; and a communist uprising resulted in a soviet republic, which survived for barely a month.

Peace agreements had to be concluded with the victorious
Allies. On May 7 the German delegation received the text
of the Treaty of Versailles. Its terms were vigorously denounced by the parties of the right, whereas the Independents
urged its acceptance and the Centrists and Majority Socialists
counseled moderation. After more than a month of indecision
the Allied ultimatum of June 16 produced a crisis. Scheidemann resigned rather than subscribe to the treaty, but a
coalition ministry of Majority Socialists and Centrists, with
Bauer as chancellor, proved more amenable. An Allied threat
to resume hostilities resulted in the German acceptance of the
treaty on June 23. Disarmed, Germany was now helpless to
defy the might of her recent adversaries.

On July 31, 1919, the new constitution of the German
Republic was accepted. It created a democratic federal gov-

*The New Framework
of Government*

ernment in which each member state had to
possess a republican administration. Popular
sovereignty was introduced, and universal,
equal, direct, and secret suffrage for men and women, and
the principle of proportional representation, were required.
Parliamentary government and ministerial responsibility were
established.

The structure of government provided for an executive
consisting of the president and his cabinet, composed of the
chancellor and other ministers. The president, elected by
popular vote for a term of seven years, was eligible for re-
election. He could be removed by an adverse popular vote if
a proposal were submitted to the people by a two-thirds

majority of the *Reichstag*. A vote favorable to the president automatically reëlected him for seven succeeding years and occasioned the dissolution of the legislature. In practice the president was little more than a figurehead, being unable to issue an executive order without a ministerial countersignature. More powerful was the chancellor, who as actual chief executive determined the policies of the cabinet. He was responsible to the *Reichstag*, and his position depended on the support of that body.

A bicameral national legislature was created, consisting of the *Reichstag* and the *Reichsrat*. The *Reichstag* enacted national laws, but the approval of the *Reichsrat* was ordinarily required. Members of the former house were elected for four years by direct vote of the people. It could be dissolved by the president, but only once for the same cause. The *Reichsrat*, or national council, represented the states, each having at least one vote and the larger ones having one for every seven hundred thousand inhabitants. To prevent a possible Prussian hegemony it was specifically provided that no state could have over two fifths of the seats. Both the initiative and the referendum were provided for in the constitution.

In certain respects the German Republic was a highly democratized version of the old empire. The boundaries of the states could be altered by the federal government, and their territories split up. The new administration was somewhat more centralized than its predecessor. With exclusive jurisdiction over certain matters, the central government could legislate over many others, which were allowed tentatively to remain in the hands of the states. National laws were to be executed by the states under the supervision of the cabinet, unless specific provision to the contrary had been made. The legal power of the central government was superior to that of the states. Disputed cases, however, were taken before the Supreme Judicial Court of the Republic.

Certain states resented the supremacy of the central government and the merging of smaller into larger units. Bavaria's objections to the abrogation of her earlier privileges gave rise to a particularistic movement. As a result Bavarian

Catholics seceded from the Centrists to form the Bavarian People's party, which advocated states' rights and the reduction of federal authority.

Moderate socialism was apparent in the new constitution. Provision was made for the ultimate nationalization of certain public utilities and industries, with compensation to the owners. A National Economic Council was created. Here were represented the local wage-earners' organization, the district workers' groups, the National Workers' Council, employers, and other interested parties. All vocational groups were accorded representation. Drafts of important laws relating to social and economic affairs had to be submitted by the cabinet to the National Economic Council before they could be sent to the *Reichstag*. Representing the corporations and great economic groups, the council could propose laws; but its capacity was purely advisory, and it wielded no executive or legislative power.

The new constitution, characterized by compromise, was a victory for the moderates and the middle classes. It was too liberal for the right and too conservative for the left. Accepted by the National Assembly, the constitution was signed by President Ebert on August 11, going into effect three days later. The president took the oath of office on August 21, and the National Assembly functioned as a provisional national legislature, meeting in Berlin after September 30.

This new governmental structure, although it was forced to resist attacks from both right and left, proved fairly durable. During 1919 the communists resorted to strikes, riots, and violent uprisings in an attempt to overthrow the newly established republic. With the restoration of law and order their influence diminished. Later, however, despite the continuance of their revolutionary activities, they entered into politics as a party, sending representatives to the *Reichstag*.

Early Opposition to the Republic

In 1920 the irreconcilable conservatives made the first of several attempts to overthrow the republic. In March of that year Lüttwitz and Kapp, two reactionaries, attempted a *coup d'état*. With eight thousand troops Lüttwitz seized Berlin and forced the government to flee. The junkers and the army failed to support these monarchists, and the so-called *Putsch* collapsed when Ebert called a general strike which paralyzed the nation. Disorders occasioned by the *Putsch* and the strike caused a poorly organized communist uprising in the industrial Ruhr valley. A Red army of some seventy or eighty thousand was created, but government forces crushed the revolt on April 6. Both reactionary and radical attempts to undermine the new government were thus frustrated.

Nevertheless the opposition parties continued to grow. The *Reichstag* elections of June 6, 1920, led to an increase of seats for the groups, both left and right, which were opposed to the permanent maintenance of the republic. During the next few years the internal disorders and the attempted fulfillment of the harsh terms imposed by the Allies led to much criticism of the republican régime. Reactionaries caused the assassinations of several prominent moderate statesmen, including Matthias Erzberger, the Centrist leader, and Walter Rathenau, an advanced social thinker. The government responded by a drastic "law for the protection of the republic," designed to crush revolutionary movements.

During the French invasion of the Ruhr in 1923, monarchical plots came to a head. Conspirators in Bavaria determined to take advantage of the situation to overthrow the republic. Ludendorff and Adolf Hitler, the later German Fascist leader, planned to march on Berlin, overthrow the republic, and establish a military dictatorship. Another faction, under the leadership of Otto von Kahr, intended to assume control of the nation through a directory. The rival groups, however, dissipated their energies in quarreling among themselves, and the reactionary movements collapsed. An attempt, apparently supported by French officials, to detach the Rhineland from Germany and set up an independent state also failed dismally. The separatist movement in the Rhineland finally ended by February, 1924, and the unity of the republic was preserved.

After the war economic as well as political problems had to be solved. Inflation of the currency, unemployment and necessary doles, shortage of food, reparation payments, and lack of credit caused the country to be threatened with eco-

Economic Problems and the New Government

nomic chaos. In November, 1922, the German mark had dropped to 7000 to the dollar. A year later, owing to inflation and the effects of the French occupation of the Ruhr, it descended to about 2,520,000,000 to the dollar in Berlin and about 4,000,000,000 to the dollar in Cologne. This collapse of the mark dislocated social and economic life. Savings, pensions, insurance, mortgages, and bonds were rendered almost worthless. Many businesses failed, and the middle classes were practically ruined. Those who had any money, which was dropping rapidly in value, spent extravagantly. In the fall of 1923, farmers and merchants brought on serious food shortages by refusing to sell for worthless currency. On September 23 the government declared a state of siege.

By stabilizing the currency, wages, and prices the authorities sought to rehabilitate the economic order. A national bank, called the *Rentenbank,* was established in November with the sole right to issue currency. The new money was based on a nominal blanket mortgage of all German industries and production lands to the extent of 3,200,000,000 gold marks. The *Rentenmark,* as it was called, was stabilized at four and two-tenths to the dollar, and the old marks circulated at a ratio of one to one trillion. By drastic economy the government also balanced the budget, eliminating the need for further inflation.

The stabilization of the mark had both good and bad results. Reckless extravagance gave way to saving, and retrenchment led in turn to less demand, lower prices, and the breakdown of many business enterprises, especially the great vertical trusts. These organizations, dealing in everything from the raw materials to the finished product, were established at the opening of the twentieth century as a substitute for horizontal trusts, which aimed at domination in a limited field and at coöperation between firms engaged in a particular branch of industry. Hugo Stinnes and other financial giants took advantage of the fall of the powerful German government and the defeat of the movement for socialization in the early months of 1919 to reshape the economic life of the country on the basis of vertical trusts. With the scarcity of fluid capital in 1924 these tremendous enterprises crashed. But the provision of the Dawes Plan for a loan of 800,000,000 gold marks in October, 1924, bolstered the sagging economic structure.

Despite this aid social and economic life showed little immediate improvement. "There has never been so much social injustice in Germany as now," wrote the *Manchester Guardian* in 1924. "Never has the contrast between rich and poor been so glaring. At no time have entire classes been submerged by misery so desperate." To Emil Ludwig, the literary historian, the Germany of Bismarck was superior in many ways to the Fatherland of 1924. "The Germany of those days," he wrote, "was bent under a yoke, that must be admitted, but, at least, it presented a picture of material unity and mighty morale. On the other hand, the present Germany offers a spectacle of chaos." Impressed by the tremendous problems confronting the German republican government, many persons doubted the ability of the new régime to endure. "On which rock," they queried, "Communism, France, or Monarchism, will the German ship of state be shattered?"

After the death of President Ebert, on February 28, 1925, the first popular presidential election was held. German electoral procedure required that a candidate receive a clear majority of all votes cast. If *The Election of Paul von Hindenburg* no contender obtained the necessary majority, a second election would be held, in which the one receiving the greatest number of votes would be declared elected. Because of the number of parties none of the seven candidates of March 29 succeeded in securing a majority; so a second election was called. The right, disregarding earlier candidates, on April 26 elected the aged field marshal, Paul von Hindenburg. Commanding world-wide respect, the former military chieftain proved a great stabilizing force in preserving the middle-class republic from the assaults of extremists.

Although Germany suffered heavy losses in raw materials, equipment, markets, and capital, owing to the war, she made a mild economic recovery. By 1924 her industries and transportation facilities were in excellent condition, although international credit was badly needed. Later, foreign loans were secured and new techniques and methods were introduced. Then German economic life underwent a thoroughgoing "rationalization," or modernization. After the collapse of the vertical trusts in 1924, the movement toward cartels revived. These organizations, as stated before,[1] consisted of groups of independent manufacturers who engaged in contracts to control output and prices. Partly through their efficient methods industry was revived.

Economic and Educational Changes

Post-war Germany witnessed a sweeping educational and moral transformation among the youth of the land. Educational theory and practices were in a state of confusion as a result of the revolutionary disorders of 1918–1919. The old system, a creation of the Hohenzollern machine, was aggressively nationalistic and monarchical in sentiment. If the republic was to endure, therefore, it was necessary to transform the schools into centers of loyalty to the new order. To this end new textbooks became obligatory, and propaganda was introduced designed to inculcate democratic ideals. The constitution of the new republic declared, "In every school the educational aims must be moral training, public spirit, personal and vocational fitness, and, above all, the cultivation of German national character and of the spirit of international reconciliation."

The younger generation responded enthusiastically to the new conditions in which they found themselves after the war. A youth movement developed which was, in effect, a revolt against the excessive tutelage, discipline, pedagogy, coercion, and police repression of the imperial régime. Old traditions were discarded, and the bonds of industrialism and the older generation were denounced. Asserting this independence and freedom, the youngsters initiated a vigorous movement. A moral rejuvenescence, which aimed at the expression of personality, the assertion of human worth, spiritual freedom, and a return to simple life, as reflected in the nudist cult and

[1] See page 347.

the emphasis on nature, characterized the revolt of modern youth in Germany.

Germany also regained her position as one of the great European powers. After 1919 she was regarded as an outlaw nation and so was barred from the "eminently respectable" League of Nations. Although *Stresemann and German Foreign Policies* disarmed and helpless, she almost immediately instigated a campaign for readmission to the "family," but found that her late enemies regarded her with fear and suspicion.

Germany was confronted with two alternatives: a Western policy and friendship with Bolshevist Russia. In April, 1922, she alarmed her late enemies by signing the Treaty of Rapallo with the "outlaw" Soviet state. This provided for the following: (1) the German recognition of the Soviet government; (2) mutual renunciation of war claims and pre-war debts; (3) Germany to receive indemnities on debts if other states did; (4) resumption of consular and diplomatic relations; and (5) mutual trade facilities and the most-favored-nation principle. Although this agreement was not an alliance, many feared a Russo-German coalition and became much concerned. On April 24, 1926, the Rapallo settlement was supplemented by a five-year neutrality pact.

In the summer of 1923 the bourgeois Gustav Stresemann assumed control of German foreign policy. He reoriented it to the west and turned his back on Russia. It was his conciliatory program of "fulfillment" which led to the Dawes and Young plans and the evacuation of the Ruhr and the Rhineland. Stresemann desired above all else to reëstablish Germany's position in Europe. To do this he had to clarify her relations with France. The latter was suspicious and seemed to desire the permanent blight of German political and economic life. Friendly overtures from Stresemann and the conciliatory attitude of Briand, the French foreign minister, finally resulted in the famous Locarno Pact (1925), discussed in a subsequent chapter.[1]

The Locarno Pact, by which the inviolability of the fron-

[1] See page 740.

tiers between Germany, France, and Belgium was guaranteed, was a great step toward reëstablishing Germany's position in Europe. Fear and distrust on all sides were greatly decreased, and Germany made application for League membership. The session of March, 1926, was unable to grant this request and deferred a decision until the session of the Assembly on September 8, 1926. This meeting unanimously approved her application; Germany was granted a permanent seat on the League Council and became a prominent participant in League politics.

Inextricably connected with economic conditions in Germany and her post-war foreign policies was the problem of reparations. The resources of the warring *The Problem of Reparations* powers were inadequate to meet the estimated direct war costs of $186,000,000,000 and the indirect costs of some $150,000,000,000. Therefore they found themselves heavily in debt, with unbalanced budgets. Originally the Allies planned to escape this war burden by shifting the gigantic load to the defeated enemy.

Fixing the total amount of reparations, as previously indicated,[1] was no simple problem. A compromise had to be effected between the German desire to pay a minimum and the Franco-British wish to impose a maximum. In addition some attention had to be accorded to Germany's capacity to pay, which the Germans underrated and the Allies usually overestimated. Furthermore, if the reparations were too high and Germany were pushed too far, there was the danger that she might embrace Bolshevism.

In July, 1920, the first reparation conference met at Spa. As expected, the German proposals were inadequate, whereas the $56,500,000,000 demanded by the Allies, payable in forty-two annual installments, was exorbitant. In March, 1921, another conference met at London. Again the Germans made proposals which were considered entirely inadequate, arousing considerable indignation in the Allied countries. Wearied of the German tactics, the Allies decided to resort to coercion. French troops seized several industrial centers on the right

[1] See pages 589–590, 599–600.

bank of the Rhine, and German customs receipts on her western frontier were sequestered. The attempt to determine the total amount and the terms of payment was a failure.

The Reparation Commission now undertook to settle the problem arbitrarily. On April 28, 1921, Germany was notified that the total amount due, in addition to Belgium's war debt, was $33,000,000,000. By the so-called London Schedule, subsequently arranged, the annual payments were to be $500,000,000, in addition to variable annuities amounting to 26 per cent of the value of German exports. Also Germany was informed that the $650,000,000 paid up to May 1, 1921, had merely covered expenses of Allied commissions and armies of occupation. The total amount of reparations due on May 11 was demanded under pain of a threatened Allied occupation of the Ruhr valley.

Germany, at least ostensibly, tried to carry out her agreements. This was difficult to do in view of the disturbed condition of her economic life. She lacked international credit for floating loans; at the same time she was being drained of her gold supply by the necessity of buying raw materials without being able to sell much, and by the tendency of Germany's capitalists to export their wealth. The currency was hopelessly depreciated by inflation; heavier taxation provided no solution. Further, there was no will to pay, individual Germans struggling to circumvent their government's avowed policies.

On March 21, 1922, the Reparation Commission granted Germany a partial moratorium, the payments being reduced or modified. But the Germans felt themselves unable to meet even this revised schedule. By this time Allied solidarity had been destroyed, the English desiring to see the economic recovery of central Europe so that their own trade might revive. The French, on the other hand, had spent considerable money in rebuilding their war-torn sections, maintaining heavy armaments, and arranging alliances. They hoped, therefore, to compel German adherence to her obligations. Germany, however, failed to meet all her payments in kind, and the Reparation Commission declared her in default.

The French thereupon invaded the Ruhr valley. Inasmuch as this area was heavily populated and highly industrialized, France felt that its seizure would force Germany to carry out her promises. Accordingly French and Belgian troops occupied the valuable Ruhr valley from January 11, 1923, to July 31, 1925.

The Occupation of the Ruhr

Rather than submit to French dictation the German government adopted a policy of passive resistance. All the inhabitants were enjoined to strike and to assist the invaders in no wise, and were assured financial aid from the German government. It was assumed that the French could not profitably operate the industries and that military occupation would be very expensive. The French retaliated by establishing virtual martial law. Much violence resulted, and about 150,000 Germans were deported from the area. Both sides were prepared to fight it out to the bitter end.

French control of this vital industrial area was an important factor in paralyzing German economic life. The mark depreciated by leaps and bounds, unemployment mounted, and the bourgeoisie and working classes in Germany were seriously impoverished. Reactionary and monarchical nationalism also was stimulated in defiance of a republican government which was held responsible for Germany's plight. New German proposals failed before the uncompromising attitude of Poincaré. Chancellor Cuno's unwillingness to modify his course caused his downfall on August 12, and Stresemann formed a new cabinet. On September 26 the latter formally announced the termination of the policy of passive resistance.

Both Germany and France were more amenable now. The former knew that France had the upper hand, while the French realized that brute force alone could not make Germany pay her debts. Faced by a near economic collapse, Germany warned France of the danger of pressing her too far. Meanwhile two international committees of experts were created by the Reparation Commission. One was to seek ways and means of stabilizing German currency and balancing the budget, and the other

The Dawes Report

was to attempt an estimate of the amount of capital exported from Germany and to devise means of bringing it back. The latter committee of experts, headed by Reginald McKenna of Great Britain, reported that $1,687,500,000 of German capital was abroad and that some $300,000,000 of foreign currency was held in Germany.

The other group, headed by Charles G. Dawes of the United States, worked out a plan for the economic rehabilitation of Germany and urged its immediate adoption. The recommendations were as follows: (1) restoration of German economic unity by the evacuation of the Ruhr; (2) heavy mortgages on German railways and industries, and a transportation tax; (3) annual reparation payments beginning at $250,000,000, to be increased in four years to a normal payment of $625,000,000; (4) future payments to be regulated according to "index of prosperity"; (5) a foreign loan of some $200,000,000; and (6) establishment of a bank of issue with a fifty-year monopoly on the issue of currency. The bank was to be under the control of an international board of seven foreigners and seven Germans. Other recommendations were made designed to increase German revenues so that the reparation payments might be met.

Although France hesitated at first, the Dawes report was accepted by the Allies within a few weeks. Premier Poincaré's fall and the accession to office of Herriot finally resulted in French adhesion, and a London conference met in July to draft a protocol to put the plan in operation. Under pressure, France was now forced to abandon her policy of independent action. Henceforth a German default could only be proclaimed by a unanimous vote of the Reparation Commission. Sanctions were to be determined by the Allied powers.

On August 30, 1924, German laws, providing for the operation of the new plan, were promulgated. Two days later the plan went into operation, and in July, 1925, French and Belgian troops were withdrawn from the Ruhr. During the four years from September, 1924, to September, 1928, the reparation payments were met on schedule, some $1,350,000,000 being collected. The Dawes Plan, however, was not a success.

Declaring Germany unable to conform to the reparation schedule, the German government, in 1928, asked for a com-

The Young Plan plete and final settlement. In 1929 the so-called Young Committee of experts began to consider ways and means of achieving this end. The committee had to work out a plan acceptable to all interested parties. Finally they presented a report whereby it was provided (1) that Germany pay annuities averaging $512,500,000 over a period of thirty-seven years, and (2) that during the next twenty-one years they were to average $391,250,000. Reduced payments in kind were continued. It was further stipulated that, should any of the creditor powers have its war debts reduced, German reparations to that state should be cut. A Bank of International Settlement was created to receive and distribute payments, indirectly to supervise German economic life and to facilitate international finance and trade. Thus were linked the problems of inter-Allied war debts and reparations. On June 7, 1929, the final report was signed.

This Young Plan supposedly provided a lasting settlement for the vexatious problem of reparations. In the Hague conference of August, 1929, however, the British demanded a greater share of the reparations. Chancellor Snowden asked for a return to the abandoned Spa apportionments. A deadlock was finally averted, a readjustment made, and on November 1 the Young Plan went into effect. The evacuation of the Rhineland began on September 15, 1929, and by the following summer Germany was freed of foreign soldiers.

The success of the Young Plan was short-lived. In the German parliamentary elections of September, 1930, its un-

Germany and the World Economic Crisis popularity was revealed by the spectacular gains made by the National Socialists and the Communists, both opponents of the reparation settlement. Foreign investors, alarmed at the increases of the two groups of extremists, began to make extensive withdrawals of their money. As Germany succumbed to the economic blight which was gripping the whole world, production and foreign trade dwindled, unemployment increased, and business failures became more numerous. Emergency decrees, issued between July, 1930, and July, 1931, providing for reduced taxes and rigid governmental economy, failed to deflect the current of economic depression.

An Austro-German attempt, in the form of a customs union, or *Anschluss*, to arrest the paralysis which was stifling economic life was announced on March 23, 1931. This scheme, although preserving the independence of the two countries, provided for close economic coöperation. Hostility on the part of France and her allies, who contended that the *Anschluss* was a violation of Austro-German treaty obligations, together with the threat of force, finally compelled its abandonment.

Within a few months Germany was overtaken by economic disaster. The disturbing effects of Austrian financial difficulties, an adverse trade balance, an unsound financial structure, continued monetary withdrawals by foreign investors, a growing budgetary deficit, and the shrinkage of business precipitated a serious crisis. A panic swept the nation in 1931, and its whole economic structure seemed on the verge of a collapse. Appreciating the seriousness of a crisis which threatened the political and economic stability of the world, President Hoover proposed a one-year moratorium, or postponement "of all payments on inter-governmental debts, reparations, and relief debts, both principal and interest . . . not including obligations of governments held by private parties." This scheme, despite French hesitancy, went into effect on July 1, 1931. Nevertheless the Hoover moratorium, in the face of the economic difficulties which were engulfing all capitalistic states, was powerless to arrest the German decline. Finally the great powers, fearful of the German drift toward chaos, agreed to meet in an international conference at Lausanne on June 16, 1932. At this assembly the European nations consented to an almost complete cancellation of reparation payments.[1]

At a time when Germany was facing economic ruin and a revolution which threatened to overturn the newly formed republic the conservative President von Hindenburg was an

[1] See pages 804–805.

effective force in reassuring the nation. On April 10, 1932, he was reëlected president for seven years more, polling over *The Swing toward* 19,000,000 votes as compared to 13,500,000 *Autocratic Govern-* for Adolf Hitler, the very formidable National *ment* Socialist candidate. Despite disorders he endeavored to rule with an iron hand and to prevent the overturn of the *Reich*. Only virtual martial law and the frequent use of soldiers succeeded in avoiding a revolution as disaffected elements became more aggressive. Dissatisfied with the president's policies, the Centrist Heinrich Brüning, after two years as chancellor, finally resigned on May 30, 1932.

Many believed that the fall of the moderate ministry of Brüning would raise Adolf Hitler and his militant National Socialists, or Nazis, to power. This fiery leader, born in Austria in 1889, was a gifted speaker and one of the most outspoken critics of the Brüning government. He was the head of a German Fascist movement which, with its half-million "Brown Shirts," or "shock troops," in many respects imitated the doctrines, symbols, and trappings of its Italian counterpart. Militant and flamboyantly nationalistic, the Nazis advocated a program opposed alike to communism and to democracy, and designed to reëstablish internal order and regain external prestige. Hitler's program, a strange conglomerate of contradictory promises, was calculated to attract various elements. Industrialists and large landowners were won over by his condemnation of socialism and communism; the middle classes, especially the small shopkeepers, were attracted by his opposition to big business as represented by large department and chain stores; proletarians were fascinated by his denunciation of Jewish capitalism and his assurances of social and economic improvement for the masses; and an influential section of most parties succumbed to the intoxication of his promise to free the Fatherland from the Treaty of Versailles.

Germany's neighbors were alarmed at this German Fascist movement, for its nationalistic program was highly provocative. Designed to rehabilitate Germany's international position, it urged (1) the repudiation of the thesis of German war guilt, (2) the refusal to make further reparation payments, (3) a drastic revision of the Treaty of Versailles, (4) the erasure of the Polish Corridor so as to reunite Germany and East Prussia, (5) other adjustments on the eastern frontier, (6) the return of former German colonies, (7) the long-desired *Anschluss*, or union with Austria, and (8) the right of Germany to arm. In demanding a revision of the peace settlements Hitler declared: "France must free herself from the delusion that we are a second-rate power and must learn to treat us as a cultured people. We are not Carthage, nor is France Rome, and it should also be recalled that Rome subdued Carthage single-handed."

By the summer of 1932 the German people, made desperate by their economic plight, seemed to have lost faith in democracy. In view of the violently nationalistic movement which swept Germany, the Nazis' rise to power appeared imminent. Nevertheless President von Hindenburg, distrustful of Hitler, offered the chancellorship to Franz von Papen. On June 2 this former imperial army officer, an ultraconservative, representative of the militarists, the junkers, and the great industrialists of the Rhine, organized the "Blue-stocking" or "All-Monocle" cabinet. Despite popular opposition, as expressed in the adverse parliamentary election of July 31, the new ministry remained in power until November.

The Papen ministry, in its attempts to prevent the rise of Hitler and to improve the economic and political situation in Germany, adopted a large part of the Fascist program. It pursued a policy of state capitalism by which aid was granted to banks, shippers, and coal, iron, and steel industries in an effort to bolster private enterprises. Conditions steadily became worse, however; for the government, preoccupied with political difficulties, could do little to ameliorate the lot of the 5,000,000 unemployed.

By his foreign policies Papen stole much of Hitler's thunder. Adopting a highly nationalistic program, he was able to secure, at the Lausanne Conference in June, 1932, a virtual repudiation by the powers of the thesis of German war guilt. As will be described later,[1] he succeeded in arranging there a provisional settlement which practically abrogated reparation obligations by requiring one single payment of approximately $714,500,000, the whole contingent upon a secret "Gentleman's agreement" among the great powers, by which they hoped to force the United States to scale down war debts. Later Papen demanded that Germany be allowed to arm and that her colonies be returned. Under his leadership Germany threatened to withdraw from the League of Nations unless the Allies allowed her parity in arms. Symbolical of the renascence of autocratic government in Germany was a monstrous parade in Berlin of 195,000 members of the "Steel Helmets," a war veterans' organization. Believing that a new Germany was at hand, their leader, Franz Seldte, declared: "The rule of inferior spirits has been broken. The time of the soldier has come. The system of Weimar [the democratic republic] and the system of parties have collapsed."

Democratic party government received a severe setback on September 12, 1932, when the *Reichstag* was dissolved arbitrarily because of its opposition to the government. At that time Papen declared that democracy in Germany was doomed and that he proposed to inaugurate a drastic revision of the Weimar constitution. Before the projected reforms could be enacted, however, the Papen government fell from power as a result of the November elections. The inability of any single party to muster sufficient strength to control the new *Reichstag* finally impelled President von Hindenburg to appoint the former minister of war Kurt von Schleicher as chancellor on December 2, 1932. Like Papen the new chancellor, a stanch conservative, relied on militarism and dictatorial policies in order to preserve the state from the rising tide of radicalism. Unable to secure a working majority in the *Reichstag*, however, Schleicher's government was seriously embarrassed by mounting opposition, which finally, on January 28, 1933, forced the new chancellor to resign.

Two days later Hitler was appointed chancellor and became the head of a coalition Nazi-junker government. Al-

[1] See pages 804–805.

though the National Socialists constituted the most numerous single party, Hitler was forced to rely on the support of the Nationalists and other conservative elements. Therefore Papen, Neurath, Hugenberg, and other leaders of the right were included in the cabinet, where they served as brakes against drastic modifications in foreign or domestic policies on the part of the Hitlerites. Nevertheless the advent of Hitler occasioned great alarm among the Jews and Communists, his most bitter adversaries. Riots and disorders followed, and the government, to extirpate opposition, resorted to harsh policies. By "an emergency decree for the protection of nation and state," enacted on February 28, martial law was established, and Hitler was invested with vast powers as he embarked on a war against communism to save capitalism.

Within a few months of its establishment the Hitler government was converted into a dictatorship. Early in February, 1933, the *Reichstag* and the Prussian diet were dissolved, new elections being scheduled for *Hitler in Power* March 5. Decisive victories at the polls gave the Nazis political control of nearly all Germany. Regarding these victories as a mandate to reform the constitution, Hitler, repudiating democracy as well as communism and socialism, undertook to promote a "nationalistic revolution" which had as its major aim the creation of a Fascist Germany. Freedom of speech, assembly, and the press vanished. Jews, because of their alleged leadership in the "Marxist" republic, were persecuted and discriminated against in the professions and in business. On March 24 the *Reichstag* conferred upon Hitler, in an enabling act, dictatorial powers for four years, during which time the Weimar constitution and parliamentary government were suspended. Even Bismarck had not dreamed of such vast power!

To consolidate his authority further, Hitler proceeded to nationalize the economic and cultural life of Germany. From top to bottom the economic structure was reorganized, with Nazi adherents in control of agricultural organizations, trade unions, chambers of commerce, labor banks, and the consumers' coöperatives, with their vast network of factories and chain stores. Through Nazi control of local and state government, which caused a unitary nation to supplant the German federation, the government was able to reorganize the Lutheran and other churches along nationalistic lines and to permeate education with Fascism and Nordicism.

Aided by his Brown Shirts and the Steel Helmets, Hitler proceeded ruthlessly to strike down opposition and to spread Hitlerism. On June 21, 1933, the Nationalists were ordered to dissolve their shock troops (Green Shirts) and their *Bismarck-Bund*, an organization for youths. In striving to realize his aim of a totalitarian state, Hitler made many enemies. His position seemed secure, however, as he was supported by influential industrialists and by the popular President von Hindenburg. But the famous "Blood Purge" in the summer of 1934, wherein Hitler encompassed the death of many of his followers, including Ernst Roehm, head of the storm troops, and Schleicher, an ex-chancellor, who he alleged were conspiring against him, indicated the lack of solidarity in his own ranks. On August 2, 1934, the death of Hindenburg, whose powers as president Hitler assumed, increased the latter's authority. Many Germans, notwithstanding the gloomy economic outlook and the hostility of foreign powers, rallied to Hitler's support, fearful of a Communist uprising in the event of his fall.

A Cartoon of Hitler, *from Ulk, Berlin*

CHAPTER XXXVI

New States and Old: The Triumph of Nationalism

ONE of the most amazing results of the World War was the triumph in central Europe of the long-repressed principle of nationalism. On the ruins of the Romanov and Hapsburg empires national states arose, extending from Finland in the far north to the Balkans in the south.

Long before the end of the conflict the ramshackle Dual Monarchy began to manifest signs of approaching dissolution. Lacking national solidarity and internal co- *Revolutionary Move-* hesion, the government resorted to repressive *ments in the Dual* policies to avert revolutions. After 1916 the *Monarchy* grip of the imperial administration was weakened. The assassination of the despotic Austrian premier Stürgkh in October of that year indicated the drift toward revolution. In the following month the death of the aged emperor, Francis Joseph, removed another contact with the past, and the weak and incompetent Charles ascended the ancient throne. By the spring of 1918 anti-Austrian and anti-Hungarian demonstrations occurred, at which time the government's makeshift scheme to create a federal state on the basis of national self-determination was denounced.

While the revolutionary movements were developing at home the claims of the national groups were being presented abroad. Thomas Masaryk, Edward Beneš, and certain other prominent leaders estab- *National Organizations* lished Czech committees in France and other *Abroad* Allied countries to spread propaganda and to secure recognition. Yugoslavs engaged in similar steps, issuing, on July 20, 1917, the famous Declaration of Corfu, which provided for a union of the Serbs, Croats, and Slovenes under the Karageorgevich dynasty of Serbia. Polish aspirations were also represented abroad. In 1917 a national committee was organized at Lausanne, and later moved to Paris, where it carried on the struggle for an independent Poland.

At first the Allies, hoping to detach Austria-Hungary from Germany's side, were indifferent to the Czech, Yugoslav, and Polish drives for recognition, but by the summer of 1918, confident of a complete victory, they recognized the independence and the belligerency of the subject nationalities. Separate contingents of Czechoslovaks, Poles, and Yugoslavs were created in the Allied armies. Meanwhile the discontented nationalities in the Dual Monarchy shattered the morale of that state by destroying munition plants, fostering mutinies, facilitating wholesale desertions from the army and navy, and spreading Allied propaganda.

In the autumn of 1918 the actual dissolution of the empire occurred. Despite the desperate attempt of Charles of Austria to save the state by federalization, the political administration of the Dual Monarchy was supplanted by a series of national councils of Czechoslovaks, Yugoslavs, Ruthenians, German-Austrians, Magyars, Poles, and Rumanians. The ancient Hapsburg dynasty was overthrown.

National states arose in Austria-Hungary. On November 12, notwithstanding the opposition of the bourgeois parties who favored a constitutional monarchy, the *The Rise of New States* Social Democrats, supported by the workers, succeeded in having a democratic republic proclaimed in Austria. An independent Hungary also appeared. Unable to preserve the country from dismemberment and to retain the Hapsburg dynasty, the Magyars, led by the liberal aristocrat Count Michael Karolyi, established a revolutionary Hungarian National Council. On November 13, 1918, King Charles renounced all rights to participate in Hungarian affairs, and the National Council, three days later, proclaimed the Hungarian People's Republic.

A Czechoslovakian republic and a Polish state emerged in the fall of 1918. Declaring for union with the Czechs, the Slovak National Council joined the Czech National Council at Prague, which henceforth became the Czechoslovakian Provisional National Assembly. On November 14 the latter proclaimed a republic, with Masaryk as its first president and Beneš as its foreign minister. About the same time the Polish state was revived. At first Polish unity was menaced by the multiplicity of provisional governments, but the appearance of the strong and able general, Joseph Pilsudski, provided Poland with a much-needed leader. Supported by Socialists, peasants, and the Polish legions who had fought in the World War, he succeeded in having himself proclaimed head of the provisional government in Poland. The provisional Polish government in Paris, however, representing conservative elements, opposed his régime. A schism between the rival factions was averted by Paderewski, the famous musician, who effected a reconciliation. On January 16, 1919, a compromise government was created, with Pilsudski as provisional head of the state and with Paderewski as premier and foreign minister.

Other remnants of the Hapsburg empire were transferred to new owners. The Croats, who had declared their independence, created a national council at Zagreb. On November 23 they united with Serbia and Montenegro to form the kingdom of Yugoslavia, under the regency of Alexander of Serbia. By December the Rumanians in Bukowina and Transylvania had joined Rumania, and in accordance with the terms of the armistice the Italians had already acquired their share of the spoils. Recognizing the dissolution of the Dual Monarchy as a *fait accompli*, on November 11 Charles, the last Hapsburg emperor, renounced his Austrian throne.

Post-war Austria was no longer a great state. From an area of 115,832 square miles, with a diversified population of some thirty millions in 1914, Austria was reduced to 32,369 square miles, with a homogeneous popu- *Austria after the War* lation of some six millions. The coal and iron of Moravia and Bohemia, and the great industrial centers, went to Czechoslovakia; agricultural and mineral resources were taken over by Rumania; the oil of Galicia became Polish; and the seacoast was lost to Italy and Yugoslavia. Austria was now a small landlocked power, disarmed, impoverished, and forced to import foodstuffs and raw products.

After 1918 the future of the provisional government which supplanted the Hapsburg monarchy was uncertain. Taking advantage of distress resulting from unemployment and food shortages, Bolshevist agents tried to convert Austria to communism. Liberal elements were victorious, however, and the temporary administration won the workers over to a moderate socialist program. At the elections for the national constituent assembly which met in February, 1919, the Social Democrats were triumphant. Dashing bourgeois hopes of a constitutional monarchy, they declared their intention of retaining the republic, banished the Hapsburgs, and confiscated their property. Finally the assembly, invoking the principle of national self-determination, proclaimed the union of Austria and Germany. Largely because of French and Czechoslovakian insistence, however, the peace conference forbade the contemplated union, or *Anschluss*. By the Treaty of St. Germain, in September, 1919, Austria was forced to promise not to alienate her sovereignty or to permit infringement upon it without permission of the Council of the League of Nations.

The Austrian assembly, abandoning the hope of an early merger with Germany, proceeded to draft a constitution; this was formally adopted on October 1, 1920. *The New Government* Owing to the influence of the peasants and clericals in the provinces, who were fearful of being dominated by Socialist Vienna, a federal governmental structure was created. The union comprised nine provinces, each having its own local diet. A legislature consisting of a Federal Council selected by the local diets and a popularly elected National Council was established. Although a president was selected by the two houses functioning as a federal assembly, real executive authority was vested in the ministry, which was responsible to the National Council. Empowered to disregard the veto of the upper house in the enactment of legislation, the National Council was the more important body. Universal suffrage and proportional representation were characteristic features of the new state. Thus a bourgeois democracy supplanted the old autocratic régime.

Upon the foundation of the republic a conflict occurred between the radicals of Vienna and the conservatives of the provinces. Control of the government, after the elections of October 17, 1920, however, remained in the hands of the Christian Socialists, who were chiefly peasants and clericals. Representing Vienna and the factory workers, the Social Democrats constituted the chief opposition party. The Pan-Germans, who hoped for union with Germany, were also a potent element in Austrian politics. Several proletarian uprisings occurred in Vienna, where the Social Democrats, dominating the city government, had introduced political and social reforms. Suspicious of these socialistic tendencies, the provinces occasionally opposed the national government. Later, however, greater cohesion and federal coöperation developed.

The new republic was faced with difficult economic and financial problems. Vienna, with a population of nearly two millions, was formerly the nerve center of an *Problems Confronting* almost self-sufficing economic organism. After *the Austrian Govern-* the break-up of the empire, however, she found *ment* herself cut off from the markets and raw materials which had sustained her industries, and confronted by hostile neighbors. Despite the fact that Austria still possessed considerable resources, — coal, iron, abundant timberlands and water power, — economic ruin threatened the former imperial capital.

Austria, although obliged to pay but a small portion of reparations, was soon on the verge of bankruptcy. In order to bolster her finances, her late enemies, after 1918, had to furnish food supplies and loans. Nevertheless, by 1922 the Austrian currency was hopelessly inflated and an economic collapse impended. Fearing that a social upheaval might follow a currency debacle, the Allies, after failing to arrive at a satisfactory solution, appealed to the League of Nations.

On August 31, 1922, the League began to operate through the financial, economic, and legal committees, in conjunction with a committee created especially to deal with Austrian affairs. These groups of experts prepared a series of reports that became the bases for assistance to Austria. The political independence, territorial integrity, and sovereignty of that country were declared to be inalienable, and she was required to abstain from financial or economic policies which might jeopardize her status. Austria was compelled to adopt a policy of rigid economy and reform. Meanwhile a foreign loan approximating $135,000,000 was to be floated for the purpose of restabilizing economic conditions. To facilitate her recovery, a bank of issue was to be created, and the government was to renounce the rights of issuing paper money and of engaging in foreign loans without special authorization. The project was to be supervised by a commissioner-general, representing the League, and a Committee of Control of the Guaranteeing Governments. Through the adoption of these measures the economic situation in Austria was so improved that by June 30, 1926, the League was able to terminate its work of rehabilitation.

The desire for union with Germany, although it subsided temporarily during the period of economic demoralization in the two countries, did not wholly disappear. *The Proposed Union with Germany* After the establishment of the Dawes Plan in 1924, the *Anschluss* movement was revived. Austrians and Germans bound themselves closely together through exchange of professorships, uniform legislation and codes, economic and educational coöperation, and Austro-German cartels. This progressive assimilation was perhaps to be the prelude to a potential political union. At all events, on March 21, 1931, an Austro-German customs union was announced in Berlin and Vienna. Declaring Austrian independence unimpaired, this proposal provided for an economic merger of the two countries, with identical tariff rates and laws, mutually reciprocal treatment, pooling and apportionment of total customs, and separate staffs, but with uniform execution of customs laws. All vital economic disputes were to be arbitrated, and the agreement was to run for three years, subject to termination upon one year's notice.

The proposed union met with great opposition, as France, Italy, and Czechoslovakia registered protests. Eventually the matter was referred to the World Court, where a decision was rendered against it on the ground that it constituted a violation of the agreements of St. Germain and Geneva, which guaranteed Austrian independence.

Discontent persisted in Austria. Despite the partial recovery of Vienna as a commercial and banking center, economic conditions throughout Austria were bad. This situation was reflected in the growth of new political parties — the Nazis, adherents of Hitlerism, who favored the *Anschluss*, and the *Heimwehr*, a Fascist organization which received its inspiration from Italy.

Both groups, in common with the Christian Socialists, whose leader, Engelbert Dollfuss, was premier of Austria, opposed the radical Social Democrats. In February, 1934, an uprising of the latter was suppressed only after considerable bloodshed. Thereupon Dollfuss, by this time endowed with almost dictatorial powers, proceeded to organize a Fascist Austria. This policy antagonized the Nazis, who rose in rebellion in July, 1934. Dollfuss was murdered; but the uprising was crushed, and his successor, Kurt Schuschnigg, continued his policies.

Accompanying these Austrian disorders were successive war scares, as Great Britain, Italy, France, and the Little Entente, fearful of German intervention on behalf of the Nazis, warned Hitler against interference.

Hungary, like her former imperial partner, found herself, after the war, reduced to the position of a minor power. Her area was reduced from 125,641 square miles, *Hungary after the War* with a population of twenty-one millions in 1914, to 35,911 square miles and a population of about eight millions. A Hungarian People's Republic was proclaimed at Budapest on November 16, 1918. Old governmental institutions controlled by the landowning aristocracy were abolished, and a national council of the workmen's and soldiers' councils declared that a new constitution should be drafted by a constituent assembly selected by universal suffrage.

Karolyi, head of the provisional government, by adopting conciliatory policies toward both the Allied powers and the subject nationalities, sought to preserve Hungary from dismemberment. To placate disaffected classes, he hastily undertook a comprehensive program of reforms designed to democratize the government. His liberal concessions came too late, however, for the right considered his reforms too radical, while the left felt that they were inadequate. Spurning a democratic federation, the subject nationalities united with their brethren in neighboring countries.

Opposition to Karolyi's leadership developed. Continuation of the Allied blockade and the demobilization of the Magyar armies led to great unemployment and famines, which furnished opportunities for the spread of Bolshevist ideas. Influenced by these developments, the national council of workmen's and soldiers' councils, by electing him provisional president, practically shelved Karolyi and cleared the way for a more radical ministry. Thus, provoking attacks from conservative landowners and orthodox Socialists, Karolyi's attempt to weaken the radicals by securing peasant support through agrarian reform proved unsuccessful. Greatly strengthened, the Social Democrats only awaited an opportunity to supplant Karolyi and to seize supreme power.

Karolyi's policy of friendship for the hated Allies finally caused his downfall. The latter had approved the disintegration of Hungary and had ordered Magyar troops to withdraw from Transylvania. Patriotic Hungarians were vexed, and the national council refused to accept the settlement. Practically admitting the failure of his conciliatory policies, the president resigned on March 21, 1919, and left the field open for rival factions.

Combining forces, the Socialists and Communists seized control of the state. A revolutionary government was organized, with Garbai, a bricklayer, as president, and a young Jew, Bela Kun, as commissar for foreign affairs. The latter, an adherent of Bolshevism, was the real power in the new régime. In imitation of the Russian Bolshevists, with whom they had con-

The Radical Régime in Hungary

cluded an alliance, Bela Kun and his followers attempted to create a soviet government in Hungary. Assuming dictatorial powers, the new officials ordered the nationalization of industries, public utilities, and large estates. A soviet system and the dictatorship of the proletariat were established. Although they constituted but a minority of the population, the Communists created a Red Army and instigated a Red Terror. A war was now instituted against the upper and middle classes and the ecclesiastics, all of whom were regarded as enemies by the new order. Their property was seized, their newspapers suppressed, and many of their leaders imprisoned. Business was soon at a standstill, as trade and transportation broke down and a reign of terror came into being.

Bela Kun's collapse was as rapid as his rise. The Allies, opposing the Bolshevist régime, offered to support a moderate socialist government if it were set up. Meanwhile Rumanian and Czech forces under French command invaded Hungary. A counter-revolution led by Admiral Horthy developed, and a rival government was set up. In July, 1919, Bela Kun began an untimely offensive against the Rumanian troops who were invading eastern Hungary. Decisively defeated, he fled to Vienna, and Rumanian troops occupied Hungary in defiance of the orders of the Allied Supreme Council. For three months they systematically ransacked the country, carrying away live stock, machinery, railway equipment, and other property of a total estimated value of nearly $19,000,000. Finally, leaving a legacy of hatred, the Rumanians withdrew on November 11.

The Bolshevist régime being hopelessly smashed, a reaction toward the right developed. On November 14 Horthy, accompanied by a small army, entered Budapest and assumed control of the state. Early in *The Regency* 1920 a national assembly was elected which restored the monarchical constitution. In the enforced absence of Charles IV, who had never legally abdicated the Hungarian throne, Horthy, on March 1, was elected as regent. A White Terror and an anti-Semitic movement followed, resulting in the persecution of Communists and Jews.

Encouraged by the reactionary tendencies in Hungary, the exiled king Charles decided to return. His appearance, on March 26, 1921, was not greeted with the popular acclaim which he anticipated. Horthy refused to relinquish his power save at the behest of the National Assembly. Moreover, the protest of the principal Allies and the threats of Czechoslovakia and Yugoslavia, supported by Rumania, caused the National Assembly to join Horthy in requesting the departure of the unwelcome guest. Disappointed, Charles reluctantly withdrew in April.

On October 20, 1921, Charles made a second attempt to recover his throne. Landing from Switzerland by airplane, he placed himself at the head of a group of royalists and marched toward Budapest. Czechoslovakia and Yugoslavia threatened war and decreed mobilization on October 23. To avoid a foreign conflict, Horthy dispatched troops who captured the king. Charles, refusing to accede to Horthy's request for his abdication, was placed on a British monitor in the Danube for delivery to a more secure exile. He finally died in Madeira on April 1, 1922, and his young son Otto became the Hapsburg pretender to the throne. Whereas the Allies only demanded the deposition of Charles, the Little Entente obligated the Hungarian National Assembly to exclude the Hapsburg dynasty from the throne. Thus Hungary remained a kingdom without a monarch.

The National Assembly terminated its career early in 1922. It had concluded peace with the Allies by the Treaty of Trianon. No new constitution was created, nor were provisions made for a second national assembly. Later, as a phase of attempts to restore the old régime, universal suffrage and the secret ballot were abolished. Nevertheless the ultra-reactionaries desired a more complete restoration of the old order. Decisively defeated in the elections by the moderate conservatives, they formed many secret monarchist societies aiming at the restoration of the youthful Otto. As a result of their activities a Defense of the Realm Act was passed in 1922 to curb them.

A serious financial crisis jeopardized Hungary's national

existence. She appealed to the League, to which she had been admitted in 1922. After an investigation the League recommended a plan which involved (1) stabilization of the crown and termination of inflation, (2) creation of a bank of issue, (3) balancing of the budget by June 30, 1926, (4) grant of a reconstruction loan of two hundred and fifty million gold crowns secured by specific revenues, and (5) supervision of Hungarian finances by a commissioner-general responsible to the League. League control began in 1924, and by June, 1926, it had been so successful that Hungarian national finances were restored and the budget was balanced.

Hungary was little changed politically and socially from the pre-war state. Deprived of most of her forest lands and much of her agricultural and mineral resources, that landlocked country, whose industries had never been highly developed, remained dominantly agrarian. Seventy-five per cent of the peasants, however, were nearly landless, nearly 40 per cent of the land being included in estates of more than fourteen hundred acres. Meager attempts at agrarian reform did little to remedy this problem. In November, 1926, the unicameral National Assembly created a rather undemocratic upper house to replace the abolished Table of Magnates. This body enjoyed no power over the budget and but a suspensive veto over other legislation. Aristocratic agrarian Hungary remained one of the most backward states in Europe.

Although the Regent, Admiral Horthy, was perhaps the best-known Hungarian statesman, the conservative Count Bethlen was chiefly responsible for the recovery of Hungary. He headed the moderate Union party, representing the landowners and wealthier peasants. The reactionary right and the radical left made little headway against this Union party, and Bethlen became increasingly liberal. In 1927 he renounced the desire for revenge against former enemy neighbors. The following year he promised that a Hungarian monarchy should be reëstablished legitimately, without recourse to a *coup d'état*. An amnesty was also granted to all political prisoners not sentenced for more than five years. Under his leadership conditions improved in Hungary.

Of the so-called succession states of central Europe, Czecho-slovakia was most successful in avoiding the ills which beset her neighbors. On February 29, 1920, the Czechoslovak National Council adopted a constitution which provided for a democratic parliamentary government. A bicameral legislature was created, consisting of a Chamber of Deputies and a Senate, both popularly selected by universal suffrage. The more powerful of the two houses was the Chamber, which could override the Senate's veto of legislation. The president was to be selected by the National Assembly for a seven-year term, and the ministry was to be responsible to the Chamber. On May 27, 1920, Masaryk was chosen first president under the new constitution, with Beneš serving as foreign minister. Under their capable guidance most of the problems confronting the new state were ably adjusted.

The Czechoslovakian Republic

Czechoslovakia had a population of some fourteen millions living in an area of 54,207 square miles. Ethnic disunity, however, was a serious obstacle to her development. The new state consisted of the three former Austrian provinces of Bohemia, Austrian Silesia, and Moravia, as well as the former Hungarian district of Slovakia. Czechs, Germans, Slovaks, and Ruthenians had to be welded together into a unified nation, — a process which was difficult in view of the divergent development of these peoples. Whereas the Czechs and Germans were accustomed to an advanced industrial and commercial society, the Slovaks and Ruthenians, engaged primarily in agricultural and pastoral occupations, were relatively backward.

Internal Problems confronting Government

Problems exceedingly difficult to solve were those arising from the national minorities. The country lacked ethnic homogeneity, about one third of the total population consisting of Germans, Magyars, Ruthenians, Poles, and Jews. The Minorities' Treaty which the Allies obliged Czechoslovakia to sign guaranteed their national, religious, and educational freedom. Nevertheless friction developed. The Ruthenians insisted upon the creation of an autonomous régime which the government had pledged. Hostility to the more advanced

Czechs, who dominated the new state, developed among the relatively backward Slovaks. Germans, Poles, and Jews also showed signs of dissatisfaction.

Conciliatory policies of the government went far toward healing the minorities' problems. The tendency was for these elements to identify their interests with those of the state. This attitude was illustrated by the manner in which all groups stood solidly behind Masaryk and reëlected him president in 1927. A new local autonomy, dividing the country into three administrative districts, — Bohemia, Moravia and Silesia, and Slovakia,— went into effect on January 1, 1929. Each had a local council which provided some measure of decentralized administration. Ruthenia, however, was excepted and enjoyed partial autonomy under an elective diet. These tendencies toward federalism caused the minority problems to decline.

Czechoslovakia, one of the notable manufacturing countries of Europe, possessed an enviable position. Enjoying abundant coal, iron, and other raw materials, she fell heir to 80 per cent of the industry of the Dual Monarchy. Situated advantageously in central Europe, amidst a highly developed network of railways, her outlets to the sea assured by the peace treaties of 1919, Czechoslovakia was in close proximity to agricultural countries like Russia and Hungary, which needed manufactured products. Commercial treaties with neighboring states facilitated trade. Compared to her neighbors Czechoslovakia had a very promising economic outlook.

In 1919, however, the matter of land reform called for prompt attention. Czechoslovakia was a country of great landowners, much of the land belonging to Germans whose ancestors had secured it in 1620 from dispossessed Bohemian Protestants. In Slovakia a few thousand persons owned nearly half the land; in Moravia less than 1 per cent possessed nearly one third of the soil; in Bohemia 2 per cent of the landlords held over 25 per cent of the land. By a series of laws in 1919–1920 provisions were made for expropriation, with compensation to the owners, and the distribution of the property on a credit basis. By 1926 the reform was practically complete, with over 2,000,000 acres distributed among more than 500,000 peasants.

Friction with the Roman Catholic church arose as a result of the movement for the separation of church and state. Highly developed nationalism finally caused the creation of a Czech national church in January, 1920. This church, declaring its independence of the Pope, democratizing its administration, and adopting the Czech language for its services, by 1924 boasted over a million adherents.

There were other sources of disagreement. Many clerics resented the secularization of education during the early years of the republic. A great number of the people opposed the governmental decree that all church dioceses in Czechoslovakia should be confined to the national frontiers and should be under the jurisdiction of Czechoslovakian prelates. Attempts to break up the large ecclesiastical estates also caused friction. The increased strength of nationalism and socialism seemed to presage a complete separation of church and state.

The celebration, on July 6, 1925, as a national holiday, of the burning of John Hus, the Bohemian Protestant national hero of the fifteenth century, produced a crisis. The Vatican, affronted, recalled the Papal Nuncio from Prague, whereupon the Czechoslovakian minister was withdrawn from Rome, and the adversaries remained deadlocked for three years. An indecisive compromise resulted, and a complete separation of church and state did not materialize. All Czechoslovakian dioceses were placed under the jurisdiction of national prelates, the bishops were required to be nationals and to take the oath of allegiance to the republic, while the government continued to pay the salaries of the clergy. By May, 1928, both parties agreed to the arrangement, and normal diplomatic relations were resumed.

Czechoslovakia became the pivotal link between France and the chief beneficiaries of the Dual Monarchy. Czecho-

The Little Entente   slovakia, Yugoslavia, and Rumania were fearful of the recovery of Hungary and the return of the Hapsburgs. Since they were to some extent dependent upon one another for prosperity, these states found economic coöperation desirable. Furthermore, by uniting their forces they could increase their political and military prestige. They therefore formed the Little Entente to preserve the *status quo* in south-central Europe.

Resting on a number of treaties and informal understandings, this coalition, entered into by Czechoslovakia, Yugoslavia, and Rumania during 1920–1921, was especially significant. From the political and military point of view it constituted the equivalent of a great power. Through the Franco-Czech agreement of 1924 the Little Entente became an integral part of France's system of European alliances. French loans, military instructors, and diplomatic support were beneficial in strengthening this group. Both France and the Little Entente agreed upon the desirability of treaty enforcement and were also affiliated with Poland. Thus the Little Entente was linked with the French policy of maintaining a "sanitary cordon" of powers hostile to Bolshevist Russia and to Germany.

The Little Entente, by surrounding Austria and Hungary with a ring of hostile powers, did much to retard the economic recovery of the Danubian nations. Before the war the old empire was a unified organism with a single customs union. Important raw materials, production, and transportation facilities were synthetized into a well-knit economic structure. After the break-up of the empire, however, the succession states, instead of coöperating, erected tariff barriers and remained antagonistic to one another, thus hindering the economic recovery of these regions. In this way the principle of nationalism, by fostering disunity in these interdependent regions, jeopardized the political and economic security of the small nations of south-central Europe.

By the summer of 1932, with nearly all these states threatened with bankruptcy, eight countries — Bulgaria, Estonia, Czechoslovakia, Yugoslavia, Hungary, Latvia, Poland, and Rumania — held a conference. France proposed that a Danubian customs union be created in order to overcome political barriers to trade. She further suggested that these agrarian states be accorded preferential tariffs by their neighbors and that an international loan be floated. Because of Italo-German opposition, however, the scheme failed. In September a conference of seventeen powers was held at Stresa, and the earlier project was accepted with certain modifications. Fear of an Italo-Hungarian alliance prompted the members of the Little Entente, in February, 1933, to enter into a formal agreement which was designed to create a political and economic *bloc*. Italian influence was enhanced, nevertheless, when, on March 17, 1934, Italy, Austria, and Hungary signed protocols which provided for economic coöperation.

Before the war the Balkans consisted of small competitive national states as contrasted with the great powers above the Danube. As a result of the peace treaties, *The Balkans* however, the whole of central Europe south of the Carpathians, decentralized politically and economically, became "Balkanized." Violent political methods, involving frequent revolutions, *coups d'état*, assassinations, dictatorships, and border incidents, continued to prevail after 1918 in the Balkan powers, which consisted of Yugoslavia, Albania, Greece, Bulgaria, and Rumania. Although still possessing territory in the Balkans, Turkey, as related elsewhere,[1] became primarily an Asiatic power.

Overlapping both the Balkans and the territories of the former Hapsburg empire was Yugoslavia. With a population of over twelve million, this polyglot kingdom *Yugoslavia* consisted chiefly of Serbs, Croats, and Slovenes. Even though all were Slavs, long separation had resulted in distinct separatist tendencies in culture, religion, and customs. Their chief common interests were a hatred of the Hapsburgs and their Slavic affinities. The union of the three peoples had been provided for by the Corfu Manifesto of 1917, which assured "a constitutional, democratic, and parliamentary monarchy" under the Serbian dynasty. The two alphabets and the three prevalent religions were to be recognized, and suffrage was to be universal, direct, and secret. A constitution for the new kingdom was to be devised by a national assembly.

[1] See pages 604–607.

The creation of a government for Yugoslavia was a difficult undertaking. Some groups, especially the Serbs, favored
a unitary state, while others preferred a fed-
eral organization. Particularly insistent were *Political Problems*
the Croatian leaders, who demanded autonomy under a federal structure. King Alexander, however, refused to call a
constituent assembly until the boundaries of the new states
were definitely delimited. Finally elections for the constituent assembly were held, on November 28, 1920. The noncoöperation policies of the Croatian Peasant party enabled
Pashitch, the dominant political figure, to maintain a working
majority in the national assembly and to establish the constitution of June 28, 1921. In an attempt to obliterate regional
and historical boundaries a highly centralized government
was created, with a national parliament at Belgrade. Local
administration was partly under popular control, but subject
to the supervision of the national government.

After the establishment of the constitution its revision
became the outstanding domestic problem. Until March,
1924, because certain leaders refused to participate, Pashitch
and his adherents continued to dominate the government.
Upon the fall of Pashitch a series of ministries arose and collapsed with disconcerting frequency. Parliamentary government was at a standstill. Finally, after the murder of their
leader, Raditch, the Croatian deputies withdrew from Belgrade and set up a rival parliament at Zagreb in August, 1928.
Inasmuch as the latter seemed determined to boycott Serbia,
efforts of the government to effect a settlement between the
Serbs and the Croats were unavailing. The king then resolved
to adopt drastic measures. Declaring constitutional government a failure, he dissolved parliament on January 5, 1929,
abrogated the constitution of 1921, and instructed General
Zhivkovitch to form a new government pending the creation
of a constitution. The king, in taking such drastic steps,
declared his intention of carrying out a program designed
to unify and to improve the administration of the kingdom.
Furthermore, he promised to reëstablish democratic and
parliamentary government. By arrests and other repressive

measures his administration endeavored to crush the separatist movement. In September, 1931, a new constitution was placed in operation. Zhivkovitch became premier, and retained direction of the government until he was replaced by Dr. Marinkovitch.

Economic as well as political troubles beset the new kingdom. Lack of capital and raw materials, poor transportation facilities, and inadequate outlets to the sea handicapped her advancement. A free zone in Salonika failed to compensate Yugoslavia for her losses elsewhere. Consequently her commercial ambitions led to difficulties and tension with Italy over the control of Albania, Dalmatia, and the Adriatic. Fear of Italian imperialism and distrust of Hungary were largely responsible for the participation of Yugoslavia in the Little Entente.

Economic Problems

On the Adriatic coast below Yugoslavia lay the smallest and weakest of the Balkan powers. A mountainous country, isolated from the world, Albania had a population of less than one million. Although it was very backward, its economic opportunities excited the cupidity of Italians, Greeks, and Yugoslavs. Consequently the Albanian struggle for existence as an independent state was frequently complicated by the intervention of foreign powers.

Albania after the War

Despite the ambitions of grasping neighbors, Albanian independence was recognized, and admission was procured to the League of Nations in December, 1920. After some years of disorder Ahmed Zogu emerged triumphant over other rivals for the mastery of the barbaric state. Ruling as a virtual dictator, he convoked, in 1925, a national assembly which proclaimed a republic and elected him president for seven years. He then announced an ambitious program of reform. Needing capital to carry out his plans, he entered into the Treaty of Tirana, which really established an Italian protectorate in 1926. In September, 1928, the national assembly proclaimed Zogu as king, and Italian influence subsequently became all-powerful.

Little less turbulent was the career of Greece, the southernmost of the Balkan powers. After having been coerced into joining the Allies, she was dominated by Venizelos. His prestige was enhanced as Greece emerged from the conflict with handsome territorial gains. An ardent imperialist, he was about to embark on an *Greece after the War* attempt to win much of Asia Minor for Greece when an unexpected reversal of political fortunes brought about his fall.

The pro-German king Constantine of Greece had been forced into exile during the war. With the death of Alexander on October 25, 1920, a reaction developed in favor of the exiled monarch. A plebiscite held in December was favorable to his return, and great popular rejoicing greeted his arrival at Athens on December 19, 1920. Constantine, however, was forced to carry out Venizelos' Anatolian policies, and therefore he was held responsible for the crushing defeat of the Greeks in 1922 at the hands of the Turks. Jeers now greeted the ill-starred monarch, so that, on September 27, 1922, he wisely relinquished the throne in favor of his son, who became George II.

A military dictatorship under royal control followed. The parliamentary elections of December, 1923, however, resulted in a great victory for the adherents of Venizelos. Thereupon the royal family withdrew into exile, and in January, 1924, Venizelos again headed the Greek state. Unable to restore order, he resigned in March, and a republic was approved by a popular plebiscite of April 13, 1924. While the provisional government was vacillating as to its future policies the extremely nationalistic republican, General Pangalos, in June, 1925, overthrew the government by a *coup d'état*. His short-lived dictatorship was followed by eighteen months of coalition government, beginning in December, 1926. In 1928 Venizelos again emerged from retirement and headed the government, remaining in control until 1932.

Under the rule of Venizelos the position of the Greek republic was strengthened. For a time he reëstablished domestic order, but serious political unrest followed his subsequent retirement. Conciliatory relations with neighboring states restored Greek prestige, and a debt settlement was arranged with the United States. To solve the vexatious problem of

Turks and Greeks living under the rule of one another, an exchange of nationals was agreed upon in 1922–1923. Over 1,200,000 Greek refugees had to be accommodated, but their addition strengthened the national solidarity of Greece.

Bulgaria's history after the war was much less unsettled than that of Yugoslavia and Greece. Nevertheless defeat in the World War led to the fall of those respon-

Bulgaria after the War sible for Bulgaria's participation. Upon the abdication of the autocratic Ferdinand in favor of his democratic son Boris III, Alexander Stambolisky, leader of the agrarian party, became premier (1919), and ruled until 1923. During this period the government was devoted to the peasants, attempting, by repressive policies, to crush the upper classes. The premier's high-handed policies caused a number of factions to unite to overthrow him by a *coup d'état*. Finally his ministers were arrested and he was murdered. After his fall a middle-class government ruled Bulgaria, but was frequently compelled to quell serious communist uprisings.

The war left Bulgaria much dissatisfied. She was deprived of sections of Macedonia, to which she believed she had legitimate claims. Moreover, the loss of her outlets to the Ægean crippled her economic life, and a free zone in Salonika, which Greece offered her, was not adequate compensation. Like Yugoslavia she continued to seek suitable access to the sea.

Rumania emerged from the war with greatly increased territories but with serious internal problems. Partly a Balkan and partly a central-European state, she at the

Rumania after the War same time was closely linked with the Russian borderlands. By the peace treaties she secured valuable cessions from Austria-Hungary and Bessarabia from Russia, which greatly increased her size. These territories, however, brought new troubles, involving the assimilation of the peoples inhabiting these recently acquired regions.

The greater Rumania which developed after 1918 was the largest of the Balkan states. In an area of some 113,887 square miles she had a population of over seventeen millions, of which over 70 per cent were Rumanians. In the matter of natural resources the country was well endowed, possessing enormous oil reserves and some coal and iron. Transylvania brought additional mineral wealth, especially in the form of gold mines, which were among the richest in Europe. Rumania, despite the growth of manufactures and the acquisition of natural resources, remained predominantly an agricultural country. An important granary of Europe even before 1914, she produced cereals in much greater quantities during the post-war period. Demands for agrarian reform persisted, however, as numerous landless peasants urged a redistribution of the land. There was need also for the introduction of improved methods of cultivation.

Although well equipped to play an important rôle in the economic life of Europe, Rumania was hindered in her development by the turbulent nature of her politics. After the war the three chief political groups were the Liberals, led by John Bratianu, the conservative People's party, under the leadership of General Averescu, and a number of disunited peasant parties. Although numerically superior, the peasant factions failed to unite and thus enabled either Bratianu or Averescu to control the government. By 1926, however, a fusion of parties resulted in the formation of the National Peasant party led by the liberal Dr. Julius Maniu. Demands for agrarian reform resulted in riots and disorders and giant demonstrations, until finally the regency, acting for young King Michael (1927–1930), was forced to appoint Maniu as premier.

With the rise to power of the new administration the aristocratic-capitalistic class rule was finally shattered, and the peasants gained control of the government. Hoping to place Rumania on a par with Western constitutional powers, Maniu favored (1) freedom of the press, (2) free and fair elections, (3) absence of discriminations against national minorities, (4) a decentralized government with local autonomy, (5) equal opportunities for domestic and foreign capital, and (6) a peaceful foreign policy.

Maniu's administration, which lasted until 1930, was relatively successful. Under his régime the budget was balanced, the currency stabilized, foreign capital attracted, and

the economic life of the country reconditioned. But a partial
material recovery failed to satisfy Rumania; hatred of Hungary and fear of Soviet Russia clouded her future. The return
of the exiled Carol at the behest of the National Peasants'
party, in 1930, and his ascent to the throne, added a touch of
romance to an otherwise drab record. A thinly veiled dictatorship under the new king and Nicola Jorga of the National
Union party lasted until October, 1932, when the democratic
Maniu returned to power.

The World War also resulted in the creation of new states
along the Russian borderlands. Extending from the Arctic
to the Black Sea in the shape of a crescent,
The Russian Border- these regions comprised six states, with Fin-
lands land at the northern extremity and Rumania
at the southern. Largely the result of circumstances, they
owed their independence to the temporary crippling of Russia
through the revolution, and to the Allied, especially French,
encouragement inspired by fear of Bolshevism. After 1918
these countries served as buffers, holding Soviet Russia at
arms' length from the rest of Europe.

There were four so-called Baltic Republics: Finland,
Estonia, Latvia, and Lithuania. Finland, the largest and the
Finland northernmost of these states, was sparsely
populated and deficient in economic resources.
Long, cold winters, short summers, and poor soil hindered
agricultural development, although over half the population
was dependent on agriculture and stock-raising. Timber resources and abundant water power partially compensated
for the lack of mineral resources in a country whose manufactures did not develop greatly until after the war.

In spite of their handicaps the Finns had long displayed
great solidarity in their opposition to Russian rule. With
the collapse of the old order in Russia, on December 6, 1917,
they declared their independence, receiving recognition from
Russia, Germany, France, and the Scandinavian countries.

A period of disorder ensued as rival factions struggled for
control of the new state. Afforded aid in the form of arms,
munitions, and soldiers by the Russian Bolsheviks, the left

wing of the Finnish Social Democrats endeavored to introduce the soviet form of government. Alarmed at the surprisingly rapid advance of these radicals, who early in 1918 controlled all southern Finland, the upper and middle classes resorted to armed conflict, and, assisted by German troops, succeeded in quickly crushing the communist movement.

After the end of the World War the Finns established a more stable régime. By that time Teutonic influences had declined, and the Finnish Diet, supported by the victorious Allies, who feared Bolshevism, proclaimed a republic. In July, 1919, a democratic constitution was adopted which provided for a president, a diet of two hundred members, and a responsible ministry. Because Finland was on the very edge of Soviet Russia the fear of Bolshevism, on the part of the adherents of capitalism, was pronounced. Consequently a Fascist organization, called the *Lapua*, arose in opposition to communism. In February, 1932, an attempt of this group to seize power by a *coup d'état* failed, and the legal government maintained its position.

Post-war Finland enjoyed a certain measure of prosperity. At first her relations with neighboring powers were not friendly, but later they improved. After a period of strife Finland came to terms with Russia, and on October 14, 1920, the boundaries between the two countries were delimited. Finland received a strip of land which afforded her an ice-free port on the Arctic, but her attempts to secure eastern Karelia were unsuccessful. In 1920 the newly independent state was admitted to the League of Nations. Following a heated controversy between Finland and Sweden over the Åland Islands, at the mouth of the Gulf of Finland, the League, as has been noted,[1] awarded the islands to Finland.

After the war the independence of the three other Baltic states, Estonia, Latvia, and Lithuania, was recognized by the Allies as a phase of their scheme to make Russia an inland if not an Eastern power. In 1920 the Bolsheviks, preoccupied with important problems, also granted recognition to these states. In general the problems and fortunes of these small

[1] See page 615.

republics were similar. Because they were geographically and economically dependent on Russia they felt a common fear of aggression on the part of that country. In 1923, therefore, Estonia and Latvia entered into a defensive pact designed to protect them from their powerful neighbor. The harmonious relations of the Baltic nations were disturbed by the hostility of Lithuania toward Poland, owing to the latter's policy of imperialistic expansion. Internal problems due to economic backwardness in these agrarian countries, together with ethnic and religious diversity, made difficult the preservation of the existing order. Lumbering and agriculture constituted the chief occupations. Despite social, economic, and agrarian reforms, particularly in the expropriation of the large estates from their owners and the granting of these to the peasants, the future of these tiny states was uncertain. Only the sympathetic support of the capitalistic powers of the West enabled them to preserve their independence of their powerful Bolshevist neighbor.

Estonia, Latvia, and Lithuania

Poland was the pivotal center of the eastern frontier. When, after the war, this power was revived, considerable difficulty was encountered in attempting to determine her boundaries. The Fourteen Points had provided for the creation of a state which should include all territory inhabited by Poles, but the historic frontiers of Poland, which had fluctuated according to the political fortunes of the old kingdom, were difficult to determine. Ardent nationalists desired a restoration of Poland at her maximum extent, although this plan would have disregarded the ethnic diversity characteristic of neighboring districts which had formerly been Polish. A number of petty wars and border disputes were caused by the determination of extreme nationalists to restore the "historic Poland." As a result of such aggressive policies, which led to the acquisition of the Polish corridor, the seizure of Vilna, and the partition of Upper Silesia and Teschen, the enmity of Germany, Lithuania, and Czechoslovakia was aroused. Disregarding the hostility of her neighbors, Poland still insisted on retaining what she regarded as her just heritage.

The Restoration of Poland

In carrying out her plan of restoration, Poland was compelled to use force to suppress the Ruthenians of eastern Galicia in 1918–1919. Originally the Peace Conference had intended to permit the Ruthenians, who disliked the Poles, the right of self-determination, but in December, 1919, it decided to grant them autonomy for twenty-five years under a Polish protectorate. The future status of the Ruthenians was to be determined by the League of Nations. Disregarding this plan, the Poles forcibly conquered the country and ruled it as an integral part of their newly established state. Unable to unite in opposition to this illegal annexation, the Allies, by March, 1923, tacitly recognized Polish claims to eastern Galicia as well as Vilna.

A dispute between Soviet Russia and Poland eventually led to a war between those countries. Desirous of extending their boundaries far into Russia in order to regain the frontier of 1772, the Poles undertook a military conquest. After some success they were decisively defeated, and only French assistance saved Warsaw from the enemy. Both sides desired peace, and in 1921 they entered into the Treaty of Riga, which definitely created a compromise frontier.

By 1923 the boundaries were finally delimited. Lacking natural frontiers, however, Poland found herself surrounded by hostile states, who only awaited a suitable opportunity to despoil her. Particularly menacing to Polish security were Germany and Soviet Russia. The former resented the creation of a Polish corridor across German territory. This district bade fair to become an Alsace-Lorraine of the east.

Both Poland and Russia, regarding the frontier of 1921 as a provisional arrangement, seemed ready to take advantage of one another's weakness should an opportunity of readjusting the settlement arise. Moreover, the little republic of Lithuania persevered in her enmity to Poland for having deprived her of Vilna. Consequently, in view of the antagonism of her neighbors, Poland felt the need of security in the form of heavy armaments and alliances with foreign powers. Military policies burdened the new state with enormous expenditures which were partially defrayed by French capital.

Internal difficulties also handicapped the new state. Lack of experience on the part of her political leaders, and the multiplicity of parties, contributed to her political instability. The situation was further complicated by virtue of the fact that the former Austrian, German, and Russian sections of Poland had been separated so long that their interests diverged. To mold them together again, separatist tendencies had to be combated and a uniform administration established. The existence of large and dissatisfied minorities of Germans, Ruthenians, Jews, and others was not conducive to domestic harmony. An economic recovery and post-war reconstruction were made more difficult by border disputes, military campaigns, internal disorders, and financial troubles.

Domestic Troubles

Amidst domestic and foreign complications a democratic republic was created. The union of the provisional governments of Paris and Warsaw was followed, in January, 1919, by the election of a constitutional assembly on the basis of universal suffrage. Over two years elapsed, however, before a constitution, resembling that of France, was finally adopted. Conservative in nature, it provided for a bicameral legislature consisting of a Senate and a *Sejm*. The president, elected for seven years by the two houses, was little more than a figurehead; real authority rested in the *Sejm*, to which the ministry was responsible.

The New Government

Constitutional government was not a conspicuous success in Poland. Insufficiently prepared for popular rule, the people were incapable of directing the complicated affairs of the state in such turbulent times. External and domestic problems called for an iron hand, as the weakness and vacillation of the parliamentary government menaced national security. Pilsudski, therefore, generally dominated Polish politics, establishing a military dictatorship in 1926. Under his vigorous direction a partial political and economic recovery was effected.

Serious economic problems confronted Poland after the war. She was primarily an agricultural country, most of the land being held by a comparatively small number of landlords, who clung to outworn methods of cultivation. Attempts to expropriate the land and materially increase the small holders were generally unsuccessful. The lack of effi- *Economic Problems* ciency in the agriculture of Poland and the other borderland states contrasted markedly with the advance in Soviet Russia. Manufacturing, mining, and metallurgy, however, became important. Abundant coal deposits in Silesia and nearly 5 per cent of the world's oil supply in eastern Galicia strengthened Poland's economic position. Notwithstanding these advantages the suppression of the Jews and other minorities, the dissatisfaction of the peasants, a precarious financial situation which nearly resulted in a debacle in 1923, and hostility toward neighboring states which resented Polish imperialism disturbed the serenity of the resurrected nation.

During the post-war period Poland and the other states bordering on Russia were so unstable that the whole eastern frontier remained insecure. These states, like France and the capitalistic powers of the West, *Poland and the Eastern Frontier* feared not only the spread of Bolshevist principles but also future aggressions by the Soviet government. For purposes of protection from common dangers they tended to link themselves together. On March 17, 1922, a Polish-Baltic Entente was created by the Treaty of Warsaw, signed by Poland, Latvia, Estonia, and Finland. Providing for co-operation and friendship, the arrangement was designed to afford protection from Russia, although it professed to be friendly toward that country. The coalition was weakened, however, by the failure of Finland to ratify the treaty and by the refusal of Lithuania to participate.

The Polish-Baltic Entente came to be a phase of the French policy of a "sanitary cordon" against Bolshevism and Pan-Germanism. France, fearing not only Russia but also German aggressions in the east, was determined to preserve the *status quo* in central and eastern Europe. Therefore she allied herself in 1921 with Poland, who was also linked to the Little Entente by a treaty in the same year with Czechoslovakia. In 1922 a Polish-Rumanian agreement provided for mutual assistance in the event of a Russian attack on Bessarabia or Poland. By 1934, however, Poland seemed to be slipping out of the French orbit, for on January 26 she signed a non-aggression pact with Germany. This treaty improved German-Polish relations, but was regarded with suspicion by France.

After several years of mutual fear and suspicion, Russia and the border states became less hostile. The failure of the capitalistic powers of the West to organize a drive to crush Bolshevism, and the improvement of Russia's international position, dissipated some of the war clouds which had long hovered over the eastern frontier. On February 9, 1929, relations between Russia and the border states were improved by a protocol at Moscow, signed by all powers concerned except Lithuania. This provided for immediate adhesion to the Kellogg-Briand Pact for the outlawry of war. Non-aggression pacts, signed late in 1932, between Poland and Russia and between France and Russia, materially reduced the tension in eastern Europe. In July, 1933, Russia and her seven neighbors — Poland, Rumania, Turkey, Afghanistan, Persia, Estonia, and Latvia — signed a non-aggression pact.[1] In February, 1934, Turkey, Greece, Yugoslavia, and Rumania signed a Balkan pact of non-aggression.

As a result of the World War the principle of nationalism triumphed in central Europe and in the Russian borderlands.

Conclusion A number of aggressive states arose from the ruins of the great empires which formerly occupied these regions. The advantages of political freedom, however, were partially nullified by the evils of the unrestrained economic warfare which proved a handicap to trade, industry, and prosperity. Therefore, with the possible exception of Czechoslovakia, these states soon drifted into a prolonged depression, — a situation that was further aggravated by the maintenance of heavy armaments and alliances which helped to create an atmosphere of suspicion and fear.

The middle-class system apparently was on trial in central Europe. After the war, although most of these states established constitutional governments and engaged in social

[1] For further discussion of these pacts see page 650.

and agrarian reforms, unstable conditions led to the creation of veiled autocracies. Dictatorships in Poland, Hungary, Austria, Yugoslavia, Greece, and Bulgaria seemed necessary in order to preserve national unity and to protect the middle classes from the proletarians. Danger of radical uprisings persisted, however, as political turmoil and economic ruin undermined the none too stable bourgeois régimes in the regions lying between the Baltic and Ægean seas.

The THREE UNHAPPY MONARCHS of Yugoslavia, Rumania, and Bulgaria
From a cartoon in *Izvestia*, Moscow

CHAPTER XXXVII

Recovery of France: The Search for Security

AFTER 1918 the capitalistic system in France was strained to the utmost. Confronted with serious problems of reconstruction and readjustment, France found her whole economic life severely shaken. Enormous expenditures for munitions and supplies practically bankrupted the French government and necessitated internal and foreign loans. Prewar manufactures were disrupted by the struggle, which required the concentration of all energies on winning the war. The loss of some 1,260,000 men, half of whom came from the farms, was a frightful blow. Three problems had to be solved: namely, the rehabilitation of the war-devastated areas, the restoration of national finance, and provision for security against a future attack.

France faced no easy task in trying to restore her northern war-torn areas. This region, including some 12,884 square miles, had contained one eighth of her popu-
Post-war Reconstruction lation and most of her industries and mines. During the war hundreds of villages and thousands of homes had been destroyed and the population dispersed. Factories, mines, railways, orchards, forests, wells, farms, cattle, and stock were ruined or completely destroyed. The terrain was disfigured with shell holes, barbed-wire entanglements, and débris. France thus found herself confronted with the problem of rebuilding a completely devastated land.

The French government early undertook the work of restoration. In December, 1914, it promised to reimburse its citizens for material losses sustained during the war. This pledge was reiterated by the government in April, 1919, with the assurance of reparation. In each canton of the devastated area a commission was created for the purpose of ascertaining the amount of damages. By May 1, 1921, claims had been presented totaling 34,000,000,000 francs for actual losses and 106,000,000,000 francs for indemnities. The cost of replacement, partly because of the decline of the franc, averaged five times the appraised valuation of 1914. For the rehabilitation of the area a special "Budget of Recoverable Expenditure" was established, and reconstruction expenses were charged thereto. Special loans were floated with the understanding that they should be retired as German reparation payments were received. The government immediately proceeded to spend billions in restoring northern France, and in a few years order and prosperity had returned to the war-torn areas.

Closely associated with the problem of reparation was the revival of prosperity. The reconstruction of northern France, the recovery of national finances, the restoration of credit, and the rehabilitation of the *The Problem of Reparation* economic structure depended chiefly upon the extraction of payments from Germany. Consequently politics in France were largely concerned with this vital problem.

During the early post-war period the conservatives were in control. The fear of Bolshevism was reflected in the parliamentary elections of 1919, wherein the conservatives united in a National Bloc and gained a decisive victory. The retirement of Clemenceau in January, 1920, was followed by the elevation to the premiership of Alexandre Millerand. Chief architect of the National Bloc, the latter became president upon the resignation of President Deschanel in September.

A few months later Aristide Briand (1862–1932), the ardent French internationalist, became premier. Throughout the year 1921, during which he directed French foreign policy, European politics were convulsed by the problem of reparations. Germany was essaying to make an economic recovery and desired leniency. The British favored moderation, while the French insisted on tangible results. Briand, wishing to retain British support in regard to reparations and security, tried to reconcile the French demands with British policy. His conciliatory attitude toward the British and the Germans caused popular disapproval. When, late in 1921, he agreed in collaboration with Great Britain to grant a partial moratorium to the German government, the ardent nationalists became aroused. Raymond Poincaré and André Tardieu, his protégé, denounced the premier's feeble foreign policies and demanded the full execution of the Treaty of Versailles.

To satisfy the militant spirit of French public opinion, Briand, in January, 1922, was replaced as premier by the nationalistic Poincaré. As a result French policy toward Germany was stiffened. When Germany failed to live up to the reparation schedule, she was declared in default. The Ruhr was occupied on January 11, 1923, by French and Belgian troops, and an attempt was made to coerce Germany. As discussed previously,[1] the invasion of the Ruhr proved a fiasco, and the Dawes report concerning the economic situation in Germany presaged its ultimate termination. During this period domestic conditions in France were becoming worse. Despite loans and increased taxes the franc was falling rapidly, the government was unable to balance its budget, and the cost of living increased steadily. Hopes of alleviating the situation in France by extracting enormous reparation payments from the Germans had been frustrated, temporarily at least, by Germany's policy of passive resistance. Although Germany was ultimately forced to accede to French demands, nevertheless the futility of Poincaré's coercive methods was demonstrated.

In 1923, as public opinion became less chauvinistic, the Radical Socialists and other parties of the left became vehement in making new demands. A general *The Left Bloc in Power* amnesty for all but rebels and traitors, extension of direct taxation, fiscal and budgetary reforms, and a reduction of the term of military service were requested. The left urged the suppression of the Vatican embassy, reëstablished in 1921, and also of the alleged clericalism of the conservative government. A more conciliatory foreign policy was advocated, based on friendly relations with Great Britain, recognition of Russia, rapprochement with Germany, and coöperation with the League of Nations.

[1] See pages 690–691.

The government was soon overthrown as Briand organized a left *bloc* which triumphed in the parliamentary elections of May 11, 1924. The defeated premier Poincaré immediately resigned. President Millerand thereupon invited Édouard Herriot, leader of the Radical Socialists, to form a government. The latter declined, declaring that it was impossible for him to create a cabinet acceptable to the Chamber of Deputies. He asserted that the president had overstepped his presidential prerogatives and that his removal was vital. On June 11 Millerand, after failing to secure a premier and a responsible cabinet, resigned. Gaston Doumergue, president of the Senate, was elected as his successor two days later, and Édouard Herriot accepted the new president's invitation to form a cabinet.

For the ensuing eighteen months the left *bloc* controlled French politics. The bellicose aggressive foreign policies of Poincaré gave way to the conciliatory attitude of Herriot and Painlevé. Coöperation with the British at the London Conference in August, 1924, and a more lenient attitude toward Germany resulted. The Dawes Plan, which temporarily settled the reparation problem, was approved, and French troops evacuated the Ruhr the following year. The consequent improvement of Franco-German relations made possible the success of the negotiations which led to the Locarno Pact of 1925. Meanwhile recognition was accorded the Russian Soviet government, and friendlier relations were established with the new states of central Europe.

A deep-rooted anticlericalism characterized the parties of the left. They regarded the Roman Catholic church as the implacable foe of the republic. Therefore they *Religious Policies* saw with misgivings Briand's revival of the French embassy at the Vatican and the reappearance of unauthorized religious orders. Adhering to the avowed election pledges of May, 1924, Herriot undertook to weaken the position of the church. He planned to enforce more rigidly the laws against religious congregations, to abolish the embassy at the Vatican, and to extend the religious and educational régime of France into Alsace-Lorraine.

The ecclesiastical policies of the left *bloc*, however, did not result in a break with the church. A beginning was made toward the expulsion of unauthorized religious orders, and provision for the Vatican embassy was omitted from the national budget of 1925; but public opinion forced the government to maintain its ambassador at the papal court. At the same time the church endeavored to demonstrate its friendly regard for the republic. *L'Action Française*, a monarchical publication, was placed on the papal index in January, 1927. The following year a decree of the archbishop of Paris practically excommunicated all French Catholics belonging to the monarchist party.

Attempts to assimilate Alsace-Lorraine furnished the left *bloc* with one of its most difficult problems. In these provinces the religious and educational settlement *Alsace-Lorraine after the War* effected by the Concordat of 1801 of Napoleon had been continued by the German government. Salaries of the clergy were paid by the local government, and children attended Catholic, Jewish, or Protestant schools in accordance with the faith of their parents. When these territories were regained by France, President Poincaré had pledged the undisturbed continuation of their religious system.

Nevertheless the anticlerical left wished to make Alsace-Lorraine conform to the rest of France. Earlier legislation had completely altered the situation in the republic. France had severed connections between church and state by removing religious instruction from the schools and by forbidding religious orders to teach in private institutions. The leaders of the left therefore favored the enforcement of these laws in Alsace-Lorraine. In an effort to assimilate the provinces by the disestablishment of the church and by the introduction of secular schools Herriot tried to efface all legislative and administrative differences. Violent Catholic protests forced the government to adopt a compromise solution by which children were to receive academic instruction in common schools but were separated for purposes of religious instruction.

There were other causes for friction in Alsace-Lorraine. After 1911 Germany had permitted a certain degree of autonomy in the form of a local legislature with considerable authority. The French unitary system did not provide for an autonomous administration. Therefore, in 1919, the legislature was superseded by an arrangement whereby the two provinces were split into three departments. Furthermore, the government discouraged the use of the German language. Popular disapproval greeted these restrictions on political and linguistic freedom. A serious separatist movement developed, which culminated, in 1929, in demands for autonomy. Although the government rejected these requests, it decided to abandon the attempts to coördinate the provinces with France proper.

The financial problem almost wrecked the French government. During the World War the debt had risen to over 180,000,000,000 francs, and the vast expenditures involved in keeping up heavy armaments on land, air, and sea, and in rehabilitating the *The Restoration of National Finance* war-torn areas, made economy impossible. In the early postwar years the debt mounted steadily by virtue of annual deficits. Heavy taxes and some reparation payments were not sufficient to balance the budget. Long-term loans, short-term bills, and loans from the Bank of France had proved but temporary expedients. By March, 1924, the inflation of the national currency had reduced the value of the franc to less than five cents. The government experienced increasing difficulty in floating additional loans or in securing renewals on the short-term bills. Unwilling to impose the heavy income or excess-profit taxes advocated by the extreme Socialists, the administration resorted to further issues of currency and consequent inflation. Foreign credit was complicated by the delay in making definite arrangements for the repayment of the loans from Great Britain and the United States.

A series of ministerial crises resulted. The refusal of the Chamber to sanction further inflation caused the fall of Herriot on April 10, 1925. His colleague and successor, Painlevé, fared little better. The latter's finance minister, Caillaux, failed to conclude a satisfactory debt settlement with the United States and preferred further inflation to a capital levy. A second Painlevé ministry fell on November 22, 1925, after a month's duration. Governmental instability became more pronounced during the next eight months as four ministries wrestled with the serious fiscal problem. Even the astute Briand, who headed three of them, could devise no solution. By July, 1926, the treasury was depleted, the government's credit practically destroyed, the budget still unbalanced, while the enormous floating debt was maturing at the rate of 7,500,000,000 francs a month. The value of the franc had fallen to 48 to the dollar, and public confidence in the soundness of governmental finance was seriously impaired.

The acute financial crisis produced a political readjustment. Party lines were practically obliterated as a National Union ministry was organized. It included six former premiers under the leadership of Poincaré, who was endowed with almost dictatorial powers in affairs relating to finance.

Under Poincaré's leadership an amazing transformation occurred. The national budget was reorganized, administrative reforms reduced expenditures, and new taxes increased the state's revenue by 9,300,000,000 francs. At the close of the year 1926 there was a surplus of over 1,500,000,000 in the treasury. Furthermore, a definite arrangement was made for the funding of the French debt to the United States. By the restoration of French credit the value of the franc was steadily raised until it stood at 25.19 to the dollar, at which point it was stabilized on December 20, 1926. This value was confirmed by *de jure* stabilization on June 24, 1928. As investors' confidence in the government was revived the latter was enabled to readjust its floating debt so as to postpone the dates of maturities and to decrease the service charges. In time the extraordinary expenditures in the devastated areas had become negligible, while the Dawes Plan increased the income from the reparation payments. Fixing the franc at approximately one fifth of its pre-war value further reduced the actual value of pre-war bonds and was tantamount to a capital levy.

In 1928 party politics were temporarily laid aside during the serious financial crisis. The election of that year resulted in a spectacular victory for Poincaré and the government of the National Union. The right generally gained in strength, while the parties of the left lost, with the exception of the Republican Socialists headed by Briand and Painlevé. Later attempts of the Radicals and Socialists to overthrow Poincaré's government resulted in the resignation of the entire cabinet. But the left *bloc* was not strong enough to form a new ministry, and on November 11, 1928, the able minister again returned to power. Ill health resulted in his final retirement on July 26, 1929. Briand once more assumed the premiership, later giving way to ministries headed by Laval and Tardieu. The principles and methods of Poincaré still dominated the French state, although he himself was unable to resume an active part.

On May 6, 1932, an unfortunate event occurred,— the assassination of the aged Paul Doumer, president of the French Republic. After this attack another conservative, Albert Lebrun, was elected as his successor. Later there came a shift toward the left, when, on June 4, Herriot supplanted Tardieu as premier. Although the new premier had by this time discarded many of his more radical ideas, the return to power of the liberal groups resulted in definite changes of domestic and foreign policies. In December, 1932, largely as a result of his insistence on the payment of the war-debt installment to the United States, Herriot fell. The ministry headed by Joseph Paul-Boncour, embarrassed by tax and budgetary difficulties, fared little better, and on January 28, 1933, was supplanted by a cabinet under the leadership of Édouard Daladier.

In 1931 France was economically the soundest state in Europe. She was able to employ and to feed her population, which, unlike those of other European nations, was practically stationary. Although her national wealth declined from $64,000,000,000 in 1913 to $48,000,000,000 in 1927, a few years later the monetary gold reserve of France, over one quarter of the world's supply, was second only to that of the United States. Taxes were unusually heavy, to be sure, equaling from 20 to 22 per cent of the national income; nevertheless the French people, relatively prosperous, were able to shoulder the burden without undue suffering. French industry had staged a great revival after the war because of the modernization of processes, large-scale production, and the invaluable metallurgical industries of Alsace-Lorraine and the Saar Basin. An extensive foreign trade had also revived. French production was greater than ever before, and foreign exports had increased to such an extent that France enjoyed a favorable balance of trade.

By 1933, however, France began to succumb to the paralysis of the world depression. Economic unrest was reflected in increased ministerial instability, demands for tax relief, class antagonism, and tendencies toward political extremism. The Stavisky "pawnshop" scandal, involving high French officials, brought matters to a head. Stavisky was a Pole who had opened a "pawnshop" in Bayonne, where he exchanged worthless bonds for various articles or sold these "securities" for cash. Finally the public discovered that the bonds were worthless and that Stavisky had relieved them of over two hundred million francs. As certain government officials seemed to be involved in the affair, opponents of the bourgeois republic claimed that this Stavisky matter was another example of republican corruption. In February, 1934, royalist and communist riots and disorders swept France. Recalled from retirement, Doumergue, as premier, proclaimed a political truce and organized a nonpartisan cabinet of "strong men," the major object of which was the preservation of the republic.

After the conflict French leaders devised many types of safeguards, in the form of powerful armaments, policies designed to weaken Germany, security pacts, alliances, international pacts, and international machinery. The possession of an enormous gold reserve enabled France, through loans and investments, to gain a dominant position in the commercial and industrial enterprises of most of the new states in central Europe. Through alliances she attained political hegemony as well as economic and financial leadership.

French security plans at the Peace Conference met with but partial success. A Rhine policy aimed at military control and the creation of an independent buffer state on the left bank was not realized. Instead a compromise was effected by which the left bank was permanently demilitarized and subjected to Allied military occupation for fifteen years, and the right bank was demilitarized to a depth of fifty kilometers. A tripartite Guarantee Treaty was devised whereby the United States and Great Britain promised to come to the assistance of France in the event of an unprovoked German attack. Although the arrangement was ratified by Great Britain, the refusal of the United States to adhere to it caused the collapse of the whole scheme.

The failure of the Guarantee Treaty caused the French to resort to a series of bilateral treaties for protection. In common with France, Belgium feared future German attacks and also desired to enforce the collection of reparation payments. After a series of military conversations France and Belgium entered into an alliance on September 7, 1920. This agreement was registered with the Secretariat of the League of Nations, but the specific terms were not divulged. Although the two states would presumably support one another, their combined strength was by no means equal to that of Germany.

French security seemed to be menaced by two factors: namely, German revenge and Bolshevism. Fearful of a German attack and of the spread of communism farther into Europe, France, in her desire to attain security, urged the establishment of a "sanitary cordon" against Bolshevism. To France, Germany and Russia were the two great states most dissatisfied with the peace settlements and were therefore the most dangerous to her safety.

Like France the new republic of Poland also was menaced by Russia and Germany. Largely built on the border provinces of those two states, Poland needed security on both her eastern and her western frontier. Common interests, therefore, brought the two countries together. By May, 1922, diplomatic negotiations finally culminated in a Franco-Polish alliance aimed against a German attempt to revise the settlement on the western frontier or to erase the Polish Corridor. This treaty assured France and Belgium of Polish support in the event of German aggression, but did not as yet apply to Russia or to other powers.

Regarding the existing alliances as inadequate, French statesmen tried to obtain a political agreement with Great Britain. At Cannes, on January 12, 1922, Lloyd George, the British prime minister, offered to Briand, the French premier, a treaty whereby Great Britain would actively assist France in the event of direct and unprovoked aggression; but he refused to guarantee the existing Polish-German frontier. Poincaré, who succeeded Briand as premier on the following day, demanded that the proposed treaty should be reciprocal, should guarantee French security for thirty years rather than ten, and should be supplemented by a definite military agreement. British opposition to a military convention and the incompatibility of French and English policies created an impasse, and the negotiations finally lapsed.

Poincaré next determined to obtain security for France by the occupation of the Ruhr. Reverting to the earlier French policy, he tried to force the late enemy into paying the heavy reparations. At the same time he deliberately retarded German economic recovery by taking possession of Germany's great industrial region. He hoped thereby to create an independent buffer state in the Rhineland which would be dependent upon France. The loyalty of the people living in this region to Germany, and the heavy cost of the occupation, however, contributed to the failure of this undertaking.

In 1923–1924 Poincaré also revived the French policy of encirclement. Plans were made to bring the Little Entente into the French scheme to isolate Germany. Ensuing negotiations finally resulted in the signing of a treaty by Czechoslovakia and France on January 25, 1924, in which they practically agreed to coöperate in matters of foreign policy and to preserve the *status quo*. Specifically they decided to oppose the union of Germany and Austria and the restoration of either the Hohenzollerns or the Hapsburgs.

France also turned to the League of Nations in her attempt
to obtain security. Largely because of her influence the
fourth assembly of the League, in September,
1923, adopted the draft Treaty of Mutual   *Disarmament and
Assistance, which embodied the idea that mu-   Security*
tual security must be given in exchange for reduction of arms.
This League scheme for joint disarmament and security,
therefore, was definitely linked with French aims. It virtually
guaranteed the preservation of the *status quo*, which France,
the new countries in central Europe, and the small states along
the Baltic desired. Inasmuch as the powers not directly concerned with the situation in middle Europe refused to increase
their obligations by being involved in such an international
guarantee, the treaty failed of adoption.

In the spring of 1924, political shake-ups both in Great
Britain and in France helped to revive the French problem of
security. The Socialist Édouard Herriot and the Laborite
Ramsay MacDonald, as heads of their respective governments, now tried to improve Anglo-French relations by bringing about a settlement of the problem of security and disarmament by the League of Nations. At the fifth meeting of
the Assembly, therefore, an Anglo-French resolution for the
linking of arbitration with disarmament and security was
adopted, and the so-called Geneva Protocol was prepared.
According to this agreement all legal disputes must be taken
to the Permanent Court of International Justice, all nonlegal
cases must be submitted to arbitration, and aggressive war
was declared illegal. Since the state first resorting to war
in violation of the provisions of the Covenant or of the
Protocol was defined as the aggressor, the League sanction
of an economic boycott or military action could be invoked.
Again France failed to gain security, for most of the states
refused to increase the authority of the League, and so the
Geneva Protocol failed of adoption.

A conciliatory spirit developed in European politics after
the rejection of the League plan. French hostility and suspicion of Germany declined as the latter renewed her offer to
enter into a mutual guarantee and nonaggression pact. As a

result of this general friendly feeling, representatives of Germany, Great Britain, Italy, Poland, Czechoslovakia, and Belgium gathered at Locarno, Switzerland, on October 4, 1925.

The Locarno treaties, which they signed, marked a great advance in the French search for security. On October 16 the Treaty of Mutual Guarantee was approved. Thereby Germany, France, Belgium, Great Britain, and Italy guaranteed the inviolability of the frontier between Germany, France, and Belgium. The German border districts were to remain demilitarized to a depth of fifty kilometers east of the Rhine. With certain exceptions Germany and France and Germany and Belgium mutually agreed to refrain from war against one another. The exceptions were a legitimate defense, a flagrant violation of the provisions for a demilitarized zone, and League instructions to resort to hostilities. The signatory powers guaranteed the settlement, and any alleged doubtful violation was to be submitted to the League Council. They were required to fulfill their obligations should the Council decide that a breach had been committed. The treaty did not modify the signatory powers' obligations under the Treaty of Versailles, nor did it restrict the League of Nations. It was to go into operation as soon as Germany became a member of the League.

The Locarno Treaties

In addition to the Treaty of Mutual Guarantee, Germany signed four arbitration pacts with France, Belgium, Poland, and Czechoslovakia, and also two treaties of guarantee between France, on the one hand, and Poland and Czechoslovakia, on the other. The result of the Locarno agreements was to guarantee the *status quo* in south-central Europe, assuring France and her allies security from German aggression.

During the next few years the pacific Briand dominated French foreign policy. Somewhat reassured by the doctrines of nonaggression, arbitration, and the renunciation of war, suggested by various statesmen, he nevertheless continued the old game of checkerboard diplomacy. An arbitration pact with Rumania, signed June 10, 1926, was made another link in the French system. It provided for mutual consultation should

French Foreign Policy after Locarno

danger threaten the external security or the treaties of peace relating to either state. France signed an identical agreement with Yugoslavia on November 11, 1927. As a result of these pacts the Little Entente became a part of the French international system. Diplomatic support and loans further strengthened the relations of France with her various satellites, which included Belgium, Poland, Czechoslovakia, Rumania, and Yugoslavia. In practice the series of bilateral treaties upon which these relationships were based, together with economic penetration in the form of investments, provided France with greater security than did the more imposing international projects such as the Treaty of Mutual Assistance, the Geneva Protocol, and the Locarno treaties.

In 1927 Premier Briand, to strengthen the security of France against war, proposed a Franco-American arbitration agreement which should renounce armed conflict as "an instrument of national policy." *The Pact of Paris* At the suggestion of Frank B. Kellogg, the American Secretary of State, the original scheme was elaborated into a multilateral treaty, and all states of the world were invited to join in the renunciation of war. Since resort to war was justified in certain cases such as self-defense, execution of treaty obligations, and fulfillment of obligations incurred by League membership or the Locarno treaties, the Kellogg-Briand Pact of 1928 was little more than a pious ideal; but over thirty states, including Russia, accepted it within a few weeks, and on July 24, 1929, it was promulgated by President Hoover.

The French quest for security was not limited, however, to international pacts and alliances. France became the most conspicuous advocate of large armaments. Maintaining one of the world's most powerful *French Militarism and Imperialism* military forces, she also encouraged her allies and satellites to remain heavily armed. France, perhaps more than any other European power, was responsible for the failure of effective military or air disarmament. Contending that treaties were not sufficient security, and sincerely believing that more tangible forms of protection were necessary, she maintained the world's most powerful army and air force.

The Washington Conference of 1922 allowed her to maintain the fourth-ranking navy. After that meeting she devoted special attention to naval aviation and submarines. Her resistance of Italy's attempts to secure naval parity produced a deadlock in the London Naval Conference of 1930.

France encouraged the economic development of her huge colonial empire by protective tariffs and export duties and by military protection of colonists; after the war she provided military training for the natives.

The French search for security was very successful. A formidable system of alliances compensated France for the loss of her Russian ally. She also resisted successfully the disunited opposition of Great Britain, Italy, Germany, Russia, and other powers, who resented her dominance. The might of her armaments on land, air, and sea, in addition to her financial and economic power, enabled France to assume a rôle in European affairs such as no state had enjoyed since the days of Bismarck. This ascendancy, assured by the Treaty of Versailles, she was determined to maintain.

The EXCHANGE ASYLUM

After a cartoon in *Punch*

ROUBLE. What's your name? MARK. Mark.
ROUBLE. What are you doing? MARK. Falling.
ROUBLE. What's your face value? MARK. A shilling.
ROUBLE. What are you worth now? MARK. Twenty million to the pound.
ROUBLE. Come inside.
FRANC. (*Nervously*) I'm not feeling too sane myself.

CHAPTER XXXVIII

Great Britain after the War: Labor in Power

GREAT BRITAIN underwent a serious trial after the war. She found herself confronted with a number of problems which demanded early solutions, such as unemployment, the status of India, imperial relations, and the revival of trade. Some of these had been temporarily solved or shelved during the conflict; others, notably the Irish question, had been seriously aggravated. New ones arose as a result of a war which seriously disrupted the economic structure of the insular kingdom.

The cessation of hostilities practically terminated the demand for war materials and led to the demobilization of millions of men who could not find employment. *Great Britain in 1918* Entering the war a creditor state, Great Britain emerged a debtor, having lent billions to her allies and borrowed more from the United States. Enormous war-time expenditures also caused heavy taxation during and after the conflict, which almost ruined the agrarian aristocracy and the middle classes.

Perhaps the most serious problem concerned Great Britain's inability to restore her foreign trade to its pre-war level. After the conflict she found many of her former customers ruined, while others had been won over by the United States. Chaotic conditions in Russia, Germany, and elsewhere, inflated currencies in many countries, and high protective tariffs were disastrous to British commerce and industry. Nevertheless Great Britain made a temporary recovery. Restoring her pre-war currency to its earlier exchange value, she returned to the gold standard. The budget was again balanced, and her enormous debt to the United States was funded, payable in sixty-two annual installments at a favorable rate of interest. Despite the decline of foreign trade, industrial depression, chronic unemployment, large debts, and high taxes, before 1921 it appeared that prosperity might return to the British Isles.

Post-war economic conditions left their imprint on politics. Conservatives, Liberals, and Laborites struggled without avail to find the key to Britain's dilemma. In order to win the war it had been necessary to erase party lines and to create a coalition government under the premiership of Lloyd George. The end of the conflict found this ministry still in power. As eight years had elapsed since the last general election, Lloyd George, riding on the crest of his war-time popularity, felt it desirable to consult the electorate without delay. By this time he had abandoned his earlier radical tendencies and advocated an "enlightened conservatism."

The dissolution of Parliament was followed, December 14, 1918, by elections which afforded some 13,000,000 new voters the first opportunity to express their views. Earlier in the year the Representation of the People Act had further democratized the British government, admitting to the electorate, with minor exceptions, all men twenty-one years of age who could show six months' residence or occupation of business premises, and all women of thirty years of age who were electors or wives of electors in local government. Representatives were redistributed in accordance with the principle of single-member constituencies of nearly equal size. Plural voting was not abolished, but an elector was allowed to cast ballots in but two constituencies.

A spectacular victory for the coalition government of Lloyd George was recorded in the elections of 1918. His platform called for (1) punishment of German "war criminals," (2) payment of Allied war costs by defeated powers, (3) protection for the essential industries of Great Britain, particularly from the dumping of goods produced by cheap foreign labor, (4) better labor and housing conditions, and (5) settlement of the vexatious Irish question. In contrast to the 467 seats won by Lloyd George's coalition, Asquith's Independent Liberals and the irreconcilable Conservatives, who had quit

The Coalition Government of Lloyd George

the coalition, secured but 28 and 23 seats respectively. The representation of the Labor party was increased to 63, while the Sinn Feiners, who demanded complete independence for Ireland, won 73. The Irish delegates, however, refused to take their seats. Therefore, enjoying an overwhelming majority, the triumphant Lloyd George reorganized the ministry, which became predominantly Conservative, in January, 1919.

A serious economic depression soon required the attention of the government. The short-lived revival of commerce and industry which immediately followed the war led to the workers to demand shorter hours and *The Economic Depression* higher wages in view of the increased cost of living. After numerous strikes an eight-hour day and better wages were secured. Toward the end of 1920, however, the boom collapsed because of the inability of foreigners to purchase British goods, serious competition from the United States and Germany, and a nonrecognition policy which prevented the resumption of commerce with Soviet Russia. Foreign trade fell off some 50 per cent during 1921, and the pre-war level was never again attained.

The decline of export business produced serious repercussions in Great Britain. Production was sharply curtailed, and industrial and business stagnation set in. The decline of business and the growth of the working classes, through the increase of population and the participation of women and former leisure classes in industrial and business life, led to increased unemployment. Over 1,000,000 men and women were out of work early in 1921, and this number had more than doubled by summer. To alleviate the resultant distress, the Unemployment Insurance Act of 1920 was modified so as to afford relief through a system of doles.

Steps were taken to rejuvenate British trade. In the hope of reëstablishing markets in Russia an agreement was signed with the Soviet government on March 16, 1921. This provided for the resumption of commerce pending a formal treaty which should define more accurately the political relations. Each side promised to refrain from propaganda and intrigue detrimental to the other. In the same year, to protect British key industries and workmen from cheap foreign commodities, an act was passed which levied a 33⅓ per cent duty on certain goods and also a tax on imports from countries whose currencies were depreciated. This was actually a step toward the abandonment of traditional free trade.

During the war the unsettled Irish problem disturbed the British Isles. In 1914 Ireland was on the verge of civil war over the impending introduction of the third Home Rule Bill. For economic and religious reasons the Protestants of Ulster and the northeast were opposed to any scheme which provided for their inclusion with the rest of Ireland under home rule. On the other hand, the majority of the Irish were determined that the whole island should be united under a restored Irish parliament. During the conflict both sides became more determined and their claims became more extreme, the Sinn Feiners demanding full independence, while the Irish Nationalists were still content with home rule. An abortive revolt, aided by German support and characterized by the proclamation of a republic in 1916, was decisively crushed.

The Irish Problem

After the war the parliamentary elections resulted in an overwhelming victory for the Sinn Feiners, who secured 73 seats as opposed to 6 for the Nationalists. Styling themselves the Irish Republican party, the Sinn Fein representatives constituted themselves an Irish parliament, the *Dail Eireann*, which first met at Dublin on January 21, 1919. Delegates were selected for the Peace Conference, but failed to secure recognition. Under the leadership of Eamon de Valera, elected president on January 22, a ministry was created, and the Irish republic was in a state of virtual war with Great Britain.

In 1920 Lloyd George undertook to settle Anglo-Irish relations. Opposed to full independence, he was willing to grant home rule but felt that Ulster should not be forced to submit unwillingly to the Catholic south. Accordingly a Government of Ireland Bill was prepared, which became a law on December 23, 1920. This act separated Ulster from the rest of Ireland and gave each a parliament and home rule. Certain powers and imperial services were reserved for the British Parliament, wherein both Ireland and Ulster were to be represented. There was to be a Council of Ireland, elected by the two Irish parliaments, for the purpose of harmonizing the relationships and interests of the two sections. Ulster accepted this new arrangement, but the rest of Ireland rejected the scheme and flared into open revolt.

Great Britain was prepared to offer even further concessions. Therefore, after months of fighting and fruitless negotiations, the Sinn Feiners, on December 6, 1921, accepted a treaty which created the Irish *The Irish Free State* Free State. By this plan Ireland, except for Ulster, was placed on the same constitutional and imperial basis as the self-governing dominions. Northeastern Ireland was allowed to continue under the Act of 1920. The Anglo-Irish treaty created a schism in the ranks of the Sinn Feiners. When the *Dail Eireann* approved it, President de Valera resigned, and Arthur Griffiths was finally chosen to succeed him. After the *Dail Eireann* was transformed into the Parliament of Southern Ireland, De Valera and his followers withdrew. A provisional government under the chairmanship of Michael Collins continued to function, and it appointed a constitutional committee in January, 1922. Rather than submit to the new arrangement De Valera plunged the country into a sanguinary civil war, which was finally crushed in the spring of 1923.

The coalition government of Lloyd George soon began to encounter difficulties as a result of its Irish policies. The Conservatives, although they approved of its partial adoption of protectionism, were dissatisfied with its Anglo-Irish treaty, which recognized the Irish Free State. Their disapproval and outspoken criticisms nearly led to the overthrow of the government early in 1922, when the cabinet threatened to resign. In October the Conservatives declared their independence and withdrew from the coalition. The lack of a workable majority forced the resignation of Lloyd George, and Great Britain at last returned to government along party lines.

In 1922 the Conservatives came into power. The new prime minister, Bonar Law, organized a purely party ministry.

The Conservatives in Power

Parliament was dissolved, and elections were scheduled for November. The Conservatives won a decisive victory over Lloyd George's National Liberals, Asquith's Independent Liberals, and the Laborites. Economic unrest and industrial strife led to a great influx of workers into the Labor party, however, and it polled over 4,000,000 votes, securing 142 seats,— second only to the victorious Conservatives. Internal dissension in its ranks seemed to have shattered the Liberal party, and the Laborites were now strong enough to be regarded as "His Majesty's Opposition."

Short-lived was the triumph of the Conservatives. Great Britain's economic dilemma proved to be a Juggernaut which overthrew them within a year. Ill health forced the retirement of the astute Bonar Law, who was succeeded by the rather inexperienced Stanley Baldwin in May, 1923. Seeking a remedy for the commercial and industrial depression, the unemployment, heavy taxes, and high cost of living, which afflicted Great Britain, Baldwin determined to resort to protection. This unexpected renunciation of the traditional free-trade principles alarmed and alienated many supporters. Although Baldwin held that a tariff on manufactured goods would relieve unemployment and preserve wage levels, many feared that it would result in higher prices. Baldwin decided to take the issue to the people, dissolved Parliament, and scheduled new elections.

At the polls the Conservatives encountered a decisive reverse. Baldwin's argument for a protective tariff on manufactured goods, and for a policy of imperial preference, failed to convince the electorate. In opposition to the Conservatives the Asquith and Lloyd George forces were amalgamated to restore the old Liberal party, which stood for traditional free trade and industrial insurance and coöperation. More serious, however, was the growing strength of the Labor party, under the leadership of Ramsay MacDonald. The Laborites were moderate socialists, advocating free trade, beneficial labor and industrial legislation, better housing facilities, the nationalization of mines and railways, a capital levy on all fortunes of £5000 and above, pensions for the people, and a revision of the Treaty of Versailles. Although most of the electorate was opposed to the more radical of the Laborite proposals, such as the capital levy, popular disapproval of Baldwin's protectionism led to a great increase of strength in both opposition parties.

The immediate result of the election of 1923 was the fall of the Baldwin government. The Conservatives secured more seats than either of their rivals, but their working majority was obliterated. The Labor- *The First Labor Ministry* ites retained second place, with 192 seats, and the Liberals were third, with 158. Perceiving his decisive defeat on the issue of protection, Premier Baldwin resigned, and Ramsay MacDonald was invited to form the first Labor government in British history. He did so with the support of the Liberals, who preferred his moderate socialism to the protective policies of the Baldwin ministry.

Premier MacDonald's Labor government did not prove to be a thunderbolt in the political atmosphere. It believed in legal methods and parliamentary practices. Mildly socialistic, the party accepted class consciousness as a desirable working-class ideology, but rejected the principle of class warfare. Dependent on Liberal support, it was in no position to introduce any radical proposals. In financial affairs MacDonald pursued moderate policies. The tax on cheap amusements was repealed, and the McKenna war duties were abolished. Duties on tea, coffee, and chocolate were lowered. Unable to reduce unemployment materially, MacDonald continued the dole with slight modifications. Through the Wheatley Bill he encouraged the building of homes, utilizing government subsidies for the purpose. Despite party convictions the Labor government made no attempt to introduce a capital levy. Its relatively conservative policy in domestic affairs was justified by MacDonald when he said, "Our Labor government has never had the least inclination to try short cuts to the millennium."

The Labor government's achievements in foreign affairs were more outstanding. England's relations with the Continental powers, which had been rendered somewhat unsatisfactory by the chauvinistic policies of the Conservatives, were now decidedly improved by the new government. More friendly bonds were established with France and with the League of Nations. MacDonald coöperated with Herriot of France in assisting the League in its attempt to achieve disarmament and to provide security. To lessen mutual suspicions and naval competition in the Far East, construction on the great war base at Singapore was discontinued. Coöperation with France assured the adoption of the Dawes Plan. An amicable spirit in European international affairs, engendered by MacDonald's foreign policies, helped to prepare the way for the Locarno treaties. England's Labor government was indeed a boon to British foreign policy.

Foreign Policies of the Labor Government

In conformity with MacDonald's policy of international conciliation was his *de jure* recognition of the Soviet government on February 1, 1924. He thereby expected to bolster British trade with Russia and to relieve the depression which had set in after the war. In April an Anglo-Russian conference met in London to prepare for the renewal of commercial relations and to settle the claims. The British delegates hoped to secure Russian recognition of debts aggregating more than £1,000,000,000, while the Soviet representatives sought a loan of £60,000,000 to finance the purchase of manufactured goods. Two treaties evolved from the negotiations. One accorded the British goods unconditional most-favored-nation treatment, thus reopening the Russian markets. Concerning the debt claims and the desired loan, the latter remained contingent upon the findings of a joint commission which was to investigate the claims and to prepare a subsequent treaty. The significant feature of the negotiations, however, was the clearing of the way for renewed trade with Russia.

Another general election soon followed the consummation of the Russian treaties. The Liberals disapproved of the arrangements with the Soviet government, and this led them to withdraw their support from the Laborites. As a result Premier MacDonald's working majority disappeared. Rather than resign, however, he determined to take the issue to the people. Both Conservatives and Liberals denounced the Laborite policy of friendly relations with Russia and harangued the electorate on the danger of communist influence in England. Color was lent to their fears by the publication, in October, 1924, of the so-called Zinoviev letter, which urged the British communists to prepare for a revolution in Great Britain. Fear of Bolshevism and the inability of MacDonald's government to effect an economic rehabilitation of Great Britain caused the defeat of the Labor party. An overwhelming victory at the polls swept the Conservatives into power with a majority of over 200 seats. Labor representation numbered 155, while the Liberal party elected only 36. Subsequently the MacDonald government resigned, and the Conservatives, led by Baldwin, returned to power.

Five years of Conservative government now followed. Efforts to curb the depression during this period proved ineffectual. In order to expand the domestic markets, Baldwin succeeded in having a bill *Conservative Rule (1924–1929)* enacted providing for partial protection. By this act certain duties might be authorized, subject to the approval of the Board of Trade and Parliament. Designed to curtail foreign competition in domestic markets, the scheme failed to achieve signal success.

The coal industry was hard hit by the depression. Because of the development of new sources of power the demand for raw coal had decreased. Moreover, England had lost markets for coal in France and in *The Coal Situation* Italy as a result of German deliveries of coal to these countries as partial reparation payments. Consequently the price of coal fell, and British producers asked the miners to lengthen the working day from seven to eight hours and to accept a wage cut as part of a program designed to reduce production costs. Upon the miners' refusal to accept their proposals the operators, on July 31, 1925, announced the termination of the existing wage agreement.

Governmental intervention now followed. Fearful of the consequences of the complete cessation of operations, the state determined to subsidize the coal industry temporarily, and declared that the wage scale of June, 1925, had to be kept in effect until May 1, 1926. It utilized nearly £20,000,000 of public funds to reimburse the coal operators for the amounts paid out in excess of the wages which they were willing to grant. After a thorough investigation of the industry a royal commission, headed by Sir Herbert Samuel, issued a report on March 11, 1926. The commission recommended that, in order to prevent a disastrous collapse of the entire industry, national ownership and an extensive reorganization should be effected. Pointing out that 75 per cent of the coal was being produced at a loss, it advocated a reduction of wages and the abolition of the state subsidies. The existing wage agreement expired on May 1, 1926, with owners and miners unable to effect a compromise.

A so-called "general strike" followed. The miners "walked out," and the Trades Union Congress called a sympathetic strike in certain vital industries, such as the transport service and the printing trade. Actually it was not a general strike, since less than half the 6,000,000 trade-union members were called out. Food, gas, electric, sanitary, and health services, despite occasional difficulties, remained available. The seriousness of the situation, however, caused the government to proclaim a state of emergency and to appeal for volunteers to maintain essential activities. A prompt response on the part of volunteers contributed to the failure of the strike, which lasted but a few days. On May 12 the Trades Union Congress called a halt and indicated its willingness to resume negotiations. In July Parliament passed a law establishing the eight-hour day in mines. Finally, after seven months of fruitless negotiations, the miners' unions were forced to give way and accept the wage cut. The strike was terminated on November 19, 1926. Nevertheless a solution of the fundamental problems of the coal industry, which was vital to the economic welfare of Great Britain, was not attained.

The General Strike

Partly as a result of the great strike of 1926 the Conservatives determined to undermine the power of the labor groups. In 1927 they passed the Trades Disputes and Trades Union Act. This law made a general strike illegal, prohibited picketing, and forbade the disciplining of a union member for refusing to participate in an illegal walkout. Trade-unions were no longer exempt from legal suits, and the attorney-general had the right to attach their funds. Political levies, on the other hand, might be made upon members only if the latter provided specific permission in writing.

The Baldwin government undertook to bring about additional changes. In June, 1927, the premier introduced a plan for the reorganization and strengthening of the House of Lords. He desired to curtail its *Political and Social Reforms* membership from 800 to about 350 and to make it less aristocratic and more democratic in character. Opposition of progressive Conservatives and Liberals led to the failure of the project. More successful was the attempt further to enlarge the electorate. A new suffrage law, in 1928, extended the franchise to all women twenty-one years of age on an identical basis with men.

A series of miscellaneous social reforms were also enacted. These provided pensions for retired workers, widows, and orphans. Contributions of the state, the employer, and the worker created a retirement fund for the employee. At the age of sixty-five an insured wage-earner could retire on a pension, but in the event of his prior decease this pension was to go to his widow and children. A reform and reduction of local taxation helped the basic industries, which, it is estimated, were relieved of 75 per cent of their local tax burdens.

In foreign affairs the Conservatives generally continued the conciliatory policies of MacDonald. Friendly relations were maintained with the League of Nations *Foreign Policies* and with all the European powers save Russia. In 1925 the Conservatives discovered the close connections existing between the Bolshevist Third International and the British Communist party. During the great coal strike of 1926 the strikers were allegedly subsidized by Russian funds. Furthermore, Russian propaganda was allegedly carried on in the British Isles and in China, causing British trade with the latter to fall off. Suspecting the Russian trade headquarters, Arcos, Ltd., of the possession of secret documents stolen from the war office, the British raided their offices on May 12, 1927. The documents were not found, but evidences of Russian military espionage and revolutionary activities were obtained, which caused Parliament to sever relations with Russia shortly afterward.

Despite the government's attempts to bring about economic recovery the unemployment situation became worse. *Decline of Foreign Trade* The foundation of many new industries and the shift of population to southern England did not materially help matters. By 1928 over two millions were unemployed, and their economic plight was desperate. Soon the British began to realize that their plight was due not to temporary conditions but to more fundamental factors, especially the decline of foreign trade. With the spread of the Industrial Revolution the British had lost their former dominance of world markets. After the war the increased economic competition abroad, especially from the United States, and the unsettled conditions throughout the world, led to a much greater reduction in British trade.

Not only was Great Britain's commerce diminishing, but her industry was in need of modernization. The unification, expansion, and coöperation of industrial activities were vital if Great Britain was to meet the keen competition of the United States, Germany, France, and other countries. A "rationalization" was therefore effected which led to partial modernization of chemical, tin-plate, electrical, and other industries. Out-of-date machinery was discarded, and replaced by labor-saving and cost-saving machinery. Economy and efficiency also were introduced, in an effort to eliminate waste of materials, money, and labor. Although in need of modernization the more staple industries, perhaps owing to the expenditures involved, were not greatly improved.

Uppermost in the general election of May 30, 1929, was the imperative necessity for economic rehabilitation. For the first time since the war a Parliament had been able to complete a full legal life of five years. The three parties were well organized and proceeded to conduct energetic campaigns to win over the electorate. In con- *The Election of 1929* trast to the Liberals and Laborites the Conservatives desired to preserve the *status quo*. They denounced socialist experiments, urging the solution of the economic problem through the rationalization of industry and through a *laissez faire* policy. The Liberals, under the leadership of Lloyd George, recommended a colossal program of public works and reconstruction as a solution for the problem of unemployment.

Much more detailed than rival schemes was the Labor program. It planned to solve Britain's dilemma by transforming the capitalistic system into socialism by legal parliamentary methods. The Laborites desired the nationalization of the coal, power, and transport industries and of life insurance. They recommended other reforms designed to transform the social and economic life of the land and to eliminate unemployment. To satisfy the wage-earners, they promised to secure the repeal of the Mines Act of 1926 and the Trades Disputes and Trades Union Act of 1927. They also advocated the introduction of a steeply graded inheritance tax and high supertaxes on the wealthy.

Foreign affairs were stressed in the campaign of 1929. The Conservatives recommended coöperation with the League of Nations and the reduction of arms. Both Liberals and Laborites favored (1) the strengthening of treaties designed to prevent war, (2) free trade, (3) the resumption of relations with Soviet Russia, and (4) the evacuation of the Rhineland. Labor leaders also desired a naval agreement with the United States.

The elections resulted in a decisive victory for the Labor party. It secured 289 seats as compared with 259 for the Conservatives and a meager 58 for the Liberals. Premier Baldwin immediately resigned, *The Second Labor Government* and on June 5, 1929, Ramsay MacDonald organized England's second Labor government. By this time the continued eclipse of the Liberal party seemed to indicate that its traditional progressive position had been usurped by the Labor party, which maintained control of the government until 1931. The economic life of Great Britain was not materially modified, however, the combined strength of Conservative and Liberal opposition preventing socialistic experimentation. To ameliorate conditions in foreign affairs, steps were taken in the fall of 1929 to reëstablish relations with Soviet Russia, and on October 7 invitations were issued to the United States, France, Italy, and Japan for a five-power naval conference to be held in London during 1930. The earlier visits of Premier MacDonald to the League's tenth Assembly in September, 1929, and to Washington in the following month, were designed to promote friendly relations with foreign powers.

By the summer of 1931 the inability of the Laborites to effect a solution of Great Britain's economic impasse culminated in a serious situation. Confronted by the danger of revolution, the three parties combined in a national coalition under the leadership of Premier MacDonald. Many of the Labor delegates became dissatisfied because of the prime minister's plans to reduce taxes and cut the dole; consequently, repudiating the leadership of Premier MacDonald, they refused to participate in the coalition. Their desertion and the formation of an independent organization practically disrupted the Labor party and left its future uncertain. Notwithstanding the dissatisfaction of certain of the Labor leaders the coalition party took the issue to the people, and the Parliamentary elections of October, 1931, resulted in a landslide victory for the Conservatives. Relying chiefly on Conservative support, the government continued under the direction of the popular MacDonald.

The government, on September 21, 1931, partly because of the drain on its reserves and partly to stimulate trade, abandoned the gold standard. As was anticipated, *The Coalition Government* this step reduced domestic sterling prices below the gold prices prevailing among foreign competitors. It was hoped that this temporary disparity in price levels would encourage home consumption of domestic commodities, which would be cheaper than imported goods. Furthermore, those who favored the discarding of the gold standard believed that this situation would result in a decline of imports and an increase of exports, since English producers would be enabled to undersell their rivals. Therefore they held out to English business leaders most alluring prospects of a stimulation of industry and a consequent gradual rise in prices.

Protection policies were again revived, and on March 1, 1932, a system of protective and imperial preferential tariffs was put into effect. These provided for a 10 per cent *ad valorem* tax on manufactured goods, but exempted certain raw products and other materials. Later a special tariff commission was empowered to raise duties 100 per cent on imports from countries that discriminated against British goods. To encourage domestic consumption, "Buy British" and "Buy Empire" propaganda was disseminated. To counteract foreign gold withdrawals, people were urged to pay income taxes in advance and to turn in their gold supplies.

Actually, however, the anticipated prosperity did not return. A number of other nations, including some of England's competitors, followed her lead in abandoning the gold standard. Consequently the advantages which she expected to gain from this shift did not materialize. Furthermore, forced to import certain foods and raw materials, England was unable to escape from dependence on overseas supplies. An Anglo-Russian dispute over the trial in 1933 of several Englishmen found guilty of espionage in Russia resulted in a temporary suspension of commercial relations. Nevertheless the erection of tariffs, the creation of commercial treaties in 1933 with Germany, Denmark, and Argentina, the signing of a new Anglo-Russian trade agreement in February, 1934, the grant of imperial preferences, and the campaign to promote the purchase of English or empire goods were all phases of the attempts of the National Union government to revive prosperity in Great Britain.

Despite these measures the economic depression persisted. England's industries remained stagnant. Coal exports fell from the pre-war level of some 62,500,000 tons to slightly under 42,000,000 by 1932. The decline of the cotton exports was even more alarming; they fell from 7,075,252,000 square yards in 1913 to a meager 1,716,249,000 in 1931. This unsatisfactory economic situation, responsible for the persistence of extensive unemployment, necessitated the continuation of the doles. Efforts on the part of the government to reduce or entirely abandon payments to those out of work encountered serious resentment on the part of the unemployed. During the summer and fall of 1932 the economic situation became steadily worse; bread riots and disorders occurred in London and other industrial centers. Denunciations of royalty and the upper and capitalistic classes became more frequent as unemployment figures swelled to 3,000,000, the highest in British history. Although a slight economic improvement was apparent in 1933, conditions were far from normal.

In recent years the British Empire has undergone a process of readjustment and transformation. From the welter of divergent types of possessions which constituted *Imperial Decentralization versus Imperial Centralization* the British Empire there have arisen six self-governing dominions: Canada, Australia, New Zealand, South Africa, Newfoundland, and the Irish Free State. These dominions, politically self-conscious, tended to develop distinct nationalities. As a result the British Empire was gradually transformed into a federation in which the dominions were on an equal footing with the former mother country.

After the World War the autonomous dominions made rapid strides toward independence. In practice most of them had enjoyed self-government for some time. Each nation secured separate and distinct membership in the League. Although there was a conflict of opinion as to the treaty-making capacity of the dominions, they nevertheless entered into treaties, and none were regarded as being bound by any of the proposed Anglo-French security pacts. The dominions had their own diplomats and were represented in the peace and post-war conferences. Both in foreign and in domestic affairs their status verged on independence.

In many respects the interests of the dominions diverged from those of the empire. Opposed to the traditional British practice of free trade was their desire for tariff protection for their infant industries. Furthermore, some of them wanted preferential treatment for their agricultural products in British markets. Many British imperialists also felt that the empire should be converted into a self-sufficing economic unit in which all the political entities would be held together by common interests. Hence they favored the raising of tariff barriers, and preferential treatment for members of the empire.

An important step toward imperial economic solidarity was taken at the Ottawa Conference of 1932. At this meeting, on August 20, several bilateral treaties were signed between Great Britain and the dominions and among the dominions themselves. Through the creation of preferential tariffs and special concessions the signatories hoped to check alleged "dumping" by Russia and to retaliate against the high-tariff policies of the United States. The exact extent of trade losses to the Americans was not apparent, but it was estimated that they might run to several hundred million dollars a year. Indeed, at that time it appeared that the Ottawa treaties were planned as a practical British lever to force the United States to revise the tariff schedule and to coöperate more willingly at the World Economic Conference planned to be held in London in the summer of 1933.

Certain factors, however, acted as barriers to imperial unity. Relations within the empire were not uniformly friendly. India had for some time been seething with dissension and revolution, and the Nationalists there, led by Mahatma Gandhi, demanded independence. Furthermore, the white dominions raised bars against Indian and other Oriental immigration, thereby causing great indignation in India.

Rule over much of the Islamic world also brought its train of troubles. British participation in the dismemberment of Turkey, the alleged betrayal of Arab nationalism, and the support of the Zionist movement made conciliation of the Moslem populations difficult. The desire for raw commodities, especially oil, led to flagrant disregard of the rights of certain

Moslem peoples, — in Persia, Mosul, and elsewhere. However, the grant of practical independence to Egypt and Iraq, and a benevolent attitude toward the Hejaz, partially placated the Moslems.

After the creation of a self-governing Irish Free State the Irish seemed reconciled to remaining in the empire. Submission to imperial regulation was accepted during the administration of President Cosgrave, but the election of the fiery De Valera as president in 1932 revived the movement for complete independence. His denunciation of the oath of allegiance to the British crown and of land annuities totaling several million dollars provoked economic retaliation by England which threatened to result in bloodshed. On July 15 a 20 per cent *ad valorem* duty was imposed by England on certain Irish imports, thereby provoking an Irish reprisal tariff. The Anglo-Irish economic war continued. On February 8, 1933, the policies of De Valera were upheld by the *Dail Eireann* when it reëlected him as president.

As a result of these difficulties some Englishmen believed that the empire had reached its twilight. They regarded as inevitable the ultimate secession of the dominions and of India. Therefore they desired to anticipate such eventualities by voluntarily casting them adrift and concentrating on other possessions. Although the latter had vast potentialities, the British unfortunately lacked the capital necessary for their development. Perhaps this need for money explained England's desire to retain her financial strength by canceling the debt owed the United States.

On the other hand, many were of the opinion that the empire was beneficial to England, and favored a policy designed to strengthen the bonds between the colonies and the mother country. Despite the drift toward independence they held that there was a counter-tendency toward imperial solidarity. British attempts to conciliate the dominions of Canada and Australia were reflected in the termination, in 1922, of the Anglo-Japanese alliance. Great Britain also felt constrained to deal more leniently with the Turks and other Moslem peoples in order to placate their co-religionists in India. Later an effort was made to stimulate imperial loyalty and pride. British statesmen began to welcome the participation of the dominions in the formulation of imperial policies. This tendency was demonstrated by the increasing frequency of imperial conferences and the consultation of dominion premiers. At the imperial conference of 1926 Great Britain and the dominions were declared autonomous and equal, and in the absence of a written constitution the crown was the chief bond of unity. Characteristic of the dominions' foreign policy was their tendency to prefer reliance on the League of Nations to formal alliances. In practice the British Empire was tending to become a league of nations within the League.

An important aspect of the empire was the problem of defense. For the protection of their commerce and colonies, and to maintain accessibility to raw products and markets, the British relied chiefly on their great sea power. Although they had formerly rejected all suggestions for naval equality or freedom of the seas, they relinquished their traditional position of supremacy in 1922 at the Washington Conference. Financial difficulties and the virtual rapprochement with the United States at that time caused them to consent to parity with the latter power in certain types of ships. Great Britain later became a strong propagandist of effective disarmament, being particularly desirous of curbing the development of submarines and naval aviation. But the British navy retained first place, chiefly because of the failure of the United States to build up to the limits established by the London Treaty of 1930, which reiterated the principle of Anglo-American naval parity.

Of outstanding importance to the British Empire were Anglo-American relations after the war. The rise of the United States as the world's leading producer, exporter, banker, and creditor was an impor- *Anglo-American Relations* tant factor in retarding a British recovery. Therefore relations between the two powers were largely concerned with trade rivalry, naval competition, and war debts. Commercial antagonism was reflected in a terrific contest for oil in Persia, Mosul, Mexico, and parts of South America. Similar competition was apparent, shortly after the war, in the conflict for supplies of raw rubber. Prior to the depression of 1929 the United States steadily forged ahead, while Great Britain slipped back in the struggle for markets and profits.

After some years of economic warfare the United States and Great Britain tended to effect a rapprochement. They settled temporarily the problems of debts and naval competition, and reached an accord in their Far-Eastern policies. Friendship between the two countries appeared further strengthened, during the administration of President Herbert Hoover, by the visits of Premier MacDonald to the United States and the appointment, in 1932, of Andrew W. Mellon, influential American financier and ex-Secretary of the Treasury, as ambassador to the Court of St. James's. In the summer of 1932 Great Britain attempted to procure a substantial reduction, if not a total cancellation, of her debts to the United States. To this supposed end Montague Norman, president of the Bank of England, visited the United States. Strong public opinion against readjustment of the debts, however, discouraged, at least until after the presidential election, any official pronouncement in favor of drastic slashes.

Particularly alarming to Great Britain was the military and diplomatic strength of France. The latter power, through *Anglo-French Relations* her armaments and alliances, threatened to overturn the Continental balance of power. Her enormous forces on land, air, and sea gave her an overwhelming military supremacy on the Continent. This situation was partly responsible for the British support of the League of Nations and its disarmament policies. Moreover, French industrial, commercial, and imperial interests repeatedly clashed with Britain's. Nevertheless, at the Lausanne Conference of 1932, which will be discussed later,[1] an Anglo-French entente emerged the principal aim of which was to force the United States to consent to a readjustment of war debts.

[1] See pages 804–805.

In 1933 the fate of Britain as a great power was in the balance. The war eliminated Germany as her chief rival, but resulted in the rise of France and the United States as serious competitors. After 1918 Lloyd George, Baldwin, MacDonald, and other patriots all struggled fruitlessly to revive prosperity. Fearing internal uprisings, however, they did not dare seriously to disturb the *status quo.* As a result their domestic policies were weak. Norman's statement of October, 1932, that the economic situation seemed hopeless,— although perhaps a phase of the debt-cancellationist propaganda,— together with the fall of the English pound, appeared to indicate that England was still on the decline. Fundamentally, hopes of a British recovery seemed to depend on the restoration of world-wide prosperity.

THE LION'S CUBS GROW UP

By James Harrison Donahey, in the *Cleveland Plain Dealer*

CHAPTER XXXIX

The Pacific and the Revolt of Asia

MORE and more did the problems of the Pacific and its borderlands tend to project themselves into the forefront of world politics. Before the World War the rapid introduction of bourgeois culture had reoriented the Pacific world; new nations had arisen, and old ones were stimulated into self-consciousness. In the post-war period the progressive Americas, a nascent Australasia, an awakened Asia, the competitive imperial powers, all came upon the stage of the international drama.

During the nineteenth century the United States gradually emerged as the most powerful of the American nations in the Pacific. By 1914 she held two important wedges which approached Asia: gigantic Alaska, with its frozen fastnesses, pointing toward the Old World, and the insular empire, with the Philippines as its extremity. In 1914 the opening of the Panama Canal, which provided a shorter route for the interocean transfer of merchant ships and war vessels, and the outbreak of the World War, which forced her leading competitors to concentrate on winning the war rather than on commerce, enabled the United States to become the world's greatest producer, exporter, and banker. By 1917 the colossus of North America appeared capable of dominating the world's economic life.

To the north of the United States a friendly neighbor, Canada, although still a part of the British Empire, became virtually an independent nation. Like the United States this country had important interests in the Pacific. Both nations, in fact, aroused by the influx of Oriental laborers, who were able to overcome the competition of white workers, and alarmed at the amazing advance of Japanese imperialism, which threatened to dominate the markets and resources of the Far East, found it expedient to legislate against the un-restricted immigration of Orientals.

In Hispanic America political, economic, and social stability was, by 1914, largely a hope rather than a reality. In contrast to the United States and Canada most of the states in this region welcomed foreign economic penetration and immigration. Only the Monroe Doctrine and subsequent American protective policies shielded them from the inroads of European imperialism. Many of the South American states never-theless resented American interference and were openly hostile toward the United States.

After the World War the Hispanic-American countries, with abundant resources but scanty capital, continued to offer a fertile field for foreign business enterprise. American financial and commercial interests outdistanced foreign competition in the race for profits. The nations of Central and South America, still lacking political, social, and economic order, ran the risk of becoming the victims of imperialistic aggressions, inasmuch as their markets, raw products, economic opportunities, and foreign trade were of great value. The future of Hispanic America was important, since its stability was necessary for the serenity of the Americas and the Pacific world.

Australia and Oceania, in the Pacific, constituted almost another world in themselves. Thousands of miles in width and extending from the Antarctic to the Arc-tic, the Pacific was dotted with innumerable *Australia and the Islands of the Pacific* islands, varying in size from tiny coral reefs to the continent of Australia. The East Indies, the Philippines, and parts of Australia had passed under European rule during the older colonial movement. Most of the isolated islands and groups, however, remained under native control much longer. Strategic motives caused them to be regarded as potential naval bases by the great powers of the world. Valuable too was the copra, or dried coconut kernel, from which coconut oil was extracted. Although the native cultures persisted in many cases, the Oceanian world was almost entirely under European control in 1914.

Analogous to the development of Canada was the rise of the autonomous dominions of Australia and New Zealand. From a wilderness inhabited by dark-skinned natives two "white" nations emerged. These states were particularly jealous of their interests and desired to protect themselves from foreign competition by the erection of tariff barriers. They adopted exclusionist policies, designed to keep out all Oriental immigrants. Fearful lest their unoccupied expanses be overrun, the Australians were alarmed at the rapid expansion of Japanese interests. They began, therefore, to share in the problem of imperial defense by building a navy and by occupying former German islands below the equator in order to hold the Japanese at arm's length. In common with the United States and Canada, Australia and New Zealand stood firmly against Nipponese expansion in the Pacific; as a result Oceania and most regions marginal to the Pacific were closed both to private Asiatic immigration and to Japanese imperialism.

After the World War the struggle for the Pacific centered in Asia. By that time the native peoples, most of whom (except those in China and Japan) lived under *Coming of the Revolt of Asia* European control, were beginning to assimilate Western ideas, institutions, and techniques. Opposition to alien influences developed and generally took the form of nationalist movements whose aims were independence and the expulsion of foreigners. This Asiatic revolt against alien domination was later encouraged and stimulated by Soviet Russia. Bitterly opposed to both imperialism and capitalism, the Bolshevist movement aimed at the establishment of communist states in the East. Consequently the revolt of Asia was complicated by the intrusion of the forces of the newer revolution which were challenging the supremacy of capitalism in Western civilization.

The three chief theaters of war in the dramatic conflict between European imperialism and Oriental nationalism were the Near East, chiefly the home of Moslem populations; India, the "jewel of the British Empire"; and China, a republic. In addition Siam, Indo-China, Korea, the Philippines, and other marginal regions were stirred by revolutionary nationalistic movements.

Before the close of the World War the revolt began against European imperialism in the Near East. Moslem Asiatic peoples were in a state of turmoil as a result of the decline of the Ottoman Empire and the aggressions of the European powers. North Africa was already under the control of European states, Morocco, Algeria, and Tunis being ruled by France, Tripoli by Italy, and Egypt, although technically under Turkish suzerainty, by Great Britain. The populations of these districts were dissatisfied with alien rule even before the war, and the great conflict gave them an opportunity to revolt. *The Moslem World in the Near East*

Post-war Africa, from the Mediterranean to the Cape of Good Hope, was in a state of potential revolt. Native dissatisfaction with alien rule had been aggravated by such factors as foreign oppression, economic competition between blacks and whites, and dislocative educational and religious influences. Labor troubles and uprisings developed in Kenya, the Belgian Congo, the Union of South Africa, and elsewhere. In response to the discontent of their compatriots, several native leaders held meetings, under the auspices of the Pan-African Congress, in which they prepared a charter of liberties for the blacks. Therein demands were made for political, educational, and economic equality; for the termination of industrial and concessionary exploitation; and for the restoration of confiscated native lands. "Africa for the Africans" became their slogan as they strove to release the black man from the bondage of the imperialistic Europeans. *Revolutionary Africa*

A number of uprisings in North Africa formed a phase in the conflict between East and West. They were attempts on the part of the Moslem populations to resist the relentless march of Western middle-class civilization. Hostility to their conquerors was enhanced in 1914 by the fact that the Turkish Sultan, who as Caliph was also the head of the Moslem faith, had joined the Central Powers and was being assailed by the Allies. Furthermore, the Allied powers, especially Great

Britain and France, were the chief oppressors of Moslem peoples. After joining the Central Powers the Turkish Sultan proclaimed a holy war against the Allied infidels.

Concerted action against the Allies in the form of a holy war, however, did not materialize. Nevertheless the Arabs and Berbers, unreconciled to Italian rule in Tripoli, practically drove the aliens out of the interior, and by 1918 the Italians were hard pressed to retain the coast towns. A number of years elapsed before the interior was again brought under Italian control. Farther to the west, in the Spanish zone of Morocco, the Riffs, resenting foreign encroachments, seriously damaged the aspirations of the Spaniards in regard to military penetration. By 1923, as the result of a Riffian offensive, the Spaniards retained merely the seacoast towns. Spanish imperialism was thoroughly discredited.

The French were more successful than the Italians and the Spaniards. During the war, order was generally maintained among the Moslem populations under French rule. After the conflict the restlessness of the peoples of Tunisia and Algeria was assuaged by the extension of a share in the government and by other liberal reforms. Later the Riff revolt spread into the French zone in Morocco, where, after a severe conflict, the leader Abd-el-Krim and his forces surrendered on May 27, 1926. But the smoldering resentment of the native tribesmen remained ready to flare into another revolt whenever a general Moslem uprising might occur.

A serious challenge to Western imperialism was also experienced by the British in Egypt. Although occupied by the English in 1882, Egypt was not proclaimed a *The Egyptian Struggle for Independence* protectorate until December 18, 1914. This proclamation, together with native opposition to the British policy of forced labor and the commandeering of grain and animals during the war, strengthened the nationalist and anti-Christian movements in that country. In 1919 the outburst of violence forced the British government to send a commission of investigation which recommended Egyptian independence, with special safeguards for British interests.

The British government, harrassed by the disorders which continued, terminated the protectorate and abolished martial law on February 28, 1922. Although the independence of Egypt was recognized, certain matters were temporarily reserved for future consideration. These concerned British imperial communications and the Suez Canal, the problem of the defense of Egypt, the disposition of the Anglo-Egyptian Sudan, and protection for minorities and foreigners in Egypt. On March 15 the Sultan assumed the title of "King," and in April, 1923, a constitution provided for a parliamentary government. Enjoying quasi-independence, the state still remained under the guidance of imperial Britain.

Despite these concessions the nationalists demanded complete independence. In 1924 the assassination of Sir Lee Stack, the British governor-general of the Sudan, precipitated a crisis. Great Britain demanded an apology, punishment of the murderers, an indemnity of $2,500,000, and the cessation of political demonstrations. She forced the Egyptian government to accept these requirements. In August, 1927, the death of the able Egyptian premier Zaghlul removed the most outstanding nationalist leader, but the movement for complete freedom continued.

The myth of Egyptian independence was exploded by the British ultimatum of April, 1928, which demanded the immediate withdrawal of all bills granting Egyptians the right to assemble, to carry arms, and to engage in demonstrations. Vainly protesting, the Egyptian government quashed the legislation, and the king, suspending parliament for three years, ruled through his ministers under the virtual supervision of the British. Freedom of speech, of the press, and of assembly disappeared, and nationalist agitation was prohibited in the delta.

In 1929 a treaty of alliance defining Anglo-Egyptian relations was prepared. This agreement provided for mutual assistance in the event of war, and prohibited a political understanding with a third power. Except in the region of the Suez Canal, British troops were to be withdrawn. Relations between the states were to be conducted through ambassadors, but Egypt agreed to use only British subjects if foreign officials or military instructors were required. According to the terms of the settlement Great Britain also promised to facilitate Egypt's entrance into the League of Nations and to help abolish the capitulations by which foreigners remained under alien jurisdiction. The Sudan, however, was to continue under the Anglo-Egyptian condominium which had been established by the conventions of 1899. Apparently Great Britain was unwilling to relinquish Egypt, the key to her African and Asiatic possessions.

One of the most spectacular results of the World War was the dissolution of the Ottoman Empire. Turkey was deprived *The Scramble for Oil* of her vast possessions and reduced to a relatively tiny Asiatic national state extending from Thrace into the Anatolian uplands. Her sovereignty was seriously impaired by the foreign control of her financial and economic life, and her territory was being converted into spheres of influence. The principle of national self-determination in her former imperial possessions was ignored. By the Treaty of Sèvres (1920) the imperialistic, oil-minded powers of the West glutted themselves with their new acquisitions in the Near East. British mandates were established in Mesopotamia and Palestine, and France became a trustee for Syria. The Greeks held western Thrace and Smyrna, while the Italians possessed the Dodecanese Islands and Rhodes. The Turkish government was forced to relinquish all claims to former African possessions, and the Hejaz and Armenia were granted independence.

More significant, perhaps, than the political and territorial arrangements was the international scramble for oil concessions in the Near and Middle East. Even before the World War the great powers had sensed the importance of petroleum. Several foreign interests had endeavored to obtain oil concessions in Persia and the Ottoman Empire before the war. In 1914, however, the Turkish government had granted to the British-controlled Turkish Petroleum Company exclusive rights to exploit the oil resources in Mesopotamia as far north as Mosul. German and Dutch interests, although greatly inferior to those of the British, were represented in the company which enjoyed a monopoly in the Tigris-Euphrates valley. Nevertheless it was not until the outbreak of the struggle that the capitalistic nations could give free rein to their imperialistic desires in this respect.

In no theater of the war did we see this better illustrated than in the Near East between 1914 and 1918. In that side-show of the World War, where movements on a large scale afforded the Powers wider opportunities of revealing their appetites than did the close trench warfare in France, the imperialistic aims of Great Britain appeared long before the peace treaties of Versailles and Sèvres gave them legal and honorable sanction. Palestine, Mesopotamia, the Caucasus, North Persia, South Persia — to the English this broad belt, stretching from the Mediterranean to India, with the 35th parallel of latitude as its axis, meant empire as well as oil. The two can hardly be judged apart.[1]

After 1918, despite vigorous competition from the United States and France, Great Britain controlled the petroleum reserves of Palestine, Mesopotamia, and Persia. Only in the Baku oil fields of the Caucasus was she thwarted. Subsequent efforts to gain a foothold in these, the richest petroleum regions of the world, proved futile, inasmuch as Soviet Russia refused to grant oil concessions to the capitalistic powers except on her own stringent terms.

France and the United States achieved only meager success in the attempt to obtain the open door in Mosul and Mesopotamia. Diplomatic notes and negotiations between the powers finally resulted in small grants to the United States and France. England nevertheless emerged from the general struggle in control of a major part of the world's petroleum reserves,— possibly a partial compensation for her war losses.

While this scramble for concessions in the Near and Middle East was occupying the Allied powers a congress of Turkish notables met at Sivas, in the hills of Anatolia, far beyond the range of Allied guns. Their *Revival of Nationalism in Turkey* spirit of national religious pride inflamed by Mustafa Kemal, a clever and energetic army officer, they determined to resist Allied attempts to seize truly Turkish

[1] Fischer, *Oil Imperialism*, p. 19.

territory, and provided the inspiration for the National Pact which was accepted on January 28, 1920, by the delegates of the Turkish parliament.

The nationalists then proceeded to tear up the execrated Treaty of Sèvres. Although reconciled to the loss of the non-Turkish provinces, the opening of the Straits to international commerce, and the minorities treaties, they refused to accede to the cession of truly Turkish regions or to limitations on Turkish sovereignty. They demanded a plebiscite in Thrace, control of Constantinople, and the abolition of the capitulations. Under Allied pressure the Sultan denounced the revolutionaries and dissolved parliament. The nationalists then held a Grand Assembly at Angora, where they renounced the authority of the Sultan and proclaimed a new government, with the astute Mustafa Kemal at the head.

During 1920–1922 the nationalists met with a series of military successes which insured the victory of their cause. By June, 1920, their armies menaced the French in Cilicia, the Greeks near Smyrna, and the British on the Ismid peninsula. Alarm at the Turkish advance prompted the British to support Venizelos' project for a Greek offensive against the Turks. After a series of victories the Greeks occupied large sections of Anatolia. Recognizing that the Treaty of Sèvres would have to be revised, the London Conference of the great powers invited representatives of the Sultan, the provisional government at Angora, and Greece to discuss modifications. Their inability to effect a compromise caused hostilities to continue, but the solidarity of the Allied front was broken as France and Italy entered into secret negotiations with the Turkish nationalists.

Encouraged by these developments, the nationalists overran Armenia and reunited it with Turkey. In March, 1921, they concluded a treaty of amity with Soviet Russia whereby the Bolshevist government indorsed the Turkish National Pact and agreed upon a boundary settlement. Defeats in Cilicia, jealousy of Great Britain, and hostility to their Greek protégé caused the French to sign the Treaty of Angora with Turkey on October 20, 1921. In exchange for the return of

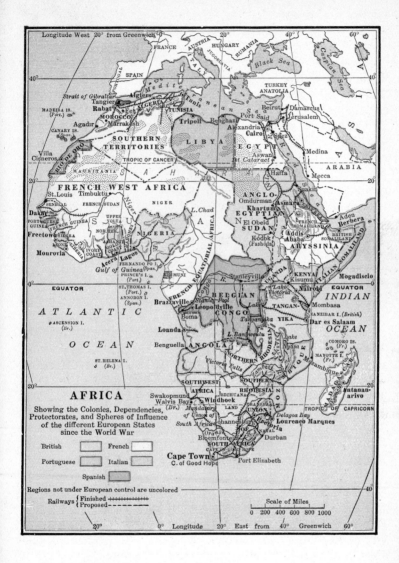

AFRICA

Showing the Colonies, Dependencies, Protectorates, and Spheres of Influence of the different European States since the World War

British ☐ French ☐

Portuguese ☐ Italian ☐

Spanish ☐

Regions not under European control are uncolored

Railways { Finished ++++++++++++ Proposed ----------

Scale of Miles
0 200 400 600 800 1000

Cilicia and a strip of northern Syria extensive economic concessions were assured to the French. The Italian government had already entered into a secret treaty providing for the evacuation of Turkish soil by Italian troops in exchange for economic privileges. The Turks were now free to concentrate their attention on the Greeks, whose imperial pretensions in Asia Minor were being supported by Great Britain.

Flushed with success, the Greek troops, seemingly irresistible, had surged back into Turkish territory. During 1921 they marched to within 200 miles of Angora, but their supreme attempt to take the capital was a complete failure. In the late summer of 1922 the tide turned; a decisive defeat was followed by a retreat which became a rout, and on September 9 the victorious Turks entered the burning Smyrna in triumph. Within a short time Anatolia was cleared of all Greek troops. Only the menace of British military and naval power prevented the Turkish nationalists from occupying the neutral zone along the Straits.

Hostilities finally terminated in Anatolia. In September the great powers addressed a note to Greece and Turkey inviting them to a peace conference. The restoration of Turkish sovereignty in Thrace to the Maritsa River and the abstention of Turkey from military occupation of Thrace or the neutral zone were accepted as bases for further discussion. Mustafa Kemal, ignoring the bellicose impetuosity of many nationalist leaders who wished to continue the conflict, entered into the armistice convention of Mudania on October 11, 1922.

The conference to revise the discredited Treaty of Sèvres met at Lausanne on November 20 and was attended by delegates of the great powers, of certain Balkan states, and of Greece and Turkey. On *The New Turkey* several occasions the success of the conference was jeopardized when the Turks refused to accept the terms offered, and demanded further modifications. Finally, on July 24, 1923, the Turks were satisfied and signed the Treaty of Lausanne. Thus Turkey became the only one of the Central Powers to reject a dictated peace and to procure a negotiated treaty.

The terms of this pact were more favorable to Turkey than those of Sèvres. The Turks recovered Armenia in the East, Thrace up to the Maritsa River, and a section beyond; they preserved a clear title to Constantinople, the Straits, and certain Ægean islands; the Turkish-Syrian frontier was to remain as designated by the earlier agreement with France; and the frontier between Turkey and Iraq was to be settled by direct negotiations with Great Britain, or, should these fail, by the Council of the League. Turkey reiterated her renunciation of claims on her imperial possessions in Africa, on most of the Ægean islands, and on the Arab provinces.

Turkey emerged from the peace settlement with unimpaired sovereignty. She accepted minorities treaties, similar to those signed by certain European states, and agreed to their guarantee by the League. The powers, however, renounced their projected spheres of influence on Turkish soil, and the capitulations were abolished. Turkey's military and naval forces suffered no restrictions, and she was released from reparation payments.

A series of other agreements was also entered into by the new Turkish government. Some of these provided for the permanent opening of the Straits and the Sea of Marmara to international trade; others demilitarized the Dardanelles, the Bosporus, and all but one of the neighboring Turkish islands in the Sea of Marmara.

The Greco-Turkish and the Turko-Bulgarian frontier were also demilitarized on both sides, and upon the ratification of the treaty all foreign soldiers were withdrawn from Turkish territory. A Greco-Turkish convention provided for a compulsory exchange of Turkish and Greek nationals residing respectively in Greece and Turkey. Certain exceptions were stipulated, but there occurred subsequently one of the greatest compulsory transfers of populations in history. Although considerable suffering was entailed at the time, the transfer led to greater ethnic unity both in Greece and in Turkey. Thus, as a result of the nationalist revival, Turkey finally emerged from the war an ethnically unified nation, freed from foreign political and economic control.

Mustafa Kemal's rise to power ushered in an age of Westernizing policies. After the defeat of the Greeks and the deposition of the Sultan Mohammed VI the republic was proclaimed, in October, 1923, by the Grand National Assembly at Angora. A new constitution providing for representative democratic government was created, and Mustafa Kemal was elected the first president. In March, 1924, the National Assembly abolished the Caliphate, thus officially terminating the leadership of Turkey in the Moslem world. New legislation provided for the secularization of education and for the abolition of ecclesiastical courts. The development of a feminist movement helped to enact laws which abolished polygamy in favor of universal monogamy and required the registration of marriages. New criminal, civil, and commercial codes, copied after European models, were also adopted. The wearing of the fez, the turban, and the veil was prohibited, and dervish monasteries were closed.

Other measures were introduced designed to modernize Turkish life. Sweeping educational reforms were effected, which provided for compulsory education of all children from seven to sixteen years of age. Adult education was also encouraged, and a literary test for citizenship rights was established. As a result of these efforts adult illiteracy declined from the 1914 level of 85 per cent to 42 per cent in 1932. The Gregorian calendar, the twenty-four hour day, the Latin alphabet, European numerals, and the metric system were all adopted. Turks were encouraged to control labor, capital, ownership, and production, and to these ends the government resorted to protective tariffs, entered into commercial treaties, encouraged agricultural improvements, and embarked on a vast program of public works. Soon Turkey possessed replicas of European cities, with statues, movies, dance halls, tramways, sewer systems, and modern buildings.

Despite the strong opposition of the conservatives, Mustafa Kemal continued to Westernize his Oriental people. While renovating and modernizing the new Turkish republic he also preserved its independence by avoiding financial and diplomatic dependence on foreign powers and by maintaining friendly relations with the capitalist states of the West on the one hand and with Bolshevist Russia on the other.

Other Moslem peoples were not so fortunate as the Turks in their attempts to obtain freedom. After the war the Moslem world, from the Mediterranean to the borders of India, was in a state of revolt against the West. Arab support against the Turks had been secured by Great Britain upon promises to promote the Arab nationalist movement, but with the restoration of peace the Allies conveniently forgot those pledges and proceeded to partition western Asia among themselves. The French, disregarding the opposition of the native populations, established a mandate in Syria, while British administrations were set up in Mesopotamia (Iraq) and Palestine. The Arabs felt themselves betrayed when they found their hope of national unity shattered and were forced to content themselves with independent states in Arabia and Hejaz. The latter, which occupied a strip of the Red Sea coast including the holy cities of Mecca and Medina, under the rule of King Hussein, was submerged by puritanical Wahabite reformers from the desert. The rest of Arabia remained decentralized under the rule of native tribesmen.

Revolt of the Arab World

Great Britain soon found herself beset with troubles in Palestine. The Balfour Declaration, which was committed to the establishment of a Jewish national home there, had added to the smoldering discontent of the Arabs, who considered Palestine included in the unfulfilled promise of a united Arabia. Although the Arabs did not object to Zionism on racial or religious grounds, they were bitterly opposed to the aspirations of conquest and empire held by the Jews coming into the country after 1919 from Asia and eastern Europe. Antagonism to the Balfour Declaration culminated in a series of brutal assaults upon the Jews in the fall of 1929. A dispute over the Wailing Wall in Jerusalem furnished the religious pretext for the attacks which were interpreted by many as a veiled thrust against the British government and its Zionist policies. British forces finally quelled the disorders, but Arab unrest persisted, capable at any time of blazing into revolt.

In Syria the French encountered serious difficulties. Hostility to the Christians, and the unpopularity of French institutions which were forced upon the inhabitants, caused protests from the Druses, and the imprisonment of native delegates by the French, in July, 1925, provoked a revolt. A long-drawn-out war followed, in which the French opposed the Druses with the most modern methods of warfare. So fierce were the tribesmen that at times the French controlled only the cities, being unable to suppress the guerrilla warfare in the rural districts. Twice the ancient city of Damascus was bombarded by the French.

By the middle of 1927 the Druse revolt was finally crushed. In 1928 the French permitted the holding of general elections for a representative constitutional assembly. This body met on June 9, 1928, with the Syrian nationalists wielding a substantial majority. Their determination to establish a republic independent of both France and the League, and the conflicting desire of the French government to create a Franco-Syrian treaty which would define their relations, produced a deadlock. Opposition of the Syrian nationalists finally resulted in the adjournment of the assembly by the high commissioner on February 5, 1929. Thereafter Syria remained under French control and martial law, but the revolutionary movement appeared to be merely awaiting a more suitable opportunity for expression.

If the British encountered little serious opposition in Transjordan, they were less fortunate in Iraq. In Transjordan the local government was intrusted to Abdullah, a son of Hussein, the first king of the Hejaz. This helped to allay native discontent. In Iraq, however, a revolt against the British occurred in the summer of 1920. Emir Feisal, another son of the king of the Hejaz, had been made king. Although the revolt in Iraq was suppressed, the persistence of dissatisfaction with alien rule caused the British to transform the mandate into a quasi-independent country by an Anglo-Iraq treaty. This was accepted by a constituent assembly at Bagdad, and Iraq became an "independent" state in 1932. Feisal died in 1933 and was succeeded by the youthful Ghazi I.

Farther to the east the Moslem populations of Persia and Afghanistan were more successful in throwing off foreign rule. Like their co-religionists to the west the Persians had become deeply imbued with a national spirit. The treaties of 1907 and 1915 had actually partitioned Persia between Great Britain and Russia. But the Bolshevist Revolution caused the withdrawal of the Russians, and their place was taken by the British, who in 1919 imposed an Anglo-Persian treaty on the weak government. Her independence practically nullified, Persia became a dependency of Great Britain.

Persia and Afghanistan

A strong Persian nationalist movement soon developed. Led by Riza Khan Pahlevi, the patriots overthrew the government in February, 1921. Determined to reconstruct the Persian nation, he denounced the treaty with Great Britain. As the dominant figure in the Persian state he held various posts until he became premier in October, 1923. While the Shah was abroad plans were made to declare Riza Khan first president of a Persian republic; but an anti-republican reaction which swept the country upset the scheme, and on December 12, 1925, he was proclaimed hereditary Shah by the Persian constituent assembly.

Riza Khan's rule marked a renascence of political and social life in modern Persia. A well-organized army reëstablished order and restored the authority of the central government over the local tribesmen. The foreign irregulars who had been disturbing Persia were expelled or subdued. In 1921 the services of Dr. Arthur Chester Millspaugh, an American financial adviser, were procured, and the national finances were reorganized. Great improvement was made in the fields of public hygiene, sanitation, education, and public works. Foreign capitulations were terminated on May 10, 1928. Partially Westernized, Persia began to reassert her national independence.

The persistence of British interests in the ancient land of Persia, however, caused considerable trouble. For example, at the end of 1932 and the beginning of 1933 Great Britain and Persia engaged in a sharp conflict over the question of the

Anglo-Persian oil concession. Because of the world over-production of oil the Anglo-Persian company had curtailed its Persian flow, and the consequent reduction in royalties angered the Persians. Therefore the Shah canceled the concession. The British government, thoroughly angered, sent an "oily ultimatum," which was ignored. Persia then referred the dispute to the Council of the League of Nations, whereupon the latter, under Dr. Edward Beneš, "perennial Foreign Minister of Czechoslovakia and 'Europe's smartest little statesman,'" persuaded the two parties to negotiate a new concession. Pending another arrangement, which was finally accepted, the Anglo-Persian Oil Company continued to work the oil fields.

In Afghanistan the anti-Western reaction was much stronger than in Persia. Before the war the fear of the Russian advance in central Asia induced Afghanistan to submit to British control of its foreign policies. The temporary collapse of Russian imperialism in 1917 removed the need for British assistance. Amanullah Khan, Amir after February, 1919, therefore inaugurated an anti-British program in April, hoping to reëstablish the complete independence of Afghanistan, and launched an offensive against the British in India; but his forces encountered a crushing defeat in May. In response to his request Great Britain entered into a treaty on November 22, 1922, which restored peace, and recognized the complete independence of Afghanistan.

Amanullah now attempted the Westernization of his people and introduced foreign experts to establish Western methods of administration, education, and economic life. His modernizing policies provoked an uprising among the orthodox Afghan tribes in 1923, which was not quelled until 1925. The attempted introduction of additional innovations caused another backfire, and on January 14, 1929, he was forced to abdicate. Eventually the throne passed to Habibullah Khan, the leader of the rebels, whose opposition to sweeping changes was decidedly attractive to the conservative tribesmen.

From the Mediterranean to the borders of India there

was a general ebb of European prestige. Moslem opposition to the West found a ready ally in Soviet Russia. In 1921 representatives of Russia, Turkey, Persia, and Afghanistan gathered at Moscow to work out a joint policy designed to safeguard their interests. Bilateral treaties of amity were signed among the various Oriental states during the next few years. Among the most significant results of these new diplomatic alignments in western Asia was the increased prestige of Bolshevist Russia and the decline of British influence in the Near East and in central Asia. Western imperialism was undoubtedly on the defensive before the rising tide of Asiatic nationalism.

The great nationalist revolution against British rule in India had been brewing since the latter half of the nineteenth *The Revolt of India* century. It was only after the World War, however, that forces and events conspired to lead to a serious upheaval, for it was then that the advent of a real nationalist leader, Mohandas Karamchand Gandhi (1869–   ), furnished the movement for revolution with effective direction and a unified program.

Throughout the war India remained loyal to the British Empire. Nearly 1,500,000 men were sent overseas, a third of that number took part in the fighting, and India assumed a financial burden of some $700,000,000 as her share of the war costs. As a counteraction against enemy attempts to stir up a revolution in India, Great Britain made extensive promises of political reforms and of increased native participation in the government.

Despite numerous material benefits derived from British rule, economic and social life in India remained relatively *Social and Economic Conditions* backward. In an area equal to half that of Europe there lived over three hundred million people, three fourths of whom depended directly or indirectly upon agriculture for their existence. Agricultural methods, "the most obsolete and least effective" in all Asia, together with the uncertainty of rainfall, a heavy land tax, and high rents, kept most of these people living in squalor on the verge of starvation. Through the development

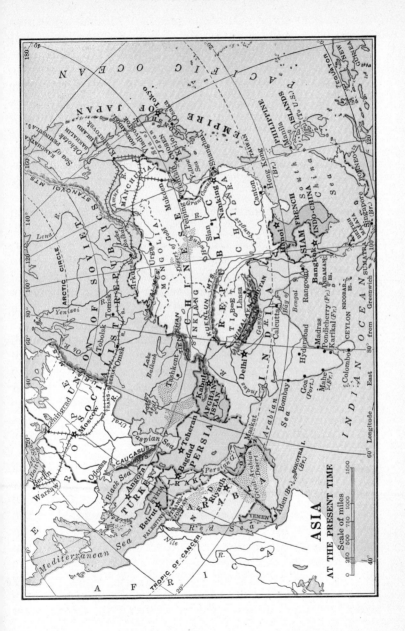

ASIA

AT THE PRESENT TIME

Scale of miles

0 250 500 750 1000   1500

of an extensive system of irrigation, however, a water supply was assured for over 71,000 square miles of land. This irrigation system, in conjunction with improved facilities for transportation, reduced the danger of food shortages and consequent famines. Cotton and wheat were the principal crops, being produced in sufficient quantities to provide surpluses for export. Nevertheless the mass of the natives achieved only a precarious existence.

India, with teeming millions and vast natural resources, offered Great Britain an unexampled opportunity to invest surplus capital, to dispose of manufactured goods, and to secure raw materials. To these ends the British were primarily concerned with maintaining order and security; they developed and extended the machinery of commercial life, such as ports, shipping, railways, irrigation, and agriculture, and they brought about a limited industrialization of India by introducing machinery and establishing banks. The spinning of cotton became one of the leading occupations. By the end of the World War, India stood on the threshold of an industrial age.

As long as the British market for manufactured products in India was not threatened by this industrialization England was not very much concerned; but when many of the so-called "infant industries," often owned by native capitalists, began to compete with English industry and to seek tariff protection from foreign and even English competitors, trouble ensued. Great Britain, realizing that the development of Indian manufactures would undoubtedly injure English industry and commerce by enabling the natives to substitute home goods for British manufactures, not only refused to protect native enterprise but also discouraged industrial development as a whole. This policy of the British government aroused the bitter opposition of the Indian bourgeoisie. Constituting less than 10 per cent of the population, this minority group, living for the most part in the cities, furnished the nuclei for the nationalist movement.

The nationalists, determined to gain economic justice and political freedom, maintained that the British had purposely allowed over two fifths of India to remain under feudal dynasts who were dependent upon the British government, in order that she might more easily keep India subjugated. They therefore held England responsible for the paralyzing provincialism which hindered unity of thought and of action.

In reply to these accusations the British asserted that they had attempted to improve material and cultural conditions. In addition to the development of trade, transportation, and irrigation they had spent vast sums on educational and humanitarian work. It was true, they admitted, that the educational system served only a small portion of the population, but this was because of social antagonisms between the upper and lower castes (there being some 2400 castes in India) and between the Moslem and Hindu religious factions; a real renascence in India could not be expected till these diverse groups subordinated their sectional and class interests and coöperated with their English overlords.

During the World War the British seemed to be losing their hold on India. The Indian people, acquiring from the conflict a heightened sense of national self-consciousness, believed that self-determination was their just and promised reward. Although it still moved in the orbit of British imperial policy and aimed at home rule rather than independence, the Indian nationalist movement had become a powerful force. Representatives of both Moslems and Hindus met in December, 1916, and drafted a reform program for the National party. Recognizing the unifying tendencies of the nationalist movement, the British government then included two native delegates in the Imperial Conference of 1917 and promised political reforms. In July, 1918, Edwin Samuel Montague, Secretary of State for India, and Lord Chelmsford, viceroy of India, prepared a report which proposed the development of self-governing institutions and responsible government in India.

The Nationalist Movement

On the other hand, during 1918–1919 the British government engaged in imperialistic policies which had disquieting effects on India. Expansion of British interests in Tibet, Persia, and Afghanistan, the projected control of Transcaucasia, and the oppressive treatment of Moslem populations in Egypt and Western Asia aroused active resentment.

Suspicious of British imperialism and despising niggardly concessions, the extreme nationalists rejected the Montague-Chelmsford plan. They demanded immediate and complete autonomy rather than the partial concessions which were acceptable to the moderates. A revolutionary clamor for reform of the British administration and its personnel swept the country. The government determined to adopt a "strong hand" and appointed a sedition committee under the chairmanship of Justice Rowlatt, which, in January, 1919, proposed emergency measures to deal with the situation. The leaders and press of the nationalists thereupon denounced the reactionary policies of the government, but the Rowlatt Acts, which sharply curtailed native freedom of action, were passed on March 18, 1919, and an official reign of terror was inaugurated. The disorders became more grave as strikes, reprisals, and national days of mourning brought about the establishment of martial law in parts of India. When the Rowlatt Acts became law, Gandhi declared a day of national humiliation and called for prayer. Great excitement prevailed in the Punjab, and on April 13 British military forces, in dispersing an alleged unlawful gathering at Amritsar, killed some 400 natives.

Inclined to simplicity and asceticism and opposed to the Westernization of India, Gandhi came to be the recognized champion of Indian nationalism. In 1919 the whole attitude of India toward Great Britain *Mohandas Gandhi* underwent a transformation. Coming before the Nationalist Congress at Amritsar in April, "Saint Gandhi" presented his program of noncoöperation and passive resistance. The Nationalists enthusiastically adopted his scheme of civil disobedience and pledged themselves: (1) to resign all official titles and positions in the administration, army, and police forces; (2) to boycott law courts, elections, government schools, and foreign goods, especially British textiles; and (3) to refuse to pay taxes. An amazing revolution was under way, — one of passive resistance, not of violence.

The British government, alarmed at the trend of events, hoped to alleviate conditions by the early grant of reforms. Admitting Indian claims to self-government, the Montague-Chelmsford scheme of constitutional government was approved by Parliament in December, 1919, and became the Government of India Act. Applying to British India and not to the several hundred neighboring India principalities, this statute modified the existing political structure and increased native participation in the central and provincial governments. In this new system, known as a dyarchy, there was a division of governmental functions into "reserved subjects" and "transferred subjects," the former being almost entirely under British control and the latter partially under native officials. These reforms, however, merely granted the Indians limited political rights. Designed to train native leaders in practical administration under British tutelage, they were to be a temporary experimental stage prior to the grant of home rule. Actually, however, India remained subjected to direct British rule under the guise of democratic concessions.

Establishment of the Dyarchy

In January, 1921, the new system of government went into operation. Native opposition continued, however, and the Nationalists boycotted the administration by declining to pay taxes and refusing to purchase European manufactured goods. In spite of Gandhi's opposition to the use of violence some disorders occurred during the period of his imprisonment, from March, 1922, to January, 1924; the policy of noncoöperation seemed to be a failure. Although the British textile industries were suffering from the effects of the boycott, the British government refused to meet the demands of the Nationalists.

This dyarchy was not a success. Some of the Nationalists repudiated Gandhi's program in 1924 and organized the All-India *Swaraj*, which aimed at home rule. Participating in the government, the Swarajist leaders denounced the dyarchy and demanded complete self-government in the provinces and in the national government, except in relation to foreign and military affairs.

Great Britain, aroused by the situation, decided to make a thorough investigation. In 1928 Sir John Simon headed a commission for this purpose, but the absence of native representatives caused it to be boycotted on its first visit. In the fall, however, the natives abandoned their boycott, and eight of the nine provincial governments pledged coöperation. The Indians, relaxing their demands for complete independence, seemed to be willing to accept dominion status for India. The All-India Congress reiterated its demands for autonomy, and Gandhi, formerly an advocate of complete independence, acquiesced in a dominion status provided it were created by 1930.

On April 11, 1929, the Simon Commission completed its investigations. Despite the strength of the movement for home rule in the form of dominion status, however, Indian radicals sowed dissension and distrust of the commission. Gandhi again resorted to a "revolution in homespun," urging the boycott of British cloth and other manufactures. Strikes, disorders, riots, many of which were allegedly fomented by Bolshevist emissaries, characterized the ensuing stage in the genesis of the Indian revolution.

In 1930 a strange revolution began. In fulfillment of an earlier promise the Nationalist Congress authorized a campaign of nonviolent disobedience. After a conference with Gandhi its executive com- *The Uprising of 1930* mittee empowered him to launch the revolt when he deemed it expedient. Anticipating a violent uprising, the British rushed troop ships and began to concentrate soldiers.

The revolution opened March 12, 1930. On that day Gandhi began a pilgrimage of 170 miles afoot to the Gulf of Cambay, where he made salt from the sea in defiance of the governmental monopoly. British derision turned to alarm as Gandhi's example of civil disobedience caused a revolutionary wave to sweep the country. Throughout India his example was enthusiastically imitated. Nationalist committees were formed, attacks were made upon the governmental control of the liquor traffic, a boycott of British goods developed, and women renounced their traditional seclusion and joined the rebels. Police were embarrassed in their attempts to suppress a revolution characterized by the absence of violence. The arrest of Gandhi and other leaders failed to check the revolution, and by summer India was in a state of pandemonium.

England at first found herself at a loss to deal with this unusual revolution. The Nationalists, having rejected as inadequate the Simon report, with its meager promises of reform, boycotted the Round Table Conference in the autumn of 1930. Even the former stanch supporters of Great Britain, the native dynasts, flayed the character of British rule in India. Suffering heavily from the boycott and the unsettled conditions, certain British business interests urged their government to seek an early settlement of the serious problems.

The Indian Nationalists consistently refused to accept the compromise proposals of the British government. They demanded the cessation of martial law and the grant of full home rule. With affairs at an impasse Gandhi consented to go to England in the fall of 1931 to attend discussions of the problems and the future status of India. The conference failed to achieve any notable success, and the Nationalist leader returned home to promote the revolution. In the spring of 1932 passive resistance still continued, although marred by serious disorders which led to the imprisonment of Gandhi and many of his followers. Influenced by this opposition, England endeavored unsuccessfully to solve the Indian problem by catering to the selfish demands of the upper classes in India. Informed of British proposals to effect undemocratic changes in the electorate as a result of which millions of "untouchables," or outcastes, would be debarred from political life, Gandhi announced from his prison his intention of going on a hunger strike. After six days of fasting he abandoned his opposition when the British gave up the proposed plan. The revolutionary movement, however, did not abate.

A Chinese nationalist movement had likewise developed years before the World War. It was in a large measure the expression of an antiforeign sentiment which had frequently

manifested itself in sporadic outbursts against the Westerners and their civilization. Opposition to the aliens was engendered by the influence they exerted on China's political and economic life. Not only had the *The Far East: China*
Celestial Empire been deprived of many of her border provinces, vassal states, and ports, but she had also lost much of her economic independence. Most of her banks, mines, railways, steamship lines, ship yards, factories, and mills were controlled, directly or indirectly, by foreign interests. She was not free to modify her own tariffs, nor could she interfere in the treaty ports, foreign concessions, and international settlements which had been established on Chinese soil. By the practice of extraterritoriality, foreigners enjoyed the right to live under their own laws as administered by their nations' officials. Furthermore, although scorning political partition, the foreign powers had subdivided China into spheres of influence, which, despite the assurances of the open-door policy, afforded their traders a privileged position in the exploitation of the vast economic resources of the ancient empire.

Chinese patriots began to hold their decadent government responsible for the ills which beset them. Conjointly with the nationalist movement there developed a liberal movement among the intelligentsia, especially in the south. The innate corruption and weakness of the old imperial administration were painfully apparent. Unable to control the Chinese provinces, the government was forced to submit to the demands and inroads of the hated Westerners. Before it could recover national independence the Chinese nation needed to engage in a process of political rehabilitation and internal consolidation to which the imperial government seemed the greatest obstacle.

The political renascence of China began in 1911. In that year a dispute over railway concessions resulted in open warfare between the Peking government and
two rebellious provinces. The imperial armies *Civil War in China*
were defeated, and the civil war spread throughout southern China. On February 12, 1912, the last of the Manchu em-

perors was forced to abdicate, and the dynasty came to an inglorious end after two and one-half centuries of rule.

While the imperial government was being overturned by the revolutionists a republican movement was steadily gaining strength. Dr. Sun Yat-sen, an enlightened liberal who had been educated abroad, had become the leader of a party in Canton which desired the establishment of a democratic republic. A constitution was created, and, to win the support of moderates in other parts of China, Dr. Sun Yat-sen effaced himself and enabled Yuan Shih-k'ai, the last of the imperial prime ministers, to become president. Suspicious of the new executive, the liberals organized the Nationalist party known as the *Kuomintang*.

The ascendancy of Yuan Shih-k'ai was but an interlude in the political regeneration of China. A dictator at heart, he soon defied the Kuomintang and discarded the constitution. To bolster up his authority he now proceeded to grant privileges and concessions in order to gain the support of foreign bankers and diplomats. In 1913 he suspended parliament, exiled certain Kuomintang leaders, and apparently contemplated a restoration of the monarchy, with himself as emperor at Peking.

Representing young China, the Nationalists now organized a revolt against the Peking dictatorship. A provisional government under the leadership of Dr. Sun Yat-sen was established in 1913 at Canton. China was then thrown into tumult as the progressive elements supported the Kuomintang in its unsuccessful endeavors to resist the reactionary conservatism of Yuan Shih-k'ai.

While China was engaged in civil strife the World War broke out. The Japanese, joining the Allies in the fall of 1914, seized the German concessions in Shantung, *China during the World War* which they claimed as spoils of victory despite the Chinese contention that these rights were not transferable. The preoccupation of the Western states gave the Japanese a golden opportunity for further aggrandizement in China. In 1915 they presented to the Peking government a secret ultimatum which embraced twenty-one demands. The principal provisions included therein were (1) transfer of the province of Shantung to Japanese control; (2) extension to 1997 of the lease on the Liaotung Peninsula; (3) refusal of further concessions to other powers in Manchuria; (4) exclusion of powers other than Japan from securing territory on the Chinese coast; (5) exclusive use of Japanese capital in major developments in China; (6) monopolistic rights for Japanese citizens in railways, mines, industrial enterprises, and loans; (7) exclusive Japanese right to furnish China with military, political, or financial advisers; (8) control by Japanese of Chinese arms, arsenals, and munition factories; and (9) opening of all property and trade rights in China to Japanese nationals. The Japanese demands were tantamount to the establishment of a protectorate over China.

The publication of the "twenty-one demands" provoked an uproar throughout the world. Thereupon the Japanese shifted tactics; consenting to postpone indefinitely five of their demands, they forced China to accept the remaining sixteen by May, 1915. In 1916 Yuan Shih-k'ai, who was driven from power and died the same year, was followed by a line of weak presidents. The Japanese, now controlling the puppet rulers at Peking, signed secret agreements with Russia, Great Britain, France, and Italy. Inasmuch as these arrangements guaranteed her a free hand in northern China, she awaited the end of the conflict to claim her reward.

Before the conclusion of the war the American government had persuaded China to join the Allies. Participation on the victorious side was expected to raise Chinese prestige and improve China's international *China after the War* standing. These aims, however, were not fully realized. Both the official Peking and the revolutionary Cantonese government sent delegations to Versailles and demanded the recovery of Chinese independence, including tariff autonomy, abolition of spheres of influence and extraterritoriality, surrender of leased territories, and withdrawal of foreign troops. Denying its competency to deal with such matters, the Paris Peace Conference brushed aside the Chinese demands. Angered by this rebuff China refused to sign the Treaty of Versailles.

Though the peace conference failed to assist her, China's membership in the League of Nations seemed to strengthen her international position. A separate treaty with Germany provided for the cancellation of extraterritoriality, and in agreements with the new states of Europe no such concession was granted. A shock to Chinese hopes, however, came in April, 1919, with the award of former German rights in Shantung to Japan. In protest a violent antiforeign reaction resulted, and a Chinese national federation at Shanghai became a nucleus for a patriotic movement. A vigorous boycott of Japanese goods had adverse effects on Nipponese business in China. Scorning direct negotiations with Japan, the official Chinese delegates refused to sign the peace treaty. Later, however, at the Washington Conference on the limitations of armaments in 1921–1922, the Chinese gained several points: they secured from Japan the promise to restore Shantung to China,— a promise which Japan fulfilled by evacuating the province; China was permitted to increase her tariff rates and to assume greater control of the expenditure of the proceeds; and provision was made for the creation of two commissions to investigate the problems of extraterritoriality and tariff autonomy. At the conference the Nine-Power Pact, adhered to by Great Britain, France, Italy, Japan, the Netherlands, Belgium, China, Portugal, and the United States, guaranteed the sovereign independence and integrity of China as well as the *status quo* in the Far East.

After 1911 China, lacking a stable government, was torn with chronic civil wars. Rival factions (often subsidized by foreign interests) and selfish war lords struggled among themselves for mastery. After 1916 the tendency of the war lords to rule as independent sovereigns became more pronounced. In 1921, therefore, the Cantonese denounced the Peking government as illegal, declared their own the sole constitutional authority, and elected Sun Yat-sen as president.

Rise of the Cantonese Nationalists

The Cantonese Nationalists, planning to suppress the northern war lords and to terminate the foreign restrictions on Chinese sovereignty, undertook to extend their sway over all China. Assistance was secured from Soviet Russia, since the Bolsheviks were anxious to combat Western imperialism in Asia and to spread communist doctrines in China. Although Bolshevist activities produced frequent disorders in southern China, the communist ideas were not generally accepted. In 1925 the death of Sun Yat-sen and the succession to power of Chiang Kai-shek, who definitely repudiated communism, caused the capitalistic Western powers to look with favor on the Nationalist government.

By 1928 most of China was under the control of the Nationalists. Their northern advance in 1926 resulted in the capture of Hankow, and early in the following year they took Shanghai and Nanking. Peking was captured in June, 1928, and most of the war lords had been crushed or won over to the Nationalist cause. In August the League of Nations recognized the Nationalist as the *de jure* government.

The triumph of the new administration saw the breakdown of many foreign restrictions. It was accompanied by anti-foreign movements and some looting and violence. Alien warships and troops were called upon to protect their nationals and property, especially in 1927, when Shanghai fell. The spheres of influence in the vast interior of China, however, were partially obliterated. In July, 1928, the Nationalists denounced unequal treaties and announced that they would be abrogated upon expiration. Imitating the example of the United States, the powers entered into agreements which restored Chinese tariff autonomy during 1928. A revised national tariff went into effect early in 1929, which raised the basic rate from 5 per cent to 12½ per cent. The introduction of a new criminal code in September, 1928, presaged the end of extraterritoriality. Upon Chinese requests certain states abandoned their rights of extraterritoriality, but the majority of the great powers refused to relinquish these special privileges.

Among the most serious problems confronting the new government was that of national consolidation. Although foreign restrictions had been reduced, they were by no means abolished. To establish a policy of financial self-sufficiency and escape foreign entanglements, a National Bank of China was created, with the minister of finance as director-general. The policy of national unification and democracy soon aroused the hostility of independent militarists in the provinces. Fearing to lose their freedom of action, these war lords became restless as President Chiang Kai-shek built up an enormous federal army and continued his policy of nationalizing and unifying China.

In the late spring of 1929 the authority of Chiang Kai-shek and the republican government at Nanking was seriously challenged. Revolts occurred in Shantung, southern China, and the western provinces. The Kuomintang extremists, sympathetic toward communism, withdrew their support from the Nanking régime because of its coolness toward Soviet Russia. General Feng Yu-hsiang, a former National-ist leader, then precipitated a civil war by repudiating the government. Epidemics of banditry reduced large sections of the country to anarchy. The Nanking régime seemed to be crumbling.

Complications in Manchuria soon threatened to involve China in a foreign war. The decision of its governor, Chang Hsueh-liang, to bring the three Manchurian provinces into the Nanking federation met with latent Japanese hostility. A war with Russia nearly broke out in 1929, when the gover-nor attempted to seize the Chinese Eastern Railway, owned and operated jointly by China and Russia. The Manchurian forces were defeated, however, and the crisis was passed with-out recourse to war.

China was confronted by more civil strife in 1930–1931. The Cantonese radicals, opposed to the president's moderate policies, accused him of being too autocratic and of attempt-ing to curry favor with capitalist powers. Accordingly they denounced the Nanking government, set up a new one at Canton, and embarked on another civil war. Such was the situation by the summer of 1931. At this time China found herself afflicted with two new ills: devastating floods, which brought death, famine, and disease; and Japanese aggression in Manchuria, which threatened to disrupt the whole republic.

The economic situation in Japan was conducive to a policy of continental expansion. A prolonged depression, which had begun in 1921, had subjected the capitalistic system to severe strain. Unemployment be- *Japanese Aggression in* came serious, and there was great discontent *Manchuria* in the rural districts. A subsequent decline in the prices of silk and rice further contributed to already unsatisfactory conditions. By 1931 the economic blight which had swept the world resulted in a decline of Japanese markets and a sharp reduction of both exports and imports. As the suffering in Japan became intense, expansion seemed imperative. Therefore the Japanese decided to exploit the mineral and other resources of Manchuria and to utilize it as an outlet for surplus goods and population. Another motive caused the " Land of the Rising Sun " to extend its interests into Manchuria : the determination to check the possible advance of the Bolsheviks in China by establishing a buffer outpost.

Manchuria was a land of great potentialities. With an area of 382,000 square miles, divided into three provinces by the Chinese for administrative purposes, this region had a population of some 30,000,000, of whom about 96 per cent were Chinese. It was chiefly an agricultural country, the principal crops being soya beans, kaoliang, wheat, millet, cotton, and sugar beets. Characterized as "the milk and meat of Far-Eastern peoples," the soya bean was the food item of second importance in China, Japan, and Korea. The economic life of Manchuria hinged largely on this bean. Numerous varieties were produced, being utilized in the form of oils, lard, pastes, sauces, beverages, flour, and bean curds. Approximately 40 per cent was exported to Japan, of whose total imports it constituted 3 per cent. The fact that Manchuria could support a much larger population had resulted in heavy immigration from China, especially after 1918, as the region afforded the Chinese peasant the chief escape from the civil wars and crowded conditions of China proper.

Excepting the Shanghai area, Manchuria was the most highly industrialized section of China. It possessed abundant resources of coal and iron, estimated at 1,500,000,000 and 700,000,000 metric tons respectively. Transportation was facilitated by a network of rivers, which drained the country and at the intersections of which thriving cities had developed. In addition to these natural advantages 3700 miles of railway had been built, chiefly with Chinese, Russian, and Japanese capital.

Extensive Japanese interests had long existed in Manchuria, and consisted chiefly in the ownership of coal and iron mines and railways (especially the South Manchurian), the Kwantung leased area, and the presence of over a million Japanese nationals in Manchuria, of whom some 80 per cent were Koreans. According to the Nipponese government incessant civil strife in Manchuria had menaced Japanese lives and property there. That fact, together with the desires of Japanese imperialists to control the food supplies, timber, and mineral resources, and in general to exploit the economic life of this region, largely accounted for the Japanese thrust of 1931.

In the fall of 1931 an opportunity arose for the Nipponese to extend their interest in China. At that time the Nanking government was distressed by civil war, floods, and famines, and the western states were preoccupied with domestic problems resulting from the world economic depression after 1929. At all events the Japanese, directed by the military clique in Tokyo, found suitable pretexts for entering, and began the conquest of Manchuria on September 18, 1931. By January, 1932, the whole country, including the Russian sphere, was in the hands of the invaders.

The seizure of Manchuria produced a serious crisis in the Far East. Accusing Japan of unjustifiable aggression and violation of treaty obligations, the Nanking government appealed to the League of Nations. The Japanese, however, proclaimed the disinterestedness of their policies and contended that their invasion of Manchuria was actuated by the desire to protect the lives and property of Japanese and Koreans there. Thereupon, in default of tangible assistance from the League, the Chinese resorted to their most effective instrument in dealing with foreign powers,— the economic boycott.

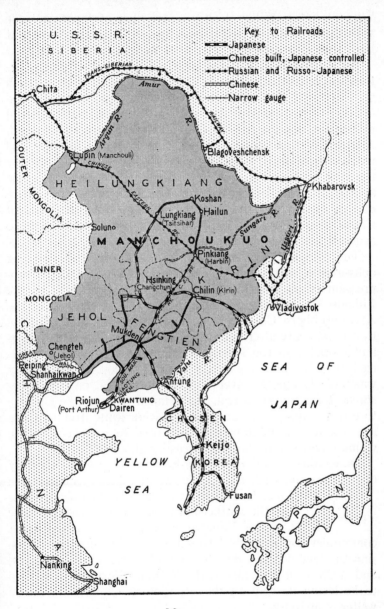

MANCHOUKUO

This retaliatory policy dealt a severe blow at Japanese trade with the republic. The Japanese in China began to feel that both their property and their lives were in danger.

Although China had not declared war, her economic retaliation had an adverse effect on conditions in Japan. Such ills as resulted from the depression and unemployment were aggravated, and financial difficulties soon forced the island empire off the gold standard. Alarmed at the trend of events, leaders of the military and naval cliques urged a "strong policy" in China. Accordingly the civil government, bowing to their will, consented to the attack on Shanghai. It was widely believed that the seizure of this metropolis, the commercial and industrial heart of China, would force the latter to abandon the boycott and to acquiesce in the loss of Manchuria.

The Shanghai Gesture

The conquest of Shanghai proved no easy task. Having delivered an ultimatum demanding an apology and the suppression of all anti-Japanese movements, the forces of the Mikado, on January 28, 1932, began the investment of the city. Stubborn Chinese resistance so delayed their progress that it was only after many weeks, during which foreign lives and property in the International Settlement were jeopardized, that the Japanese finally took Shanghai. Their victory was a costly one, however; for not only did it provoke widespread foreign disapproval, but it failed to bring the Chinese to terms. Apparently desirous of withdrawing from so fruitless a venture, the Japanese consented to a truce with the Chinese and withdrew their forces by June, 1932.

Dangerous tension in the Far East was created by the fury of Japanese imperialism. The future of China was uncertain; menaced with political disintegration, some of the southern provinces, and especially those in the Yangtze valley, set up independent communist governments. To many, a Red China under Russian tutelage was not remote. Torn by civil strife, banditry, and antiforeign movements, the Nanking government seemed to be losing its grip on the situation as China sank into a welter of anarchy.

International Crisis in the Far East

Regardless of revolutionary disturbances in the East the great powers displayed little readiness to abandon their stakes in China. Economic exploitation remained the underlying factor in the relations between the imperialistic states and the newly founded republic, whose vast population and resources made her the largest potential market for the surplus capital and goods of the expanding capitalistic states. In 1931–1932 estimates showed that although aliens residing in China numbered less than half a million, foreign investments totaled over $4,000,000,000. Great Britain and Japan were credited with interests of approximately $1,250,000,000 each; those of the United States and Soviet Russia totaled between $250,000,000 and $300,000,000 each; and France, Germany, Italy, the Netherlands, and Belgium had considerable, though lesser, stakes.

In the decade following the World War, American interests in the Far East expanded rapidly. Trade between the United States and China grew by leaps and bounds; whereas in 1913 the total value of exports and imports between these states amounted to only about $53,650,000, in the year 1928 it totaled nearly $230,000,000. The same period witnessed an influx of American publications, cinemas, automobiles, and schools. Missionary activities of the Americans increased to a considerable extent.

Despite these advances the United States, scorning territorial acquisitions and concessions, advocated the maintenance of the open-door policy and the preservation of China's territorial integrity. By adhering to this traditional foreign policy the United States continued her attempts to keep the great Asiatic nation open to American interests, to prevent the disintegration of China, and to check the establishment of economic monopolies by rival states.

The Sino-Japanese crisis in 1932 had an unfortunate effect on international relations in the Far East. In the Shanghai and Manchurian crises Japan threatened the *status quo*. The United States, Soviet Russia, *Japan in Manchuria* Great Britain, and the Pacific dominions, fearful lest decisive action provoke a world war, avoided undue interference.

From the United States came the most persistent challenge to Japanese aggressions. Asserting that the doctrine of neutrality was no longer tenable, Secretary of State Henry M. Stimson attempted to provide "teeth" for the Kellogg-Briand Pact by declaring that any war was the concern of all powers. Reiterating a policy of nonrecognition toward all modifications of the *status quo* effected by force, he said that the moral opinion of the world should be aroused against aggressor states. The so-called Hoover-Stimson doctrine provoked great indignation in Japan, against whom it was apparently aimed. Foreign Minister Uchida, denouncing the meddling of Western powers, asserted that such international commitments as the Nine-Power Treaty, the Pact of Paris, and the League Covenant were not applicable to the kaleidoscopic politics of the Orient. Therefore, in defiance of world opinion, he granted recognition to Manchoukuo in September, 1932. This Japanese puppet state in Manchuria had been organized in the preceding March under the nominal rule of Henry Pu Yi, last of the Chinese emperors.

During the winter of 1932–1933 the Japanese endeavored to complete the organization and pacification of the new régime which they had set up in Manchuria. For many months Chinese irregulars and bandits had thwarted the attempts of the intruders to reëstablish order, but by the middle of January, 1933, the country was practically cleared of the insurrectionists. By this time the forces of the Mikado had already begun the subjugation of Jehol, a Chinese province lying within the Great Wall, which they claimed was part of Manchoukuo. In March the entire province was in the hands of the invaders, and in the spring of 1933 continued hostilities resulted in a Japanese drive toward Tientsin and Peiping. Unable to check the Nipponese advance the Nanking government on May 31 signed a formal truce at Tangku. This armistice provided for a withdrawal of the military forces of both powers from the area bounded by the Great Wall, the Peiping-Mukden railway, and the Peiping-Suiyuan railway; the dissolution of Chinese irregulars; and the initiation of peace measures. While negotiations were in progress the

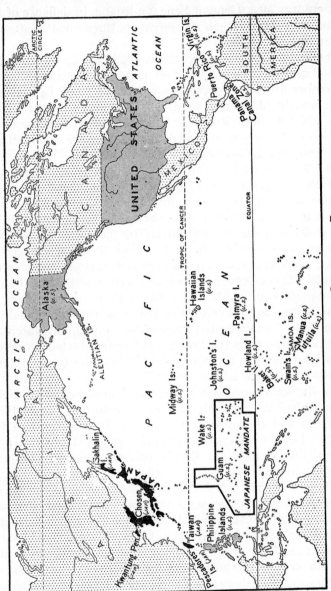

THE UNITED STATES AND JAPAN IN THE PACIFIC

Chinese war lord, General Feng Yu-hsiang, in defiance of the Nanking authorities and the Japanese, threatened to attempt the reconquest of Jehol.

While the war clouds were darkening in the East the League of Nations was hoping to effect a peaceful settlement. On December 10, 1931, a commission under Lord Lytton had been sent to Manchuria to study conditions there. Its findings, which in the fall of 1932 had been referred to the Commission of Nineteen, furnished the basis for the report of the latter which was adopted by the League on February 24, 1933. Reiterating its faith in the Kellogg-Briand Pact, the Nine-Power Treaty, and the obligations incumbent on a League member, the report invited the United States and Russia to concur in a policy of nonrecognition of Manchoukuo and insisted upon the withdrawal of the Japanese to their position of September 18, 1931 (before their alleged aggressions), the creation of an autonomous régime under international supervision in Manchuria, and a settlement of the Sino-Japanese difficulties in collaboration with the League. Offended by the League's active policy in having branded her as guilty of "unwarranted aggression," Japan, on March 27, 1933, withdrew from the League, and again asserted her determination to pursue an independent policy and to maintain a "Monroe Doctrine of the Orient."

By the spring of 1933 Japan was threatened with diplomatic isolation. Not only did she have to face the hostility of China and the opposition of the United States and the League, but she also had to struggle against the increasingly unfavorable attitude of Russia and the western-European powers. Nonaggression pacts signed by Russia with France and Poland during the winter somewhat reassured the Soviet government as to the security of its western frontier and stiffened its attitude toward Japan in the Far East. A Russo-Chinese entente on December 12 occasioned considerable alarm in the East, many regarding it as the prelude to a military alliance for the purpose of thrusting back the Japanese. A serious dispute between Russia and Manchoukuo, backed by Japan, over the control and operation of the Chinese Eastern Railway nearly embroiled the states in war.

Japan's break with the League gave rise to a number of complicated problems. One of these concerned the disposition of the former German islands of the Pacific which Japan held as a mandate. Because of the strategic importance of these islands, which numbered some 1600 spread out over an area of about 100,000 square miles in the western Pacific, Japan, despite her withdrawal from the League, was loath to relinquish them to their legal trustee. Even the menace of League sanctions in the form of an arms embargo, boycott, or military intervention did not suffice to deter the Japanese leaders from their policies.

American prestige in the Pacific showed signs of waning as the United States began to return to a policy of isolation. Because she neglected to fortify her Pacific islands (prohibited by the Washington treaties), and failed to build the navy up to the treaty limits established at London in 1930, American interests in the Pacific and in the Far East were jeopardized. On January 17, 1933, the United States showed a tendency to recede from Eastern politics when Congress passed the Hawes-Cutting bill over the veto of President Hoover. This act provided for ultimate Philippine independence, which, with certain restrictions, was to be accomplished by stages. Within two years the Philippines were expected to prepare a constitution, which, subject to the approval of the Philippine people and the American Congress, was to go into operation. The Philippine legislature, however, rejected this half measure of freedom and demanded full independence. Partially in response to this request the American government in March, 1934, passed the McDuffie-Tydings bill. This act, although very similar to the Hawes-Cutting bill, by the grant of additional concessions such as the agreement to abandon all American military posts in the islands upon their attainment of freedom, proved more acceptable to native leaders. Apparently the way had been paved for the rise of an independent nation in the turbulent Far East.

Thus the revolt of Asia continued. The Orient was in a state of flux. It was agitated from without and within: from without by avaricious Westernizing forces, imperialistic in desire and often brutally shortsighted, which caused the Asiatic nations to flare up with hatred and fear; from within it seethed as the coals of civil war, rebellion, communism, and anarchy fed the flames of that desire which actuated all peoples — the determination of their own national destiny, political, social, and economic. Indeed, the fate of Asia hung in the balance.

The MANCHURIAN CRISIS

From a cartoon in the *Glasgow Evening Times*

CHAPTER XL

The Twentieth Century: Culmination of the Bourgeois Order?

T HE World War had no victors. Fought "to make the world safe for democracy," it made it *unsafe*: disaster, not democracy, seemed to be the bitter spoils of the smallest as well as of the greatest nation.

Capitalism received a terrific assault, from which, say its opponents, it may never recover. Blow after blow struck against its armor,— armor forged by a century of economic experiment, hardened by decades of political pressure, battered by years of social strife,— and now at last it threatened to crack beneath the impact of discontent and dissatisfaction. Would its integral weaknesses be exposed? Would it become vulnerable to radical attack? Was this to be the culmination of the bourgeois order?

For the inherent defects of capitalism were truly brought out with grim reality after four years of war. Traditional trends in business, science, arts, and other activities were changed or diverted. Conventions, standards, and traditions were altered or discarded. The bubbles of idealism and patriotism had burst in the trenches of No Man's Land. A new age had dawned,— an age of skepticism, iconoclasm, and hard-headed realism.

With industries hopelessly dislocated and disorganized by war demands, with tremendous losses of man power and property, and with enormous inflation of finan- *Post-war Governmental* cial systems, the world in 1918 was indeed in *Policies* a lamentable state. After the war, governments did little to improve conditions; in fact, in many instances they made them worse. Selfish interests dictated policies harmful to public and political improvement. High protective tariffs, burdensome armaments, imperialistic designs, the tangle of reparations and war debts, inflation and depreciated currencies, and unrestricted play of big business groups,— all these were conspicuous in post-war history.

Instead of stimulating international trade and business, states tended, after the war, to throttle it by the erection of high tariff barriers for the protection of home *Erection of High Tariff Walls* products. This policy, in which the United States assumed undisputed leadership, had a dual effect. In the United States, although by favoring certain industries the tariff supposedly increased wages and the standard of living of the people as a whole, in reality it had the effect of raising commodity prices even with respect to increased earnings; in other words, a few privileged individuals in the state were favored at the expense of the rest. Abroad the high protective policy had even more disastrous results. Many nations, such as Great Britain, France, Italy, and Canada, faced with an ever-decreasing gold reserve and a declining export trade, were forced to retaliate by building up tariff walls of their own. Only the largest of American industrialists were able to nullify the effects of retaliation; they did this by erecting factories in foreign lands.

Another financial phase of post-war governmental policies was the problem of reparations and war debts. The near-collapse of Germany's economic life in 1932, *Reparations and War Debts* partially as a result of reparation payments, led to the grant of the Hoover moratorium, which suspended all intergovernmental payments for one year ending June 30, 1932. Nevertheless Germany, faced with bankruptcy and still resenting the thesis of German war guilt, decided to break the chains of her financial bondage. Accordingly she repudiated the Young Plan and declared her intentions of withholding further reparation payments.[1] The other European nations, confronted with the collapse of some of the most important provisions of the Treaty of Versailles, held a conference at Lausanne in June, 1932, to thrash out the debt problem. There they made a provisional agree-

[1] See above, p. 692.

ment to cancel reparation obligations, in lieu of which Germany was to pay a lump sum of $714,500,000 for the reconstruction of Europe. This settlement was contingent upon a so-called "gentlemen's agreement," whereby Great Britain, Italy, and other countries undertook to get the United States to lower war debts in proportion to the reduction of reparation payments.

A movement for the cancellation of European debts to the United States paralleled the reparation negotiations. After the end of the war the indebted Allied countries were aiming at a complete release from their obligations. They appealed to the United States on the ground that their losses in man power more than offset the latter's financial outlay and that economic conditions did not warrant Europe's paying her war debts when Germany was failing to conform to the reparation settlement. The United States refused to cancel the war debts, chiefly on two grounds: first, because she did not see why the American taxpayers should bear the brunt of the war losses; and, second, because she had no desire to finance the European nations in their expensive projects of maintaining powerful armies and navies.

The American government, however, did agree to ease Europe's financial burdens. Arrangements were concluded in 1925 and 1926 whereby most of the governments funded their debts to the United States, payments being spread out over a longer number of years. Thus, although future generations were "generously" inflicted with a portion of the war cost, European countries, because of the fall of interest rates, got off rather cheaply. Nevertheless persistent refusal by the American government to annul war debts won for it the enmity of France, England, Italy, and the other debtor nations; all looked upon the United States as an Uncle Shylock who was determined to exact his pound of flesh.

A new impetus was given to the cancellationist agitation by the world crisis (1929–   ). As already mentioned, President Hoover, in 1931, proclaimed a one-year moratorium of all intergovernmental obligations. The reparation settlement concluded at Lausanne in June, 1932, was, as stated above, dependent upon the success of the "League of Debtors" in negotiating for a reduction or cancellation of the obligations to the United States. America's debtors were prepared, therefore, to reopen this question; but tacitly, so as not to embarrass the American administration, they agreed to let the matter slide until after the presidential campaign of 1932. Shortly after the overwhelming victory of the Democrats at the polls on November 8, Great Britain, France, Belgium, Poland, and other minor powers requested the United States to suspend the payments due on December 15, probably as a prelude to complete cancellation.

By 1932, of over $10,000,000,000 lent to European powers, less than one third had been repaid. Nevertheless certain American financial interests, to safeguard their investments, would have welcomed a settlement of the debt question, even by cancellation. Backed by a strong public opinion, the American government, however, insisted upon the payments without reservation. The complete discarding of the war debts at this time, it was said, would have placed upon the United States a relatively large portion of the total cost of the war.

Great Britain reluctantly agreed to pay the installment, but desired that her remittance be treated as "a capital payment of which account should be taken in a final settlement." Italy, Finland, Czechoslovakia, Lithuania, and Latvia followed England's example. France, Belgium, Poland, Hungary, and Estonia, however, defaulted. On June 15, 1933, another payment on the war debts fell due. Great Britain this time paid $10,000,000, or about 8 per cent of her obligation, "as an acknowledgment of the debt pending a final settlement." Italy, Czechoslovakia, Rumania, Latvia, and Lithuania followed suit with token payments. The other debtors, however, defaulted with the exception of Finland, who alone met her payment.

On June 12, 1933, the World Monetary and Economic Conference convened in the new Geological Museum at London. The delegates, numbering one hundred and sixty-eight, from sixty-six countries, were welcomed by King George V and by Prime Minister MacDonald. Almost every known economic creed and fad seemed to be represented; but the outstanding problems which pervaded the assembly concerned the stabilization of currencies, the return to the gold standard, the reduction of tariffs and other trade barriers, the raising of world commodity prices, and the settlement of intergovernmental debts. Although all nations desired a revival of international trade and business, there was, from the first, bitter disagreement as to the soundest method of attaining such ends. France, Germany, and certain other states — the so-called "Gold Bloc" — insisted on the immediate stabilization of currencies, especially the pound and the dollar, and an early return to the gold standard. The United States and, to a lesser extent, Great Britain — whose position was not well defined, however — preferred to begin with the raising of prices and the reduction of trade barriers. As every country, primarily intent upon its particular welfare, pursued a policy of economic nationalism, affairs quickly reached an impasse, especially when the United States refused to agree to stabilize her currency until the policy of domestic inflation had been successfully carried out. Consequently, instead of promoting international solidarity, the conference had the reverse effect of portraying in bold relief the political animosities and economic antagonisms of the participating states. Although the conference dragged on for six weeks, it was in a spirit of disillusionment that the assembly was adjourned indefinitely on July 27, 1933. Positive achievements in the direction of economic recovery had escaped the highly nationalistic diplomats, and the nations of the world found themselves confronted with the prospect of an international trade war.

Unwilling to meet their comparatively small debts, the European states nevertheless found it expedient, because of national and imperial rivalries, to expend billions on armaments. In 1931 Italy spent *Militarism and Disarmament* 25 per cent of her annual budget on military, naval, and air forces; France, 22 per cent; and Great Britain, almost 14 per cent. The total yearly expenditure for war preparations was over $4,000,000,000. Europe was indeed, even more than in 1914, an armed camp.

Fear lest the maintenance of overburdening armaments should lead to war or financial insolvency caused many nations to look with favor upon proposals for disarmament. By the peace of Paris in 1919 the defeated powers had been compelled to disarm, and the victors obligated to do so. Under League leadership numerous conferences were held for the purpose of curtailing the military and air forces of the great powers. All were unsuccessful; at the one which met at Geneva in 1932–1933 France and her satellites rejected practical plans for disarmament except in exchange for additional security pacts.

Elimination of unrestricted naval competition, however, was effected by the major powers. At the Washington Conference of 1921–1922 the great naval states entered into a five-power treaty in which Great Britain, the United States, and Japan accepted, respectively, a 5–5–3 ratio for capital ships, and France and Italy agreed to a 1.67 ratio. Construction of aircraft carriers was also limited, but attempts to restrict the building of cruisers, submarines, and destroyers failed. The Washington Conference succeeded, however, in allaying suspicions and in reducing naval competition.

To effect a certain amount of real naval disarmament, subsequent conferences were held. One was planned for Geneva in 1927, but failed miserably when France and Italy refused to attend and the United States and Great Britain could not adjust their differences. In 1930 a conference at London achieved a slight degree of success. Great Britain and Japan agreed to reduce the tonnage of their cruisers, destroyers, and submarines, and, with the United States, decided to scrap certain battleships which were obsolete anyway. France and Italy, however, failed to adhere to the London agreement, largely because Great Britain refused to guarantee French security and France was unwilling to accord Italy naval parity. An American weekly aptly summed up the importance of this meeting when it stated: "As a whole it may be said that the mountain labored at London and brought forth a mouse. A mouse is something, but nothing more than a mouse." The attempts in 1933 to bring about disarmament again proved ineffectual. The opposition of France to military disarmament without security, the determination of Japan to build a navy as large as that of Great Britain and of the United States, and the latter's decision to build her fleet up to the treaty limits,— all these factors indicated the failure of the conference.

In May, 1933, a war scare, caused by Germany's threat to rearm, jeopardized the success of the disarmament conference at Geneva. On May 16 the President of the United States appealed to the nations of the world, asking them to disarm partially, to abstain from aggressive war, and to coöperate in a peaceful solution of the world's economic dilemma. The refusal of the states, however, to grant Germany arms equality culminated in her withdrawal from the conference on October 14. Five days later she resigned from the League. The impasse between Germany and the powers created a real danger of war.

One reason for the failure of the victorious powers to effect a general disarmament was the continuance, after the war, of imperialist policies. The industrial nations of the world did not throw imperial designs and ambitions into the junk pile of pre-war anachronisms. Japan, in 1932, "defended itself against Chinese aggression" by setting up a puppet state in Manchuria. Great Britain continued to hold India in subjection despite vigorous nationalist strivings. The United States still retained the Philippines, persisted in her "dollar diplomacy" in the Caribbean, and competed with England for the profitable South American markets. France held on to her enormous and expensive colonial empire and engaged in a vigorous rivalry with Italy for the control of the Mediterranean. Finally Japan, the United States, and to a lesser extent Great Britain and France, had yet to settle a long-standing dispute for the dominion of the Pacific. Indeed, imperialism was still rife.

After the World War, political ferment challenged, often successfully, the existence of governments in some of the

Persistence of Imperialism

industrially undeveloped countries. Most conspicuous was the overthrow, in 1931, of the Spanish monarchy and the *Bourgeois Movements* establishment of the youngest republic in Eu-*in Nonindustrial Na-* rope. Despite the enlightened dictatorships of *tions* Miguel Primo de Rivera and General Berenguer, which lasted from 1923 to 1931, the decadent Spanish monarchy fell. This collapse was caused by such factors as economic backwardness, an adverse trade balance, growing radicalism among the lower classes, the development of regionalism, or separatism, in the provinces (especially Catalonia), the interference of the military authorities in politics, and difficulties in Morocco. Under the leadership of Zamora, the new president, a movement was initiated to destroy all the vestiges of the old régime and to establish an enlightened, liberal middle-class order. Education was secularized, the church was deprived of its holdings and was subordinated to the state, the army was reorganized so as to give more opportunity to the "common man," and economic reforms were realized. Also, by a special Catalan Statute of Autonomy (1932), Catalonia was permitted to maintain a separate administration, with its own flag, anthem, language, and officials. Other provinces clamored for similar privileges. This presaged an ultimate federation of states rather than a centralized Spanish republic.

The spirit of revolution was also rampant in many Hispanic-American countries. Boundary disputes resulted in armed aggression in the Gran Chaco, between Bolivia and Paraguay, and at Leticia, between Colombia and Peru; civil strife arising out of social and economic unrest occurred in Argentina, Cuba, Chile, Brazil, and many other countries. At the same time most of Asia, especially India and China, seethed with nationalist discontent.

Economic conditions were not greatly improved in Europe after 1918. Some pretense was made at recovery; but, on the whole, economic depression continued. Millions of men and women were unemployed, industry and trade almost collapsed, and monetary systems were completely disorganized. By 1929 certain nations, notably Germany, dependent on borrowed capital, suffered severely as the United States ceased to make loans and began to absorb gold and short-term credits. At about the same time France, determined to prevent a proposed economic union between Austria and Germany, decided to weaken the financial structure of these countries by drawing in gold. England and other states were subsequently forced off the gold standard. Bankruptcy and revolution, it was said, were narrowly averted in many European countries.

The United States, youngest and strongest of the great capitalistic powers, was the last to succumb to the disaster of an economic crisis.[1] In 1929 came "the time-honored signal of approaching depression," namely, "a tightening of money and investment rates." Credit was restricted, and business activity *The World Economic Crisis (1929–)* slowed down almost to a standstill. Widespread unemployment resulted, conservative estimates placing the number of men and women seeking jobs in 1930 at 6,000,000, and in 1933 at 13,000,000. Bread lines were longer than ever before as men from all walks of life faced starvation. In many cases farmers found themselves unable to pay their bills or to meet the interest on their mortgages, merchants were unable to satisfy their obligations to the banks, investors received reduced dividends, and bond coupons were not paid. The wheels of industry ran slowly and the business machine functioned poorly. In March, 1933, economic conditions became so critical that President Roosevelt proclaimed a national "bank holiday," whereby all banking operations were suspended pending the enactment of financial legislation by Congress. So tense was the situation that the assumption of war-time powers by the President seemed imminent.

This depression was no usual crisis. It was world-wide. Unprecedented was its severity, and unexampled its length. It was "characterized by other than the usual cyclical features."

[1] In discussing the problems confronting the bourgeois nations after the World War this chapter tends to emphasize the United States. Inasmuch as that country was the leading defender of the bourgeois system, which, as we have seen, had its origin in Europe, this emphasis, it is believed, is justifiable.

In the past, depressions were followed by prosperity on a larger scale, because of undeveloped forces within capitalism — the expansion of home and foreign markets and the growth of new industries. In the United States the undeveloped lands out west were an additional stimulus to expansion. But these lands are no more, there are no new industries in sight, home markets are saturated, and the competition for foreign markets is enormously aggravated.

What brought about this economic debacle? A more debatable question could not be asked. Economists, politicians, teachers, ministers, all had their pet theories. Contained therein were explanations for all depressions, past, present, and future. Lack of economic planning, individual control and direction of industry chiefly for profit incentives, high tariff walls, the inability of the central banks to coöperate in making the world's gold supply more productive, insufficient flexibility in the banking system, the maintenance of crushing armaments, the establishment of impossible reparation payments, the virtual refusal of the former Allied countries to pay war debts, disorganization wrought by the World War, and, finally, capitalism itself,— all were advanced at one time or another as the real reasons for the depression. Which ones were most pertinent was difficult to say; probably all played a smaller or a larger share in "the many known chains of influences to bring on a business slump."

The inauguration, on March 4, 1933, of Franklin Delano Roosevelt as the president of the United States, with a Democratic administration, ushered in a new era in this post-war problem. Laying the foundations of a "planned society" in the United States through governmental programs of reforestation, public works, agricultural relief, financial legislation, and governmental supervision of business and commerce, he endeavored to fulfill his campaign pledge of a "new deal." With the passage of the Farm Relief Act (the F.R.A.) the administration instituted its program of raising agricultural prices by regulating or limiting production. Industry and commerce were to be revived by means of a National Industrial Recovery Act (the N.I.R.A.). This bill provided for an emergency program aimed at the elimination of destructive competition, improved working conditions, and a fair living wage. To achieve these ends the government inaugurated public-works projects and offered to coöperate with business. Industrial codes were drawn up by various groups, such as the steel, textile, and oil industries, and were submitted to the government. When the administration approved of the proposed schedules of working hours and wages, the codes were to be adopted by all concerns within given groups. Meanwhile, pending the approval of the codes, the National Recovery Administration (the N. R. A.) attempted to obtain a nation-wide blanket agreement to shorten hours and to raise wages, and thereby to increase the amount of money in circulation and the corresponding purchasing power of the American people. "Controlled capitalism" instead of "rugged individualism," many believed, had become the order of the day.

As a phase of this attempt to create and diffuse prosperity President Roosevelt had been willing to consider war-debt readjustments and tariff reductions in exchange for economic concessions from foreign powers. To prepare the way for the World Economic Conference at London, he invited delegates from Great Britain, France, Italy, Japan, Germany, China, and other leading powers to confer with him at Washington. On April 19, the eve of these conversations, the United States, in order to boost domestic prices and to avoid the disadvantage of competing against rivals with depreciated currencies, abandoned the gold standard. This action led to an immediate fall in the value of the dollar on the foreign exchanges, and left France, Germany, Italy, Switzerland, Holland, and Belgium as the "gold nations." During April and May, 1933, Roosevelt discussed with MacDonald, Herriot, and other notables such matters as tariffs, monetary stabilization, war debts, world prices, bank policies, the status of silver, trade discriminations, and unemployment.

Out of the economic depression arose social and political criticism of the established order. Present at the opening of the twentieth century, attacks gained momentum after the upheaval of 1914–1918 and were in full swing during the lean years of 1929–1933. Subjected to increasing and sharper scrutiny were the economy, politics, culture, and morality of the bourgeois state. The middle-class order, however, although somewhat altered to meet new demands and conditions, managed to survive this scorching examination and cross-examination of its predominating philosophies.

Growth of Discontent

Attacked by both radical and bourgeois elements was the economic organization of society. Socialists and communists blamed capitalism for all the existing economic evils, and particularly condemned in that system private property, the inequitable distribution of wealth, the running of industry and distribution for private profit, the exploitation of wage-earners by employers, and the lack of a well-ordered economic plan for the benefit of society as a whole. As discussed in a previous chapter,[1] they proposed a new order based upon social control of the means of production, distribution, and exchange, — a system which in their opinion would rest upon the principles of human justice.

Criticism of Bourgeois Economy

Severe, too, in the widespread disapprobation were certain bourgeois intellectuals. But they, unlike the radicals, did not attack the very system of capitalism; they only "observed" its inherent contradictions and its apparent decline. Thus, Dr. Harry Fosdick declared:

Our whole capitalistic society is on trial, for obviously there is something the matter with the operation of a system that over the world leaves millions upon millions of people out of work who want work, and millions in the sinister shade of poverty.

Professor James Harvey Rogers wrote in a more ominous vein:

Thus while the human caterpillars go round and round, the golden spiral winds ever higher and tighter its rapidly encircling coils. The dying gasps of capitalism in the constrictor's grasp can all but be heard by one of the world's leading bankers [Montague Norman], while its most renowned dramatist [Bernard Shaw] plumed and

[1] See Chapter XVI.

painted, awaits the dance at the funeral pyre. Just as each major expansion period is a new era, so is each violent and prolonged depression the end of our modern industrial civilization.[1]

Moreover, Professors Frank W. Taussig and Carl S. Joslyn declared, with apparent substantiation, that "business leadership is in the hands of a caste, selected by birth and connections." Pope Pius XI (1922–   ), in his encyclicals, criticized the prevailing economic individualism and declared that cooperation between capital and labor was vital if the existing order was to survive.

Another evidence of unrest manifested itself in 1932. A group of American engineers and scientists, termed *Technocrats*, disclosed findings which were supposedly the result of twelve years of research. Asserting that machinery was responsible for the increase of unemployment, they proposed a drastic cut in the hours of labor, the abolition of the price system, and the establishment of an economy based on units of energy instead of money.

Onslaughts upon the political order were decidedly pronounced. By 1933 the principle of democracy itself was under fire. In Italy, Poland, Yugoslavia, Russia, Turkey, and Germany there were unconcealed dictators. In other countries dictatorial governments were concealed by democratic labels. Woodrow Wilson's ideal of "making the world safe for democracy" had not been realized. In the opinion of many, democracy, which offered numerous opportunities for demagogy, was the underlying cause for the sorry state of the world's affairs. Too often, these critics asserted, incompetent politicians surrendered to the whims and prejudices of the multitude, or to selfish interests, instead of heeding the judgment of competent experts. In France a publicist denounced democracy as "the cult of the incompetent." In Italy, Mussolini declared:

Criticism of Bourgeois Democracy

When the sheep lead the shepherd, when the soldiers of an army can conduct a campaign better than an experienced and technically trained general, when the sailors can command a battleship in action, then democracy will be accepted as an efficient form of government.

[1] Rogers, *America Weighs her Gold*, p. 125.

Disturbing indeed were the prophecies concerning existing society expounded in certain post-war literature. The German writer Oswald Spengler, in his *Decline of the West,* ushered in a "new pessimism." Arguing from historical analogy, he maintained in this work that Western civilization had reached its apex and was beginning to descend. Charles A. Beard, in his preface to *Whither Mankind?* reiterated Spengler's theme when he asked whether civilization was still rising to a zenith or had already begun to crumble into ruin.

Criticism of the order of things was not limited to economics and politics. Science, religion, and morality were also sub-*Cultural Skepticism* jected to incessant challenges. Scientific conceptions especially underwent severe scrutiny and revolution. Einstein, Jeans, and other learned men, although not in agreement among themselves, completely upset earlier ideas concerning the size and nature of the universe, and in many instances revolutionized certain physical and astronomical theories. In the field of chemistry, scientists, ever investigating the mysteries of nature, discovered new elements, although the number was theretofore supposed to have been fixed. Millikan, by his momentous discovery of cosmic rays, evolved the theory that creation, formerly considered complete, is still in progress, and that new chemical elements are constantly being born.

In a period of scientific changes a renewed questioning of the values and fundamentals of religion was only natural. A committee of orthodox laymen in the United States raised doubts as to the worth of missions in foreign lands. In Soviet Russia the authorities discouraged religious faiths and propagandized atheism as an official doctrine. The growing acceptance of the evolutionary theory, as already mentioned, had caused many men to question the story of creation as related in the Bible. This fact, together with the intense and widespread suffering occasioned by the economic depression, it is said, led to a growing loss of religious faith.

Coincident with this increasing skepticism was a break-away from the traditional morality. Questions of right and wrong were no longer to be decided by set standards. Individual acts were now to be judged not by the church but by society. Walter Lippmann, in his *Preface to Morals*, declared that religious sanctions of morality were no longer sacred and that the existing moral structure must find a philosophy based on a rational foundation. Judge Ben Lindsey proposed his scheme for "companionate marriage"; and although this plan did not receive any great support, the new temper of the times was indicated by the tranquillity with which most Americans viewed the orgy of divorces.

The fine arts too refused to be bound by tradition and convention. Of these literature, art, and music, long stirred by the spirit of revolt, suffered the most radical attacks. Consequently, there arose changed artistic standards which were peculiarly characteristic of the bourgeois twentieth century. *New Trends in the Fine Arts and Literature*

In literature one of the outstanding characteristics, about 1900, was the revolt against the romanticism of the nineteenth century and the so-called bourgeois respectability. Through fantasy, satire, psychological analysis, and realism verging on cynicism, various authors tried to analyze society. The influence of the social sciences and that of psychology were apparent especially in the works of such writers as Carl Sandburg (1878–   ), the American poet who reflected the trend toward grim realism and "big business" when he wrote of Chicago:

> Hog Butcher for the World
> Tool Maker, Stacker of Wheat,
> Player with Railroads and the Nation's Freight Handler;
> Stormy, husky, brawling,
> City of the Big Shoulders.

During an age of realistic reaction against nineteenth-century romanticism many prominent writers, besides Shaw, France, Wells, and others already mentioned, satirized existing social and economic conditions. In England the death of Thomas Hardy (1840–1928), the "last of the great Victorians," broke the final surviving direct literary link with the earlier period. John Galsworthy (1867–1933), in his *Forsyte*

Saga and social dramas, analyzed various ethical and social problems which confront a person of today. In Russia, Maxim Gorki (1868–   ), formerly an advocate of revolution and later an ardent exponent of Bolshevism, became noted for his plastic realism. Sinclair Lewis (1885– ?), author of *Main Street, Babbitt, Arrowsmith,* and other books, wrote realistically of life in the middle-western portion of the United States. Knut Hamsun (1859–   ), a Norwegian with a great love of nature and an unusually analytical mind, contributed morbidly realistic novels of the Scandinavian peoples.

In contrast to the grim realism of most of their contemporaries might be mentioned Joseph Conrad (1857–1924) and James Branch Cabell (1879–   ). The former, Polish-born, became a master of English prose. Opposing both the "squalor" of realism and the exaggerated sentimentality of the earlier romanticists, he was the outstanding romantic author of the period. Cabell, a keen satirist, wrote ironic romances wherein he aimed "to write perfectly of beautiful happenings." After years of writing, fame came to him with the suppression of his extremely satirical *Jurgen.*

Late nineteenth-century art had been dominated by painters such as Renoir, Manet, and Degas, who employed a principle in art known as impressionism, a form of realism. They aimed to preserve the vividness and force of the first impression made by nature on the painter's vision and to convey the sensation of movement and light.

Art and Artists

One of the outstanding impressionists was Paul Cézanne (1839–1906), a French master. By his interest in primitive art and his emphasis on simple lines he virtually became the founder of a new school. Another painter, Pablo Picasso, established, about 1908, a movement known as cubism. Going beyond the followers of Cézanne, he believed that art was not representation at all, but expression. He and his disciples, through arbitrary proportion, distorted symmetry, and geometrical simplicity, produced pictures which were divested of all realistic traits. The futurists, emerging in Italy, went even farther than the impressionists and cubists in the revolt against realistic representation.

Even more than in literature did the twentieth century witness a rebellion in the realm of music. In the earlier period there was a general attempt to imitate Richard Wagner, which prompted a wit to write that *The Baton in Rebellion* he "was a great and good man, but he left behind him the Wagnerites, which was most unkind." In a revolt against the dominant Wagnerism the French composer Claude Achille Debussy (1862–1918) became the founder of a school which espoused musical impressionism. Made fashionable by him, the new type consisted in the avoidance of set forms and patterns. By using the joyous major and the sad minor which had been in vogue in the medieval days of the Gregorian chants, and also by adopting numerous Oriental scales, he created a new harmonic atmosphere in music. This permitted the music to "flow on like ever-changing clouds, with a sunset sky," represented by an orchestral coloring, as a background.

Other notable figures, especially Stravinsky and Scriabin, by departing from established standards, created works which, to many conservatives, seemed bizarre. Certain composers flaunted their unconventionalism. Defying all standards, Leo Ornstein, a young Russian, wrote the *Dance of Wild Men, Marche Grotesque*, and other extravagances. One of his critics queried, "If we have the music of butterflies, why not of toads?" To the scandalized orthodox musician, however, chaos was reached when American jazz appeared. A derivative of primitive Negro rhythms, it became the dominant type of lighter music in the United States and in many European countries.

Confronted with this turbulent unrest, the leaking bourgeois ship seemed to many in imminent danger of capsizing. It was forced, on numerous occasions, to calk its hulk, to strengthen the ebbing spirit of its *Compensating Features of the Bourgeois Order* crew, and at times to send out signals of distress. The question loomed, How much longer could it weather the storm?

Many believed that it could do so indefinitely; they looked upon the manifold benefits and blessings of the day as a sign of the usefulness and permanency of the existing order. In fact, Herbert Hoover, president of the United States, summed up the case for capitalism when he declared in a 1932 campaign speech:

> If it can be demonstrated that by means of this, our unequaled political, social, and economic system, we have secured a lift in the standards of living and a diffusion of comfort and hope to men and women, the growth of equal opportunity, the widening of all opportunity, such as had never been seen in the history of the world, then we should not tamper with it or destroy it, but on the contrary we should restore it and, by its gradual improvement and perfection, foster it into new performance for our country and for our children.

The first three decades of the twentieth century saw a tremendous improvement in the standard of living and the diffusion of culture. A rising flood of inventions and a supreme ingenuity in applied sciences revolutionized the daily life of the average middle-class person by placing at his command innumerable appliances for making life more comfortable, more enjoyable, and more economical of time and effort than it had ever been before. More than most persons realized, the increase of electrical power and the diversity of its application in transportation, industry, and agriculture reduced hours of labor and increased real wages.

In transportation and in communication marked progress was made. The wireless telegraph and the radio transmitter encircled the globe; television, practicable already to a degree, seemed likely to become a common domestic feature within an appreciably short time. As the ether was being conquered, so too was the transport aspect of distance. Highway, railway, steamboat, and airplane transportation continued to cut down schedules and to increase convenience. Fine roads not only stimulated automobile travel but also led to better truck and bus services. Greatly improved machinery and structure enabled floating palaces far to surpass their predecessors in the transatlantic traffic. In travel by rail too, speed and comfort increased. Finally there was the airplane, constantly transforming its potentialities into actualities. From a mechanical curiosity it became a practical servant, carrying passengers, mail, and freight. Constant improvement decreased the element of risk. Various types of aircraft, such as the autogiro and the dirigible, promised further improvement, and regular transoceanic air voyages were considered not far distant. Spectacular flights tested new devices and kept aviation always before the public.

Knowledge was more widely distributed than in any other period during the history of mankind. Books, newspapers, and periodicals, radios, motion pictures, churches, and clubs helped to dispel ignorance. Most civilized states maintained schools for the free and compulsory education of children. Illiteracy generally disappeared except in the more backward countries. The importance of mass education was manifested in the construction of beautiful school buildings, the wide variety of subjects taught, and the astonishing increase in the number of students attending universities. In the United States such organizations as the Rockefeller and Carnegie foundations, by subsidizing research, also contributed greatly to the expansion of human knowledge.

Barriers of race, nationality, and religion declined. In addition to these the political inequalities of sex were practically removed. At the opening of the twentieth century women had been regarded as the "weaker sex." Deprived of political rights and of social and educational opportunities, and dependent for support, they were expected to stay in the home. As a result of the feminist movement, however, women shattered these earlier prejudices, reasserted their individuality, and began to take an active part in politics and business. By the first decade of the twentieth century the movement to emancipate women was steadily gaining ground as the "suffragettes" in England, inspired by Mrs. Emmeline Pankhurst, resorted to violence and sabotage. In 1918, largely as a result of their assistance in the war, English women over thirty secured the suffrage. Later, in 1928, the franchise was granted to all women over twenty-one years of age. Other countries, notably Norway (1913), Denmark (1915), and the United States (1920), extended political equality to women, and most of the new governments in post-war Europe did likewise. The tendency of women to participate in business, politics, sports, and other activities became more and more pronounced as the century advanced.

Notwithstanding the remarkable achievements of the twentieth century the middle-class régime, largely responsible for them, suffered a distinct setback. Before 1914 the bourgeoisie, optimistic and dominant in both Europe and America, encountered pressure from both extremes of the social system, — the wealthy and the poor. Sympathetic toward labor's demand for higher wages, this middle class, in common with the wage-earners, opposed the increasing concentration of wealth in the hands of a few. The need for continuous production during the conflict, however, forced the bourgeoisie to acquiesce in this accumulation of gigantic fortunes and in the rapid rise of wages. Largely dependent upon salaries and upon the returns from investments, which increased more slowly than wages and prices, the middle classes suffered from the abnormal conditions engendered by the conflict.

The Middle Classes after the War

Post-war tendencies toward deflation subjected the middle-class system to a serious strain. Continued inflation in Germany, France, and Italy, moreover, together with depreciated currencies, caused the ruin or impoverishment of thousands of investors in those countries. In the United States and Great Britain the persistence of high prices and the slashing of salaries jeopardized the living conditions of the bourgeoisie. Even the small capitalists, like their salaried compatriots, began "to feel the pinch." The growth of large-scale production lowered costs and prices to levels which prohibited competition from the individual producer or distributor. In contrast to this decline of the erstwhile flourishing middle classes was the continued prosperity of the large capitalists and the improved position of organized labor. These groups fought stubbornly to retain what they had gained during the war.

The bourgeoisie, alarmed at the rise of proletariat radicalism, which threatened the very existence of the established order, allied themselves, however, with the big capitalists against labor. Self-constituted apostles of nationalism and capitalism, both groups in common combated socialism and communism by identifying existing economic institutions with national security. Thus a *bloc* of propertied classes arose in bourgeois countries, having as its chief object the preservation of the *status quo*. To this end, in such states as Italy and Germany, the middle classes willingly submitted to the iron rule of dictators; in Great Britain they accepted the leadership of Premier MacDonald, formerly head of the Labor party; while in the United States they welcomed the directed society sponsored by President Roosevelt. Millions believed that drastic political and social changes were preferable to the threatened collapse of middle-class society.

The Four Horsemen *who haunted the Second Quarter of the Twentieth Century*
From a cartoon by Daniel R. Fitzpatrick in the *Saint Louis Post-Dispatch*

SELECTED BOOKS

CHAPTER I · *The Founding of the New Order*

Introductory Note. The following list of selected readings and books is designed for persons who do not care to read detailed and often technical monographs and works on limited subjects. An attempt has been made to select reliable and readable accounts written in English. Should one desire additional information not included in the works cited in this volume, he should consult two large coöperative histories: one, the *Cambridge Modern History*, edited by Lord Acton and others (13 vols.) (Macmillan, 1902–1913), is in English; the other, *Histoire générale du IVe siècle à nos jours*, edited by E. Lavisse and A. Rambaud (12 vols.) (A. Colin & Cie., 1893–1901), is in French. Accurate and thorough, both works contain stores of information and excellent bibliographies. A critical bibliography of the whole field of history is available in *A Guide to Historical Literature*, compiled by W. H. Allison, G. M. Dutcher, and others (Macmillan, 1931). There are also special bibliographies, of which the *Foreign Affairs Bibliography, 1919–1932*, compiled by W. L. Langer and H. F. Armstrong (Harper, 1933), is of particular value. To secure information on specific subjects one may very profitably resort to the generally excellent articles to be found in the *Encyclopædia Britannica* (14th ed.) (24 vols.) (Encyclopædia Britannica, Inc., 1929) and in the *Encyclopædia of the Social Sciences*, edited by E. R. A. Seligman and A. Johnson (15 vols.) (Macmillan, 1930–). For reviews of recent books the reader should consult such publications as the *American Historical Review*, the *Journal of Modern History*, and other scholarly periodicals in the fields of history, economics, political science, sociology, literature, and philosophy. W. R. Shepherd's *Historical Atlas* (7th ed.) (Holt, 1929), the *Cambridge Modern History Atlas* (2d ed.) (Macmillan, 1925), J. G. Bartholomew's *Atlas of Economic Geography* (Hammond, 1914), and *Ploetz's Manual of Universal History* (rev. ed.) (Houghton, 1925), a compendium of historical dates, are also valuable works of reference.

The Rise of the Middle Classes. W. J. ASHLEY, *Economic Organization of England, an Outline History*. Longmans, 1914. See chaps. vii, ix. A. BIRNIE, *An Economic History of Europe, 1760–1930*. Methuen & Co., 1930. See chaps. i–v. R. H. GRETTON, *The English Middle Class*. G. Bell & Sons, 1917. F. L. NUSSBAUM, *A History of the Economic Institutions of Modern Europe: an Introduction to Der Moderne Kapitalismus*. Crofts, 1933. W. SOMBART, *The Quintessence of Capitalism*. Dutton, 1915.

The Idea of Progress. H. E. BARNES, *Living in the Twentieth Century*. Bobbs, 1928. See pp. 62–150. H. E. BARNES, *World Politics in Modern Civilization*. Knopf, 1930. See pp. 33–125. J. B. BURY, *The Idea of Progress:*

an Inquiry into its Origin and Growth (new ed.). Macmillan, 1932. C. GIDE and C. RIST, *A History of Economic Doctrines from the Time of the Physiocrats to the Present Day* (rev. ed.). Heath, 1915. G. SLATER, *The Making of Modern England* (rev. ed.). Houghton, 1915. F. J. TEGGART, *Theory of History.* Yale Univ. Press, 1925.

Economic Revolutions. W. H. R. CURTLER, *A Short History of English Agriculture.* Oxford, 1909. C. DAY, *Economic Development of Modern Europe.* Macmillan, 1933. F. C. DIETZ, *The Industrial Revolution.* Holt, 1927. M. E. FORDHAM, *A Short History of English Rural Life, from the Anglo-Saxon Invasion to the Present Time.* Scribner, 1916. See chaps. viii–x. H. DE B. GIBBINS, *Economic and Industrial Progress of the Century.* Linscott Pub. Co., 1903. See chaps. i–v. H. DE B. GIBBINS, *Industry in England* (11th ed.), Methuen & Co., 1925. J. L. and B. HAMMOND, *The Rise of Modern Industry.* Harcourt, 1926. J. A. HOBSON, *The Evolution of Modern Capitalism: a Study of Machine Production* (rev. ed.). Scribner, 1926. M. M. KNIGHT, H. E. BARNES, and F. FLÜGEL, *Economic History of Europe in Modern Times.* Houghton, 1928. P. MANTOUX, *The Industrial Revolution in the Eighteenth Century; an Outline of the Beginnings of the Modern Factory System in England* (rev. ed.). Harcourt, 1927. L. B. PACKARD, *The Commercial Revolution, 1400–1776.* Holt, 1927. H. SÉE, *Modern Capitalism, its Origin and Evolution.* Adelphi Co., 1928.

Contemporary Accounts. A. E. BLAND, P. A. BROWN, and R. H. TAWNEY, *English Economic History: Select Documents* (2d ed.). G. Bell & Sons, 1915. See Part III. J. H. ROBINSON and C. A. BEARD, *Readings in Modern European History.* 2 vols. Ginn, 1908–1909. See Vol. I, pp. 45–72. J. F. SCOTT and A. BALTZLY, *Readings in European History since 1814.* Crofts, 1931. See pp. 52–70, 113–139.

CHAPTER II · *The World in 1815*

Geographical Accounts. J. F. UNSTEAD and E. G. R. TAYLOR, *General and Regional Geography for Students* (9th ed.). Geo. Philip & Son, 1926. J. K. WRIGHT, *The Geographical Basis of European History.* Holt, 1928.

Nationalism. L. DOMINIAN, *The Frontiers of Language and Nationality in Europe.* Holt, 1917. G. P. GOOCH, *History and Historians in the Nineteenth Century* (2d ed.). Longmans, 1928. G. P. GOOCH, *Nationalism.* Harcourt, 1920. A. C. HADDON, *The Races of Man and their Distribution.* Macmillan, 1925. C. J. H. HAYES, *Essays on Nationalism.* Macmillan, 1926. C. J. H. HAYES, *The Historical Evolution of Modern Nationalism.* Ray Long & Richard R. Smith, 1931. P. T. MOON, *Syllabus on International Relations.* Macmillan, 1925. See Part II. R. MUIR, *Nationalism and Internationalism: the Culmination of Modern History.* Constable & Co., 1916. E. H. REISNER, *Nationalism and Education since 1789.* Macmillan, 1922. W. Z. RIPLEY, *The Races of Europe.* Appleton, 1910. J. H. ROSE, *Nationality in Modern History.* Macmillan, 1916. See chaps. i–iii, vii–ix. J. F. SCOTT, *Patriots in the Making.* Appleton, 1916.

CHAPTER III · *The Congress of Vienna, 1815:*
Triumph of Conservatism

The Age of Metternich. W. P. CRESSON, *The Holy Alliance*. Oxford, 1922.
A. J. MAY, *The Age of Metternich, 1815–1848*. Holt, 1933. A. H. OAKES and
R. B. MOWAT, *The Great European Treaties of the Nineteenth Century*. Oxford,
1918. See chap. ii. D. PERKINS, *The Monroe Doctrine, 1823–1826*. Harvard
Univ. Press, 1927. W. A. PHILLIPS, *Confederation of Europe* (2d ed.). Long-
mans, 1920. H. W. V. TEMPERLEY, *The Foreign Policy of Canning, 1822–1827*.
Harcourt, 1925. C. K. WEBSTER, *Congress of Vienna, 1814–1815*. Oxford,
1919. C. K. WEBSTER, *The Foreign Policy of Castlereagh, 1815–1822*. Harcourt,
1925. E. L. WOODWARD, *Three Studies in European Conservatism*. Richard
R. Smith, Inc., 1930.

Biographies. A. CECIL, *Metternich, 1773–1859; a Study of his Period and
Personality*. Macmillan, 1933. A. D. COOPER, *Talleyrand*. Harper, 1932.
W. P. CRESSON, *Diplomatic Portraits*. Houghton, 1923. J. W. FORTESCUE,
Wellington. Dodd, 1925. A. HERMAN, *Metternich*. Century, 1932. G. B.
MALLESON, *Life of Prince Metternich*. W. H. Allen, 1888. J. McCABE, *Tal-
leyrand*. Hutchinson & Co., 1906. G. A. C. SANDEMAN, *Metternich*. Methuen
& Co., 1911.

Contemporary Accounts. J. H. ROBINSON and C. A. BEARD, *Readings*. See
Vol. I, pp. 372–387. J. F. SCOTT and A. BALTZLY, *Readings*. See pp. 3–12,
15–17, 29–31.

CHAPTER IV · *The Spread of the Revolutionary Movement, 1815–1848*

National Histories. C. E. CHAPMAN, *A History of Spain*. Macmillan, 1918.
J. H. CLAPHAM, *The Economic Development of France and Germany, 1815–1914*.
Macmillan, 1923. See chaps. i–vi. R. C. K. ENSOR, *Belgium*. Holt, 1915. See
pp. 117–165. A. L. GUÉRARD, *French Civilization in the Nineteenth Century, a
Historical Introduction*. Century, 1914. See pp. 89–120. C. A. H. GUIGNEBERT,
A Short History of the French People. 2 vols. Macmillan, 1930. See pp. 520–
575. W. A. PHILLIPS, *Poland*. Holt, 1915. See pp. 101–125. G. YOUNG,
Portugal, Old and Young, an Historical Study. Oxford, 1917. See pp. 217–234.

General Accounts of Revolutionary Movements. F. B. ARTZ, *France under
the Bourbon Restoration, 1814–1830*. Harvard Univ. Press, 1931. G. L. DICK-
INSON, *Revolution and Reaction in Modern France* (2d ed.). George Allen &
Unwin, 1927. J. R. HALL, *The Bourbon Restoration*. Alston Rivers, Ltd., 1909.
J. HALLER, *The Epochs of German History*. Harcourt, 1930. See chaps. xi–xii.
B. KING, *A History of Italian Unity, being a Political History of Italy from 1814
to 1871*. 2 vols. Scribner, 1899. J. G. LEGGE, *Rhyme and Revolution in Ger-
many*. Constable & Co., 1918. See pp. 13–231. J. LUCAS-DUBRETON, *The
Restoration and the July Monarchy*. Putnam, 1929. See Part I, chaps. i–vii.

Biographies. E. S. BAGGER, *Francis Joseph, Emperor of Austria — King of
Hungary*. Putnam, 1927. A. CECIL, *Metternich, 1773–1859; a Study of his
Period and Personality*. Macmillan, 1933. B. KING, *The Life of Mazzini*.
Dutton, 1911. J. LUCAS-DUBRETON, *Louis XVIII*. Putnam, 1927.

Histories of Music and Literature. J. F. COAR, *Studies in German Literature in the Nineteenth Century.* Macmillan, 1903. K. FRANCKE, *A History of German Literature as determined by Social Forces* (4th ed.). Holt, 1901. G. P. GOOCH, *History and Historians in the Nineteenth Century* (2d ed.). Longmans, 1928. P. C. R. LANDORMY, *A History of Music.* Scribner, 1923. C. H. C. WRIGHT, *Background of Modern French Literature.* Ginn, 1926.

Contemporary Accounts. J. H. ROBINSON and C. A. BEARD, *Readings.* See Vol. II, pp. 2–44. J. F. SCOTT and A. BALTZLY, *Readings.* See pp. 13–15, 17–28, 44–51.

CHAPTER V · *The Crisis: 1848*

The Revolutions of 1848. J. M. S. ALLISON, *Thiers and the French Monarchy, 1797–1848.* Houghton, 1926. A. R. CALMAN, *Ledru-Rollin and the Second French Republic.* Columbia Univ. Press, 1923. F. H. CHEETHAM, *Louis Napoleon and the Genesis of the Second Empire.* John Lane, 1908. G. ELTON, *The Revolutionary Idea in France, 1789–1871.* Longmans, 1923. See chap. vii. E. F. HENDERSON, *A Short History of Germany* (2d ed.). 2 vols. in 1. Macmillan, 1916. See chap. viii. J. G. LEGGE, *Rhyme and Revolution in Germany.* Constable & Co., 1918. See pp. 235–504. J. LUCAS-DUBRETON, *The Restoration and the July Monarchy.* Putnam, 1929. See Part I, chap. viii, and Part II, chaps. i–viii. J. A. R. MARRIOTT, *The French Revolution of 1848 in its Economic Aspect.* 2 vols. Oxford, 1913. J. REDLICH, *Emperor Francis Joseph of Austria.* Macmillan, 1929. F. SCHEVILL, *The Making of Modern Germany.* McClurg, 1916. See pp. 115–123. G. M. TREVELYAN, *Garibaldi's Defence of the Roman Republic.* Longmans, 1907. G. M. TREVELYAN, *Manin and the Venetian Revolution of 1848.* Longmans, 1923. H. C. M. WENDEL, *The Evolution of Industrial Freedom in Prussia, 1845–1849.* New York Univ. Press, 1921.

Contemporary Accounts. K. MARX, *Revolution and Counter-revolution; or Germany in 1848* (edited by E. M. Aveling). Scribner, 1896. J. H. ROBINSON and C. A. BEARD, *Readings.* See Vol. II, pp. 73–84, 95–114. J. F. SCOTT and A. BALTZLY, *Readings.* See pp. 144–172. A. C. H. C. DE TOCQUEVILLE, *Recollections.* Macmillan, 1896.

For additional references consult the works cited in the bibliography for Chapter IV.

CHAPTER VI · *England, 1815–1848: Decline of the Aristocratic Oligarchy*

General Histories of England. J. H. CLAPHAM, *An Economic History of Modern Britain* (2d ed.). 2 vols. Macmillan, 1931–1932. See Vol. I. É. HALÉVY, *A History of the English People in 1815.* Harcourt, 1924. W. E. LUNT, *A History of England.* Harper, 1928. See chaps. xxiv–xxv. F. S. MARVIN, *The Century of Hope: a Sketch of Western Progress from 1815 to the Great War.* Oxford, 1919. C. E. ROBINSON, *England, a History of British Progress from the Early Ages to the Present Day.* Crowell, 1928. See pp. 533–581. G. SLATER, *The Making of Modern England* (rev. ed.). Houghton, 1915. See chaps. i–xiii. H. D. TRAILL, *Social England* (new ed.). 6 vols in 12. Putnam, 1909. See Vol. VI. G. M. TREVELYAN, *British History in the Nineteenth Century, 1782–1901.* Longmans, 1922. See chaps. ix–xviii. E. C. WINGFIELD-STRATFORD, *The History of British Civilization.* 2 vols. Harcourt, 1928. See Vol. II, Book 4, chap. i.

Special Works. J. R. M. BUTLER, *The Passing of the Great Reform Bill.* Longmans, 1914. O. F. CHRISTIE, *Transition from Aristocracy, 1832–1867.* Putnam, 1928. G. D. H. COLE, *A Short History of the British Working-Class Movement.* 2 vols. in 1. Macmillan, 1927. G. D. H. COLE, *Robert Owen.* Little, 1925. W. H. R. CURTLER, *A Short History of English Agriculture.* Oxford, 1909. See chaps. xviii–xx. H. DE B. GIBBINS, *Industry in England* (11th ed.). Methuen & Co., 1925. J. L. and B. HAMMOND, *The Age of the Chartists, 1832–1854.* Longmans, 1930. G. M. TREVELYAN, *Lord Grey of the Reform Bill, being the Life of Charles, Second Earl Grey.* Longmans, 1920.

Contemporary Accounts. A. E. BLAND, P. A. BROWN, and R. H. TAWNEY, *English Economic History: Select Documents* (2d ed.). Harcourt, 1915. See Part III. J. H. ROBINSON and C. A. BEARD, *Readings.* See Vol. II, pp. 239–250, 266–296. J. F. SCOTT and A. BALTZLY, *Readings.* See pp. 52–112.

CHAPTER VII · *Napoleon III and the Second Empire*

Works on the Second Empire. F. W. H. CAVENDISH, *Society, Politics, and Diplomacy, 1820–1864.* T. F. Unwin, 1913. H. R. C. W. COWLEY, *Secrets of the Second Empire; Private Letters from the Paris Embassy.* Harper, 1929. H. A. L. FISHER, *Bonapartism.* Oxford, 1908. P. GUEDALLA, *The Second Empire: Bonapartism, the Prince, the President, the Emperor.* Putnam, 1922. L. C. A. KNOWLES, *Economic Development in the Nineteenth Century: France, Germany, Russia, and the United States.* George Routledge & Sons, 1932. P. F. MARTIN, *Maximilian in Mexico; the Story of the French Intervention, 1861–1867.* Constable & Co., 1914. H. ONCKEN, *Napoleon III and the Rhine: Origin of the War of 1870–1871.* Knopf, 1928. F. A. SIMPSON, *Louis Napoleon and the Recovery of France, 1848–1856.* Longmans, 1923. F. A. SIMPSON, *Rise of Louis Napoleon* (2d ed.). Longmans, 1925. C. H. C. WRIGHT, *The Background of Modern French Literature.* Ginn, 1926.

Biographies. E. B. F. D'AUVERGNE, *Napoleon the Third, a Biography.* Dodd, 1929. E. C. CORTI, *Maximilian and Charlotte of Mexico.* 2 vols. Knopf, 1929. B. JERROLD, *Life of Napoleon III.* 4 vols. Longmans, 1874–1882.

Contemporary Accounts. J. H. ROBINSON and C. A. BEARD, *Readings.* See Vol. II, pp. 84–94. J. F. SCOTT and A. BALTZLY, *Readings.* See pp. 228–237.

For additional references consult the works cited in the bibliography for Chapter IV.

CHAPTER VIII · *Cavour: Architect of a United Italy*

Works dealing with Italian Unity. C. S. FORESTER, *Victor Emmanuel II and the Union of Italy.* Dodd, 1927. R. S. HOLLAND, *Builders of United Italy.* Holt, 1908. B. KING, *A History of Italian Unity, being a Political History of Italy from 1814 to 1871.* 2 vols. Scribner, 1899. E. L. H. MARTINENGO-

CESARESCO, *The Liberation of Italy, 1815–1870* (3d ed.). Seeley & Co., 1910. P. K. O'CLERY, *The Making of Italy, 1856–1870.* K. Paul, Trench, Trübner & Co., 1892. W. J. STILLMAN, *The Union of Italy, 1815–1895* (rev. ed.). Cambridge Univ. Press, 1909. G. M. TREVELYAN, *Garibaldi and the Making of Italy.* Longmans, 1911. G. M. TREVELYAN, *Manin and the Venetian Revolution of 1848.* Longmans, 1923.

Biographies. J. A. R. MARRIOTT, *Makers of Modern Italy; Napoleon–Mussolini.* Oxford, 1931. E. L. H. MARTINENGO-CESARESCO, *Life of Cavour.* Macmillan, 1898. G. M. PALÉOLOGUE, *Cavour.* Harper, 1927. W. R. THAYER, *The Life and Times of Cavour.* 2 vols. Houghton, 1914.

Contemporary Accounts. J. H. ROBINSON and C. A. BEARD, *Readings.* See Vol. II, pp. 115–141. J. A. SCOTT and A. BALTZLY, *Readings.* See pp. 255–267. A. J. B. WHYTE, *The Early Life and Letters of Cavour, 1810–1848.* Oxford, 1925. A. J. B. WHYTE, *The Political Life and Letters of Cavour, 1848–1861.* Oxford, 1930.

CHAPTER IX · *Bismarck: Founder of the German Empire*

Works dealing with the Unification of Germany. J. H. CLAPHAM, *The Economic Development of France and Germany, 1815–1914.* Macmillan, 1923. W. H. DAWSON, *The German Empire, 1867–1914, and the Unity Movement.* 2 vols. Macmillan, 1919. B. E. HOWARD, *The German Empire.* Macmillan, 1906. See chap. i. R. H. LORD, *Origins of the War of 1870.* Harvard Univ. Press, 1924. G. B. MALLESON, *The Refounding of the German Empire, 1848–1871.* Seeley & Co., 1892. H. VON MOLTKE, *The Franco-German War of 1870–1871* (rev. ed.). Harper, 1907. E. OLLIVIER, *The Franco-Prussian War and its Hidden Causes.* Little, 1912. F. SCHEVILL, *The Making of Modern Germany.* McClurg, 1916. See chaps. iii–v. M. SMITH, *Bismarck and German Unity* (3d ed.). Columbia Univ. Press, 1923. C. L. H. VON SYBEL, *Founding of the German Empire by William I.* 7 vols. Crowell, 1890–1898. C. TOWER, *Germany of Today.* Holt, 1913.

Biographies. J. W. HEADLAM-MORLEY, *Bismarck and the Foundation of the German Empire.* Putnam, 1899. C. LOWE, *Prince Bismarck: an Historical Biography.* 2 vols. Cassell & Co., 1887. E. LUDWIG, *Bismarck, the Story of a Fighter.* Little, 1927. C. G. ROBERTSON, *Bismarck.* Holt, 1919.

Contemporary Accounts. O. VON BISMARCK, *Bismarck, the Man and the Statesman* (Bismarck's Autobiography). 2 vols. Harper, 1899. O. VON BISMARCK, *The Kaiser vs. Bismarck.* Harper, 1921. J. H. ROBINSON and C. A. BEARD, *Readings.* See Vol. II, pp. 142–165. J. F. SCOTT and A. BALTZLY, *Readings.* See pp. 238–255.

CHAPTER X · *Imperial Russia: Infiltration of Liberalism*

Histories of Russia. V. BERARD, *The Russian Empire and Czarism.* David Nutt, 1905. M. M. KARPOVICH, *Imperial Russia, 1801–1917.* Holt, 1932. See pp. 1–50. V. O. KLIUCHEVSKY, *A History of Russia.* 5 vols. Dutton, 1911–1931. A. KORNILOV, *Modern Russian History* (rev. ed.). Knopf, 1924.

D. S. MIRSKY, *Russia: a Social History.* Cresset Press, 1931. B. PARES, *A History of Russia.* Knopf, 1926. See chaps. xvii–xx. G. V. VERNADSKY, *A History of Russia* (rev. ed.). Yale Univ. Press, 1930. See chaps. vii–x. D. M. WALLACE, *Russia* (rev. ed.). Cassell & Co., 1912.

Social and Economic Accounts. M. BARING, *The Russian People* (2d ed.). Methuen & Co., 1914. G. KENNAN, *Siberia and the Exile System.* 2 vols. Century, 1891. T. G. MASARYK, *The Spirit of Russia: Studies in History, Literature, and Philosophy.* 2 vols. Macmillan, 1919. J. MAVOR, *An Economic History of Russia* (2d rev. ed.). 2 vols. Dutton, 1925. W. A. PHILLIPS, *Poland.* Holt, 1915. See pp. 101–156. A. N. RAMBAUD, *Expansion of Russia: Problems of the East and Problems of the Far East* (2d rev. ed.). Scott-Thaw Co., 1904. H. Y. REYBURN, *The Story of the Russian Church.* A. Melrose, 1924. F. H. B. SKRINE, *The Expansion of Russia, 1815–1900* (3d ed.). Cambridge Univ. Press, 1915.

Books on Russian Literature and Music. P. A. KROPOTKIN, *Ideals and Realities in Russian Literature* (3d ed.). Knopf, 1915. D. S. MIRSKY, *A History of Russian Literature.* Knopf, 1927. M. MONTAGU-NATHAN, *A History of Russian Music.* Scribner, 1914. W. L. PHELPS, *Essays on Russian Novelists.* Macmillan, 1911.

Contemporary Accounts. A. I. HERZEN, *My Past and Thoughts.* 6 vols. Knopf, 1924–1928. P. A. KROPOTKIN, *Memoirs of a Revolutionist.* Houghton, 1899. J. H. ROBINSON and C. A. BEARD, *Readings.* See Vol. II, pp. 338–371. J. F. SCOTT and A. BALTZLY, *Readings.* See pp. 31–44, 268–303.

CHAPTER XI · *The Rise of the Bourgeois System in the Americas*

History of the Americas. H. E. BOLTON, *History of the Americas.* Ginn, 1928.

The United States. C. A. and M. BEARD, *The Rise of American Civilization.* 2 vols. Macmillan, 1927. See Vol. I, and Vol. II, chaps. xvii–xviii. A. J. BEVERIDGE, *Abraham Lincoln, 1809–1858.* 2 vols. Houghton, 1928. G. R. B. CHARNWOOD, *Abraham Lincoln* (3d ed.). Holt, 1917. W. E. DODD, *Expansion and Conflict.* Houghton, 1915. W. A. DUNNING, *Reconstruction, Political and Economic, 1865–1877.* Harper, 1907. H. U. FAULKNER, *American Economic History.* Harper, 1924. C. R. FISH, *The Rise of the Common Man.* Macmillan, 1927. G. P. GARRISON, *Westward Extension, 1841–1850.* Harper, 1906. R. HOLDEN, *Abraham Lincoln, the Politician and the Man.* Minton, 1929. S. E. MORISON, *The Oxford History of the United States, 1783–1917.* 2 vols. Oxford, 1927. See Vol. I, and Vol. II, chaps. xxxiii–xxxv. S. E. MORISON and H. S. COMMAGER, *The Growth of the American Republic.* Oxford, 1930. See chaps. i–xxxiv. D. S. MUZZEY, *The United States of America.* 2 vols. Ginn, 1922–1924. See Vol. I. F. L. PAXSON, *History of the American Frontier, 1763–1893.* Houghton, 1924. I. M. TARBELL, *Life of Abraham Lincoln* (new ed.). 2 vols. Macmillan, 1917. F. J. TURNER, *Rise of the New West, 1819–1829.* Harper, 1906. F. J. TURNER, *The Frontier in American History.* Holt, 1921.

Hispanic America. H. ANGELL, *Simón Bolívar, South American Liberator.* Norton, 1930. J. B. BRYCE, *South America: Observations and Impressions* (rev. ed.). Macmillan, 1914. C. E. CHAPMAN, *Colonial Hispanic America: a History*. Macmillan, 1933. F. L. PAXSON, *The Independence of the South American Republics, a Study in Recognition and Foreign Policy* (2d ed.). Ferris & Leach, 1916. H. I. PRIESTLEY, *The Mexican Nation: a History*. Macmillan, 1923. See chaps. i–xxi. J. F. RIPPY, *Historical Evolution of Latin America*. Crofts, 1932. W. S. ROBERTSON, *History of the Latin-American Nations* (rev. ed.). Appleton, 1925. W. R. SHEPHERD, *Latin America*. Holt, 1914. E. L. WHITE, *El Supremo: a Romance of the Great Dictator of Paraguay*. Dutton, 1916. M. W. WILLIAMS, *The People and Politics of Latin America*. Ginn, 1930.

Canada. *Cambridge History of the British Empire*. 8 vols. Macmillan, 1929– . Consult Vol. VI. J. H. ROBINSON and C. A. BEARD, *Readings*. See Vol. II, pp. 316–322. C. WITTKE, *A History of Canada*. Knopf, 1928.

CHAPTER XII · *The Spread of Liberalism in Austria-Hungary and among the Lesser Powers*

National Histories. R. N. BAIN, *Scandinavia, a Political History of Denmark, Norway, and Sweden from 1513 to 1900*. Cambridge Univ. Press, 1905. See chaps. xvi–xvii. P. J. BLOK, *History of the People of the Netherlands*. 5 vols. Putnam, 1898–1912. See Vol. V, chaps. xxiii–xxxiv. G. DRAGE, *Austria-Hungary*. J. MURRAY, 1909. R. C. K. ENSOR, *Belgium*. Holt, 1915. K. GJERSET, *History of the Norwegian People*. Macmillan, 1927. See Vol. I, pp. 446–544. C. J. H. HALLENDORF and A. SCHUCK, *History of Sweden*. C. E. Fritze, 1929. F. C. HOWE, *Denmark: a Coöperative Commonwealth*. Harcourt, 1921. H. VAN DER LINDEN, *Belgium: the Making of a Nation*. Oxford, 1920. W. OECHSLI, *The History of Switzerland, 1499–1914*. Macmillan, 1922. W. A. PHILLIPS, *Poland*. Holt, 1915. See chaps. viii–xii. A. A. STOMBERG, *History of Sweden*. Macmillan, 1931.

Special Works and Contemporary Accounts. E. S. BAGGER, *Francis Joseph, Emperor of Austria — King of Hungary*. Putnam, 1927. P. DRACHMANN and H. WESTERGAARD, *The Industrial Development and Commercial Policies of the Three Scandinavian Countries*. Oxford, 1915. O. JÁSZI, *The Dissolution of the Habsburg Monarchy*. Univ. of Chicago Press, 1929. J. REDLICH, *Emperor Francis Joseph of Austria*. Macmillan, 1929. J. H. ROBINSON and C. A. BEARD, *Readings*. See Vol. II, pp. 165–171. H. WESTERGAARD, *Economic Development in Denmark Before and During the World War*. Oxford, 1922.

CHAPTER XIII · *England's Golden Age: the Mid-Victorian Period, 1848-1878*

Histories of England. W. E. LUNT, *A History of England*. Harper, 1928. See chaps. xxxvi–xxxvii. C. E. ROBINSON, *England, a History of British Progress from the Early Ages to the Present Day*. Crowell, 1928. See pp. 590–669. G. M. TREVELYAN, *British History in the Nineteenth Century, 1782–1901*. Longmans, 1922. See chaps. xix–xxiii. E. C. WINGFIELD-STRATFORD, *The History of British Civilization*. 2 vols. Harcourt, 1928. See Vol. II, Book 4, chap. ii.

Special Works. E. BARKER, *Political Thought in England from Herbert Spencer to the Present Day.* Holt, 1915. E. W. BYRN, *The Progress of Invention in the Nineteenth Century.* Munn & Co., 1900. T. CARLYLE, *Past and Present.* Macmillan, 1927. F. E. GREEN, *A History of the English Agricultural Labourer, 1870–1920.* P. S. King & Son, 1920. S. L. GWYNN, *Ireland.* Scribner, 1925. L. C. A. KNOWLES, *The Industrial and Commercial Revolutions in England during the Nineteenth Century* (4th ed.). Dutton, 1921. F. S. MARVIN, *The Century of Hope: a Sketch of Western Progress from 1815 to the Great War.* Oxford, 1919. H. O. MEREDITH, *Outlines of the Economic History of England, a Study in Social Development.* Sir I. Pitman & Sons, 1908. J. T. MERZ, *A History of European Thought in the Nineteenth Century* (new ed.). 4 vols. Univ. of Chicago Press, 1924. See Part I. L. PAUL-DUBOIS, *Contemporary Ireland.* Maunsel & Co., 1908. G. H. PERRIS, *Industrial History of Modern England.* Holt, 1914. W. B. SCOTT, *The Theory of Evolution, with Special Reference to the Evidence upon which it is Founded.* Macmillan, 1917. C. J. SINGER, *A Short History of Medicine.* Oxford, 1928. E. E. SLOSSON, *Creative Chemistry.* Century, 1921. H. A. TAINE, *History of English Literature.* Henry Altemus Company, 1908. J. A. THOMSON (ed.), *Outline of Science.* 4 vols. Putnam, 1922. A. P. USHER, *An Introduction to the Industrial History of England.* Houghton, 1920. S. and B. WEBB, *A History of Trade-Unionism* (rev. ed.). Longmans, 1920. H. B. WOODWARD, *History of Geology.* Putnam, 1911.

Biographies. G. T. BETTANY, *Life of Charles Darwin.* W. Scott, 1887. O. BURDETT, *W. E. Gladstone: a Psychological Study.* Houghton, 1928. E. G. CLARKE, *Benjamin Disraeli — the Romance of a Great Career, 1804–1881.* Macmillan, 1926. P. GUEDALLA, *Palmerston, 1784–1865.* Putnam, 1927. W. P. HALL, *Mr. Gladstone.* Norton, 1931. S. LEE, *Queen Victoria* (new ed.), Smith, Elder & Co., 1904. A. MAUROIS, *Disraeli: a Picture of the Victorian Age.* Appleton, 1928. W. F. MONYPENNY and G. E. BUCKLE, *Life of Benjamin Disraeli, Earl of Beaconsfield* (new rev. ed.). 2 vols. Macmillan, 1929. J. MORLEY, *The Life of William Ewart Gladstone* (new ed.). 3 vols. Macmillan, 1911. D. C. SOMERVELL, *Disraeli and Gladstone, a Duo-biographical Sketch.* Doran, 1926. G. L. STRACHEY, *Queen Victoria.* Harcourt, 1924.

Histories of Literature. G. K. CHESTERTON, *The Victorian Age in Literature.* Holt, 1913. O. ELTON, *A Survey of English Literature, 1780–1880.* 4 vols. Macmillan, 1920. G. P. GOOCH, *History and Historians in the Nineteenth Century* (2d ed.). Longmans, 1928.

Contemporary Accounts. J. H. ROBINSON and C. A. BEARD, *Readings.* See Vol. II, pp. 251–254. J. F. SCOTT and A. BALTZLY, *Readings.* See pp. 173–175, 181–186.

CHAPTER XIV · *The Near-Eastern Question: Cross Roads of Interests*

National Histories. C. U. CLARK, *United Roumania.* Dodd, 1932. See chaps. i–viii. W. S. DAVIS, *A Short History of the Near East, A.D. 330–1922.* Macmillan, 1922. See chaps. xxv–xxxi. C. J. S. EVERSLEY and V. CHIROL, *The Turkish Empire* (2d ed.). T. F. Unwin, 1924. S. LANE-POOLE, *The Story of Turkey* (new ed.). Putnam, 1899. See chaps. xiv–xvii. E. G. MEARS,

Modern Turkey: a *Politico-economic Interpretation, 1908–1923.* Macmillan, 1924. W. MILLER, *A History of the Greek People, 1821–1921.* Dutton, 1913. W. MILLER, *The Balkans: Roumania, Bulgaria, Servia, and Montenegro* (3d rev. ed.). T. F. Unwin, 1923. W. MILLER, *The Ottoman Empire and its Successors, 1801–1927* (rev. ed.). Macmillan, 1928. W. S. MURRAY, *The Making of the Balkan States.* Columbia Univ. Press, 1910. V. M. PETROVITCH, *Serbia, her People, History, and Aspirations.* George G. Harrap & Co., 1915. F. SCHEVILL and W. M. GEWEHR, *The History of the Balkan Peninsula, from the Earliest Times to the Present Day* (rev. ed.). Harcourt, 1933. See chaps. xix–xxvii. W. M. SLOANE, *The Balkans; a Laboratory of History* (rev. ed.). Abingdon Press, 1920. F. S. STEVENSON, *A History of Montenegro.* Jarrold & Sons, 1912. A. J. TOYNBEE and K. P. KIRKWOOD, *Turkey.* Scribner, 1927. G. YOUNG, *Egypt.* Scribner, 1927.

Special Accounts. G. F. ABBOTT, *Turkey in Transition.* Longmans, 1909. C. R. BUXTON, *Turkey in Revolution.* T. F. Unwin, 1909. C. W. CRAWLEY, *The Question of Greek Independence.* Macmillan, 1931. E. DICEY, *The Peasant State: an Account of Bulgaria in 1894.* J. Murray, 1894. H. H. DODWELL, *The Founder of Modern Egypt: a Study of Muhammad 'Ali.* Macmillan, 1931. N. D. HARRIS, *Europe and the East.* Houghton, 1926. See chaps. ii–iii. T. E. HOLLAND, *The European Concert in the Eastern Question.* Oxford, 1885. J. A. R. MARRIOTT, *The Eastern Question, an Historical Study of European Diplomacy* (3d rev. ed.). Oxford, 1925. E. PEARS, *Life of Abdul Hamid II.* Holt, 1917. R. W. SETON-WATSON, *The Rise of Nationality in the Balkans.* Constable & Co., 1917.

Contemporary Accounts. J. H. ROBINSON and C. A. BEARD, *Readings.* See Vol. II, pp. 382–405. J. F. SCOTT and A. BALTZLY, *Readings.* See pp. 352–381.

CHAPTER XV · *Pope Pius IX and the New Régime*

Special Works. G. BAGNANI, *Rome and the Papacy.* Methuen & Co., 1929. W. F. BARRY, *The Papacy and Modern Times, a Political Sketch, 1303–1870.* Holt, 1911. G. T. BETTANY, *Life of Charles Darwin.* W. Scott, 1887. L. M. CASE, *Franco-Italian Relations, 1860–1865.* Press of the Univ. of Pennsylvania, 1932. W. CUNNINGHAM, *Christianity and Politics.* Houghton, 1915. W. CUNNINGHAM, *Christianity and Social Questions.* Scribner, 1910. J. MACCAFFREY, *History of the Catholic Church in the Nineteenth Century* (2d rev. ed.). 2 vols. M. H. Gill, 1910. A. C. McGIFFERT, *The Rise of Modern Religious Ideas.* Macmillan, 1915. L. F. MOTT, *Ernest Renan.* Appleton, 1921. F. NIELSEN, *History of the Papacy in the Nineteenth Century.* J. Murray, 1906. J. A. O'BRIEN, *Evolution and Religion.* Century, 1932. H. F. OSBORN, *Evolution and Religion in Education.* Scribner, 1926. A. R. WALLACE and others. *The Progress of the Century.* Harper, 1901. J. J. WALSH, "Church and the Experimental Method," *American Catholic Quarterly* (January, 1908).

Contemporary Accounts. J. H. ROBINSON and C. A. BEARD, *Readings.* See Vol. II, pp. 505–519. J. F. SCOTT and A. BALTZLY, *Readings.* See pp. 414–424. *Catholic Encyclopedia* (edited by G. G. Herbermann and others). 17 vols. Universal Knowledge Foundation, 1907–1912. See article on Pius IX.

CHAPTER XVI · *The New Revolution: Rise of the Proletariat*

Works dealing with Socialism. M. BEER, *History of British Socialism.* 2 vols. Harcourt, 1919–1920. M. BEER, *The Life and Teaching of Karl Marx.* Small, Maynard, 1924. E. BERNSTEIN, *Evolutionary Socialism: a Criticism and Affirmation.* Independent Labour Party, 1909. F. ENGELS, *Socialism: Utopian and Scientific.* Kerr, 1900. F. J. C. HEARNSHAW, *A Survey of Socialism, Analytical, Historical, and Critical.* Macmillan, 1928. A. W. HUMPHREY, *The Modern Case for Socialism.* Macmillan, 1928. T. KIRKUP, *History of Socialism* (5th rev. ed., by E. R. Pease). Longmans, 1913. H. W. LAIDLER, *A History of Socialist Thought.* Crowell, 1927. H. W. LAIDLER, *Socialism in Thought and Action.* Macmillan, 1920. J. R. MACDONALD, *Socialism: Critical and Constructive.* Bobbs, 1924. J. R. MACDONALD, *The Socialist Movement.* Holt, 1911. K. MARX, *Capital: a Critique of Political Economy.* International Publishers, 1929. K. MARX and F. ENGELS, *The Communist Manifesto.* International Publishers, 1930. O. RÜHLE, *Karl Marx: his Life and Work.* Viking Press, 1929. F. R. SALTER, *Karl Marx and Modern Socialism.* Macmillan, 1921. W. SOMBART, *Socialism and the Social Movement.* J. M. Dent & Sons, 1909. J. SPARGO, *Karl Marx: his Life and Work.* National Labour Press, 1911.

Special Accounts. H. E. BARNES, *Living in the Twentieth Century.* Bobbs, 1928. See pp. 191–199, 238–275. A. J. BOOTH, *Saint-Simon and Saint Simonism: a Chapter in the History of Socialism in France.* Longmans, 1871. L. L. LORWIN, *Labor and Internationalism.* Brookings Institution, 1929. E. S. MASON, *The Paris Commune.* Macmillan, 1930. L. MUMFORD, The Story *of Utopias.* Boni & Liveright, 1922. R. W. POSTGATE, *Out of the Past.* Houghton, 1922. P. J. PROUDHON, *What is Property?* B. R. Tucker, 1876. J. H. ROBINSON and C. A. BEARD, *Readings.* See Vol. II, pp. 478–505. B. A. W. RUSSELL, *German Social Democracy.* Longmans, 1896. J. F. SCOTT and A. BALTZLY, *Readings.* See pp. 396–414. G. B. SHAW, *The Intelligent Woman's Guide to Socialism and Capitalism.* Brentano's, 1928. W. K. WALLACE, *The Trend of History: Origins of Twentieth Century Problems.* Macmillan, 1922. S. and B. WEBB, *A Constitution for the Socialist Commonwealth of Great Britain.* Longmans, 1920.

CHAPTER XVII · *Great Britain: Twilight of the Victorian Age*

General Histories of England. W. E. LUNT, *A History of England.* Harper, 1928. See chaps. xxxviii–xxxix. C. E. ROBINSON, *England, a History of British Progress from the Early Ages to the Present Day.* Crowell, 1928. See pp. 655–710. G. SLATER, *The Making of Modern England.* Houghton, 1915. See chaps. xviii–xxiii. E. C. WINGFIELD-STRATFORD, *The History of British Civilization.* 2 vols. Harcourt, 1928. See Vol. II, Book 4, chaps. iii–iv.

Special Political and Economic Accounts. W. F. ADAMS, *Ireland and Irish Emigration to the New World, from 1815 to the Present.* Yale Univ. Press, 1932. W. J. ASHLEY, *British Industries.* Longmans, 1903. W. CUNNINGHAM, *Rise and Decline of the Free Trade Movement.* C. J. Clay & Sons, 1904. W. H. R. CURT-

LER, *A Short History of English Agriculture.* Oxford, 1909. See chap. xxi.
C. J. S. EVERSLEY, *Gladstone and Ireland.* Methuen & Co., 1912. J. A.
FARRER, *England under Edward VII.* George Allen & Unwin, 1922. R. H.
GRETTON, *Imperialism and Mr. Gladstone, 1876–1887.* Harcourt, 1913.
W. P. HALL, *Empire to Commonwealth: Thirty Years of British Imperial History.* Holt, 1928. P. KNAPLUND, *Gladstone and Britain's Imperial Policy.*
Macmillan, 1927. A. L. LOWELL, *The Government of England* (rev. ed.). 2 vols.
Macmillan, 1912. H. O. MEREDITH, *Outlines of the Economic History of England.* Sir I. Pitman & Sons, 1908. G. H. PERRIS, *Industrial History of Modern England.* Holt, 1914. See chaps. vii–ix. J. W. ROOT, *The Trade Relations of the British Empire.* J. W. Root, 1904. J. W. SWAIN, *Beginning of the Twentieth Century.* Norton, 1933. See chap. ii. A. P. USHER, *An Introduction to the Industrial History of England.* Houghton, 1920.

Biographies. J. H. EDWARDS, *David Lloyd George.* Sears Publishing Co.,
1929. S. LEE, *King Edward VII: a Biography.* 2 vols. Macmillan, 1925–1927.
For biographies of Gladstone, Disraeli, and Queen Victoria consult works
cited in the bibliography for Chapter XIII.

Contemporary Accounts. H. H. ASQUITH, *Fifty Years of British Parliament.* 2 vols. Little, 1926. G. E. BUCKLE, *Letters of Queen Victoria,* second
series. 3 vols. Longmans, 1928. H. J. GLADSTONE, *After Thirty Years.* Macmillan, 1928. J. H. ROBINSON and C. A. BEARD, *Readings.* See Vol. II,
pp. 255–266, 289–292, 296–305. J. F. SCOTT and A. BALTZLY, *Readings.* See
pp. 176–181, 187–227.

CHAPTER XVIII · *Liberalism in France, Italy, and the Iberian Peninsula*

Works dealing with France. J. H. CLAPHAM, *The Economic Development of France and Germany, 1815–1914.* Macmillan, 1923. See chaps. viii, x.
P. DE COUBERTIN, *The Evolution of France under the Third Republic.* Crowell,
1897. P. E. L. DESCHANEL, *Gambetta.* Dodd, 1920. A. L. GUÉRARD, *French Civilization in the Nineteenth Century; a Historical Introduction.* Century,
1914. C. A. H. GUIGNEBERT, *A Short History of the French People.* 2 vols.
Macmillan, 1930. See Vol. II, pp. 622–672. C. J. H. HAYES, *France, a Nation of Patriots.* Columbia Univ. Press, 1930. L. C. A. KNOWLES, *Economic Development in the Nineteenth Century: France, Germany, Russia, and the United States.* George Routledge & Sons, 1932. F. LAWTON, *The Third French Republic.* G. Richards, 1909. A. LIESSE, *Evolution of Credit and Banks in France from the Founding of the Bank of France to the Present Time.* U. S. Government Printing Office, 1910. L. L. LORWIN, *The Labor Movement in France; a Study in Revolutionary Syndicalism.* Longmans, 1912. E. S. MASON, *The Paris Commune.* Macmillan, 1930. R. POINCARÉ, *How France is Governed.* McBride,
1919. F. L. SCHUMAN, *War and Diplomacy in the French Republic.* McGraw,
1931. C. SEIGNOBOS, *Evolution of the French People.* Knopf, 1932. A. SIEGFRIED, *France, a Study in Nationality.* Yale Univ. Press, 1930. R. H. SOLTAU,
French Parties and Politics. Oxford, 1922. J. W. SWAIN, *Beginning of the Twentieth Century.* Norton, 1933. See chap. iv.

Italy, Spain, and Portugal. C. E. CHAPMAN, *History of Spain*. Macmillan, 1918. See chaps. xxxix–xl. F. B. DEAKIN, *Spain Today*. Knopf, 1924. R. F. FOERSTER, *The Italian Emigration of our Times*. Harvard Univ. Press, 1919. B. KING and T. OKEY, *Italy Today* (rev. ed.). Nisbet, 1909. E. MÉRIMÉE, *History of Spanish Literature* (translated and enlarged by S. G. MORLEY). Holt, 1930. F. A. OGG and W. R. SHARP, *Economic Development of Modern Europe* (rev. ed.). Macmillan, 1926. See pp. 92–103, 187–200. A. ROBERTSON, *Victor Emmanuel III*. Stokes, 1925. H. D. SEDGWICK, *Spain: a Short History of its Politics, Literature, and Art from the Earliest Times to the Present*. Little, 1925. See pp. 329–368. J. W. SWAIN, *Beginning of the Twentieth Century*. Norton, 1933. See chap. v. F. M. UNDERWOOD, *United Italy*. Methuen & Co., 1912. W. K. WALLACE, *Greater Italy*. Scribner, 1917. G. YOUNG, *Portugal, Old and Young, an Historical Study*. Oxford, 1917.

Contemporary Accounts. J. H. ROBINSON and C. A. BEARD, *Readings*. See Vol. II, pp. 208–238. J. F. SCOTT and A. BALTZLY, *Readings*. See pp. 304–315, 324–326.

CHAPTER XIX · *The German Empire: Enlightened Despotism*

Works dealing with Germany. J. E. BARKER, *The Foundations of Germany* (rev. ed.). J. Murray, 1918. B. H. M. K. VON BÜLOW, *Imperial Germany*. Dodd, 1914. J. H. CLAPHAM, *The Economic Development of France and Germany, 1815–1914*. Macmillan, 1923. See chaps. ix, xi. W. H. DAWSON, *The Evolution of Modern Germany*. Scribner, 1914. See Vol. I, chaps. x–xii, and Vol. II. W. H. DAWSON, *The German Empire, 1867–1914, and the Unity Movement*. 2 vols. Macmillan, 1919. B. E. HOWARD, *The German Empire*. Macmillan, 1906. J. W. SWAIN, *Beginning of the Twentieth Century*. Norton, 1933. See chap. iii. T. VEBLEN, *Imperial Germany and the Industrial Revolution*. Macmillan, 1915.

Special Works. P. W. L. ASHLEY, *Modern Tariff History: Germany — United States — France* (3d rev. ed.). Dutton, 1926. W. J. ASHLEY, *The Progress of the German Working Classes in the Last Quarter of a Century*. Longmans, 1904. E. B. BAX, *German Culture, Past and Present*. George Allen & Unwin, 1915. B. CERF, *Alsace-Lorraine since 1871*. Macmillan, 1919. W. H. DAWSON, *Bismarck and State Socialism* (2d ed.). S. Sonnenschein & Co., 1890. W. H. DAWSON, *Protection in Germany: a History of German Fiscal Policy during the Nineteenth Century*. P. S. King & Son, 1904. F. C. HOWE, *Socialized Germany*. Scribner, 1915. L. C. A. KNOWLES, *Economic Development in the Nineteenth Century: France, Germany, Russia, and the United States*. George Routledge & Sons, 1932. H. H. O'FARRELL, *The Franco-German War Indemnity and its Economic Results*. Harrison & Sons, 1913. W. P. PATERSON (ed.), *German Culture*. T. C. and E. C. Jack, 1915. C. G. ROBERTSON, *Bismarck*. Holt, 1919. K. WIEDENFELD, *Cartels and Combines*. World Peace Foundation, 1927.

Contemporary Accounts. F. E. G. PONSONBY (ed.), *Letters of the Empress Frederick*. Macmillan, 1928. J. H. ROBINSON and C. A. BEARD, *Readings*. See Vol. II, pp. 176–207. J. F. SCOTT and A. BALTZLY, *Readings*. See pp. 315–323. WILLIAM II, *The Kaiser's Memoirs, 1888–1918*. Harper, 1922.

CHAPTER XX · *Imperial Russia: Decline of an Old Order*

Histories of Russia. M. M. KARPOVICH, *Imperial Russia, 1801–1917.* Holt, 1932. See pp. 50–95. A. KORNILOV, *Modern Russian History* (rev. ed.). Knopf, 1924. N. MAKEEF and V. O'HARA, *Russia.* Scribner, 1925. See chaps. i–ii. J. MAVOR, *An Economic History of Russia* (2d rev. ed.). 2 vols. Dutton, 1925. D. S. MIRSKY, *Russia: a Social History.* Cresset Press, 1931. B. PARES, *History of Russia.* Knopf, 1926. See pp. 391–448. M. N. POKROVSKY, *History of Russia.* International Publishers, 1931. J. W. SWAIN, *Beginning of the Twentieth Century.* Norton, 1933. See chap. vi. G. V. VERNADSKY, *History of Russia* (rev. ed.). Yale Univ. Press, 1930. See chaps. xi–xii.

Special Works. L. C. A. KNOWLES, *Economic Development in the Nineteenth Century: France, Germany, Russia, and the United States.* George Routledge & Sons, 1932. M. M. KOVALEVSKY, *Russian Political Institutions.* Univ. of Chicago Press, 1902. C. LOWE, *Alexander III of Russia.* William Heinemann, 1895. P. N. MILIUKOV, *Russia and its Crisis.* Univ. of Chicago Press, 1905. H. W. NEVINSON, *The Dawn in Russia.* Harper, 1906. M. J. OLGIN, *The Soul of the Russian Revolution.* Holt, 1917. B. PARES, *Russia and Reform.* Constable & Co., 1907. G. H. PERRIS, *Russia in Revolution* (2d ed.). Chapman & Hall, 1905. F. H. B. SKRINE, *The Expansion of Russia, 1815–1900* (3d ed.). Cambridge Univ. Press, 1915.

Contemporary Accounts. K. P. POBIEDONOSTSEV, *Reflections of a Russian Statesman.* G. Richards, 1898. J. H. ROBINSON and C. A. BEARD, *Readings.* See Vol. II, pp. 371–381. J. F. SCOTT and A. BALTZLY, *Readings.* See pp. 329–351. S. J. WITTE, *Memoirs.* William Heinemann, 1921.

CHAPTER XXI · *Austria-Hungary: the Multinational State*

General Histories of the Dual Monarchy. G. DRAGE, *Austria-Hungary.* J. Murray, 1909. V. GAYDA, *Modern Austria: her Racial and Social Problems, with a Study of Italia Irredenta.* Dodd, 1915. O. JÁSZI, *Dissolution of the Habsburg Monarchy.* Univ. of Chicago Press, 1929. H. W. STEED, *The Hapsburg Monarchy* (4th ed.). Constable & Co., 1919. J. W. SWAIN, *Beginning of the Twentieth Century.* Norton, 1933. See chap. vii.

Special Works. E. S. BAGGER, *Francis Joseph, Emperor of Austria — King of Hungary.* Putnam, 1927. O. ERNST, *Franz Joseph as revealed by his Letters.* Stokes, 1927. E. KETTERL, *The Emperor Francis Joseph I.* Stratford, 1929. C. M. KNATCHBULL-HUGESSON, *The Political Evolution of the Hungarian Nation.* 2 vols. National Review Office, 1908. See Vol. II, chaps. xvii–xx. A. L. LOWELL, *Governments and Parties in Continental Europe* (rev. ed.). 2 vols. Houghton, 1900. See Vol. II, chaps. viii–x. A. MARGUTTI, *The Emperor Francis Joseph and his Times.* Hutchinson & Co., 1921. F. A. OGG, *The Governments of Europe.* Macmillan, 1913. See chaps. xxiv–xxvii. J. REDLICH, *Emperor Francis Joseph of Austria.* Macmillan, 1929. R. W. SETON-WATSON, *Corruption and Reform in Hungary: a Study of Electoral Practice.* Constable & Co., 1911. R. W. SETON-WATSON, *German, Slav, and Magyar: a Study in the Origins of the Great War.* Williams & Norgate,

1916. R. W. SETON-WATSON, *The Southern Slav Question and the Haps-burg Monarchy.* Constable & Co., 1911. K. TSCHUPPIK, *Francis Joseph I.* Harcourt, 1930. L. VOINOVITCH, *Dalmatia and the Jugoslav Movement.* George Allen & Unwin, 1920.

Contemporary Accounts. J. F. SCOTT and A. BALTZLY, *Readings.* See pp. 326–329.

CHAPTER XXII · *The Old and the New Imperialism*

Works dealing with Economic Imperialism. W. S. CULBERTSON, *Raw Materials and Foodstuffs in the Commercial Policies of Nations.* American Academy of Political and Social Science, 1924. J. A. HOBSON, *Imperialism: a Study* (rev. ed.). Constable & Co., 1905. A. G. KELLER, *Colonization: a Study of the Founding of New Societies.* Ginn, 1908. P. T. MOON, *Imperialism and World Politics.* Macmillan, 1926. See chaps. i–iv. P. T. MOON, *Syllabus on International Relations.* Macmillan, 1925. See Part III. E. D. MOREL, *The Black Man's Burden.* National Labour Press, 1920. F. A. OGG and W. R. SHARP, *Economic Development of Modern Europe* (rev. ed.). Macmillan, 1926. P. S. REINSCH, *Colonial Government.* Macmillan, 1902. H. ROBINSON, *The Development of the British Empire.* Houghton, 1922. A. VIALLATE, *Economic Imperialism and International Relations during the Last Fifty Years.* Macmillan, 1923. J. A. WILLIAMSON, *Europe Overseas.* Oxford, 1925. L. S. WOOLF, *Economic Imperialism.* Harcourt, 1920.

Imperialism and Christianity. J. S. DENNIS, *Christian Missions and Social Progress.* 3 vols. Revell, 1897–1906. C. H. PATTON, *The Business of Missions.* Macmillan, 1924.

Contemporary Accounts. J. H. ROBINSON and C. A. BEARD, *Readings.* See Vol. II, pp. 406–419. J. F. SCOTT and A. BALTZLY, *Readings.* See pp. 430–435.

CHAPTER XXIII · *The Partition of Africa*

Works dealing with the Colonization of Africa. R. BROWN, *The Story of Africa and its Explorers.* 4 vols. Cassell & Co., 1911. N. D. HARRIS, *Europe and Africa.* Houghton, 1927. N. D. HARRIS, *Intervention and Colonization in Africa.* Houghton, 1914. H. L. HOSKINS, *European Imperialism in Africa.* Holt, 1930. H. H. JOHNSTON, *History of the Colonization of Africa by Alien Races* (2d rev. ed.). Macmillan, 1913. H. H. JOHNSTON, *The Opening up of Africa.* Holt, 1911. A. G. KELLER, *Colonization: a Study of the Founding of New Societies.* Ginn, 1908. See chap. xiv. J. S. KELTIE, *Partition of Africa* (2d ed.). E. Stanford, 1895. P. T. MOON, *Imperialism and World Politics.* Macmillan, 1926. See chaps. v–x.

Special Works. R. L. BUELL, *The Native Problem in Africa.* 2 vols. Macmillan, 1928. LORD CROMER, *Modern Egypt.* 2 vols. in 1. Macmillan, 1916. H. H. DODWELL, *The Founder of Modern Egypt: a Study of Muhammad 'Ali.* Macmillan, 1931. I. L. EVANS, *The British in Tropical Africa, an Historical Outline.* Macmillan, 1929. H. A. GIBBONS, *The New Map of Africa, 1900–1916.* Century, 1916. A. GIRAULT, *The Colonial Tariff Policy of France.*

Oxford, 1916. A. B. KEITH, *The Belgian Congo and the Berlin Act.* Oxford, 1919. E. D. MOREL, *Red Rubber* (new and rev. ed.). Viking Press, 1920. M. E. TOWNSEND, *The Rise and Fall of Germany's Colonial Empire, 1884–1918.* Macmillan, 1930. J. A. WILLIAMSON, *A Short History of British Expansion* (2d ed.). 2 vols in 1. Macmillan, 1931. See Vol. II, pp. 116–130, 196–204, 214–224, 229–235. L. WOOLF, *Empire and Commerce in Africa, a Study in Economic Imperialism.* George Allen & Unwin, 1920. G. YOUNG, *Egypt.* Scribner, 1927.

Contemporary Accounts. D. LIVINGSTONE, *Missionary Travels and Researches in South Africa* (new ed.). J. Murray, 1899. D. LIVINGSTONE, *The Last Journals of David Livingstone in Central Africa* (edited by H. Waller). 2 vols. Harper, 1875. J. H. ROBINSON and C. A. BEARD, *Readings.* See Vol. II, pp. 327–336, 447–458. J. F. SCOTT and A. BALTZLY, *Readings.* See pp. 461–468. H. M. STANLEY, *Through the Dark Continent, or The Sources of the Nile.* 2 vols. Harper, 1906.

CHAPTER XXIV · *The Exploitation of Asia and Oceania*

Accounts dealing with the Pacific Area. T. DUNBABIN, *The Making of Australasia, a Brief History of the Origin and Development of the British Dominions in the South Pacific.* Macmillan, 1922. C. B. FLETCHER, *The Problem of the Pacific.* Holt, 1919. J. F. RIPPY, *Latin America in World Politics, an Outline Survey* (rev. ed.). Crofts, 1931. J. A. WILLIAMSON, *A Short History of British Expansion* (2d ed.). 2 vols. in 1. Macmillan, 1931. See Vol. II, pp. 193–196, 204–214.

The Near East and Middle Asia. V. CHIROL, *India: Old and New.* Macmillan, 1921. V. CHIROL, *The Occident and the Orient.* Univ. of Chicago Press, 1924. H. H. GOWEN, *Asia: a Short History from the Earliest Times to the Present Day.* Little, 1926. N. D. HARRIS, *Europe and the East.* Houghton, 1926. See chaps. i–iii, vi–vii. P. T. MOON, *Imperialism and World Politics.* Macmillan, 1926. See chaps. xi–xiii. P. M. SYKES, *A History of Persia* (2d ed.). 2 vols. Macmillan, 1921.

The Far East. H. F. BAIN, *Ores and Industry in the Far East.* Council on Foreign Relations, Inc., 1927. M. J. BAU, *The Foreign Relations of China: a History and a Survey* (rev. ed.). Revell, 1921. M. J. BAU, *The Open Door Doctrine in Relation to China.* Macmillan, 1923. G. H. DANTON, *Culture Contacts of the United States and China.* Columbia Univ. Press, 1931. R. K. DOUGLAS, *Europe and the Far East, 1506–1912* (rev. ed.). Putnam, 1913. H. A. GILES, *China and the Manchus.* Macmillan, 1912. H. H. GOWEN and J. W. HALL, *An Outline History of China.* Appleton, 1926. See chaps. xxi–xxvii. K. S. LATOURETTE, *The Development of China* (4th ed.). Houghton, 1929. A. LOBANOV–ROSTOVSKY, *Russia and Asia.* Macmillan, 1933. See chaps. i–xi. R. S. McCORDOCK, *British Far Eastern Policy, 1894–1900.* Columbia Univ. Press, 1931. H. B. MORSE and H. F. MacNAIR, *Far Eastern International Relations.* Houghton, 1931. See pp. 1–544. P. S. REINSCH, *World Politics at the End of the Nineteenth Century as influenced by the Oriental Situation.* Macmillan, 1900. See Parts II–III, V. P. J. TREAT, *The Far East. A Political and*

Diplomatic History. Harper, 1928. H. M. VINACKE, *A History of the Far East in Modern Times*. Knopf, 1928. P. WEALE, *The Vanished Empire*. Macmillan, 1926. E. T. WILLIAMS, *China: Yesterday and To-day* (rev. ed.). Crowell, 1927. W. W. WILLOUGHBY, *Foreign Rights and Interests in China* (2d ed.). 2 vols. Johns Hopkins Press, 1927.

Contemporary Accounts. J. H. ROBINSON and C. A. BEARD, *Readings*. See Vol. II, pp. 306–316, 322–327, 419–423, 435–444. J. F. SCOTT and A. BALTZLY, *Readings*. See pp. 435–453. W. M. SHUSTER, *The Strangling of Persia: a Story of European Diplomacy and Oriental Intrigue*. Century, 1912.

CHAPTER XXV · *The Young Capitalistic Powers: the United States and Japan*

Accounts dealing with the United States. J. T. ADAMS, *The Epic of America*. Little, 1931. C. A. and M. BEARD, *The Rise of American Civilization*. 2 vols. Macmillan, 1927. See Vol. II, chaps. xix–xxvii. J. B. BISHOP, *Theodore Roosevelt and his Time shown in his Own Letters*. 2 vols. Scribner, 1920. T. DENNETT, *Roosevelt and the Russo-Japanese War*. Doubleday, Page, 1925. A. L. P. DENNIS, *Adventures in American Diplomacy, 1896–1906*. Dutton, 1928. F. R. DULLES, *America in the Pacific: a Century of Expansion*. Houghton, 1932. C. R. FISH, *American Diplomacy* (5th ed.). Holt, 1929. J. H. LATANÉ, *From Isolation to Leadership: a Review of American Foreign Policy* (rev. ed.). Doubleday, Page, 1925. J. H. LATANÉ, *The United States and Latin America*. Doubleday, Page, 1920. G. PEEL, *The Economic Impact of America*. Macmillan, 1928. J. F. RIPPY, *Historical Evolution of Hispanic America*. Crofts, 1932. G. H. STUART, *Latin America and the United States* (2d ed.). Century, 1928. J. W. SWAIN, *Beginning of the Twentieth Century*. Norton, 1933. See chap. ix.

Japan. H. DYER, *Japan in World Politics*. Blackie & Son, 1909. H. H. GOWEN, *An Outline History of Japan*. Appleton, 1927. K. S. LATOURETTE, *The Development of Japan* (2d ed.). Macmillan, 1926. J. MURDOCH, *A History of Japan*. 3 vols. Greenberg, 1926. A. M. POOLEY, *Japan's Foreign Policies*. Dodd, 1920. R. P. PORTER, *Japan, the Rise of a Modern Power*. Oxford, 1918. P. J. TREAT, *Japan and the United States, 1853–1928* (rev. ed.). Stanford Univ. Press, 1928. H. M. VINACKE, *A History of the Far East in Modern Times*. Knopf, 1928. See chaps. iv–vi, viii, xvi–xvii.

Contemporary Accounts. J. H. ROBINSON and C. A. BEARD, *Readings*. See Vol. II, pp. 425–435, 444–447.

CHAPTER XXVI · *Internationalism before the World War*

Works dealing with Pacifism. D. ALLEN, *The Fight for Peace*. Macmillan, 1930. NORMAN ANGELL, *The Great Illusion*. Putnam, 1910. C. G. COULTON, *The Main Illusions of Pacificism*. Bowes & Bowes Co., 1916. P. T. MOON, *Syllabus on International Relations*. Macmillan, 1925. See Parts IV, IX–X. R. B. MOWAT, *Concert of Europe*. Macmillan, 1930. R. B. MOWAT, *History of European Diplomacy, 1815–1924*. Longmans, 1922. K. PEARSON,

National Life from the Standpoint of Science (2d ed.). A. & C. Black, 1905. J. B. SCOTT, *The Hague Peace Conferences of 1899 and 1907*. 2 vols. Johns Hopkins Press, 1909.

War. J. BAKELESS, *The Economic Causes of Modern War: a Study of the Period 1878–1918*. Moffat, 1921. H. N. BRAILSFORD, *The War of Steel and Gold: a Study of the Armed Peace* (3d ed.). Harcourt, 1915. G. L. DICKINSON, *War: its Nature, Cause, and Cure*. Macmillan, 1923. F. W. HIRST, *The Political Economy of War*. Dutton, 1915. J. H. JONES, *The Economics of War and Conquest*. P. S. King & Son, 1915. D. S. JORDAN, *War and Waste: a Series of Discussions of War and War Accessories*. Doubleday, Page, 1913. S. NEARING, *War: Organized Destruction and Mass Murder by Civilized Nations*. Vanguard Press, 1931.

Contemporary Accounts. W. H. COOKE and E. P. STICKNEY, *Readings in European International Relations since 1879*. Harper, 1931. See pp. 119–127. J. H. ROBINSON and C. A. BEARD, *Readings*. See Vol. II, pp. 458–466.

CHAPTER XXVII · *The Precarious Equilibrium*

General Accounts of European Diplomacy. S. B. FAY, *Origins of the World War* (rev. ed.). 2 vols. in 1. Macmillan, 1930. See Vol. I, chap. ii. G. P. GOOCH, *Franco-German Relations, 1871–1914*. Longmans, 1923. R. B. MOWAT, *History of European Diplomacy, 1815–1914*. Longmans, 1922. B. E. SCHMITT, *The Coming of the War, 1914*. 2 vols. Scribner, 1930. R. J. SONTAG, *European Diplomatic History, 1871–1932*. Century, 1933. See chaps. i–iii. J. W. SWAIN, *Beginning of the Twentieth Century*. Norton, 1933. See chaps. x–xv.

Special Works. J. V. FULLER, *Bismarck's Diplomacy at its Zenith*. Harvard Univ. Press, 1922. O. HAMMANN, *The World Policy of Germany, 1890–1912*. Knopf, 1927. W. L. LANGER, *European Alliances and Alignments, 1871–1890*. Knopf, 1931. W. L. LANGER, *The Franco-Russian Alliance, 1890–1894*. Harvard Univ. Press, 1929. G. MICHON, *The Franco-Russian Alliance, 1891–1917*. Macmillan, 1929. K. F. NOWAK, *Germany's Road to Ruin*. Macmillan, 1932. K. F. NOWAK, *Kaiser and Chancellor: the Opening Years of the Reign of Kaiser Wilhelm II*. Macmillan, 1930. A. F. PRIBRAM, *England and the International Policies of the European Powers, 1871–1914*. Oxford, 1931. F. L. SCHUMAN, *War and Diplomacy in the French Republic*. McGraw, 1931.

Contemporary Accounts. W. H. COOKE and E. P. STICKNEY, *Readings.* See pp. 3–95. G. B. MANHART, *Alliance and Entente, 1871–1914*. Crofts, 1932. A. F. PRIBRAM, *The Secret Treaties of Austria-Hungary, 1879–1914*. 2 vols. Harvard Univ. Press, 1920–1921. J. F. SCOTT and A. BALTZLY, *Readings.* See pp. 469–492. William II, *Letters from the Kaiser to the Czar*. Stokes, 1920.

CHAPTER XXVIII · *The Drift toward War*

General Accounts of European Diplomacy. E. BRANDENBURG, *From Bismarck to the World War: History of German Foreign Policy, 1870–1914*. Oxford, 1927. G. L. DICKINSON, *International Anarchy, 1904–1914*. Century,

1926. S. B. FAY, *Origins of the World War* (rev. ed.). 2 vols. in 1. Macmillan, 1930. B. E. SCHMITT, *Coming of the War, 1914.* 2 vols. Scribner, 1930. R. J. SONTAG, *European Diplomatic History, 1871–1932.* Century, 1933. See chaps. iv–v. J. W. SWAIN, *Beginning of the Twentieth Century.* Norton, 1933. See chaps. xvi–xviii.

Special Works. W. L. S. CHURCHILL, *The World Crisis, 1911–1914.* 2 vols. Scribner, 1923. E. M. EARLE, *Turkey, the Great Powers, and the Bagdad Railway.* Macmillan, 1923. A. FABRE-LUCE, *Limitations of Victory.* Knopf, 1926. See Part I. G. P. GOOCH, *Recent Revelations in European Diplomacy.* Longmans, 1927. R. B. HALDANE, *Before the War.* Funk, 1920. O. J. HALE, *Germany and the Diplomatic Revolution, 1904–1906.* Press of the Univ. of Pennsylvania, 1931. O. HAMMANN, *The World Policy of Germany, 1890–1912.* Knopf, 1927. See pp. 139–257. K. M. LICHNOWSKY, *Heading for the Abyss: Reminiscences.* Payson & Clarke, 1928. H. LUTZ, *Lord Grey and the World War.* Knopf, 1928. G. MICHON, *The Franco-Russian Alliance, 1891–1917.* Macmillan, 1929. See chaps. vi–xv. A. F. PRIBRAM, *Austrian Foreign Policy, 1908–1918.* George Allen & Unwin, 1923. P. RENOUVIN, *Immediate Origins of the War.* Yale Univ. Press, 1928. R. W. SETON-WATSON, *Sarajevo: a Study in the Origins of the Great War.* Hutchinson & Co., 1926. O. WEDEL, *Austro-German Diplomatic Relations, 1908–1914.* Stanford Univ. Press, 1932. A. VON WEGERER, *A Refutation of the Versailles War Guilt Thesis.* Knopf, 1930.

Contemporary Documents. W. H. COOKE and E. P. STICKNEY, *Readings.* See pp. 95–119, 127–385. R. H. LUTZ, *Fall of the German Empire.* 2 vols. Stanford Univ. Press, 1932. See Vol. I, chap. i. J. F. SCOTT, *Five Weeks: the Surge of Public Opinion on the Eve of the Great War.* Day, 1927. J. F. SCOTT and A. BALTZLY, *Readings.* See pp. 380–395, 492–518. B. VON SIEBERT and G. A. SCHREINER (eds.), *Entente Diplomacy and the World War, Matrix of the History of Europe, 1909–1914.* Putnam, 1921. F. STIEVE (ed.), *Izvolski and the World War.* Knopf, 1926.

CHAPTER XXIX · *The World War, 1914–1916: the Deadlock*

Histories of the War. F. M. BRIDGE, *A Short History of the Great World War.* Year Book Press, 1920. J. BUCHAN, *A History of the Great War.* 4 vols. Houghton, 1922. G. V. CAREY, *An Outline History of the Great War.* Macmillan, 1928. W. L. S. CHURCHILL, *The World Crisis, 1916–1918.* 2 vols. Scribner, 1927. B. H. L. HART, *The Real War.* Little, 1930. C. J. H. HAYES, *A Brief History of the Great War.* Macmillan, 1920. A. F. POLLARD, *A Short History of the Great War.* Methuen & Co., 1920. F. H. SIMONDS, *The Great War.* 5 vols. Doubleday, Page, 1917–1920.

Special Works. W. L. S. CHURCHILL, *The Unknown War: the Eastern Front.* Scribner, 1931. F. S. COCKS (ed.), *The Secret Treaties and Understandings.* Union of Democratic Control, 1918. J. S. CORBETT, *Naval Operations.* 5 vols. Longmans, 1920–1931. G. A. R. DEWAR, *The Great Munition Feat, 1914–1918.* Constable & Co., 1921. C. W. DOMVILLE-FIFE, *Submarine Warfare of Today.* Lippincott, 1920. C. R. GIBSON, *War Inventions and How they were Invented.* Lippincott, 1916. B. H. L. HART, *Reputations Ten Years After.* Little, 1928.

H. D. LASSWELL, *Propaganda Technique in the World War*. Knopf, 1927. H. J. NEWBOLT, *A Naval History of the War, 1914–1918*. Hodder & Stoughton, Ltd., 1920. W. D. PULESTON, *The Dardanelles Expedition: a Condensed Study*. U. S. Naval Inst., 1927. W. R. ROBERTSON, *Soldiers and Statesmen, 1914–1918*. 2 vols. Scribner, 1926. L. STALLINGS (ed.), *The First World War, a Photographic Study*. Simon & Schuster, 1933. C. C. TURNER, *The Struggle in the Air, 1914–1918*. Longmans, 1919.

Contemporary Accounts. W. H. COOKE and E. P. STICKNEY, *Readings*. See pp. 389–472. P. VON HINDENBURG, *Out of my Life*. Cassell & Co., 1920. J. R. JELLICOE, *The Grand Fleet, 1914–1916: its Creation, Development, and Work*. Doran, 1919. E. VON LUDENDORFF, *Ludendorff's Own Story*. 2 vols. Harper, 1920. R. H. LUTZ, *Fall of the German Empire*. 2 vols. Stanford Univ. Press, 1932. See Vol. I, chaps. iii–xviii. H. P. Pétain, *The Battle of Verdun*. Dial Press, 1930. J. F. SCOTT and A. BALTZLY, *Readings*. See pp. 518–521. A. P. F. VON TIRPITZ, *My Memoirs*. 2 vols. Dodd, 1919.

CHAPTER XXX · *The Allied Triumph, 1917–1918*

Special Works. J. S. BASSETT, *Our War with Germany: a History*. Knopf, 1919. E. L. BOGART, *Direct and Indirect Cost of the Great World War* (2d rev. ed.). Oxford, 1920. G. P. CLARKSON, *Industrial America in the World War, the Strategy behind the Line, 1917–1918*. Houghton, 1923. E. T. COOK, *The Press in War Time, with some Account of the Official Press Bureau*. Macmillan, 1920. H. D. LASSWELL, *Propaganda Technique in the World War*. Knopf, 1927. T. E. LAWRENCE, *Revolt in the Desert*. Doran, 1927. A. L. LOWELL, *Public Opinion in War and Peace* (rev. ed.). Longmans, 1926. J. B. McMASTER, *The United States in the World War*. 2 vols. Appleton, 1927. W. T. MASSEY, *How Jerusalem was Won: the Record of Allenby's Campaign in Palestine*. Constable & Co., 1919. E. M. REMARQUE, *All Quiet on the Western Front*. Little, 1929. B. A. W. RUSSELL, *Free Thought and Official Propaganda*. Viking Press, 1922. C. SEYMOUR, *Woodrow Wilson and the World War*. Yale Univ. Press, 1921. J. W. SWAIN, *Beginning of the Twentieth Century*. Norton, 1933. See chaps. xxiii, xxv–xxvi. L. J. THOMAS, *Raiders of the Deep*. Doubleday, Doran, 1929.

Contemporary Accounts. R. S. BAKER, *Woodrow Wilson, Life and Letters*. 4 vols. Doubleday, Doran, 1927–1931. W. H. COOKE and E. P. STICKNEY, *Readings*. See pp. 473–564. J. F. SCOTT and A. BALTZLY, *Readings*. See pp. 518–538.

For general accounts of the war consult works cited for Chapter XXIX.

CHAPTER XXXI · *The Conference of Paris and the Peace Settlements*

Books dealing with the Peace Conference. F. L. BENNS, *Europe since 1914*. Crofts, 1930. See chaps. vii–viii. W. C. LANGSAM, *The World since 1914*. Macmillan, 1933. See chaps. iv–v. D. H. MILLER, *The Drafting of the Covenant*. 2 vols. Putnam, 1928. H. W. V. TEMPERLEY, *A History of the Peace Conference of Paris*. 6 vols. Oxford, 1920–1924.

Special Works. R. S. Baker, *Woodrow Wilson and the World Settlement.* 3 vols. Doubleday, Page, 1922. B. M. Baruch, *The Making of the Reparation and Economic Sections of the Treaty.* Harper, 1920. G. L. Beer, *African Questions at the Paris Peace Conference.* Macmillan, 1923. A. H. Brooks and M. F. Lacroix, *The Iron and Associated Industries of Lorraine, the Saare District, Luxemburg, and Belgium.* U. S. Government Office, 1920. W. L. S. Churchill, *The Aftermath.* Scribner, 1929. C. H. Haskins and R. H. Lord, *Some Problems of the Peace Conference.* Harvard Univ. Press, 1920. E. M. House and C. Seymour (eds.), *What Really Happened at Paris: the Story of the Peace Conference, 1918–1919, by American Delegates.* Scribner, 1921. J. M. Keynes, *The Economic Consequences of the Peace.* Harcourt, 1920. J. Martet, *Georges Clemenceau.* Longmans, 1930. K. F. Nowak, *Versailles.* V. Gollancz, 1928. A. P. G. A. Tardieu, *The Truth about the Treaty.* Bobbs, 1921. *The Treaties of Peace, 1919–1923.* 2 vols. Carnegie Endowment for International Peace, 1924.

Contemporary Accounts. W. H. Cooke and E. P. Stickney, *Readings.* See pp. 589–758. J. F. Scott and A. Baltzly, *Readings.* See pp. 539–552.

Chapter XXXII · *The League of Nations: In Quest of an Ideal*

General Accounts of the League. J. S. Bassett. *The League of Nations: a Chapter in World Politics.* Longmans, 1928. F. L. Benns, *Europe since 1914.* Crofts, 1930. See chap. ix. R. B. Mowat, *History of European Diplomacy, 1914–1925.* Longmans, 1927. P. B. Potter, *The World of Nations: Foundations, Institutions, Practice.* Macmillan, 1929.

Special Works. P. M. Baker, *The League of Nations at Work.* Nisbet, 1926. G. N. Barnes, *History of the International Labor Office.* Williams & Norgate, Ltd., 1926. P. M. Brown, *International Society: its Nature and Interests.* Macmillan, 1923. A. S. de Bustamante y Sirvén, *The World Court.* Macmillan, 1925. A. P. Fachiri, *The Permanent Court of International Justice: its Constitution, Procedure, and Work.* Oxford, 1925. A. S. Hershey, *Essentials of International Public Law and Organization* (rev. ed.). Macmillan, 1927. M. O. Hudson, *The World Court, 1921–1931.* World Peace Foundation, 1931. E. S. Lindsey, *The International Court.* Crowell, 1931. T. Marburg, *The Development of the League of Nations Idea* (documents and correspondence of Theodore Marburg, edited by J. H. Latané). 2 vols. Macmillan, 1932. F. Morley, *The Society of Nations.* Brookings Institution, 1932. D. P. Myers, *Nine Years of the League of Nations, 1920–1928.* World Peace Foundation, 1929. S. Nearing, *War: Organized Destruction and Mass Murder by Civilized Nations.* Vanguard Press, 1931. P. B. Potter, *An Introduction to the Study of International Organization* (3d ed.). Century, 1928. H. S. Quigley, *From Versailles to Locarno: a Sketch of the Recent Development of International Organization.* Univ. of Minnesota Press, 1927. *Ten Years of World Coöperation* (edited by E. Drummond). World Peace Foundation, 1930.

Contemporary Accounts. W. H. Cooke and E. P. Stickney, *Readings.* See pp. 761–851, 887–892, 927–938, 971–991. J. F. Scott and A. Baltzly, *Readings.* See pp. 553–563.

CHAPTER XXXIII · *Bolshevist Russia: The New Revolution*

Works dealing with the Russian Revolution. I. BOWMAN, *The New World* (4th ed.). World Book Co., 1928. See pp. 450–481. L. LAWTON, *The Russian Revolution, 1917–1926*. Macmillan, 1927. N. MAKEEF and V. O'HARA, *Russia*. Scribner, 1925. See chaps. v–xii. J. MAVOR, *The Russian Revolution*. Macmillan, 1928. P. MILIUKOV, *Russia Today and Tomorrow*. Macmillan, 1922. M. J. OLGIN, *Soul of the Russian Revolution*. Holt, 1917. G. V. VERNADSKY, *Russian Revolution, 1917–1931*. Holt, 1932.

Economic and Social Accounts. S. CHASE, R. DUNN, and R. G. TUGWELL (eds.), *Soviet Russia in the Second Decade: a Joint Survey by the Technical Staff of the First American Trade Union Delegation*. Day, 1928. M. DOBB and H. C. STEVENS, *Russian Economic Development since the Revolution*. Dutton, 1928. R. FÜLÖP-MILLER, *The Mind and Face of Bolshevism: an Examination of Cultural Life in Soviet Russia*. Knopf, 1928. M. G. HINDUS, *The Russian Peasant and the Revolution*. Holt, 1920. C. B. HOOVER, *The Economic Life of Soviet Russia*. Macmillan, 1931. H. R. KNICKERBOCKER, *The Red Trade Menace: Progress of the Soviet Five-Year Plan*. Dodd, 1931. I. L. LEE, *Present-Day Russia* (2d ed.). Macmillan, 1928. D. S. MIRSKY, *Russia: a Social History*. Cresset Press, 1931. V. M. MOLOTOV, *The Success of the Five-Year Plan*. International Publishers, 1931. S. NEARING and J. HARDY, *The Economic Organization of the Soviet Union*. Vanguard Press, 1927. L. PASVOLSKY and H. G. MOULTON, *Russian Debts and Russian Reconstruction: a Study of the Relation of Russia's Foreign Debts to her Economic Recovery*. McGraw, 1924. S. N. PROKOPOVICH, *The Economic Condition of Soviet Russia*. P. S. King & Son, 1924. S. ZIMAND, *State Capitalism in Russia; the Soviet Economic System in Operation, 1917–1926*. Foreign Policy Association, 1926.

Miscellaneous Works. R. P. ARNOT, *Soviet Russia and her Neighbors*. Vanguard Press, 1927. W. R. BATSELL, *Soviet Rule in Russia*. Macmillan, 1929. W. H. CHAMBERLIN, *Soviet Russia: a Living Record and a History*. Little, 1930. E. T. COLTON, *The X-Y-Z of Communism*. Macmillan, 1931. A. L. P. DENNIS, *The Foreign Policies of Soviet Russia*. Dutton, 1924. G. P. FEDOTOFF, *The Russian Church since the Revolution*. Macmillan, 1928. M. T. FLORINSKY, *End of the Russian Empire*. Yale Univ. Press, 1931. R. FÜLÖP-MILLER, *Rasputin: the Holy Devil*. Viking Press, 1928. S. N. HARPER, *Making Bolsheviks*. Univ. of Chicago Press, 1931. V. MARCU, *Lenin*. Macmillan, 1928. D. S. MIRSKY, *Lenin*. Little, 1931. G. V. VERNADSKY, *Lenin: Red Dictator*. Yale Univ. Press, 1931.

Contemporary Accounts. W. H. COOKE and E. P. STICKNEY, *Readings*. See pp. 849–872. F. A. GOLDER, *Documents of Russian History, 1914–1917*. Century, 1927. M. ILN, *New Russia's Primer*. Houghton, 1931. N. LENIN (V. I. ULIANOV), *The Soviets at Work*. Rand Book Store, 1919. J. F. SCOTT and A. BALTZLY, *Readings*. See pp. 564–587, 633–662, 677–680. J. STALIN, *Leninism*. International Publishers, 1928. L. D. TROTSKY, *History of the Russian Revolution*. 3 vols. Simon & Schuster, 1932–1933.

CHAPTER XXXIV · *Fascism in Italy: The New Cæsarism*

Works on Fascism. J. S. BARNES, *Fascism.* T. Butterworth, 1931. J. S. BARNES, *The Universal Aspects of Fascism.* Williams & Norgate, 1928. F. L. BENNS, *Europe since 1914.* Crofts, 1930. See chap. xvi. I. BOWMAN, *The New World* (4th ed.). World Book Co., 1928. See pp. 231–247. G. FERRERO, *Four Years of Fascism.* P. S. King & Son, 1924. E. W. HULLINGER, *The New Fascist State.* Rae D. Henkle, 1928. C. E. McGUIRE, *Italy's International Economic Position.* Macmillan, 1926. F. NITTI, *Bolshevism, Fascism, and Democracy.* Macmillan, 1927. A. PENNACHIO, *The Corporative State.* Italian Historical Society, 1927. G. PREZZOLINI, *Fascism.* Dutton, 1927. G. SALVEMINI, *The Fascist Dictatorship in Italy*, Vol. I. Holt, 1927. H. W. SCHNEIDER, *Making the Fascist State.* Oxford, 1928, T. SILLANI (ed.), *What is Fascism and Why?* Ernest Benn, 1931.

Biographies of Mussolini. W. BOLITHO, *Italy under Mussolini.* Macmillan, 1926. V. J. BORDEUX, *Benito Mussolini — the Man.* Doran, 1927. E. LUDWIG, *Talks with Mussolini.* Little, 1933. B. MUSSOLINI, *My Autobiography.* Scribner, 1928.

Special Accounts. W. PARSONS, *The Pope and Italy.* The America Press, 1929. J. F. SCOTT and A. BALTZLY, *Readings.* See pp. 601–609, 680–682.

CHAPTER XXXV · *The German Republic: An Experiment in Democracy*

Books on the German Republic. I. BOWMAN, *The New World* (4th ed.). World Book Co., 1928. See pp. 260–296. R. BRUNET, *The New German Constitution.* Knopf, 1922. H. G. DANIELS, *The Rise of the German Republic.* Scribner, 1928. W. C. LANGSAM. *The World since 1914.* Macmillan, 1933. See chaps. vii, xv. E. LUEHR, *The New German Republic.* Minton, 1929. H. QUIGLEY and R. T. CLARK, *Republican Germany.* Dodd, 1928.

Special Works. J. W. ANGELL, *The Recovery of Germany.* Yale Univ. Press, 1929. H. F. ARMSTRONG, *Hitler's Reich.* Macmillan, 1933. G. P. AULD, *The Dawes Plan and the New Economics.* Doubleday, Page, 1927. M. BAUMONT, *The Fall of the Kaiser.* Knopf, 1931. K. BERGMANN, *The History of Reparations.* Houghton, 1927. G. H. DANTON, *Germany Ten Years After.* Houghton, 1928. P. DAWSON, *Germany's Industrial Revival.* Macmillan, 1926. K. FRANCKE, *German After-War Problems.* Harvard Univ. Press, 1927. G. P. GOOCH, *Germany.* Scribner, 1925. C. B. HOOVER, *Germany enters the Third Reich.* Macmillan, 1933. R. H. LUTZ, *The German Revolution, 1918–1919.* Stanford Univ. Press, 1922. H. G. MOULTON and C. E. McGUIRE, *Germany's Capacity to Pay: a Study of the Reparation Problem.* McGraw, 1923. R. A. K. RHEINHABEN, *Stresemann, the Man and the Statesman.* Appleton, 1929. H. SCHACHT, *The End of Reparations.* Jonathan Cape & Harrison Smith, 1931. M. SERING, *Germany under the Dawes Plan.* P. S. KING & SON, 1929. A. VALLENTIN, *Stresemann.* Constable & Co., 1931. P. VIENOT, *Is Germany Finished?* Macmillan, 1932. R. WETERSTETTEN, *The Biography of President von Hindenburg.* Macmillan, 1930.

Contemporary Accounts. W. H. COOKE and E. P. STICKNEY, *Readings.*
See pp. 892–915, 938–946, 1017–1029. A. HITLER, *My Battle.* Houghton,
1933. R. H. LUTZ, *Fall of the German Empire.* 2 vols. Stanford Univ. Press,
1932. See Vol. II. P. SCHEIDEMANN, *The Making of New Germany.* 2 vols.
Appleton, 1929. J. F. SCOTT and A. BALTZLY, *Readings.* See pp. 587–593,
668–673.

CHAPTER XXXVI · *New States and Old: The Triumph of Nationalism*

Books dealing with the New States of Europe. H. F. ARMSTRONG, *The
New Balkans.* Harper, 1926. C. A. BEARD and G. RADIN, *The Balkan Pivot:
Yugoslavia, a Study in Government and Administration.* Macmillan, 1929.
F. L. BENNS, *Europe since 1914.* Crofts, 1930. See chaps. v, xviii–xx.
I. BOWMAN, *The New World* (4th ed.). World Book Co., 1928. See pp. 307–
449. J. O. CRANE, *The Little Entente.* Macmillan, 1931. M. W. GRAHAM,
New Governments of Eastern Europe. Holt, 1927. M. W. GRAHAM and R. C.
BINKLEY, *New Governments of Central Europe.* Holt, 1924. J. GRUBER, *Czecho-
slovakia: a Survey of Economic and Social Conditions.* Macmillan, 1924.
N. IORGA, *A History of Roumania: Land, People, Civilization.* Dodd, 1926.
W. C. LANGSAM, *The World since 1914.* Macmillan, 1933. See chaps. xvi–
xvii, xix. K. F. NOWAK, *The Collapse of Central Europe.* Dutton, 1924.
C. PHILLIPS, *The New Poland.* George Allen & Unwin, 1923. O. RUTTER,
*The New Baltic States and their Future: an Account of Lithuania, Latvia, and
Estonia.* Houghton, 1926.

Special Works. E. S. BAGGER, *Eminent Europeans: Studies in Continental
Reality.* Putnam, 1922. I. L. EVANS, *The Agrarian Revolution in Roumania.*
Macmillan, 1924. O. JÁSZI, *Revolution and Counter-revolution in Hungary.*
P. S. King & Son, 1924. R. LANDAU, *Pilsudski and Poland.* Dial Press, 1929.
C. A. MACARTNEY, *The Social Revolution in Austria.* Cambridge Univ. Press,
1926. J. MAVROGORDATO, *Modern Greece: a Chronicle and a Survey, 1800–1931.*
Macmillan, 1931. W. MILLER, *Greece.* Scribner, 1928. M. I. NEWBIGIN, *Geo-
graphical Aspects of Balkan Problems in Relation to the Great European War.*
Putnam, 1915. L. PASVOLSKY, *Economic Nationalism of the Danubian States.*
Brookings Institution, 1928. J. H. WUORINEN, *Nationalism in Modern Fin-
land.* Columbia Univ. Press, 1931.

Contemporary Accounts. J. F. SCOTT and A. BALTZLY, *Readings.* See
pp. 593–601, 662–668.

CHAPTER XXXVII · *Recovery of France: the Search for Security*

Books dealing with Post-war France. F. L. BENNS, *Europe since 1914.*
Crofts, 1930. See chap. xiii. I. BOWMAN, *The New World* (4th ed.). World
Book Co., 1928. See pp. 148–193. R. L. BUELL, *Contemporary French Politics.*
Appleton, 1920. C. J. H. HAYES, *France, a Nation of Patriots.* Columbia
Univ. Press, 1930. R. B. MOWAT, *History of European Diplomacy, 1914–1925.*
Longmans, 1927. W. F. OGBURN and W. JAFFÉ, *The Economic Development
of Post-war France: a Survey of Production.* Columbia Univ. Press, 1929.

J. H. ROGERS, *The Process of Inflation in France, 1914–1927*. Columbia Univ. Press, 1929. D. J. SAPOSS, *The Labor Movement in Post-war France*. Columbia Univ. Press, 1931. F. L. SCHUMAN, *War and Diplomacy in the French Republic*. McGraw, 1931. A. SIEGFRIED, *France: a Study in Nationality*. Yale Univ. Press, 1930.

Special Works. V. DE BALLA, *The New Balance of Power in Europe*. Johns Hopkins Press, 1932. A. FABRE-LUCE, *Locarno the Reality*. Knopf, 1928. S. HUDDLESTON, *Poincaré: a Biographical Portrait*. Little, 1924. F. A. KELLOR, *Security against War*. Macmillan, 1924. D. H. MILLER, *The Geneva Protocol*. Macmillan, 1925. D. H. MILLER, *The Peace Pact of Paris: a Study of the Briand-Kellogg Treaty*. Putnam, 1928. R. J. SONTAG, *European Diplomatic History, 1871–1932*. Century, 1933. See chaps. vii–ix. J. W. WHEELER-BENNETT, *Disarmament and Security since Locarno, 1925–1931*. Macmillan, 1932.

Contemporary Accounts. W. H. COOKE and E. P. STICKNEY, *Readings*. See pp. 924–927, 946–971, 998–1007. J. F. SCOTT and A. BALTZLY, *Readings*. See pp. 682–689.

CHAPTER XXXVIII · *Great Britain after the War: Labor in Power*

Economic and Social Books. I. BOWMAN, *The New World* (4th ed.). World Book Co., 1928. See pp. 34–123. H. CLAY, *The Post-war Unemployment Problem*. Macmillan, 1929. H. CLAY, *The Problem of Industrial Relations*. Macmillan, 1929. G. D. H. COLE, *British Trade and Industry: Past and Future*. Macmillan, 1932. G. D. H. COLE, *The Next Ten Years in British Social and Economic Policy*. Macmillan, 1929. W. C. DAMPIER-WHETHAM, *Politics and the Land*. Macmillan, 1927. R. C. DAVISON, *The Unemployed; Old Policies and New*. Longmans, 1929. W. DIBELIUS, *England*. Harper, 1930. P. FITZGERALD, *Industrial Combination in England*. Sir I. Pitman & Sons, 1927. A. H. JOHNSON, *Disappearance of the Small Landowner*. Oxford, 1909. H. LEVY, *Monopolies, Cartels, and Trusts in British Industry*. Macmillan, 1927. A. LOVEDAY, *Britain and World Trade*. Longmans, 1931. J. ORR, *A Short History of British Agriculture*. Oxford, 1922. A. SIEGFRIED, *England's Crisis*. Harcourt, 1931. A. SIEGFRIED, *Post-war Britain*. Dutton, 1925. Liberal Industrial Inquiry, *Britain's Industrial Future*. Ernest Benn, 1928.

Miscellaneous Works. D. R. GWYNN, *The Irish Free State, 1922–1927*. Macmillan, 1928. M. A. HAMILTON, *J. Ramsay MacDonald*. Jonathan Cape, 1930. A. B. KEITH, *Sovereignty of the British Dominions*. Macmillan, 1929. J. M. KEYNES, *Essays in Persuasion*. Harcourt, 1932. W. C. LANGSAM, *The World since 1914*. Macmillan, 1933. See chaps. x–xi. G. PEEL, *The Economic War*. Macmillan, 1930. R. E. PROTHERO, *English Farming, Past and Present* (4th ed.). Longmans, 1927. J. W. ROOT, *The Trade Relations of the British Empire*. J. W. Root, 1904.

Contemporary Accounts. J. F. SCOTT and A. BALTZLY, *Readings*. See pp. 616–633.

CHAPTER XXXIX · *The Pacific and the Revolt of Asia*

Books dealing with the Americas and the Pacific. C. A. and M. BEARD, *Rise of American Civilization.* 2 vols. Macmillan, 1927. See Vol. II, chaps. xxviii–xxx. J. M. CALLAHAN, *American Foreign Policy in Mexican Relations.* Macmillan, 1932. L. FISCHER, *Oil Imperialism, the International Struggle for Petroleum.* International Publishers, 1926. W. C. LANGSAM, *The World Since 1914.* Macmillan, 1933. See chap. xxii. J. C. MALIN, *The United States after the World War.* Ginn, 1930. P. W. SLOSSON, *The Great Crusade and After, 1914–1928.* Macmillan, 1930. B. H. WILLIAMS, *The Economic Foreign Policy of the United States.* McGraw, 1929.

Africa, the Near East, and Middle Asia. R. L. BUELL, *The Native Problem in Africa.* 2 vols. Macmillan, 1928. I. BOWMAN, *The New World* (4th ed.). World Book Co., 1928. See pp. 482–564. V. CHIROL, *The Egyptian Problem.* Macmillan, 1920. M. K. GANDHI, *Young India, 1924–1926.* Viking Press, 1927. H. H. GOWEN, *Asia: a Short History from the Earliest Times to the Present Day.* Little, 1926. J. W. HALL, *The Revolt of Asia.* Putnam, 1927. M. HARRIS, *Egypt under the Egyptians.* Chapman & Hall, 1925. N. D. HARRIS, *Europe and the East.* Houghton, 1926. W. B. HARRIS, *France, Spain, and the Riffs.* Longmans, 1927. H. KOHN, *History of Nationalism in the East.* Harcourt, 1929. S. P. LADAS, *The Exchange of Minorities: Bulgaria, Greece, and Turkey.* Macmillan, 1932. W. C. LANGSAM, *The World since 1914.* Macmillan, 1933. See chaps. ix, xx. W. MILLER, *The Ottoman Empire and its Successors (1801–1927)* (rev. ed.). Macmillan, 1928. See pp. 540–563. A. J. TOYNBEE, *The Western Question in Greece and Turkey: a Study in the Contact of Civilizations* (2d ed.). Houghton, 1923. A. J. TOYNBEE and K. P. KIRKWOOD, *Turkey.* Scribner, 1927.

The Far East. I. BOWMAN, *The New World* (4th ed.). World Book Co., 1928. See pp. 565–626, 656–746. L. CURTIS, *The Capital Question of China.* Macmillan, 1932. G. M. DUTCHER, *The Political Awakening of the East.* Abingdon Press, 1925. H. H. GOWEN, *An Outline History of Japan.* Appleton, 1927. H. H. GOWEN and J. W. HALL, *An Outline History of China.* Appleton, 1926. See chaps. xxviii–xxxvi. A. N. HOLCOMBE, *The Chinese Revolution: a Phase in the Regeneration of a World Power.* Harvard Univ. Press, 1930. S. KING-HALL, *Western Civilization and the Far East.* Scribner, 1924. O. LATTIMORE, *Manchuria, Cradle of Conflict.* Macmillan, 1932. A. LOBANOV-ROSTOVSKY, *Russia and Asia.* Macmillan, 1933. See chaps. xii–xiv. H. F. MACNAIR, *China in Revolution.* Univ. of Chicago Press, 1931. H. B. MORSE and H. F. MACNAIR, *Far Eastern International Relations.* Houghton, 1931. See pp. 545–780. H. G. MOULTON and J. Ko, *Japan, an Economic and Financial Appraisal.* Brookings Institution, 1931. J. E. and D. ORCHARD, *Japan's Economic Position: the Progress of Industrialization.* McGraw, 1930. H. B. RESTARICK, *Sun Yat Sen, Liberator of China.* Yale Univ. Press, 1931. P. W. SLOSSON, *The Great Crusade and After, 1914–1928.* Macmillan, 1930. G. E. SOKOLSKY, *The Tinder Box of Asia.* Doubleday, Doran, 1932. J. A. SPENDER, *The Changing East.* Stokes, 1926. Y. TAKEKOSHI, *The Economic Aspects of the History of the Civilization of Japan.* 3 vols. Macmillan, 1930. P. J. TREAT, *Japan and* *the United States, 1853–1928* (rev. ed.). Stanford Univ. Press, 1928. H. M. VINACKE, *History of the Far East in Modern Times.* Knopf, 1928. See chaps. xviii–xxii. W. W. WILLOUGHBY, *Foreign Rights and Interests in China* (rev. ed.). 2 vols. Johns Hopkins Press, 1927. C. W. YOUNG, *Japan's Special Position in Manchuria: its Assertion, Legal Interpretation, and Present Meaning.* Johns Hopkins Press, 1931.

Contemporary Accounts. W. H. COOKE and E. P. STICKNEY, *Readings.* See pp. 872–887, 918–924. J. F. SCOTT and A. BALTZLY, *Readings.* See pp. 453–460, 610–616.

CHAPTER XL · *The Twentieth Century: Culmination of the Bourgeois Order?*

Books dealing with Economic and Social Conditions. M. J. BONN, *The Crisis of Capitalism in America.* Martin Hopkinson, 1931. S. CHASE, *A New Deal.* Macmillan, 1932. G. D. H. COLE, *A Guide through World Chaos.* Knopf, 1932. G. D. H. COLE, *Economic Tracts for the Times.* Macmillan, 1932. L. DENNIS, *Is Capitalism Doomed?* Harper, 1932. M. H. DOBB, *Capitalist Enterprise and Social Progress.* George Routledge & Sons, 1925. W. B. DONHAM, *Business Adrift.* McGraw, 1931. W. B. DONHAM, *Business Looks at the Unforeseen.* McGraw, 1932. P. EINZIG, *The World Economic Crisis, 1929–1931* (2d ed.). Macmillan, 1932. A. H. HANSEN, *Economic Stabilization in an Unbalanced World.* Harcourt, 1932. H. W. LAIDLER, *Concentration of Control in American Industry.* Crowell, 1931. H. G. MOULTON and L. PASVOLSKY, *War Debts and World Prosperity.* Century, 1932. J. H. ROGERS, *America Weighs her Gold.* Yale Univ. Press, 1931. A. SALTER, *Recovery: Second Effort.* Century, 1932. F. SOMARY, *Changes in the Structure of World Economics since the War.* P. S. King & Son, 1931. G. H. SOULE, *A Planned Society.* Macmillan, 1932. H. G. WELLS, *The Work, Wealth, and Happiness of Mankind.* Doubleday, Doran, 1931. Q. WRIGHT (ed.), *Unemployment as a World Problem.* Univ. of Chicago Press, 1931. League of Nations, *The Course and Phases of the World Economic Depression.* World Peace Foundation, 1931. Royal Institute of International Affairs, *The International Gold Problem.* Oxford, 1931. *The International Financial Position of the United States.* National Industrial Conference Board, 1929. *Recent Economic Changes in the United States,* Report of the President's Conference on Unemployment. 2 vols. McGraw, 1929.

Political Problems. H. E. BARNES, *World Politics in Modern Civilization.* Knopf, 1930. See Part V. C. A. BEARD, *Whither Mankind?* Longmans, 1928. G. A. DORSEY, *Man's Own Show: Civilization.* Harper, 1931. W. E. HOCKING, *The Spirit of World Politics, with Special Studies of the Near East.* Macmillan, 1932. W. C. LANGSAM, *The World since 1914.* Macmillan, 1933. V. LEFEBURE, *Scientific Disarmament.* Macmillan, 1931. W. LIPPMAN, *Interpretations, 1931–1932.* Macmillan, 1932. P. T. MOON, *Syllabus on International Relations.* Macmillan, 1925. See Parts VII–X. S. NEARING, *War: Organized Destruction and Mass Murder by Civilized Nations.* Vanguard Press, 1931. F. L. PAXSON, *Recent History of the United States, 1865–1929.* Houghton,

1929. J. H. RANDALL, *Making of the Modern Mind; a Survey of the Intellectual Background of the Present Age.* Houghton, 1926. B. H. WILLIAMS, *The United States and Disarmament.* McGraw, 1931.

Art, Science, Literature, and Religion. O. W. CALDWELL and E. E. SLOSSON (eds.), *Science Remaking the World.* Doubleday, Page, 1923. E. FRIEDELL, *Cultural History of the Modern Age.* 2 vols. Knopf, 1930. H. GARDNER, *Art through the Ages: an Introduction to its History and Significance.* Harcourt, 1926. F. H. HOOPER (ed.), *These Eventful Years: the Twentieth Century in the Making, as told by Many of its Makers.* 2 vols. Encyclopædia Britannica, Inc., 1924. P. C. R. LANDORMY, *History of Music.* Scribner, 1923. L. MAGNUS, *Dictionary of European Literature, designed as a Companion to English Studies.* Dutton, 1926. F. S. MARVIN (ed.), *Science and Civilization.* Oxford, 1923. J. PIJOAN Y SOTERAS, *History of Art.* 3 vols. Harper, 1927. W. S. PRATT, *The History of Music* (rev. ed.). Schirmer, N. Y., 1927. J. H. ROBINSON and C. A. BEARD, *Development of Modern Europe.* 2 vols. Ginn, 1929–1930. See Vol. II, chaps. xviii–xx. W. T. SEDGWICK and H. W. TYLER, *Short History of Science.* Macmillan, 1917. O. SPENGLER, *Decline of the West.* 2 vols. Knopf, 1926–1928. *Introduction to Contemporary Civilization in the West* (edited by the faculty, Columbia University; 8th ed.). Columbia Univ. Press, 1930. See pp. 353–444.

INDEX

Abd-el-Kader, 403

Abd-el-Krim, 768

Abdul Hamid II (Sultan of Turkey), policies of, 250; fall of, 257, 507; and Germany, 500, 501, 502

Abdullah, 777

Abolitionists, 418

Absolutism, and nationalism, 33; and Russia, 158; and mercantilism, 386

Abyssinia, and Italy, 328, 407–408; Bruce in, 399; independence of, 401, 416, 418

Accident Insurance Law of 1884, Germany, 341

Acerbo law, 660

Acre, 605

Action Libérale, 314

Adalia, 605, 655

Adams, Henry, 279

Adana, 605

Aden, Gulf of, 406, 408

Adowa, 407

Adriatic Sea, and Austria, 134, 370; and Italy, 208, 325, 329, 592–593, 653–654, 716

Ægean Sea, 329; and Bulgaria, 604, 718, 727; and Greece, 605; and Turkey, 774

Aehrenthal, Aloys Lexa von, 508

Afghanistan, and Anglo-Russian rivalry, 440, 441, 442; and Soviet Russia, 650, 726, 780; anti-Western reaction in, 778, 779, 782

Africa, in 1815, 25–26, 28; and France, 58, 59, 402–404; and the Netherlands, 213; and the Near-Eastern question, 246; and Italy, 329, 407–408; physical nature of, 397–398; partition of, 397–419; and old imperialism, 398–399; explorations in, 399–401; in 1875, 401–402; and Egypt, 404–406, 768–770; Anglo-French rivalry in the Sudan, 406–407; Congo Free State, 408–410; and Berlin Conference, 410–411; division of the interior, 411–412; partition of West, 411–412; and Treaty of Sèvres, 606, 607; revolts in North, 767–770; and Turkey, 774

"Africa for the Africans," 767

African Association, 399

Agadir affair, 417, 506–507

Agamemnon, 46

Agriculture, in France, 58, 120, 315; in Italy, 132, 323; in the United States, 183–184; in Switzerland, 211; in Belgium, 212; in Denmark, 215–216; in England, 291; in Germany, 343; in Russia, 357–358, 367, 644, 645–646, 647; in Czechoslovakia, 711–712; in Poland, 725; in India, 780–781

Agricultural Revolution, 13, 16–18

Aguinaldo, 452

Ahmed Zogu, 716

Airplanes, 25, 531, 820–821

Aisne, battle of the, 538

Aix-la-Chapelle, 47

Alabama, 181

Alabama case, 470

Åland Islands, controversy over, 615, 721; and Russia, 636

Alaska, and Russia, 421, 422; and United States, 453, 470, 764

Albania, and Greece, 241, 251; and Balkan wars, 510–511; and Italy, 533, 654, 671, 716; and World War, 547; independence of, 616–617, 654; frontiers of, 618

Albert I (king of Belgium), 212–213

Alberta, 203

Aleppo, 578

Aleutian Islands, 421, 453

Alexander I (king of Greece), 717

Alexander VI (Pope), 466

Alexander I (prince of Rumania), 245

Alexander I (Czar of Russia), and Holy Alliance, 43, 45–46, 47; Quadruple Alliance, 47–48, 49; and France, 52; and Poland, 70; and Napoleon III, 122; and Congress of Vienna, 157; reign of, 161–163; and serfdom, 164, 165; and education, 165; and Sweden, 216; and world peace, 467

Alexander II (Czar of Russia), and Napoleon III, 128, 129; reign of, 169–177, 353; and Russo-Turkish War, 251; and Bulgaria, 254; and Austria-Hungary, 378; and Three Emperors' League, 478

Alexander III (Czar of Russia), conservatism of, 176; reign of, 353–358

Alexander I (king of Serbia), 255

Alexander I (king of Yugoslavia), regency of, 701; dictatorship of, 715–716

Alexander of Bulgaria, 254

Alexiev, Michael, 460, 637